THE
KINGFISHER
JUNIOR
ILLUSTRATED
DICTIONARY

KING*fisher*

Dictionary Editor	Heather Crossley
Dictionary Editorial Consultants	John Grisewood and Anne Soukhanov
Dictionary Editorial Development	Angela Crawley
Dictionary Definitions	Allene Tuck, Penny Stock, Anne Soukhanov, and Elizabeth Longley
Dictionary Pronunciation Consultant	Sheila Dignen
Thesaurus Author	George Marshall
Thesaurus Editor	John Grisewood
Thesaurus Revised By	John Bollard
Designer	Malcolm Smythe
Photographers	Tim Ridley, Nick Goodall, Steve Gorton
Cover Design	Tracey McNerney
Art Archivists	Wendy Allison, Steve Robinson
Artwork Researcher	Vicky Guilder
Prop Organizer	Sarah Wilson
Production Managers	Susan Wilmot and Oonagh Phelan

KINGFISHER
New Penderel House
283-288 High Holborn
London WC1V 7HZ
www.kingfisherpub.com

Material in this edition previously published by
Kingfisher Publications Plc as *The Kingfisher Junior Illustrated Dictionary*
and *The Kingfisher Children's Illustrated Thesaurus*

This edition published by Kingfisher Publications Plc 2001
This edition produced for S. Webb & Son Ltd by Kingfisher Publications Plc

2 4 6 8 10 9 7 5 3 1

1 Webbs/0801/TIM/HBM(UD.UNV)/150GPM

Copyright © Kingfisher Publications Plc 1994, 1996, 1997

A CIP catalogue record for this book is available from the British Library.

ISBN 0 7534 0650 0

Printed in China

Contents

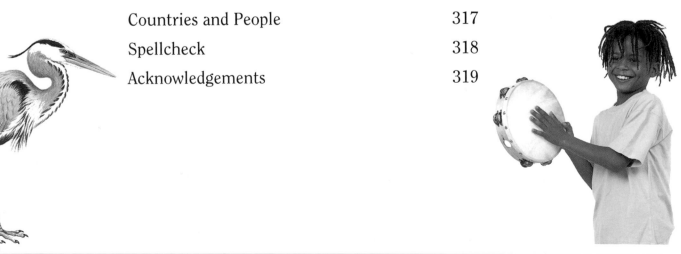

Your Guide to the Dictionary

a b c d e f g h i j k l m n o p q r s t u v w x y z

How to find a word
All headwords (entries) in this dictionary are listed in the order of the alphabet. Words that begin with **A** are followed by those which begin with **B**, and so on until you reach **Z**. All the words under each letter of the alphabet are themselves in alphabetical order, so **admit** follows **admire**; **form** follows **fork** and **vampire** follows **value**.

guide words
show first headword on left-hand page and last headword on the right-hand page.

headword
all entries begin with a coloured headword showing how the word is spelt.

entry
a headword plus all its information including any different definitions and related words.

alpha rule
helps you find the right letter section. The highlighted **b** shows that you are in the **b** section.

definition
what the word means.

different senses
some words have more than one meaning. Each different sense or definition is numbered.

example sentence
how a word is used to make the meaning clearer.

part of speech
what a word does in a sentence. It shows whether the word is a noun, verb, adjective, adverb, conjunction or preposition (see page 8).

changed form
spelling changes when words are used in different ways. All plurals of nouns, verb inflections and the comparatives and superlatives of adjectives are shown.

tenses of verbs
this shows how the verb is written in the present, continuous present and past tenses.

related word
belonging to the same word family.

picture topic pages and panels
here words and pictures are grouped by topic – birds, fruit or space, for example. With their word boxes, these pages extend vocabulary and knowledge about the topic.

new letter section
a big, coloured letter starts each section of the alphabet.

Bb

4

Useful features to help you explore words

thesaurus box

this shows how you can vary and enrich your vocabulary by choosing a different word with a similar meaning to express yourself. The *Kingfisher Junior Illustrated Dictionary* has thesaurus boxes for the following words:
bad, big, eat, fast, good, happy, like, nice, piece, small.

happy

Some words that you can use instead of happy:

I'm happy I've finished my homework.
☞ **contented, pleased, glad** ☜

They are happy with their wedding presents.
☞ **delighted, pleased, thrilled** ☜

Christmas is a happy time of year.
☞ **merry, cheerful** ☜

small

Some words you can use instead of small:

All small animals look sweet.
☞ **baby, young** ☜

The writing is so small you need a magnifying glass to read it.
☞ **minute, tiny** ☜

Don't worry. It's only a small mistake.
☞ **unimportant, slight, minor** ☜

homophones

words which sound the same but have different meanings are marked with this sign ●

fair fairs *noun*
a place outside where rides and roundabouts and competitions are set up for people to have fun. ● A word that sounds like **fair** is **fare**.

pronunciation and rhyming words

words that are difficult or awkward to say have this sign ▲

fracture fractures *noun*
a break or crack in something, especially a bone. *Her arm is in plaster because she has a fracture.* ▲ Say *frak*-cher.

opposites

the opposite meaning of some words is shown by this sign ■

fill fills filling filled *verb*
If you fill something you put as much into it as it can hold. *Fiona filled the bottles with water.* ■ The opposite is **empty**.

Spellcheck

The Spellcheck on page 188 lists many of the commonest little words in the language. These are words that are not likely to be looked up for their meaning, but which may be difficult to spell. Also listed are some words in the dictionary which are difficult to spell – such as address, handkerchief and jewellery.

spelling tips

If you cannot find a word under one letter, it may be under another letter. For instance the correct spelling for "cangaroo is "kangaroo"!

Spelling tip:
Some words that begin with a "co" sound are spelt with a "ko", for example koala.

vocabulary boxes

Many topic pages have a list of special words connected to the topic.

> **VOCABULARY**
>
> **bailey**
> *the courtyard inside the walls.*
>
> **battering ram**
> *a heavy, wooden pole that was rammed against an enemy castle wall or gate.*
>
> **battlement**
> *top of a castle wall with gaps through which people could fire on the enemy.*
>
> **buttress**
> *a pillar strengthening a wall.*
>
> **drawbridge**
> *a bridge over the moat that could be pulled up to stop the enemy getting into the castle.*
>
> **dungeon**
> *a prison under the castle.*
>
> **keep**
> *the main tower.*
>
> **loophole**
> *a slit in a wall for light, air or for shooting through.*

First Writing

At first people would just draw a picture of a thing they wanted to record – a woman, a horse, a bird for instance. The people of ancient Egypt could write quite complicated messages using these kinds of pictures. The people of ancient China also drew pictures of things they wanted us to know about. In time these pictures became much simpler – just a few brush strokes known as "characters". Chinese is still written in characters to this day.

About 3000 years ago a way of writing was developed which used signs for each sound in a word. A letter stood for a sound. We call letters that stand for sounds an alphabet. These are the "bricks" we use to build our language.

A B C D E F G H I J K L M N O P Q R S T U V W X Y Z

A a

abandon abandons abandoning abandoned *verb*
If you abandon somebody or something, you leave them behind. *The puppies had been abandoned by their mother.*

abbreviation abbreviations *noun*
a short way of writing a word or a group of words. *"Rd" is an abbreviation for "Road".*

ability abilities *noun*
If you have the ability to do something, you can do it. *Sarah has the ability to draw well.*

aboard *adverb, preposition*
If you are aboard a train, bus, ship or plane, you are on it or in it.

above *adverb, preposition*
higher than something. *My bedroom is above the kitchen.* ■ The opposite is **below** or **beneath**.

abroad *adverb, preposition*
If you go abroad, you go to another country. *We went abroad for our summer holiday.*

absent *adjective*
If somebody is absent, they are not here. *Katie was absent from school yesterday.* ■ The opposite is **present**.

absorb absorbs absorbing absorbed *verb*
When a cloth or sponge absorbs water, it soaks it up.

accelerator accelerators *noun*
the pedal that you press with your foot to make a car go faster.

accent accents *noun*
1 the way that a person from a certain place speaks. *He spoke with a Yorkshire accent.*
2 a mark on a word that shows you how to pronounce it. *"Café" has an accent on the "e".*

accept accepts accepting accepted *verb*
1 If you accept something that somebody gives you, you take it. *She accepted the gift.*
2 If you accept an invitation to a party, you say that you will come.
■ The opposite is **refuse**.

accident accidents *noun*
something bad that happens without being planned. *Ella dropped the drinks. It was an accident.*
accidentally *adverb*.

accompany accompanies accompanying accompanied *verb*
If you accompany somebody, you go with them. *The teacher accompanied the children to the sports centre.*

account accounts *noun*
1 If you give an account of something, you describe what happened. *He wrote an account of the bank robbery in the local newspaper.*
2 money that you keep in the bank.

accurate *adjective*
exactly right. *Is your watch accurate?*
▲ Say *ak-yoo-rut*.

accuse accuses accusing accused *verb*
If you accuse somebody, you say that they have done something wrong. *The man was accused of stealing the money.*

ace aces *noun*
a playing-card with one symbol on it. *the ace of hearts.*

ache aches *noun*
a pain in your body that goes on hurting, such as earache. ▲ Rhymes with **take**.

achieve achieves achieving achieved *verb*
If you achieve something, you get it after trying very hard.

acid acids *noun*
a liquid that tastes sour such as lemon juice or vinegar. Some strong acids can burn your skin.

acid rain *noun*
rain that has chemicals in it from factories and cars. Acid rain damages trees, rivers and buildings.

acorn acorns *noun*
the nut that grows on an oak tree.

acrobat acrobats *noun*
a person who can do difficult and clever balancing tricks. You can see acrobats in a circus.

across *adverb, preposition*
If you walk across something such as a field, you walk from one side to the other.

act acts *noun*
1 one part of a play. *This play has three acts.*
2 something that you do. *an act of kindness.*

act acts acting acted *verb*
1 When you act, you do something. *She acted quickly to save the boy from drowning.*
2 If you act in a play or film, you play a part in it.

action actions *noun*
something that you do. *Frankie's fast actions saved the man's life.*

active *adjective*
If you are active, you are always busy and able to do lots of things.

activity activities *noun*
1 something that you do. *Playing football is his favourite activity.*
2 a lot of things happening and people doing things. *During the carnival there is a lot of activity on the streets.*

actor actors *noun*
a person who acts in a play or film.

add adds adding added *verb*
1 When you add numbers, you put them together to find an answer. *If you add 2 and 3, you get 5.* ■ The opposite is **subtract**.
2 If you add something to something else, you put the two things together. *She put coffee in a mug and added hot water and milk.*
addition *noun*.

address addresses *noun*
Your address is the number or name of the building where you live, and the street and town where it is. *My address is 21 Morris Road, Southampton.*

adjective adjectives *noun*
a word that tells you what somebody or something is like. In the sentence "Tom has a new, red bike", "new" and "red" are adjectives.

admire admires admiring admired *verb*
If you admire somebody or something, you think they are very good. *Everyone admired Katie's painting.*

admit admits admitting admitted *verb*
If you admit something, you agree that you have done something wrong. *Matthew admitted that he had broken the glass.*

adopt adopts adopting adopted *verb*
When somebody adopts a child, they take the child to live with them as part of their family.

adult adults *noun*
a person or an animal that is fully grown. *an adult bear.*

advance advances advancing advanced *verb*
When something advances, it moves forward. *The army advanced towards the enemy.*

advantage advantages *noun*
something that can help you to do better than other people. *In a game of basketball, it is an advantage to be tall.* ■ The opposite is **disadvantage**.

adventure adventures *noun*
something exciting that happens to you. *We got lost in the snow. It was a real adventure!*

adverb adverbs *noun*
a word that tells you more about a *verb, adjective* or another *adverb*. In the sentence "Ewen quickly opened the parcel", "quickly" is an adverb.

advertise advertises advertising advertised *verb*
If you advertise, you tell people about things that you are selling. *This poster is advertising a coach service.*

advertisement advertisements *noun*
information on a poster, in a newspaper or on television that tells you about something to buy or something to do. ▲ Say *ad-ver-tiss-ment.*

advice *noun*
If somebody gives you advice, they tell you what they think you should do.

advise advises advising advised *verb*
If you advise somebody, you tell them what you think they should do.

aerial aerials *noun*
a wire that sends out or receives radio or television signals. ▲ Say *air-ee-al.*

aeroplane aeroplanes *noun*
a flying machine with wings and an engine.

aerosol aerosols *noun*
a can with liquid inside. You press a button to send out the liquid in a spray. ▲ Say *air-o-sol.*

affect affects affecting affected *verb*
If something affects you, it makes you different in some way. *Smoking affects your health.*

affection *noun*
the feeling of loving or liking somebody. *Samantha shows great affection for her little sister Josephine.*
affectionate *adjective.*

afford affords affording afforded *verb*
If you can afford something, you have enough money to buy it. *I can't afford any more sweets this week.*

A
B
C
D
E
F
G
H
I
J
K
L
M
N
O
P
Q
R
S
T
U
V
W
X
Y
Z

a
b
c
d
e
f
g
h
i
j
k
l
m
n
o
p
q
r
s
t
u
v
w
x
y
z

afraid *adjective*
If you are afraid, you think something nasty will happen to you. *Are you afraid of the dark?*

afternoon afternoons *noun*
the part of the day between midday and the evening. *I'm going swimming on Saturday afternoon.*

again *adverb*
If you do something again, you do it once more. *Tell me that story again.*

against *preposition*
1 If you play against somebody in a match, you are on the other side to them. *We played against a team from another school.*
2 next to, or touching something. *The ladder was against the wall.*
3 If you are against something, you do not agree with it. *I'm against testing drugs on animals.*

age ages *noun*
1 Your age is how old you are.
2 a certain time in history. *Bronze Age.*

agree agrees agreeing agreed *verb*
If you agree with somebody, you think the same about something. ■ The opposite is **disagree**.
agreement *noun*.

agriculture *noun*
Agriculture is keeping animals and growing plants for food.
agricultural *adjective*.

ahead *adverb*
in front of somebody or something. *We walked slowly, but the dog ran ahead.*

aim aims aiming aimed *verb*
1 If you aim at something, you point something such as a gun at the thing you want to hit.
2 If you aim to do something, you try to do it. *We aimed to get home by 6 o'clock.*

air *noun*
the mixture of gases that we breathe.

aircraft aircraft *noun*
any machine that can fly. Aeroplanes and helicopters are aircraft.

airport airports *noun*
a place where aeroplanes take off and land. *Heathrow is a very large airport near London.*

aisle aisles *noun*
a place where you can walk between rows of seats, such as in a theatre or a church. *The bride and groom walked down the aisle.* ▲ Say **eye-l**.

alarm alarms *noun*
1 something such as a bell or a flashing light that warns you of something. *a burglar alarm.*
2 a sudden feeling of fear.

album albums *noun*
1 a book that you keep things such as photographs or stamps in.
2 a CD, tape or record with several different pieces of music on it.

alcohol *noun*
Drinks such as wine and beer have alcohol in them. If people drink too much alcohol, they get drunk.
alcoholic *adjective*
Wine and beer are alcoholic.

alien aliens *noun*
a creature from another planet. ▲ Say **ay-lee-en**.

alike *adjective*
If two things or people are alike, they are the same in some way. *The twins are not identical, but they are alike.*

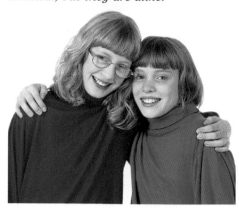

alive *adjective*
A person, an animal or a plant that is alive is living now. *Plants need water to stay alive.* ■ The opposite is **dead**.

allergy allergies *noun*
an illness caused by something that does not normally make people ill. *Some people have an allergy to dust.*
allergic *adjective*.

alley alleys *noun*
a narrow path between buildings.

alligator alligators *noun*
a large reptile similar to a crocodile but with shorter, wider jaws. Alligators live in rivers in the southern United States and in China.❖ *Look below*

allow allows allowing allowed *verb*
If you are allowed to do something, somebody lets you do it. *I'm allowed to stay up later at weekends.* ■ The opposite is **forbid**.

alone *adjective, adverb*
by yourself, with nobody else. *Sophie walked home alone.*

Aircraft

single-engined trainer

multi-engined short-haul jet

twin-engined executive jet

airborne early warning turboprop

VOCABULARY

aileron
a flap on the back of a wing that makes the plane roll sideways.

cabin
the part of a plane where the passengers sit.

elevator
a panel on the tailplane that makes the plane climb or descend.

flight deck
the part where the pilot and crew sit.

fuselage
the main part of a plane carrying passengers and crew.

galley
the kitchen.

rudder
a vertical piece on the tailplane that turns the plane left or right.

tailplane
a small horizontal wing at the back of the plane.

wing
one of the long, flat parts that keep the plane in the air.

"Stealth" bomber

fighter

special-purpose transport plane

seven-seat utility helicopter

tailplane

rudder

elevator

multi-engined, long-haul passenger aircraft

fuselage

flight deck

galley

cabin

aileron

cargo hold

fuel tank

wing

engine

A B C D E F G H I J K L M N O P Q R S T U V W X Y Z

a
b
c
d
e
f
g
h
i
j
k
l
m
n
o
p
q
r
s
t
u
v
w
x
y
z

aloud *adverb*
If you read or speak aloud, you do it so that other people can hear. ● A word that sounds like **aloud** is **allowed**.

alphabet **alphabets** *noun*
all the letters from A to Z that we use to write words.
alphabetical *adjective*.

A a	A α	ა გ	A	а	اﺄ
B b	В β	ბ ბ	Б	б	بﺐ
C c	Γ γ	გ გ	В	в	تﺖ
D d	Δ δ	დ დ	Г	г	ثﺚ
E e	Ε ε	ე ე	Д	д	جﺞ
F f	Ζ ζ	ჳ ჳ	Е	е	حﺢ
G g	Η η	ჱ ჱ	Ж	ж	خﺦ
H h	Θ θ	თ თ	З	з	دﺪ
I i	Ι ι	ი ი	И	и	ذﺬ
J j	Κ κ	კ კ	Й	й	رﺮ
K k	Λ λ	ლ ლ	К	к	زﺰ
L l	Μ μ	მ მ	Л	л	شﺶ
M m	Ν ν	ნ ნ	М	м	سﺲ
N n	Ξ ξ	ო ო	Н	н	صﺺ

parts of different alphabets

already *adverb*
before this time. *We ran to the bus stop but the bus had already gone.*

alter **alters altering altered** *verb*
If you alter something, you change it in some way. *My dad has altered his working hours so he can pick me up from school.*
alteration *noun*.

altogether *adverb*
counting everybody or everything. *My uncle gave me £5 and my aunt gave me £10, so I've got £15 altogether.*

aluminium *noun*
a light, silver-coloured metal. Aluminium is used to make cans and tin foil. ▲ Say *al-yoo-**min**-yum*.

amateur **amateurs** *noun*
a person who does something such as a sport because they enjoy it, but does not get paid for it. ▲ Say *am-at-ur*.

amaze **amazes amazing amazed** *verb*
If something amazes you, it surprises you very much.
amazement *noun*
We watched the acrobat in amazement.
amazing *adjective*
She told us an amazing story.

ambition **ambitions** *noun*
If you have an ambition to do something, you want to do it very much. *My ambition is to learn to fly an aeroplane.*

ambulance **ambulances** *noun*
a special van that takes people who are hurt or ill to hospital.

among *preposition*
1 in the middle of. *The house stood among the trees.*
2 shared between two or more people. *She divided the sweets among the children.*

amount **amounts** *noun*
An amount of something is how much there is. *I get the same amount of pocket money as my friend.*

amphibian **amphibians** *noun*
an animal that lives on land but breeds in water. Toads, newts and axolotls are amphibians. ▲ Say *am-fib-ee-an*.

amplifier **amplifiers** *noun*
a machine that makes sounds louder. CD players and cassette players have amplifiers.

amuse **amuses amusing amused** *verb*
If you amuse somebody, you make them laugh or smile, or you keep them happy and busy. *The joke amused my sister.* ◆ *We played games to amuse ourselves on the long journey.*

ancestor **ancestors** *noun*
Your ancestors are members of your family who lived a long time ago.

anchor **anchors** *noun*
a heavy, metal hook on a long chain that you drop into the water from a ship or boat to stop the ship or boat from floating away. ▲ Say *ang-ker*.

ancient *adjective*
very old. *an ancient castle.*

anger *noun*
Anger is the strong feeling you have when you think something is unfair.
angrily *adverb*.

angle **angles** *noun*
the corner where two lines meet.

right angle   **obtuse angle**

acute angle

no angles

warty newt

common toad

axolotl

angry **angrier angriest** *adjective*
If you are angry, you feel anger.

animal **animals** *noun*
any living thing that is not a plant.
Birds, fish, insects, frogs, snakes, rabbits
and elephants are all animals.

ankle **ankles** *noun*
Your ankle is the part of your leg where
it joins your foot.

anniversary **anniversaries** *noun*
a day when you remember something
special that happened on the same date
in another year. *Today is my parents'
11th wedding anniversary.*

announce **announces**
announcing announced *verb*
If you announce something, you say it in
front of a lot of people. *Miss Burton
announced to the class that she was
leaving at the end of term.*

annoy **annoys annoying annoyed**
verb
If you annoy somebody, you make them
angry.
annoyance *noun*.

annual *adjective*
If something is annual, it happens once
every year. *The town carnival is an
annual event.*

answer **answers answering
answered** *verb*
When you answer, you say something to
somebody who has asked you a question
or said something to you. *"What's the
capital of France?" "Paris," she
answered.* ▲ Say **an**-*sur*.
answer *noun*.

ant **ants** *noun*
a tiny insect. Ants live in large groups
called colonies.

antelope **antelopes** *noun*
an animal like a deer with
horns and long legs that
can run fast. Antelopes live
in Africa and parts of Asia.

an eland (back) and a nilgar (front)

antenna **antennas** or **antennae**
noun
1 a long, thin part on the head of an
insect that it uses for feeling with.
2 an aerial.

anticlockwise *adjective, adverb*
If you turn anticlockwise, you move in
the opposite direction to the hands on a
clock. ■ The opposite is **clockwise**.

antique **antiques** *noun*
a thing that is very old and may be
worth a lot of money. *My grandma
collects antiques.* ▲ Say *an-t***eek**.

antiseptic **antiseptics** *noun*
a cream or liquid that you put on a
wound to keep it clean and germ-free.

antler **antlers** *noun*
one of two large horns that grow on the
head of a male deer. The male deer,
called a stag, loses its antlers every year
and grows new ones.

anxious *adjective*
If you are anxious about something, you
worry about it. *Mum was anxious
because we were late home.* ▲ Say
ank-shuss.

ape **apes** *noun*
an animal like a big monkey with no tail.
Gorillas, chimpanzees, orangutans and
gibbons are all apes. ❖ *Look below*

apologize **apologizes**
apologizing apologized *verb*
If you apologize, you say you are sorry.
Billy apologized for being late.
apology *noun*.

apostrophe **apostrophes** *noun*
1 a mark that you use in writing to show
that something belongs to somebody.
Lucy's book. ◆ *my parent's house.*
2 a mark that you use in writing to show
that a letter has been missed out. In
the word "I'm", which is short for "I
am", the apostrophe shows that the
letter "a" has been missed out.
▲ Say *a-***poss**-*trof-ee*.

different types of ape

gibbon

gorilla

chimpanzee

orangutan

A
B
C
D
E
F
G
H
I
J
K
L
M
N
O
P
Q
R
S
T
U
V
W
X
Y
Z

apparatus *noun*
1 the pieces of equipment that you need to do a scientific experiment.
2 things such as bars and ropes that you use in gymnastics.

appear appears appearing appeared *verb*
1 If somebody or something appears, they come to a place where you can see them. *He appeared from behind a tree.* ■ The opposite is **disappear**.
2 If something appears to be a certain way, it seems to be that way. *A magnifying glass makes things appear bigger than they really are.*

appearance appearances *noun*
1 If you make an appearance, you come to a place where people can see you. *We all sat down when the teacher made a sudden appearance.*
2 Your appearance is what you look like. *Having her hair cut really changed her appearance.*

appendix appendixes *noun*
Your appendix is a small, closed tube inside your body. It is part of the long tube called the intestine that carries food out of your stomach.

appetite appetites *noun*
If you have an appetite, you are ready to eat something. *I hope you've got a big appetite because I've cooked a lot of food for dinner.*

applause *noun*
Applause is when people clap their hands together to show that they liked something.

apple apples *noun*
a hard, round, green, red or yellow fruit that grows on a tree. Apples have seeds called pips inside.

apply applies applying applied *verb*
1 If something such as a rule applies to you, you must do what it says. *School rules apply to everyone in the school.*
2 If you apply for something such as a job, you write to somebody to ask for it.
application *noun*.

appointment appointments *noun*
a time that you have arranged to see somebody. *I have a doctor's appointment at 4 o'clock.*

appreciate appreciates appreciating appreciated *verb*
If you appreciate something, you are grateful for it. *I appreciate all your help.*
appreciation *noun*.

approach approaches approaching approached *verb*
If something approaches, it comes nearer to you. *The train is approaching the station.*

approve approves approving approved *verb*
If you approve of something, you think it is good and right. *Mum doesn't approve of my new haircut.*

apricot apricots *noun*
a soft, round, orange-yellow fruit with a large stone in the middle.

apron aprons *noun*
a piece of clothing that you wear over your clothes to keep them clean when you are cooking.

aquarium aquariums or **aquaria** *noun*
1 a glass tank where fish and other water animals are kept.
2 a building with lots of glass tanks where people can look at fish.

arch arches *noun*
a part of a bridge, building or wall that has a curved shape. Arches support buildings and let people, trains, boats, cars and other vehicles pass underneath.

archery *noun*
the sport of shooting with a bow and arrow. You shoot the arrow at a circular target.

architect architects *noun*
a person whose job is to design buildings. ▲ Say *ar-kee-tekt*.

area areas *noun*
1 a part of a country, a town or the world. *My uncle comes from this area.*
2 the size of a flat place. *If a room is 3 metres wide and 4 metres long, it has an area of 12 square metres.*
3 a place that you use for something special. *a play area.*

arena arenas *noun*
a place with rows of seats around it where you can watch sport or concerts.

argue argues arguing argued *verb*
If you argue with somebody, you speak in an angry way because you do not agree with them.
argument *noun*.

arithmetic *noun*
doing sums and working with numbers to find an answer.

arm arms *noun*
Your arm is the part of your body between your shoulder and your hand.

armed *adjective*
If somebody is armed, they have a weapon, such as a sword or a gun and they are ready to fight.

armour *noun*
a suit of strong metal that soldiers used to wear to protect their bodies in battle.

arms *noun*
Arms are guns, swords, bombs and other weapons used in fighting.

army armies *noun*
a large group of soldiers who are trained to fight on land in a war.

arrange arranges arranging arranged *verb*
1 If you arrange something such as a party, you plan it. *We are arranging a birthday party for my sister.*
2 If you arrange things such as flowers or your belongings, you set them out in a certain way or put them in order. *We arranged the books on the shelf in alphabetical order.*
arrangement *noun*.

arrest arrests arresting arrested *verb*
When the police arrest somebody, they catch them and accuse them of breaking the law.

arrive arrives arriving arrived *verb*
If you arrive somewhere, you get there. *She arrived at 3 o'clock.* ■ The opposite is **depart** or **leave**.
arrival *noun*.

arrow arrows *noun*
1 a thin stick with a sharp point at one end, that you shoot from a bow.
2 a sign that points to tell you the way.

art *noun*
Art is something beautiful that somebody has made, such as a painting or a statue.

artery arteries *noun*
An artery is one of the large tubes that carries blood from your heart to all parts of your body.

artificial *adjective*
If something is artificial, it is made by people and is not natural. *These are artificial flowers.*

artist artists *noun*
a person who draws or paints pictures or makes other beautiful things.

ash ashes *noun*
1 the grey powder that is left after something has been burnt.
2 a tree with grey bark that loses its leaves in winter.

ashamed *adjective*
If you are ashamed of something you have done, you are sorry and unhappy about it. *William was ashamed that he had told a lie.*

ask asks asking asked *verb*
1 If you ask a question, you say that you want to know something. *"What time is it?" she asked.*
2 If you ask for something, you tell somebody that you want it. *Tom asked for a bike for his birthday.*

asleep *adjective*
sleeping. *The cat was asleep by the fire.* ■ The opposite is **awake**.

assembly assemblies *noun*
a meeting of a big group of people for something special. *We have a school assembly every morning.*

assist assists assisting assisted *verb*
If you assist somebody, you help them.
assistance *noun*, **assistant** *noun*.

assorted *adjective*
If things such as sweets or biscuits are assorted, all different kinds are mixed together.

asthma *noun*
an illness that makes it difficult for a person to breathe. ▲ Say *ass-ma*.

astonish astonishes astonishing astonished *verb*
If something astonishes you, it surprises you very much. *She was astonished to hear the parrot talk.*

astronaut astronauts *noun*
a person who travels in space.

astronomy *noun*
the study of the Sun, Moon, planets and stars.

ate past of **eat**.

A
B
C
D
E
F
G
H
I
J
K
L
M
N
O
P
Q
R
S
T
U
V
W
X
Y
Z

athlete **athletes** *noun*
a person who is good at sports such as
running, jumping and throwing.

athletics *noun*
sports such as running, high jump, long
jump and throwing.

atlas **atlases** *noun*
a book of maps.

atmosphere *noun*
1 the layer of gases that surrounds the
Earth.
2 the feeling that a room or a place has.
*The lounge had a warm, cosy
atmosphere.*

atom **atoms** *noun*
a very tiny part of something.
Everything is made of atoms. *Water is
made of hydrogen and oxygen atoms.*

attach **attaches attaching
attached** *verb*
If you attach something to something
else, you join or fasten them together.
We attached the rope to a tree.

attack **attacks attacking attacked**
verb
If somebody attacks another person, they
try to hurt them.
attack *noun.*

attempt **attempts** *noun*
a try. *After two attempts, I managed to
get over the wall.*
attempt *verb.*

attention *noun*
If you pay attention to somebody, you
listen to them or watch them carefully.

attic **attics** *noun*
a room or space under the roof of a
house. *We keep our old toys in the attic.*

attract **attracts attracting
attracted** *verb*
1 If somebody or
something attracts
you, you like
them or find
them interesting.
*Katie was
attracted to the
red car.*
2 To attract also
means to
make
somebody
or
something
come nearer.
Magnets attract iron.

attractive *adjective*
very nice to look at. *an attractive scarf.*

audience **audiences** *noun*
a group of people who are watching a
play, film or concert. *At the end of the
play the audience applauded loudly.*

aunt **aunts** *noun*
Your aunt is the sister of your mother or
your father, or the wife of your uncle.

author **authors** *noun*
a person who writes stories or books.

autograph **autographs** *noun*
the signature of somebody famous.

automatic *adjective*
If a machine is automatic, it works by
itself instead of a person doing the work.
A lot of trains have automatic doors.

autumn **autumns** *noun*
the season of the year between summer
and winter. *Leaves fall off the trees in
autumn.*

available *adjective*
If something is available, you can have
it. *The video is only available in
America.*

avenue **avenues** *noun*
a street. Avenues are often wide with
trees along both sides.

average *noun*
1 a usual or normal amount. *Ben's exam
results were above average.*

2 In maths, to find the average of three
numbers, 5, 9 and 10, add them up
and divide by 3. $5 + 9 + 10 = 24$, and
$24 \div 3 = 8$.

avoid **avoids avoiding avoided**
verb
If you avoid something, you stay away
from it. *The driver swerved to avoid the
boy and his dog.*

awake *adjective*
If you are awake, you are not asleep.

award **awards** *noun*
a prize for something you have done
well. *I won a gold award for swimming.*
award *verb.*

awful *adjective*
very bad. *This cake is stale. It tastes
awful.*

awkward *adjective*
1 If you move in an awkward way, you
are clumsy.
2 difficult or not convenient. *Our village
is awkward to get to if you don't have
a car.*

axe **axes** *noun*
a tool with a long handle
and a sharp blade for
cutting down trees and
chopping wood.

B b

baboon baboons *noun*
a large African monkey with a nose and mouth the same shape as a dog's.

a family of baboons

baby babies *noun*
a very young child.

babysitter babysitters *noun*
a person who looks after children when their parents are out.
babysit *verb*.

back backs *noun*
1 Your back is the part of your body behind you, between your neck and your bottom.
2 The back of something is the opposite part to the front. *We keep our bikes at the back of the house.*

background backgrounds *noun*
The background is everything behind the main thing you are looking at. *This picture shows some camels with pyramids in the background.*

bacon *noun*
meat from the back or sides of a pig which has been prepared over smoke or treated with salt.

bacteria *noun*
Bacteria are living things so tiny that you cannot see them without a microscope. Bacteria live in air, soil, water and inside people and animals, and some kinds can make you ill.

bad worse worst *adjective*
1 not good.
2 If you are bad at something, you cannot do it very well.
3 If food goes bad, it starts to smell or to go mouldy, so that you cannot eat it.

b a d

Some words you can use instead of bad:

The weather was very bad last week.
☞ **unpleasant, nasty** ☜

You've been a bad girl.
☞ **naughty, disobedient** ☜

Sweets are bad for your teeth.
☞ **harmful, damaging** ☜

Is the pain bad?
☞ **severe** ☜

Her car is in bad condition.
☞ **poor** ☜

The food has gone bad.
☞ **rotten** ☜

badge badges *noun*
a piece of metal, plastic or material with a picture or words on it. A badge is pinned or sewn to your clothes.

badger badgers *noun*
a wild animal with grey fur, and black and white stripes on its head. Badgers live in holes called sets underground, and come out to feed at night.

badminton *noun*
a game in which players use rackets to hit a light object called a shuttlecock over a high net.

bag bags *noun*
a thing that you use for carrying other things in.

bait *noun*
a piece of food that you fix to a hook or put in a trap to catch fish or animals.

bake bakes baking baked *verb*
When you bake food, you cook it in an oven. *I love the smell of freshly baked bread, don't you?*

balance balances balancing balanced *verb*
If you balance, you keep steady and do not fall over. *Connie balances on the box.*

balcony balconies *noun*
a platform joined to the wall of a building upstairs, with a wall or railing around it.

bald balder baldest *adjective*
A man who is bald has no hair on his head.

ball balls *noun*
1 a round thing that you use to play games. *a tennis ball.*
2 something made into a round shape. *a ball of wool.*
3 a very grand party where people dance.

ballet ballets *noun*
a kind of dancing that tells a story.
▲ Say *bal-ay.*

balloon balloons *noun*
a round bag made of rubber or other material and filled with air or gas so that it floats.

bamboo *noun*
a tropical plant with hollow stems, used to make things such as furniture.

ban bans banning banned *verb*
If somebody bans something, they say it is not allowed. *My parents have banned us from watching TV in the morning.*

banana bananas *noun*
a long, curved fruit with yellow skin. Bananas grow in hot countries.
❖ *Look at page 69*

A B C D E F G H I J K L M N O P Q R S T U V W X Y Z

band bands *noun*
1 a group of people who play music together.
2 a group of people who do something together. *a band of robbers.*
3 a narrow piece of material that goes around something. *Tennis players often wear wrist bands.*

bandage bandages *noun*
a long strip of material that can be wrapped around a part of your body that is injured in order to protect it.

bang bangs *noun*
a sudden and very loud noise.
bang *verb.*

bank banks *noun*
1 a building where people can keep their money safely.
2 the ground at the side of a river.

banner banners *noun*
a long piece of cloth with writing on it that people can carry in a crowd or procession to show what they think about something. *The people in the crowd carried banners saying "Stop animal experiments".*

bar bars *noun*
1 a long, straight piece of metal.
2 a flat, solid piece of something. *a bar of soap.*
3 a place where you can buy and have a drink.
4 one of the short groups of notes that a piece of music can be divided into. When music is written down, the bars are shown by lines between the groups of notes.

barbecue barbecues *noun*
a kind of cooker on which you can grill things like sausages or meat over hot charcoal outdoors. ▲ Say *bar-bi-kyoo.*

bare bare barest *adjective*
1 without any clothes on. *bare feet.*
2 A bare cupboard or shelf is empty.
● A word that sounds like **bare** is **bear**.

bargain bargains *noun*
a thing being sold which is much cheaper than you expected.

barge barges *noun*
a long boat with a flat bottom, used on canals and rivers.

bark barks barking barked *verb*
When a dog barks, it makes a sudden loud noise.

bark *noun*
the rough outside covering of a tree's trunk and branches.

barley *noun*
a plant whose grain is used as food and for making beer.

barn barns *noun*
a large farm building for storing crops such as hay or keeping animals inside.

barrel barrels *noun*
a large container with curved sides that is used for storing liquids.

barrier barriers *noun*
a thing like a wall or fence, that stops people or things getting past.

base bases *noun*
The base of a thing is the bottom part or the part that it stands on. *The lamp has a heavy metal base.*

baseball *noun*
a game played with a bat and ball by two teams of nine players. Each player has to hit the ball and run around four points on the field before the ball is caught.

safety helmet
face mask
bat
Batter
Pitcher
catcher's mitt
Catcher
ribbed shoes

basement basements *noun*
a room or rooms below the ground floor in a building.

basic *adjective*
Basic things are the important things that you cannot do without. *The one basic piece of equipment you need for football is a ball.*

basket baskets *noun*
a stiff bag made from cane or wire, for carrying things in.

basketball *noun*
a game played by two teams of five players with a large ball. The teams have to get the ball through a net fixed to a high metal ring at each end of the court.

bat bats *noun*
1 a small animal like a mouse with wings. Bats hunt for food at night.
2 a piece of wood or metal that you use for hitting the ball in sports such as baseball, cricket or table tennis.

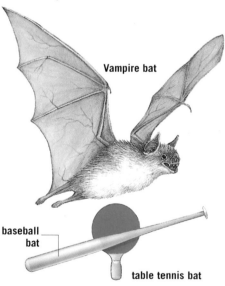

Vampire bat

baseball bat

table tennis bat

bat bats batting batted *verb*
When you bat, you have a turn at hitting the ball in games like cricket or baseball. *Jennifer batted the ball to Lucy.*

bath baths *noun*
1 a very large container for water that you get into to wash your whole body.
2 When you have a bath, you get into a bath and wash yourself.

battery batteries *noun*
a metal object that makes and stores electricity. You put batteries in things such as radios, cameras and torches to make them work.

battle battles *noun*
a fight between two armies.

bay bays *noun*
a part of the sea which has land curving around it on three sides.

beach beaches *noun*
the land beside the sea that is covered with sand or pebbles.

bead beads *noun*
a small, round piece of glass, wood or plastic with a hole through the middle. A piece of string can be threaded through the holes of lots of beads to make a necklace or bracelet.

beak beaks *noun*
the hard, pointed part of a bird's mouth.

beam beams *noun*
1 a thick, strong piece of wood or metal that holds up a roof.
2 a line of bright light.

roof beam

torch beam

beam beams beaming beamed *verb*
If you are beaming, you have a big, happy smile on your face.

bean beans *noun*
a large seed that grows inside a pod. Sometimes you eat the whole pod and sometimes you eat the seed.
runner beans ◆ *baked beans*.
● A word that sounds like **bean** is **been**.

bear bears *noun*
a big, wild animal with thick fur.
● A word that sounds like **bear** is **bare**.

bear bears bearing bore borne *verb*
1 If you cannot bear something, you cannot put up with it. *She couldn't bear the pain any longer.*
2 If you bear something, you carry or support it. *The cart bore a heavy load.*
● A word that sounds like **bear** is **bare**.

beard beards *noun*
the hair on a man's chin and face.

beast beasts *noun*
a wild animal.

beat beats beating beat beaten *verb*
1 If you beat somebody in a game or competition, you win.
2 To beat somebody or something means to hit them very hard again and again, especially with your hand or a stick.
3 If you beat eggs or cream, you stir them fast with a fork, spoon or whisk.
4 When your heart is beating, it is pushing the blood around your body regularly and keeping you alive.

beat beats *noun*
the regular rhythm of your heart or of a piece of music. *the beat of a drum.*

beautiful *adjective*
very lovely to look at, or listen to or smell. *a beautiful painting.* ■ The opposite is **ugly**.

beaver beavers *noun*
a furry animal with strong teeth and a flat tail. Beavers live by rivers or streams where they build homes called lodges.

become becomes becoming became *verb*
1 When one thing becomes another thing, it changes into it. *Caterpillars eventually become butterflies.*
2 When a person becomes something, they change to be it. *She became worried about her son when he didn't come home at the usual time.*

bed beds *noun*
1 the piece of furniture that you sleep on. The room where your bed is and where you sleep is called a bedroom.
2 The sea bed is the bottom of the sea.

bee bees *noun*
an insect with a yellow and black body that makes honey. ● A word that sounds like **bee** is **be**.

beef *noun*
meat from a cow.

beer *noun*
an alcoholic drink made from grain.

beetle beetles *noun*
an insect with hard, shiny wings.

beetroot beetroots *noun*
a round, purple vegetable that grows in the ground.

beg begs begging begged *verb*
1 If somebody begs, they ask people for money in the street.
2 If you beg for something, you ask for it in a way that shows you want it very badly. *Ali begged for a kitten.*

begin begins beginning began begun *verb*
When something begins, it starts.
■ The opposite is **finish** or **end**.
beginning *noun*.

behave behaves behaving behaved *verb*
The way you behave is the way you act. *The children behaved very badly.*
behaviour *noun*.

believe believes believing believed *verb*
1 If you believe something, you are sure that it is true or real even though you cannot prove it. *Do you believe in fairies?*
2 If you believe somebody, you think they are telling the truth. *My mum believed I didn't break the window.*
belief *noun*.

A B C D E F G H I J K L M N O P Q R S T U V W X Y Z

bell bells *noun*
a metal instrument like a large upside-down cup which has a thin piece of metal hanging inside called the clapper. When the clapper hits the side of the bell it makes a ringing sound.

belong belongs belonging belonged *verb*
1 If something belongs to you, it is yours.
2 If you belong to a club or society, you are a member of it.

below *preposition*
If something is below something else, it is underneath it.
■ The opposite is **above**.

belt belts *noun*
a strip of material or leather that you wear around your waist.

bench benches *noun*
1 a long, hard seat made of wood or metal that more than one person can sit on. *a garden bench.*
2 a wooden table that people put things on when they work. *She was working at a bench in the laboratory.*

work bench

garden bench

bend bends bending bent *verb*
1 If you bend, you move the top part of your body downwards. *He bent down and stroked the dog.*
2 If you bend something, you make it curved instead of straight.

beneath *preposition*
If something is beneath something else, it is below it. ■ The opposite is **above**, **over** or **on top of**.

raspberry huckleberry cranberry

blackberry blueberry strawberry grape gooseberry redcurrant blackcurrant

berry berries *noun*
a small, soft fruit with seeds in it. ● A word that sounds like **berry** is **bury**.

beside *preposition*
If something is beside something else, it is next to it or at the side of it.

bet bets betting bet *verb*
1 If you bet that something is going to happen, you are sure that it is going to happen. *I bet it will rain tomorrow.*
2 If you bet on a race, you risk some money and guess who will win the race. If you are right, you get some money but if you are wrong you lose some.

betray betrays betraying betrayed *verb*
If you betray somebody, you harm them on purpose even though they trusted you. *I thought he was my friend but he betrayed me by telling lies about me.* **betrayal** *noun*.

between *preposition*
If something is between two other things, it is in the middle with the other things on each side.

BICYCLE

safety helmet

reflective jacket

handlebar

brake lever

elbow pads

front reflector

saddle

rear reflector

fork

tyre

hub

spoke

pedal

knee pads

beware *verb*
If somebody tells you to beware of something, they are warning you to be careful because it is dangerous. *The sign said "Beware of the dog".*

bewildered *adjective*
If you are bewildered, you are confused.

beyond *preposition*
If something is beyond something else, it is on the far side of it. *The car park is beyond the station.*

bicycle **bicycles** *noun*
a vehicle with two wheels that you ride by sitting on it and pushing two pedals with your feet. ▲ Say *by-sik-ul.*

bid **bids bidding bid** *verb*
If you bid for something, you offer an amount of money for it. Other people also offer an amount of money for it and the person who offers the most gets it.

big **bigger biggest** *adjective*
large in size, or important. ■ The opposite is **small** or **little**.

VOCABULARY

chain: *a series of metal rings called links.*

hub: *the centre of a wheel.*

gears: *a set of toothed wheels (sprockets) over which the chain fits and which changes the power and speed of the bicycle.*

reflector: *a red object that makes the bicycle visible in the dark by reflecting lights from vehicles behind it and in front of it.*

spoke: *one of the rods connecting the hub to the rim of a wheel.*

tandem: *a bicycle with seats and pedals for two riders.*

gears

chain

---

big

Some words you can use instead of big:

There is a big crowd.
☞ **huge, large, great** ☜

This case is too big for me to lift.
☞ **heavy, weighty** ☜

Canada is a big country.
☞ **vast, huge** ☜

The wedding was a big occasion.
☞ **grand, impressive** ☜

As we sailed close, we saw a big iceberg.
☞ **huge, great, gigantic** ☜

This was a big decision for her to make.
☞ **important, serious** ☜

---

bike **bikes** *noun*
a bicycle.

bill **bills** *noun*
1 a piece of paper showing how much money you have to pay for something. *After we had finished our meal, the waiter brought the bill.*
2 a bird's beak.

bin **bins** *noun*
a container that you put rubbish in.

bind **binds binding bound** *verb*
If you bind something, you tie it up very firmly.

binoculars *noun*
An instrument with two lenses that you look through to make things that are far away look closer.

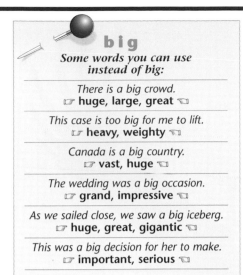

biodegradable *adjective*
Something which is biodegradable will decay naturally. Paper is biodegradable but a lot of plastic is not. ▲ Say *by-oh-dee-gray-da-bul.*

biology *noun*
the scientific study of people, plants and animals.
biological *adjective.*

bird **birds** *noun*
a creature that has wings, feathers and a beak. Most birds can fly.
❖ *Look at page 24*

---

birth **births** *noun*
The birth of a baby is when it comes out of its mother's body.

birthday **birthdays** *noun*
Your birthday is a day that you remember each year because it is the same day as the day you were born.

biscuit **biscuits** *noun*
a small, flat food like a crisp, dry cake. ▲ Say *bis-kit.*

bit **bits** *noun*
1 a piece. *a bit of paper.*
2 a little. *These shoes are a bit too small.*
3 the smallest unit of memory in a computer.

bite **bites biting bit bitten** *verb*
If you bite something, you close your teeth on it. *The dog won't bite you.*
● A word that sounds like **bite** is **byte**.

bitter **bitterest** *adjective*
1 Food which is bitter has a sharp, nasty taste. *bitter medicine.* ■ The opposite is **sweet**.
2 If you are bitter about something, you go on being angry and upset about it a long time after it happened.
3 If the weather is bitter, it is very cold.

blackbird **blackbirds** *noun*
a bird that can often be seen in gardens. The female has brown feathers.

blackboard **blackboards** *noun*
a large, dark-coloured board that you write on with chalk.

blade **blades** *noun*
the sharp edge of a knife or sword.

blame **blames blaming blamed** *verb*
If you blame somebody for something, you say that it is their fault. *My brother blamed me for breaking his computer.*

blank **blanker blankest** *adjective*
If something is blank, it has nothing on it. *a blank sheet of paper.*

blanket **blankets** *noun*
a thick woollen cover for a bed.

A B C D E F G H I J K L M N O P Q R S T U V W X Y Z

BIRDS

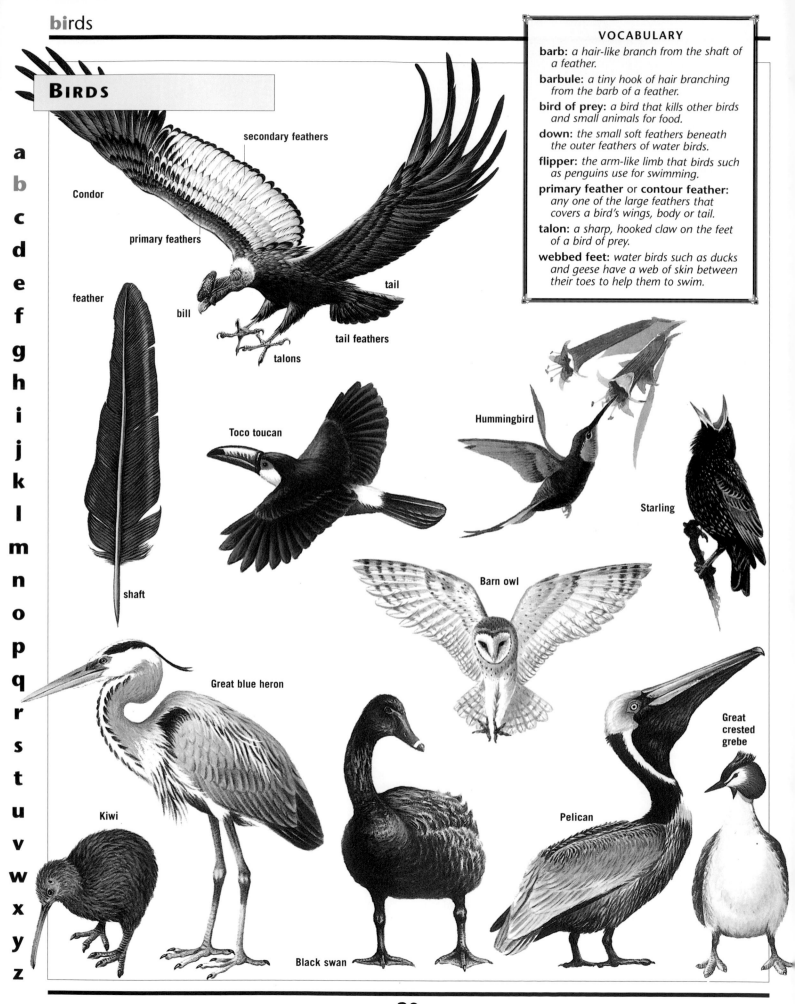

a b c d e f g h i j k l m n o p q r s t u v w x y z

VOCABULARY

barb: *a hair-like branch from the shaft of a feather.*

barbule: *a tiny hook of hair branching from the barb of a feather.*

bird of prey: *a bird that kills other birds and small animals for food.*

down: *the small soft feathers beneath the outer feathers of water birds.*

flipper: *the arm-like limb that birds such as penguins use for swimming.*

primary feather or **contour feather:** *any one of the large feathers that covers a bird's wings, body or tail.*

talon: *a sharp, hooked claw on the feet of a bird of prey.*

webbed feet: *water birds such as ducks and geese have a web of skin between their toes to help them to swim.*

Condor

secondary feathers

primary feathers

tail

bill

talons

tail feathers

feather

shaft

Toco toucan

Hummingbird

Starling

Barn owl

Great blue heron

Kiwi

Black swan

Pelican

Great crested grebe

blast blasts *noun*
an explosion. *One person was injured in the blast when the bomb went off.*

blaze blazes blazing blazed *verb*
When a fire blazes, it burns very strongly. *The forest fire blazed for more than a week.*

bleed bleeds bleeding bled *verb*
When a part of your body bleeds, blood flows out. *Mohammed cut his arm and it started bleeding.*

blew past of **blow**
● A word that sounds like **blew** is **blue**.

blind *adjective*
A person who is blind cannot see.

blind blinds *noun*
a roll of material that you pull down to cover a window.

blindfold blindfolds *noun*
a piece of material tied over somebody's eyes so that they cannot see.

blink blinks blinking blinked *verb*
When you blink, you shut both your eyes and open them again very quickly.

blister blisters *noun*
a small bubble of liquid just under your skin that you get if something has rubbed your skin a lot or if you get burned. *Rosamund's new shoes have given her two large blisters.*

blizzard blizzards *noun*
a snow storm with very strong winds.

block blocks *noun*
1 a thick piece of something solid, with flat sides. *a block of wood.*

2 A block of flats is a large building divided into flats. An office block is a large building divided into offices.

block blocks blocking blocked *verb*
If something blocks a place, it is in the way and nothing can get past. *A fallen tree blocked the road to the school.*

blond, blonde blonder blondest *adjective*
A person who is blond or blonde has light-coloured hair. We use the spelling **blond** for men and boys, and **blonde** for women and girls.

blood *noun*
the red liquid that flows all around your body through your arteries and veins.

bloom blooms blooming bloomed *verb*
When a plant blooms, its flowers come out. *Daffodils bloom in March.*

blossom *noun*
flowers on a tree. *cherry blossom.*

blot blots *noun*
a drop of ink that has spilt on to something and left a mark.

When the clapper hits the side of the bell it makes a ringing sound.

belong belongs belonging belonged *verb*
1 If something belongs to you, it is yours.
2 If you belong to a club or society, you are a member of it.

below *preposition*
If something is below something else, it is underneath it.
■ The opposite is **above**.

belt belts *noun*

blouse blouses *noun*
a piece of clothing like a shirt worn by a girl or woman.

blow blows blowing blew blown *verb*
1 If you blow, you breathe a lot of air out of your mouth at once. *He blew all nine candles out in one go.*
2 When you blow your nose, you breathe out through your nose very hard into a handkerchief.
3 If something blows somewhere, the wind is pushing it along. *Leaves were blowing about in the street.*
blow up If somebody blows something up, they destroy it with an explosion.

blow blows *noun*
a hard hit. *a blow to the head.*

blunt blunter bluntest *adjective*
1 A blunt knife does not cut very well because it is not sharp any more.
2 A blunt object has a rounded or flat end instead of a pointed one. *My pencil is blunt, I'll have to sharpen it.*
3 If you are blunt, you say exactly what you think even if it is not polite or kind.

blur blurs blurring blurred *verb*
When something blurs, you cannot see it clearly. *My eyes were so tired that the TV was beginning to blur.*

blush blushes blushing blushed *verb*
to become red in the face because you are embarrassed or ashamed.
blush *noun*
A blush spread over his cheeks.

board boards *noun*
1 a flat piece of wood or stiff card with straight sides.
2 a blackboard.
● A word that sounds like **board** is **bored**.

boarding-school boarding-schools *noun*
a school where the pupils eat and sleep during the term.

A B C D E F G H I J K L M N O P Q R S T U V W X Y Z

boast boasts boasting boasted *verb*
If you boast about something you have or something you have done, you talk in a way that shows you are too proud of it. *John boasted that his parents had an expensive new car.*

boat boats *noun*
Boats carry people and things across water. Some boats have engines, some have sails, and some you row by using oars or paddles. ❖ *Look at page 147*

body bodies *noun*
1 all of the parts of a person or of an animal that can be seen or touched.
2 a dead person.

boil boils boiling boiled *verb*
1 When liquid boils, it gets so hot that bubbles appear on the surface and it starts to change into steam.
2 When you boil food, you cook it in boiling water. *boiled potatoes.*

boil boils *noun*
a big, painful spot on your skin.

bold bolder boldest *adjective*
A person who is bold is not afraid to do dangerous things.
boldness *noun.*

bolt bolts *noun*
1 a metal bar that slides across to lock a door or window.
2 a metal pin that screws into a metal nut to fasten things together.

door bolt

bolt

nut

bolt bolts bolting bolted *verb*
1 When you bolt a door, you slide a bolt across it so that it cannot be opened.
2 When a person or an animal bolts, they suddenly run away. *The horse was frightened by the noise and bolted across the field.*

bomb bombs *noun*
a weapon containing chemicals that can be made to explode, damaging or destroying everything around it.

bone bones *noun*
A bone is one of the hard parts inside your body that make up your skeleton.

bonfire bonfires *noun*
a fire that is made outdoors to burn rubbish.

bonnet bonnets *noun*
1 the part of a car that covers the engine.
2 a kind of hat that is tied with strings under the chin. Babies sometimes wear bonnets.

book books *noun*
sheets of printed paper fastened together inside a cover.

book books booking booked *verb*
When you book something, you ask somebody to keep it for you. *My Mum phoned the restaurant to book a table for tomorrow evening.*

boomerang boomerangs *noun*
a curved stick that comes back to the person who throws it. The first people who lived in Australia, called Aboriginals, used the boomerang as a weapon for hunting.

boot boots *noun*
1 a shoe that covers your foot and ankle, and sometimes part of your leg.
2 a space usually at the back of a car where you can put luggage.

border borders *noun*
1 the line that separates two countries.
2 a strip around the edge of something which is a different colour or has a different pattern.

bore bores boring bored *verb*
1 If something bores you, you are not interested in it.
2 If you bore into something, you make a hole in it using a drill. *The engineer bored a hole in the rock.*
boredom *noun,* **boring** *adjective.*

bore past of **bear.**

born *adjective*
When a baby is born, it comes out of its mother's body.

borrow borrows borrowing borrowed *verb*
If you borrow something from somebody, they let you have it for a time and then you give it back. *I borrowed some books from the library.* ■ The opposite is **lend.**

boss bosses *noun*
The boss is the person who is in charge.

both *pronoun*
When something is true about two people or things, you can say it is true about both of them. *Both my sister and my aunt are called Mary.*

bother bothers bothering bothered *verb*
1 If something bothers you, it makes you feel worried or uncomfortable.
2 If you bother about something you care about it and take trouble with it.

bottle bottles *noun*
a tall container made of glass or plastic that liquid is kept in. *a milk bottle.*

bottom bottoms *noun*
1 the lowest part of something. ■ The opposite is **top.**
2 Your bottom is the part of your body that you sit on.

bought past of **buy**
▲ Say *bort.*

boulder boulders *noun*
a large, smooth rock.

bounce bounces bouncing bounced *verb*
When something bounces, it hits the ground or another hard surface and moves back up again. *In basketball you have to bounce the ball.*

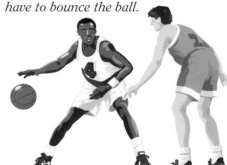

bound bounds bounding bounded *verb*
To bound is to move along by making big jumps. *The dogs were bounding in all directions.*
bound to If something is bound to happen, it will definitely happen.

bound past of **bind**.

bouquet bouquets *noun*
a bunch of flowers. ▲ Say *boo-kay*.

bow bows bowing bowed *verb*
If you bow, you bend your head or body forward. *Actors bow at the end of a play when people clap them.*
▲ Rhymes with **cow**.

bow bows *noun*
1 a long piece of wood with a string fastened at each end that is used to shoot arrows.
2 a knot with two loops.
3 a long, straight piece of wood with horse hair stretched along it and fastened at each end. A bow is used to play a musical instrument such as a violin or double bass.
▲ Rhymes with **no**.

different types of bow

bowl bowls *noun*
a deep, round dish for food or liquids.

bowl bowls bowling bowled *verb*
When you bowl in a game like cricket, you throw the ball towards the person who is batting.

box boxes *noun*
a container, usually with a lid, that is used for packing or storing things.

box boxes boxing boxed *verb*
When people box, they fight with their fists as a sport called boxing.

boy boys *noun*
a male child. ● A word that sounds like **boy** is **buoy**.

brace braces *noun*
a piece of wire that a dentist can fit over your teeth to make them straighter.

bracelet bracelets *noun*
a piece of jewellery that you wear around your wrist.

Braille *noun*
a form of writing made of patterns of raised dots that blind people can read by touching.

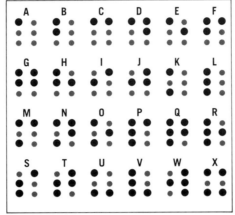

the Braille alphabet

brain brains *noun*
the part inside your head that you use to think and that controls all the parts of your body.

brake brakes *noun*
the part of a bicycle or car which you use to make it go slower or stop. ● A word that sounds like **brake** is **break**.

brake brakes braking braked *verb*
When you brake, you make a bicycle or car go slower or stop by using the brake.
● A word that sounds like **brake** is **break**.

branch branches *noun*
a part of a tree that grows out from the trunk.

brass *noun*
a yellow metal made from copper and another metal called zinc. *This trumpet is made of brass.*

brave braver bravest *adjective*
If you are brave, you will do something frightening or dangerous without showing fear.

bread *noun*
a food made from flour, water and often yeast, and baked in an oven.

break breaks breaking broke broken *verb*
1 If you break something, you damage it so that it is in pieces or does not work any more. *I think I've broken the CD player.* ◆ *He broke the dish.*
2 If you break a promise, you do not do what you promised you would.
3 If you break the law, you do something that is not allowed by law.
● A word that sounds like **break** is **brake**.

break breaks *noun*
a short rest from work. *She's having a tea break.* ● A word that sounds like **break** is **brake**.

breakfast breakfasts *noun*
the first meal of the day.

breast breasts *noun*
A woman's breasts are the two round parts on the front of her chest that can make milk to feed a baby.

breath breaths *noun*
the air that goes in and out of your lungs through your nose or mouth when you breathe.

breathe breathes breathing breathed *verb*
When you breathe, you take air into your lungs through your nose or mouth and then let it out again.

breed breeds *noun*
one kind of an animal. *Spaniels and labradors are different breeds of dog.*

breed breeds breeding bred *verb*
1 If you breed animals, you keep them in order to produce young ones.
2 When animals breed, they produce young ones.

breeze breezes *noun*
a gentle wind.

A B C D E F G H I J K L M N O P Q R S T U V W X Y Z

brick bricks *noun*
a block made out of baked clay that is used for building houses and walls.

bride brides *noun*
a woman on her wedding day.

bridegroom bridegrooms *noun*
a man on his wedding day.

bridesmaid bridesmaids *noun*
a girl or young woman who helps the bride on her wedding day.

bridge bridges *noun*
something built over a river, railway line or road so that people and vehicles can travel from one side to the other.

cantilever bridge

suspension bridge

arch bridge

cable-stayed bridge

brief briefer briefest *adjective*
Something that is brief lasts only a short time. *We had a brief chat.*

bright brighter brightest *adjective*
1 A bright light shines very strongly. ■ The opposite is **dim**.
2 Bright colours are clear and strong. ■ The opposite is **dull** or **dark**.
3 A bright person is clever. ■ The opposite is **stupid**.
▲ Say *brite*.
brightness *noun*.

brilliant *adjective*
1 A brilliant person is very clever.
2 Brilliant light is very bright.
3 very good. *We went to a brilliant disco last night.*

brim brims *noun*
1 If you fill a cup or glass to the brim, you fill it right up to the top.
2 the flat part that sticks out from the edge of a hat.

bristle bristles *noun*
1 a short, stiff hair on an animal.
2 Bristles are the stiff hairs fastened to the handle of a brush.

brittle *adjective*
If something is brittle, it is hard but easy to break. *Eggshells are brittle.*

broad broader broadest *adjective*
wide. *a broad street.* ▲ Rhymes with *cord*. ■ The opposite is **narrow**.

broadcast broadcasts broadcasting broadcast *verb*
When a radio or TV programme is broadcast, it is sent out so that you can hear it on the radio or see it on the TV.

broke, broken past of **break**.

bronze
noun
a brown metal made from a mixture of copper and tin. *All these ancient objects are made of bronze.*

brooch brooches *noun*
a piece of jewellery with a pin that you can fasten on to your clothes. ▲ Rhymes with *coach*.

brook brooks *noun*
a small stream.

broom brooms *noun*
a brush with a long handle for sweeping.

broth *noun*
a clear, thin soup made by boiling meat, fish or vegetables.

brother brothers *noun*
A person's brother is a boy or man who has the same mother and father.

brow brows *noun*
1 a person's forehead.
2 the top of a hill.
▲ Rhymes with *cow*.

bruise bruises *noun*
a dark mark on your skin where something has hit it or you have fallen over and banged it.

brush brushes *noun*
a set of bristles fastened to a handle. You use different sizes and shapes of brush for different jobs like painting, cleaning your teeth or sweeping the floor.

brush brushes brushing brushed *verb*
If you brush something, you clean or tidy it with a brush. *Don't forget to brush your hair.*

bubble bubbles *noun*
a little ball of air or gas that you get in fizzy drinks or boiling water.

bucket buckets *noun*
a large container with a handle used for carrying liquid. *Ned filled a bucket with water and cleaned his bike.*

buckle buckles *noun*
a fastening on a belt or strap. *My belt has a silver buckle.*

bud buds *noun*
a part of a plant that opens up to become a flower or a leaf.

Buddhist Buddhists *noun*
a person who follows a religion started by a religious teacher called Buddha.
▲ Say *buh-dist*.

buffalo buffalo or **buffaloes** *noun*
a large kind of cow that has long, curved horns.

bug bugs *noun*
1 an insect.
2 an illness such as a cold or flu. *There's a nasty bug going around.*

build builds building built *verb*
When you build something, you make it by putting different parts together.

building buildings *noun*
any place which has walls and a roof, like a house, a shop or an office block.

bulb bulbs *noun*
1 the thick, round part of a plant such as a daffodil or tulip that is under the ground, from which the plant grows.
2 the round glass part of a lamp or light.

bull bulls *noun*
the male of the cattle family. Male elephants and whales are also called bulls.

bulldozer bulldozers *noun*
a tractor with a wide blade in front of it which is used to move earth or knock down buildings.

bullet bullets *noun*
a small piece of metal that is fired from a gun.

bully bullies *noun*
a person who hurts or frightens other, weaker people.

bump bumps bumping bumped *verb*
If you bump into something, you hit it by accident. *I wasn't looking where I was going and I bumped into the wall.*

bump bumps *noun*
1 the sound that something makes when it hits something else. *She fell off the chair and landed on the floor with a loud bump.*
2 a round lump or swelling on a surface. *Dad has a bump on his head where he banged it on the ceiling.*
bumpy *adjective*.

bunch bunches *noun*
a group of things. *a bunch of flowers.* ◆ *a bunch of grapes.*

bundle bundles *noun*
a group of things tied together. *Katie tied the stkicks into a bundle.*

bungalow bungalows *noun*
a low house that has only a ground floor.

bunkbeds *noun*
two beds, one above the other.

buoy buoys *noun*
a floating object fastened to the bottom of the sea or a river. A buoy shows a ship where it is dangerous to go. ▲ Say **boy**.

burglar burglars *noun*
a person who gets into a house or shop to steal things.
burgle *verb*.

burglary burglaries *noun*
getting into a house or shop to steal things.

burn burns burning burnt or **burned** *verb*
1 If something is burning, it is on fire.
2 If you burn something, you damage it with fire or heat. *What's that smell? Have you burnt the potatoes?*

burn burns *noun*
a sore place on your skin, or a mark on something caused by fire or heat.

burrow burrows *noun*
a hole or tunnel under the ground where an animal lives. *Prairie dogs live in burrows.*

burst bursts bursting burst *verb*
When something bursts, it breaks open suddenly, especially because there is too much inside. *The little boy was crying because his balloon had burst.*

bury buries burying buried *verb*
When you bury something, you put it in a hole in the ground and cover it up. *Squirrels bury their nuts to store them for winter.* ▲ Say **ber-ee**. ● A word that sounds like **bury** is **berry**.

bus buses *noun*
a large vehicle that carries a lot of passengers by road.

bush bushes *noun*
1 a large plant like a small tree with a lot of branches.
2 The bush is a wild part of the countryside in Australia or Africa.

A B C D E F G H I J K L M N O P Q R S T U V W X Y Z

business businesses *noun*
1 the work of making, buying or selling things. *The company does a lot of business with the United States.*
2 a company or shop that makes or sells things. *a hairdressing business.*
▲ Say *biz-niss.*

busy busier busiest *adjective*
1 If you are busy, you have a lot to do.
2 A place that is busy is full of people doing things. *a busy supermarket.*
▲ Say *biz-ee.*

butcher butchers *noun*
a person whose job is to sell meat.

butter *noun*
a yellow fat made from cream. You spread it on bread and use it in cooking.

butterfly butterflies *noun*
an insect with large, white or coloured wings and a thin body.

button buttons *noun*
1 a small disc for fastening clothes.
2 a small thing that you press to make a machine work.

buy buys buying bought *verb*
When you buy something, you pay somebody money for it. ● Words that sound like **buy** are **by** and **bye**.

byte bytes *noun*
a unit of memory in a computer. One letter or one number takes up one byte.
● A word that sounds like **byte** is **bite**.

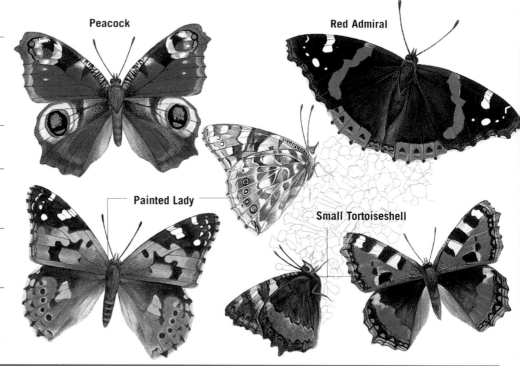

Peacock

Red Admiral

Painted Lady

Small Tortoiseshell

C c

cab cabs *noun*
1 a taxi.
2 the part of a lorry, train or bus where the driver sits.

cabbage cabbages *noun*
a large, round vegetable with green, white or dark-red leaves.
❖ *Look at page 178*

cabin cabins *noun*
1 a bedroom on a ship.
2 the part of a plane where the passengers travel.
3 a small house made of wood. *a log cabin in the forest.*

cable cables *noun*
1 a set of wires that carry electricity, television or radio signals. *an underwater telephone cable.*
2 strong, thick wire or rope.

cable television *noun*
a way of sending television programmes using wires. You have to pay to get cable television.

cactus cactuses or cacti *noun*
a plant with no leaves. Cactuses are covered in sharp spikes. Cactuses store water in their stems and grow in hot, dry places like deserts.

café cafés *noun*
a place where you can buy a drink and something to eat, and sit down to eat it.
▲ Say *kaf-ay.*

cage cages *noun*
a box or room with metal bars for keeping animals or birds in. *a hamster cage.* ◆ *a parrot cage.*

cake cakes *noun*
a sweet food that you usually make by mixing flour, butter, eggs and sugar, and baking it in the oven.

calculator calculators *noun*
a small machine for doing sums quickly. You work a calculator by pressing buttons with numbers on.

calendar calendars *noun*
a list of all the days, weeks and months of one year.

calf calves *noun*
1 a young cow. Young elephants, whales and seals are also called calves.
2 the thick part at the back of your leg, between your knee and your ankle.

call calls calling called *verb*
1 If you call somebody, you shout to them. *"Dinner's ready," he called.*
2 If you call somebody something, you give them that name. *She called the dog Spot.*
3 To call also means to telephone somebody or go to see them. *Did anyone call when we were out?*
call *noun.*

calm calmer calmest *adjective*
1 If you are calm, you are quiet and not afraid.
2 If the sea is calm, there are no big waves on it.
▲ Say *karm.*

camcorder camcorders *noun*
a camera that can take moving pictures and record sound.

camel camels *noun*
an animal with one or two humps on its back. Camels are used to carry people and things in the desert because they can travel for a long time without water.

camera cameras *noun*
a machine for taking photographs or making films.

camouflage camouflages camouflaging camouflaged *verb*
If somebody or something is camouflaged, you cannot see it because it is the same colour or shape as things around it. *This gecko is camouflaged by the ground it is sitting on.*
▲ Say *kam-o-flaj.*
camouflage *noun.*

a camouflaged gecko

camp camps *noun*
a place where people live in tents or stay in tents on holiday.

Spelling tip:
....
Some words that begin with a "ca" sound are spelt with "ka", for example kangaroo, karate.

camp camps camping camped *verb*
When you camp, you live in a tent or have a holiday in a tent.
go camping *We're going camping this summer in Scotland.*

can cans *noun*
a metal container for food, drink or paint. *a can of fizzy drink.*

canal canals *noun*
a long, narrow strip of water made for boats and barges to travel along.

cancel cancels cancelling cancelled *verb*
If you cancel something that you have planned, you stop it from happening. *We cancelled our trip because Mum was ill.*

cancer *noun*
a serious illness that makes some cells inside the body grow too fast.

candle candles *noun*
a stick made of wax with a string called a wick inside. You light the wick and the candle burns to give light.

cane canes *noun*
1 the hard, hollow stem of some plants such as sugar cane. You can make chairs and tables out of cane.
2 a long, thin stick, sometimes used as a walking stick.

cannon cannons *noun*
a big gun that fires heavy metal balls, or shells that explode.

canoe canoes *noun*
a light, thin boat that you move with a paddle. ▲ Say *kan-oo.*

canopy canopies *noun*
1 a piece of material over a door or window that keeps the sun out.
2 a cover over something. *Tall trees form a canopy over the rainforest floor.*

canvas canvases *noun*
strong material that is used for making sails, tents or shoes.

canyon canyons *noun*
a deep, rocky valley. *In the United States the Colorado river flows through the famous Grand Canyon.*

cap caps *noun*
1 a flat hat with a peak at the front. *a baseball cap.*
2 the top of a jar, bottle or pen.

cape capes *noun*
1 a piece of land that sticks out into the sea. *Cape Horn.* ◆ *Cape Canaveral.*
2 a loose coat with no sleeves that you wrap around your shoulders.

capital capitals *noun*
1 the most important city in a country. *Rome is the capital of Italy.*
2 a big letter in the alphabet. *The name Mark starts with a capital M.*

captain captains *noun*
1 the person in charge of a ship or an aircraft.
2 an officer in the army or navy.
3 the leader of a sports team. *a football captain.*

capture captures capturing captured *verb*
If you capture a person or an animal, you catch them and keep them in a place where they cannot escape. *The police captured the robbers.*

A B C D E F G H I J K L M N O P Q R S T U V W X Y Z

car **cars** *noun*
a machine with an engine and four wheels for travelling on the road. The driver uses the steering wheel to turn the car, and stops it by putting a foot on the brake.

caravan **caravans** *noun*
1 a vehicle that you can live in or use for holidays. Some caravans can be pulled along by a car.
2 a group of people, and animals, such as camels, that travel together.

card **cards** *noun*
1 stiff, thick paper.
2 a piece of stiff, thick paper with a picture and message on it. We send cards on birthdays and other special occasions.
3 one of a pack of 52 cards that you play games with. Each pack has four groups of cards called suits. These are hearts, diamonds, clubs and spades.

cardboard *noun*
very thick card. *It's made of cardboard.*

cardigan **cardigans** *noun*
a knitted jacket with buttons down the front.

care **cares caring cared** *verb*
1 If you care about somebody or something, you think they are important. *Jimmy cared for his puppy a great deal.*
2 If you care for somebody or something, you look after them.

care *noun*
If you do something with care, you try not to make a mistake or break something. *Wash the glasses with care.*

career **careers** *noun*
a job that you learn to do and then do for a long time. *a career in teaching.*

careful *adjective*
If you are careful, you think about what you are doing so that you do it safely and well. *Be careful when you cross the road.* ■ The opposite is **careless**. **carefully** *adverb*.

careless *adjective*
If you are careless, you make mistakes because you are not thinking about what you are doing. ■ The opposite is **careful**.

carnival **carnivals** *noun*
a special time when people dress up in colourful clothes and sing, dance and play music as they move through the streets. *a dancer at a carnival.*

carpenter **carpenters** *noun*
a person who makes or mends wooden things such as chairs, tables or doors.

carpet **carpets** *noun*
a thick cover for the floor. Carpets are often made of wool.

carriage **carriages** *noun*
1 one of the separate parts of a train where the passengers travel.
2 an old-fashioned vehicle with wheels that is pulled by horses.

carrot **carrots** *noun*
a long, orange-coloured vegetable that grows under the ground.

carry **carries carrying carried** *verb*
When you carry something, you pick it up and take it to another place. *Tom carried the books upstairs.*

cart **carts** *noun*
a wooden vehicle with two or four wheels that is pulled by a horse or donkey.

carton **cartons** *noun*
a cardboard or plastic box for holding food or drink. *a carton of milk.*

cartoon **cartoons** *noun*
1 a film that uses drawings instead of real people or animals.
2 a drawing in a newspaper or magazine that is funny or makes a joke.

cartwheel **cartwheels** *noun*
If you do a cartwheel, you put your hands on the ground and swing your legs over sideways in a complete circle, ending up standing on your feet again.

carve **carves carving carved** *verb*
1 If you carve wood or stone, you cut it to make a shape out of it.
2 If you carve cooked meat, you cut it into slices.

case **cases** *noun*
1 a bag that you carry things in when you go on holiday. *a suitcase.*
2 a container such as a pencil case.
3 a crime that the police are trying to solve. *The detective was working on a murder case.*

cash *noun*
money in coins and paper notes.

cassette **cassettes** *noun*
a plastic box with magnetic tape inside it which you can use to record and play music and other sounds. You can record and play moving pictures on a video cassette.

cast **casts** *noun*
1 all the actors in a play or film.
2 a hard plaster covering that holds a broken arm or leg in place while it is healing.

cast casts casting cast *verb*
1 If you cast something like a fishing line, you throw it.
2 If somebody in a story casts a spell, they use magic to trick somebody. *The wicked witch cast a spell on the prince and changed him into a frog.*

castle castles *noun*
a large building with thick, high walls. Castles were built long ago to keep the people who lived inside them safe from their enemies.
❖ *Look at page 34*

casualty casualties *noun*
1 a person who is hurt or killed in an accident or a war. *There were three casualties in the road accident.*
2 a department in a hospital where people go for emergency treatment when they have an accident or suddenly become ill.

cat cats *noun*
a furry mammal with sharp claws. Small cats are kept as pets. Big cats such as lions and tigers live in the wild.

catalogue catalogues *noun*
1 a book listing all the things that a company or shop sells.
2 a list of all the books or other things in a library.

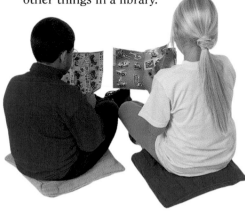

catapult catapults *noun*
a stick, shaped like a Y, with a piece of elastic stretched over it. You pull the elastic to shoot small stones.

catch catches catching caught *verb*
1 If you catch a ball, you take hold of it when it is moving.

2 If you catch a person or an animal, you stop them from running away.
3 If you catch a train or bus, you get on it to go somewhere.
4 If you catch an illness, you get it. *He caught a cold.*

caterpillar caterpillars *noun*
a small animal like a hairy worm that will turn into a butterfly or moth.

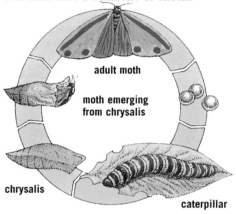

adult moth

moth emerging from chrysalis

chrysalis

caterpillar

cathedral cathedrals *noun*
a large, important church. *St Paul's Cathedral is in London.*

A B C D E F G H I J K L M N O P Q R S T U V W X Y Z

CATS

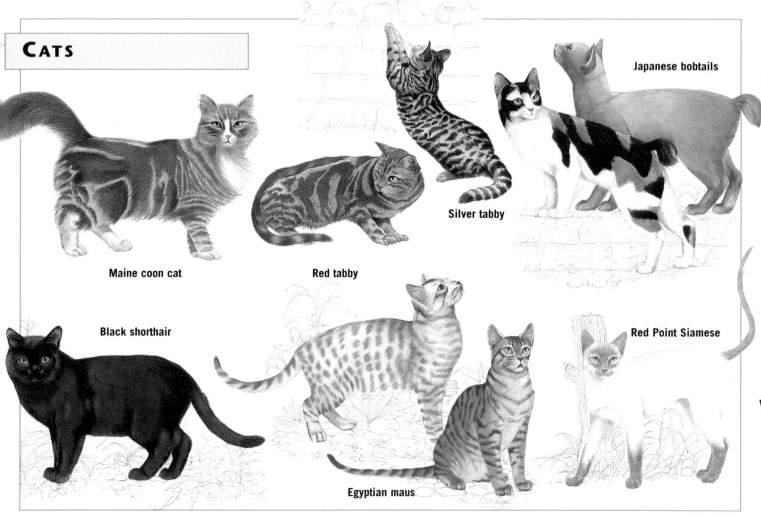

Maine coon cat

Red tabby

Silver tabby

Japanese bobtails

Black shorthair

Red Point Siamese

Egyptian maus

CASTLE

a b c d e f g h i j k l m n o p q r s t u v w x y z

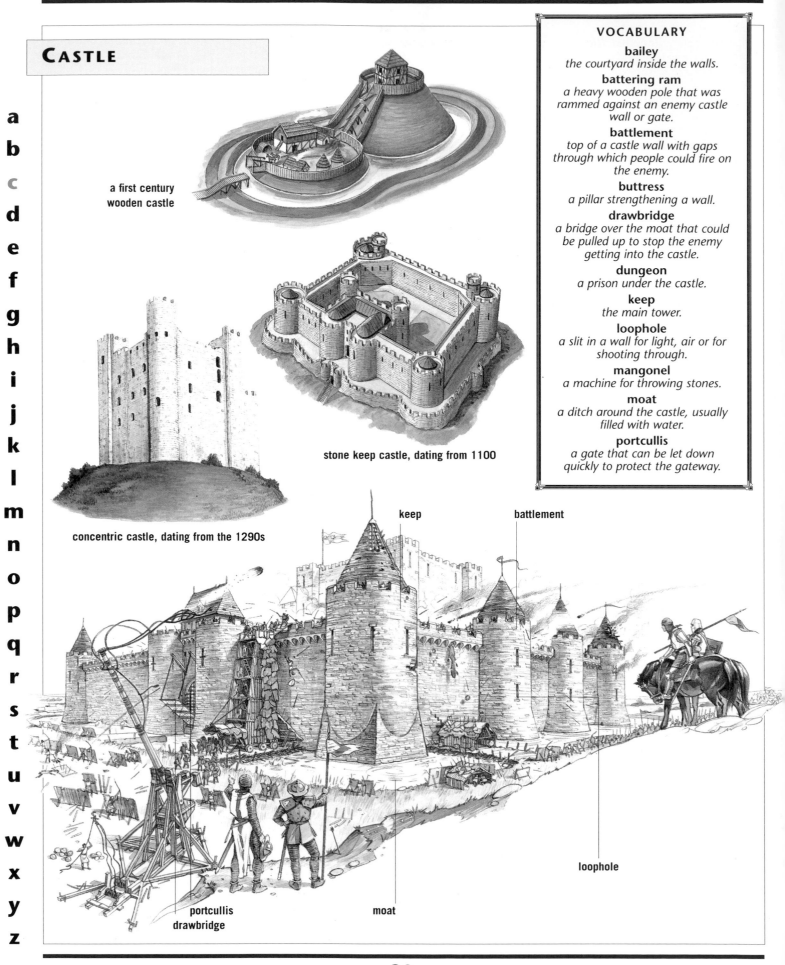

a first century wooden castle

concentric castle, dating from the 1290s

stone keep castle, dating from 1100

keep

battlement

loophole

portcullis
drawbridge

moat

cattle *noun*
cows and bulls. *a herd of cattle.*

caught past of **catch.**

cauliflower **cauliflowers** *noun*
a large, round white vegetable with green leaves on the outside.

cause **causes causing caused** *verb*
If you cause something, you make it happen. *Keep your dog on a lead or you'll cause an accident.*

cautious *adjective*
If you are cautious, you are very careful because of danger.

cave **caves** *noun*
a big hole under the ground, or in the side of a mountain or cliff.

CD **CDs** *noun*
a flat, round piece of plastic which can store music or information. CD is short for **compact disc.**

CD-ROM **CD-ROMs** *noun*
a disc that you use with a computer or a television to show words and pictures. CD-ROM is short for **compact disc read-only memory.**

ceiling **ceilings** *noun*
the top part of a room over your head. *The light is hanging from the ceiling.*

celebrate **celebrates celebrating celebrated** *verb*
When you celebrate something, you do something that you enjoy at a special time. *Let's have a party to celebrate your birthday.*
celebration *noun.*

celery *noun*
a vegetable with a white or pale green stem that you can eat raw or cooked.

cell **cells** *noun*
1 one of the tiny parts that make up all animals and plants. The human body contains millions of red blood cells.

2 a small room in a prison or police station where people are locked up.
● A word that sounds like **cell** is **sell.**

cellar **cellars** *noun*
a room under a building where you store things such as wine or coal.

cello **cellos** *noun*
a musical instrument like a big violin that you sit and hold between your knees. You play it by sliding a bow across the strings. ▲ Say **chell**-oh.
cellist *noun.*

cement *noun*
a grey powder that becomes hard like stone when you mix it with water and leave it to dry. Cement is used for building.

cemetery **cemeteries** *noun*
a place where dead people are buried.

centipede **centipedes** *noun*
a tiny animal like a worm but with many sets of legs.

central *adjective*
in the middle. *I live in central London.*

centre **centres** *noun*
1 the middle of something. *The table was in the centre of the room.*
2 a place where people go to do something special, such as a sports centre or a shopping centre.

century **centuries** *noun*
1 100 years.
2 a time of 100 years that we use in dates. The 20th century is the time between 1900 and 1999.

cereal **cereals** *noun*
Cereals are plants such as rice and wheat that produce grain. We use the grain of cereal plants to make flour and bread. The cereal that you eat for breakfast is also made from cereals such as rice and wheat. ● A word that sounds like **cereal** is **serial.**

rice   wheat   rye   oats   barley

ceremony **ceremonies** *noun*
the actions and words that are used at a special and important event such as a wedding.

certain *adjective*
1 If you are certain about something, you are sure it is true. *I'm certain I saw him yesterday.*
2 If something happens at a certain time, it happens then and not at other times. *The swimming pool is open all day at weekends, but only at certain times during the week.*

certificate **certificates** *noun*
an important piece of paper that shows that something is true. *birth certificate.*

chain **chains** *noun*
A chain is made from rings of metal joined together. *a bicycle chain.*

chair **chairs** *noun*
a seat with four legs and a back, for one person to sit on.

chalk **chalks** *noun*
1 soft, white rock.
2 a stick of soft, white or coloured material used for writing on a blackboard.
▲ Say **chork.**

challenge **challenges challenging challenged** *verb*
If you challenge somebody, you ask them to try to do something better than you. *Tom challenged Paul to a race.*

challenge **challenges** *noun*
If something is a challenge, it is difficult to do. *These sums are a real challenge!*

champion **champions** *noun*
a person who is the best at a sport or game. *Jazz is the champion.*

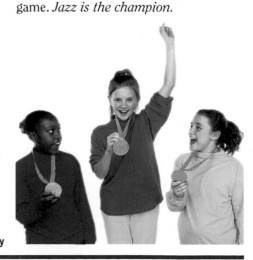

31

chance chances *noun*
1 a time when you can do something. *It was their last chance to escape.*
2 If there is a chance that something will happen, it might happen. *There's a chance it will rain today.*
by chance If something happens by chance, it happens without being planned.

change changes changing changed *verb*
1 When something changes, it becomes different. *Tadpoles change into frogs.*
2 If you change your clothes, you put on different ones. *Katie changed into her jeans.*

change changes *noun*
1 If there is a change in something, it is different now.
2 the money that you get back if you have paid too much for something.
3 coins like £1, 50p, 20p, 10p and 5p. *Do you have change for the phone?*

channel channels *noun*
1 a narrow sea.
2 a television station. *Which channel is the programme on?*

chapter chapters *noun*
a part of a book.

character characters *noun*
1 the way a person or thing is. *She has a kind and loving character.*
2 a person in a play, film or book.

charge charges charging charged *verb*
1 If somebody charges you a certain amount of money for something, they are asking you to pay that amount. *He charged me 50p for the fruit.*
2 When the police charge somebody, they say that person has done something wrong.
3 If you charge at somebody or something, you run towards them very fast. *The bull charged at the fence.*
4 If you charge a battery, you pass an electric current through it to make it work. *She charged the battery in her mobile phone to keep it working.*

charge charges *noun*
the money that you have to pay for something. *There is a charge of £1 to get into the museum.*
in charge If you are in charge, you are the leader of a group of people. *The headteacher is in charge of the school.*

chariot chariots *noun*
a vehicle with two wheels pulled by a horse. Chariots were used in wars and races a long time ago.

charity charities *noun*
an organization which collects money to help people who need it.

chart charts *noun*
1 a drawing that shows important dates or numbers. *The chart shows how long different animals live.*
2 a map of the sea or the stars.

Animal lifespans

Turtle

Elephant

Chimpanzee

Lion

Dog

10 20 30 40 50 60 70 80 90 100
Numbers of years

chase chases chasing chased *verb*
If you chase somebody, you run after them and try to catch them.

cheap cheaper cheapest *adjective*
Something that is cheap does not cost a lot of money. ■ The opposite is **expensive** or **dear**.

cheat cheats cheating cheated *verb*
If somebody cheats, they do something that is not fair, or that breaks the rules. *Play the game without cheating!*

check checks checking checked *verb*
When you check something, you look at it again to make sure that it is right. *Check your spellings in the dictionary.*
● A word that sounds like **check** is **cheque**.

check *noun*
a pattern of squares. ● A word that sounds like **check** is **cheque**.
checked *adjective*
a checked shirt.

cheek cheeks *noun*
Your cheeks are the soft parts on each side of your face.

cheerful *adjective*
If you are cheerful, you feel happy.
cheerfully *adverb*.

cheese cheeses *noun*
a white or yellow food made from milk. *Some cheese has a strong flavour.*

cheetah cheetahs *noun*
a large, wild cat that can run very fast.

chef chefs *noun*
a person who cooks food in a restaurant. ▲ Say *sheff*.

chemical chemicals *noun*
a substance that is made by chemistry or used in chemistry.

chemist chemists *noun*
1 The chemist's is a shop where you can buy medicine and things such as soap and toothbrushes.
2 a person who prepares and sells medicines.
3 a scientist who works with chemicals.

chemistry *noun*
the scientific study of what substances are made of and how they work together.

cheque cheques *noun*
a piece of paper that people use to pay for things. When you pay by cheque, you write the price and sign your name on it. ● A word that sounds like **cheque** is **check**.

cherry cherries *noun*
a small, round, red, yellow or black fruit. Cherries have a hard seed called a stone in the middle.

chess *noun*
a game that two people play with 16 chesspieces on a board with black and white squares.

chest chests *noun*
1 Your chest is the front part of your body between your neck and your waist.
2 a big, strong box with a lid. *The pirates stored gold in a wooden chest.*

chew chews chewing chewed *verb*
When you chew food, you use your teeth to make it soft and to break it into smaller pieces.

chick chicks *noun*
a baby bird.

chicken chickens *noun*
a bird that people keep on farms for its eggs and meat.

chickenpox *noun*
an illness that gives you lots of itchy spots.

chief chiefs *noun*
the leader of a group of people.

child children *noun*
1 a young boy or girl.
2 a son or daughter. *They have two children.*

childhood *noun*
the time when you are a boy or girl, before you grow up. *He had a happy childhood.*

childish *adjective*
If you are childish, you are being silly and acting younger than your age.

chilli chillies *noun*
a small, red or green vegetable. Chillies have a very hot taste.

chilly chillier chilliest *adjective*
If you are chilly, you feel quite cold.

chime chimes chiming chimed *verb*
When a bell or a clock chimes, it makes a ringing sound. *The clock chimed midnight.*

chimney chimneys *noun*
a large pipe above a fire that lets smoke and gas go outside into the air.

chimpanzee chimpanzees *noun*
a small African ape. Chimpanzees are clever animals.

chin chins *noun*
Your chin is the part of your face below your mouth.

china *noun*
things such as cups and jugs made from a kind of white clay. It breaks easily.

chip chips *noun*
1 a long, thin piece of fried potato.
2 a tiny piece of a material called silicon that has an electronic circuit on it. Chips are used in computers.
3 a small piece that has broken off something, or the gap that is left. *This plate has a small chip in it.*

chip chips chipping chipped *verb*
If you chip something, you accidentally break a small part off. *a chipped plate.*

chisel chisels *noun*
a long, thin tool with a sharp, flat edge at one end. You use it to cut wood or stone.

chocolate chocolates *noun*
1 sweet, brown food made from cocoa.
2 a sweet made of chocolate. *a box of chocolates.*

choice choices *noun*
1 all the things you can choose from. *There's a wide choice of books in the library.*
2 a person or thing that you choose.

choir choirs *noun*
a group of singers. ▲ Say *kwire*.

choke chokes choking choked *verb*
If you choke, you cannot breathe because something is blocking your throat. *Tom choked on a fish bone.*

choose chooses choosing chose chosen *verb*
When you choose something, you take it because it is the thing you want.

chop chops chopping chopped *verb*
If you chop something, you cut it with a knife or an axe. *Ricky is chopping carrots with his mum.*

chord chords *noun*
a group of notes that you play at the same time in a piece of music. ▲ Say *kord*. ● A word that sounds like chord is cord.

chorus choruses *noun*
the part of a song that you repeat at the end of each verse. ▲ Say *kor-uss*.

chose, chosen past of **choose**.

Christian Christians *noun*
a person who believes in and follows the teachings of Jesus Christ. *Italy is a Christian country.* **Christianity** *noun*.

chrysalis chrysalises *noun*
a moth or a butterfly at the stage between a caterpillar and an adult, when it has a hard case around it. ▲ Say *kriss-e-liss*. ❖ *Look at page 33*

chuckle chuckles chuckling chuckled *verb*
When you chuckle, you laugh quietly to yourself.

church churches *noun*
a building where Christians hold religious services.

cinema cinemas *noun*
a building where people go to watch films.

A B C D E F G H I J K L M N O P Q R S T U V W X Y Z

a b c d e f g h i j k l m n o p q r s t u v w x y z

circle circles *noun*
1 a flat, round shape like a ring.
2 a part of a theatre or cinema where you sit upstairs.
circle *verb*
The plane circled the airport.

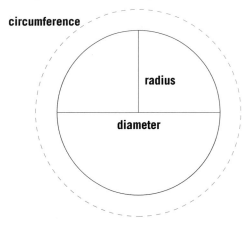

circumference

radius

diameter

circuit circuits *noun*
1 a complete path that an electric current can flow around.
2 a path or road in the shape of a circle. *a motor racing circuit.*

circular *adjective*
round like a circle. *a circular table.*

circulation *noun*
the movement of blood around the body. Blood is pumped by the heart and travels in arteries and veins.

circumference circumferences *noun*
the distance around the edge of a circle.

circus circuses *noun*
a travelling show with people such as acrobats and clowns. A circus is held in a big, round tent.

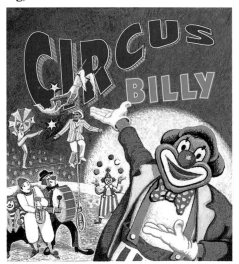

city cities *noun*
a big and important town.

civilization civilizations *noun*
1 the way people live in a certain place and at a certain time. *We're learning about civilization in ancient Greece.*
2 living in a group with lots of laws and certain ways of doing things, not living wild in a forest.

claim claims claiming claimed *verb*
1 If you claim something, you say it is yours. *Nobody has claimed the watch I found.*
2 If you claim that something is true, you say it is true. *She claimed the dog had eaten her homework.*

clap claps clapping clapped *verb*
When you clap, you hit your hands together to make a noise. You clap to show you have enjoyed something.

clash clashes clashing clashed *verb*
1 When metal objects clash, they hit together making a loud, banging sound. *cymbals clash.*
2 If colours clash, they do not look good together. *Do you think red and orange clash?*

class classes *noun*
1 a group of people who learn together. *Sam and I are in the same class at school.*
2 a group of people, animals or things that are the same in some way.

classical *adjective*
in a style that has been used for a long time because people think it is good. *classical music.*

classroom classrooms *noun*
a room in a school where you have lessons.

claw claws *noun*
the long, sharp nails that an animal or bird has on its feet.

clay *noun*
sticky red or grey earth that becomes hard when it is dry. Clay is used to make pots and bricks.

clean cleaner cleanest *adjective*
Something that is clean does not have any dirt or marks on it. *clean clothes.*

clean cleans cleaning cleaned *verb*
When you clean something, you make it clean. *Don't forget to clean your teeth.*
■ *The opposite is* **dirty.**

clear clearer clearest *adjective*
1 easy to see, hear or understand. *a clear photograph.*
2 easy to see through. Most glass is clear.
3 free from things that are blocking the way or covering something. *A clear sky does not have any clouds.*

clear clears clearing cleared *verb*
When you clear something, you take away things that you do not want or need. *We cleared the snow from the path.*

clever cleverer cleverest *adjective*
A person who is clever can learn and understand things quickly.

cliff cliffs *noun*
the high, steep side of a hill by the sea.

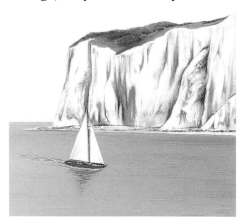

climate climates *noun*
the kind of weather that a place usually has. *India has a hot climate.*

climb climbs climbing climbed *verb*
When you climb something, you move up using your hands and feet. *Ella is climbing up Rishi's back.*
climber *noun*.

cling clings clinging clung *verb*
If you cling to somebody or something, you hold on to them very tightly. *I clung to my mum because I was afraid.*

clinic clinics *noun*
a place where you go to see a doctor.

clip clips *noun*
a small metal or plastic object used for holding things together. *a paper-clip.*

clip clips clipping clipped *verb*
If you clip something, such as a hedge or your fingernails, you cut small pieces off to make it neater.

cloak cloaks *noun*
a long, loose coat with no sleeves. *The king wore a velvet cloak.*

clock clocks *noun*
a machine that tells you the time.

clockwise *adjective, adverb*
If you turn clockwise, you move in the same direction as the hands on a clock.
■ The opposite is **anticlockwise**.

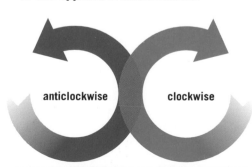

anticlockwise   clockwise

.......Spelling tip:.......
Some words that begin with a "co" sound are spelt with a "ko", for example koala.

close closes closing closed *verb*
When you close something, you shut it. *He closed the drawer quietly.*
▲ Rhymes with **nose**. ■ The opposite is **open**.

close closer closest *adjective*
1 near, not remote. *I live close to school.*
2 If you are close to someone, you like them very much. *Richard and Raj are close friends.*
▲ Rhymes with **dose**.

cloth cloths *noun*
1 material made from something such as cotton or wool that we use to make clothes and other things.
2 a piece of material used for cleaning. *She wiped the table with a cloth.*

clothes *noun*
Clothes are things such as jeans, skirts, jumpers and coats that you wear.

cloud clouds *noun*
Clouds are made of millions of drops of water which sometimes fall as rain. On a cloudy day, the sky is full of white or grey clouds.

clown clowns *noun*
a person in a circus who wears funny clothes and makes people laugh.

club clubs *noun*
a group of people who meet to do something that they are all interested in. *a swimming club.*◆ *a chess club.*

clue clues *noun*
something that helps you to find the answer to a puzzle or a mystery. *I can't guess who it is. Give me a clue.*

clump clumps *noun*
a group of plants growing together. *a clump of grass.*

---

clumsy clumsier clumsiest *adjective*
If somebody is clumsy, they often fall over and drop things.
clumsily *adverb*.

clung past of **cling**.

clutch clutches clutching clutched *verb*
If you clutch something, you hold it tightly. *The child clutched her mother's hand when they crossed the road.*

clutch clutches *noun*
the pedal in a car or other vehicle that you press when you change gear.

coach coaches *noun*
1 a bus that takes people on long journeys.
2 a large carriage that is pulled along by horses.
3 a person who teaches people a sport. *a tennis coach.*

coal *noun*
a hard, black substance that is dug out of the ground and burnt to give heat. Coal is made from plants that died millions of years ago.

coast coasts *noun*
the part of the land that is next to the sea. *a day trip to the coast.*

coat coats *noun*
1 You wear a coat on top of your other clothes to go out when it is cold.
2 The fur that an animal has is called a coat. *A leopard has a spotted coat.*

cobweb cobwebs *noun*
a net that a spider makes to catch insects.

cock cocks *noun*
1 a male bird.
2 a fully grown male chicken.

cockerel cockerels *noun*
a young male chicken.

A B C D E F G H I J K L M N O P Q R S T U V W X Y Z

cockpit cockpits *noun*
the front part of a plane where the pilot sits. The part of a racing car where the driver sits is also called a cockpit.

cocoa *noun*
1 a brown powder made from the beans of the cacao tree and used to make chocolate.
2 a drink made from cocoa powder mixed with hot milk.

coconut coconuts *noun*
a large, round fruit with a hard, hairy brown shell. Inside there is a milky juice and sweet, white flesh that you can eat. Coconuts grow on palm trees in hot countries.

coconut shell and edible seed

cocoon cocoons *noun*
a bundle of silky threads that some young insects make to cover themselves while they are developing into adults.

cod cod *noun*
a large sea fish that you can eat.

code codes *noun*
1 If you write something in code, you mix up the letters or change them into special signs. Only the people who know the code can read the message.
2 a group of letters or numbers that give information about something. *The postcode for this area of London is W1P 7AD.*
3 a collection of laws or rules. *the Highway code.*

coffee *noun*
1 a brown powder made from the roasted and ground beans of the coffee tree. You use coffee to make drinks.
2 a hot drink that you make by mixing coffee powder with hot water.

coffin coffins *noun*
a box in which a dead person is buried.

cog cogs *noun*
1 a wheel with teeth around the edge. Cogs are used in machines to turn other things.
2 The teeth around the edge of the wheel are also called cogs.

coil coils *noun*
a thing that is twisted around into circles. *a coil of rope.*
coil *verb*
The snake coiled around the branch.

coin coins *noun*
a flat, usually round piece of metal that we use as money.

coincidence coincidences *noun*
A coincidence is when two things happen at the same time or in the same place by chance. ▲ Say *koh-in-si-denss.*

cold colder coldest *adjective*
1 not hot or warm. Ice and snow are cold.
2 unfriendly. *He gave me a cold look.*

cold colds *noun*
an illness that makes you sneeze and cough. *Lucy caught a cold.*

collage collages *noun*
a picture that you make by sticking lots of bits of material or paper on to a surface. ▲ Say *kol-arj.*

collapse collapses collapsing collapsed *verb*
1 If something collapses, it falls down suddenly. *The tent collapsed.*
2 If somebody collapses, they fall over because they are ill. *She collapsed in the street and was taken to hospital.*

collar collars *noun*
1 the part of a shirt or coat that goes around your neck.
2 a band that you put around the neck of a pet dog or cat.

collect collects collecting collected *verb*
1 When you collect things, you bring them together. *Please collect the dirty plates and put them in the sink.*
2 If you collect things such as stamps, you keep a lot of them because you like them. *I collect shells.*
3 When you collect somebody, you go and bring them back from somewhere. *Mum collects me from school.*
collection *noun*
a stamp collection.

college colleges *noun*
a place where people go to study when they have left school.

collide collides colliding collided *verb*
If something collides with another thing, it crashes into it. *The bus collided with a lorry.*
collision *noun.*

colour colours *noun*
Red, blue, yellow and green are colours.
colourful *adjective.*
❖ *Look at page 145*

column columns *noun*
1 a tall piece of stone that holds up part of a building or stands on its own.
2 a long, thin strip of writing in a book or newspaper.

coma comas *noun*
If somebody is in a coma, they are in a very deep sleep and cannot wake up for a long time. People who have had a serious accident sometimes go into a coma.

comb **combs** *noun*
a flat piece of metal or plastic with teeth along one edge. You use it to make your hair tidy. ▲ Rhymes with **home**.
comb *verb*.

combine **combines combining combined** *verb*
When you combine things, you join or mix them together.
combination *noun*.

combine harvester **combine harvesters** *noun*
a large machine that is used on a farm. It cuts corn and collects the seeds.

comedy **comedies** *noun*
a funny play, film or TV programme.

comet **comets** *noun*
a thing in space that looks like a star with a tail and moves around the Sun.

comfortable *adjective*
If something is comfortable, it is nice to wear, sit in or lie on. *a comfortable bed.*
comfortably *adverb*.

comic **comics** *noun*
1 a magazine that tells stories in pictures.
2 a person who tells jokes and makes people laugh.

comma **commas** *noun*
a mark (**,**) that you use in writing. You put commas between words in a list. *Katie, Tom, Lucy and I went to the park.*

command **commands commanding commanded** *verb*
If somebody commands you to do something, they tell you that you must do it. *He commanded the soldiers to march to the village.*

comment **comments** *noun*
If you make a comment about something, you say what you think about it.

common *adjective*
1 If a thing is common, it exists in large numbers. *Robins and sparrows are common birds.*
2 Something that happens often is common. *These days it is common for people to have computers at home.*
■ The opposite is **rare**.

communicate **communicates communicating communicated** *verb*
If you communicate with somebody, you talk or write to them. *Pilots communicate with the airport by radio.*

communications *noun*
Communications are ways of sending information to people, or ways of moving from one place to another. Roads, railways and telephones are communications.

compact disc **compact discs** *noun*
a flat, round piece of plastic which can store music or information. Also known as a **CD**.

company **companies** *noun*
1 a group of people who work together to make or sell something.
2 being with others so that you are not alone. *My granny lives alone so she has a cat for company.*

compare **compares comparing compared** *verb*
When you compare two things, you look at them both together so that you can see in what ways they are the same or different. *When you have finished the sums, compare your answers with the ones in the back of the book.*
comparison *noun*.

compartment **compartments** *noun*
1 a small room in a train where people sit or sleep.
2 a part of a container. *My bag has separate compartments for my pencil case and hair brush.*

compass **compasses** *noun*
A compass helps walkers and sailors tell which direction they are going in. It has a magnetic needle that always points north.

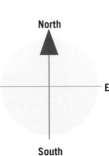

compasses *noun*
a tool that you use for drawing circles. One arm has a sharp point and the other holds a pencil. You hold the pointed arm still and move the other around it.

competition **competitions** *noun*
a game or test that people try to win. *Sophie won first prize in the painting competition.*

complain **complains complaining complained** *verb*
If you complain about something, you say that you are not happy about it or that it makes you angry. *He complained about having to tidy his room.*
complaint *noun*.

complete *adjective*
1 If something is complete, it has no parts missing. *a complete pack of cards.*
2 in every way. *a complete surprise.*
completely *adverb*, **complete** *verb*.

complicated *adjective*
If something is complicated, it is difficult to do or understand. *The story had a very complicated plot.*

compliment **compliments** *noun*
If somebody pays you a compliment, they say something nice about you.

compose **composes composing composed** *verb*
To compose means to write music or poetry. *Beethoven composed nine symphonies.*
composer *noun*.

compulsory *adjective*
having to be done. *Studying maths is compulsory in all schools.*

computer **computers** *noun*
a machine that can solve problems quickly, store information or control other machines.

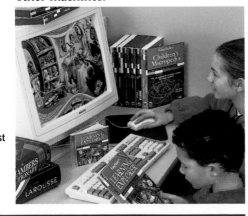

A B C D E F G H I J K L M N O P Q R S T U V W X Y Z

a b c d e f g h i j k l m n o p q r s t u v w x y z

conceal conceals concealing concealed *verb*
If you conceal something, you hide it. *She concealed the box under the bed.*

concentrate concentrates concentrating concentrated *verb*
If you concentrate on something, you give all your attention to it. *Please be quiet, I can't concentrate on my book.*

concerned *adjective*
If you are concerned about something, you worry about it.

concert concerts *noun*
a performance of music to a big group of people.

conclusion conclusions *noun*
1 the end of something. *The story had a sad conclusion.*
2 If you come to a conclusion about something, you decide what happened and why it happened. *We came to the conclusion that she went home because she was very ill.*

concrete *noun*
a building material made from cement, sand and small stones mixed with water that goes hard when it dries.

condition conditions *noun*
1 how somebody or something is. *The car is old, but it's still in good condition.*
2 how things are around you. *The animals in the zoo lived in terrible conditions.*
3 something that you must do before you are allowed to do something else. *You can go out on condition that you tidy your room first.*

conductor conductors *noun*
a person who stands in front of a group of musicians and controls how they play a piece of music.

cone cones *noun*
1 a solid shape that is pointed at the top and rounded at the bottom.
2 the hard fruit of a pine or fir tree.

confess confesses confessing confessed *verb*
If you confess something, you say that you have done something wrong. *Luke confessed that he had broken the fence.* **confession** *noun*.

confidence *noun*
the feeling that you can do something well. *She climbed the tree with confidence.*
confident *adjective*.

confuse confuses confusing confused *verb*
1 If you confuse somebody, you mix up their ideas so that they cannot understand. *My sister tried to explain the rules of the game to me but she went too quickly and I got confused.*
2 If you confuse two things, you mix them up so that you cannot tell the difference between them. *I always confuse the words "there" and "their" because they sound the same.*
confusing *adjective*, **confusion** *noun*.

congratulate congratulates congratulating congratulated *verb*
When you congratulate somebody, you tell them that you are pleased about something they have done. *I congratulated Lucy on passing her dancing exam.*
congratulations *noun*.

conifer conifers *noun*
a tree with long, thin leaves called needles that stay green in winter. Conifers have hard brown fruit called cones. Pine trees are conifers.

conjunction conjunctions *noun*
a word that joins words or groups of words in a sentence. "And", "but" and "if" are conjunctions.

conker conkers *noun*
a hard, shiny brown fruit of the horse-chestnut tree. ● A word that sounds like **conker** is **conquer**.

connect connects connecting connected *verb*
When you connect things, you join them together. *Ella and Neil connect the pieces to make a vehicle.*

conquer conquers conquering conquered *verb*
If an army conquers its enemies, it wins the war and takes control of them. ● A word that sounds like **conquer** is **conker**.
conqueror *noun*.

conscience consciences *noun*
Your conscience is a feeling inside you that tells you about right and wrong. *Mazy didn't steal any sweets, so she has a clear conscience.* ▲ Say **kon-shunss**.

conscious *adjective*
If you are conscious, you are awake and you know what is happening around you. ▲ Say **kon-shuss**. ■ The opposite is **unconscious**.

consider considers considering considered *verb*
When you consider something, you think carefully about it. *We must consider what to do next.*

considerate *adjective*
If you are considerate, you think about other people's feelings and you are not selfish.

consist consists consisting consisted *verb*
If something consists of different things, it is made up of those things. *This cake consists of flour, eggs, butter and sugar.*

consonant consonants *noun*
any letter of the alphabet except a, e, i, o or u, which are vowels.

construct constructs
constructing constructed *verb*
If you construct something, you build or put it together. *Tara is constructing a tractor.*

contact contacts contacting
contacted *verb*
If you contact somebody, you write to them or telephone them.

contact *noun*
If two things make contact, they touch each other. *The spaceship made contact with the shuttle.*

contain contains containing
contained *verb*
To contain something is to have something inside. *This tin contains coffee powder.*

container containers *noun*
A container is something that you put things in. Boxes, bottles and tins are containers.

content *adjective*
If you are content, you feel happy. ▲ Say kon-**tent**.

contents *noun*
The contents of something are all the things inside. *Yasmin dropped her bag and all the contents fell on the floor.*
▲ Say kon-*tents*.

contest contests *noun*
a competition or game that people try to win. *a judo contest.*

continent continents *noun*
one of the seven big pieces of land in the world. The continents are: Africa, Asia, Europe, North America, South America, Australia and Antarctica.

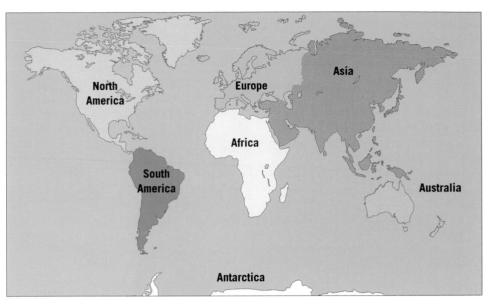

continue continues continuing
continued *verb*
When you continue doing something, you keep on doing it. *We continued playing outside until it got dark.*

contract contracts *noun*
a written agreement between two people or groups. *an employment contract.*

control *noun*
If you have control over somebody or something, you can make them do what you want. *You should have more control over your dog and not let it run into the road like that.*
control *verb*.

convenient *adjective*
If something is convenient, it is easy to do or use. *The cinema is very convenient; it is just around the corner.*
■ The opposite is **inconvenient**.

conversation conversations *noun*
If you have a conversation with somebody, you talk to them. *Hugo and Toby are having a conversation.*

convince convinces convincing
convinced *verb*
If somebody or something convinces you, they make you believe something.

cook cooks cooking cooked *verb*
When you cook food, you prepare and heat it, ready to eat.

cook cooks *noun*
a person who prepares and cooks food.

cooker cookers *noun*
A cooker is used to heat food. It has an oven inside for baking and roasting, and metal parts on the top that heat up for boiling and frying.

cool cooler coolest *adjective*
If something like water or the weather is cool, it is quite cold, but not very cold.

cool cools cooling cooled *verb*
When something cools, it becomes colder. *Take the cake out of the oven and leave it to cool.*

copper *noun*
a red-brown metal that is dug out of the ground. Copper wire is used to carry electricity.

copy copies copying copied *verb*
1 If you copy somebody, you try to do the same things or look the same as them. *Lucy copied her sister's way of talking.*
2 If you copy something, you write or draw something that is exactly the same as another thing. *The teacher asked us to copy the questions into our books for homework.*

A B C D E F G H I J K L M N O P Q R S T U V W X Y Z

copy copies *noun*
a thing that is made to look exactly the same as another thing.

coral *noun*
Coral is found at the bottom of the sea. It is the skeletons of small sea creatures that are left when the animals have died. Most coral is pink, white or red.

cord cords *noun*
strong, thick string. ● A word that sounds like **cord** is **chord**.

core cores *noun*
1 the middle part of some kinds of fruit where the seeds are. *an apple core.*
2 the centre of the Earth. *The Earth's core is very hot.*

cork corks *noun*
1 the light bark of the cork oak tree. Cork is used to make things such as tiles and table mats.
2 a piece of cork that is pushed into the top of a bottle to close it. You use a corkscrew to get a cork out of a bottle.

corn *noun*
plants such as wheat or oats that farmers grow for their seeds called grain. Corn can be made into flour.

corner corners *noun*
the place where two walls, roads or edges meet.

correct *adjective*
If something is correct, it is right and there are no mistakes. *Are all your spellings correct?*
correction *noun.*

corridor corridors *noun*
a long, narrow space inside a building with rooms on each side of it.

cost costs *noun*
the amount of money that you must pay to buy something. *The cost of the cinema tickets was £3.50 each.*

cost costs costing cost *verb*
If something costs £5, you have to pay £5 to buy it. *How much did it cost?*

costume costumes *noun*
the clothes that actors wear or that people wear at special times. *They wore fancy dress costumes to the party.*

cosy cosier cosiest *adjective*
If a place is cosy, it is warm and comfortable.

cot cots *noun*
a small bed with high sides that a baby sleeps in.

cottage cottages *noun*
a small house in the country.

cotton *noun*
1 material that is made by weaving the soft white fibres of the cotton plant. *a cotton shirt.*
2 thread that people use for sewing.

cough coughs coughing coughed *verb*
When you cough, you make a sudden loud noise in your throat. *The smoke made me cough.*
cough *noun*
I've got a bad cough.
▲ Say **koff**.

council councils *noun*
a group of people who are chosen to plan and decide things for other people. *The town council is planning to build a new sports centre.*

count counts counting counted *verb*
1 When you count, you say numbers one after another in the right order. *I can count from one to a million!*
2 When you count things, you add them up to find out how many there are. *Can you count the spoons and see if we have enough?*

counter counters *noun*
1 a long, high table in a shop or bank between the people who work there and the people who want to buy things.
2 a small, round piece of plastic that you use in some games.

country countries *noun*
1 an area of land in the world with its own people and government. *France, Spain and Japan are countries.*
2 the land outside towns and cities.

county counties *noun*
one of the parts of Britain and Ireland that can make some rules for the people who live in it. *Lancashire and Dorset are counties in England.*

couple couples *noun*
1 two people who are together. *A young couple live next door.*
2 two things. *a couple of oranges.*

courage *noun*
If you show courage, you are being brave.
courageous *adjective.*

course courses *noun*
1 an area of ground used for some games and sports. *Horses race on a race course.* ◆ *People play golf on a golf course.*
2 a set of lessons that you have when you learn something new. *My mum is doing a computing course.*
3 one of the parts of a meal. *We had chicken for the main course.*

abcdefghijklmnopqrstuvwxyz

court courts *noun*
1 a place where a group of people, called a jury, and a judge, decide if a person has done something wrong and what their punishment should be.
2 a piece of ground where you can play a certain sport. *a tennis court.*
3 a place where a king or queen lives.

courtyard courtyards *noun*
an area surrounded by walls.

cousin cousins *noun*
Your cousin is the child of your aunt or uncle.

cover covers *noun*
1 a thing that you put over another thing. *She got into bed and pulled the covers over her head.*
2 the outside of a book or magazine.

cover covers covering covered *verb*
1 to put something over something else to hide it or keep it warm.
2 When something covers another thing, it is all over it. *The grass was covered with snow.*

cow cows *noun*
a big, female farm animal that gives us milk. Female whales, seals and elephants are also called cows.

coward cowards *noun*
a person who is easily frightened.

cowboy cowboys, **cowgirl** cowgirls *noun*
a person whose job is to look after cattle in the USA.

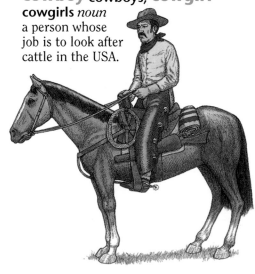

crab crabs *noun*
a sea animal with a flat, hard shell and ten legs. The two front legs have big claws called pincers on the end.

crack cracks *noun*
1 a thin line on something where it has nearly broken. *This cup has a tiny crack in it.*
2 a sudden loud noise. *a crack of thunder.*

crack cracks cracking cracked *verb*
If something cracks, it has a thin split in it, but it does not break in pieces. *Hot water will crack the glasses.*

cracker crackers *noun*
1 a tube covered with coloured paper that has a small toy and a hat inside. It makes a loud bang when two people pull it apart.
2 a thin biscuit that you eat with cheese.

cradle cradles *noun*
a small, wooden bed for a baby.

craft crafts *noun*
work or a hobby where you make things carefully and cleverly with your hands. Pottery and wood carving are crafts.

crane cranes *noun*
1 a tall machine that lifts and moves heavy things.
2 a large water bird with a long neck and long legs.

crash crashes *noun*
1 an accident when something that is moving hits another thing. *a serious car crash.*
2 a loud noise like the sound of thunder. *There was a loud crash as he dropped the plates on the floor.*

crash crashes crashing crashed *verb*
When something crashes, it hits another thing very hard and makes a loud noise. *The car crashed into a wall.*

crate crates *noun*
a wooden or plastic box for carrying things in. *a crate of bananas.*

crater craters *noun*
1 a huge hole in the ground that is made by something like a bomb landing on it.
2 the hole at the top of a volcano where fire and hot, liquid rock called lava come out.

crawl crawls crawling crawled *verb*
When a baby crawls, it moves slowly along the ground on its hands and knees. When an insect crawls, it moves with its body close to the ground.

The baby is crawling over the floor.

crayon crayons *noun*
a coloured pencil or wax stick that you draw with.

creak creaks creaking creaked *verb*
If something like a door creaks, it makes a strange squeaking sound. *Don't step on that floorboard, it creaks.*

cream *noun*
the thick, pale yellow liquid on the top of milk. *Would you like cream?*

crease creases creasing creased *verb*
If you crease something, you put lots of untidy lines in it by crushing it, or not folding it carefully. *If you sit on your jacket you will crease it.*

create creates creating created *verb*
If you create something, you make something new.
creator *noun,* **creation** *noun.*

A B C D E F G H I J K L M N O P Q R S T U V W X Y Z

creature creatures *noun*
any animal, fish or bird. *Ants are very tiny creatures.*

creep creeps creeping crept *verb*
If something creeps along, it moves slowly and quietly. *The cat crept towards the birds.*

crescent crescents *noun*
1 the curved shape of a new Moon.
2 a street that has a curved shape.

crew crews *noun*
all the people who work on a ship or an aeroplane.

cricket *noun*
1 a game played by two teams of 11 players with bats and a ball.
2 an insect like a grasshopper with wings and long legs that can jump quite high.

cried past of **cry**.

crime crimes *noun*
something that is against the law. *Murder is a very serious crime.*

criminal criminals *noun*
a person who does something that is against the law.

crisp crisper crispest *adjective*
If something such as a biscuit is crisp, it is hard and crunchy and easy to break.

crisp crisps *noun*
a very thin slice of potato that is fried in hot oil. *a bag of salted crisps.*

criticize criticizes criticizing criticized *verb*
If somebody criticizes you, they say you have done something badly or wrong. *Mrs Cobb criticized my handwriting for being untidy.* ■ The opposite is **praise**.

croak croaks croaking croaked *verb*
To croak is to make a deep rough sound like a frog makes. *"I've got a sore throat," she croaked.*

crocodile crocodiles *noun*
a large reptile with a long body and sharp teeth. Crocodiles live in rivers in some hot countries.

crooked *adjective*
not straight. *a crooked path through the trees.* ▲ Say *krook-id*.

crop crops *noun*
Crops are plants that farmers grow as food. Wheat, rice and oats are all crops.

cross crosses *noun*
a mark like this + or this x.

cross crosses crossing crossed *verb*
When you cross something such as a road or a river, you go from one side to the other.

cross crosser crossest *adjective*
If you are cross, you are angry about something.

crouch crouches crouching crouched *verb*
When you crouch, you bend your knees so that your body is close to the ground. *Hugo crouched to look at the plant.*

crow crows *noun*
a big, black bird that makes a loud noise.

crow crows crowing crowed *verb*
To crow means to make a noise like a cock makes in the early morning.

crowd crowds *noun*
a lot of people together in one place. *There was a huge crowd at the football match.*

crowded *adjective*
If a place is crowded, it is full of people. *The swimming pool gets very crowded.*

crown crowns *noun*
a ring of precious metal and jewels that kings and queens wear on their heads.

cruel crueller cruellest *adjective*
A person who is cruel hurts people or animals on purpose.

cruise cruises *noun*
If you go on a cruise, you have a holiday on a ship that travels to different places.

crumb crumbs *noun*
a tiny piece of bread, cake or biscuit. *After the party there were a lot of crumbs on the table.*

crunch crunches crunching crunched *verb*
If you crunch something hard and firm like a biscuit, you make a loud noise when you eat it. *She crunched a carrot.* **crunchy** *adjective*.

crush crushes crushing crushed *verb*
If you crush something, you press it hard so that you break or squash it.

a nile crocodile

crust crusts *noun*
1 the hard layer on the outside of a loaf of bread or pastry.
2 The Earth's crust is the thin outer layer.

crutch crutches *noun*
one or two long sticks that fit under your arms to help you walk if you have hurt your foot or leg.

cry cries crying cried *verb*
1 When you cry, you have tears falling from your eyes. *The baby is crying because he is hungry.*
2 To cry also means to shout or make a loud noise. *"Help!" she cried.*

crystal crystals *noun*
1 a hard kind of rock that looks like glass.
2 a small, hard piece of something such as salt or ice that has a regular shape.
▲ Say **kriss**-tal.

cub cubs *noun*
a young bear, lion, tiger, fox or wolf.

cube cubes *noun*
a solid shape with six square sides. *a cube of sugar.*

cuckoo cuckoos *noun*
a bird that makes a sound like its name. Cuckoos lay their eggs in the nests of other birds.

cucumber cucumbers *noun*
a long vegetable that is dark green on the outside and pale green inside. You can eat it raw in salads.

cuddle cuddles cuddling cuddled *verb*
When you cuddle somebody, you put your arms around them and hold them. *Dad cuddled the baby.*

cup cups *noun*
1 a small container with a handle. You drink liquids such as tea and coffee from a cup.
2 a metal container with two handles, that you can win as a prize. *He won a silver cup for coming first in the race.*

cupboard cupboards *noun*
a piece of furniture or a space in a wall with shelves and doors where you can keep things such as clothes or food.
▲ Say **kub**-erd.

cure cures curing cured *verb*
If something cures somebody, it makes their illness go away.
cure *noun.*

curious *adjective*
If you are curious about something, you want to know more about it. *I was curious to know what the noise was.*

curl curls *noun*
a piece of hair in a curved shape.
curly *adjective*
My sister has curly hair.

curl curls curling curled *verb*
If something curls or curls up, it bends into a curved shape. *The hedgehog curled up into a ball.*

currant currants *noun*
a small, dried grape. ● A word that sounds like **currant** is **current**.

current currents *noun*
1 air or water that is moving. *It is too dangerous to swim here because of the strong currents.*
2 electricity that is passing through a wire.
● A word that sounds like **current** is **currant**.

cursor cursors *noun*
a little sign on a computer screen that shows you where to type the next letter.

curtain curtains *noun*
Curtains are pieces of cloth that you pull across a window or the front of the stage in a theatre to cover it.

curve curves *noun*
a line that bends smoothly. *The letter "S" has two curves in it.*

curved *adjective*
If something is curved, it has the shape of a curve.

cushion cushions *noun*
a bag filled with soft material that you put on a chair to make it more comfortable.

custom customs *noun*
something that people usually do. *It is the custom to give people presents on their birthday.*

customer customers *noun*
a person who buys something from a shop.

cut cuts cutting cut *verb*
1 You use scissors or a knife to cut things into pieces.
2 If you cut yourself, you hurt yourself by accident with something sharp. *Katie cut her hand on a piece of glass.*
cut *noun.*

cute cuter cutest *adjective*
If something like a kitten is cute, you like it because it looks pretty and sweet.

cutlery *noun*
Knives, forks and spoons.

cycle cycles *noun*
a bicycle. *Jason rides his cycle to school.*

cycle cycles cycling cycled *verb*
When you cycle, you ride a bicycle. *Tom cycles to school every day.*
cyclist *noun.*

cylinder cylinders *noun*
a long, round shape like a tube or a can.

cymbals *noun*
two round metal plates that you use as a musical instrument. Cymbals make a loud clashing sound when you hit them together.

A B C D E F G H I J K L M N O P Q R S T U V W X Y Z

D d

daffodil **daffodils** *noun*
a bright-yellow, trumpet-shaped flower that blooms in the spring.

dagger **daggers** *noun*
a short sword with two sharp edges.

daily *adjective, adverb*
every day. *a daily newspaper.*

dainty **daintier daintiest** *adjective*
small and neat. *We had some dainty little sandwiches with the crusts cut off.*

dairy **dairies** *noun*
a company that sells milk and other foods made from milk such as butter and cheese.

dairy *adjective*
Dairy foods are milk, butter and cheese, and foods made from milk.

daisy **daisies** *noun*
a small flower with narrow, white petals around a yellow centre.

dam **dams** *noun*
a wall built across a river to hold back the water.

damage **damages damaging damaged** *verb*
If you damage something, you break it or harm it. *A car hit the wall and*

damaged it. ▲ Say *dam-ij.*
damage *noun.*

damp **damper dampest** *adjective*
a little wet.

dance **dances dancing danced** *verb*
When you dance, you move your body in time to music.
dance *noun.*

dandelion **dandelions** *noun*
a wild flower with a lot of bright-yellow petals.

danger **dangers** *noun*
1 If you are in danger, you are in a situation where something bad could happen to you. *The notice on the fence said: "Danger! Keep out!"*
2 something that might harm you. *Cigarettes are a danger to your health.*

dangerous *adjective*
Something that is dangerous might harm you. *It's dangerous to go near the edge of the cliff.* ■ The opposite is **safe**.

dare **dares daring dared** *verb*
1 If you dare to do something, you are brave enough to do it even though it is dangerous. *Shona wouldn't dare touch the angry swan.*
2 If you dare somebody, you ask them if they are brave enough to do something. *I dare you to walk along the top of that wall.*
dare *noun.*

dark **darker darkest** *adjective*
1 without any light. *Open the curtains. It's dark in here.* ■ The opposite is **light** or **bright**.
2 Dark colours are nearer to black than to white. *Ricky is wearing a dark coloured T-shirt, Lucy's is light.* ■ The opposite is **light**, **pale** or **fair**.
darkness *noun.*

dart **darts** *noun*
a short arrow that you throw at a round target called a dartboard in a game called darts.

dart **darts darting darted** *verb*
If you dart somewhere, you run there very quickly and suddenly. *Dad darted into the shop and came out with ice-creams for everybody.*

dash **dashes dashing dashed** *verb*
If you dash somewhere, you run there very quickly. *She put her umbrella up and dashed across the road.*

data *noun*
facts and information. Information stored in a computer is called data. ▲ Say *day-ta.*

date **dates** *noun*
1 the day, the month and sometimes the year when something happens. *What's the date today?*
2 a brown, sticky fruit with a stone inside. Dates grow on a type of palm tree.

daughter **daughters** *noun*
Somebody's daughter is a girl or woman who is their child. ▲ Say *dor-ter.*

dawdle **dawdles dawdling dawdled** *verb*
If you dawdle, you walk very slowly, taking more time than you should.

dawn **dawns** *noun*
the beginning of the day when the Sun is just starting to come up.

day **days** *noun*
1 the time when it is light. ■ The opposite is **night**.
2 a measure of time. The 24 hours of a day start at midnight and end the next midnight.

daze *noun*
If you are in a daze, you cannot think clearly and you are confused. *He's hit his head and he's in a bit of a daze.*

dazzle dazzles dazzling dazzled *verb*
If a light dazzles you, it is very bright and shining straight in your eyes so that you cannot see.

dead *adjective*
no longer alive. *a dead bird*.

deaf *adjective*
A person who is deaf cannot hear very well or cannot hear at all.

dear dearer dearest *adjective*
1 Something that is dear costs a lot of money. ■ The opposite is **cheap**.
2 You write "dear" at the beginning of a letter, before the person's name.
● A word that sounds like **dear** is **deer**.

death deaths *noun*
the end of a person's or an animal's life, when they die.

debt debts *noun*
money that you owe somebody and have to pay them back. ▲ Say *det*.

decade decades *noun*
a measure of time. There are ten years in a decade.

decay decays decaying decayed *verb*
When something decays, it goes bad or becomes rotten. *Eating sweets can make your teeth decay*.

deceive deceives deceiving deceived *verb*
If you deceive somebody, you trick them by making them believe something that is not true.

decide decides deciding decided *verb*
If you decide something, you make up your mind about what you are going to do. *I'm trying to decide what to buy my brother for his birthday*.

deciduous *adjective*
A deciduous tree loses its leaves in winter and gets new ones in spring. ▲ Say *dis-id-yoo-us*. ■ The opposite is **evergreen**.

decimal decimals *noun*
a fraction that you write as a number, with amounts less than one written after the dot, called a decimal point. 2.5 is a decimal. It is the same as 2½.

decimal *adjective*
A decimal system counts numbers in tens.

decision decisions *noun*
If you make a decision, you make up your mind about what you are going to do. *Have you made a decision yet?*

deck decks *noun*
a floor on a ship or bus.

declare declares declaring declared *verb*
If you declare something, you say something important to a lot of people. *I declare that the winner is Ben Watson*.

decorate decorates decorating decorated *verb*
1 If you decorate something, you add things to it to make it look more beautiful. *Sam decorated the cake*.
2 If you decorate a room, you paint it or put wallpaper on the walls.
decoration *noun*.

decrease decreases decreasing decreased *verb*
If something decreases, it gets smaller or less. *The number of trees in the rainforests of South America has decreased over the last few years*. ■ The opposite is **increase**.

Rainforest losses

deep deeper deepest *adjective*
1 Something that is deep goes a long way down from the top. *The river is very deep*. ■ The opposite is **shallow**.
2 A deep sleep is sleep that is hard to wake somebody from.
3 A deep voice is very low. *Men's voices are usually deeper than women's*.

deer deer *noun*
a wild animal that eats grass and can run very fast. Male deer (stags) have big horns called antlers on their head. ● A word that sounds like **deer** is **dear**.

defeat defeats defeating defeated *verb*
If you defeat somebody, you beat them in a game, competition or battle. **defeat** *noun*.

defend defends defending defended *verb*
When you defend somebody or something, you protect them when somebody else is attacking them. *Jamie defended the goal*. **defence** *noun*.

definite *adjective*
certain and not likely to change. *We haven't fixed a definite date for the trip*. **definitely** *adverb*
I'm definitely going to do my homework this evening.

defrost defrosts defrosting defrosted *verb*
To defrost is to unfreeze frozen food.

degree degrees *noun*
1 a measurement of temperature. Degree is sometimes written as ° 10°C is ten degrees Celsius.
2 a measurement of angles. *A right angle is 90°*.
3 a qualification that you can get after you have studied at university.

A B C D E F G H I J K L M N O P Q R S T U V W X Y Z

delay delays delaying delayed *verb*
1 If you delay doing something, you put it off until later. *We had to delay our holiday for a week because my sister was very ill.*
2 To delay somebody is to make them late. *The bus was delayed for an hour because of the accident.*

delete deletes deleting deleted *verb*
If you delete something, you remove it from a piece of writing or from a computer's memory.

deliberate *adjective*
If something you do is deliberate, you do it on purpose.

delicate *adjective*
1 Something that is delicate is small and lovely but it can be broken or damaged quite easily. *a spider's web is very delicate.*
2 A person who is delicate gets ill quite easily. *He's a delicate child.*

delicious *adjective*
Food that is delicious tastes very nice. ▲ Say *dee-lish-us.*

delight delights delighting delighted *verb*
If something delights you, it makes you feel very pleased. *She was delighted with the beautiful present.*

deliver delivers delivering delivered *verb*
When you deliver something, you take it to the person it is supposed to go to. *A postman or postwoman delivers letters and parcels to your home.*

demand demands demanding demanded *verb*
If you demand something, you ask for it very strongly. *Dad demanded to know why I was so late getting home.*
demand *noun.*

demolish demolishes demolishing demolished *verb*
To demolish something is to destroy it completely. *The council is demolishing the old houses.*
demolition *noun.*

den dens *noun*
the home of a wild animal such as a lion.

dent dents denting dented *verb*
If you dent something that is made of metal, you damage it so that part of it is pushed in slightly instead of flat. *a dented tin.*

dentist dentists *noun*
a person whose job is to look after people's teeth.

deny denies denying denied *verb*
If you deny something, you say it is not true. *Tom denied taking the money.*

depart departs departing departed *verb*
If you depart, you leave. *The plane departs at 6.25.* ■ The opposite is **arrive.**
departure *noun.*

depend depends depending depended *verb*
1 If you depend on somebody or something, you need them. *The school depends on parents to raise money.*
2 If you depend on somebody, you trust them to do what they say they will. *I'm depending on you to help me.*
3 To depend also means to be decided by something. *Whether we have a picnic tomorrow depends on the weather.*
dependent *adjective*
■ The opposite is **independent.**

depth depths *noun*
The depth of something is how deep it is. *What is the depth of the lake?*

deputy deputies *noun*
a person who does another person's job when that person is not there. *a deputy headteacher.*

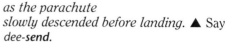

descend descends descending descended *verb*
If something descends, it goes down. *We watched as the parachute slowly descended before landing.* ▲ Say *dee-send.*

describe describes describing described *verb*
When you describe something, you say what it is like.
description *noun*
The woman gave the police a description of the man she had seen.

desert deserts *noun*
an area where it is very dry and hardly any plants can grow. ▲ Say *dez-ert.*

deserted *adjective*
If a place is deserted, there is nobody there. *The house was deserted.*

deserve deserves deserving deserved *verb*
If you deserve something, it is fair that it should happen to you. *He trained very hard and he deserved to win the medal.*

design designs designing designed *verb*
If you design something, you decide what it will be like and then you draw it to show how it should be made. ▲ Say *dee-zine.*

design designs *noun*
a pattern. *Each of these jumpers has a different design.* ▲ Say *dee-zine.*

desire desires *noun*
a very strong wish for something. *She had a great desire to become an artist.*
desirable *adjective*
worth having. *a desirable house.*

a b c d e f g h i j k l m n o p q r s t u v w x y z

desk desks *noun*
a table that you sit at to write or read. Desks often have drawers.

despair despairs despairing despaired *verb*
If you despair, you feel no hope that something good will happen.

desperate *adjective*
If you are desperate, you are in a very bad situation and you will do almost anything to change it. *She was so desperate for food that she started begging on the streets.*

destination destinations *noun*
the place you are going to.

destroy destroys destroying destroyed *verb*
If you destroy something, you damage it or break it so badly that it cannot be mended. *Fire destroyed the house.*
destruction *noun*
The storm caused a lot of destruction.

detail details *noun*
one of many small pieces of information about something. *I can give you some idea of what happened but I don't know all the details yet.*

detective detectives *noun*
a person who tries to find out who did a crime. *Detectives are police officers.*

detergent *noun*
a powder or liquid that you use to clean clothes or dishes.

determined *adjective*
If you are determined to do something, you are going to do it and nothing can stop you. *Alex had trained very hard, he was determined to win the race.*

detest detests detesting detested *verb*
If you detest somebody or something, you hate them very much.

develop develops developing developed *verb*
When something develops, it changes as it grows. *Here we see a photograph developing.*
development *noun*
the new housing development.

dew *noun*
Small drops of water that form in the night on grass and plants. ● A word that sounds like **dew** is **due**.

diagonal *adjective*
a line that slants from one corner of something to the opposite corner.

diagram diagrams *noun*
a simple picture explaining something. *a diagram about plant growth.*

dial dials *noun*
the part of something such as a clock or speedometer that has numbers on it.

diameter diameters *noun*
a line drawn straight across a circle, through the centre.
❖ *Look at page 38*

diamond diamonds *noun*
1 a very hard, clear, precious jewel.
2 a shape like a rectangle turned so that it is standing on one of its corners.

diary diaries *noun*
a book where you can write what has happened during the day or what you plan to do.

dice *noun*
small cubes with a different number of dots on each side. You use dice when you play some games. The word for one of the dice is a **die**.

dictionary dictionaries *noun*
a book that gives the meanings of words and how to spell them in the order of the alphabet. *If you don't understand a word, you look it up in a dictionary.*

die dies dying died *verb*
When a person, an animal or a plant dies, they come to the end of their life and stop living. ■ The opposite is **live**. ● A word that sounds like **die** is **dye**.
death *noun*.

diesel *noun*
a kind of oil that is used as fuel in bus and lorry engines. Some cars use diesel too. ▲ Say *dee-zel*.

diet diets *noun*
1 Your diet is the food that you normally eat. *A healthy diet includes plenty of fresh fruit and vegetables.*
2 If you go on a diet, you eat only certain foods because you have an illness or because you are trying to lose weight.

different *adjective*
If something is different from another thing, it is not like it.
difference *noun*
Can you tell the difference between these two horses?

difficult *adjective*
hard to do. ■ The opposite is **easy** or **simple**.
difficulty *noun*.

dig digs digging dug *verb*
If you dig, you use something such as a spade or fork to move earth or make a hole in the ground. Animals dig using their claws.

digest digests digesting digested *verb*
When you digest food, it passes through your body and gets broken up so that your body can use it to make energy.
digestion *noun*.

A B C D E F G H I J K L M N O P Q R S T U V W X Y Z

a b c d e f g h i j k l m n o p q r s t u v w x y z

digit digits *noun*
1 one of the numbers from 0 to 9.
2 a finger or a toe.

dilute dilutes diluting diluted *verb*
When you dilute a liquid, you make it weaker by adding water.
dilution *noun*.

dim dimmer dimmest *adjective*
A dim light is not very strong or bright.

dinghy dinghies *noun*
a small, open boat that you row or sail.
▲ Say *ding-ee*.

dinner dinners *noun*
the main meal that you eat in the day, either in the evening or in the middle of the day.

dinosaur dinosaurs *noun*
a large reptile that lived millions of years ago and then became extinct.

dip dips dipping dipped *verb*
1 If you dip something into a liquid, you put it in for a moment. *He dipped his brush into the paint.*
2 If something dips, it slopes down. *The road dipped suddenly after the bridge.*
■ The opposite is **rise**.

direct *adjective*
The direct way to go somewhere is by the shortest way and without stopping.

direct directs directing directed *verb*
1 If you direct somebody to a place, you tell them the way to go.
2 A person who directs a film or television programme tells the actors what to do.

direction directions *noun*
1 the way that something is pointing or moving. *Am I going in the right direction for the old castle?*
2 Directions are instructions telling you how to do something.

dirt *noun*
mud, dust or marks on something.

dirty dirtier dirtiest *adjective*
covered with dirt or marks. ■ The opposite is **clean**.

Word Builder

Dis – is a little word called a prefix that you can add to the beginning of certain words, often to change their meaning.
1 Not, or the opposite of – disloyal, dishonest.
2 To do the opposite of – disagree, dislike.

---

disabled *adjective*
A disabled person has a part of their body that does not work properly.
disability *noun*.

disagree disagrees disagreeing disagreed *verb*
When people disagree, they do not think the same way about something. *My brother and I often disagree about what to watch on TV.*
■ The opposite is **agree**.

disappear disappears disappearing disappeared *verb*
If something disappears, it goes out of sight. *We waved at the boat until it disappeared in the distance.* ■ The opposite is **appear**.
disappearance *noun*.

disappointed *adjective*
You feel disappointed when something you were looking forward to does not happen or when what happens is not as good as you hoped. *My parents were disappointed with my exam results.*
disappointment *noun*.

disaster disasters *noun*
a really terrible thing that happens. *An earthquake is a natural disaster.*

disc discs *noun*
a round, flat object.

discover discovers discovering discovered *verb*
If you discover something, you find out about it or see it for the first time. *We discovered a secret hiding place in the hollow trunk of a tree.*
discovery *noun*.

discuss discusses discussing discussed *verb*
If you discuss something, you talk about it with other people.
discussion *noun*.

disease diseases *noun*
an illness.

disguise disguises *noun*
something that you do to change the way you look so that other people do not know who you are. ▲ Say *dis-gize*.

disgust *noun*
a very strong feeling of not liking something that is really nasty or bad.
disgusting *adjective*.

dish dishes *noun*
a plate or a bowl used for cooking or for putting food on.

disk disks *noun*
a flat plastic case with a magnetic metal part inside that stores information from a computer.

dislike dislikes disliking disliked *verb*
If you dislike somebody or something, you do not like them.

distance distances *noun*
Distance is how far apart two things are.
distant *adjective*.

distract distracts distracting distracted *verb*
If something distracts you, it takes your attention away from what you are doing. *I can't do my homework with the radio on because I get distracted by it.*
distraction *noun*.

disturb disturbs disturbing disturbed *verb*
If you disturb somebody, you stop them doing something such as working or sleeping. *Don't disturb her, she's asleep.*
disturbance *noun*.

ditch ditches *noun*
a long hole in the ground that has been dug along the side of a road so that water can drain away.

dive dives diving dived *verb*

1 When you dive, you jump into water with your arms and head first.
2 To dive also means to go swimming underwater with special equipment that lets you breathe.
3 To dive is to go under water. *We watched the submarine dive.*
diver *noun*.

divide divides dividing divided *verb*

1 If you divide something, you separate it into smaller parts.
2 When you divide one number by another number, you see how many times the smaller number goes into the larger one. *8 divided by 2 is 4 (8 ÷ 2= 4).* ■ The opposite is **multiply**.

Joe divides the liquid into four equal amounts.

division *noun*
I am not very good at long division.

divorce divorces *noun*
the ending of a marriage.
divorce *verb*
She divorced her husband.

dizzy dizzier dizziest *adjective*
If you feel dizzy, you feel as if everything is spinning around and you are going to fall over.

dock docks *noun*
a place where ships stop to load or unload goods or to get repaired.
dock *verb*.

doctor doctors *noun*
a person whose job is to help people who are ill to get better by giving them medicines or advice. We usually write "doctor" as "Dr" before a name.

document documents *noun*
a piece of paper with important information on it.

dog dogs *noun*
an animal that is often kept as a pet or for hunting or guarding things. A young dog is called a puppy. ❖ *Look below*

doll dolls *noun*
a toy in the shape of a very small person.

A B C D E F G H I J K L M N O P Q R S T U V W X Y Z

DOGS

Labrador retriever

Dogue de Bordeaux (mastiff)

Basenji

Bull terrier

Black and tan coonhound

Beagle

dolphin dolphins *noun*
a mammal that lives in the sea but breathes air. Dolphins look like very large fish. ▲ Say **dol**-fin.

domino dominoes *noun*
Dominoes are small, rectangular blocks of wood or plastic with different numbers of dots on them, used to play a game.

donation donations *noun*
an amount of money that you give, often to a charity.

donkey donkeys *noun*
an animal like a small horse but with longer ears.

door doors *noun*
a large piece of wood or glass that moves to open and close the way into a room, building or cupboard.

dose doses *noun*
an amount of medicine that you have to take at one time.

dot dots *noun*
a small, round spot. *a blue shirt with white dots.*

double *adjective*
twice as large or twice as many. *Natasha has double the number of bricks that Jazz has.* ▲ Say **dub**-l.

doubt doubts *noun*
If you have a doubt about something, you are not sure about it. *I don't have any doubt that our team will win.* ▲ Say **dowt**.

dough *noun*
a mixture of flour, water and other things that you cook to make bread, cakes or pastry. ▲ Say **doh**.

dove doves *noun*
a kind of pigeon. ▲ Say **duv**.

doze dozes dozing dozed *verb*
When you doze, you sleep very lightly and you can wake up easily. *Granddad was dozing in his chair.*

dozen *noun*
twelve. *We made two dozen sandwiches for the party.* ▲ Say **duz**-en.

drag drags dragging dragged *verb*
If you drag something, you pull it along the ground. *Freddie dragged his coat across the floor.*

dragon dragons *noun*
a very large animal in stories with a long body covered in scales. Dragons have wings and can breathe fire.

dragonfly dragonflies *noun*
an insect with a long, thin body and two sets of wings. Dragonflies live near ponds and rivers.

drain drains draining drained *verb*
1 When water drains away, it flows slowly away.
2 When you drain food, you pour away the water that it was cooked in. *Drain the pasta and serve with a sauce.*

drain drains *noun*
a pipe that carries water away.

drama dramas *noun*
1 a serious play.
2 an interesting or exciting thing that happens. *There was a great drama when Anya won the lottery.*

drank past of **drink**.

drastic *adjective*
severe or harsh.

draught draughts *noun*
cold air coming into a room because there is a slight gap between a window or door and the wall. ▲ Say **draft**.
draughty *adjective*.

draw draws drawing drew drawn *verb*
1 When you draw, you use a pencil, pen or crayon to make a picture.
2 If you draw the curtains, you move them together by pulling.
3 If two teams of people draw in a game, both have the same score.
drawing *noun*.

drawer drawers *noun*
a wooden box that slides in and out of a piece of furniture.

dream dreams dreaming dreamt or **dreamed** *verb*
1 When you dream, you see pictures and hear sounds in your mind while you are sleeping. *I dreamt I could fly.*
2 When you dream of something, you think about how much you would love to do it. *She dreams of becoming a famous ballet dancer.*
dream *noun*.

dress dresses dressing dressed *verb*
When you dress you put on clothes. ■ The opposite is **undress**.

dress dresses *noun*
a piece of clothing that a woman or girl wears. A dress has a top part and a skirt joined together.

drew past of **draw**.

drift drifts drifting drifted *verb*
When something drifts, it is carried slowly along by the wind or by the movement of water. *She stopped the engine and let the boat drift.*

drill drills *noun*
a tool that is used for making holes.
drill *verb*.

drink drinks drinking drank drunk *verb*
When you drink, you take liquid into your mouth and swallow it.
drink *noun*.

drip drips dripping dripped *verb*
When liquid drips, it falls in drops. *Rain dripped off the roof.*

drive drives driving drove driven *verb*
When somebody drives, they control something such as a car or bus and make it go where they want.

drizzle *noun*
light rain in very small drops.

droop droops drooping drooped *verb*
When something droops, it hangs or bends down because it is weak or tired. *The flower drooped because it had no water.*

drop drops *noun*
a tiny amount of liquid. *a drop of water.*

drop drops dropping dropped *verb*
If you drop something, you let it fall. *I dropped the plate.*

drought droughts *noun*
a long period of time when there is no rain. ▲ Say **drowt.**

drove past of **drive.**

drown drowns drowning drowned *verb*
If somebody drowns, they die because they cannot breathe under water.

drug drugs *noun*
1 a pill or medicine that a doctor gives you to treat an illness.
2 an illegal pill or chemical that someone takes.

drum drums *noun*
a musical instrument that you beat with a stick or your hands. A drum is made from a round frame with a piece of material stretched across it.
drummer *noun*
Jed is a drummer in a band.

drunk *adjective*
When somebody is drunk, they have drunk too much alcohol and cannot speak clearly or act sensibly.

drunk past of **drink.**

dry drier driest *adjective*
If something is dry, there is no water or liquid in it. ■ The opposite is **wet.**

dry dries drying dried *verb*
If you dry something, you make it dry. *Jordan is drying himself with a towel.*

duck ducks *noun*
a water bird with webbed feet and a flat, broad beak. A male duck is called a drake, and a young duck is called a duckling.

Northern pintail
Steller's eider
Garganey
Shelduck
Mandarin

due *adjective*
When something is due at a particular time, it should happen at that time. *They are due to arrive at 10 o'clock .*
● A word that sounds like **due** is **dew.**

dug past of **dig.**

dull duller dullest *adjective*
1 A dull colour is not very bright.
2 A dull day is cloudy and the Sun is not shining.
3 If something such as a film or book is dull, it is not interesting.
4 not sharp. *a dull ache.*

dumb *adjective*
1 completely unable to speak.
2 stupid.

dummy dummies *noun*
1 a model of a person that clothes can be put on. *I like the trousers on the dummy in the shop window.*
2 a rubber thing that a baby sucks.

dump dumps dumping dumped *verb*
If you dump something, you put it down quickly and carelessly. *My parents get cross when my sister just dumps her clothes on the floor.*

dune dunes *noun*
a low hill of sand by the sea or in a desert.

models of sand dunes

dungeon dungeons *noun*
an underground prison in a castle.
▲ Say **dun-jun.**

dusk *noun*
the time in the evening when it is nearly dark but not quite.

dust *noun*
dirt that is like powder. *The furniture was covered in dust.*
dusty *adjective.*

dustbin dustbins *noun*
a large container with a lid that you keep outside your house to put your rubbish in.

duty duties *noun*
a job that you have to do. *The dog belongs to my brother, so it's his duty to take it for walks.*

duvet duvets *noun*
a thick cover that keeps you warm in bed. Some duvets are filled with feathers. ▲ Say **doo-vay.**

dye dyes *noun*
a liquid that you soak cloth or your hair in to change its colour. ● A word that sounds like **dye** is **die.**
dye *verb.*

dyslexia *noun*
a learning difficulty that causes problems with reading and spelling.
▲ Say *dis-lex-ee-a.*

A
B
C
D
E
F
G
H
I
J
K
L
M
N
O
P
Q
R
S
T
U
V
W
X
Y
Z

E e

a
b
c
d
e
f
g
h
i
j
k
l
m
n
o
p
q
r
s
t
u
v
w
x
y
z

eager *adjective*
If you are eager to do something, you want to do it very much. *Ben was eager to help with the cooking.*

eagle eagles *noun*
a large bird with a curved beak and broad wings. Eagles are called birds of prey because they catch and eat small animals and other birds.

ear ears *noun*
Your ears are the part of your body that you hear with.

early earlier earliest *adjective, adverb*
1 near the beginning of a period of time. *Early cars had solid tyres.*
2 before the usual time or the time that you are expected. *We went to the swimming pool early before it got crowded.*
■ The opposite is **late**.

earn earns earning earned *verb*
If you earn money, you get money for work that you do. *Lauren sometimes earns extra pocket money by washing her mother's car.*

earring earrings *noun*
a piece of jewellery that you wear on your ear.

earth *noun*
1 The Earth is the planet that we live on. Our Earth moves around the Sun.
2 the ground that plants grow in.

earthquake earthquakes *noun*
An earthquake happens when part of the ground suddenly begins to shake. Earthquakes happen when rocks beneath the surface of the Earth move.

easel easels *noun*
a stand for a blackboard or an artist's painting.

east *noun*
1 the direction from which the Sun rises in the morning.
2 the East is where countries such as China and Japan are.
east *adjective*, **eastern** *adjective*
Norfolk is in eastern England.

easy easier easiest *adjective*
not difficult. *These sums are easy!*
■ The opposite is **hard** or **difficult**.

eat eats eating ate eaten *verb*
When you eat something, you chew food in your mouth and swallow it.

e a t
Some words you can use instead of eat:

Rabbits eat carrots.
☞ **nibble** ☜

Apples make a crunchy sound when you eat them.
☞ **chew, munch, bite** ☜

We ate at the new Italian restaurant.
☞ **dined** ☜

echo echoes *noun*
An echo is the sound that comes back to you when you shout in a place such as a cave. ▲ Say *ek-oh*.

eclipse eclipses *noun*
1 An eclipse of the Sun is when the Moon comes between the Earth and the Sun so that you cannot see all the Sun's light (**a**).

a   Earth
Moon

Moon
b   Earth

2 An eclipse of the Moon is when the Earth comes between the Sun and the Moon so that you cannot see all the Moon's light (**b**).

edge edges *noun*
An edge is the end or side of something. *Don't stand on the edge of the cliff.*

education *noun*
Education is teaching people to read, write and learn about all kinds of things in a school or college.

eel eels *noun*
a long, thin fish that lives in rivers or in the sea.

effect effects *noun*
An effect is a change that is caused by somebody or something. *The rubbish in the river had a bad effect on the fish.*

effort efforts *noun*
If you make an effort, you try hard to do something. *It takes a lot of effort to pull Angelina off the floor.*

egg eggs *noun*
1 Birds, fish, some reptiles and some other animals lay eggs. The young of these animals live inside the eggs until they are ready to hatch.
2 a hen's egg with a hard shell that you can cook and eat.

elastic *noun*
a rubber material that stretches when you pull it. *elastic around the waist.*

elbow elbows *noun*
Your elbow is the joint in the middle of your arm where it bends.

Sun

Sun

elderly *adjective*
rather old. *an elderly man.*

election **elections** *noun*
An election is when people choose who they want to be their leader by voting. *an election for a new President.*

electric *adjective*
A machine that is electric works by using electricity. *an electric cooker.*

electricity *noun*
the form of energy that travels along wires. Rubbing a balloon on hair creates a form of electricity called "static electricity".
electrical *adjective*.

electronic *adjective*
An electronic machine, such as a computer, uses a piece of material called a silicon chip that has a tiny electric circuit on it.

elephant **elephants** *noun*
a very big, grey animal with a long trunk and two long teeth called tusks. Elephants live in Africa and Asia. They eat grass, and parts of trees which they tear off with their trunks.

embarrassed *adjective*
If you are embarrassed, you feel shy or ashamed, and worried about what people think of you. *I was so embarrassed when I fell over and everyone laughed.*
embarrassment *noun*.

embroidery *noun*
sewing that you do with pretty colours and small stitches, to decorate cloth.
embroider *verb*.

embryo **embryos** *noun*
a tiny person or animal that has only just begun to develop inside its mother and has not been born yet. ▲ Say *em-bree-oh.*

emerald **emeralds** *noun*
a bright green jewel.

emergency **emergencies** *noun*
An emergency is when somebody is in danger and needs help immediately. *In an emergency, you should call 999.*

emotion **emotions** *noun*
a strong feeling such as love, anger or sadness. ▲ Say *ee-moh-shun.*

emperor **emperors** *noun*
a man who rules over a group of countries, called an empire.

a Chinese emperor

employ **employs employing employed** *verb*
If you employ somebody, you pay them to work for you.

empress **empresses** *noun*
a woman who rules over a group of countries, called an empire.

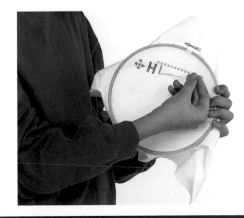

empty *adjective*
If something is empty, there is nothing in it. *She drank all the milk and left the empty glass on the table.*
■ The opposite is **full**.

empty **empties emptying emptied** *verb*
If you empty something, you take out or throw away everything that is in it. *He emptied the jug of juice.* ■ The opposite is **fill**.

enchanted *adjective*
A place that is enchanted has been put under a magic spell. *The story is about an enchanted wood where the trees come to life.*

encourage **encourages encouraging encouraged** *verb*
If you encourage somebody, you make them feel that what they are doing is good and help them to go on doing it. *We encouraged my brother to swim a length of the pool.*
encouragement *noun*.

encyclopedia **encyclopedias** *noun*
a book that tells you about all kinds of facts and subjects from A to Z. ▲ Say *en-sye-kloh-pee-dee-a.*

end **ends** *noun*
1 the last part of something. *I'm almost at the end of my book.* ■ The opposite is **beginning** or **start**.
2 one of the short edges of something long. *They sat at opposite ends of the table.*

end **ends ending ended** *verb*
When something ends, it finishes. *What time does the film end?* ■ The opposite is **begin** or **start**.

enemy **enemies** *noun*
Your enemy is a person who hates you or a person that you fight against.

energy *noun*
1 Energy is the power that makes machines work and gives us heat and light. Electricity is one kind of energy.
2 Your energy is the strength that your body has to do things. *You need a lot of energy to run 1,000 metres.*
energetic *adjective*.

engaged *adjective*
1 If two people are engaged, they have agreed to get married.
2 If a telephone number is engaged, you cannot talk to the person you want because they are already talking to somebody else.

engine **engines** *noun*
1 a machine that makes things move. *a car engine.*
2 the front part of a train that pulls it along.

a model engine

enjoy **enjoys enjoying enjoyed** *verb*
If you enjoy something, you like doing it. *I enjoy playing football.*
enjoyable *adjective*, **enjoyment** *noun*.

enormous *adjective*
very, very big. *China is an enormous country.* ■ The opposite is **tiny**.

enough *adjective, adverb, noun*
If you have enough of something, you have as much as you need. *Have you had enough to eat?*

enter **enters entering entered** *verb*
1 If you enter a place, you go into it. *She entered the room quietly.*
2 If you enter a race or competition, you take part in it. *Did you enter the egg and spoon race?*

entertain **entertains entertaining entertained** *verb*
If you entertain somebody, you do things that they find interesting or amusing. *The clown entertained the crowd while the acrobats changed their costumes.*
entertainment *noun*.

enthusiasm *noun*
a strong feeling of liking something or wanting to do something. *The children were full of enthusiasm for the party.*
enthusiastic *adjective*.

entrance **entrances** *noun*
the way into a place. *I'll meet you at the entrance to the shop.* ■ The opposite is **exit**.

envelope **envelopes** *noun*
a folded paper cover for a letter or card. You write the address of the person you are writing to on the front of the envelope.

environment *noun*
The environment is the air, water, land, and all the plants and animals around us. *We must all try to protect the environment.*
environmental *adjective*.

envy **envies envying envied** *verb*
If you envy somebody, you wish you had the same things that they have. *I envied Della because she had a new bike.*
envious *adjective*.

episode **episodes** *noun*
An episode is one part of a long story in a book, or on television or radio that you read, watch or listen to in several parts.

equal *adjective*
If things are equal, they are the same in size, amount or number. *The children had an equal number of sweets each.*
equally *adverb*.

equator *noun*
The equator is an imaginary line on maps that goes around the Earth at an equal distance between the North and South Poles. Countries near the equator are very hot.

equipment *noun*
all the things you need to do something. *sports equipment.* ◆ *kitchen equipment.*

shoulder pads

helmet

thigh pads

arm pads

hip pads

knee pads

shin pads

error **errors** *noun*
a mistake.

erupt **erupts erupting erupted** *verb*
When a volcano erupts, it explodes and very hot liquid rock called lava shoots out of the top.
eruption *noun*.

escalator **escalators** *noun*
a staircase with moving steps.

escape **escapes escaping escaped** *verb*
When a person or an animal escapes, they get away from somebody or something. *The bird has escaped from its cage.*

especially *adverb*
most of all. *I like animals, especially cats and rabbits.*

essential *adjective*
If something is essential, it is absolutely necessary. *Warm clothes are essential in very cold weather.*

evaporate **evaporates evaporating evaporated** *verb*
When a liquid evaporates, it changes into a gas or vapour and seems to disappear. *Water evaporates when it is heated.*
evaporation *noun*.

even *adjective*
1 flat and smooth. *an even floor.* ■ The opposite is **uneven**.
2 Even numbers can be divided exactly by two. *2, 4, 6 and 8 are even numbers.* ■ The opposite is **odd**.

evening **evenings** *noun*
the part of the day between afternoon and night. *The Sun goes down in the evening.*

event **events** *noun*
something that happens, especially something important or unusual. *The school sports day is a big event.*

eventually *adverb*
after a very long time. *I waited for ages, then eventually the bus came.*

evergreen *adjective*
An evergreen tree does not lose its leaves in the winter. Pine trees are evergreen. ■ The opposite is **deciduous**.

evidence *noun*
proof of something that happened. *The paw marks were evidence that the cat had jumped on the table.*

evil *adjective*
A person who is evil is very bad and cruel. *an evil emperor.*

exact *adjective*
correct. *What is the exact time?*
exactly *adverb*.

exaggerate **exaggerates exaggerating exaggerated** *verb*
If you exaggerate, you pretend something is bigger, better or worse that it really is. *Tom was exaggerating when he said he saw a spider as big as a cat.*
exaggeration *noun*.

exam **exams** *noun*
a short word for examination. *a maths exam.* ◆ *a ballet exam.*

examination **examinations** *noun*
1 an important test that you are given to see how much you have learnt.
2 looking at somebody or something closely and carefully. *a medical examination.*

examine **examines examining examined** *verb*
If you examine something, you look at it closely and carefully. *Freddie examined the fossil with a magnifying glass.*

example **examples** *noun*
a thing that shows what other things of the same kind are like. *At the school open day, we showed our parents examples of our work.*

excellent *adjective*
Something that is excellent is very good. *We had an excellent holiday.*

except *preposition*
but not. *We all went shopping except Peter who stayed at home.*
exception *noun*.

exchange **exchanges exchanging exchanged** *verb*
If you exchange something, you give one thing and get something else in return. *At the end of the holiday we exchanged addresses with our new friends.*

excited *adjective*
If you are excited, you are so happy that you cannot keep quiet or calm. *Freddie is so excited that he is jumping for joy!*
excitement *noun*,
exciting *adjective*.

exclaim **exclaims exclaiming exclaimed** *verb*
To exclaim means to say something in a loud voice because you are surprised or angry. *"What a mess!" she exclaimed.*
exclamation *noun*
He gave an exclamation of surprise when he saw the huge present.

exclamation mark **exclamation marks** *noun*
a mark (**!**) that you use in writing. You put an exclamation mark to show that somebody is surprised or angry. *Oh no!*

excuse **excuses** *noun*
If you make an excuse, you try to explain why you did something wrong. *What's your excuse for being late this time?*
▲ Say *ex-kyoos*.

excuse **excuses excusing excused** *verb*
If you excuse somebody, you forgive them for something they did wrong. *I'll excuse you for forgetting your sports kit this time, but don't do it again.*
▲ Say *ex-kyooz*.

exercise **exercises** *noun*
1 Exercise is something such as running or jumping that you do to keep your body strong and well. *The children are doing different kinds of exercise.*
2 An exercise is a piece of work that you do to help you learn something. *Our teacher asked us to finish exercise 2 for homework.*

exhausted *adjective*
very tired. *After running all the way up the hill, I was exhausted.*

exhibition **exhibitions** *noun*
a collection of things in a place such as a museum or gallery for people to come and look at. ▲ Say *ex-i-bish-un*.

A B C D E F G H I J K L M N O P Q R S T U V W X Y Z

a
b
c
d
e
f
g
h
i
j
k
l
m
n
o
p
q
r
s
t
u
v
w
x
y
z

exist exists existing existed *verb*
If something exists, you can find it in the real world now. *Do you think fairies really exist?*
existence *noun*.

exit exits *noun*
the way out of a building. *The exit is at the back of the cinema.* ■ The opposite is **entrance**.

expand expands expanding expanded *verb*
If something expands, it gets bigger. *When you blow air into a balloon it expands.*

expect expects expecting expected *verb*
If you expect something to happen, you think it will happen. *I expect they will be here soon.*

expedition expeditions *noun*
a long journey to find or do something special. *Robert Peary led an expedition to the South Pole.*

expensive *adjective*
Something that is expensive costs a lot of money. ■ The opposite is **cheap**.

experience experiences *noun*
1 An experience is something that has happened to you. *What's the most frightening experience you've had?*
2 Experience is knowing about something because you have done it for a long time. *I can cycle to school when I've had more experience of riding my bike on the road.*

experiment experiments *noun*
a test that you do to find out something. *We did an experiment to see which objects are magnetic.*

expert experts *noun*
a person who knows a lot about something. *a computer expert.*

explain explains explaining explained *verb*
1 If you explain how to do something, you tell somebody about it so they can understand it. *My brother explained how to mend my bike.*
2 If you explain something that happened, you give reasons why it happened. *We explained that we were late because we had missed the bus.*
explanation *noun*.

explode explodes exploding exploded *verb*
If something such as a bomb explodes, it bursts suddenly with a very loud noise.
explosion *noun*.

explore explores exploring explored *verb*
When you explore, you look carefully around a place you have never seen before.
exploration *noun*.

express expresses expressing expressed *verb*
If you express what you think or feel, you show it in words or actions.

expression expressions *noun*
Your expression is the look on your face that shows how you feel. *A smile is a happy expression.*

extensive *adjective*
covering a wide area. *an extensive park.*
extent *noun*.

extinct *adjective*
An animal or plant that is extinct does not exist now. *Dinosaurs became extinct millions of years ago.*
extinction *noun*.

extinguish extinguishes extinguishing extinguished *verb*
If you extinguish a fire, you put it out. *He extinguished the flames with a bucket of water.* ▲ Say *ex-ting-gwish*.

extra *adjective*
more than you usually have. *I took an extra jumper because I was cold.*

extraordinary *adjective*
very special or unusual. *I read an extraordinary story about a horse that could talk.*

extremely *adverb*
very. *Elephants are extremely big animals.*

eye eyes *noun*
Your eyes are the parts of your face that you use to see with. In the middle of the eye is a hole called a pupil that lets light on to the lens behind. ● A word that sounds like **eye** is **I**.

eyebrow
eyelid
eyelash

F f

fable fables *noun*
a story, usually about animal characters, that teaches you something.

face faces *noun*
Your face is the front part of your head where your eyes, nose and mouth are.

fact facts *noun*
something that is known to be true and that you can prove.

factory factories *noun*
a building where people use machines to make things. *a car factory.*

fade fades fading faded *verb*
1 If something fades, it becomes paler so that you can no longer see it properly. *The ink on the document had faded so much that we could hardly read it.*
2 If a sound fades away, it slowly becomes quieter. *The music faded away until you couldn't hear it.*

fail fails failing failed *verb*
If you fail at something, you do not succeed in doing it. *She failed to get into the team because she had injured her knee.*
failure *noun.*

faint faints fainting fainted *verb*
If you faint, you become unconscious for a short time. *Sam fainted when he saw blood coming from the cut on his finger.*

faint fainter faintest *adjective*
Something that is faint is not very strong or clear. *There is a faint smell of burning.*

fair fairer fairest *adjective*
1 A person who is fair has light-coloured hair and skin. ■ The opposite is **dark**.
2 Something that is fair seems right or treats everybody the same. *It's not fair that I have to go to bed when Ben is allowed to stay up.* ■ The opposite is **unfair**.
● A word that sounds like **fair** is **fare**.

fair fairs *noun*
a place outside where rides and roundabouts and competitions are set up for people to have fun. ● A word that sounds like **fair** is **fare**.

fairy fairies *noun*
a magical creature in stories like a very small person with wings.

faith *noun*
If you have faith in somebody, you trust them to do what they say.

faithful *adjective*
If you are faithful to somebody who trusts you, you do not do anything to hurt that person. *She's very faithful to her friends.*

fake fakes *noun*
a copy of something that looks like the real thing. *It's not a real diamond – it's just a fake.*

fall falls falling fell fallen *verb*
When something falls, it goes down or drops from a higher to a lower place. *Sam fell off the skateboard.*
fall *noun.*

false *adjective*
1 not true. *The man gave a false name to the police instead of his real name.*

2 not the real thing. *Tom is wearing a false beard and glasses.*

fame *noun*
being famous.

familiar *adjective*
If something is familiar to you, you know it well. *Her face was familiar but I couldn't remember her name.* ■ The opposite is **unfamiliar** or **strange**.

family families *noun*
1 a group of people made up of parents, grandparents and children. Aunts, uncles and cousins are also part of your family.
2 a group of animals or plants that are like each other in certain ways. *Polar bears are members of the bear family.*

Grizzly bear
Black bear
Sun bear   Asiatic black bear   Polar bear

famine famines *noun*
a time when there is not enough food for the people in a country to eat. ▲ Say *fam-in.*

famous *adjective*
known by lots of people. *a famous film star.* ▲ Say *fay-muss.*

fan fans *noun*
1 a machine with blades that turn around fast to keep a room cool in hot weather.
2 a flat object, often made of paper, that you wave in front of your face to keep you cool in hot weather.
3 a person who really admires somebody famous such as a singer or an actor, or who likes a certain sport very much. *football fans.*

fancy dress *noun*
clothes that you wear to a party that make you look like somebody or something different. *Jed's having a fancy dress party and I'm going to go as a gorilla. What are you wearing?*

A B C D E F G H I J K L M N O P Q R S T U V W X Y Z

fang fangs *noun*
a long, sharp, pointed tooth. Many animals that eat meat have fangs.

fantastic *adjective*
amazing or really good.

fare fares *noun*
the money that you pay to go on a bus, train or plane. ● A word that sounds like **fare** is **fair**.

farm farms *noun*
a place where people grow crops or keep animals to sell as food.
farmer *noun*.

fascinate fascinates fascinating fascinated *verb*
If something fascinates you, you feel very interested in it. *Snakes fascinate me.* ▲ Say *fas-in-ate.*
fascination *noun*, **fascinating** *adjective*.

fashion fashions *noun*
a way of dressing or behaving that is very popular for a time and that everyone wants to copy.

fast faster fastest *adjective*
1 very quick. *She's a fast runner.*
2 If a watch is fast, it shows a time that is later than the real time. *My watch says five past two but it's five minutes fast, because it's only two o'clock.*
■ The opposite is **slow**.
fast *adverb*.

fast

Some words you can use instead of fast:

We caught a fast train to Edinburgh.
☞ **express, high speed** ☜

She's a very fast talker.
☞ **quick, rapid** ☜

The news spread fast.
☞ **quickly, swiftly, speedily, rapidly** ☜

fasten fastens fastening fastened *verb*
If you fasten something, you do it up or fix it firmly.

fat fatter fattest *adjective*
A person who is fat has a large, heavy body. *a fat Vietnamese pot-bellied pig.* ■ The opposite is **thin**.

fat fats *noun*
oil, butter or margarine that you can use to cook with.

father fathers *noun*
a man who has children.

fault faults *noun*
1 a thing that is wrong with a machine. *We had to take the camera back to the shop because it had a fault.*
2 If something bad is your fault, it happened because of you. *It's your fault we were late because you wouldn't get out of bed.*

favour favours *noun*
a kind and helpful thing that you do for somebody. *Could you do me a favour and carry this box for me?*

favourite *adjective*
Your favourite thing is the one you like best. *Jenny is watching her favourite television programme.*

fax faxes *noun*
1 a machine which sends a picture or message along a telephone wire to another machine which prints it out.
2 a message or picture sent on a fax machine.

an original document and a fax copy

fear *noun*
the feeling that you have when you are afraid. *He has a fear of heights.*

feast feasts *noun*
a large, special meal for a lot of people.

feather feathers *noun*
one of the light, soft parts that cover a bird's body.

feeble feebler feeblest *adjective*
weak. *a feeble old man.*

feed feeds feeding fed *verb*
1 If you feed a person or an animal, you give them food. *We fed the ducks.*
2 When an animal feeds, it eats. *Cows and sheep feed on grass.*

feel feels feeling felt *verb*
1 When you feel something, you touch it and know what it is like against your skin. *Feel my bear – it's so soft.*
2 If you feel sad, happy or angry, you are that way at the moment. *I feel quite hungry.*

feeling feelings *noun*
A feeling is what you feel, like happiness, anger or worry.

feet plural of **foot**.

fell past of **fall**.

felt past of **feel**.

female *adjective*
A female person or animal belongs to the sex that can have babies or lay eggs. Girls and women are female. ■ The opposite is **male**.

fence fences *noun*
a kind of wall made of wood or wire around a piece of land such as a garden or field. *a wooden fence.*

fern ferns *noun*
a plant that has leaves like feathers and no flowers.

ferocious *adjective*
fierce and violent. *The dog was ferocious and bit anybody who went near it.*
▲ Say *fer-oh-shuss.*

ferry **ferries** *noun*
a boat that carries passengers, cars and other vehicles across a river or a narrow bit of sea.

fertile *adjective*
Fertile land is land where plants grow well.

festival **festivals** *noun*
a special day or a religious day that people have as a holiday so they can celebrate it. *During the festival of Chinese New Year, dragons dance to celebrate.*

fetch **fetches fetching fetched** *verb*
When you fetch something, you go to get it and bring it back. *Can you fetch me my coat from the hall, please?*

fever **fevers** *noun*
an illness that makes the temperature of your body higher than usual.

fibre **fibres** *noun*
a thread of wool, cotton or something similar that is used to make cloth.

fiction *noun*
stories that have been made up by somebody and are not about people that really exist. *The novels and stories of Dickens and Andersen are fiction.*

field **fields** *noun*
an area of land where farmers grow crops or keep animals.

fierce **fiercer fiercest** *adjective*
An animal that is fierce is angry and likely to attack you.

fight **fights fighting fought** *verb*
When people or animals fight, they attack and try to hurt each other. *Two boys were fighting in the playground.*
fight *noun.*

figure **figures** *noun*
1 one of the signs that we use to write numbers, such as 1, 2 and 3.
2 the shape of a person. *I could just make out the figure of a tall man in the fog.*

file **files** *noun*
1 a box or cardboard cover for keeping papers in.
2 a set of information on a computer.
3 a tool with a rough surface that you use to make things smooth. *a nail file.*
single file a line of people or animals, one behind the other. *The children walked in single file into the school hall.*

different types of file

fill **fills filling filled** *verb*
If you fill something, you put as much into it as it can hold. *Fiona filled the bottles with water.* ■ The opposite is **empty.**

film **films** *noun*
1 a story in moving pictures that you watch in a cinema or on television.
2 a long, thin strip of plastic that you put in a camera for taking photographs. *I need a new film for my camera.*

fin **fins** *noun*
A fin is one of the thin, flat parts on a fish's body that help it to swim and balance.

final *adjective*
last. *The final episode of the TV series is on tonight.*
finally *adverb.*

find **finds finding found** *verb*
When you find something, you see it again after it has been lost or you did not know where it was. *I've found my old trainers. They were at the back of the cupboard.* ■ The opposite is **lose.**

fine **finer finest** *adjective*
1 healthy. *"How are you?" "I'm fine, thanks."*
2 bright and sunny. *We'll go to the beach if it's fine tomorrow.*
3 good enough. *There's nothing wrong with your work – it's fine.*
4 very thin. *You need a sharp pencil to draw a fine line.*
5 very good. *She's a fine athlete.*

fine **fines** *noun*
Money that you have to pay as a punishment. *Mum had to pay a fine for parking on a double yellow line.*

finger **fingers** *noun*
Your fingers are the long, thin parts at the end of your hands.

fingerprint **fingerprints** *noun*
the mark made by the tip of your finger showing the lines on your skin. *The police couldn't find any fingerprints because the thief had worn gloves.*

finish **finishes finishing finished** *verb*
When you finish something, you come to the end of it. ■ The opposite is **start** or **begin.**
finish *noun.*

fir **firs** *noun*
an evergreen tree with cones and leaves that are the shape of needles. ● A word that sounds like **fir** is **fur.**

fire **fires** *noun*
the hot, bright flames that come from something that is burning.

fire **fires firing fired** *verb*
1 to shoot bullets from a gun. *The thief fired at the policeman.*
2 to dismiss or sack somebody from their job. *Get out; you're fired!*

A B C D E F G H I J K L M N O P Q R S T U V W X Y Z

fire engine **fire engines** *noun*
a large lorry with hoses and ladders that fire-fighters travel in to get to a fire.

fire extinguisher **fire extinguishers** *noun*
a metal container full of chemicals or water that you use to put out a fire.

fire-fighter **fire-fighters** *noun*
a person whose job is to put out dangerous fires and to rescue people who are in danger.

fireplace **fireplaces** *noun*
a hole in a wall in a room beneath a chimney where you can light a fire.

fireworks *noun*
small objects containing chemicals that explode noisily and make brightly coloured sparks when you light them.

firm **firmer firmest** *adjective*
1 Something that is firm is quite hard and does not change its shape when you press it. *Bananas are firm when they are green but get softer when they are ripe.*
2 If you are firm about something, you are sure and you are not going to change your mind. *We haven't made a firm decision yet about where we are going on holiday.*

firm **firms** *noun*
a business company. *Figgy works for a large publishing firm.*

first aid *noun*
medical help or treatment that is given to a sick or hurt person before the doctor arrives.

fish **fish** or **fishes** *noun*
an animal that lives in water and breathes through gills. A fish has fins and a tail for swimming, and its body is covered in scales. ❖ *Look opposite*

fish **fishes fishing fished** *verb*
To fish is to try to catch fish. *My uncle taught us how to fish with a fishing-rod.*

fishmonger **fishmongers** *noun*
a person in a shop or market, who sells fresh fish to eat.

fist **fists** *noun*
You make a fist when you curl your fingers and thumb into your palm. *The boys were punching each other with their fists.*

fit **fits fitting fitted** *verb*
1 If something fits, it is the right size or shape. *These jeans don't fit me any more.*
2 If you fit things together, you join one thing to another. *I fitted the jigsaw puzzle together.*

fit **fitter fittest** *adjective*
If you are fit, your body is well and strong. *My dad does exercises to keep himself fit.*

fix **fixes fixing fixed** *verb*
1 When you fix something to another thing, you join the two things firmly. *She fixed the shelf to the wall.*
2 When you fix something that was broken, you make it useful again. *I've fixed your bike.*

fizzy **fizzier fizziest** *adjective*
A fizzy drink is full of small bubbles.

flag **flags** *noun*
a piece of cloth with a pattern on it, on the end of a pole. Each country has its own flag.

flake **flakes** *noun*
a small, thin, light piece of something. *a snowflake.*

flame **flames** *noun*
the hot, bright, burning gas that comes from a fire.

flap **flaps flapping flapped** *verb*
When a bird flaps its wings, it moves them up and down quickly.

flap **flaps** *noun*
a flat piece that hangs down to cover an opening. *a cat flap.*

flare **flares** *noun*
a bright flame or light used as a signal.

flash **flashes** *noun*
a sudden, bright light that lasts a short time. *a flash of lightning.*

flask **flasks** *noun*
1 a container with a lid for keeping hot drinks hot and cold drinks cold.
2 a glass container for liquids that is used for doing scientific experiments.

flat **flatter flattest** *adjective*
1 level and completely smooth and even, with no parts that are higher than the rest. *A table has a flat top.*
2 A flat tyre does not have enough air in it. *My bike has a flat tyre.*

flat **flats** *noun*
a set of rooms for living in on one floor of a building.

flavour **flavours** *noun*
The flavour of something is what it tastes like. *different flavours of ice-cream.*

flea **fleas** *noun*
a tiny jumping insect with no wings. Fleas bite people and animals.

fleece **fleeces** *noun*
a sheep's coat of wool.

flesh *noun*
1 the soft part of your body that is under your skin, covering your bones.
2 the soft part of fruit or vegetables.

flew past of **fly**
● A word that sounds like **flew** is **flu**.

flight **flights** *noun*
1 a journey in a plane.
2 flying through the air. *Have you ever seen swans in flight?*
3 A flight of stairs is a set of stairs.

float **floats floating floated** *verb*
1 When something floats in a liquid, it stays on the top and does not sink. *an experiment to see what floats.*
2 When something floats in air, it moves along gently in the air without falling to the ground. *floating balloons.*

flock flocks *noun*
a group of animals of one kind. *a flock of sheep.* ◆ *a flock of geese.*

flood floods *noun*
A flood happens when a lot of water covers an area that is usually dry. Floods often happen when there has been a lot of rain. *A burst pipe flooded the kitchen.* **flood** *verb.*

floodlight floodlights *noun*
very bright lights that light up a sports ground or a building at night.

floor floors *noun*
1 the flat part that you walk on inside a building.
2 a level of a building. *We live on the third floor of a block of flats.*

floppy disk floppy disks *noun*
a magnetic disk in a square case that stores information from a computer.

flour *noun*
white or brown powder that is made by grinding grains such as wheat. We use flour to make bread, cakes and pastry. ● A word that sounds like **flour** is **flower**.

flow flows flowing flowed *verb*
When a liquid flows, it moves smoothly along. *Rivers flow into the sea.* ◆ *The water flowed down the drain.*

flower flowers *noun*
the part of a plant at the end of the stem that has coloured or white petals. ● A word that sounds like **flower** is **flour**.

flown past of **fly**.

flu *noun*
an illness that gives you a high temperature and makes your body ache all over. Flu is short for **influenza**. ● A word that sounds like **flu** is **flew**.

fluffy fluffier fluffiest *adjective*
soft and light, like wool or hair. *Baby chickens are fluffy.*

fluid fluids *noun*
a substance that flows. *Liquids and gases are fluids.*

fluorescent *adjective*
A fluorescent object glows in the dark when you shine a light on it. *Cyclists wear fluorescent strips so that car drivers can see them in the dark more easily.* ▲ Say flor-**es**-ent.

flush flushes flushing flushed *verb*
1 If you flush, your face goes red. *Thomas flushed with embarrassment.*
2 When you flush the toilet, you make a lot of water flow through it to clean it.

flute flutes *noun*
a musical instrument like a long, thin pipe. You hold it sideways and blow into the end, covering holes with your fingers to play different notes.

flutter flutters fluttering fluttered *verb*
When something flutters, it makes quick, light, flapping movements. *A moth was fluttering against the window.*

fly flies *noun*
a small insect with two wings.

fly flies flying flew flown *verb*
1 When something flies, it moves through the air. *A flock of geese was flying overhead.*
2 When you fly, you make a journey in a plane.

foal foals *noun*
a young horse.

foam *noun*
a mass of small air bubbles. *If you use washing-up liquid, you get a lot of foam.*

focus focuses focusing focused *verb*
When you focus a camera or a telescope, you move a part of it so that what you see through it is clear.

fog *noun*
thick cloud near the ground that makes it difficult to see anything. **foggy** *adjective.*

foil *noun*
a very thin sheet of metal used to wrap food.

fold folds folding folded *verb*
When you fold something, you bend one part so that it covers another. *Fred folded his jumper before putting it in his suitcase.* ■ The opposite is **unfold**. **fold** *noun.*

follow follows following followed *verb*
1 If you follow somebody, you go along behind them. ■ The opposite is **lead**.
2 If one thing follows another, it comes after it. *Night always follows day.*

fond fonder fondest *adjective*
If you are fond of somebody, you like them very much and care about what happens to them.

food *noun*
all the things that people and animals can eat.

foolish *adjective*
very silly. ■ The opposite is **sensible**.

foot feet *noun*
Your foot is the part of your body at the bottom of your leg that you stand on.

football footballs *noun*
1 a game played by two teams who try to kick a ball into the other team's goal. The game is also called soccer.
2 the ball that you use to play football.

footprint footprints *noun*
the mark that your foot or shoe leaves on a surface.

footstep footsteps *noun*
the sound that a person who is walking makes when each foot touches the ground. *I could hear footsteps coming up the path.*

forbid forbids forbidding forbade forbidden *verb*
If somebody forbids you to do something, they are telling you that you are not allowed to do it. *Our teacher has forbidden us to bring our pets to school.*
■ The opposite is **permit** or **allow**.

force forces forcing forced *verb*
1 If somebody forces you to do something, they make you do it. *He forced me to give him the money.*
2 If you force something somewhere, you use your strength to make it go there. *She tried to force a parcel through the letter box.*

force forces *noun*
power or strength. *A lot of trees were blown down by the force of the wind.*

forecast forecasts forecasting forecast or forecasted *verb*
If you forecast something, you say it is going to happen in the future. *She forecasts that the weather will become warmer at the weekend.*
forecast *noun*
the weather forecast.

forehead foreheads *noun*
Your forehead is the part of your face above your eyes and below your hair.

foreign *adjective*
A person or thing that is foreign belongs to a country that is not your own. *Jane collects foreign stamps.* ▲ Say *for-en.*

forest forests *noun*
a very large group of trees.

forge forges forging forged *verb*
If somebody forges something, such as money, they make an exact copy of it in order to deceive people. *He was put in prison for forging passports to sell to criminals.* ▲ Say *forj.*
forgery *noun.*

forget forgets forgetting forgot forgotten *verb*
When you forget something, you do not remember it. *Don't forget your keys.*

forgive forgives forgiving forgave forgiven *verb*
When you forgive somebody, you do not mind any more about something bad they did to you. *Lily finally forgave me for losing her pen.*

fork forks *noun*
1 a tool with long, pointed parts called prongs at one end. You use a small fork for putting food in your mouth. Large forks are used for digging.
2 the place where something divides into two parts. *a fork in the road.*

form forms *noun*
1 the shape of something. *a birthday cake in the form of a dog.*
2 a kind of something. *Gas and coal are forms of fuel.*
3 a printed paper with questions and spaces for you to write the answers.
4 a class in a school.

form forms forming formed *verb*
1 When things form a certain shape, they are arranged in that shape. *The chairs formed a half circle.*
2 When something forms, it starts to appear. *A crowd was forming outside the theatre.*

fortnight fortnights *noun*
two weeks. *a fortnight's holiday in Italy.*

fortress fortresses *noun*
a big, strong building such as a castle that can be defended against enemies.

fortune fortunes *noun*
1 good or bad luck.
2 a lot of money. *They won a fortune in the lottery.*

fossil fossils *noun*
what remains of a plant or animal that died millions of years ago and that has become part of a piece of rock.
fossilized *adjective.*

foster fosters fostering fostered *verb*
When somebody fosters a child, they take the child into their home and look after them for a while.

fought past of **fight**.

found past of **find**.

fountain fountains *noun*
a statue or object that sprays water up into the air.

fox foxes *noun*
a wild animal that looks like a small dog with red-brown fur and a long, thick tail.

fraction fractions *noun*
1 a part of a whole number. $\frac{1}{2}$ and $\frac{2}{5}$ are fractions.
2 a tiny part. *She opened the cage door a fraction but the hamster escaped.*

fracture fractures *noun*
a break or crack in something, especially a bone. *Her arm is in plaster because she has a fracture.* ▲ Say *frak-cher.*
fracture *verb.*

fragile *adjective*
Something that is fragile can break easily. *Be careful not to drop that vase, it's quite fragile.* ▲ Say *fraj-ile.*

frame frames *noun*
1 an edge around something such as a picture or window.
2 the shape of something such as a building or vehicle that is built first out of metal or wood, so that the rest can be built over it. *An aeroplane has a strong steel frame.*
frame *verb*
The pictures are being framed.

freckle freckles *noun*
a small brown spot on a person's skin.

free *adjective*
1 If you are free, you are able to do what you want or go where you want without anybody stopping you.
2 Something that is free does not cost any money.
3 Free also means not busy. *I'm busy now but I'll be free after supper.*
freedom *noun*.

freeze freezes freezing froze frozen *verb*
1 When water freezes, it gets so cold that it turns into ice.
2 When you freeze food, you make it very cold by storing it at a very low temperature so that it stays fresh for a long time.
3 If you are freezing, you are very cold.
● A word that sounds like freeze is frieze.

freezer freezers *noun*
a large metal chest or cupboard that freezes food so that it stays fresh for a long time.

freight *noun*
goods that a lorry, train, ship or plane is carrying. ▲ Rhymes with **late**.

frequent *adjective*
Something that is frequent happens or comes often. *There are frequent buses to the city centre from here.*

fresh fresher freshest *adjective*
1 Food that is fresh has been made or picked recently and is not old or bad. *fresh eggs.* ◆ *fresh fruit.*
2 Fresh air is air that is clean and good to breathe. *We went outside to get some fresh air.*
3 Fresh water is water that is not salty.

fridge fridges *noun*
A kind of metal cupboard that is cold inside, where food can be kept fresh for a time. Fridge is short for **refrigerator**.

friend friends *noun*
a person that you know well and like a lot. *Jazz, Tash and Sam are best friends.*
friendship *noun*.

friendly friendlier friendliest *adjective*
A friendly person gets to know other people easily and acts like a friend towards them. *Erica is friendly to everybody.*

frieze friezes *noun*
a strip along the top of a wall that has coloured decorations or pictures on it.
● A word that sounds like frieze is freeze.

frighten frightens frightening frightened *verb*
If you frighten somebody, you make them feel afraid.
frightened *adjective*, **frightening** *adjective*.

frill frills *noun*
a strip of material with a lot of folds in it that is sewn on to the edge of something to decorate it. *a blouse with frills down the front.*
frilly *adverb*.

fringe fringes *noun*
1 a strip of hanging threads decorating the edge of something.
2 the front part of a person's hair that hangs down over their forehead.

frog frogs *noun*
a small animal with long, powerful back legs that it uses to jump. Frogs lay their eggs in water and these eggs develop into tadpoles.

front fronts *noun*
the part of something that faces forward or that you usually see first. ■ The opposite is **back** or **rear**.
in front of not behind. *There is a small garden in front of our house.*

frost *noun*
a layer of ice crystals like white powder that forms at night when the weather is very cold.
frosty *adjective*.

froth *noun*
a mass of small bubbles on the surface of a liquid.
frothy *adjective*.

frown frowns frowning frowned *verb*
When you frown, you pull your eyebrows down and make your forehead wrinkle, often because you are cross or worried. *He was frowning because he wasn't allowed to go to the football match.*

froze, frozen past of freeze.

fruit fruits *noun*
the part of a plant that contains seeds or a stone. You can eat many kinds of fruit.
❖ *Look opposite*

fry fries frying fried *verb*
When you fry food, you cook it in hot fat. You fry food in a frying-pan.

fuel fuels *noun*
something such as coal, wood, gas or petrol that we burn to make heat or power. *Cars and aeroplanes cannot run without fuel.*

full fuller fullest *adjective*
If something is full, there is so much inside it that there is no room for any more. *The bus was full of people.* ■ The opposite is **empty**.

full stop full stops *noun*
a dot (.) that you use in writing. You must always put a full stop at the end of a sentence.

A B C D E F G H I J K L M N O P Q R S T U V W X Y Z

fumes *noun*
smelly or poisonous smoke or gases that come from something that is burning or from chemicals. *petrol fumes.*

fun *noun*
When you have fun, you enjoy yourself.

fund funds *noun*
an amount of money that is going to be used for a special purpose. *The school is raising funds to build a new gym.*

funeral funerals *noun*
a ceremony in which a dead body is buried or burned.

fungus funguses or **fungi** *noun*
a kind of plant that is not green and does not have leaves or flowers. Fungi grow in damp, dark places. Mushrooms and toadstools are kinds of fungi.

funnel funnels *noun*
1 a tube that is wide at one end and narrow at the other. A funnel is used for pouring liquid into a narrow container such as a bottle.
2 a chimney on a ship.

funny funnier funniest *adjective*
1 If something is funny, it makes you laugh or smile. *a funny story.*
2 Funny also means strange. *There was a funny smell coming from the kitchen.*

fur *noun*
the soft, thick hair that covers the body of many animals such as cats and hamsters. ● A word that sounds like **fur** is **fir**.
furry *adjective*.

a furry hamster

furious *adjective*
very angry. *She was furious when she lost her keys.*

furniture *noun*
large things such as chairs, tables, beds and desks that people have in their homes and other buildings.

fuse fuses *noun*
a small piece of wire in electrical equipment that melts if too much electricity flows through it. Fuses prevent things from getting damaged and prevent fires from starting.

fuss *noun*
If you make a fuss about something, you keep being worried about it and talking about it although it is not very important. *What a lot of fuss you are making about nothing.*
fuss *verb*.

future *noun*
the time that has not happened yet. Nobody can be sure what will happen in the future. ■ The opposite is **past**.

G g

gadget gadgets *noun*
a tool that you use to do a special job. *different kitchen gadgets.*

useful kitchen gadgets

gain gains gaining gained *verb*
1 To gain means to get or win something. *By the end of the game, our team had gained 10 points.*
2 To gain also means to get more of something. *The bicycle gained speed as it went down the hill.*

galaxy galaxies *noun*
a very large group of stars and planets in space. *The Earth is part of one galaxy.*

gale gales *noun*
a very strong wind. *Gales can blow down trees and damage buildings.*

galleon galleons *noun*
a big sailing ship that was used a long time ago. *a large galleon carrying treasure.*

gallery galleries *noun*
a place where you can go to look at paintings, sculptures or photographs.

gallop gallops galloping galloped *verb*
When a horse gallops, it runs very fast.

gamble gambles gambling gambled *verb*
When somebody gambles on something such as a horse race, they pay to choose a horse that they think will win. If that horse wins the race, that person will get their money back and win more money.

game games *noun*
A game is something that you play for fun. Games often have rules.

gang gangs *noun*
a group of people who do things together. *There was a big fight between the two gangs.*

gaol gaols *noun*
a prison. ▲ Say *jail*.

gap gaps *noun*
a space between two things. *We climbed through the gap in the fence.*

garage garages *noun*
1 a building where somebody can keep their car.
2 a place that sells petrol or where people mend cars.

garden gardens *noun*
a piece of land near a house, where people grow flowers and vegetables.

garlic *noun*
a plant similar to a small onion with a very strong taste and smell. Garlic is used in cooking.

gas gases *noun*
A gas is something like air that is not liquid or solid and that you cannot see. Air is made of several gases mixed together. We use another kind of gas for cooking and heating.

gasp gasps gasping gasped *verb*
When you gasp, you take in a short, quick breath of air through your mouth. People gasp when they are surprised or hurt. *He was gasping for air when they pulled him out of the river.*

gate gates *noun*
a gate is a kind of door in a wall or fence. *a garden gate.*

gather gathers gathering gathered *verb*
1 If you gather things, you collect them. *We gathered wood for the camp fire.*
2 If people gather, they come together in a group. *The children gathered around the ice-cream van.*

gaze gazes gazing gazed *verb*
If you gaze at something, you look at it for a long time. *He stood on the shore gazing out to sea.*

gear gears *noun*
1 a set of wheels that work together in a car, bicycle or model to make it go faster or slower.
2 the special clothes or things that you need for something. *camping gear.*

geese plural of **goose**.

gem gems *noun*
a precious stone or jewel.

gene genes *noun*
Genes are the tiny parts of the cells of plants and animals that control what they look like. Genes are passed from parents to children. ▲ Say *jeen*.

general *adjective*
Something that is general is to do with most people or things. *The general feeling is that exercise is good for you.* **generally** *adverb*.

generation generations *noun*
all the people who were born at about the same time. *This photo shows three different generations of my family: my grandparents, my parents and me.*

generous *adjective*
If you are generous, you are kind and always ready to give money and other things. *a generous act.* **generosity** *noun*.

model helicopter gears

genius geniuses *noun*
an unusually clever and intelligent person. ▲ Say *jee-nee-us*.

gentle gentler gentlest *adjective*
a gentle person is kind and careful, not rough. *Be gentle with the baby.*

genuine *adjective*
real, not fake. *Is this a genuine dinosaur fossil?* ▲ Say *jen-yoo-in*.

geography *noun*
the study of the countries of the world, and of things such as its mountains, rivers and people.

gerbil gerbils *noun*
a small, furry animal with long back legs. Some people keep gerbils in cages as pets.

germ germs *noun*
a very small living thing that can make you ill. *flu germs.*

ghost ghosts *noun*
the figure of a dead person that some people say they have seen.

giant giants *noun*
a very big, strong person in stories.

gift gifts *noun*
1 a present. *birthday gifts.*
2 If you have a gift for something, you are very good at it. *Harry has a gift for music.*

gigantic *adjective*
very, very big. *a gigantic mountain.*
▲ Say *jye-gan-tik.*

giggle giggles giggling giggled *verb*
If you giggle, you laugh in a silly way. *We couldn't stop giggling at our teacher's funny hat.*

gill gills *noun*
Gills are the parts of a fish that it breathes through. A fish has a pair of gills, one on each side of its head.

ginger *noun*
1 a plant with a strong, hot taste. You can use the root, or powder made from the root in cooking. *root ginger.*
2 an orange colour. *a ginger haired boy.*

giraffe giraffes *noun*
a tall African animal with a very long neck. Giraffes feed on leaves and twigs from trees.

girl girls *noun*
a female child or a young woman.

ice fields

ice moves downwards creating cracks called crevasses

ice falls from the slope of the glacier and melts to form rivers

glacier glaciers *noun*
a huge river of ice that moves very slowly down a mountain valley.

glad *adjective*
happy. *I'm glad you can come to my birthday party.*

glance glances glancing glanced *verb*
If you glance at something, you look at it quickly. *She glanced at her watch.*

gland glands *noun*
one of the parts of your body that make the chemicals that your body needs. *Sweat glands produce sweat to help your body cool down when you are hot.*

glare glares glaring glared *verb*
If you glare at somebody, you look at them in an angry way.

glass glasses *noun*
1 Glass is a hard material that you can see through and that breaks easily. Windows and bottles are made of glass. *A greenhouse is made of glass.*
2 A glass is a container that you drink from, made of glass.

glasses *noun*
Glasses are two pieces of special glass, called lenses, in a frame. Some people wear glasses to help them see better. *She wears glasses to help her see more clearly.*

gleam gleams gleaming gleamed *verb*
To gleam means to shine with a soft light. *The lake gleamed in the moonlight.*

glide glides gliding glided *verb*
If something glides, it moves smoothly along. *The dancers glided gracefully around the floor.*

glider gliders *noun*
a very light aircraft that does not have an engine. Gliders fly by floating on currents of air.

glimpse glimpses glimpsing glimpsed *verb*
If you glimpse somebody or something, you only see them for a very short time. *We just glimpsed the rabbit as it ran into the wood.*

glitter glitters glittering glittered *verb*
If something glitters, it shines brightly with lots of flashes of light. *a ring with many glittering diamonds.*
glitter *noun.*

globe globes *noun*
a ball with a map of the world on it.

gloomy gloomier gloomiest
adjective
1 If a room or a day is gloomy, it is dark and dull.
2 If you are gloomy, you feel sad.

glossy glossier glossiest *adjective*
shiny. *a dog with a glossy coat.*

glove gloves *noun*
a piece of clothing that you wear on your hand. *woollen gloves.*

glow glows glowing glowed *verb*
If something glows, it shines with a steady light. *The fire glowed in the dark.*

glue *noun*
a thick liquid that you use for sticking things together. *Jazz and Sajni used glue to mend the broken pottery.*
glue
verb.

gnat gnats *noun*
a small, flying insect that bites people.
▲ Say *nat*.

gnaw gnaws gnawing gnawed
verb
If you gnaw something hard, you keep biting it for a long time. *The dog was gnawing at a bone.* ▲ Say *nor*.

gnome gnomes *noun*
a little old man in fairy stories who lives underground. Gnomes usually have long beards and pointed hats. ▲ Say *nome*.

goal goals *noun*
1 A goal is the place where you have to make the ball go to score a point in games such as football or hockey.
2 A goal is also the point that you score when the ball goes into the goal.
3 A goal can also be something important that you want to do in your life. *My goal is to run the marathon in the Olympic Games.*

goat goats *noun*
an animal with horns and short, rough hair. A male goat is called a billy-goat, a female is a nanny-goat and a young goat is a kid.
Goats are kept on farms for their milk.

gobble gobbles gobbling gobbled
verb
If you gobble food, you eat it very quickly and greedily. *She gobbled up all the biscuits and cakes before anyone else could eat them.*

god gods *noun*
a being that people believe controls them and nature. Some people pray to many different gods. *Brahma, Vishnu and Shiva are the three main gods of the Hindu religion.*

goggles *noun*
special glasses that you wear to protect your eyes from water or dust. *He wears goggles when he's making models.*

go-kart go-karts *noun*
a small, low, open racing car. *go-kart racing.*

gold *noun*
a shiny, yellow metal that is used to make rings and other jewellery.

goldfish goldfish or goldfishes
noun
a small, orange fish you keep as a pet.

golf *noun*
a game that you play by using long sticks called golf clubs to hit a ball into holes around a golf course.

gong gongs *noun*
a round piece of metal that you hit to make a loud noise.

good better best *adjective*
1 If something is good, people like it. *a good story.*
2 If you are good, you do as you are told.
3 If you are good at something, you can do it well. *Yasmin is good at spelling.*
4 If something is good for you, it makes you healthy. *Fruit is good for you.*

> **good**
>
> *Some words you can use instead of good:*
>
> We need a good plumber to mend the broken pipes.
> ☞ **skilled, expert** ☜
>
> He's a good pianist.
> ☞ **talented** ☜
>
> The weather is good today.
> ☞ **marvellous** ☜

goods *noun*
things that can be bought and sold.

goose geese *noun*
a large bird with a long neck and webbed feet that lives near water. Some geese are wild but others are kept on farms for their eggs, meat and feathers. A male goose is called a gander, and a young goose is a gosling.

Canada Goose

Barnacle Goose *Egyptian Goose*

gorge **gorges** *noun*
a deep, narrow valley. *The river runs through the gorge.*

gorgeous *adjective*
very beautiful. *a gorgeous day.* ◆ *a gorgeous view of the sea.* ▲ Say **gor**-*juss.*

gorilla **gorillas** *noun*
a very big African ape with dark fur.

gorse *noun*
a prickly bush with yellow flowers.

government **governments** *noun*
a group of people who are in charge of a country. *In Britain, the Prime Minister is the head of the government.* ▲ Say **guv**-er-ment.

gown **gowns** *noun*
1 a long dress that women wear at special times. *a ball gown.*
2 a long, loose piece of clothing that judges and some teachers wear.

grab **grabs grabbing grabbed** *verb*
If you grab something, you take it quickly and roughly. *The robber grabbed the money and ran away.*

graceful *adjective*
If somebody or something is graceful, they move in a beautiful way. *a graceful skater.*

grade **grades** *noun*
a mark that a teacher gives you to show how good your work is. *I got grade A for my story and B for art.*

gradual *adjective*
If something is gradual, it happens slowly and steadily. *I'm making gradual progress at swimming.*
gradually *adverb*.

graffiti *noun*
writing and drawing on walls in public places. ▲ Say gra-**fee**-tee.

grain **grains** *noun*
1 Grain is the seeds of plants such as wheat and rice that we eat.
2 Grains are tiny, hard bits of something such as salt, sugar or sand.

grand **grander grandest** *adjective*
big and important. *a grand country house.* ◆ *a grand party.*

grandchild **grandchildren** *noun*
A grandchild is the child of a person's son or daughter.

grandparent **grandparents** *noun*
Your grandparents are the mother and father of your mother or father.

grape **grapes** *noun*
a small, green or black fruit that grows in bunches on a vine. Wine is made from grapes. Raisins are dried grapes.

grapefruit **grapefruit** *noun*
a large, round yellow fruit that is similar to an orange but not as sweet.

graph **graphs** *noun*
a diagram that shows how numbers and amounts compare with each other. *We drew a graph to show how much rain there was in each month of the year.*

grasp **grasps grasping grasped** *verb*
If you grasp something, you hold it tightly. *She grasped the child's hand as they crossed the road.*

grass **grasses** *noun*
the thin, green leaves that cover fields and lawns. *Sheep and cows eat grass.*
grassy *adjective*.

grasshopper **grasshoppers** *noun*
a jumping insect with strong back legs and two pairs of wings. Grasshoppers feed on plants.

grate **grates grating grated** *verb*
If you grate food, you rub it over a metal tool called a grater to shred it into very small pieces. *grated cheese.* ● A word that sounds like **grate** is **great**.

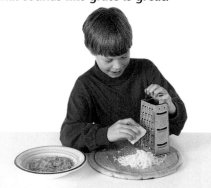

grateful *adjective*
If you feel grateful to somebody, you want to thank them because they have done something for you. *I was very grateful to her for finding my purse.* ■ The opposite is **ungrateful**.
gratefully *adverb*.

grave **graves** *noun*
a hole in the ground where a dead person is buried.

grave **graver gravest** *adjective*
very serious and important. *a grave mistake.* ◆ *a grave illness.*

gravel *noun*
small stones that are used to cover paths and roads.

gravity *noun*
the natural force that pulls everything down towards the Earth.

gravy *noun*
a sauce made from the juices that come out of meat when you cook it.

graze grazes grazing grazed *verb*
1 When animals graze, they move around eating grass. *The sheep were grazing in the field.*
2 If you graze your skin, you cut it slightly by scraping it against something. *When she fell over she grazed her knee quite badly.*

grease *noun*
thick oil or soft fat. *You will need very hot water to wash the grease off those dirty plates.*
greasy *adjective.*

great greater greatest *adjective*
1 very good. *a great film.*
2 very important. *a great king.*
3 very big. *a great crowd of people.*
● A word that sounds like **great** is **grate**.

greedy greedier greediest *adjective*
A person who is greedy wants more of something than they really need. *Don't be so greedy – leave some cake for your brother and sister.*

greenhouse greenhouses *noun*
a building made of glass, used for growing plants.

greet greets greeting greeted *verb*
When you greet somebody, you do something friendly when you meet them, such as saying "hello" or kissing. *They greeted each other by shaking hands.*

greeting greetings *noun*
words such as "hello", "good morning" or "Happy New Year" that you say when you meet somebody.

grew past of **grow**.

grief *noun*
great sadness. *She was filled with grief when her dog died.*

grill grills grilling grilled *verb*
If you grill food, you cook it on metal bars under or over strong heat. *the smell of grilled sausages.*
grill *noun.*

grin grins grinning grinned *verb*
If you grin, you have a big smile. *She grinned at me when I said hello.*
grin *noun.*

grind grinds grinding ground *verb*
If you grind something, you crush it into tiny pieces or into a powder. *grinding peppercorns.*

grip grips gripping gripped *verb*
If you grip something, you hold it very firmly. *She gripped the branch and swung from it.*

groan groans groaning groaned *verb*
If you groan, you make a long, deep sound because you are unhappy or in pain. *"My leg hurts," he groaned.*

groom grooms *noun*
1 a person who looks after horses.
2 a man on his wedding day.

groom grooms grooming groomed *verb*
If you groom an animal, you clean and brush it. *The children are grooming their horse before riding it.*

groove grooves *noun*
a long, thin line that is cut into a flat surface.

grope gropes groping groped *verb*
If you grope for something, you try to find it by feeling with your hands when you cannot see. *It was dark so she had to grope about for the door handle.*

ground grounds *noun*
1 The ground is what you walk on when you are outside. *We sat on the ground to eat our picnic.*
2 a piece of land that is used for something special. *a playground.*

ground past of **grind**.

group groups *noun*
1 a number of people or things that are together in one place. *A group of children stood near the ice-cream van.*
2 a group of musicians who play or sing together.

grow grows growing grew grown *verb*
1 When something grows, it gets bigger. *The puppies are growing very fast.*
2 If you grow something, you plant it so that it will develop. *Flora grew this plant from seed.*
3 To grow also means to become. *We are all growing older.*

growl growls growling growled *verb*
To growl is to make the low, rough noise that a dog or a bear makes when it is angry or frightened.
growl *noun.*

A B C D E F G H I J K L M N O P Q R S T U V W X Y Z

grown-up grown-ups *noun*
an adult. *Parents are grown-ups.*

growth *noun*
growing. *We measured the tree every month to check its growth.*

grumble grumbles grumbling grumbled *verb*
If you grumble, you complain about something in a cross way. *My sister often grumbles about having to do her homework.*

grunt grunts grunting grunted *verb*
To grunt is to make the short, deep, rough sound that a pig makes.

guarantee guarantees *noun*
1 a promise made by the makers of something, that they will mend or replace it if it goes wrong.
2 a promise that something will happen. *I want a guarantee that you will all behave yourselves.*
▲ Say ga-ran-**tee**.
guarantee *verb*.

guard guards
noun
a person who keeps somebody or something safe, or who stops people from escaping. *a Swiss guard.*

guard
guards
guarding
guarded *verb*
If you guard somebody or something, you keep them safe, or stop them from escaping. *The house was guarded by two fierce dogs.*

guess guesses guessing guessed *verb*
When you guess, you try to give an answer to something when you do not really know if it is right. *Can you guess what's in the box?*
guess *noun*.
Have a guess at how much the birthday cake weighs.

guest guests *noun*
a person who is staying in your home because you have invited them. *We have guests staying with us this weekend.*
▲ Rhymes with **best**.

guide guides guiding guided *verb*
If you guide somebody, you show them where to go or what to do. *Her job is to guide people around the city.* ▲ Rhymes with **wide**.
guide *noun*.

guilty *adjective*
1 If you are guilty, you have done something wrong. ■ The opposite is **innocent**.
2 If you feel guilty, you feel sorry because you have done something wrong. *She felt guilty for being rude to her aunt.*

guinea-pig guinea-pigs *noun*
a small, furry animal with short ears and no tail. Some people keep guinea-pigs as pets.

guitar guitars *noun*
a musical instrument with six strings that you play with your fingers.

gull gulls *noun*
a large, grey or white sea bird.

gulp gulps gulping gulped *verb*
If you gulp, you swallow something very quickly. *Katie gulped down the orange juice because she was thirsty.*

gum gums *noun*
1 Your gums are the firm, pink flesh around your teeth.
2 a kind of glue.

gun guns *noun*
a weapon that shoots bullets. *He aimed the gun and fired two shots.*

gunpowder *noun*
powder that explodes. Gunpowder is used in guns and fireworks.

gutter gutters *noun*
an open pipe along the edge of a roof or a narrow ditch at the side of a road for carrying away rainwater.

gym gyms *noun*
a large room where you can do exercises, often using special equipment. Gym is short for **gymnasium**.

gymnast gymnasts *noun*
a person who does difficult and carefully controlled movements with their body in competitions. *an Olympic gymnast.*

gymnastics *noun*
1 exercises for your body.
2 a sport in which people do difficult and carefully controlled movements with their body in competitions.

H h

habit habits *noun*
something that you do often, usually without thinking about it. *Biting your nails is a bad habit.*

habitat habitats *noun*
The habitat of an animal or a plant is the kind of place where it lives. *This monkey's natural habitat is the jungle.*

hail *noun*
frozen rain falling as little balls of ice, called hailstones.

hair hairs *noun*
Your hair is made up of lots of thin threads which grow on your head. Hair can also grow on other parts of your body. ● A word that sounds like **hair** is **hare**.

straight, curly and wavy hair

hairdresser hairdressers *noun*
a person whose job is to cut and arrange people's hair.

hairy hairier hairiest *adjective*
covered with hair. *The book is about a big, hairy monster.*

half halves *noun*
one of two equal parts of something. You can write half as ½. *Half of ten is five.*
◆ *Two halves make a whole.*

hall halls *noun*
1 the part just inside the door of a house or flat with doors leading to other rooms.
2 a large room or a building where events such as concerts and meetings take place. *a school hall.*

halt halts halting halted *verb*
When something halts, it stops. *The lorry halted at the traffic lights.*

halve halves halving halved *verb*
If you halve something, you divide it into two equal parts. *Halve the fruit and remove the stone.*

ham *noun*
meat from a pig's leg which has been treated with salt so it can be kept for a long time. *a ham and cheese sandwich.*

hamburger hamburgers *noun*
chopped beef pressed into a flat, round shape and eaten in a bread roll.

hammer hammers *noun*
a tool with a heavy part at one end that you use for hitting nails into things.

hammock hammocks *noun*
a bed made of strong cloth or pieces of rope which is hung at each end from something such as a tree or post.

hamster hamsters *noun*
a small animal that is often kept as a pet. It is similar to a large mouse with a very short tail. Hamsters can store food in pouches inside their cheeks.

hand hands *noun*
Your hand is the part of your body at the end of your arm.

hand hands handing handed *verb*
If you hand something to somebody, you give it to them. *Hand me that book.*

handicap *noun*
something that makes it more difficult to do things. *Being tall can be a handicap in small cars.*

handkerchief handkerchiefs *noun*
a small square of cloth or paper tissue that you use for blowing your nose.
▲ Say **hang**-ker-cheef.

handle handles *noun*
1 The handle of something such as a cup or a bag is the part that you take in your hand to carry it or pick it up.
2 The handle of a door is the lever or knob that you move with your hand to open and close it.

different types of handle

handlebar handlebars *noun*
the curved bar at the front of a bicycle or a motorbike that you use for steering.

handsome *adjective*
A man who is handsome has an attractive face.

handwriting *noun*
Your handwriting is the way you write with a pen or pencil.

hang hangs hanging hung *verb*
If you hang something somewhere, you fix it from the top to something above it. *Hang your coat up in the wardrobe.*

hang-glider hang-gliders *noun*
a kind of large kite with a harness underneath, in which you fly through the air in the sport of hang-gliding.

happen happens happening happened *verb*
1 Something that happens or occurs takes place. *The accident happened because she was not paying attention.*
2 If you happen to do something, you do it by chance. *I happened to find your ball when I was in the garden.*

A
B
C
D
E
F
G
H
I
J
K
L
M
N
O
P
Q
R
S
T
U
V
W
X
Y
Z

happy happier happiest *adjective*
If you are happy, you feel good because something nice has happened or because you are enjoying yourself. ■ The opposite is **unhappy** or **sad**.
happily *adverb*, **happiness** *noun*.

---

happy

Some words that you can use instead of happy:

I'm happy I've finished my homework.
☞ **contented, pleased, glad** ☜

They are happy with their wedding presents.
☞ **delighted, pleased, thrilled** ☜

Christmas is a happy time of year.
☞ **merry, cheerful** ☜

---

harbour harbours *noun*
an area of sea by the coast where ships can shelter.

hard harder hardest *adjective*
1 If something is hard, you cannot break, cut or bend it easily. *Stones, nuts and bolts are hard.* ■ The opposite is **soft**.
2 Something that is hard to do is difficult. *a hard puzzle.* ■ The opposite is **easy**.

hard harder hardest *adverb*
Hard means a lot. *Sarita works hard.*

hard disk hard disks *noun*
the part inside a computer where a large amount of information is stored.

harden hardens hardening hardened *verb*
When something hardens, it becomes hard. *Hold the pieces together until the glue has hardened.* ■ The opposite is **soften**.

hare hares *noun*
an animal that looks like a large rabbit with long

ears and long legs. ● A word that sounds like **hare** is **hair**.

harm harms harming harmed *verb*
1 If you harm somebody, you hurt them. *The dog won't harm you.*
2 If you harm something, you damage it.

harmful *adjective*
If something is harmful, it could hurt you or make you ill. *Looking straight at the Sun is harmful to your eyes.* ■ The opposite is **harmless**.

harmless *adjective*
If something is harmless, it will not hurt you. *Our dog is harmless – she wouldn't bite anybody.* ■ The opposite is **harmful**.

harmony harmonies *noun*
a group of musical notes that sound nice when you hear them together.

harness harnesses *noun*
1 a set of straps and metal parts that go around a horse's head or body so that you can control it.
2 a set of straps for fastening something such as a parachute to a person's body.

harp harps *noun*
a musical instrument. It has a large frame with strings which you play (pluck) with your fingers.
harpist *noun*.

harsh harsher harshest *adjective*
1 If somebody behaves in a harsh way, they are cruel or unkind. *That was a very harsh punishment.*
2 A harsh winter is very cold and difficult.
3 Harsh sounds are loud and unpleasant. *a harsh voice.*

harvest harvests *noun*
the time when farmers pick or cut their crops because they are ripe.

hat hats *noun*
a covering that you wear on your head.

hatch hatches hatching hatched *verb*
When a baby bird or other animal hatches, it breaks out of its egg.

hatchet hatchets *noun*
a small axe.

hate hates hating hated *verb*
If you hate somebody or something, you have a very strong feeling of not liking them. *I hate getting up early in the morning.* ■ The opposite is **love**.

haunted *adjective*
If a place is haunted, there is supposed to be a ghost there. *a haunted house.* ▲ Say **horn-ted**.

hawk hawks *noun*
a large bird with a curved beak and strong claws, that eats other birds and small animals.

hay *noun*
grass that has been cut and dried and is used to feed horses and cattle in the winter months.

hazard hazards *noun*
a danger or risk. *Patches of oil on the sea from leaking tankers are a hazard to sea birds and fish.*
hazardous *adjective*.

head **heads** *noun*
1 Your head is the top part of you, where your hair and face are.
2 the person who is in charge of a group. *the head of a large company.*

headache **headaches** *noun*
a pain in your head.

headlight **headlights** *noun*
Headlights are the bright lights on the front of a car or other vehicle.

headline **headlines** *noun*
words in larger print at the top of a story in a newspaper.

DAILY GLOBE

BOOKS STILL REIGN SUPREME!

by John Grisewood
Dictionary Correspondent

headphones *noun*
small speakers that fit on your ears and that are joined together by a band over the top of your head. Headphones let you hear music and other sounds without other people hearing them.

headquarters *noun*
the building where the people in charge of in an organization work. *The company's headquarters are in Paris.*

headteacher **headteachers** *noun*
the teacher who is in charge of a school.

heal **heals healing healed** *verb*
If something heals, it gets better after being ill or injured. *I hurt my ankle two weeks ago but it's healed now.* ● A word that sounds like **heal** is **heel**.

health *noun*
Your health is how well you are. If your health is bad, you are ill. If your health is good, you are well. ▲ Say **helth.**

healthy **healthier healthiest** *adjective*
1 If you are healthy, you are well and fit.
2 Something that is healthy is good for you and helps you to stay well. *Fresh fruit and vegetables are healthy foods.*
▲ *Say* **helth-ee.** ■ The opposite is **unhealthy.**

heap **heaps** *noun*
a large, untidy pile of things. *She left her clothes in a heap on the floor.*

hear **hears hearing heard** *verb*
When you hear a sound, you notice it through your ears. ● A word that sounds like **hear** is **here.**

heart **hearts** *noun*
Your heart is the part of you, inside your chest, that pumps the blood around your body.
▲ Say *hart.*

heat *noun*
warmth. *I can feel the heat from the Sun on my skin.*

heat **heats heating heated** *verb*
If you heat something, you make it hot. *He heated some water to make coffee.*

heave **heaves heaving heaved** *verb*
If you heave something somewhere, you use a lot of energy to lift, push or pull it. *Ben and Joe heaved the rope together.*

heavy **heavier heaviest** *adjective*
Something that is heavy weighs a lot. *The suitcase was too heavy for me to lift.* ■ The opposite is **light.**

hedge **hedges** *noun*
a line of bushes or small trees growing close together at the edge of a garden, road or field.

hedgehog **hedgehogs** *noun*
a small, brown animal with sharp spikes, called spines, all over its back.

Hedgehogs come out to feed on insects at night and curl up into a ball to protect themselves when they are in danger. ❖ **Look at page 154**

heel **heels** *noun*
1 Your heel is the back part of your foot.
2 the part of a shoe or boot that is under the back part of your foot.
● A word that sounds like **heel** is **heal.**

height **heights** *noun*
The height of something is how high it is from the bottom to the top. *The height of the tree is six metres.*
▲ Rhymes with **kite.**

held past of **hold.**

helicopter **helicopters** *noun*
an aircraft without wings that is kept in the air by long blades attached to its roof, which turn round very fast.

helmet **helmets** *noun*
a hard hat that protects your head.

help **helps helping helped** *verb*
If you help somebody, you make it easier for them to do something. *Sam helped me with my maths homework.*
help *noun.*

helpful *adjective*
1 If you are helpful, you do what you can to help other people.
2 Something that is helpful is useful. *Thank you for your helpful advice.*

helpless *adjective*
If you are helpless, you cannot look after yourself. *A baby is completely helpless when it is born.*

hem **hems** *noun*
the edge of a piece of material that is folded over and sewn to make it neat.

A B C D E F G H I J K L M N O P Q R S T U V W X Y Z

hen **hens** *noun*
1 a female chicken that lays eggs that we eat.
2 any female bird.

herb **herbs** *noun*
a plant that we use to give flavour to food or to make medicines. *Marjoram, rosemary and mint are all herbs.*

yarrow

marjoram

herd **herds** *noun*
a large group of animals of one kind that live together. *Elephants live in herds.*

hero **heroes** *noun*
1 a person who is very brave or very good.
2 the main male character in a book, play or film.

heroine **heroines** *noun*
1 a woman who is very brave or very good.
2 the main female character in a book, play or film.
▲ Say *herr-oh-in.*

heron **herons** *noun*
a large, grey bird with long legs and a long neck. Herons live near water and eat fish.

hesitate **hesitates hesitating hesitated** *verb*
If you hesitate, you stop for a short time before you do something, often because you are not sure what to do. *She hesitated before answering me.*
hesitation *noun.*

hexagon **hexagons** *noun*
a flat shape with six sides.
❖ *Look at page 145*
hexagonal *adjective.*

hibernate **hibernates hibernating hibernated** *verb*
When an animal hibernates, it stays in a deep sleep all through the winter. *Bears, dormice and hedgehogs hibernate.*
hibernation *noun.*

hiccup **hiccups** *noun*
a sudden, short breath in and a noise that sounds like "hic", that you cannot help making. You sometimes get hiccups when you eat or drink too quickly.
hiccup *verb.*

hide **hides hiding hid hidden** *verb*
1 If you hide, you go where nobody can find you. *You hide, and I'll come and look for you.*
2 If you hide something, you put it where nobody can find it. *She hid the present under the bed.*

hieroglyphics *noun*
a kind of writing that uses pictures instead of letters and words. Hieroglyphics were used in ancient Egypt. ▲ Say *hye-row-glif-iks.*

high **higher highest** *adjective*
1 Something that is high goes up a long way from the bottom to the top. *a high wall.*
2 High also means a long way above the ground. *We were high up in the mountains.* ■ The opposite is **low.**

hijack **hijacks hijacking hijacked** *verb*
If somebody hijacks a plane or ship, they take control of it by threatening the passengers and crew and then try to make it go where they want it to.
hijacker *noun.*

hill **hills** *noun*
an area of land that is higher than the land around it.
hilly *adjective.*

hind *adjective*
An animal's hind legs are its back legs.

Hindu **Hindus** *noun*
a person who follows a religion called Hinduism. Hindus worship several different gods and believe that after you die you are born again in a different body.
Hinduism *noun.*

hinge **hinges** *noun*
a piece of metal that fixes a door to its frame at one side, so that it can open and close.

hint **hints hinting hinted** *verb*
When you hint, you let somebody know something without actually saying it. *Ben hinted that he wanted a new bike.*
hint *noun.*

hip **hips** *noun*
Your hips are at the side of your body between your waist and the top of your legs.

hippopotamus **hippopotamuses** *noun*
a large animal with a thick skin and very short legs. Hippopotamuses live by lakes and rivers in Africa. A hippopotamus is sometimes called a **hippo** for short.

African hippo

Pygmy hippo

hire hires hiring hired *verb*
If you hire something, you pay to have it for a certain time. *We'll hire a boat for the afternoon and go out on the lake.*

hiss hisses hissing hissed *verb*
If something hisses, it makes a sound that is like saying a very long "s". *Snakes hiss when they are angry.*

history *noun*
the study of things that happened in the past. *At school we are learning about the history of our town.*
historical *adjective.*

hit hits hitting hit *verb*
When you hit something, you touch it quickly and with force. *I hit the ball with the bat.*

hive hives *noun*
a special box for bees to live in and where you can collect their honey.

hoarse hoarser hoarsest *adjective*
If you are hoarse, your voice sounds rough. *He yelled at the top of his voice all through the match until he was hoarse.* ● A word that sounds like **hoarse** is **horse.**

hobble hobbles hobbling hobbled *verb*
If you hobble, you walk with difficulty because your feet hurt. *He was hobbling along slowly because his feet were covered in blisters.*

hobby hobbies *noun*
something that you enjoy doing in your spare time. *My hobbies are swimming, reading and collecting shells.*

hockey *noun*
a game played outdoors by two teams of eleven players who try to get a hard ball into a goal by hitting it with a long, curved stick.

hold holds holding held *verb*
1 If you hold something, you have it in your hand or hands. *Can you please hold the baby?*
2 If a container holds a certain amount, it can have that amount in it but no more. *The bottle holds a litre of water*

hole holes *noun*
a gap or space in something. *These jeans have a hole in the knee.* ● A word that sounds like **hole** is **whole.**

holiday holidays *noun*
a time when you do not have to go to school or work. *How long are the summer holidays?* ◆ *Heather is going to Mexico for her holiday.*

hollow *adjective*
Something that is hollow has an empty space inside it. *Chocolate eggs are hollow.* ■ The opposite is **solid.**

holly *noun*
an evergreen tree that has red berries and leaves with sharp points.

hologram holograms *noun*
a three-dimensional image made by laser beams.

holy holier holiest *adjective*
Something that is holy is very special because it is to do with religion. *Monks and nuns are holy people.*

home homes *noun*
Your home is the place where you live. *When does Max get home from school?*

homework *noun*
work for school done at home.

honest *adjective*
If you are honest, you tell the truth and people can trust you. ▲ Say *on-est.* ■ The opposite is **dishonest.**
honesty *noun.*

honey *noun*
a sweet, sticky food that is made by bees. ▲ Rhymes with *funny.*

honeymoon honeymoons *noun*
a holiday that a man and woman take when they have just got married.

hood hoods *noun*
a part of a coat or jacket that you can pull over your head.

hoof hooves or hoofs *noun*
the hard covering on the foot of some animals such as a horse or deer.

hoof   horse shoe

water
deer   deer   wild boar   reindeer   elk

horse   rhino   tapir

hook hooks *noun*
a curved piece of metal or plastic that is used for hanging things on or for holding or fastening things. *There is a hook on the back of the door for hanging your coat on.* ◆ *A fish-hook is tied to the end of a fishing-line for catching fish.*

hoop hoops *noun*
a large ring made of wood, metal or plastic.

hoot hoots hooting hooted *verb*
1 To hoot is to make the long "oo" sound that an owl makes.
2 When drivers hoot, they make a loud noise with a car horn. *The driver hooted impatiently at the car in front.*

hop hops hopping hopped *verb*
1 If you hop, you jump on one leg.
2 When an animal or insect hops, it moves along by jumping. *The frog hopped away.*

hope hopes hoping hoped *verb*
If you hope something will happen, you want it to happen and you think it probably will. *I hope you will be able to come to my party.*
hope *noun,* **hopeless** *adjective*
He's hopeless at diving.

hopeful *adjective*
If you are hopeful, you think that what you want will probably happen. *The police are hopeful that they will soon be able to solve the crime.*

horizon horizons *noun*
the line in the far distance where the land or the sea seems to meet the sky.
▲ Say *hor-eye-zon*.

horizontal *adjective*
Something that is horizontal goes from side to side, parallel to the ground, not up and down. *The top of the table is horizontal with the floor.* ■ The opposite is **vertical**.

horizontally *adverb*
The smoke spread out horizontally over the town.

horn horns *noun*
1 Horns are the hard, pointed, bony parts that grow out of the head of some animals such as cows and goats.
2 A horn is a brass musical instrument that you blow into to make sounds.
3 A horn is also an instrument in a car or other vehicle that the driver uses to make a loud noise as a warning.

horrible *adjective*
terrible, or very unpleasant. *What a horrible thing to say!*
horribly *adverb*.

horror *noun*
1 a feeling that you get when you are very shocked and upset at something terrible. *We were filled with horror at the news of the famine in Africa.*
2 A horror story is a story that is meant to frighten you.

horse horses *noun*
a large animal with a long tail and a mane. People ride horses or use them to pull carts or carriages. A female horse is called a mare, a male horse is a stallion and a young horse is a foal. ● A word that sounds like **horse** is **hoarse**.

horse chestnut *noun*
a large tree that produces a large nut called a conker.

hose hoses *noun*
a long, plastic pipe that is used for spraying water. *You can use a hose to water the garden or clean a car.*

HORSES

Przewalski's horse

Wild ass

Clydesdale horse

Arab stallion

Shetland pony

> **VOCABULARY**
> **aids**
> *the signals a rider gives to tell the horse what to do.*
>
> **bit**
> *the metal or rubber device attached to the bridle and placed in the horse's mouth.*
>
> **bridle**
> *the part of saddle that is placed over a horse's head and to which the bit and reins are attached.*
>
> **colt**
> *a male foal.*
>
> **filly**
> *a female foal.*
>
> **gait**
> *the pace of a horse: walk, trot, canter, gallop.*

HOUSES

Polynesian stilt house

Native American tepee

Mongolian "yurt"

modern American family home

A B C D E F G H I J K L M N O P Q R S T U V W X Y Z

hospital hospitals *noun*
a building where people who are ill or injured are looked after by doctors and nurses.

host hosts *noun*
a person who invites guests and looks after them when they come.

hostage hostages *noun*
a person who is held prisoner by somebody who threatens to hurt or kill the prisoner if they do not get what they want.

hot hotter hottest *adjective*
1 Something that is hot has a high temperature. *Careful! Those chips are hot!* ■ The opposite is **cold**.
2 Hot foods have a strong taste and make your mouth feel as if it is burning when you eat them. *Chillies are hot.*

hotel hotels *noun*
a building with bedrooms where people pay to stay for a few nights.

hour hours *noun*
a period of 60 minutes. There are 24 hours in a day. ▲ Rhymes with *tower*.
● A word that sounds like **hour** is **our**.

house houses *noun*
a building where people live.
❖ *Look at page 83*

hover hovers hovering hovered *verb*
If something hovers, it stays in one place in the air. *A rescue helicopter hovered over the boat.*

hovercraft hovercrafts *noun*
a vehicle that can move over land and water. A hovercraft floats on a cushion of air as it travels along.

howl howls howling howled *verb*
When an animal howls, it makes a long, loud, crying sound. *Wolves were howling in the distance.*

hug hugs hugging hugged *verb*
When you hug somebody, you put your arms around them and hold them tight.
hug *noun.*

huge *adjective*
very, very big. ■ The opposite is **tiny**.

hum hums humming hummed *verb*
When you hum, you make a singing sound with your lips closed. *He was humming a tune while he worked.*

human humans *noun*
a person. *A lot of animals are afraid of humans.*

humid *adjective*
Humid weather is hot, sticky and damp.
▲ Say **hyoo-mid**.

humour *noun*
the ability to make people laugh or to see when something is funny. *She has a good sense of humour.* ▲ Say **hyoo-mer**.
humorous *adjective.*

hump humps *noun*
1 a large, round lump, on a camel's back, for example.
2 a bump in the road.

a Bactrian camel (two humps) and a dromedary camel (one hump)

hung past of **hang**.

hungry hungrier hungriest *adjective*
If you are hungry, you want to eat.
hunger *noun.*

hunt hunts hunting hunted *verb*
1 To hunt is to chase and catch wild animals to kill them, either to eat or as a sport.
2 If you hunt for something, you look everywhere for it. *I've been hunting for my watch all morning.*
hunt *noun.*

hurl hurls hurling hurled *verb*
If you hurl something, you throw it as far and as hard as you can. *She hurled the stone at the wall.*

hurricane hurricanes *noun*
a powerful storm with winds that are strong enough to blow down trees or damage roofs.

hurry hurries hurrying hurried *verb*
If you hurry, you try to get somewhere or do something as quickly as possible. *You'd better hurry or you'll miss the match.*
hurry *noun.*

hurt hurts hurting hurt *verb*
1 If you hurt yourself, you cause pain to a part of your body. *Did you hurt yourself when you fell over?*
2 If a part of your body hurts, it feels pain. *I've got a sore knee. It really hurts.*
3 To hurt somebody is also to upset them. *I think Arabella was really hurt when you didn't invite her to your birthday party.*

husband husbands *noun*
A woman's husband is the man she is married to.

hut huts *noun*
a small building, usually with one room.

hutch hutches *noun*
a wooden and wire cage for a rabbit.

hydrogen *noun*
a gas that is lighter than air. Oxygen and hydrogen together make up water.

hyphen hyphens *noun*
a mark in writing (-) that you use to show that two parts of a word belong together. *grown-up.* ▲ Say **hye-fen**.

I i

ice *noun*
frozen water. *There was ice on the pond last winter.*
icy *adjective*.

iceberg **icebergs** *noun*
a huge piece of ice floating in the sea. Icebergs are dangerous to ships because most of the ice is under the water where you cannot see it.

ice-cream **ice-creams** *noun*
a sweet, frozen food made from milk or cream.

ice-skating *noun*
sliding on ice in special boots called ice-skates that have thin, metal blades on the bottom.

icicle **icicles** *noun*
a hanging, pointed piece of ice made of dripping water that has frozen.

icing *noun*
a smooth, sweet covering for cakes, made of sugar mixed with water or egg whites.

icy **icier** **iciest** *adjective*
very cold. *an icy wind.*

idea **ideas** *noun*
1 a new thought about something. *I've got an idea. Let's go to the beach!*
2 a picture in your mind. *The film gives you a good idea of what India is like.*

ideal *adjective*
If something is ideal, it is perfect and just what you want. *The weather was ideal for a picnic.*
ideally *adverb*.

identical *adjective*
exactly the same. *Ben and Jason are identical twins.*

identify **identifies** **identifying** **identified** *verb*
If you identify somebody or something, you know who or what they are and can name them. *Can you identify this wild flower?*
identification *noun*.

idle *adjective*
lazy, or not working.

igloo **igloos** *noun*
a round house, built by Inuit people out of blocks of hard snow or ice.

ignorant *adjective*
not knowing about something.
ignorance *noun*.

ignore **ignores** **ignoring** **ignored** *verb*
If you ignore somebody, you take no notice of them. *She ignored me when I said hello.*

ill *adjective*
If you are ill, you are not well. *I didn't go to school today because I was ill.*

illegal *adjective*
If something is illegal, it is not allowed by law. ■ The opposite is **legal**.

illness **illnesses** *noun*
something such as measles or a cold that makes you feel unwell.

illusion **illusions** *noun*
something that you think you can see, but that is not really there.

illustration **illustrations** *noun*
a picture in a book or magazine. *This dictionary has lots of illustrations.*

image **images** *noun*
1 a picture on paper, on a screen or in a mirror. *A ghostly image appeared in the mirror.*
2 a picture in your mind. *I have an image of how I want to look when I'm a grown-up.*

imaginary *adjective*
Something that is imaginary is not real and exists only in your mind. *I read a story about a boy who had an imaginary friend.* ▲ Say *i-maj-in-ar-ee.*

imagination *noun*
Your imagination is your ability to think of new ideas or create pictures in your mind. *Use your imagination and draw whatever you like.*
imaginative *adjective*.

imagine **imagines** **imagining** **imagined** *verb*
When you imagine something, you create a picture of it in your mind. *Can you imagine living in a cave like people in the Stone Age?*

imitate **imitates** **imitating** **imitated** *verb*
If you imitate somebody, you copy the way they talk or act. *Domenic imitates Nick taking a photograph of the magician.*
imitation *noun*
It is not a real Christmas tree, but a plastic imitation.

immediately *adverb*
now. *The ambulance arrived immediately after we telephoned.*

immune *adjective*
If you are immune to a disease, you cannot catch it. *The doctor said that I should be immune to measles because I've already had it.*
immunize *verb*.

impatient *adjective*
If you are impatient, you do not like waiting for things. *I get very impatient waiting for the bus.* ■ The opposite is **patient.**
impatience *noun.*

important *adjective*
1 If something is important, it matters a lot. *It is important to look both ways before you cross the road.*
2 A person who is important has a lot of power. *The king is an important man.*
importance *noun.*

impossible *adjective*
If something is impossible, you cannot do it, or it cannot happen. *You can't walk on water - it's impossible.* ■ The opposite is **possible.**

impress **impresses impressing impressed** *verb*
If you impress somebody, they think that what you have done is very good. *Her drawings impressed me.*

impression **impressions** *noun*
1 thoughts and feelings that you have about somebody or something. *My first impressions of the new school were that it was very large and noisy.*
2 If you make an impression on somebody, they remember what you are like and what you have done. *The ballet dancer made a great impression on all of us.*

impressive *adjective*
If something is impressive, people admire it, especially because it is very good or very big. *an impressive castle.*

improve **improves improving improved** *verb*
If something improves, it gets better. *With practice my spelling will improve.*
improvement *noun.*

include **includes including included** *verb*
To include is to have somebody or something as part of a group or as part of the whole thing. *Depti was pleased to be included in the football team.*

increase **increases increasing increased** *verb*
If something increases, it gets bigger in size or amount. *The number of cars on the roads has increased.* ■ The opposite is **decrease.**
increase *noun.*

incredible *adjective*
If something is incredible, it is difficult to believe. *an incredible story.*

incubator **incubators** *noun*
1 a container where babies who are born early are kept until they grow bigger and stronger.
2 a container where eggs are kept warm until they hatch.

independent *adjective*
If you are independent, you do not want or need help from other people. ■ The opposite is **dependent.**
independence *noun.*

index **indexes** *noun*
a list of words from A to Z at the end of a book. The index tells you what things are in the book and where they are.

indigestion *noun*
an uncomfortable feeling that you have in your stomach when you have eaten too much or eaten the wrong food. *If you eat those apples before they are ripe, you'll get indigestion.*

individual *adjective*
to do with one person or thing, not a whole group. *individual flowers.*

individual **individuals** *noun*
one person. *Every individual is different.*

indoors *adverb*
inside a building. *We went indoors when it started to rain.* ■ The opposite is **outdoors.**

industry **industries** *noun*
the work of making things in factories. *the car industry.*
industrial *adjective*
an industrial area.

infant **infants** *noun*
a baby or young child.

infection **infections** *noun*
an illness that is caused by germs. *a throat infection.*

infectious *adjective*
If an illness is infectious, it goes easily from one person to another. *Measles is a very infectious disease.*

inflate **inflates inflating inflated** *verb*
If you inflate something such as a balloon or a tyre, you blow it up with air or gas.
inflatable *adjective.*

influence *noun*
If somebody or something has an influence over you, they have a certain effect on you so that you change the way you think or behave. *My parents don't like me playing with Daniel because they say he is a bad influence on me.*
influence *verb,* **influential** *adjective.*

inform **informs informing informed** *verb*
If you inform somebody about something, you tell them about it. *The teacher informed us that there would be a history test next week.*

information *noun*
the facts about something. *This dictionary gives you information about words and how to spell them.*

ingredient **ingredients** *noun*
Ingredients are all the things that you put in when you make something. *The ingredients for making a cake are butter, sugar, flour and eggs.*

inhabitant **inhabitants** *noun*
The inhabitants of a place are the people or animals that live there. *The inhabitants of the island are mainly fishermen and their families.*
inhabit *verb.*

initial **initials** *noun*
the first letters of each of your names. *Tom Jackson's initials are T.J.*

injection injections *noun*
If a doctor or nurse gives you an injection, they put medicine into your body through a special needle.
inject *verb*.

injure injures injuring injured *verb*
If you injure yourself, you hurt a part of your body. *He injured his leg playing football.*
injury *noun*.

ink inks *noun*
a coloured liquid that is used for writing or printing. *The words on this page were printed with ink.*

inland *adjective, adverb*
towards the middle of a country, away from the sea. *an inland lake.*

inner *adjective*
1 in the middle of a place. *He lives in inner London.*
2 inside something. *A bicycle tyre has an inner tube.*
■ The opposite is **outer**.

innocent *adjective*
If you are innocent, you have not done anything wrong. *The police have accused him of stealing the money but he says he is innocent.* ■ The opposite is **guilty**.
innocence *noun*.

inquire inquires inquiring inquired *verb*
If you inquire about something, you ask about it. *We inquired about the times of trains to Hull.*
inquiry *noun*
an official inquiry into the disaster.

insect insects *noun*
a small creature with six legs and a body that is divided into three sections. Many insects have wings. *Ants, grasshoppers and butterflies are insects.*
❖ *Look at page 89*

insert inserts inserting inserted *verb*
If you insert a thing into something else, you put it inside it. *She inserted the key into the lock and opened the door.*

insist insists insisting insisted *verb*
If you insist on doing something, you say very firmly that you want to do it so that no one can stop you. *Eleanor insisted on wearing her new trainers.*
insistence *noun*.

inspect inspects inspecting inspected *verb*
to look at something carefully.
inspection *noun*.

instant *adjective*
If something is instant, it happens very quickly, or you can make it very quickly. *instant coffee.*

instead *adverb*
in the place of somebody or something else. *I don't like ice-cream. May I have fruit instead?*

instinct instincts *noun*
something that makes people and animals do things without having to think or learn about them. *Birds build their nests by instinct.*

instructions *noun*
words that tell you how to do something. *She gave us instructions on how to look after the puppies.*

instrument instruments *noun*
1 a thing that is used for doing a special job. *A telescope is an instrument for looking at things, such as stars.*
2 A musical instrument is something that you play to make music. *Recorders and pianos are instruments.*

insulate insulates insulating insulated *verb*
to cover something with a material so that electricity cannot pass through it.

insult insults insulting insulted *verb*
If somebody insults you, they upset you by saying nasty or rude things to you.
insult *noun*.

intelligent *adjective*
A person who is intelligent is able to learn and understand things quickly.
intelligence *noun*.

intend intends intending intended *verb*
If you intend to do something, you plan to do it. *What do you intend to do now?*
intention *noun*.

interest interests interesting interested *verb*
If something interests you, you like it and want to know more about it. *Football doesn't interest my gran at all.*
interesting *adjective*.

interfere interferes interfering interfered *verb*
If you interfere, you try to do something for somebody when they do not want your help.
interference *noun*.

interior *noun*
The interior of something is the part inside it. *The interior of the castle was dark and gloomy.*

international *adjective*
If something is international, it has to do with more than one country. *an international football match.*

interrupt interrupts interrupting interrupted *verb*
If you interrupt somebody, you stop them while they are saying or doing something. *Please don't interrupt me.*
interruption *noun*.

interval intervals *noun*
a break between two parts of a play or concert.

interview interviews *noun*
a meeting when you answer questions about yourself. *a job interview.*

intestine intestines *noun*
Your intestine is the long tube inside your body that carries food from your stomach.

introduce introduces introducing introduced *verb*
If you introduce two people who have never met before, you tell them each other's names so they can get to know one another. *Tim introduced me to Bob.*
introduction *noun*.

invade invades invading invaded *verb*
When an army invades, it goes into another country to attack it.
invasion *noun*.

A
B
C
D
E
F
G
H
I
J
K
L
M
N
O
P
Q
R
S
T
U
V
W
X
Y
Z

invent **invents inventing invented** *verb*
If you invent something, you make something that has never been made or thought of before.
invention *noun*.

inventor **inventors** *noun*
a person who invents something.

investigate **investigates investigating investigated** *verb*
When you investigate something, you try to find out all about it. *The police investigated the theft.*
investigation *noun*.

invisible *adjective*
If something is invisible, you cannot see it. ■ The opposite is **visible**.

invitation **invitations** *noun*
If somebody has given you an invitation, they have written or spoken to you to ask you to go somewhere.

invite **invites inviting invited** *verb*
If you invite somebody, you ask them to come to your home, to a party or a meal.

involve **involves involving involved** *verb*
1 If you are involved in something, you take part in it. *Are you involved in the school play?*
2 If something is involved in an activity, it is part of it. *Tennis involves a lot of skill.*

iron *noun*
1 Iron is a strong, hard metal that is found in rocks. Iron is used for making tools, gates and other things.
2 An iron is an electrical tool that you use to make clothes smooth.
▲ Say *eye-un*.

irritate **irritates irritating irritated** *verb*
If something irritates you, it annoys you.
irritation *noun*.

Islam *noun*
the religion that Muslims follow.

island **islands** *noun*
a piece of land with water all around it.
▲ Say *eye-land*.

itch **itches itching itched** *verb*
When a part of your body itches, you have a feeling on your skin that you want to scratch it.
itch *noun*, **itchy** *adjective*.

ivy **ivies** *noun*
a plant with shiny, pointed leaves that stay green in winter. Ivy climbs up walls and trees.

Jj

jack **jacks** *noun*
the playing-card that comes between the ten and the queen and has a picture of a young man on it.

jacket **jackets** *noun*
a short coat.

jagged *adjective*
Something that is jagged has a lot of sharp points along the edges. *a jagged piece of broken glass.*

jaguar **jaguars** *noun*
a wild cat that has brown and yellow fur with black spots. Jaguars live in North and South America.

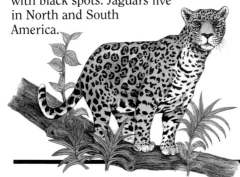

jail **jails** *noun*
a prison.

jam *noun*
1 a food made by cooking fruit with sugar. *Billie loves strawberry jam on toast.*
2 a traffic jam is a large number of vehicles unable to move.

jam **jams jamming jammed** *verb*
If something jams, it cannot move. *The paper has jammed in the printer.*

jar **jars** *noun*
a glass container for jam or other foods. *a jar of pickles.*

jaw **jaws** *noun*
Your jaws are the two large bones in your mouth that hold your teeth. Your jaws move up and down when you speak and eat.

jealous *adjective*
If you are jealous, you want what somebody else has and it makes you angry and unhappy. *Joe was jealous of his little sister because she always seemed to get what she wanted.*
▲ Say *jel-uss*.
jealousy *noun*.

jeans *noun*
trousers made from thick, strong, cotton material called denim. ● A word that sounds like **jeans** is **genes**.

jelly **jellies** *noun*
a clear, slightly wobbly food with a fruit flavour. *At Amanda's party we had orange jelly and ice-cream.*

jellyfish **jellyfish** or **jellyfishes** *noun*
a sea animal that has a clear, round body and long tentacles that sting.

jerk **jerks jerking jerked** *verb*
To jerk is to make a sudden, sharp movement. *She jerked her hand away from the flame.*

jet jets *noun*
1 a fast, thin stream of liquid. *A jet of water was coming out of the burst pipe.*
2 a fast plane with an engine that sucks air in and then forces it out at the back.

Jew Jews *noun*
a person who belongs to the race of people who in ancient times lived in Israel, or a person who follows the religion called Judaism.
Jewish *adjective*.

jewel jewels *noun*
a beautiful and valuable stone such as a diamond, ruby or emerald.

jewellery *noun*
rings, bracelets, necklaces, brooches and other things that people wear to decorate their bodies. Jewellery is often made of valuable metals such as gold or silver, and jewels such as diamonds or rubies.

jigsaw
jigsaws *noun*
a puzzle made up of a lot of small pieces of wood or thick card that fit together to make a picture.

job jobs *noun*
1 the work that a person does to get money. *My mum is looking for a job at the moment.*
2 a piece of work that you have to do. *My sister and I were given the job of washing the car.*

jockey jockeys *noun*
a person who rides a horse in races.

jog jogs jogging jogged *verb*
If you jog, you run quite slowly, for exercise.

join joins joining joined *verb*
1 When you join things, you put or fix them together. *I joined the pieces of the jigsaw puzzle.*
2 If you join a group, you become a member of it. *Maria has joined the school band.*

joint joints *noun*
1 A joint is part of your body where two bones are joined together, such as your elbow or knee.
2 a large piece of meat with a bone in it.

joke jokes *noun*
something that somebody says or does to make people laugh.

journalist journalists *noun*
a person who writes news and stories for newspapers. ▲ Say *jer-na-list*.
journalism *noun*.

journey journeys *noun*
When you go on a journey, you travel from one place to another. *It's a three-hour journey by car from here to the coast.* ▲ Say *jer-nee*.

joy *noun*
a feeling of great happiness. ■ The opposite is **sorrow**.
joyful *adjective*.

Judaism *noun*
the religion of the Jews.

judge judges *noun*
1 A judge is the person who controls what happens in a court of law and who decides what a guilty person's punishment should be.
2 a person who decides who is the winner in a competition.

judo *noun*
a sport from Japan in which two people try to throw each other down using various special movements.

jug jugs *noun*
a container with a handle and a shaped part at the top that is used for pouring liquids.

juggle juggles juggling juggled *verb*
If you juggle, you throw several things into the air and catch them, one after another, so there is more than one thing in the air at once. *Jazz is juggling.*
juggler *noun*.

juice juices *noun*
the liquid from fruit, vegetables or meat. *orange juice.* ◆ *carrot juice.*
juicy *adjective*.

jump jumps jumping jumped *verb*
When you jump, you push your body quickly and suddenly up into the air.
jump *noun*.

jumper jumpers *noun*
a piece of knitted clothing that covers your arms and the top part of your body.

junction junctions *noun*
a place where roads or railway lines meet. ▲ Say *junk-shun*.

jungle jungles *noun*
a thick forest in a tropical country.

junior *adjective*
younger. ■ The opposite is **senior**.

jury juries *noun*
a group of 12 ordinary people in a court of law who have to decide whether the person on trial is guilty or innocent.

justice *noun*
a way of treating people that is both fair and right.

A
B
C
D
E
F
G
H
I
J
K
L
M
N
O
P
Q
R
S
T
U
V
W
X
Y
Z

K k

kaleidoscope kaleidoscopes
noun
a tube that you look through and see lots of coloured patterns as you turn it. ▲ Say ka-*lie*-do-scope.

kangaroo kangaroos *noun*
a wild animal that lives in Australia. It has strong back legs and moves by making long jumps. A female kangaroo has a kind of pocket called a pouch at the front where she keeps her baby.

a kangaroo and her joey (baby)

karate *noun*
a sport from Japan in which two people fight with their hands and feet using special movements. ▲ Say ka-*rah*-tee.

keen keener keenest *adjective*
If you are keen on something, you like it very much. *Joe is keen on football.*

kennel kennels *noun*
a small house for a dog.

kerb kerbs *noun*
the edge of a pavement next to a road. *They stood on the kerb waiting to cross the road.*

kettle kettles *noun*
a container with a handle and a spout, that is used for heating water. *Put the kettle on and make some tea.*

key keys *noun*
1 a piece of metal that is shaped so that when you turn it, it locks or unlocks something such as a door or padlock.

2 The keys of a piano are the parts that you press when you play to make different musical notes.
3 The keys of a computer are the parts with letters and numbers on that you press when you work at the computer.
4 The key to a map is a list that tells you what the symbols on the map mean.

keyboard keyboards *noun*
1 the part of the computer with buttons, called keys, that have letters and numbers on them.
2 the row of keys on a piano or other musical instrument.
3 an electronic keyboard makes musical sounds.

kick kicks kicking kicked *verb*
If you kick something, you hit it with your foot. *Ben kicked the ball.*

kid kids *noun*
1 a young goat.
2 a child.

kidnap kidnaps kidnapping kidnapped *verb*
When somebody kidnaps another person, they take them away and hide them so that their family or friends will have to pay money to free them.

kidney kidneys *noun*
Your kidneys are the two parts inside your body that help to clean your blood.

kill kills killing killed *verb*
To kill somebody or something means to make them die.

kind kinder kindest *adjective*
A person who is kind is friendly and gentle and likes to help other people. ■ The opposite is **unkind**.

kind kinds *noun*
a sort or type. *There are thousands of different kinds of insects.*

king kings *noun*
A king is a man who leads his people and belongs to a royal family.

kingfisher kingfishers *noun*
a bird with bright-blue and orange feathers that lives near rivers and streams and eats fish.

kiss kisses kissing kissed *verb*
When you kiss somebody, you touch them with your lips in a friendly way. **kiss** *noun*.

kit kits *noun*
1 all the clothes and things that you need to do something. *a football kit.*
◆ *a tool kit.*
2 a set of pieces that you put together to make something. *a model ship kit.*

kitchen kitchens *noun*
a room where food is kept and cooked.

kite kites *noun*
a toy that you fly in the wind. It is made of a light frame covered with paper or cloth, attached to a long piece of string.

kitten kittens *noun*
a very young cat.

knee knees *noun*
Your knees are the parts in the middle of your legs where they bend. *He fell over and grazed his knee.* ▲ Say **nee**.

kneel kneels kneeling knelt *verb*
When you kneel, you go down on your knees. ▲ Say **neel**.

knew past of know
● A word that sounds like **knew** is **new**.

knife knives *noun*
A knife is a tool for cutting. It has a handle and a long, sharp piece of metal called a blade. ▲ Say **nife**.

knight knights *noun*
a soldier who wore armour and rode a horse hundreds of years ago. Knights fought in battles for their king or queen.
● A word that sounds like **knight** is **night**.

knit knits knitting knitted *verb*
When you knit, you use wool and two long needles to make clothes. *My grandmother knitted this jumper for me.* ▲ Say **nit**.

knob knobs *noun*
1 a round handle that you use to open a door or a drawer.
2 A knob is also a button that you turn or press to make a machine work.
▲ Say **nob**.

knock knocks knocking knocked *verb*
1 If you knock on something such as a door, you hit it hard so that people will hear you.
2 If you knock something over, you hit it so that it falls. *I knocked over the vase and it broke.*
▲ Say **nok**.

knot knots *noun*
a place where a piece of string, thread or rope is tied. *Can you undo this knot?*
● A word that sounds like **knot** is **not**.

know knows knowing knew known *verb*
1 If you know something, you have it in your mind and you are sure that it is true because you have learnt it. *Do you know what the capital of Peru is?*
2 If you know somebody, you have met them before. *I know her because she is in my class.*
● A word that sounds like **know** is **no**.

knowledge *noun*
what you know and understand about something. *She has a good knowledge of computers.* ▲ Say **nol**-*ij*.

different types of knot

knuckle knuckles *noun*
Your knuckles are the bony parts where your fingers join your hands, and the bony parts in the middle of your fingers where they bend. ▲ Say **nuk**-*l*.

koala
koalas *noun*
an animal that looks like a small bear with thick, grey fur. It lives in trees in Australia, and feeds on their leaves and bark. A female koala has a kind of pocket called a pouch at the front where she keeps her baby.

L l

label labels *noun*
a small piece of paper fixed to something that gives you information about it. *different types of label.*

laboratory laboratories *noun*
a room where scientists work and do experiments using special equipment.
▲ Say *la-**bor**-a-tree.*

lace *noun*
thin, delicate material with a pretty pattern of tiny holes in it. *a pair of lace gloves.*

laces *noun*
pieces of cord or string that you use to fasten shoes or boots.

lack *noun*
If there is a lack of something, it is missing or there is not enough of it. *The lack of rain meant that the crops did not grow properly.*

ladder ladders *noun*
two long, metal or wooden poles with bars, called rungs, between them that you can use to climb up or down.

ladle ladles *noun*
a big, deep spoon with a long handle, used for serving soup.

ladybird
ladybirds *noun*
a small, round beetle. Ladybirds are usually red with black spots on their wings.

laid past of **lay**.

lain past of **lie**
● A word that sounds like **lain** is **lane**.

lake lakes *noun*
a large area of water with land all around it.

lamb lambs *noun*
1 a young sheep.
2 meat from a young sheep.

lame *adjective*
If a person or an animal is lame, they cannot walk properly because one of their legs has been hurt. *The dog was lame in one leg after it was hit by a car.*

lamp lamps *noun*
an object that uses electricity, gas or oil to give light.

land lands *noun*
1 the solid, dry part of the world that is not covered by sea. *The sailors were glad to be on land again after spending three months at sea.*
2 a country. *He told the children tales of the foreign lands he had visited.*

land lands landing landed *verb*
When a plane lands, it comes down to the ground and stops. ■ The opposite is **take off**.

lane lanes *noun*
1 a narrow road.
2 part of a main road or motorway that is wide enough for one car at a time. *Drivers should always signal before they change lanes.*
● A word that sounds like **lane** is **lain**.

A B C D E F G H I J K L M N O P Q R S T U V W X Y Z

language languages *noun*
the words that people use to talk and write to each other. *These books are written in different languages.* ▲ Say *lang-gwij.*

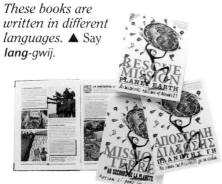

lantern lanterns *noun*
a light inside a glass and metal case that you can carry.

lap laps *noun*
1 Your lap is the top half of your legs when you are sitting down. *His little grandson was sitting on his lap.*
2 one journey around a race track.

laptop laptops *noun*
a small computer that you can open and use on your lap.

large larger largest *adjective*
big in size or amount. ■ The opposite is **small** or **little**.

larva larvae *noun*
an insect after it has come out of an egg but before it has become an adult.

laser lasers *noun*
a machine that produces a very powerful beam of light. People use laser beams for many different things such as surgery.

lasso lassos *noun*
a piece of rope with a large loop at one end that you can make bigger or smaller. Cowboys use lassos to catch cattle. ▲ Say *lass-oo.*

late later latest
adjective, adverb
If you are late, you come after the time that you were supposed to. *I was late for the dentist because I missed the bus.* ■ The opposite is **early**.

lather *noun*
a lot of small bubbles that you make when you mix water with soap or washing powder. ▲ Say *lah-ther.*

laugh laughs laughing laughed *verb*
When you laugh, you make sounds that show that you find something funny. ▲ Say *larf.*

laughter *noun*
the sound of somebody laughing. ▲ Say *larf-ter.*

launch launches launching launched *verb*
1 When somebody launches a ship or boat, they make it go into the water.
2 When a rocket or missile is launched, it is sent up into the sky.

launderette launderettes *noun*
a place where you can take your dirty washing and wash and dry it in a machine yourself.

lava *noun*
hot, liquid rock that flows from a volcano when it erupts.

lavatory lavatories *noun*
a toilet. ▲ Say *lav-a-tree.*

law laws *noun*
a rule or a set of rules made by the government, that everybody in a country has to obey. *Stealing is against the law.*

lawn lawns *noun*
an area of short grass in a garden or park.

lawyer lawyers *noun*
a person whose job is to advise people about the law and sometimes to speak for them in a court of law. ▲ Say *loy-er.*

lay lays laying laid *verb*
1 If you lay something down, you put it down carefully.
2 When you lay a table, you put knives, forks, spoons and other things on it, ready for a meal.
3 When a hen lays an egg, it produces it.

lay past of **lie**.

layer layers *noun*
a flat piece of something that lies between two other pieces of it or that lies on the top. *A sandwich usually has three layers, two slices of bread and the filling in between – this one has seven.*

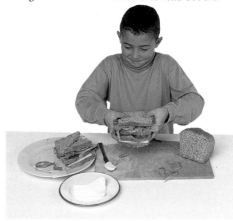

lazy lazier laziest *adjective*
Somebody who is lazy does not want to work or do very much. *She gets a lift to school every morning because she's too lazy to walk.*
laziness *noun*.

lead leads leading led *verb*
1 If you lead somebody, you go in front of them to show them the way. *Follow me and I'll lead you to the church.* ■ The opposite is **follow**.
2 If you lead a group of people, you are in charge of them. *The general led his troops to the battle.*
3 If you are leading in a race or game, you are winning at the time *John was leading for most of the race.* ▲ Say *leed.*
leader *noun*.

lead leads *noun*
a long, thin piece of leather or a chain that you attach to a dog's collar to stop it running away. ▲ Say *leed.*

lead *noun*
a soft, heavy, grey metal. ▲ Rhymes with *bed.* ● A word that sounds like **lead** is **led**.

leaf leaves *noun*
Leaves are the thin, flat parts of a plant that grow from the stem or from branches or twigs. Leaves are usually green.

leaflet leaflets *noun*
a piece of paper with information or advertisements printed on it.

leak leaks leaking leaked *verb*
If something leaks, liquid or gas escapes from it through a crack or hole. *The washing machine is leaking and there's water all over the floor.*

lean leans leaning leant or **leaned** *verb*
1 If you lean against something, you rest against it so that part of your weight is on it. *She leant against the wall.*
2 If you lean somewhere, you bend your body in that direction. *Raj leant across the table to talk to me.*

leap leaps leaping leapt or **leaped** *verb*
If you leap, you jump high or a long way. *The dog leapt over the fence.*
leap *noun.*

leap year leap years *noun*
a year that has an extra day, the 29th February, so that the year has 366 days instead of 365. Leap years happen once every four years.

learn learns learning learnt or **learned** *verb*
When you learn something, you find out about it or how to do it. *I am learning to play the piano.*

leather *noun*
a strong material made from an animal's skin. Leather is used to make things such as shoes and bags.

leave leaves leaving left *verb*
1 When you leave, you go away from somewhere. ■ The opposite is **arrive**.
2 When you leave something, you let it stay where it is. *I left my hat and coat at Jo's house.*

led past of **lead**.

left *noun, adjective, adverb*
When you write the word "left", the "l" is to the left of the "e". *Carla writes with her left hand.* ■ The opposite is **right**.

leg legs *noun*
1 Your legs are the two long parts of your body that you use for walking.
2 The legs of a table or chair are the long, narrow parts that stand on the floor and support the top part.

legal *adjective*
If something is legal, the law says you can do it. ▲ Say *lee-gul.* ■ The opposite is **illegal**.

legend legends *noun*
a story from long ago, that may or may not be true. *Do you know the legend of King Arthur?* ▲ Say *lej-end.*

leisure *noun*
a time when you do not have to work and you can do what you enjoy. ▲ Say *lesh-er.*

lemon lemons *noun*
a bright-yellow fruit with sour juice.

lend lends lending lent *verb*
If you lend something to somebody, you let them have it for a while and then they give it back to you. *Can you lend me a pen?* ■ The opposite is **borrow**.

length *noun*
The length of something is how long it is. *My desk is two metres in length.*
lengthen *verb*
to make or become longer.

lens lenses *noun*
a curved piece of glass or transparent plastic used in a camera, a pair of glasses, a telescope, or something similar to help you see more clearly.

light source   focused beam
concave lens

light source   focused beam
convex lens

lent past of **lend**.

leopard leopards *noun*
a wild cat that has yellow fur with black spots. Leopards live in Africa and South Asia. ▲ Say *lep-erd.*

leotard leotards *noun*
a tight piece of clothing that covers you from your shoulders to your thighs, made of material that stretches. Dancers wear leotards. ▲ Say *lee-o-tard.*

lesson lessons *noun*
a period of time when you are taught something by a teacher.

let lets letting let *verb*
If you let somebody do something, you do not stop them from doing it. *Will you let me stroke your dog?*

letter letters *noun*
1 one of the signs that we use to write words, such as a, b and c.
2 a written message that you send or receive by post.

lettuce lettuces *noun*
a plant with large, green leaves that we eat raw in salads. ▲ Say *let-iss.*

level *adjective*
flat and not sloping. *The table keeps shaking because the floor isn't level.*

lever levers *noun*
1 a long bar that you put under something heavy at one end so that you can lift the heavy object by pushing on the bar at the other end.
2 a long handle like a stick that you use to make a machine work. ▲ Say *lee-ver.*

liar liars *noun*
a person who tells lies.

library libraries *noun*
a building or room that has books, tapes, CDs and videos for people to borrow.

A B C D E F G H I J K L M N O P Q R S T U V W X Y Z

licence licences *noun*
an official piece of paper that gives you permission to do something. *a driving licence.* ▲ Say **lie-sens**.

lick licks licking licked *verb*
If you lick something, you move your tongue over it. *The dog licked my hand.*

lid lids *noun*
a cover for a box, pot, tin or jar.

lie lies lying lied *verb*
If you lie, you say something that you know is not true.
lie *noun*.

lie lies lying lay lain *verb*
When you lie down, you rest your body in a flat position, for example on the floor or on a bed.

life lives *noun*
A person's or an animal's life is the time they are alive, until they die. *I'll remember today for the rest of my life.*

lifeboat lifeboats *noun*
a boat that is used for rescuing people who are in danger at sea.

lift lifts lifting lifted *verb*
If you lift something, you pick it up or raise it. *I can't lift this case – it's too heavy.*

lift lifts *noun*
1 a machine like a large box that carries people or goods up and down between floors in a building.
2 If somebody gives you a lift, they take you somewhere in their car. *Can you give me a lift home from the party?*

light lights *noun*
1 Light is the bright rays that come from the Sun, the Moon, or from a lamp, that lets you see things.
2 A light is a thing that produces light. *Can you turn on the light?*

light lighter lightest *adjective*
1 Something that is light does not weigh very much and you can pick it up easily. *A feather is light.* ■ The opposite is **heavy**.
2 Light also means not dark. *My room is very light because it has two big windows.*
3 Light also means pale in colour. *light green.* ■ The opposite is **dark**.

light lights lighting lit *verb*
If you light something, you make it start burning. *Mum lit the candles on the birthday cake.*

lighthouse lighthouses *noun*
a tower with a very bright light on top that flashes to warn ships that they are near rocks or to show them the safe way to go.

lightning *noun*
a flash of very bright light that you see in the sky when there is a storm.

like likes liking liked *verb*
1 If you like somebody or something, you think they are nice.
2 If you like doing something, you enjoy it. *I like swimming more than any other sport.*
■ The opposite is **dislike**.

like

Some words you can use instead of like:

I like fire-fighters because they help people.
☞ **admire, respect** ☜

I would like an ice-cream.
☞ **enjoy, want** ☜

He's a vet because he likes animals.
☞ **fond of, loves** ☜

like *preposition*
very similar to somebody or something. *Jack looks just like his dad.* ■ The opposite is **unlike**.

likely likelier likeliest *adjective*
If something is likely, it is probably going to happen. ■ The opposite is **unlikely**.

limb limbs *noun*
an arm or a leg. ▲ Rhymes with **him**.

lime limes *noun*
a fruit similar to a lemon, with green skin and sour juice.

limit limits *noun*
the largest amount of something that is allowed. *The speed limit on this road is 80 kilometres per hour.*

limp limps limping limped *verb*
If a person or an animal limps, they walk in an uneven way because one of their legs or feet has been hurt.

line lines *noun*
1 a long, thin mark on something. *Draw a line under the title of your story.*
2 a number of people or things next to each other or one behind the other. *There was a long line of people queuing to get into the film.*
3 a long piece of rope or string. *My father is hanging the washing on the line to dry.*

link links *noun*
1 a ring in a chain.
2 a connection between things or people. *The police believe there is a link between the two crimes.*

lion lions *noun*
a large wild cat that has light-brown fur and lives in parts of Africa and Asia. The male lion has a large mane. A female lion is called a lioness and a young lion is a cub.

lip lips *noun*
Your lips are the two soft parts that form the edges of your mouth.

liquid liquids *noun*
water or anything else that flows like water. ■ The opposite is **solid**.
liquid *adjective*.

list lists *noun*
a line of things that are written down one under the other. *a shopping list.*
list *verb*.

listen listens listening listened *verb*
When you listen, you pay attention to sounds so you can hear them. *Listen carefully to the instructions.*

lit past of **light**.

litter *noun*
1 rubbish such as bits of paper and cans that are thrown away in the street or in a public place instead of being put in a bin.
2 a group of baby animals that are born at the same time to one mother. *Our cat had a litter of four kittens.*

little adjective
1 small in size. ■ The opposite is **big** or **large**.
2 A little child is a young child. *I loved drawing when I was little.*
3 small in amount. *There's only a little bit of cake left.*

live lives living lived verb
1 To live means to be alive. ■ The opposite is **die**.
2 If you live somewhere, that is where your home is. *I live with my granny.*
▲ Rhymes with **give**.

live adjective
1 A live animal is alive. *Have you ever seen a real, live crocodile?* ■ The opposite is **dead**.
2 A live TV or radio programme is being broadcast as it is happening.
▲ Rhymes with **five**.

lively livelier liveliest adjective
full of energy or excitement. *The old man is lively for his age.*

liver livers noun
Your liver is the large part inside your body that helps to clean your blood.

living noun
When you do something for a living, you earn money by doing it. *She earned her living as a journalist.*

lizard lizards noun
a reptile with four very short legs, rough skin and a long tail.

a thorny devil lizard

load loads noun
something that is being carried somewhere. *The donkey carried a very heavy load of wood.*

load loads loading loaded verb
1 If you load a car or other vehicle, you put a lot of things into it to take somewhere. *The men loaded the furniture into the lorry.* ■ The opposite is **unload**.
2 If you load a gun, you put bullets in it. *Soldiers can load their guns quickly.*

3 If you load a camera, you put a film in it. *Have you loaded the film?*
4 If you load a computer, you put information or a program into it.

loaf loaves noun
bread that is cooked in one piece and then cut up into slices.

loan loans noun
money or something else that somebody lends you and that you have to pay or give back later.

lobster lobsters noun
a sea animal with a hard shell, eight legs and two large claws in front. Lobsters can be eaten.

local adjective
close to where you live. *We go to the local school.*
locally adverb.

lock locks noun
an object that fastens a door or lid so that you cannot open it without a key.

lock locks locking locked verb
If you lock something such as a door, you fasten it with a key. *Remember to lock your bike.* ■ The opposite is **unlock**.

locomotive locomotives noun
a railway engine.

loft lofts noun
a space under the roof of a house where you can store things.

log logs noun
a piece of a thick branch cut from a tree. *We need some logs to put on the fire.*

lonely lonelier loneliest adjective
If you are lonely, you are sad because you are on your own or because you do not have any friends. *Patsy feels lonely in her new school.*

long longer longest adjective
1 far between one end and the other. *a long bridge.*
2 for more time than usual. *The film was very long and we got bored.*
■ The opposite is **short**.

long longs longing longed verb
If you long for something, you want it very much. *She longed to have a pony of her own.*

look looks looking looked verb
1 When you look at something, you use your eyes to see it.
2 If somebody or something looks a certain way, they seem that way to you. *You look tired.*
3 If you look for something, you try to find it.
4 If you look after somebody or something, you take care of them. *Dad looked after us when mum was ill.*

loop loops noun
a circle made in a piece of string, rope, thread or wire.

loose looser loosest adjective
1 not fixed firmly in place. *a loose tooth.*
2 too big to fit properly. *My trousers are loose.* ■ The opposite is **tight**.

lorry lorries noun
a large motor vehicle that is used for carrying goods by road.

lose loses losing lost verb
1 If you lose something, you do not know where to find it.
2 If you lose a competition, game or fight, you do not win it.
3 If you have lost weight, you now weigh less than you did before. *My dad is on a diet; he is trying to lose weight.*

loss losses noun
The loss of something is not having it any more. *Emily felt sad about the loss of her necklace because her gran had given it to her.*

lottery lotteries noun
a game in which you choose some numbers, or buy tickets with numbers on them, and if they are the right ones, you win a prize.

loud louder loudest adjective
Something that is loud makes a lot of noise. *loud music.* ■ The opposite is **quiet** or **soft**.
loudness noun.

A B C D E F G H I J K L M N O P Q R S T U V W X Y Z

a
b
c
d
e
f
g
h
i
j
k
l
m
n
o
p
q
r
s
t
u
v
w
x
y
z

loudspeaker loudspeakers *noun*
a piece of equipment that makes sounds louder. When a singer sings into a microphone, the audience can hear his or her voice through loudspeakers.

love loves *noun*
a very strong feeling of liking somebody or something. ■ The opposite is **hate**.

lovely lovelier loveliest *adjective*
beautiful, or very pleasant. *The park looks lovely in the spring when all the trees are in blossom.*

low lower lowest *adjective*
1 not very far from the ground. *There was a low wall between the houses.*
2 deep in sound. *He has a very low voice.*
■ The opposite is **high**.

lower lowers lowering lowered *verb*
If you lower something, you bring it slowly down. *They lowered the flag.*
■ The opposite is **raise**.

loyal *adjective*
If you are loyal to somebody, you always support them. *She is a loyal friend.*
■ The opposite is **disloyal**.
loyally *adverb*.

luck *noun*
1 Luck is when something happens by chance instead of when you plan it or make it happen. *There is no skill needed to play this game. It's just luck whether you win or not.*
2 Luck is also good things that happen to you by chance. *Wish me luck for my piano exam!*

lucky luckier luckiest *adjective*
If you are lucky, you have good things happening to you by chance. *What is your lucky number?* ■ The opposite is **unlucky**.

luggage *noun*
all the bags, cases and boxes that you take with you when you are travelling. *Have you packed your luggage yet?*
▲ Say **lug**-*ij*.

luminous *adjective*
Something that is luminous glows in the dark. *My watch has luminous hands.*

lump lumps *noun*
1 a solid bit of something. *a lump of cheese.* ◆ *This sauce has lumps in it.*
2 a swelling. *I've got a lump on my head where I banged it.*
lumpy *adjective*

lunch lunches *noun*
a meal that you eat in the middle of the day.

lung lungs *noun*
Your lungs are the two parts like bags inside your chest that fill up when you breathe in and then empty again when you breathe out.

luxury luxuries *noun*
something that is expensive and very nice to have, but that you do not need. *Mum says we can't afford the luxury of a holiday this year.* ▲ Say **luk**-*sher-ee*.
luxurious *adjective*.

M m

machine machines *noun*
a thing with parts that move to do work or to make something. We use machines in the home to help us sew, cook and clean. A washing-machine cleans our clothes and a machine called a vacuum cleaner sucks up dirt from carpets.
machinery *noun*.

mad madder maddest *adjective*
1 A person who is mad has an illness in their mind.
2 Mad also means very silly. *You're mad if you jump off this wall.*

madness *noun*
ill in your mind.

magazine magazines *noun*
a thin book with pictures, stories and information about things in it. Magazines come out every week or every month.

maggot maggots *noun*
a creature that looks like a worm and grows up to become a fly. People use maggots to catch fish.

magic *noun*
1 a power that makes strange and wonderful things happen. *The witch made the frog disappear by magic.*
2 the skill of doing clever tricks, such as making things disappear.
magic *adjective*
a magic spell.

magical *adjective*
1 produced by magic. *A magical hat that makes you disappear.*
2 strange or very exciting. *a magical fireworks display.*

magician magicians *noun*
a person who can do magic tricks.

magnet magnets *noun*
a piece of metal that makes iron or steel move towards it.
magnetic *adjective*.

magnificent *adjective*
very beautiful or grand. *a magnificent view.*

magnify magnifies magnifying magnified *verb*
When you magnify something, you make it look bigger. *We magnified the insect under the microscope.*

magnifying glass magnifying glasses *noun*
a special piece of glass called a lens that can makes things look bigger.

mail *noun*
letters, postcards and parcels that you send by post. ● A word that sounds like **mail** is **male**.

main *adjective*
most important. *the main entrance to the church.*

major *adjective, noun*
1 large, important or serious. *Paris is a major city.* ◆ *Cancer is a major illness.* ■ The opposite is **minor**.
2 an officer in the army.

make makes making made *verb*
1 If you make something, you put things together so that you have a new thing. *Mandy is making a cake.*
2 to cause something to happen. *The balloon made a loud bang when it burst.*
3 to do something. *I made a mistake.*
4 If you make somebody do something, you force them to do it. *Dad makes me go to bed at 9 o'clock.*

make-up *noun*
special powders, paints and creams that women and actors put on their faces. Face powder and lipstick are kinds of make-up.

male males *adjective*
a person or animal that belongs to the sex that cannot have babies or lay eggs. Boys and men are male. ■ The opposite is **female**. ● A word that sounds like **male** is **mail**.

malt *noun*
Malt is made from a grain called barley that has been dried. Malt is used to make whisky, beer and vinegar.

mammal mammals *noun*
an animal that drinks milk from its mother's body when it is young. People, horses and whales are all mammals.

man men *noun*
a grown-up male person.

manage manages managing managed *verb*
1 If you manage to do something difficult, you do it well. *Those sums were hard, but I managed to do them.*
2 If you manage people at work, you tell them what to do.

manager managers *noun*
a person whose job is to run or control such things as a bank, a shop or a hotel.

mane manes *noun*
the long hair on the neck of a horse or a male lion.

manner manners *noun*
1 the way that you do something. *She smiled in a friendly manner.*
2 Your manners are the way you behave when you are eating or talking to other people. *It's bad manners to talk with your mouth full.*

map maps *noun*
a drawing that shows you what a place looks like from above. Maps show things such as roads, mountains and rivers. *Will you draw me a map of how to get to your house?*

A
B
C
D
E
F
G
H
I
J
K
L
M
N
O
P
Q
R
S
T
U
V
W
X
Y
Z

MAMMALS

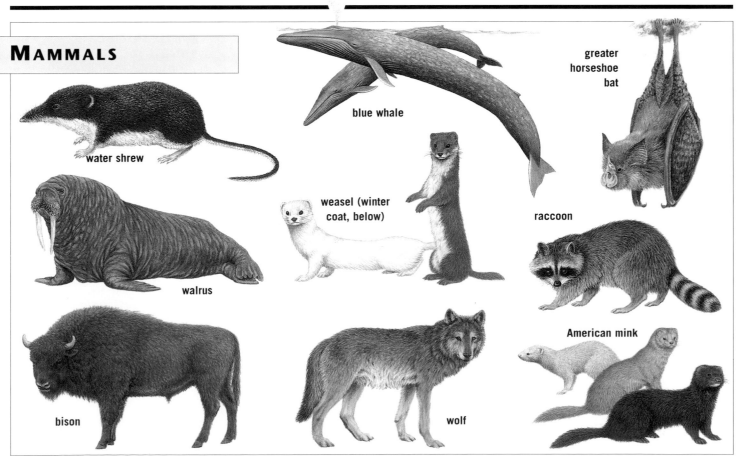

water shrew

blue whale

weasel (winter coat, below)

greater horseshoe bat

raccoon

walrus

American mink

bison

wolf

marathon **marathons** *noun*
a race when people have to run a very long way. A marathon is 42km (26 miles) long.

marble *noun*
a kind of very hard stone that can be polished until it is shiny. Marble is used to make statues and buildings.

marbles *noun*
small, coloured glass balls that you use in some games.

march **marches marching marched** *verb*
When you march, you walk like a soldier with regular steps.
march *noun*.

margarine *noun*
a soft, yellow fat that looks like butter, but is not made from milk.

margin **margins** *noun*
a space around the writing or printing on a page.

mark **marks** *noun*
1 a spot, stain or line on something that spoils it. *Your shoes have left a dirty mark on the carpet.*
2 Marks are numbers or letters that your teacher gives you to show how good your work is. *Ben got the highest marks in the class.*
mark *verb*.

market **markets** *noun*
a place, usually in the open air, with lots of little shops called stalls, where you can buy things such as fruit and vegetables or clothes.

marmalade *noun*
a jam made from oranges or lemons.

marriage **marriages** *noun*
1 the special ceremony or wedding when a man and a woman become husband and wife.
2 the time a man and woman live together as husband and wife. *Grandma and Granddad have had a long and happy marriage.*

marry **marries marrying married** *verb*
When a man and a woman marry, they become husband and wife.

marsh **marshes** *noun*
an area of land that is soft and wet.

marsupial **marsupials** *noun*
a mammal, the female of which has a pouch for carrying her young. Kangaroos and koalas are marsupials.

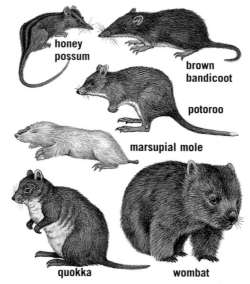

honey possum | brown bandicoot | potoroo | marsupial mole | quokka | wombat

marvellous *adjective*
very good, wonderful. *We had a marvellous day at the seaside.* ◆ *What a marvellous idea!*

mascot **mascots** *noun*
a toy or doll that people keep because they think it will bring them good luck.

mask **masks** *noun*
something you wear on your face to hide it or to protect it. Doctors in a hospital wear masks so that they do not breathe germs over patients.

mass **masses** *noun*
1 a large number of people or things. *There were masses of people at the football match.*
2 a large amount of something solid. *a mass of rock.*
3 A Mass is a service in some Christian churches.

massacre **massacres** *noun*
the violent killing of a lot of people.

massive *adjective*
very big, strong and heavy. *massive castle walls.*

mast **masts** *noun*
a tall pole that holds a flag or the sails on a boat.

mat **mats** *noun*
1 a small carpet. *Please wipe your feet on the doormat.*
2 a piece of wood or material that you put on the table under a plate. *Put the hot dishes on a table-mat.*

match **matches matching matched** *verb*
If two things match, they are the same colour, shape or pattern, or they look good together. *Jazz's hat matches her scarf.*

match **matches** *noun*
1 a small, thin stick of wood or thick card that makes fire when you rub it against something rough. *He struck a match and lit the bonfire.*
2 a game that is played between two teams or two players. *a football match.* ◆ *a tennis match.*

mate **mates** *noun*
1 a friend. *Joe was playing cricket with his mates.*
2 one of two animals that have come together to have young ones. *Most birds choose a mate in the spring.*
mate *verb*.

material **materials** *noun*
1 things that you use to make other things with. Glass, wood and stone are materials that we use to build houses.
2 a cloth that we use to make things such as clothes. *Jack bought material to make new curtains.*

maternal *adjective*
to do with being a mother. *Mothers have maternal feelings.*

maths *noun*
sums or working with shapes, sizes and measurements. Maths is short for mathematics.

a b c d e f g h i j k l m n o p q r s t u v w x y z

matter *noun*
1 something that you must talk about or do. *Mum said there were some important matters she had to see to.*
2 a problem or difficulty. *What's the matter with your computer?*
3 a thing that you can see or touch. *The world is made of matter.*

matter **matters mattering mattered** *verb*
If something matters, it is important. *Ben has lost my ruler, but it doesn't matter because I have got another one.*

mattress **mattresses** *noun*
the thick part of the bed that you lie on.

mature *adjective*
If you are mature, you are grown-up, or you behave in a grown-up way.

maximum *noun*
the most you can have of something. *Yasmin got 98 marks out of a maximum of a 100.*
maximum *adjective*
What's the maximum speed of this car?
■ The opposite is **minimum**.

mayor **mayors** *noun*
a person who is in charge of the council or government of a town or city.

maze **mazes** *noun*
a kind of puzzle made out of hedges or paths. You go into the maze at one end and have to find your way out.

meadow **meadows** *noun*
a field of grass. Wild flowers often grow in meadows. ▲ Say *med-oh.*

meal **meals** *noun*
the food that you eat at certain times of the day. Breakfast, lunch, tea, dinner and supper are all meals.

mean *adjective*
Somebody who is mean does not like giving things or spending money. *She's really mean - she ate all those sweets and didn't give us any.*

mean **means meaning meant** *verb*
1 If you ask what something means, you want somebody to explain it so that you can understand it. *What does this word mean?*
2 If you mean to do something, you plan and want to do it. *I meant to tidy my room, but I forgot.*
meaning *noun.*

meanwhile *adverb*
If something happens meanwhile, it happens at the same time as something else, or before something else happens. *I'm getting a new bike next week, meanwhile I'll have to borrow my sister's bike.*

measles *noun*
an illness that gives you little, red spots all over your skin. *Jim wasn't at school today because he has measles.*

measure **measures measuring measured** *verb*
When you measure something, you find out how big, tall, long, wide or heavy it is. *Angelina is being measured by Marianne.*
measurement *noun.*

meat *noun*
the part of an animal that we eat.

mechanical *adjective*
If something is mechanical, it is done, made or works by a machine. *a mechanical clock.*

medal **medals** *noun*
a kind of badge that somebody gives you when you win something or when you do something very brave or special. *She won a gold medal in the swimming contest.*

bronze, silver and gold medals

meddle **meddles meddling meddled** *verb*
If you meddle with something, you touch or move it when you have been told not to. *The teacher told us not to meddle with the computer.*

media *noun*
newspapers, radio and television.

medicine **medicines** *noun*
the tablets, liquid and drugs a doctor gives you when you are ill to make you feel better.

medium *adjective*
not large or small but a size in between. *Do you want a small, medium or large T-shirt?*

meet **meets meeting met** *verb*
When you meet somebody, you go to the same place at the same time as them. *Meet me at the gym at 3 o'clock.*
meeting *noun.*

melody **melodies** *noun*
a tune that you sing or play on a musical instrument.

melon **melons** *noun*
a big, round, yellow or green fruit with lots of seeds inside.

melt **melts melting melted** *verb*
When something melts, it changes into a liquid. *Flora's ice-cream is beginning to melt in the sunshine.*

member **members** *noun*
a person who belongs to something such as a club or a sports team. *Ben is a member of the school football team.*

memorize **memorizes memorizing memorized** *verb*
To memorize is to learn something so that you can remember it exactly. *Have you memorized all the names of the players in the team?*

memory **memories** *noun*
1 being able to remember things. *It is easy to learn spellings, if you have a good memory.*
2 Your memories are the things that happened to you a long time ago and that you can still remember. *My grandmother has lots of happy memories of her childhood.*
3 the part of a computer where it stores information.

men plural of **man**.

mend **mends mending mended** *verb*
When you mend something that is broken, you make it useful again. *Katie is mending her bike.*

mental *adjective*
If something is mental, it is in your mind or you do it in your mind. *mental arithmetic.*

mention **mentions mentioning mentioned** *verb*
If you mention something, you say a little bit about it. *Did Ben mention where they were going?*

menu **menus** *noun*
1 a list of things that you can eat in a café or restaurant.
2 a list on a computer that tells you what you can do.

Menu
Breakfast
Fruit Juice
Toast
Boiled eggs
Cereal
Tea or coffee

mercury *noun*
a metal that has a silver colour and is usually liquid. Mercury is used in thermometers.

Style
Edit
File
New...
Open...
Close
Save
Save As...
Revert to Saved
Get Text...
Save Text...
Save Page...

mercy *noun*
If you show mercy to somebody, you do not hurt them or punish them.

mermaid **mermaids** *noun*
a sea creature in stories that has the head and body of a woman and the tail of a fish.

merry **merrier merriest** *adjective*
happy and full of fun. *Merry Christmas!*

mess *noun*
Things are a mess when they are dirty or not where they belong. *Your bedroom is in a mess - please tidy it up!* ■ The opposite is **neat**.
messy *adjective*.

message **messages** *noun*
words that you say or write when the person you want to speak to is not there. *Tom isn't in. Leave a message for him.*

messenger **messengers** *noun*
a person who brings a message. *We sent a messenger to get help.*

met past of **meet**.

metal **metals** *noun*
a hard material that is used for making things such as cars and aeroplanes. Metal goes soft or liquid when it is heated. Silver, iron and copper are different kinds of metals.

meteor **meteors** *noun*
a piece of rock or metal that travels in space and burns when it nears the Earth.

meteorite **meteorites** *noun*
a piece of rock or metal from space that has landed on the Earth.

meter **meters** *noun*
an instrument that measures how much gas, electricity or water has been used. *a gas meter.* ◆ *a parking meter.*

method **methods** *noun*
a way of doing something. Baking, frying and boiling are methods of cooking.

metre **metres** *noun*
a measure of length. There are 100 centimetres in a metre. The short way of writing metre is m.

metric *adjective*
metres, litres and kilograms are all part of the metric system.

mice plural of **mouse**.

microphone **microphones** *noun*
an instrument that is used to record sound or to make sounds louder than they really are. *She sang with a microphone.*

microscope **microscopes** *noun*
an instrument that makes very small things look much bigger. *We looked at the insect under the microscope.*

microwave oven **microwave ovens** *noun*
a kind of oven that cooks food very quickly using waves called electromagnetic waves.

midday *noun*
12 o'clock in the middle of the day. ■ The opposite is **midnight**.

middle *noun*
the part of something that is not near the outside edges. *There is a vase of flowers in the middle of the table.*

midnight *noun*
12 o'clock in the middle of the night. ■ The opposite is **midday** or **noon**.

migrate **migrates migrating migrated** *verb*
When birds and animals migrate, they move to another country for part of the year so that they can find food. Some British birds migrate to Africa for the winter.
migration *noun*.

milk *noun*
the white liquid that mothers and female mammals make in their bodies to feed their babies. People drink the milk that cows make.
milky *adjective*.

mill **mills** *noun*
1 a building where a machine grinds grain into flour.
2 a factory for making things such as steel, paper, or materials such as wool or cotton.
3 a small tool that grinds or crushes things. *a pepper mill.*

millionaire **millionaires** *noun*
a very rich person who has more than a million pounds or dollars.

mime mimes miming mimed *verb*
If you mime something, you use actions but you do not speak. *Tom mimed blowing up a balloon and we had to guess what he was doing.*

mind minds *noun*
Your mind is the part of you that thinks, feels, learns and remembers things.

mind minds minding minded *verb*
1 If you mind about something, you feel unhappy or angry about it. *"Do you mind if I borrow your bike?" "No. I don't."*
2 To mind also means to be careful of something. *Mind the steps!*

mine mines *noun*
a place where people dig under the ground to get things such as coal, gold or diamonds. *a saltmine.*

mineral minerals *noun*
Minerals are things such as coal, gold, salt or oil that are found in rocks or under the ground.

miniature miniatures *noun*
a very small copy of something much bigger.
miniature *adjective*
miniature furniture. ▲ Say **min**-i-cher.

minimum *noun*
the smallest amount you can have of something. *We need a minimum of four people to play this game.*
minimum *adjective*
Seventeen is the minimum age for driving. ■ The opposite is **maximum**.

minister ministers *noun*
1 a person who holds services in a church.
2 an important person in the government. *the Minister of Education.*

minor *adjective*
not very serious or important. *a minor injury.* ■ The opposite is **major**.

mint *noun*
1 a plant called a herb. It is used to add flavour to things such as meat, toothpaste and sweets. *mint chocolate.*
2 a sweet with a strong mint flavour. *peppermints.*
3 the place where coins are made.

minus *noun, preposition*
1 You use the minus sign (-) to show that you have taken one number away from another. *Seven minus four is three (7 − 4 = 3).*
2 Minus also means below zero. *The temperature was minus ten degrees.*

minute minutes *noun*
a measure of time. There are 60 seconds in a minute and 60 minutes in an hour. ▲ Say **min**-it.

minute *adjective*
very, very small. *a minute insect.* ▲ Say **my**-nyoot.

miracle miracles *noun*
a wonderful thing that happens that seems impossible and that you cannot explain. *It would be a miracle if pigs could fly.* ▲ Say **mir**-i-kul.

mirror mirrors *noun*
a piece of special glass that you can see yourself in. Mirrors reflect light.

some mirrors can make you look funny

mischief *noun*
naughty or annoying behaviour.
mischievous *adjective*
Mike played a mischievous trick on his uncle.

miserable *adjective*
If you are miserable, you feel very unhappy or sad. *Katie is miserable because she can't go on holiday.*

miss misses missing missed *verb*
1 If you miss a ball, you do not hit or catch it.
2 If you miss a bus or a train, you are not there in time to catch it.
3 If you miss somebody, you are sad because they are not there. *I really missed my friend when he moved house.*

mist mists *noun*
a low cloud of tiny drops of water that is difficult to see through. *In the early morning, the fields were covered in mist.*

mistake mistakes *noun*
something that you do wrong. *I only made one spelling mistake.*

mix mixes mixing mixed *verb*
1 When you mix things, you stir them or put them together so that sometimes they make something new. *If you mix blue and red paint, you get purple.* ◆ *Oil and water do not mix.*
2 When people mix, they come together and talk to each other. *I mix with lots of different people at school.*

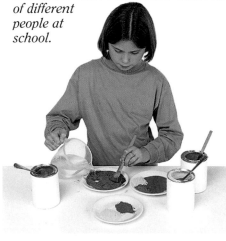

mixture mixtures *noun*
something that is made when two or more things are mixed together. *Butter, flour and sugar go into this cake mixture.*

moan moans moaning moaned *verb*
1 If you moan, you keep talking in a cross way about something that you do not like. *He was moaning about having to tidy his room.*
2 When a person or an animal moans, they make a low, sad sound because they are in pain or unhappy. *The dog was moaning because it was shut in the car.*

mobile *adjective*
If something is mobile, it can move or you can move it easily. *a mobile phone.*

mock **mocks mocking mocked** *verb*
If you mock somebody or something, you make fun of them.

model **models** *noun*
1 a small copy of something. *a model ship.*
2 a person who sits or stands so that an artist can draw them.
3 a person who wears new clothes so that people can see what the clothes look like before they buy them.

modern *adjective*
new or happening now. *We live in a modern house.*

modest *adjective*
If you are modest, you do not boast about how good or clever you are.

moist *adjective*
damp or a little wet. *The ground was moist after the rain.*
moisten *verb.*

moisture *noun*
small drops of water on something or in the air.

mole **moles** *noun*
a small animal with dark fur that lives under the ground and digs tunnels with its strong claws. Where moles have been digging they leave piles of earth called molehills.

moment **moments** *noun*
a very short time. *I'll be back in a moment.*

money *noun*
the coins and notes that we use to buy things with.

mongrel **mongrels** *noun*
a dog whose mother and father are of different types of dog.

monk **monks** *noun*
Monks are a group of men who obey rules and live and pray together in a building called a monastery because of the religion that they believe in.

monkey **monkeys** *noun*
an animal with long arms and legs and a long tail that lives mainly in trees in hot countries.

monster **monsters** *noun*
a big, frightening creature that you can read about in stories.

month **months** *noun*
a measure of time. There are twelve months in a year. *January is the first month of the year.*
monthly *adjective, adverb*
a monthly magazine.

monument **monuments** *noun*
a large statue or building that people have made to remember an important person or event. *Nelson's Column is a famous monument in London.*

mood **moods** *noun*
the way that you feel at different times. *Ben was in an angry mood today, but Katie was in a cheerful mood.*

moon **moons** *noun*
The Moon is a small satellite that travels around the Earth once every four weeks. You can often see it in the sky at night.
❖ **look below**

mop **mops** *noun*
a mop is a tool with a long handle for washing floors. It is made of sponge or bundles of cloth.

moor **moors** *noun*
an open area, often covered with grass and a spiky, low-growing plant called heather.

morning **mornings** *noun*
the early part of the day before midday. *What time do you get up in the morning?*

mosque **mosques** *noun*
a building where Muslims go to pray.
▲ Say *mosk.*

mosquito **mosquitoes** *noun*
a small, flying insect that lives in hot, wet places. Female mosquitoes bite people and animals. People can get a serious illness called malaria from mosquito bites. ▲ Say *mos-kee-toe.*

moss **mosses** *noun*
a soft, green plant that grows like a carpet on trees and damp ground.

moth **moths** *noun*
an insect that looks like a butterfly but that usually flies around at night.

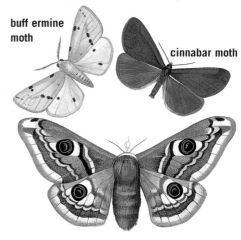

buff ermine moth

cinnabar moth

common emperor moth

mother **mothers** *noun*
a woman who has children.

motion *noun*
movement or the way of moving. *The motion of the boat on the rough sea made him feel sick.*

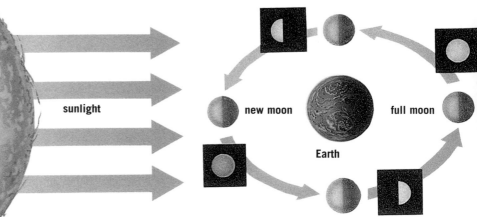

sunlight

new moon

full moon

Earth

motor motors *noun*
the part inside a machine that makes it move or work. Fridges and washing machines have electric motors.

a small motor for a model

motorbike motorbikes *noun*
a kind of bicycle with an engine.

motorway motorways *noun*
a long, wide road where cars, lorries and coaches can go fast. You cannot walk or ride a bike along a motorway.

mould moulds *noun*
1 the green or grey fungus that grows on food that has gone bad. *This cheese is covered in mould.*
2 a container for making things into a certain shape. *a jelly mould in the shape of a mouse.*

mountain mountains *noun*
a very high piece of ground. The highest mountain in the world is Mount Everest.

mouse mice *noun*
1 a small furry animal with sharp teeth and a long tail. Mice are rodents.
2 a small instrument on your desk that you use to make the cursor on your computer screen move.

moustache moustaches *noun*
hair that grows above a man's top lip.
▲ Say *mus-tash*.

mouth mouths *noun*
1 the part of your face that you open and close to talk and eat.
2 The mouth of a cave is the way into it.
3 The mouth of a river is the place where it enters the sea.

move moves moving moved *verb*
1 When you move, you go from one place to another. *Don't move - I want to take your photograph.*
2 If you move something, you put it in another place. *We moved the piano into the sitting room.*
movement *noun*.

mow mows mowing mowed *verb*
When you mow grass, you cut it with a machine called a lawnmower. ▲ Rhymes with *low*.

mud *noun*
soft, wet earth. *After playing football, Tom was covered in mud.*
muddy *adjective*.

muddle muddles muddling muddled *verb*
1 If you muddle things, you make them untidy. *Don't muddle up my clothes!*
2 If somebody muddles you, they mix things up so that you cannot understand them. *My teacher muddles me when she asks so many questions.*
muddle *noun*.

mug mugs *noun*
a big, tall cup that you use without a saucer. *a mug of hot chocolate.*

multiply multiplies multiplying multiplied *verb*
When you multiply a number, you add the number to itself several times. Four multiplied by three is twelve
$(4 + 4 + 4 = 12, \text{ or } 4 \times 3 = 12)$.
■ The opposite is **divide**.
multiplication *noun*.

munch munches munching munched *verb*
When you munch something hard, you bite and chew it in a noisy way. *Ben was munching an apple.*

murder murders murdering murdered *verb*
To murder somebody means to kill somebody on purpose.
murder *noun*, **murderer** *noun*.

murmur murmurs murmuring murmured *verb*
If you murmur, you say something softly and quietly.
murmur *noun*.

muscle muscles *noun*
Your muscles are the parts inside your body that stretch so that you can bend and move. Muscles are attached to your bones.
muscular *noun*.

museum museums *noun*
a building where lots of interesting things are kept for people to look at. *We saw a model of a dinosaur at the museum.*

mushroom mushrooms *noun*
a small plant without leaves that looks like a tiny umbrella. People eat some kinds of mushrooms, though some are poisonous. A mushroom is a fungus.

music *noun*
the sounds that come from somebody singing or playing a musical instrument, like a piano, flute or guitar.
musical *adjective*.

musical instrument musical instruments *noun*
something that you play to make music. *Violins are musical instruments.*
❖ *Look at page 106*

musician musicians *noun*
a person who plays a musical instrument well. *Sheri is a musician in a band.*

Muslim Muslims *noun*
a person who follows the religion of Islam. The religion is based on the teachings of the prophet Muhammad.

mustard *noun*
a yellow sauce with a hot taste that is made from the seeds of a plant.

mutter mutters muttering muttered *verb*
If you mutter, you speak in a quiet and angry way. *"I don't want to go home," she muttered.*

muzzle muzzles *noun*
1 the nose and mouth of an animal such as a dog or a fox.
2 something that you can put over a dog's mouth to stop it biting.

mystery mysteries *noun*
something strange that has happened and that you cannot explain.

myth myths *noun*
1 a very old story with a special meaning. Greek myths are about gods and goddesses.
2 a story that is not true.

biceps
triceps

A
B
C
D
E
F
G
H
I
J
K
L
M
N
O
P
Q
R
S
T
U
V
W
X
Y
Z

MUSICAL INSTRUMENTS

timpani

tabla drums

tuned stones

VOCABULARY

brass
metal wind instruments that you play by making your lips vibrate. Horns, trumpets and trombones are brass instruments.

keyboard
instruments with keys that you press to make notes. Pianos, harpsichords, organs and synthesizers are keyboard instruments.

percussion
instruments that are struck to produce a sound. Cymbals and drums are percussion instruments.

strings
instruments with tightly stretched strings that you pluck or stroke with a bow. Cellos, guitars and violins are string instruments.

wind instruments
that work by making a column of air vibrate inside a tube.

woodwind
wind instruments with holes along the tube that change the note.

Chinese stick fiddle

bull roarer

hurdy-gurdy

Korean piba

lira da braccio

Wagner tuba

recorder

square piano

a b c d e f g h i j k l m n o p q r s t u v w x y z

N n

nail **nails** *noun*
1 a thin piece of metal with one pointed end and a flat end, like a very large pin. *She's hammering a nail into the wall to hang the picture on.*
2 Your nails are the hard part at the end of your fingers and toes.

naked *adjective*
with no clothes on. ▲ Say *nay-kid*.

name **names** *noun*
the word we use to call somebody or something. *The dog's name is Jim.*

nap **naps** *noun*
a short sleep.

nappy **nappies** *noun*
a thick piece of soft material that you put around a baby's bottom when they are too young to be able to go to the toilet.

narrator **narrators** *noun*
a person who tells a story out loud or explains to somebody. ▲ Say *na-rate-or*.

narrow **narrower narrowest** *adjective*
If something is narrow, it is thin and does not measure very much from one side to the other. *narrow and broad leaves.* ■ The opposite is **broad** or **wide**. **narrowness** *noun*.

nasty **nastier nastiest** *adjective*
1 horrible or not nice. *a nasty smell.*
2 unkind or cruel. *He was really nasty to me.*
nastily *adverb*, **nastiness** *noun*.

nation **nations** *noun*
a country with its own laws and government. The people of a nation share the same history and language.

national *adjective*
to do with the whole of a nation or the people in a nation. *the national news.*

natural *adjective*
If something is natural, it is made by nature and not by human beings. *the natural beauty of the Scottish mountains.* ■ The opposite is **artificial**. **naturally** *adverb*.

nature *noun*
animals, plants and all the things that are not made by human beings. ▲ Say *nay-cher*.

naughty **naughtier naughtiest** *adjective*
If you are naughty, you have behaved badly or done something you should not have done. *"You naughty girl, stop hitting your brother!"* ▲ Say *nor-tee*.

navigate **navigates navigating navigated** *verb*
If you navigate a ship or aircraft, you find out and say which way to go.

navy **navies** *noun*
the ships and the sailors that are used to defend a country or fight an enemy.

near **nearer nearest** *adjective, preposition*
close by or a short distance from something or somebody. *Where's the nearest underground station?* ◆ *In the picture, I'm standing near the statue.* ■ The opposite is **far**.

nearly *adverb*
almost but not quite. *She nearly won.*

neat **neater neatest** *adjective*
clean and tidy with everything in its proper place. ■ The opposite is **messy**.

necessary *adjective*
If something is necessary, it is needed or has to happen. *It is necessary to have a passport when you go abroad.* **necessarily** *adverb*.

neck **necks** *noun*
the part of a person or animal that joins their head to their body. *The giraffe has a very long neck.*

necklace **necklaces** *noun*
a piece of jewellery such as a chain that you wear around your neck.

nectar *noun*
a sweet liquid in flowers that insects collect and that bees make into honey.

need **needs needing needed** *verb*
If you need something, you have to have it in order to live or to do a job. *People and animals need air and water or they die.* ◆ *I need some more green thread to finish my embroidery.*

needle **needles** *noun*
1 a thin, pointed piece of metal with a hole at one end for thread that is used for sewing.
2 a long, thin stick used for knitting.
3 a long, thin leaf on a pine tree.
4 a short tube with a thin, sharp point at one end that doctors use to give injections.

negative *adjective, noun*
1 meaning "no". *She gave a negative answer.*
2 A negative number is less than zero. *–20.*
3 film from a camera from which photographs are printed.
■ The opposite is **positive**.

neglect **neglects neglecting neglected** *verb*
1 If you neglect something or somebody, you do not look after them and give them the time and attention they need. *He neglected the garden.*
2 to fail to do something. *He neglected to answer the letter.*

A B C D E F G H I J K L M N O P Q R S T U V W X Y Z

neighbour neighbours *noun*
a person who lives near or next to you. *We have very friendly neighbours.* ▲ Say *nay-ber.*

neighbourhood neighbourhoods *noun*
the area where you live. *I've lived in this neighbourhood all my life.* ▲ Say *nay-ber-hood.*

nephew nephews *noun*
the son of your brother or sister. ▲ Say *nef-yoo.*

nerve nerves *noun*
1 Your nerves are the long, thin parts inside your body that link your brain to other parts of your body. They carry the messages to and from your brain that make your body move and feel.
2 brave and calm when something is difficult or frightening.

nervous *adjective*
1 worried about something that is going to happen. *I'm nervous about the test.*
2 easily frightened. *a nervous horse.*
■ The opposite is **calm**.

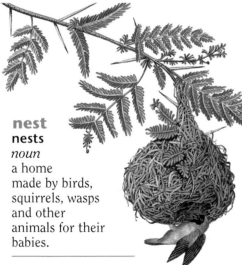

nest nests *noun*
a home made by birds, squirrels, wasps and other animals for their babies.

net nets *noun*
material made of thread, string or rope joined with knots so as to leave small holes between.

netball *noun*
a game played by two teams of seven players who have to try to get a ball through a big, round net at each end of the court.

nettle nettles *noun*
a wild plant with hairy leaves that sting you if you touch them.

network networks *noun*
1 a system of things that are connected at many different points. *the railway network.*
2 a company or group of companies that broadcast the same radio or television programmes.

never *adverb*
at no time ever in the past or the future. *He is a beautiful horse but he has never won a race.*

new newer newest *adjective*
1 If something is new, it has only just been made, or you have only just bought it. *I got some new games for my birthday.*
2 different from somebody or something you knew before. *We've got a new headteacher.*
■ The opposite is **old**.

news *noun*
information about what is going on or has just happened.

newspaper newspapers *noun*
sheets of folded paper that have news stories and pictures and other information printed on them.

newt newts *noun*
a small amphibian with short legs and a long tail that lays its eggs in water.

nib nibs *noun*
the pointed part of a pen that touches the paper when you write.

nibble nibbles nibbling nibbled *verb*
If you nibble, you eat something slowly, taking very small bites of it.

nice nicer nicest *adjective*
1 If you think something is nice, you like it or enjoy it.
2 kind and easy to like. *a nice person.*

📌 **n i c e**

Some words you can use instead of nice:

We had a nice supper.
☞ **delicious, tasty** ☜

The nice woman next door.
☞ **kind, friendly, likeable** ☜

We had a nice time on holiday.
☞ **enjoyable, pleasant, wonderful** ☜

What nice weather we are having.
☞ **good, fine, beautiful, mild** ☜

---

nickname nicknames *noun*
a short or special name that people call you instead of your real name.

niece nieces *noun*
the daughter of your brother or sister. ▲ Say *nees.*

night nights *noun*
the time when it is dark and most people are asleep. ■ The opposite is **day**. ● A word that sounds like **night** is **knight**.

nightmare nightmares *noun*
a frightening dream.

nocturnal *adjective*
awake and active mostly at night rather than during the day. *The owl is a nocturnal creature.*

nod nods nodding nodded *verb*
When you nod, you move your head up and down to show you agree with something or to say "yes".

noise noises *noun*
1 a sound. *I heard a strange noise.*
2 sounds that are too loud and unpleasant. *Please stop making so much noise!*
■ The opposite is **silence**.
noisily *adverb*, **noisy** *adjective*.

noodle noodles *noun*
a long, thin strip of pasta. *Domenic is eating a big bowl of noodles.*

noon *noun*
12 o'clock in the middle of the day. ■ The opposite is **midnight**.

noose nooses *noun*
a loop made in rope with a special knot so that when you pull on the rope the noose gets smaller.

normal *adjective*
ordinary, the same as usual. *Cold weather is normal in winter.* ■ The opposite is **unusual**.
normally *adverb*
I normally go to bed at 10 o'clock.

north *noun*
a direction that is to your left if you face the Sun as it is rising in the morning. ■ The opposite is **south**.
north *adjective*, **northern** *adjective*
a north wind. ◆ *a northern accent.*

nose noses *noun*
Your nose is the part sticking out in the middle of your face that you use for breathing and smelling. At the end of your nose there are two holes called nostrils.
❖ *Look below*

note notes *noun*
1 a few words that you write down to remind yourself of something. *I've made a note of your phone number.*
2 a short letter. *I'll send a note to the school to explain that you have to go to the dentist.*
3 a single sound in music or a symbol written to show a sound.
4 a piece of paper money. *He paid with a £10 note.*

notice notices noticing noticed *verb*
If you notice something, you start to see it or hear it or smell it. *I suddenly noticed that there were lots of people in the garden.*

Spelling tip:
....
Some words that begin with an "n" sound are spelt with "gn" or "kn" such as gnat, gnome, knee.

---

notice notices *noun*
a written message that is put in a public place so that many people can read it.

nought *noun*
the number 0. ▲ Say *nort*.

noun nouns *noun*
a word that gives the name of a thing, a state, a feeling, an idea, a person or a place. *Table, talent, happiness, sadness, Ben and London are all different nouns.*

nourishment *noun*
food that is good for you and makes you strong and healthy. ▲ Say *nur-ish-ment*.
nourishing *adjective*.

novel novels *noun*
a long written story that has been made up by somebody about people and events that do not really exist.
novelist *noun*.

nude *adjective*
without any clothes, naked.

nudge nudges nudging nudged *verb*
If you nudge somebody, you push them with your elbow to make them notice something.

---

nuisance nuisances *noun*
a person or something that annoys you.
▲ Say *new-sense*.

numb *adjective*
unable to feel anything in a part of your body. *It was so cold my feet went numb.*
▲ Say *num*.

number numbers *noun*
a word or sign that shows you how many of something there are.

Arabic	Roman	Binary	Mayan
1	I	1	•
2	II	10	••
3	III	11	•••
4	IV	100	••••
5	V	101	———
6	VI	110	•
7	VII	111	••
8	VIII	1000	•••
9	IX	1001	••••
10	X	1010	═══
15	XV	1111	≡≡≡
20	XX	10100	≣≣≣
50	L		
100	C		
500	D		
1000	M		

numerous *adjective*
very many. *Numerous people were invited.* ■ The opposite is **few**.

nun nuns *noun*
nuns are a group of women who obey rules and live and pray together in a building called a convent because of the religion that they believe in.

nurse nurses *noun*
a person whose job is to look after people who are ill or injured.

nursery nurseries *noun*
1 a place where young children can go during the day when they are too young to start school.
2 a place where plants and flowers are grown to be sold.

nut nuts *noun*
the fruit of a tree that has a seed inside a hard shell.

elephant

snow leopard

duck-billed platypus

giant anteater

elephant seal   mandrill   spear-nosed bat   proboscis monkey

A B C D E F G H I J K L M N O P Q R S T U V W X Y Z

O o

oak oaks *noun*
1 a large tree that acorns grow on.
2 the wood from this tree.

oar oars *noun*
a long pole with one flat end that you use to row a boat. ▲ Say *or*.

oasis oases *noun*
a place in a desert with water, plants and trees. ▲ Say *oh-**ay**-sis*.

oats *noun*
Oats are plants that farmers grow for their seeds called grain.

obey obeys obeying obeyed *verb*
If you obey somebody, you do what they tell you to do. ■ The opposite is **disobey**.
obedient *adjective*.

object objects *noun*
1 a thing that you can see and touch. *The box was full of objects of all shapes and sizes.*
2 the purpose or thing that you are trying to achieve. *Her object was to win the contest.*
3 in the sentence, *"Jim hit the ball"*, the object of the sentence is "the ball"
▲ Say *ob-jekt*

object objects objecting objected *verb*
If somebody objects to something, they do not like it or agree with it. *The teacher objects to noisy children.*
▲ Say *ob-jekt*.

oblong oblongs *noun*
a shape with two long, opposite sides and two short, opposite sides.
oblong *adjective*
The pages of this dictionary are oblong.

observe observes observing observed *verb*
When you observe somebody or something, you watch them carefully. *We observed a bird feeding its babies.*

obstacle obstacles *noun*
something that is in your way and stops you from doing something. *The fallen tree was an obstacle in the road.*

obstinate *adjective*
An obstinate person does not like to change what they think, or do what other people want them to do. *Oliver is so obstinate that he will only do what he wants to do.*

obvious *adjective*
If something is obvious, it is easy to see or understand. *The answers to the quiz were obvious.*

occasion occasions *noun*
a time when something happens. *A wedding is an important occasion.* ◆ *We've been to Canada on many occasions.*

occasionally *adverb*
If something happens occasionally, it happens but not very often. *I usually walk to school, but occasionally I go by bicycle.*

occupant occupants *noun*
somebody who lives or works in a place.

occupy occupies occupying occupied *verb*
1 If you occupy a house, you live in it.
2 If somebody or something occupies a space, they are in it. *All the parking spaces were occupied.*
3 If you are occupied, you are busy. *I was occupied with my computer.*

occupation occupations *noun*
a job. *What's your occupation? I'm a vet.*

occur occurs occurring occurred *verb*
1 When something occurs, it happens. *The storm occurred last night.*
2 If something occurs to you, you suddenly think about it. *It occurred to me that I had been rude to my aunt.*

ocean oceans *noun*
any of the very large areas of sea. *the Atlantic Ocean.*

octagon octagons *noun*
a shape with eight straight sides.

octopus octopuses *noun*
an animal that lives in the sea. It has eight long arms called tentacles.

odd odder oddest *adjective*
1 strange or unusual. *She was wearing a very odd hat.*
2 Odd things do not belong together in a pair or a set. *I'm wearing odd socks, one is red and the other is brown.*
3 An odd number is any number that ends in 1, 3, 5, 7, or 9. You cannot divide these numbers by two without leaving something over. ■ The opposite is **even**.
4 The **odd one out** is something that is different from the rest. *Out of apple, orange, potato and banana, potato is the odd one out because it is a vegetable. All the others are fruits.*

odour odours *noun*
a strong smell. *Domenic's socks have a strong odour!*

offend offends offending offended *verb*
If you offend somebody, you upset them and hurt their feelings. *She offended me because she said I was fat.*
offence *noun*, **offensive** *adjective*
offensive behaviour.

offer offers offering offered *verb*
1 If you offer somebody something, you ask them if they would like it. *She offered me a biscuit.*
2 If you offer to do something, you say you are willing to do it. *He offered to do the washing up.*

office offices *noun*
1 a place where people go to work. Offices have things such as desks, chairs, computers and telephones.
2 a place where you can buy something or get information. *the post office.*

officer officers *noun*
1 a person in the army, navy or air force who gives orders to other people. *an army officer.*
2 a person who does important work. *a police officer.*

official *adjective*
If something is official, it is important and people must believe it or do it. *an official report from the government.*
▲ Say o-**fish**-al.

oil *noun*
1 a smooth, thick liquid that comes from the ground. You can burn oil to make heat or to make machines work.
2 Oil is also a smooth liquid that comes from plants and animals. Some people use it for cooking. *olive oil.* ◆ *vegetable oil.*
oily *adjective*.

ointment *noun*
a cream that you put on a cut or sore skin to heal it.

old older oldest *adjective*
1 Somebody who is old has lived for a long time. *My great grandfather is very old - he is ninety!*
2 Something that is old was made a long time ago. *This castle is very old - it was built five hundred years ago.*
■ The opposite is **new**.
3 having a certain age. *My mum is thirty five years old.*
4 Something that you had or knew before. *Yesterday I saw an old friend from my old school.*

olive olives *noun*
a small green or black fruit. Olives are used to make olive oil that is used in cooking.

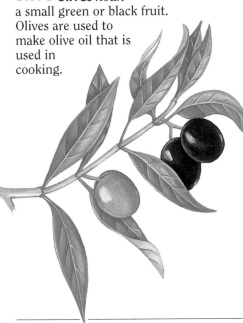

Olympic *adjective*
of the Olympic Games or the Olympics, international sports contests held every four years in a different country.

onion onions *noun*
a round vegetable with a strong taste and smell that grows under the ground.

only *adjective, adverb*
1 with no others. *This is the only photo I have of her.*
2 no more than. *I've only got one brother.* ◆ *It will only take five minutes to prepare the food.*
3 but. *This is a good story, only it's a bit long.*

open *adjective*
1 not closed or covered. *The dog escaped through the open gate.*
2 ready for people to come in. *The shop is open at nine o'clock.*

open opens opening opened *verb*
1 If you open a door, you let people or things go through.
2 To open means to move something so that it is not closed or covered. *Open your eyes!* ◆ *He opened the box and found a present inside.*
3 If you open a shop or office, you make it ready for people to come in. *The museum opens at nine o'clock.*
opening *noun*.

opera operas *noun*
a play where actors sing most of the words. *"The Magic Flute" is an opera by Mozart.*

operate operates operating operated *verb*
1 When surgeons operate, they take away or mend part of a patient's body to make them well again.
2 If you operate a machine, you use it or make it work. *Can you operate this computer?*

operation operations *noun*
When somebody has an operation, a surgeon takes away or mends a part of their body.

opinion opinions *noun*
what you think about something. *In my opinion, people should always be kind to animals.*

opportunity opportunities *noun*
a time or chance that is right for doing something. *On holiday, we had the opportunity to go sailing.*

opposite opposites *noun*
something that is different from another thing in every way. *Bad is the opposite of good.*

opposite *adjective, adverb*
1 different in every way. *North is in the opposite direction to South.*
2 across or on the other side. *The women stood opposite each other.*

optician opticians *noun*
a person who tests your eyes to see if you need glasses.

orbit orbits *noun*
the invisible path that something such as a planet or a spaceship follows as it travels around the Earth, another planet or the Sun.
orbit *verb*.

A B C D E F G H I J K L M N O P Q R S T U V W X Y Z

orchard orchards *noun*
an area of land where fruit trees grow.

orchestra orchestras *noun*
a group of people who play different musical instruments together.
▲ Say *or-kes-tra*.

order orders *noun*
1 Order means the way that things follow one another. *The letters of the alphabet always come in the same order.*
2 An order is something that you must do because somebody tells you to do it. *The officer gave the soldier an order to march.*

order orders ordering ordered *verb*
1 If you order something, you say you would like it. *We ordered bacon, sausages and eggs.*
2 If you order somebody to do something, you say that they must do it. *The doctor ordered Tom to stay in bed for a week.*

ordinary *adjective*
not exciting or special. *Yesterday was my birthday, but today is just an ordinary day.*

organ organs *noun*
1 An organ is a part of your body that does something special. Your heart, liver and kidneys are all organs.
2 a big musical instrument like a piano with pipes that air goes through to make sounds. *a church organ.*

organization organizations *noun*
a group of people who work together.

organize organizes organizing organized *verb*
If you organize something you arrange or plan it. *The school has organized a trip to London.*

origin origins *noun*
1 the beginning of something and how and why it began. *We are learning about the origins of life on Earth.*
2 where somebody or something came from. *a vase of ancient Greek origin.*

original *adjective*
1 Something that is original is the first to be made. *This is an original painting. All the others are copies.*
2 different and exciting. *What an original idea!*

a Gamelan orchestra from Indonesia

ornament ornaments *noun*
an object that you like and use to make a place look pretty. *china ornaments.*

orphan orphans *noun*
a child whose mother and father are dead.

ostrich ostriches *noun*
a very large bird with long legs and a long neck that lives in Africa. Ostriches can run fast, but they cannot fly.

otter otters *noun*
a small animal with brown fur. Otters can swim well and catch fish to eat.

ought *verb*
If you ought to do something, you should do it because it is important. *You ought to clean your teeth before you go to bed.*

outdoors *noun*
the open air or outside a building. *The outdoors is the best place to practise the violin!* ■ The opposite is **indoors**.

outer *adjective*
1 not in the middle of a place. *I live in outer London.*
2 the outside of something. *His outer clothes were covered with mud.*
■ The opposite is **inner**.

outing outings *noun*
a short trip that you go on to enjoy yourself. *We had an outing to the seaside.*

outline outlines *noun*
1 a line around the edge of something that shows its shape. *As it grew dark, we could just see the outline of the house against the sky.*
2 a drawing where you just draw a line to show the shape of something. *Tom drew the outline of a car.*

oval ovals *noun*
An oval is a shape like an egg.
oval *adjective*
an oval rugby ball.

oven ovens *noun*
the part like a box inside a cooker where you cook food. *Chris baked a chocolate cake in the oven.*

overalls *noun*
clothes that you wear to keep your other clothes clean when you do things such as painting.

overflow overflows overflowing overflowed *verb*
If something like a bath overflows, the water comes over the top of it. *I forgot to turn off the taps and the basin is overflowing!*

overgrown *adjective*
If a garden is overgrown, it is covered with weeds and the plants look untidy.

overhead *adjective, adverb*
above your head. *an overhead light.*
◆ *A plane flew overhead.*

overhear overhears overhearing overheard *verb*
When you overhear something, you hear what somebody says when they are speaking to someone else. *Jessie overheard Rachel and Sarah talking.*

overlap overlaps overlapping overlapped *verb*
When two things overlap, part of one thing covers part of the other thing. *The tiles on the roof overlap.*

overtake overtakes overtaking overtook overtaken *verb*
When drivers overtake, they pass a car, a bus or a lorry that is going more slowly. *The car overtook a bus.*

owe owes owing owed *verb*
If you owe money, you have to give the money back to the person who lent it to you. *I owe you 50p for the sweets.*

owl owls *noun*
a bird with large eyes that can see well in the dark and hunts small animals, such as mice, at night.

own owns owning owned *verb*
If you own something, you have something that belongs to you. *Do you own that bike or did you borrow it?*

owner owners *noun*
a person who has or owns something. *Who is the owner of this pencil case?*

ox oxen *noun*
a bull that is used in some countries for pulling carts.

oxygen *noun*
a gas in the air we breathe. People, animals and plants need oxygen to live and things cannot burn without it.

oyster oysters *noun*
a sea animal that lives inside a pair of shells. A few oysters produce a pearl inside their shells.

ozone *noun*
a gas in the air. Ozone forms a layer, called the ozone layer, around the Earth. It protects us from the harmful rays of the sun.
ozone friendly not harmful to the ozone layer. *We buy only ozone friendly aerosols.*

P p

pace *noun*
the speed at which something happens or moves. *They started off at a fast pace.*

pack packs packing packed *verb*
When you pack, you put clothes and other things you need in a case or container to take away with you.

package packages *noun*
a parcel.

packet packets *noun*
a box, bag or envelope containing things. *a packet of cornflakes.* ◆ *a seed packet.*

pad pads *noun*
1 a thick piece of soft material that can be used to protect something.
2 a lot of pieces of paper to write or draw on that are fixed together at one edge.
3 the soft part on the underneath of an animal's paw.

paddle paddles paddling paddled *verb*
1 If you paddle, you walk in the shallow water at the edge of the sea or a lake.
2 When you paddle a canoe, you move it through the water.

paddle paddles *noun*
a short, flat oar for a boat or canoe. *Hold the paddle in both hands.*

padlock padlocks *noun*
a small, metal block with a bar in the shape of a U at the top which you can use to lock things such as gates and bicycles.

page pages *noun*
one side of a piece of paper in a book or newspaper. *This dictionary has lots of pages.*

paid past of **pay**.

pain *noun*
the feeling that you have in a part of your body when it hurts. *I have a bad headache and a stomach pain as well.* ●
A word that sounds like **pain** is **pane**.

painful *adjective*
When something is painful, it hurts a lot. *I fell over and my knee is quite painful.*
painfully *adverb.*

paint paints *noun*
a liquid that you use to make coloured pictures or to give a new colour to the walls and ceilings in a house.
paint *verb*
I am going to paint a picture.

painter painters *noun*
1 a person whose job it is to put paint on walls, doors and window frames.
2 an artist who paints pictures. *Monet was a French painter.*

painting paintings *noun*
a picture made using paint. *We pinned our painting to the wall.*

A B C D E F G H I J K L M N O P Q R S T U V W X Y Z

pair pairs noun
1 two things that go together or that you use together. *a pair of gloves.*
2 We also talk about pairs of things such as trousers, scissors or binoculars that have two parts the same joined together.
● A word that sounds like **pair** is **pear**.

palace palaces noun
a large building for somebody very important to live in. *The queen lives in Buckingham Palace.*

pale paler palest adjective
Something that is pale is almost white. *pale blue.* ■ The opposite is **dark**.

palm palms noun
1 a tree with no branches but that has long leaves that grow from the top of the trunk. *Palm trees grow where the weather is hot.*
2 the flat part inside your hand between your wrist and your fingers.
▲ Say *parm*.

European fan palm

coconut palm

date palm

pan pans noun
a container with a handle that you use for cooking food in. *a frying-pan.*

pancake pancakes noun
a thin, flat cake made from flour, eggs and milk that is fried in a pan in hot oil.

panda pandas noun
a large animal that looks like a black and white bear. *Pandas live in China and are very rare.*

black and white panda

red panda

pane panes noun
a flat piece of glass. *a window pane.* ● A word that sounds like **pane** is **pain**.

panel panels noun
a long, flat piece of wood or glass that is part of a door or fence.

panic panics panicking panicked verb
If you panic, you feel so worried or afraid that you do not know what to do and you cannot act or think in a sensible or calm way.
panic noun.

pant pants panting panted verb
If a person or animal pants, they breathe quickly with their mouth open. *Dogs pant to cool themselves when they get hot.*

panther panthers noun
a black leopard.

pantomime pantomimes noun
a traditional Christmas show for children, with songs, jokes and dancing. The stories for pantomimes are taken from fairy tales.

pants noun
a piece of clothing or underwear that you wear at the top of your legs under trousers or a skirt. Pants have two holes for your legs.

paper noun
1 thin material that you use for writing on or wrapping things in and that books and newspapers are printed on.
2 a newspaper.

parable parables noun
a story that teaches people something.

parachute parachutes noun
a large piece of cloth fixed to a person with ropes that opens up like an umbrella so that the person can jump from a plane and float safely to the ground. ▲ Say *par-a-shoot*.

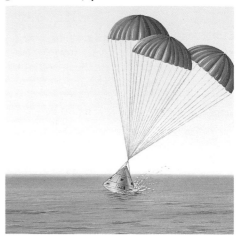

parade parades noun
a lot of people marching along, often with decorated vehicles and music to celebrate something special. *There was a big parade to celebrate the queen's visit.*

paragraph paragraphs noun
several sentences about the same idea that are written or printed together. The first sentence of a paragraph starts on a new line. ▲ Say *par-a-grarf* or *par-a-graf*.

parallel adjective
Parallel lines are straight and always the same distance from each other. *Railway lines are parallel.*

paralysed adjective
If part of somebody's body is paralysed, they cannot move it or feel anything in it. *She is paralysed from the waist down and moves around in a wheelchair.*

parcel parcels noun
something that is wrapped in paper so that it can be sent through the post.

parchment noun
a material made from the skin of a sheep or goat that was used for writing on in the past.

pardon **pardons pardoning pardoned** *verb*
If you pardon somebody, you forgive them. *The judge pardoned the criminal.*

parent **parents** *noun*
a mother or a father.

park **parks** *noun*
an area of land, usually in a town, with grass and plants where people can go to walk and children can play.

park **parks parking parked** *verb*
When you park a car, you leave it somewhere until you need it again.

parliament **parliaments** *noun*
a group of people who meet to discuss or make new laws for a country. ▲ Say *par-li-ment*.

parrot **parrots** *noun*
a tropical bird with brightly coloured feathers and a curved beak. Parrots can be taught to copy human speech.

part **parts** *noun*
1 one piece or bit of something.
2 If you have a part in a play, you act as one of the characters in the play.

part **parts parting parted** *verb*
1 to divide. *hair parted in the middle.*
2 to separate. *We parted at the crossroads.*

particular *adjective*
A particular thing or person is the one that you specially mean and not anything or anybody else. *I don't want any old kitten, I want that particular one over there.*

partner **partners** *noun*
A partner is somebody who does something with another person. *She's my partner when we go dancing.*

party **parties** *noun*
1 a group of people who get together to have fun. *a birthday party.*
2 a group of people who have the same ideas about politics. *The Democratic Party.* ◆ *The Socialist Party.*

pass **passes passing passed** *verb*
1 If you pass something, you go by it without stopping.
2 If you pass an exam, you do it well enough to succeed.
3 If you pass something to somebody, you give or hand it to them. *Pass me that pair of scissors, please.*
● A word that sounds like **passed** is **past**.

pass **passes** *noun*
a ticket or card that allows you to do something, such as travel free or enter a building.

passage **passages** *noun*
a narrow place with walls on each side like a corridor.

passenger **passengers** *noun*
a person who is travelling in a vehicle but not driving it.

passport **passports** *noun*
a small book or document that you take when you travel to another country that shows who you are and what country you come from.

password **passwords** *noun*
a secret word that you have to know to get into a place or, sometimes, to be able to work on a computer.

past *noun*
the time up until now. *In the past there were no televisions and computers.*
■ The opposite is **future**. ● A word that sounds like **past** is **passed**.

past *preposition*
farther on than something, or after it. *Go past the church and then turn left.*
● A word that sounds like **past** is **passed**.

pasta *noun*
a food made from flour that is formed into different shapes. Spaghetti and macaroni are kinds of pasta.

paste *noun*
1 a thick, soft glue.
2 a thick, soft mixture of food.

pastel **pastels** *noun*
a piece of coloured chalk that you use for drawing.

pastime **pastimes** *noun*
a hobby or sport that you do when you are not working.

pastry *noun*
a mixture of flour, fat and water that is rolled, cooked and used for making pies.

pasture **pastures** *noun*
a field with grass for animals such as cows and sheep to eat.

pat **pats patting patted** *verb*
If you pat something, you hit it gently with your hand. *He patted the dog.*

patch **patches** *noun*
1 a piece of material that you put over a hole to mend it. *His jeans have a patch on the knee.*
2 a small area that is different from the rest. *a patch of white fur.*

path **paths** *noun*
a narrow piece of ground where people can walk to get somewhere. *There's a path across the field.*

patience *noun*
If you have patience, you stay calm when something takes a long time or is very difficult. ▲ Say *pay-shens*.

patient *adjective*
If you are patient, you stay calm and do not complain when something takes a long time. ▲ Say *pay-shent*. ■ The opposite is **impatient**.
patiently *adverb*.

types of pasta

A B C D E F G H I J K L M N O P Q R S T U V W X Y Z

patient patients *noun*
a person who is being treated by a doctor or a dentist. ▲ Say *pay-shent*.

patrol patrols *noun*
a group of soldiers, guards or police officers who regularly go round an area to protect it and make sure there is no trouble or danger.

pattern patterns
noun
a design or arrangement of colours and shapes on something. *It is fun to make patterns using different colours and shapes.*

pause pauses pausing paused *verb*
If you pause, you stop what you are doing for a short time before you go on with it.
pause *noun*
● A word that sounds like **pause** is **paws**.

pavement pavements *noun*
the part with the hard surface at the side of the road where people walk and cars are not allowed to go.

paw paws *noun*
an animal's foot. ● A word that sounds like **paws** is **pause**.

pay pays paying paid *verb*
When you pay somebody, you give them money for something you have bought or for work they have done. *How much will you pay me to wash your car?*

pea peas *noun*
a small, round, green vegetable that grows in a pod.

peace *noun*
1 a time when people are not fighting. ■ The opposite is **war**.
2 a time when there is no noise or no worry.
peaceful *adjective*.

peach peaches *noun*
a soft, round fruit with a pale, furry orange skin and a large stone inside.

peacock peacocks *noun*
a large, male bird with a tail made of blue and green feathers that it can spread out like a fan. The female is called a peahen.

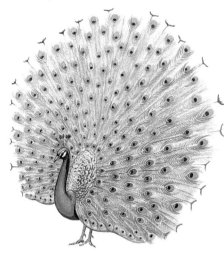

peak peaks *noun*
1 the pointed top of a mountain.
2 the part of a cap that sticks out in front above your eyes.

peanut peanuts *noun*
a small nut that grows under the ground in a covering called a pod.

pear pears *noun*
a sweet fruit that is round at the bottom but narrower at the top where the stalk is. ● A word that sounds like **pear** is **pair**.

pearl pearls *noun*
a small, hard, round, white ball that is used as jewellery and that grows inside the shell of an oyster.
▲ Rhymes with *curl*.

pebble pebbles *noun*
a small, smooth stone.

peck pecks pecking pecked *verb*
When a bird pecks, it pushes its beak at something and picks it up. *The hens were pecking at their food scattered on the ground.*

peculiar *adjective*
strange or odd. *This flower has a peculiar smell.*

pedal pedals *noun*
a part on a machine that you push with your foot. You push the pedals round on a bicycle to make it move. You push the pedals down in a car to make the car go faster or slower.

pedestrian pedestrians *noun*
a person who is walking across or along a street.

peel peels peeling peeled *verb*
If you peel a fruit or vegetable you take off the skin. *Sarah is peeling an apple.*

peel *noun*
the outside skin of a fruit or vegetable. *orange peel.*

peep peeps peeping peeped *verb*
If you peep, you look quickly at something. *The film was so frightening, he just peeped at it through his fingers.*

peer peers peering peered *verb*
You peer at something when it is difficult to see, so you have to look hard to see it. ● A word that sounds like **peer** is **pier**.

peg pegs *noun*
a piece of wood, plastic or metal that is used to hold something down or to hang something up. *a tent peg.* ◆ *a clothes peg.* ◆ *a peg to hang your coat on.*

pelican pelicans *noun*
a large water bird with a long, narrow beak with a pouch under it that it uses for holding fish. ❖ *Look at page 24*

pen pens *noun*
a long, narrow object with a point at one end that you use for writing with ink. *I have lost my pen, can I borrow yours?*

penalty penalties *noun*
a punishment given if you do not obey a rule or do something wrong.

pencil pencils *noun*
a long, thin stick made of wood with a substance called graphite in the middle that you use for writing or drawing.

pendulum pendulums *noun*
a weight on the end of a rod inside some clocks. It swings from side to side to make the clock work.

penfriend penfriends *noun*
A penfriend is a person who lives far away that you get to know by exchanging letters with them.

penguin penguins *noun*
a large, black and white bird that swims but cannot fly. Penguins mostly live in the Antarctic, the very cold land and sea in the far south of the world. Penguins feed on fish.

penis penises *noun*
the part of a man's or boy's body between their legs. Boys and men use it to get rid of waste liquid, when they go to the toilet. Men also use it to have sex and make babies with. ▲ Say *pee-nis*.

penknife penknives *noun*
a knife with blades that fold back into the handle.

pension pensions *noun*
money that people receive regularly to live on when they have retired and have stopped working.

pentagon pentagons *noun*
a shape with five sides.

people *noun*
men, women and children. *A lot of people were waiting at the bus stop.*

pepper peppers *noun*
1 a spice with a hot taste that is ground to a powder and put on food. *black pepper*.
2 a green, red or yellow vegetable that is hollow inside.

different types of pepper

per cent *noun*
a number of parts of something in every hundred. *8 per cent of people or eight people in every hundred travel to work by bike.* The sign for per cent is % *(8 %)*. ▲ Say *per sent*.

perch perches *noun*
1 a place for a bird to stand or sit.
2 a fish that lives in fresh water.
perch *verb*
The birds perched on the fence.

percussion *noun*
all the different musical instruments such as drums and tambourines that you play by hitting them.

perfect *adjective*
A perfect thing has no mistakes or faults.
perfection *noun*, **perfectly** *adverb*.

perform performs performing performed *verb*
1 If actors perform, they act, sing, dance or tell jokes in front of an audience.
2 to do or carry out. *The surgeon performed an operation.*
performer *noun*.

perfume perfumes *noun*
a liquid with a pleasant smell that you put on your skin to make you smell nice. *a bottle of perfume.*

perimeter perimeters *noun*
the outside edge of something. *the perimeter of a circle.* ▲ Say *per-im-it-er*.

period periods *noun*
1 an amount of time. *She'll be away for a period of two weeks.*
2 a particular time in history. *the Tudor period.*

periscope periscopes *noun*
a tube with mirrors inside that are arranged so that when you look in one end of the tube you can see things through the top that you would not be able to see normally. Periscopes are used in submarines to see what is happening above the surface of the water.

permanent *adjective*
lasting for ever or for a very long time. ■ The opposite is **temporary**.

permission *noun*
If somebody gives you permission to do something, they say you are allowed to do it. *My teacher gave me permission to go home early.*

permit permits permitting permitted *verb*
If somebody permits you to do something, they allow you to do it. *I'm permitted to stay up late at the weekend.* ■ The opposite is **forbid**.

person *noun*
a man, woman or child.

personal *adjective*
belonging to one person. *This is my personal CD player.*

persuade persuades persuading persuaded *verb*
If you persuade somebody to do something, you manage to make them do it, even if they did not want to. ▲ Say *per-swade*.

pest pests *noun*
1 an insect or animal that damages plants or is harmful to people.
2 a person who is annoying or causes trouble.

A B C D E F G H I J K L M N O P Q R S T U V W X Y Z

pet pets *noun*
a tame animal that you keep in the house and look after.

petal petals *noun*
one of the white or coloured parts that make the outside of a flower.

petrol *noun*
a liquid made from oil that is used as a fuel in motor vehicles to make them go.

phantom phantoms *noun*
a ghost. ▲ Say *fan-tum*.

pharmacy pharmacies *noun*
the part of a chemist's shop that sells medicines. ▲ Say *far-ma-see*.

phone phones *noun*
a telephone. ▲ Say *fone*.

photo photos *noun*
a photograph or picture that you make by using a camera. ▲ Say *foh-toh*.

photocopy photocopies *noun*
a copy of a document made by a machine called a photocopier.

physical *adjective*
to do with people's bodies rather than their minds. ▲ Say *fiz-ik-al*.
physically *adverb*
My grandmother is physically fit but she keeps forgetting things.

piano pianos *noun*
a large musical instrument with a row of black and white keys. When you press a key, a small hammer inside the piano hits a string to make a sound.
pianist *noun*.

pick picks picking picked *verb*
1 When you pick something, you take it from a group of things because it is the one that you want. *Pick your favourite tape and we'll buy it.*
2 If you pick a fruit or a flower, you take it off the plant. *We're going to the farm tomorrow to pick strawberries.*
3 When you pick something up, you lift it up from where it is lying. *Can you pick those bags up and bring them into the house?*
4 If you pick at something, you eat a little bit of it. *He picked at his food.*

pickle pickles *noun*
a mixture of vegetables or fruit kept in vinegar to preserve them. *Winston loves pickles on his sandwiches.*

picnic picnics *noun*
a meal that you take somewhere with you and eat outside.

picture pictures *noun*
a drawing, painting or photograph.

pie pies *noun*
a piece of pastry with meat, fruit, fish or vegetables cooked inside it.

piece pieces *noun*
1 a part or bit that is cut off something bigger. *Cut the pie into four equal pieces.*
2 a single thing. *a piece of paper.*

---

piece

Some words you can use instead of piece:

May I have a piece of cake?
☞ *slice, portion* ☜

She tore the paper into pieces.
☞ *bits, scraps* ☜

There were huge pieces of meat in the soup.
☞ *lumps* ☜

On this piece of land we grow roses.
☞ *part, section* ☜

---

pier piers *noun*
a long platform built out over the sea where people can walk or where boats can be tied up. ● A word that sounds like **pier** is **peer**.

pierce pierces piercing pierced *verb*
When a sharp object pierces something, it makes a hole in it. *Have you had your ears pierced?*

pig pigs *noun*
a farm animal with a flat nose, short legs and a curly tail. Male pigs are called boars and female pigs are called sows. The meat of pigs is eaten as pork, bacon and ham.

pigeon pigeons *noun*
a grey bird with a fat body. Some pigeons have been trained to carry messages and some are used for racing.

pile piles *noun*
a lot of things that have been put one on top of the other. *a pile of books.*

pill pills *noun*
A pill is a medicine that has been made into a small, round object that you swallow.

pillar pillars *noun*
a tall, round column made of stone or brick that holds up part of a building.

pillow pillows *noun*
a soft cushion that you put your head on when you are in bed.

pilot pilots *noun*
a person who flies an aircraft.

pin pins *noun*
a small, thin, metal stick with a sharp point at one end that you use for holding two pieces of cloth or paper in place.
pin *verb*
She pinned the badge to her dress.

pinch pinches pinching pinched *verb*
1 If you pinch somebody, you squeeze a little bit of their skin with your thumb and finger.
2 If you pinch something, you steal it.

pine pines *noun*
a tall, evergreen tree that has narrow, pointed leaves called needles and has its seeds held in cones.

pineapple pineapples *noun*
a large, sweet fruit that is yellow inside and has a thick, prickly skin and leaves growing out of the top. Pineapples grow in hot countries.
❖ *Look at page 69*

pip pips *noun*
a seed inside a fruit. *an orange pip.*

pipe pipes *noun*
a tube, usually made of metal or plastic, that carries things like water and gas.

pirate **pirates** *noun*
a person in the past who attacked and robbed ships.

pistol **pistols** *noun*
a small gun that is held in the hand.

pit **pits** *noun*
1 a large hole in the ground.
2 a coal mine.

pitch **pitches** *noun*
1 an area of ground for playing games such as football or cricket.
2 The pitch of a sound is how low or high the sound is. *As she got angrier, her voice rose in pitch.*

pity *noun*
If you feel pity for somebody, you feel sorry for them. *He feels pity for children who do not have enough to eat.*
pity *verb*

pixie **pixies** *noun*
a small fairy.

pizza **pizzas** *noun*
a round piece of flat dough with things on top such as tomatoes and cheese that is baked in the oven. ▲ Say *peet*-sa.

place **places** *noun*
1 an area or building. *Show me the place on your leg that hurts.*
2 a position in a race. *He was in third place.*

plague **plagues** *noun*
a serious disease that spreads quickly. Plague can be spread by rats and fleas.

plain **plainer plainest** *adjective*
1 something that is plain has no pattern or marks on it. *Take a piece of plain paper and write the essay title at the top.* ◆ *He wore a plain red tie.*
2 A plain person is ordinary and not beautiful. *She had a plain face but she was very kind.*
3 If something is plain to you, it is clear and easy to understand. *She made it plain that she expected good behaviour at all times.*
● A word that sounds like **plain** is **plane**.

plait **plaits** *noun*
hair divided into three pieces that are twisted over each other to make a tidy line like a piece of rope. *She wore her hair in two plaits.* ▲ Rhymes with *cat*.
plait *verb*

plan **plans**
noun
a set of ideas that show how you are going to do something.

plan **plans planning planned**
verb
When you plan something, you work out what you are going to do and how you are going to do it.

plane **planes** *noun*
an aeroplane or flying machine that takes people to places by air.
● A word that sounds like **plane** is **plain**.

planet **planets** *noun*
a very big, round object in space, such as Venus, Mars or the Earth, that moves around a star such as the Sun.

plank **planks** *noun*
a long, flat piece of wood. *The floors are made of planks.*

plant **plants** *noun*
a tree, flower, bush or other living thing that grows in one place and has roots and a stem and leaves.
❖ *Look at page 120*

plant **plants planting planted** *verb*
When you plant things such as flowers or trees, you put them into the ground where you want them to grow. *The council has planted trees on both sides of the road.*

plaster **plasters** *noun*
1 a small piece of sticky material that you can put over a cut to stop dirt getting into it.
2 a soft, wet mixture that you use to cover walls and ceilings inside a house and that becomes hard and smooth so that you can put paint or wallpaper on it.

plastic *noun*
a material that is made in a factory for a lot of different uses. It is light in weight and does not break easily.

plate **plates** *noun*
a flat dish that you put food on.

platform **platforms** *noun*
1 the part of a railway station where you get on and off the train.
2 a flat area that is built higher than the floor so that the people on it can be seen more easily.
3 a flat structure that is higher than the ground or built over water. *an oil platform.*

play **plays playing played** *verb*
1 When you play, you do things that you enjoy doing, such as games.
2 If you play a musical instrument, you use it to make music. *He plays the clarinet.*

play **plays** *noun*
a story that is performed in the theatre, on television or on the radio. *a play by Shakespeare.*

playful *adjective*
liking to play and have fun.

playground **playgrounds** *noun*
an area of land where children can play. *Freddie plays in the school playground.*

A B C D E F G H I J K L M N O P Q R S T U V W X Y Z

111

PLANTS

pitcher plant

broad bean

barrel cactus

potato

fly agaric

stone plant

wheat

barley

daffodil

rushes

grasses

tulip

wood lily

a b c d e f g h i j k l m n o p q r s t u v w x y z

plead pleads pleading pleaded *verb*
If you plead with somebody, you strongly ask them to do something. *She pleaded to be allowed to go home.*

pleasant pleasanter pleasantest *adjective*
A pleasant thing is something you enjoy or like. *We had a pleasant afternoon on the beach.*

please *interjection*
You say "please" to be polite when you are asking for something. *Would you pass me that magazine, please?*

pleasure *noun*
the feeling you get when you are happy and enjoying something. ▲ Say *plesh-er.*

plenty *noun*
a large amount of something and more than is needed. *There's plenty of cake, so you can all have a piece.*

plot plots *noun*
1 a secret plan by a group of people to do something, usually wrong.
2 the story in a book, film or TV programme.
3 a small area of ground. *a vegetable plot.* ◆ *a building plot.*

plough ploughs *noun*
a tool that is used for turning over the soil to make it ready for planting seeds. It is pulled along by a tractor or an animal. ▲ Rhymes with **cow**.
plough *verb*.

pluck plucks plucking plucked *verb*
1 When you pluck a musical instrument such as a guitar or a violin, you pull on the strings to make the notes sound.
2 When you pluck a flower or fruit, you pick it from the place where it was growing.

plug plugs *noun*
1 a round object that you put into the hole of a bath or basin to stop the water running out.
2 a thing at the end of a wire on a machine that fits into a socket on the wall so that the machine can be connected to the electricity supply.

plum plums *noun*
a soft, purple or yellow fruit with a thin skin and a stone in the centre.
❖ *Look at page 69*

plumber plumbers *noun*
a person whose job is to put in water pipes in a house and to mend them when they go wrong. *The plumber has come to mend the tap.* ▲ Say **plum**-er.

plump plumper plumpest *noun*
nicely fat. *The baby had plump cheeks.*
■ The opposite is **slim**.

plural plurals *noun*
the form of a word that you use when you are talking about two or more things instead of just one. The plural of "desk" is "desks" and the plural of "mouse" is "mice". ▲ Say **ploo**-ral. ■ The opposite is **singular**.

plus *preposition*
You use the word plus to talk about adding numbers together. In arithmetic, you can use the sign + to mean plus. *Six plus five equals eleven is the same as 6 + 5 = 11.*

pocket pockets *noun*
a part like a flat bag in your clothes that you can put things in.

pocket money *noun*
money that is given each week to a child to spend.

pod pods *noun*
a long, narrow part of some plants that seeds grow inside. Peas and beans grow in pods.

poem poems *noun*
a piece of writing arranged in short lines. The words in the lines make a rhythm and sometimes the words at the ends of the lines rhyme.

some poetry books

poet poets *noun*
a person who writes poetry.

poetry *noun*
poems are poetry.

point points *noun*
1 the end of something sharp like a needle or a pencil.

2 a particular place or time. *At this point, she suddenly saw that everybody had left the room.*
3 a mark that somebody gets in a game or competition.
4 the purpose for doing something. *What's the point in taking your coat off if you're going straight out again?*

point points pointing pointed *verb*
If you point, you show where something is by using your finger.

pointed *adjective*
A pointed thing has a point at one end.

poison *noun*
a substance that will make you ill or kill you if it gets into your body.
poisonous *adjective*.

poke pokes poking poked *verb*
To poke somebody is to push something into them. *She poked me in my back with her finger.*

polar bear polar bears *noun*
a large, white bear that lives near the North Pole. ❖ *Look at page 61*

pole poles *noun*
1 a long, narrow, round piece of wood or metal. *a telegraph pole.* ◆ *a flag pole.*
2 a point at each end of the Earth that is farthest from the Equator. *the North Pole and the South Pole.*

police *noun*
those whose job is to protect people and make sure that everybody obeys the law.
policeman *noun*, **policewoman** *noun*, **police officer** *noun*.

polish polishes polishing polished *verb*
If you polish something, you rub it to make it shine. *David polishes his shoes.*
polish *noun*.

A B C D E F G H I J K L M N O P Q R S T U V W X Y Z

polite politer politest *adjective*
If you are polite, you behave well towards other people and think about how to make them feel comfortable. *It is polite to say "thank you" and "please".*
■ The opposite is **rude**.
politely *adverb*.

politics *noun*
all the activities to do with the government of a country.
political *adjective*.

pollen *noun*
a fine powder inside flowers that the wind or insects take to other flowers of the same kind so that they can produce seeds.

pollution *noun*
poisonous chemicals and other forms of dangerous dirt that cause damage to the air, water and environment.

air pollution from factories

air pollution from power stations

acid rain

chemical waste

polluted rivers

pond ponds *noun*
a small area of water.

pony ponies *noun*
a small kind of horse.

pool pools *noun*
1 a small area of water.
2 a swimming pool.

poor poorer poorest *adjective*
1 A person who is poor has very little money. ■ The opposite is **rich**.
2 not good enough. *My spelling is very poor*.
3 unlucky or in a bad situation. *Poor John failed his driving test.*
● A word that sounds like **poor** is **pour**.

pop pops *noun*
1 modern, popular music.

2 a short, sharp sound like a small explosion.

poppy poppies *noun*
a plant with a large, bright flower.

popular *adjective*
liked by a lot of people. *a popular film.*
◆ *a popular girl.*
popularly *adverb*.

population populations *noun*
all the people who live in a particular area or country.

porcupine porcupines *noun*
an animal that has stiff hairs on its back, called quills.

pork *noun*
meat from a pig.

port ports *noun*
a place or town beside a large river or the sea where ships can stay and load and unload.

portable *adjective*
Something that is portable is small enough or light enough to be carried around easily. *a portable computer.*

portion portions *noun*
an amount of food for one person. *a portion of chips.*

portrait portraits *noun*
a picture of a person.

position positions *noun*
1 the place where something is. *Can you check our position on the map?*
2 the way you are sitting, standing or lying down. *Get into a comfortable position.*

positive *adjective*
1 certain about something. *I'm positive I saw him.*
2 A positive number is higher than zero. ■ The opposite is **negative**.

possess possesses possessing possessed *verb*
If you possess something, you own it and it belongs to you. *Do you possess a TV?*

possible *adjective*
If something is possible, it can be done or it can happen. *Come as soon as possible.* ■ The opposite is **impossible**.
possibility *noun* **possibly** *adverb*
Is there the possibility of rain today?

post posts *noun*
1 a long, thick, strong pole or piece of wood fixed in the ground. *a fence post.*
2 the system of sending letters and parcels from one place to another and delivering them to people's doors.

post posts posting posted *verb*
When you post a letter or a parcel, you send it through the post.

postcard postcards *noun*
a small piece of card, usually with a picture on one side, that you can use to send a short message to somebody. *They sent me a postcard with a cross drawn on it to show where their hotel is.*

postcode postcodes *noun*
a set of letters and numbers at the end of your address that tells the post office where you live. *My postcode is W1 7AD.*

poster posters *noun*
a large picture, notice or advertisement that is put up on a wall.

post office post offices *noun*
1 a place where you can send letters and parcels and buy stamps.
2 the organization or group of people who collect, sort and deliver people's letters and parcels.

postpone postpones postponing postponed *verb*
If you postpone something, you put it off until later. *The race was postponed because of bad weather.*

pot pots *noun*
1 a round container. *a pot of tea.* ◆ *a paint pot.*
2 a container for plants to grow in made of plastic or clay.

potato potatoes *noun*
a white vegetable with a thin, brown skin that grows under the ground.

pottery *noun*
dishes and other objects made out of clay and then baked hard in a special oven called a kiln.

pouch pouches *noun*
1 a small bag.
2 a bag of skin that female kangaroos and some other female animals have on their stomach and which they use for carrying their babies in.

pounce pounces pouncing pounced *verb*
To pounce is to jump forward suddenly and catch hold of something. *The kitten pounced on the ball of wool.* ◆ *He pounced on the disk saying, "I thought I'd lost this!"*

pour pours pouring poured *verb*
When you pour a liquid, you tip a container such as a jug or bottle so that the liquid flows out. *Can you pour Granny another cup of tea?*

poverty *noun*
People who live in poverty are very poor.

powder *noun*
tiny, dry grains that you get when you crush or grind something well.
powder *verb*.

power *noun*
1 the ability to do something. *Human beings have the power of speech.*
2 the force or strength of something. *The power of the wind brought the trees down.*
3 A person who has power can control what happens to a lot of people.

powerful *adjective*
A powerful person or thing has a lot of power. *a powerful king.* ◆ *a powerful engine.* ■ The opposite is **weak**.

practical *adjective*
1 to do with actually working or doing something rather than knowing or having ideas about it. *Do you have practical training in using computers?*
2 sensible, useful and likely to work. *a practical suggestion.* ◆ *He is a very practical man.*
practically *adverb*
almost. *I've practically finished eating.*

practice *noun*
doing something again and again until you can do it well. *guitar practice.*

practise practises practising practised *verb*
If you practise something, you keep doing it until you can do it well. *Rachel practises her guitar playing for three hours everyday.*

praise praises praising praised *verb*
When you praise somebody, you say how well they have done something. *Everybody praised the brave fire-fighters.* ■ The opposite is **criticize**.

pram prams *noun*
a kind of cot on wheels that people use to push a baby in.

pray prays praying prayed *verb*
If you pray, you talk to God.
● A word that sounds like **pray** is **prey**.

prayer prayers *noun*
the words somebody says when they are talking to God.

precious *adjective*
very valuable or very important to you.
▲ Say *presh-us*.

predict predicts predicting predicted *verb*
If you predict something, you say that you think it is going to happen. *The weather forecast predicts rain over the weekend.*
prediction *noun*.

prefer prefers preferred *verb*
If you prefer one thing to another thing, you like it better. *Would you prefer an apple or a peach?*
preference *noun*.

pregnant *adjective*
When a woman is pregnant, she is going to have a baby and the baby is growing inside her womb.

prehistoric *adjective*
belonging to a very long time ago before history was remembered and written down. *Dinosaurs lived in prehistoric times.* ❖ **Look at page 125**

prepare prepares preparing prepared *verb*
When you prepare something, you make it ready. *Len helped prepare lunch.*
preparation *noun*.

preposition prepositions *noun*
a word you use for such things as *where* and *how*. "Down", "on" and "in" are prepositions used in the following sentences. "He ran down the hill." "The phone was on the table." "The milk is in the jug." Prepositions show how the word before and after it are related.

prescription prescriptions *noun*
the piece of paper that a doctor uses to write down the medicines or pills you need to get from the chemist.

present *adjective*
1 being in a place or being there. *Many people were present at the concert.*
■ The opposite is **absent**.
2 happening now. *the present time.*

present presents *noun*
1 a thing that you give to somebody. *What presents did you get?*
2 the time now. *We've had no trouble up to the present.*

preserve preserves preserving preserved *verb*
1 If you preserve something, you keep it the way it is without changing it. *These foods are all preserved in different ways.*
2 If you preserve food, you do something to it so that it will not go bad.

president presidents *noun*
A person who is chosen to lead a country that does not have a king or queen.

press presses pressing pressed *verb*
If you press something, you push hard on it. *You press a button and the door slides open.*

pressure *noun*
the force of one thing pressing or pushing on another. *If you use pressure on that cut, it will stop bleeding.* ▲ Say *presh-er.*

pretend pretends pretending pretended *verb*
If you pretend, you try to make other people believe something that is not true. *He's pretending to be a tree!*

pretty prettier prettiest *adjective*
attractive and nice to look at. *Flowers are pretty.* ▲ Say *prit-ee.*

prevent prevents preventing prevented *verb*
If you prevent something, you stop it happening. *Shut the gate to prevent the horse running away.*

previous *adjective*
The previous thing is the thing that came before or earlier. *I went round to Jane's house on Wednesday as we had arranged on the phone the previous day.* ▲ Say *pree-vee-us.*
previously *adverb.*

prey *noun*
any animal that is hunted for food. *Mice are the owl's natural prey.* ▲ Rhymes with *may.* ● A word that sounds like **prey** is **pray.**

price prices *noun*
the amount of money you have to pay to buy something. *What's the price of that pair of trainers?*

prick pricks pricking pricked *verb*
If you prick something, you make a small hole in it with something sharp. *Domenic said he'd prick the balloon with a pin.*

prickle prickles *noun*
a sharp point or thorn. *Mind this bush, it's covered with prickles.*
prickly *adjective.*

pride *noun*
1 the good feeling you get when you are proud and have done something well or somebody you love has done something well.
2 a group of lions that live together.

priest priests *noun*
a person in the Christian religion who leads people in services. ▲ Say *preest.*

primary *adjective*
1 first and most important. *Our primary need is to make sure everybody has enough to eat.*
2 to do with teaching children between the ages of 5 and 11. *primary education.*

prime *adjective*
first and most important. *A matter of prime importance.*

prime number *noun*
a number that can only be divided exactly by itself or one. 7 and 17 are prime numbers.

Prime Minister Prime Ministers *noun*
the person chosen to lead a government.

prince princes *noun*
the son of a king or queen, or a man or boy who is a member of a royal family.

princess princesses *noun*
the daughter of a king or queen, or a woman or girl who is a member of a royal family.

principle principles *noun*
an important rule that you have about what is right and wrong. *It's against my principles to take drugs.*

print prints printing printed *verb*
1 When somebody prints a book, magazine or newspaper, they make copies of it on paper using a machine called a printer.
2 If you print something out from a computer, you use a machine called a printer to put information in the computer on paper.
3 If you print words, you write using letters that are not joined up.
printer *noun.*

prison prisons *noun*
a building where people who have broken the law are kept locked up.
prisoner *noun.*

private *adjective*
Something that is private is for only one person or one small group of people and not for everybody. *You can't see my letter, it's private.* ▲ Say *pry-vit.* ■ The opposite is **public.**
privately *adverb.*

prize prizes *noun*
a thing that you are given for winning a competition or for doing good work.

probably *adverb*
something will be true or likely to happen if you think it is probably true or will probably happen.

problem problems *noun*
A problem is something that is difficult to work out, understand or do.

procession processions *noun*
a number of people walking or driving in a public place as part of a ceremony. *A brass band led the procession.*

prod prods prodding prodded *verb*
If you prod something, you push at it with something such as a stick or a finger. *I prodded him in the ribs.*

PREHISTORIC ANIMALS

Maiasaura and babies

VOCABULARY

ankylosaurs
a group of dinosaurs that had body armour of bony spines.

carnosaurs
large meat-eating dinosaurs.

dinosaur
a word meaning "terrible lizard" - though not all dinosaurs were reptiles.

hadrosaurs
dinosaurs with mouths shaped like duck's bills.

icthyosaurs
big, swimming reptiles that looked like dolphins.

ornithopod
plant-eating dinosaurs that stood on their hind legs like birds.

pterosaurs
flying reptiles with wings of skin.

stegosaurs
dinosaurs that had a body armour of bony plates.

1 Apatosaurus
2 Spinosaurus
3 Iguanodon
4 Styracosaurus
5 Panoplosaurus
6 Oviraptor
7 Stygimoloch
8 Kentrosaurus

produce produces producing produced *verb*
1 To produce something is to make it. *The factory produces hundreds of new cars a week.*
2 If you produce something, you take it out and show it. *She peered in her bag and produced a clean handkerchief.*
3 To produce a play, film or TV programme is to organize the people making it and get it ready to show to the public.
▲ Say *prod-yoos.*

product products *noun*
a thing that is made to be sold. *Timber is a product of Canada.*

profession professions *noun*
a job that needs special knowledge and training, such as being a doctor or a teacher.
professional *noun*
a person who works in a profession. *A doctor is a professional.*

professor professors *noun*
a person who is a teacher at a university. *My cousin is a professor of Greek at Birmingham University.*

profit profits *noun*
money that you get when you sell something for more than it cost to buy or make.

program programs *noun*
a list of instructions that makes a computer work.

programme programmes *noun*
1 a television or radio show.
2 a printed piece of paper that gives you information about such things as a play, a concert or a football match.

progress progresses *noun*
the way something or someone moves forward or gets better. *She is making good progress learning Welsh.*

project projects *noun*
a piece of work you do in which you find out as much as you can about a subject. *We're doing a project on the Second World War at school.*

promise promises promising promised *verb*
When you promise you will do something, you say you will do it and you really mean it. *Pam promised not to make a noise.*

prompt *adjective*
When you are prompt, you do something quickly or immediately, without delay.

pronoun pronouns *noun*
a word like "you", "her", or "one" that you use when you already know the person or thing that is being talked about. "Her" and "one" are pronouns in these sentences. *Sam tossed me the ball and I threw it back to her.* ◆ *I don't want the red pen, I want the green one.*

pronounce pronounces pronouncing pronounced *verb*
When you pronounce a word right, you say the sound of the word in the correct way. *Some English words are hard for French people to pronounce correctly.*
pronunciation *noun.*

proof *noun*
To have proof of something is to have all the facts that shows that it is true.

prop props propping propped *verb*
If you prop something, you put it or lay it against something. *She propped her bike against the wall.*

propeller propellers *noun*
a set of blades that spin round to make a ship, plane or helicopter move.

proper *adjective*
The proper way to do something is the right or correct way to do it.
properly *adverb.*

property properties *noun*
1 things that you own. *Those books don't belong to the school, they're my property.*
2 a building and the land around it.

prosecute prosecutes prosecuting prosecuted *verb*
To prosecute somebody is to accuse them of a crime and make them go to court. *Trespassers will be prosecuted.*

protect protects protecting protected *verb*
If you protect somebody or something, you try to keep them from being hurt or damaged.
protection *noun.*

protest protests protesting protested *verb*
If you protest, you say that you think something is wrong and should be changed.

proud *adjective*
the good feeling of pleasure you get when you or someone else has done something very well. *I got better marks than I ever had before and I was really proud of myself.*
proudly *adverb.*

prove proves proving proved *verb*
When you prove something, you show that it is true. ▲ Rhymes with **move.**

provide provides providing provided *verb*
If you provide something, you get it and make sure that you give it when it is needed. *I'll provide the sandwiches if you bring something to drink.*

prune prunes pruning pruned *verb*
When you prune a tree or bush, you cut back its branches to keep it healthy or keep it from getting too big.

pub pubs *noun*
a place where adults can go to buy drinks and meet friends.

public *adjective*
for everybody to go to, or use, or see. *a public phone box.* ◆ *public transport.*
■ The opposite is **private.**

publish publishes publishing published *verb*
To publish a book, magazine or newspaper is to have it printed and ready for people to buy a copy.

pudding puddings *noun*
sweet food that you eat at the end of a meal. *Christmas pudding.*

puddle puddles *noun*
a pool or small area of water left on the ground after it has rained.

puff puffs *noun*
a small amount of moving air, smoke or wind. *a puff of smoke.*

puffin puffins *noun*
a black and white sea bird that has a big brightly coloured beak.

pull pulls pulling pulled *verb*
When you pull something, you hold it and move it towards you.

pulp *noun*
the soft part inside a fruit or vegetable.

pulse *noun*
the regular beat or throbbing that your blood makes as it goes through your body. You can feel your pulse by putting your fingers on your wrist.

pump pumps *noun*
a machine that is used to push air, liquid, or gas into or out of something.

pump pumps pumping pumped *verb*
to force air or liquid with a pump. *Jordan pumps up the tyre.*

pumpkin pumpkins *noun*
a large, round orange vegetable that grows on the ground.

pun puns *noun*
a joke that works because a word has two meanings. *Two pears make one pair.*

punch punches punching punched *verb*
1 If you punch somebody, you hit them with your fist.
2 If you punch something, you make a hole in it. *The guard inspected everybody's tickets and punched them.*

punctual *adjective*
arriving on time.
punctually *adverb*.

punctuation *noun*
marks such as commas, full stops and quotation marks that you use when you are writing.

puncture punctures *noun*
a hole in a bicycle tyre or a car tyre.
▲ Say *punk-cher.*

punish punishes punishing punished *verb*
To punish somebody is to make them hurt or suffer because they have done something wrong.
punishment *noun*.

pupa pupae *noun*
a stage in an insect's life after it is a larva but before it is an adult insect with wings. ▲ Say *pyoo-pa.*

pupil pupils *noun*
1 a person who is studying at school.
2 the small, round, black part at the centre of the eye.

puppet puppets *noun*
a kind of doll that you can make move by pulling strings that are fixed to the different parts of the puppet, or by putting your hand inside the puppet and moving it with your fingers.

puppy puppies *noun*
a young dog.

purchase purchases purchasing purchased *verb*
If you purchase something, you buy it.

pure purer purest *adjective*
Something that is pure is not mixed with anything else. *pure apple juice.*
▲ Say *pyoor.*

purpose purposes *noun*
the reason that something is being done or what it is meant to do. *The purpose of the trip is to see some famous paintings.*
on purpose If you do something on purpose, you mean to do it.

purr purrs purring purred *verb*
When a cat purrs, it makes a low sound to show that it is pleased.

purse purses *noun*
a small bag that you keep money in.

push pushes pushing pushed *verb*
If you push something, you move it away from you. *When the car broke down, all the family had to get out and push it.*

puzzle puzzles *noun*
a question, problem, or game that is hard to work out the answer to. *a crossword puzzle.*

pyjamas *noun*
trousers and a jacket that you wear in bed. ▲ Say *pa-jah-maz.*

pyramid pyramids *noun*
1 a solid shape with triangular sides that meet in a point at the top.
2 a building with four triangular sides that meet at the top. *There are pyramids in Egypt and Mexico and the ancient Egyptians buried their dead kings and queens, called Pharaohs, in them.*

Egyptian pyramid

Burmese pyramid

Sumerian pyramid

A
B
C
D
E
F
G
H
I
J
K
L
M
N
O
P
Q
R
S
T
U
V
W
X
Y
Z

Q q

quack quacks quacking quacked *verb*
To quack is to make the sound that a duck makes.
quack *noun*.

quaint quainter quaintest *adjective*
pretty and unusual. *a quaint old cottage.*

qualify qualifies qualifying **qualified** *verb*
1 If you qualify, you pass an exam that allows you to do a job or study at a college. *She qualified as a teacher.*
2 You qualify if you win part of a competition and are able to go on to the next part. *Our team qualified for the football final.*
qualification *noun*.

quality *noun*
1 how good or bad something is. *a dress made from material of good quality.*
2 what makes something what it is. *The quality of lemons is that they are sour.*

quantity quantities *noun*
an amount of something. *Birds need a large quantity of twigs to make a nest.*

quarrel quarrels quarrelling **quarrelled** *verb*
If you quarrel with somebody, you have an angry argument with them. *My two younger brothers are always quarrelling over their toys.*

quarry quarries *noun*
a place where things such as stone, chalk or slate are dug out of the ground.

Spelling tip:
••••••••••••••••••••••
Most words that begin with a "qu" sound as in "queen" are spelt with a "c" or "k" as in cat, kangaroo.

quarter quarters *noun*
one of four equal parts of something. Four quarters make a whole. *We cut the apple into quarters.*

quay quays
a place in a harbour where boats are tied up to be loaded or unloaded. ▲ Say *kee*.

queen queens *noun*
a woman who leads her people or who is the wife of a king and a member of a royal family.

queer *adjective*
odd or very strange. *There's a queer smell in here.*

query queries *noun*
a question. *Does anyone have any queries?*

quest quests *noun*
a long and difficult search for something important. *a quest for a cure for cancer.*

question questions *noun*
You ask a question when you want to find out about something. *I asked my teacher a question about the computer.* ■ The opposite is **answer**.

question mark question marks *noun*
a mark (**?**) that you use in writing. You put a question mark at the end of a sentence to show that somebody has asked a question. *What did you say?*

queue queues *noun*
a line of people who are waiting for something. *There is a long queue outside the cinema.* ▲ Say *kyoo*.
queue *verb*
We queued up for hours for tickets.

quick quicker quickest *adjective*
1 fast. *Be quick or we'll miss the bus.*
2 done in a short time. *We had a quick breakfast before we went out.*
quickly *adverb*
Go as quickly as you can.

quiet quieter quietest *adjective*
no noise or very little noise. *She played quiet music.* ■ The opposite is **loud**.

quilt quilts *noun*
a soft, light cover for a bed.

quit quits quitting quit or **quitted** *verb*
If you quit, you leave or stop doing something. *We quit when we started to lose the game.*

quite *adverb*
1 more than a little but not very much. *He's quite tall.*
2 completely. *You're quite right.*

quiz quizzes *noun*
a kind of game when somebody asks a lot of questions to see how much you know. *Our team won the quiz because we knew all the answers.*

quotation quotations *noun*
words that you say or write that somebody else has said before. *"To be or not to be"* is a quotation from one of Shakespeare's plays.

quotation mark quotation marks *noun*
marks (**" "**) that you use in writing. You put quotation marks before and after the words that somebody has said. *"What did you say?"* he asked.

quote quotes quoting quoted *verb*
1 If you quote something, you say or write something that somebody else has said before. *She quoted some lines from the poem.*
2 to name a price. *He quoted a price for mending the bike.*

R r

rabbi rabbis *noun*
a teacher of the Jewish religion.

rabbit rabbits *noun*
a small, wild animal with soft fur and long ears. Rabbits live in holes in the ground called burrows.

raccoon raccoons *noun*
a small animal that has black marks on its face and black-coloured rings around its tail. Raccoons live in America and in the West Indies.

race races *noun*
1 a competition to see who is the fastest. *a cycle race.*
2 a large number of human beings whose ancestors all came from the same area and who look alike in some way, for example in skin colour.

race races racing raced *verb*
If you race, you go very fast. *She was racing along the path, trying to catch her dog.*

rack racks *noun*
a frame or set of shelves that you can put things on or hang things on. *a plate rack.* ◆ *a wine rack.* ◆ *a shoe rack.*

racket rackets *noun*
a bat with an oval frame for hitting a ball in tennis, badminton or squash.

radar *noun*
a way of showing on a screen the exact position and speed of a plane or ship that cannot be seen.

Spelling tip:
....
Some words that begin with an "r" sound are spelt "wr" such as wrong, wriggle, wrestle.

radiator radiators *noun*
a flat, metal object against a wall that steam or hot water runs through to heat a room. ▲ Say *ray-dee-ay-ter.*

radio radios *noun*
a machine that receives sounds sent through the air so that you can hear them. You turn on a radio to listen to music, news and other programmes.

radius radiuses *noun*
a straight line from the centre of a circle to the edge. ❖ *Look at page 38*

raft rafts *noun*
a flat boat made of rubber or wood.

rag rags *noun*
an old piece of material that you can use to clean things.

rage *noun*
very great anger. *Benjamin was scarlet with rage.*

raid raids *noun*
a sudden attack on a place. *There was a bank raid in the centre of town today.*

rail rails *noun*
1 a bar for people to hold on to or to stop them from falling. *She held the rail as she climbed the stairs.*
2 the long, parallel metal bars (lines) that trains run on.
3 a railway system. *We travelled all round Europe by rail.*
railings *noun.*

railway railways *noun*
the system of trains, stations and track that is used when people travel by train.

rain *noun*
water that falls to the ground from clouds in small drops.
rainy *adjective,* **rain** *verb.*
rainy weather.

rainbow rainbows *noun*
an arc or curve of light of different colours that you can sometimes see in the sky when there is rain and sunshine at the same time.

rainforest rainforests *noun*
an area of thick, tropical forest where a lot of rain falls. There are rainforests in South America, Africa and Asia.

raise raises raising raised *verb*
If you raise something, you lift it up or move it so that it is higher. *Raise your hand if you know the answer.* ■ The opposite is **lower.**

raisin raisins *noun*
a dried grape.

rake rakes *noun*
a garden tool with a long handle and a row of metal teeth like a comb that you use to make the earth level or to gather leaves into a pile.
rake *verb.*

rally rallies *noun*
1 a large public meeting.
2 a car or motorcycle race that takes place over a long distance.

ram rams *noun*
a male sheep.

ran past of **run.**

A
B
C
D
E
F
G
H
I
J
K
L
M
N
O
P
Q
R
S
T
U
V
W
X
Y
Z

ranch ranches noun
a very large farm in North America for cattle, horses or sheep.

rang past of **ring**.

range ranges noun
1 a choice of things of the same kind. *The shop stocks a wide range of trainers and sports shoes.*
2 a long line of mountains.
3 the area or distance over which something can be used.

ransom ransoms noun
money that is demanded in return for letting a person who has been kidnapped go free.

rap raps noun
1 a short, sharp sound like a single knock on a door.
2 a kind of music where the words are spoken in rhythm, not sung.

rapid adjective
very quick. *a rapid heartbeat.*
rapidly adverb.

rare rarer rarest adjective
not often seen or done. *This flower is very rare.* ■ The opposite is **common**.

rash rashes noun
a lot of small, red spots that you get on your skin if you have an illness like measles.

raspberry raspberries noun
a small, sweet, red fruit that grows on a bush.
❖ Look at page 22

rat rats noun
an animal that is like a very large mouse with a long tail.

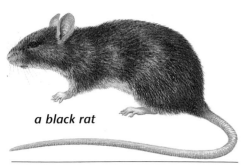

a black rat

rate rates noun
1 the speed at which something happens. *Scientists are worried by the rate at which rainforests are being cut down and destroyed.*

2 the amount of money that you pay for a service. *You pay a cheaper rate for phone calls in the evenings and at weekends.*

rattle rattles rattling rattled verb
When something rattles, it makes the noise of things knocking together. *The coins rattled when Penelope shook her money box.*

rattle rattles noun
a baby's toy that makes a noise when you shake it.

raw adjective
Food that is raw has not been cooked. *raw cabbage.* ◆ *Rose puts the raw ingredients for making vegetable soup into the pan.*

ray rays noun
a line of light. *the Sun's rays.*

razor razors noun
a tool with a very sharp blade for shaving.

reach reaches reaching reached verb
1 When you reach a place, you get there. *When we reach London, we'll stop and have lunch.*
2 When you reach for something, you stretch out your arm towards it. *I'm not tall enough to reach the books on the top shelf.*

react reacts reacting reacted verb
When you react to something, you behave in a certain way because of that thing and as a kind of answer to it. *Rose taps Freddie's knee to see if his leg reacts.*
reaction noun.

read reads reading read verb
When you read something, you look at written words and understand what they mean. ● A word that sounds like **read** is **reed**.

ready adjective
When you are ready, you are prepared and can do something straight away. *Are you ready to go yet?* ▲ Say **red-ee**.

real adjective
1 really existing and not made up. *Do you think that dinosaurs were real?*
2 not a copy. *real leather.*
■ The opposite is **fake**.
● A word that sounds like **real** is **reel**.

realize realizes realizing realized verb
When you realize something, you start to know or understand it. *I realize I can't have everything I want.*

reap reaps reaping reaped verb
When you reap crops such as wheat, you cut them and gather them up.

rear noun
the back of something. *There's a large garden at the rear of the house.* ■ The opposite is **front**.

reason reasons noun
a fact that explains why something happens. *The reason I'm afraid of geese is that I was once bitten by one.*

rebel rebels rebelling rebelled verb
When a person rebels, they refuse to obey the people who are in charge.
▲ Say **ree-bell**.

receipt receipts noun
a piece of paper that shows how much money you paid for something. ▲ Say **ree-seet**.

receive receives receiving
received *verb*
If you receive something, you get it when it has been given or sent to you. *They received a cup for winning the contest.* ▲ Say *ree-seeve.* ■ The opposite is **give**.

recent *adjective*
a short time ago. *a recent photo of my brother and mother.*
recently *adverb*.

reception receptions *noun*
the place in a building, like a hotel or hospital, where visitors go first. *Tell the nurse at reception which doctor you are going to see and then sit down.*

recipe recipes *noun*
a list of things you need to cook something and the instructions on how to cook it. ▲ Say *res-i-pee.*

reckon reckons reckoning
reckoned *verb*
If you reckon something, you think it is probably true. *I reckon our team will win on Saturday.*

recognize recognizes
recognizing recognized *verb*
If you recognize somebody, you know who they are because you have seen them before. *You look so different I didn't recognize you at first.*

recommend recommends
recommending recommended *verb*
If you recommend something, you say that you think it is good. *I recommend the apple pie and cream.*

record records recording
recorded *verb*
1 If you record something, you write down what happened. *He recorded the day's events in his diary.*
2 To record something is to store it on film, tape, a compact disc, or a record so that it can be played or shown again.
▲ Say *ree-kord.*

record records *noun*
1 a written list of what has happened. *I kept a record of everything I spent while we were on holiday.*
2 a round, black piece of plastic that has music or other sounds recorded on it.
3 the best performance so far. *She holds the record for the high jump.*
▲ Say *rek-ord.*

recorder recorders *noun*
a musical instrument that you play by blowing into it at one end.

recover recovers recovering
recovered *verb*
1 When you recover from an illness, you get better. *He's recovering from flu.*
2 If you recover something, you get it back after it has been lost or stolen.

rectangle rectangles *noun*
a shape with four sides and four corners. Each side of a rectangle is the same length as the side opposite to it.
rectangular *adjective*.

recycle recycles recycling recycled
verb
To recycle things is to make them into something new after they have already been used instead of throwing them away. *Daniella's book was printed on recycled paper.*

reduce reduces reducing reduced
verb
To reduce is to make something smaller or less. *I'm trying to reduce the amount of chocolate I eat.*

reed reeds *noun*
a plant with long, hollow stems that grows near water. ● A word that sounds like **reed** is **read**.

reef reefs *noun*
a long line of rocks, sand or coral in the sea. *In very bad weather, ships sometimes hit the reef and sink.*

reel reels *noun*
a round object that you wrap film, tape or thread around. ● A word that sounds like **reel** is **real**. *There are lots of different reels shown opposite.*

referee referees *noun*
a person who makes sure that everybody playing in a game such as football obeys the rules. *My friend's dad is usually the referee when we play hockey.*
referee *verb*.

reference book reference
books *noun*
a book with facts and information in it. *A dictionary is a reference book.*

reflect reflects reflecting reflected
verb
1 If a surface reflects light, the light hits the surface and bounces back, rather than passing through it.
2 A mirror reflects something in front of it and shows what it looks like.
reflection *noun*.

refrigerator refrigerators *noun*
a metal cupboard where you can put food to keep it cold and fresh. A refrigerator is called a **fridge** for short.
▲ Say *ree-frij-er-ay-ter.*

refund refunds *noun*
money that you are given back if you have paid too much for something.

refuse refuses refusing refused
verb
If you refuse to do something, you will not do it. *Dad refused to wash the dishes and said that somebody else would have to do it.* ■ The opposite is **accept**.

regard regards regarding
regarded *verb*
If you regard something in a certain way, that is what you think about it. *She regarded the uniform as old-fashioned.*

region regions *noun*
an area of land or part of a country. *a mountain region.* ▲ Say *ree-jun.*

register registers *noun*
a book containing a list of names or important information. *The teacher called the register at the beginning of the class.*

A
B
C
D
E
F
G
H
I
J
K
L
M
N
O
P
Q
R
S
T
U
V
W
X
Y
Z

regret regrets regretting regretted *verb*
If you regret something, you are sorry about it and wish that you had not done it or that it had not happened.

regular *adjective*
Regular things have exactly the same amount of time between them. *When you take exercise your pulse gets faster but it stays regular.*
regularly *adverb*.

rehearse rehearses rehearsing rehearsed *verb*
If you rehearse, you practise something before doing it for an audience. *We rehearsed the play every night for a week.* ▲ Say *ree-hurse*.
rehearsal *noun*.

reign reigns reigning reigned *verb*
To reign is to be the king or queen of a country. ▲ Rhymes with *pain*. ● A word that sounds like **reign** is **rain**.

reindeer *noun*
a large deer with very large antlers that lives in northern countries where it is very cold. ▲ Say *rain-deer*.

rein reins *noun*
Reins are long leather straps that you use to guide a horse. ▲ Say *rains*.

reject rejects rejecting rejected *verb*
If you reject something, you will not accept it. *He rejected my advice.*

related *adjective*
If you are related to somebody, you are in the same family as them.

relation relations *noun*
a person who is in the same family. *I've got a lot of relations.*

relative relatives *noun*
a person who is in your family.

relax relaxes relaxing relaxed *verb*
When you relax, your body becomes less tense and you feel calm and less worried.
relaxation *noun*.

relay relays *noun*
a race between teams of runners. Each member of the team takes it in turn to run a part of the race. A special stick called a baton is passed to the person whose turn it is to run.

release releases releasing released *verb*
When you release somebody or an animal that has been held in some way, you set them free. *Robert released the bird that was caught in a bush.*

reliable *adjective*
If somebody is reliable, you can trust them and depend on them. ▲ Say *ree-lie-a-bul*.

relief *noun*
the good feeling that you get when you can stop worrying. *It was such a great relief when I was told that I'd passed my exams.* ▲ Say *ree-leef*.

religion religions *noun*
believing in God or gods and a way of worshipping.
religious *adjective*.

rely relies relying relied *verb*
If you can rely on somebody, you know you can trust them and depend on them. ▲ Say *ree-lie*.

remain remains remaining remained *verb*
1 If somebody remains in a place, they stay there. *He did not go out to play but remained in the house all day.*
2 If something remains, it is still there. *The roof had gone but most of the rest of the temple remains.*

remark remarks *noun*
a thing that you say about someone or something. *She made a nasty remark about my hat.*

remedy remedies *noun*
1 an answer to a problem.
2 a way of curing an illness or making something better.
remedy *verb*.

remember remembers remembering remembered *verb*
When you remember something, you have it in your mind or bring it into your mind again. *Can you remember where you went on holiday last year?*

remind reminds reminding reminded *verb*
1 If you remind somebody, you tell them something again in case they have forgotten. *Can you remind me to phone David?*
2 If something reminds you, it makes you remember something.
3 If somebody reminds you of somebody else, they are like the other person in some way.

remote remoter remotest *adjective*
very far away. ■ The opposite is **close**.
remoteness *noun*.

remove removes removing removed *verb*
When you remove something, you take it away. *Please remove the dishes from the table.*
removal *noun*.

rendevous *noun*
an arranged time and place for a meeting. ▲ Say *rond-ay-oo*.

renew renews renewing renewed
verb

1 When you renew something, you arrange for it to go on longer.
2 When you renew something, you start doing it again.
3 To renew is to replace something old with something new.

rent rents *noun*
money that you pay to live in a place or to use something that you do not own yourself. *The rent for this house is £100 a week.*
rent *verb*.

repair repairs repairing repaired
verb
If you repair something that is broken or does not work, you mend it.

repeat repeats repeating repeated *verb*
If you repeat something, you say it or do it again. *Can you repeat the question?*
repetition *noun*.

replace replaces replacing replaced *verb*
1 If you replace something, you put it back where it came from. *She replaced the book on the shelf.*
2 When you replace something, you get a new one instead of the old one. *The school is replacing its computers with more modern ones.*

reply replies replying replied *verb*
When you reply, you give an answer. *"Must I reply to this letter?" "I don't know," he replied.*

report reports *noun*
1 Something that someone says or writes that tells you about something that has happened.

2 a piece of paper that teachers write to say how well a pupil has worked at school.

represent represents representing represented *verb*
If one thing represents another thing, it is a picture or symbol of it. *On the map crosses represent churches.*

reproduction reproductions
noun
1 a copy of something, especially a famous painting or old kind of furniture.
2 making new, young animals or plants.

reptile reptiles *noun*
an animal with cold blood that has scales on its skin. Female reptiles lay eggs. Snakes, crocodiles, tortoises and lizards are reptiles.
❖ *Look at page 134*

request requests requesting requested *verb*
If you request something, you ask for it politely. *People using the library are requested not to talk.*

require requires requiring required *verb*
If you require something, you need it.

rescue rescues rescuing rescued
verb
If you rescue somebody, you save them from danger. *The man was rescued by the mountain climbers.*

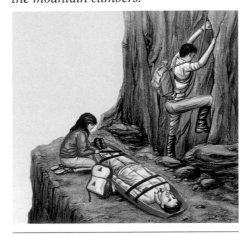

research researches researching researched *verb*
If you research a subject, you find out all the information you can about it.

resent resents resenting resented
verb
to feel injured, annoyed or insulted by.

reserve reserves reserving reserved *verb*
To reserve is to ask for something to be kept for you to use later. *Tom reserved a table for six at the restaurant.*
reservation *noun*.

reservoir reservoirs *noun*
a lake used to hold water that is sent through pipes to people's houses. ▲ Say *rez-er-vwar.*

resign resigns resigning resigned
verb
If you resign, you give up your job and leave. ▲ Say *ree-zine.*

resist resists resisting resisted *verb*
If you resist something, you fight against it or try to stop it from happening.

resources *noun*
things that are found naturally in a country, such as gas or oil, that can make the country richer.

respect *noun*
the feeling that you have for somebody you like and admire because they are a good person or know a lot or are clever.

respond responds responding responded *verb*
If you respond to somebody, you answer them.
response *noun*.

responsible *adjective*
1 A responsible person is sensible and can be trusted.
2 If you are responsible for somebody or something, you are in charge of them.

rest *noun*
1 a time when you are quiet and do not work or do anything energetic. *Jordan was having a rest reading a book.*

2 everything or everybody that is left over. *Jim and his friends went home but the rest went swimming.* ◆ *What shall we do for the rest of the day?*

A B C D E F G H I J K L M N O P Q R S T U V W X Y Z

REPTILES

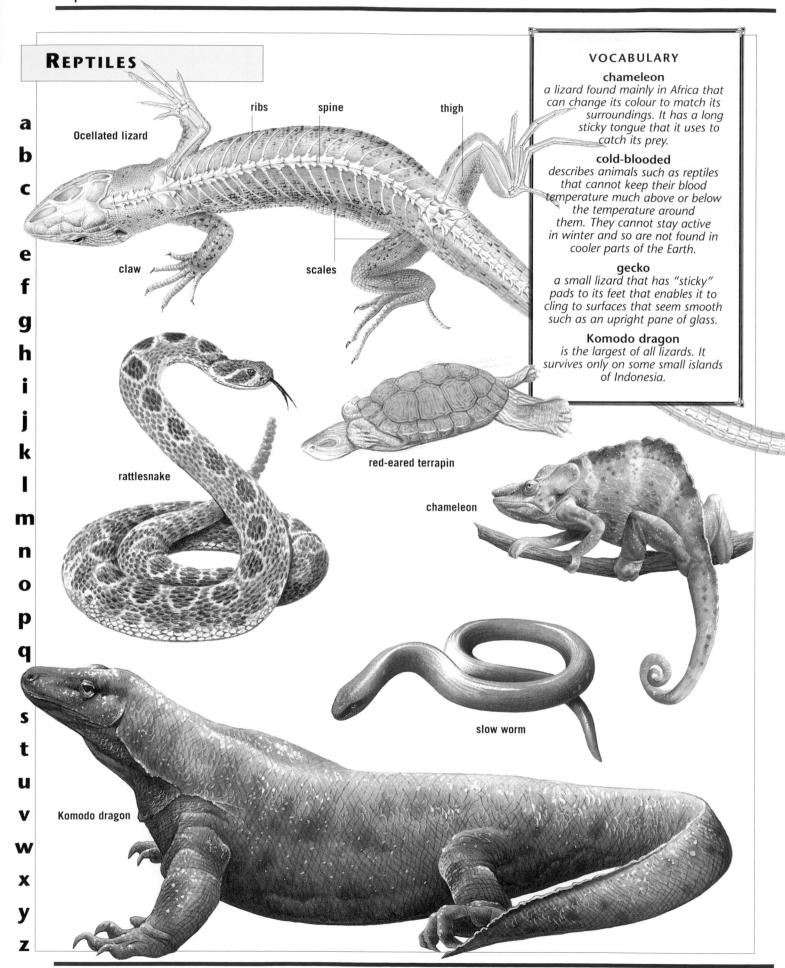

Ocellated lizard

ribs

spine

thigh

claw

scales

rattlesnake

red-eared terrapin

chameleon

slow worm

Komodo dragon

restaurant restaurants *noun*
a place where you can pay to eat a meal.
▲ Say *rest-er-ont*.

**restrict restricts restricting
restricted** *verb*
If you restrict something, you keep it
within a limit so it is not too large.

result results *noun*
1 a thing that happens because of
something else. *The fence fell down as
a result of the storm.*
2 the score at the end of a match. *the
rugby results.*

retire retires retiring retired *verb*
When somebody retires, they give up
working, usually because they are old.
retirement *noun*.

**retreat retreats retreating
retreated** *verb*
If somebody retreats, they move back
from something dangerous.

return returns returning returned
verb
1 If you return to a place after going
away, you come back or go back there.
2 If you return something, you give it
back. *James returned
his library books
after he had read
them.*

revenge *noun*
a thing that you do to hurt somebody for
being horrible to you. *Tina took revenge
on Tim for laughing at her.*

**reverse reverses reversing
reversed** *verb*
If you reverse, you go backwards. *I've
reversed my car into a tree!*

review reviews *noun*
something that somebody says or writes
in a newspaper or on radio or television
telling people what a new film, book or
TV programme is like and whether it is
good or bad.

revolting *adjective*
horrible and disgusting. *What's that
revolting smell?*

revolution revolutions *noun*
a fight to get a new kind of government.
revolutionary *noun*.

revolver revolvers *noun*
a small gun that can be fired several
times before it needs to be loaded again.

reward rewards *noun*
a nice thing that you are given because
you have done something very well or
been very helpful.
reward *verb*.

**rewind rewinds rewinding
rewound** *verb*
To rewind a tape or video is to make it
go backwards so that it can be played
again.

rhinoceros rhinoceroses *noun*
a large, heavy, wild animal with thick
skin. It has one or two horns on its nose.
Rhinoceroses live in Africa and
Asia. They are called rhinos for
short. ▲ Say *rye-noss-er-us*.

rhyme rhymes *noun*
a word that sounds the same as another
word except for the first letter. "Batter"
and "fatter" are rhymes. ▲ Say *rime*.

rhythm rhythms *noun*
a pattern of repeated sounds which is
regular. Music and poetry have rhythm.
▲ Say *rith-um*.

rib ribs *noun*
Your ribs are the bones that curve
around your chest to protect your heart
and lungs.

ribbon ribbons *noun*
a strip of coloured material that you can
use to tie hair or for decorating things.

rice *noun*
white or brown grains that you cook and
eat. Rice plants grow in wet ground in
hot regions.

rich richer richest *adjective*
A person who is rich has a lot of money.
■ The opposite is **poor**.
rich in containing a lot of. *Fruit is rich
in vitamin C.*

rid rids ridding rid *verb*
to free somebody from something
harmful or annoying.
get rid of to throw something away.
Get rid of those old comics.

riddle riddles *noun*
a question that is a puzzle and has a
clever or funny answer. *"What goes up
when the rain comes down?"* Answer:
"An umbrella."

ride rides *noun*
a journey on a horse, bicycle, bus or train. *I went for a ride on my horse.*

ride rides riding rode ridden *verb*
1 When you ride a horse or a motorbike, you sit on it and travel along.
2 When you ride in something such as a car or bus, you travel in it.

ridiculous *adjective*
very silly. *What a ridiculous hat!*

right *adjective*
1 When you write the word "right", the "i" is to the right of the "r". *I write with my right hand.* ■ The opposite is **left**.
2 If something is right, it is correct. *Congratulations, that's the right answer!* ■ The opposite is **wrong**. ● A word that sounds like **right** is **write**.

right *adverb*
correctly. *Did I guess right?* ● A word that sounds like **right** is **write**. ■ The opposite is **wrong**.

right angle right angles *noun*
an angle of 90 degrees like the corners of a square where two lines meet.

rigid *adjective*
If something is rigid, you cannot bend or stretch it. *You can't bend a rigid metal bar.*

rim rims *noun*
the edge around the top of such things as a glass, a jar or cup. *the rim of a wheel.*

ring rings *noun*
1 a round piece of metal that you wear on your finger.
2 a circle with an empty centre.
3 the noise of a bell.

ring rings ringing rang rung *verb*
1 When something rings, it makes the sound of a bell.
2 If you ring somebody, you call them on the phone.

rinse rinses rinsing rinsed *verb*
to wash in clean water, not using soap.

rip rips ripping ripped *verb*
If you rip something, you tear it. *He ripped his shirt on a nail.*

ripe riper ripest *adjective*
When a fruit is ripe, it is ready to eat. *The banana isn't ripe yet – it's green.*

ripple ripples *noun*
a very small wave or movement on the surface of water.

rise rises rising rose risen *verb*
To rise is to move upwards. *The bread dough has risen.* ■ The opposite is **dip** or **fall**.

risk risks *noun*
a danger that something bad or harmful will happen. *She took a risk when she rushed into the burning house.*
risk *verb*, **risky** *adjective*.

rival rivals *noun*
someone who is trying to win the same thing as you are.

river rivers *noun*
a large amount of water flowing across the land towards the sea or a lake.

road roads *noun*
a long piece of hard ground that cars, bicycles and lorries can travel on. ● A word that sounds like **road** is **rode**.

roam roams roaming roamed *verb*
To roam is to wander about without trying to go anywhere. *He roamed the streets at night.*

roar roars roaring roared *verb*
To roar is to make a very loud noise. *The lion roared.* ◆ *The car engine roared.*

roast roasts roasting roasted *verb*
When you roast food, you cook it in an oven or over a fire. *roast chicken.*

rob robs robbing robbed *verb*
To rob somebody is to steal from them.
robber *noun*, **robbery** *noun*.

robe robes *noun*
a long, loose piece of clothing.

robin robins *noun*
a small brown bird with red feathers on the front of its body.

European Robin

American Robin

robot robots *noun*
a machine controlled by a computer that can do jobs that people would otherwise do. *In factories, robots now do a lot of work.* ▲ Say *roe-bot.*

rock rocks *noun*
1 the very hard material that mountains and the hardest ground are made of.
2 a large piece of stone.
3 pop music with a very strong rhythm.

rock rocks rocking rocked *verb*
When you rock, you move or move something gently from side to side or backwards and forwards. *She was rocking the baby in her arms.*

rocket rockets *noun*
1 an engine in a tall metal tube that is used to send spacecraft into space or to carry bombs.

2 a firework that is sent high up into the air and then explodes in different colours.

rod rods *noun*
a long, thin, round piece of wood or metal. *a fishing rod.*

rode past of **ride**
● A word that sounds like **rode** is **road**.

rodent rodents *noun*
a small animal with sharp front teeth that gnaws things. Mice, rats and squirrels are all rodents.

roll rolls *noun*
1 a very small, round loaf of bread.
2 a long, thin tube made by rolling a piece of paper or material round and round. *a roll of wallpaper.*

roll rolls rolling rolled *verb*
1 When something rolls, it goes along the ground turning over and over. *The ball rolled slowly down the hill.*
2 To roll something is to wrap it around itself several times in the shape of a long, thin tube.
3 To roll pastry is to make it flat by pushing a wooden tube called a rolling pin over it.

rollerskate rollerskates *noun*
boots with wheels for skating on smooth, hard surfaces.

roof roofs *noun*
the part that covers the top of a building or the top of a car.

room rooms *noun*
1 a part inside a building that is separated from the other parts inside the building by walls. Bathrooms and kitchens are rooms.
2 space. *There's not enough room in our car for ten people!*
roomy *adjective*
a roomy house with pleanty of space.

root roots *noun*
1 part of a plant that grows underground and takes in water and food from the soil.
2 the part of a tooth or hair growing under the gum or skin that you cannot see.
● A word that sounds like **root** is **route**.

rope ropes *noun*
very thick, strong string that is used for tying things. *Tie the boat up with rope.*

rose roses *noun*
a plant that grows on thorny bushes.

cultivated rose   wild prairie rose

rose past of **rise**.

rot rots rotting rotted *verb*
When something rots, it goes bad or starts to get soft and weak. *The tomatoes were rotting on the ground.* ◆ *Wood rots in water.*

rotate rotates rotating rotated *verb*
If something rotates, it turns round and round like a wheel. *The Earth rotates as it goes around the Sun.*

rotten *adjective*
If something is rotten, it has rotted and is so bad that it cannot be used. *That fruit is rotten.*

rough rougher roughest *adjective*
1 bumpy or uneven, not smooth. *A cat's tongue is very rough.*
2 not exact. *a rough guess.*
3 using a lot of force. *Rugby is a rough game.* ■ The opposite is **gentle**.
▲ Say *ruff*.
roughly *adverb*, **roughness** *noun*.

this sandpaper is rough

round *adjective*
shaped like a circle or a ball. *Most coins are round.*

roundabout roundabouts *noun*
1 a round place where roads meet and where traffic goes around in a clockwise circle.

2 a machine in a playground for children to ride on that turns around and around in circles.

route routes *noun*
the way you go from one place to another place on a journey. *Please work out the best route on the map before we leave.* ▲ Rhymes with **boot**. ● A word that sounds like **route** is **root**.

row rows *noun*
1 a quarrel or angry argument. ▲ Rhymes with **cow**.
2 a number of things or people that are in a line. *a row of jars.* ▲ Rhymes with **low**.

row rows rowing rowed *verb*
When you row a boat, you make it move by pushing against the water with oars. ▲ Rhymes with **low**.

royal *adjective*
belonging to a king or queen. *the royal family.* ◆ *a royal palace.*

rub rubs rubbing rubbed *verb*
1 If you rub something, you move your hand up and down it. *She yawned and rubbed her eyes.*
2 To rub is to press one thing backwards and forwards against another. *People say that you can make a fire by rubbing two sticks together but I've never been able to do it.*

rubber *noun*
1 a strong, waterproof material that stretches and bounces. Tyres are made of black rubber.
2 a small piece of rubber that you use to make pencil marks disappear.

rubbish *noun*
things that you do not want that you throw away.

ruby rubies *noun*
a valuable red jewel. ▲ Say *roo-bee*.

A B C D E F G H I J K L M N O P Q R S T U V W X Y Z

ROAD TRANSPORT

rickshaw

off-road motorcycle

road/racing motorcycle

family car

"supercar"

"roadtrain" tanker

Terex "Titan"

VOCABULARY

bypass
a road built around a busy town so that traffic does not pass though it.

carriageway
the part of a road used by vehicles going in the same direction

crossroads
a place where two or more roads cross one another.

motorway
a wide road with several carriageways on which traffic can travel faster than on other roads.

ring road
a road that goes around a town, avoiding the busy centre.

T-junction
a place where two road meet in the shape of a T.

traffic lights
lights of changing colour for controlling traffic at road junctions and crossings.

zebra crossing
black and white stripes painted on a road to show where people may cross and where traffic must stop.

rucksack rucksacks *noun*
a bag for carrying things in that you wear on your back. *We need tents and rucksacks to take on our walking holiday.*

rude ruder rudest *adjective*
If somebody is rude, they behave in a bad way and are not polite.

rug rugs *noun*
a small piece of thick, heavy material that you put on the floor.

rugby *noun*
a game played between two teams using an oval ball. Players score points by trying to carry the ball over a line or kicking it over a bar.

ruin ruins ruining ruined *verb*
To ruin something is to completely spoil it. *The rain ruined our picnic.*
▲ Say *roo-in.*

ruins *noun*
the parts of a building that are left after the rest of it has fallen down or been destroyed. *the ruins of a castle.*
▲ Say *roo-ins.*

rule rules ruling ruled *verb*
To rule a country is to be in charge of it.

rule rules *noun*
something that says what you are allowed to do and what you are not allowed to do. *the rules of rugby.*

ruler rulers *noun*
1 a long, narrow piece of wood, metal or plastic that you use for drawing straight lines and for measuring.
2 a person who rules a country.

rumble rumbles rumbling rumbled *verb*
When something rumbles, it makes a long, low sound like thunder. *The lorries rumbled past.*

run runs running ran run *verb*
1 When a person or animal runs, they go on their feet much faster than when they walk.
2 If you run something, you are in charge of it and you make sure that it works properly.
3 When liquid runs, it flows. *Tears were running down her face.*

rung past of **ring**.

runway runways *noun*
the long, hard, level strip of land at an airport on which aeroplanes take off and land.

rush rushes rushing rushed *verb*
If you rush, you go somewhere or do something very quickly. *He was rushing to get to the bus stop before the bus.*

rust *noun*
a red-brown substance that covers iron or steel when they get wet.
rusty *adjective*.

rustle rustles rustling rustled *verb*
To rustle is to make the soft sound that leaves make as they move together in the wind. ▲ Say *russ-l.*

S s

sack sacks *noun*
a large, strong bag that you put things such as coal, potatoes or rubbish in.

sack sacks sacking sacked *verb*
If somebody is sacked from their job, they are told to leave.

sad sadder saddest *adjective*
unhappy. *Cecile was very sad when her hamster died.* ■ The opposite is **happy**.

saddle saddles *noun*
1 a seat for a rider on a horse.
2 a seat on a bicycle.

safe *adjective*
1 If you are safe, you are unharmed. *The lost kitten was found safe and well.*
2 If something is safe, it is not dangerous. *Is this ladder safe?*
safety *noun*.

safe safes *noun*
a strong box or cupboard with a lock that you keep money or jewels in.

said past of **say**.

sail sails *noun*
A sail is a big piece of cloth on a boat. When the wind blows against the sail, the boat moves along.

sail sails sailing sailed *verb*
To sail means to move along in a boat using its sails. *Sam went sailing on the river.*

sailor sailors *noun*
a person who works on a ship or boat.

salad salads *noun*
a cold food made of raw vegetables such as lettuce, beetroot and cucumbers.

salary salaries *noun*
the money that somebody is paid for the work that they do. *Teachers' salaries are paid regularly every month.*

sale sales *noun*
a time when a shop sells things at a cheaper price than usual. *Mum bought some shoes in the sale.*

saliva *noun*
the liquid in your mouth.

salmon salmon *noun*
a fish with silver skin and pink flesh that you can eat. ▲ Say *sam-un.*

salt *noun*
a white powder that you put on food to give it a stronger taste. Sea water has salt in it.
salty *adjective*
The soup that I made was too salty.

A B C D E F G H I J K L M N O P Q R S T U V W X Y Z

salute **salutes** **saluting saluted** *verb*
When soldiers salute, they make a sign by lifting their right hand to their forehead as a greeting or to show respect to somebody. *She saluted when the general walked by.*

sample **samples** *noun*
a small amount of something that shows what the rest of it is like.

sand *noun*
a white or yellow substance that is made from lots of tiny pieces of rock. You can see sand by the sea or in deserts.

sandal **sandals** *noun*
a light shoe made of a sole with straps that go over your foot.

sandwich **sandwiches** *noun*
two slices of bread with food in between them. *an egg and tomato sandwich.*

sang past of **sing**.

sank past of **sink**.

sap *noun*
the sticky liquid inside the stems of plants and the trunks of trees. Sap carries food to all parts of the plant.

sapphire **sapphires** *noun*
a bright blue jewel.

sari **saris** *noun*
a long piece of material that many Indian women and girls wrap around the body like a dress.

sat past of **sit**.

satellite **satellites** *noun*
1 a natural object in space, like a moon, that moves around a larger object, like a planet.
2 A satellite is also a machine that is sent into space to pick up and send back signals and information. Satellite television comes to us by satellite.
▲ Say *sat-ul-ite.*

satisfy **satisfies satisfying satisfied** *verb*
If you satisfy somebody, you please them and give them what they want or need. *Nothing I ever do satisfies you.*

sauce *noun*
a thick liquid that you pour over food to add to its flavour. *Do you like tomato sauce on your chips?*

saucepan **saucepans** *noun*
a metal pot with a handle and a lid for cooking food.

saucer **saucers** *noun*
A saucer is a kind of small plate for putting a cup on.

sausage **sausages** *noun*
meat that is cut up into very small pieces and made into a long, thin shape like a tube.

save **saves saving saved** *verb*
1 If you save somebody, you take them away from danger. *The man saved the child from drowning.*
2 If you save money or something else, you keep it somewhere to use later. *I'm saving for a new computer game.*

savoury *adjective*
A savoury food tastes salty instead of sweet. Cheese and crisps are savoury foods.

saw past of **see**.

saw **saws** *noun*
a tool for cutting wood. It has a metal blade with sharp points called teeth along one edge.
saw *verb*.

saxophone **saxophones** *noun*
a musical instrument made of brass that you play by blowing into it.
saxophonist *noun*.

say **says saying said** *verb*
If you say something you speak words. *My uncle said that he didn't like eating meat very often.*

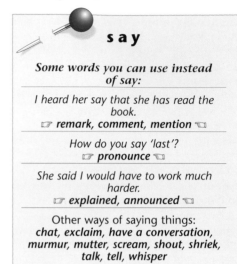

s a y

Some words you can use instead of say:

I heard her say that she has read the book.
☞ **remark, comment, mention** ✑

How do you say 'last'?
☞ **pronounce** ✑

She said I would have to work much harder.
☞ **explained, announced** ✑

Other ways of saying things:
chat, exclaim, have a conversation, murmur, mutter, scream, shout, shriek, talk, tell, whisper

scab **scabs** *noun*
a piece of dried blood that forms over a cut in your skin when it is healing.

scald **scalds scalding scalded** *verb*
If you scald yourself, you burn yourself with very hot liquid or steam.

scale **scales** *noun*
1 a row of marks on something such as a ruler that is used to measure things.
2 a way of showing distances between places on a map. *This map has a scale of one centimetre to one kilometre.*
3 one of the small, hard pieces of skin that cover the body of a fish or reptile.
4 A scale is also a series of musical notes. *You play or sing the notes of a scale one after the other.*

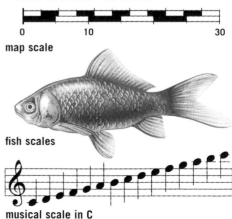

map scale

fish scales

musical scale in C

scales *noun*
You use scales to find out how heavy you are, or to weigh things such as fruit and vegetables.

scar scars *noun*
a mark on your skin left by a cut that has healed.

scarce scarcer scarcest *adjective*
If things are scarce, they are difficult to find because there are only a few of them. *Flowers are scarce in winter.*
scarcely *adverb*
I was so happy I could scarcely speak.

scare scares scaring scared *verb*
If something scares you, it frightens you. *That ghost story really scared me.*

scarecrow scarecrows *noun*
a thing that looks like a person dressed in old clothes. Farmers put scarecrows in their fields when crops are growing to frighten off birds.

scarf scarves *noun*
a long piece of material or knitted wool that you wear around your neck.

scatter scatters scattering scattered *verb*
1 If animals or things scatter, they move quickly in different directions. *The loud noise frightened the squirrels and they scattered in many different directions.*
2 If you scatter things, you throw them about in different directions. *Ben scattered some bread for the ducks.*

scene scenes *noun*
1 what you see in the countryside around you. *a mountain scene.*
2 a place where something happens. *the scene of the murder.*
3 a part of a play. *Does the hero get killed in the last scene?*

scenery *noun*
1 what you see around you in the countryside, such as mountains, forests, rivers and lakes. *What beautiful scenery!*
2 the things on the stage of a theatre that make a play more real to the audience.

scent scents *noun*
1 a nice smell. *a beautiful scent.*
2 a liquid that you can put on your skin to make you smell nice.
● A word that sounds like **scent** is **sent**.

scheme schemes *noun*
a plan for doing something. *There are many schemes for helping the environment.* ▲ Say **skeem**.

school schools *noun*
a place where children go to learn.
▲ Say **skule**.

science sciences *noun*
finding out about things such as animals, plants and natural materials.
scientific *adjective*

scientist scientists *noun*
a person who finds out about animals, plants and other things in the world by looking at them closely, writing down information about them, and doing experiments.

scissors *noun*
a small tool for cutting paper and other things. A pair of scissors has two sharp blades that are joined together.

scoop scoops scooping scooped *verb*
To scoop is to lift something up using your hands or with a kind of spoon called a scoop. *Nicky scooped some ice-cream out of the bowl.*

scooter scooters *noun*
1 a motorbike with a small engine.
2 a toy with wheels and a handlebar for a child to ride on. You stand on it with one foot and push along with the other.

scorch scorches scorching scorched *verb*
If you scorch something like a piece of material, you burn it a little, leaving a brown mark. *I scorched my shirt because the iron was too hot.*

score scores *noun*
In a game, the score is how many points each side has. *At the end of the match the score was 4-2.*

score scores scoring scored *verb*
To score means to get a point in a game. *Andy scored the winning goal in the football match.*

scowl scowls scowling scowled *verb*
If you scowl, you have an angry, bad-tempered look on your face. *She scowled at the pile of dirty clothes.*
scowl *noun.*

scramble scrambles scrambling scrambled *verb*
If you scramble over rocks or rough ground, you use your hands and feet to help you move quickly.

scrap scraps *noun*
a small piece of something such as paper or material.

scrapbook scrapbooks *noun*
a book with blank pages that you can stick pictures, postcards or pieces of writing in.

scrape scrapes scraping scraped *verb*
1 If you scrape your knee, you hurt it by rubbing it against something hard or rough.
2 If you scrape mud off your shoes, you get it off with a thing such as a knife.

A B C D E F G H I J K L M N O P Q R S T U V W X Y Z

scratch scratches scratching scratched *verb*
1 If you scratch your skin, you make thin cuts on it by rubbing something sharp against it. *Sarah scratched her hand on the thorns.*
2 If you scratch yourself, you rub your nails across your skin because it itches.
scratch *noun.*

scream screams screaming screamed *verb*
If you scream, you shout in a very loud, high voice because you are excited or frightened. *Sophie screamed when she went on the big wheel at the fair.*

screen screens *noun*
1 the flat part of a TV or computer where you see the pictures or words.
2 the place on the wall where the film is shown in a cinema.

screw screws *noun*
a thin piece of metal like a nail with a sharp point at one end and a slot in the top. Screws are used to join things such as pieces of wood together. You use a screwdriver to turn the screw into the piece of wood.

screw screws screwing screwed *verb*
1 to join things together using screws. *He screwed the shelf to the wall.*
2 If you screw things up, you squeeze them into a ball. *She screwed up the paper and threw it into the bin.*

scribble scribbles scribbling scribbled *verb*
to write quickly and without care.

script scripts *noun*
all the words that have been written for the actors to say in a play or film.

scrub scrubs scrubbing scrubbed *verb*
If you scrub something, you rub it hard to clean it. *Paul scrubbed the floor with a stiff brush.*

scruffy *adjective*
untidy and dirty. *scruffy clothes.*

sculpture sculptures *noun*
1 a person, an animal or a shape that has been made of stone, wood or metal by an artist called a sculptor.
2 Sculpture is the art of carving or modelling things.

scythe scythes *noun*
a tool with a long handle and a sharp, curved blade that you use to cut long grass. ▲ Say *sithe.*

sea seas *noun*
a large area of salt water. *We went swimming in the sea.*

sea-horse sea-horses *noun*
a tiny fish with a head shaped like a horse's head and a long curling tail.

seal seals *noun*
an animal with short, grey fur that lives near the sea. Seals spend a lot of time in the sea and catch fish to eat.

seam seams *noun*
a line made where two pieces of material are sewn together. *These two pieces of material are joined with a seam.*

search searches searching searched *verb*
If you search for somebody or something, you look very carefully for them. *We searched everywhere for the lost kitten.*

season seasons *noun*
one of the four parts of the year. They are spring, summer, autumn and winter.
seasonal *adjective*
seasonal vegetables.

seat seats *noun*
a thing you sit on. Buses and cars have seats. *We sat in the front seats at the cinema.*

seaweed *noun*
a red, green or brown plant that grows in the sea.

second seconds *noun*
a very short measure of time. There are 60 seconds in a minute.

second *adjective*
Second means next after the first. *Tom won the race and Ben came second.*

secret secrets *noun*
something that only a few people know about. *I'm not telling you what you're getting for your birthday - it's a secret!*

secretary secretaries *noun*
a person who works in an office. Secretaries answer the phone, make appointments and type letters.

section sections *noun*
one of the separate parts of something. *Rob was trying to fit together the sections of the model aeroplane.*

security *noun*
feeling safe or trying to keep things safe. *She locked the door for extra security.*

see sees seeing saw seen *verb*
1 When you see somebody or something, you look at them with your eyes.
2 To see also means to understand something. *You see what I mean?*

seed seeds *noun*
a tiny, hard part inside the flower or fruit of a plant. If you put seeds into the ground they will grow into new plants.

seek seeks seeking sought *verb*
To seek means to look for somebody or something. *The police are seeking a woman who was seen near the bank at midnight.*

seem seems seeming seemed *verb*
To seem means to look or feel like something. *Ben is tall so he seems older than he really is.*

seen past of **see**.

seesaw seesaws *noun*
a thing that you ride on in a playground. One person sits at each end of a long piece of wood and they take it in turns to go up and down.

seize seizes seizing seized *verb*
If you seize something, you take hold of it firmly and suddenly. *The thief seized the bag.* ▲ Say *seez*. ● A word that sounds like **seize** is **sees**.
seize-up to become stuck.

seldom *adverb*
not very often. *I seldom see my aunt because she lives a long way from us.*

select selects selecting selected *verb*
When you select someone or something, you choose them. *We selected the best painting to go on the wall.*
selection *noun*
a selection of chocolates.

selfish *adjective*
A selfish person does not like to help or share things with other people and only thinks of themself. *It was selfish of you to eat all the sweets yourself.*

sell sells selling sold *verb*
If somebody sells something to you, they give it to you and you pay them money.

semicircle semicircles *noun*
1 half a circle.
2 the shape of half a circle. *We put the chairs in a semicircle.*

semi-final semi-finals *noun*
in a sport, the person or team that wins each semi-final will play in the final and decide who will win the whole competition.

send sends sending sent *verb*
To send is to make somebody or something go to another place. *I am going to send a postcard to Katie.* ◆ *Mum sent me to the shops.*

senior *adjective*
older in years or more important. *the senior school.* ◆ *a senior minister in the government.* ■ The opposite is **junior**.

sense senses *noun*
1 the powers that most people have to see, hear, touch, taste and smell.
2 knowing and being careful to do the right thing. *If you had any sense, you wouldn't play with matches.*

sensible *adjective*
A sensible person thinks carefully about what they are doing and does not do anything silly or foolish. *Gita won't get lost, she's very sensible.*

sensitive *adjective*
1 A sensitive person cares about other people's feelings.
2 If your skin is sensitive, it is sore or it gets sore very easily.

sent past of **send**
● A word that sounds like **sent** is **scent**.

sentence sentences *noun*
a group of words that make sense together. A written sentence begins with a capital letter and ends with a full stop. "Jamie stroked the cat." and "Joan is late today." are both sentences.

separate *adjective*
If two things are separate they are not joined together. ▲ Say *sep-er-ut.*

separate separates separating separated *verb*
to set or keep apart. *He separates the white from the yolk.* ▲ Say *sep-er-ate.*

serial serials *noun*
a story that is told in parts on television or in a magazine. ● A word that sounds like **serial** is **cereal**.

series *noun*
1 a set of things of the same kind that follow each other.

2 a number of programmes on radio or television on the same subject, that follow each other. *I am watching a series on dinosaurs.*

serious *adjective*
1 important or very bad. *a serious accident.*
2 A serious person is quiet and does not laugh or joke very often.

servant servants *noun*
A servant is a person who works in somebody else's house, doing such things as cooking and cleaning.

serve serves serving served *verb*
1 If somebody serves you in a restaurant, they bring you food and drink.
2 If somebody serves you in a shop, they help you to look at things you want to buy. *Are you being served?*

service services *noun*
1 something useful that a person or a company does for other people. *a train service.* ◆ *the postal service.*
2 A service is also a meeting in a church where people pray and sing.

session sessions *noun*
a time when people meet to do something. *a football training session.*

set sets *noun*
a group of things that belong together. *a china tea set.* ◆ *a chess set.*

set sets setting set *verb*
1 When something liquid like cement sets, it goes hard.
2 When the Sun sets, it goes down below the horizon and then the sky gets dark.
3 When you set a table, you put all the things on it you need for a meal such as cups, plates, knives and forks.
4 When you set a clock or a watch, you move the hands to a certain time. *I set my alarm clock for 7.30.*
5 To set also means to give somebody work to do. *The teacher set a test for her pupils.*

A
B
C
D
E
F
G
H
I
J
K
L
M
N
O
P
Q
R
S
T
U
V
W
X
Y
Z

settee settees *noun*
a long, comfortable seat for two or more people, also called a sofa.

settle settles settling settled *verb*
If you settle, you go to a place and stay there. *A ladybird settled on my hand.* ◆ *Nita and Bill have settled in Australia.*

several *adjective*
more than two but not very many.

severe *adjective*
very bad. *a severe headache.*

sew sews sewing sewed sewn *verb*
When you sew, you join pieces of material together or join something to material using a needle and thread. *Can you sew this button back on my shirt, please?* ▲ Say *so*.

sewer sewers *noun*
a large pipe under the ground that takes waste away from houses and other buildings. ▲ Say *soo-er*.

sex sexes *noun*
1 the two groups that people and animals belong to. The two sexes are males and females.
2 Sex is the way that people and animals produce young ones.

shade *noun*
1 a place where the Sun cannot reach. *We sat in the shade of an oak tree.*
2 a cover for a lamp.
3 a variety of a colour. *a dark shade of blue.*
shady *adjective*.

shadow shadows *noun*
a dark shape that you see near somebody or something that is under or in front of the light. *When you place your hands in front of a light, you can have fun by making hand shadows like these.*

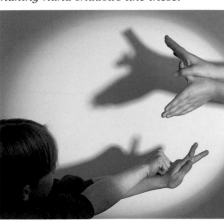

shake shakes shaking shook shaken *verb*
1 When you shake something, you move it up and down or backwards and forwards. *I shook the bottle of tomato sauce.*
2 If your body shakes because you are cold or frightened, it wobbles about.
shaky *adjective*, **shakily** *adverb*.

shallow *adjective*
not very deep. *This water is shallow, it only just covers my feet.*

shame *noun*
the guilty feeling that you have if you have done something wrong.
shameful *adjective*
shameful behaviour.

shampoo shampoos *noun*
a liquid that you use to wash your hair.

shape shapes *noun*
what you see if you draw a line around the outside of something. Circles, squares, triangles and rectangles are all different shapes. ❖ *Look at page 145*

share shares sharing shared *verb*
1 If you share something, you give some of it to somebody else. *I shared my birthday cake with my friends.*
2 To share also means to use something together with another person. *I share a bedroom with my sister.*
share *noun*.

shark sharks *noun*
a big, sea fish that has lots of very sharp teeth and a big mouth.

Great white shark

sharp sharper sharpest *adjective*
1 Something that is sharp has an edge or a point that is good for cutting. *Knives and scissors are usually sharp.*
2 sudden and severe. *a sharp pain.*
sharply *adverb*.

shatter shatters shattering shattered *verb*
If something such as glass shatters, it breaks into lots of little pieces.

shave shaves shaving shaved *verb*
To shave is to cut hair off the skin with a razor.

shawl shawls *noun*
a wide scarf that you wear around your shoulders or wrap a baby in.

shed sheds *noun*
a small building made of wood. *a tool-shed.* ◆ *a cow-shed.*

shed sheds shedding shed *verb*
1 If an animal sheds hair, some of its hair falls out.
2 When trees shed their leaves, the leaves fall off because it is autumn.

sheep sheep *noun*
an animal that farmers keep for their wool and for their meat. A male sheep is called a ram and a female sheep is called a ewe.

Soay sheep

Merino   *Oxford downs*

sheet sheets *noun*
1 a large piece of material for putting on a bed.
2 a thin, flat piece of paper, glass or metal. *a sheet of headed notepaper.* ◆ *The road was like a sheet of ice.*

SHAPES

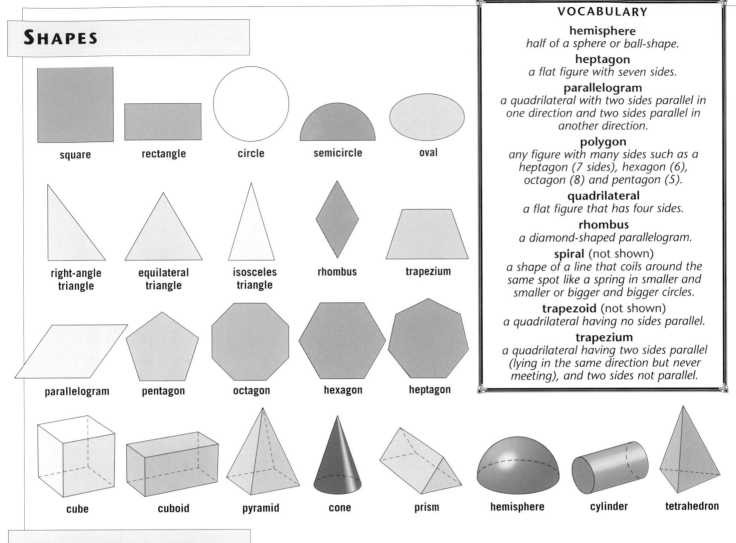

square   rectangle   circle   semicircle   oval

right-angle triangle   equilateral triangle   isosceles triangle   rhombus   trapezium

parallelogram   pentagon   octagon   hexagon   heptagon

cube   cuboid   pyramid   cone   prism   hemisphere   cylinder   tetrahedron

VOCABULARY

hemisphere
half of a sphere or ball-shape.

heptagon
a flat figure with seven sides.

parallelogram
a quadrilateral with two sides parallel in one direction and two sides parallel in another direction.

polygon
any figure with many sides such as a heptagon (7 sides), hexagon (6), octagon (8) and pentagon (5).

quadrilateral
a flat figure that has four sides.

rhombus
a diamond-shaped parallelogram.

spiral (not shown)
a shape of a line that coils around the same spot like a spring in smaller and smaller or bigger and bigger circles.

trapezoid (not shown)
a quadrilateral having no sides parallel.

trapezium
a quadrilateral having two sides parallel (lying in the same direction but never meeting), and two sides not parallel.

COLOURS

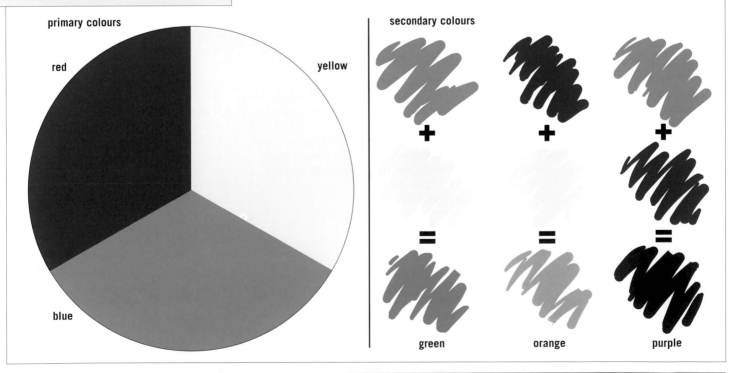

primary colours

red   yellow   blue

secondary colours

+ = green
+ = orange
+ = purple

A B C D E F G H I J K L M N O P Q R S T U V W X Y Z

a b c d e f g h i j k l m n o p q r s t u v w x y z

shelf shelves *noun*
a long, flat piece of wood or glass fixed on a wall or in a cupboard where you can put things. *a bookshelf.*

shell shells *noun*
1 the hard outside part of some living things. Eggs, nuts, snails and crabs have shells.
2 a very large kind of bullet.

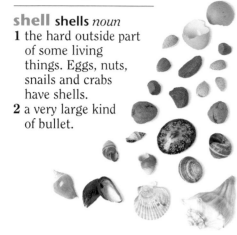

shelter shelters *noun*
a covered place where you are safe from bad weather or danger. *We stood in the bus shelter while it rained.*
shelter *verb*.

shield shields *noun*
a large piece of wood or metal that soldiers used to carry to protect their bodies from enemy weapons.

shin shins *noun*
Your shin is the front part of your leg between your knee and your ankle.

shine shines shining shone *verb*
When something shines, it gives out light, or is bright like silver. *The Sun is shining.* ◆ *She polished the silver bowl until it shone.*
shiny *adjective*
a shiny new coin.

ship ships *noun*
a big boat for carrying people and things across the sea. ❖ *Look at page 147*

shipwreck shipwrecks *noun*
a bad accident when a ship is broken up by rocks or a rough sea.

shirt shirts *noun*
a piece of clothing that you wear on the top part of your body. Shirts have a collar, sleeves and buttons down the front.

shiver shivers shivering shivered *verb*
When you shiver, you shake because you are cold or frightened. *The rabbit was shivering with fright.*

shock shocks *noun*
1 a sudden and bad thing that happens to you. *The news of the car accident gave us all a shock.*
2 An electric shock is a sharp pain that you get if electricity goes through your body.

shoe shoes *noun*
things that you wear on your feet. Shoes are usually made of leather or plastic.

shone past of **shine**
▲ Say *shon.*

shook past of **shake**.

shoot shoots shooting shot *verb*
1 To shoot means to fire bullets from a gun or to use a bow and arrow.
2 To shoot also means to kick or throw a ball at a goal in sports like football or netball.
3 To shoot can also mean to move somewhere very fast. *The kitten shot under the sofa.*

shop shops *noun*
a place where you go to buy things. *a shoe shop.*

shop shops shopping shopped *verb*
When you shop, you go to the shops to buy things. *We went shopping for food in the supermarket.*
shopper *noun*.

shore shores *noun*
the land along the edge of the sea or a lake. *We walked along the sandy shore.*

short shorter shortest *adjective*
1 not tall. *Vincent is tall and Jennifer is short, but Joe is the shortest.*
2 not long. *Gerald has short hair.*
3 not lasting long. *The queen made a short speech.*

4 short for a short way of writing or saying something. *Phone is short for telephone.*

shorts *noun*
short trousers that usually do not cover your knees. *Rose and Freddie are wearing running shorts.*

shot past of **shoot**.

shoulder shoulders *noun*
Your shoulder joins your arm to the rest of your body.

shout shouts shouting shouted *verb*
If you shout, you say something in a very loud voice. *Jill had to shout so we could hear her.*

show shows showing showed shown *verb*
1 When you show somebody something, you let them see it or you point it out to them. *Show me your photos.* ◆ *Show me the girl who hit you.*
2 When you show somebody how to do something, you explain to them how to do it. *Can you show me how to use the computer?*

show shows *noun*
1 something you see at the theatre or on television. Shows often have singing and dancing in them.
2 things arranged so that people can look at them. *a dog show.*

shower showers *noun*
1 a place where you can wash by standing under water that sprays down on you.
2 A shower is also rain that falls for only a short time.

shrank past of **shrink**.

shred shreds *noun*
a small, thin piece that has been cut or torn from something larger. *He tore the paper to shreds.* ◆ *We decorated the cake with shreds of orange peel.*

shriek shrieks shrieking shrieked *verb*
If you shriek, you shout in a high voice. *He shrieked when he saw the spider.*
▲ Say *shreek*.

shrink shrinks shrinking shrank shrunk *verb*
When something shrinks, it gets smaller. *Jordan's T-shirt shrank in the wash.*
shrunken *adjective*.

shut shuts shutting shut *verb*
1 If you shut something, you move a door, window, lid or book so that it is no longer open.
2 To shut something like a shop means that people can not go into it until it opens again. *What time do the shops shut?*
■ The opposite is **open**.

shuttle shuttles *noun*
1 an aeroplane or bus that goes backwards and forwards between two places. *the Edinburgh shuttle.*
2 A shuttle is also a kind of spaceship. *the Space Shuttle.*

shy shyer shyest *adjective*
If somebody is shy, they do not feel happy or comfortable with people they do not know very well. *She doesn't talk much because she is shy.*

sick sicker sickest *adjective*
1 When you are sick, you are ill and do not feel well.
2 If you are sick, you bring food up from your stomach through your mouth.
sickness *noun*.

side sides *noun*
1 the left or right of something. *She drew a margin down the side of the page.*
2 the flat surfaces of something. *This box has six sides.*
3 the edges of something. *A square has four sides.*
4 the two teams that are playing against each other in a game.

sieve sieves *noun*
a kitchen container or bowl with lots of tiny holes in it. You use a sieve to separate small pieces from larger pieces or a liquid from something solid.
▲ Say *siv*.

sigh sighs sighing sighed *verb*
When you sigh, you breathe out loudly because you are tired, sad or bored.

sight sights *noun*
1 the ability to see things with your eyes. *Owls have good sight in the dark.*
2 things such as interesting old buildings that people go to see are also sights. *Buckingham Palace is one of the famous sights of London.*

sign signs *noun*
1 a notice that tells you something or where to find something. *Can you see a sign to the castle?*
2 a movement you make to tell somebody something. *His sister made a sign to him to keep quiet.*
3 a mark that means something special. In maths, a sign like this + means add.

sign signs signing signed *verb*
1 When you sign your name, you write it. *He signed the cheque.*
2 **sign on** to agree to work or stay. *Uncle Jack signed on for work at the factory yesterday.*

signal signals *noun*
a sound, a light or a movement that tells you something. *The referee blew a whistle as a signal to start the game.*

signature signatures *noun*
your name written in your own writing.

Sikh Sikhs *noun*
a person who follows the religion of India called Sikhism.

silent *adjective*
not making any noise. *The house was silent and empty.*
silence *noun*, **silently** *adverb*.

silk silks *noun*
a smooth, shiny material made from threads produced by an insect called a silkworm. *a silk scarf.*
silky *adjective*.

silly sillier silliest *adjective*
stupid and not sensible or clever. *You were very silly to run across the road.*

silver *noun*
a grey, shiny metal. Rings, bracelets and necklaces are often made of silver.
silver *adjective*
a silver moon.

similar *adjective*
If two things are similar they are almost the same. *A mule, zebra and donkey are similar animals.*

simple simpler simplest *adjective*
easy to do or understand. *These questions are simple!* ■ The opposite is **difficult**.
simply *adverb*
She works simply for the money.

sing sings singing sang sung *verb*
When you sing, you make music with your voice. *Sing that song again.* ◆ *The birds started singing early in the morning.*
singer *noun*
Who's your favourite singer?

A B C D E F G H I J K L M N O P Q R S T U V W X Y Z

Skyscrapers (from left to right): 1 Sears Tower, Chicago; 2 World Trade Center (also known as the Twin Towers), New York; 3 Empire State Building, New York; 4 John Hancock Tower, Boston; 5 Bank of China, Hong Kong; 6 Library Tower, Los Angeles; 7 Chrysler Building, New York

single *adjective*
1 one. *I can't find a single sock anywhere!*
2 A person who is single is not married.
3 A single ticket on a train or a bus only takes you one way, but not back again.

singular *noun*
one person or thing. *the singular of geese is goose.* ■ The opposite is **plural**.

sink **sinks sinking sank sunk** *verb*
If something like a ship sinks, it goes under water. *The ship sank in the storm.*

sink **sinks** *noun*
a basin with taps in the kitchen where you can wash dishes.

sip **sips sipping sipped** *verb*
If you sip a drink, you drink it slowly, taking a little bit at a time. *She sipped her tea slowly because it was hot.*

sister **sisters** *noun*
A person's sister is a girl or woman who has the same mother and father.

sit **sits sitting sat** *verb*
1 When you sit somewhere you rest your bottom there. *We sat in a circle.*
2 When a bird sits on its nest, it stays there to cover its eggs.

situation **situations** *noun*
1 something that is happening in a place at a particular time. *the political situation in China.*
2 the place where something is. *The hospital is in a beautiful situation by the lake.*

size **sizes** *noun*
The size of something is how big it is. *What size shoes do you wear?*

skate **skates** *noun*
1 Rollerskates are special boots with wheels on the bottom that you wear for moving about on smooth ground.
2 Ice-skates are boots with sharp blades on the bottom that you wear for moving about on ice.
skate *verb*.

skateboard **skateboards** *noun*
a long piece of wood or plastic with wheels that you stand on to move along fast and to do clever jumps and turns.

skeleton **skeletons** *noun*
all the bones that are joined together inside the body of a person or an animal.

sketch **sketches** *noun*
a picture that you draw quickly.

ski **skis** *noun*
long, flat pieces of plastic, wood or metal that are fixed to boots for moving over snow. ▲ Say *skee*.
ski *verb*.

skid **skids skidding skidded** *verb*
When something like a car skids, it slides sideways on the road. *The van skidded on the icy road.*

skill **skills** *noun*
If you have a skill, you have the ability to do something very well. *Playing the piano is a skill you have to learn.*
skilful *adjective*.

skin *noun*
1 the natural outside covering of the bodies of people and many animals. *Goat's skin is sometime used for making coats.*
2 the outside covering of many fruits and vegetables. a *banana skin.*

skip **skips skipping skipped** *verb*
When you skip, you move with little jumps from one foot to the other. *Jonah and Ali were skipping down the street.*

skirt **skirts** *noun*
a piece of clothing that women and girls wear. A skirt hangs down from the waist.

skull **skulls** *noun*
Your skull is the round, bony part of your head. Your brain is inside your skull.

sky **skies** *noun*
the space above the Earth. *You can see the Sun and clouds in the sky in the daytime. You can often see the Moon and the stars in the sky at night.*

skyscraper **skyscrapers** *noun*
a very tall building.

slam **slams slamming slammed** *verb*
When a door slams, it closes with a bang. *She slammed the door.*

slang *noun*
words that you use in conversation, especially with people of your own age, but not when you are writing or being polite. *"Quid" is slang for "pound".*

slanted *adjective*
Something that is slanted is not straight but leans in one direction.

slap **slaps slapping slapped** *verb*
If you slap somebody, you hit them with the palm of your hand. *My sister slapped me on the arm.*

slate **slates** *noun*
a grey rock that can be split into thin flat pieces and used to cover roofs.

slave **slaves** *noun*
a person who is owned by somebody else and is forced to work very hard for them without being paid.
slavery *noun*.

sleep sleeps sleeping slept *verb*
When you sleep, you close your eyes and rest your body as you do in bed at night. *I slept for eight hours last night.*
sleep *noun.*

sleepy sleepier sleepiest *adjective*
When you are sleepy, you feel tired and it is hard to keep your eyes open.

sleeve sleeves *noun*
the part of a shirt, a coat or a dress that covers your arm.

sleigh sleighs *noun*
a vehicle that you sit on to move over snow. Sleighs are usually pulled by animals such as horses or reindeer.
▲ Say *slay.*

slept past of **sleep.**

slice slices *noun*
a thin, flat piece that has been cut from something. *a slice of cake.*

slide slides sliding slid *verb*
When something slides, it moves smoothly over a surface. *The children were sliding on the ice.*

slide slides *noun*
something that you play on. You climb up the steps on one side and slide down the other side.

slight *adjective*
small or not very important. *I've got a slight earache.*
slightly *adverb.*

slim slimmer slimmest *adjective*
If you are slim, you are thin, but not too thin. ■ The opposite is **plump.**

slimy slimier slimiest *adjective*
dirty and slippery. *The rocks were covered with slimy seaweed.*

slip slips slipping slipped *verb*
If you slip, you slide by mistake and fall down. *I slipped on the wet floor.*

slipper slippers *noun*
a soft, comfortable shoe that you wear in the house.

slippery *adjective*
Something that is slippery is very smooth and difficult to hold, or to stand on without sliding and falling over. *a slippery floor.* ◆ *a slippery, wet fish.*

slit slits *noun*
a long, thin cut in something. *They cut a slit in the material.*

slope slopes *noun*
ground that goes upwards or downwards. *We walked down the mountain slope.*

slot slots *noun*
a short, thin hole in something. *You put a coin in the slot to use the telephone.*

slow slower slowest *adjective*
Somebody or something that is slow does not move quickly. *Snails and tortoises are very slow animals.* ■ The opposite is **fast.**
slowly *adverb*
We walked home slowly.

slug slugs *noun*
a small, slimy animal like a snail without a shell. Gardeners do not like slugs because they eat plants.

sly slyer slyest *adjective*
If somebody is sly, they are clever in a secret and not very nice way. *That was a very sly trick.*

small smaller smallest *adjective*
not very big. *Ants are small insects.* ◆ *My brother is smaller than me.* ■ The opposite is **big** or **large.**

---

small

Some words you can use instead of small:

All small animals look sweet.
☞ **baby, young** ☜

The writing is so small you need a magnifying glass to read it.
☞ **minute, tiny** ☜

Don't worry. It's only a small mistake.
☞ **unimportant, slight, minor** ☜

Centipedes have lots of small legs.
☞ **short** ☜

---

smart smarter smartest *adjective*
1 neat and tidy. *Dad wears a smart suit for work.*
2 clever. *You're too smart for this quiz!*

smash smashes smashing smashed *verb*
If something smashes, it breaks into a lot of pieces. *I dropped the plate and it smashed on the floor.*

smell smells smelling smelt or smelled *verb*
1 When you smell something, you use your nose to find out about it. *I can smell food cooking in the kitchen.*
2 When something smells, you notice it with your nose. *She smells of soap.*
smelly *adjective*
smelly old socks.

smile smiles smiling smiled *verb*
When you smile, the corners of your mouth turn up to show that you are happy.
smile *noun.*

smoke smokes smoking smoked *verb*
When somebody smokes, they have a cigarette or a pipe in their mouth, and breathe the smoke in and out.

smoke smokes *noun*
the white, grey or black stuff that you see going up in the air when something is burning. *Smoke was pouring out of the chimney.*

smooth smoother smoothest *adjective*
If something is smooth, you cannot feel lumps or any rough parts when you touch it. *These vases have smooth surfaces.*
smoothly *adverb.*

smudge smudges *noun*
a dirty mark on something.

smuggle smuggles smuggling smuggled *verb*
To smuggle means to take things such as alcohol, drugs or cigarettes in to or out of a country when it is illegal.
smuggler *noun.*

A B C D E F G H I J K L M N O P Q R S T U V W X Y Z

snack snacks *noun*
a small amount of food that you eat when you are in a hurry. *We had a quick snack of cheese on toast.*

snail snails *noun*
a small creature with a hard shell on its back. Snails move along very slowly.

snake snakes *noun*
a long, thin kind of animal called a reptile. Snakes have no legs and move by sliding along the ground. *Some snakes can give a poisonous bite.*
❖ *Look at page 134*

snap snaps snapping snapped *verb*
1 When something snaps, it breaks and makes a sudden sharp sound. *The pencil snapped when I stepped on it.*
2 When a dog snaps, it tries to bite somebody or something. *The dog snapped at us when we walked by.*
3 When a person snaps, they speak in an angry way. *"Be quiet!" she snapped.*

snatch snatches snatching snatched *verb*
If you snatch something, you take it quickly and roughly. *The thief snatched her purse.*

sneak sneaks sneaking sneaked *verb*
If you sneak somewhere, you move in a quiet and secret way. *No one saw him sneak out of the room.*

sneeze sneezes sneezing sneezed *verb*
When you sneeze, you blow air out of your nose and mouth with a sudden, loud noise. *You sometimes sneeze when you have a cold.*

sniff sniffs sniffing sniffed *verb*
When you sniff, you breathe air in through your nose in a quick and noisy way. You often sniff when you are crying or when you have a cold.

snore snores snoring snored *verb*
When somebody snores, they breathe noisily when they are asleep.

snout snouts *noun*
the nose and mouth of an animal such as a pig or a badger.

snow *noun*
small, white pieces of frozen water that fall from the sky when it is very cold. **snow** *verb*, **snowy** *adjective*.

snowboarding *noun*
a sport where you move down snowy hills on a piece of wood or metal that looks like a skateboard without wheels.

snowflake snowflakes *noun*
a small piece of falling snow. Snowflakes are star-shaped ice crystals.

soak soaks soaking soaked *verb*
1 When you soak something, you put it in water and leave it for a long time.
2 If you get soaked, you get very wet. *We got soaked in the rain.*

soap *noun*
a substance that can be solid, liquid or powder that you use with water for washing. *This bar of soap smells nice.*

sob sobs sobbing sobbed *verb*
When you sob, you cry loudly.

soccer *noun*
a game of football, played by two teams of eleven players. The teams try to score goals by kicking a ball into a net at each end of a field called a pitch.

society societies *noun*
1 all the people who live in the same country or area and have the same laws and customs.
2 a kind of club for people who like the same things. *a drama society.*

sock socks *noun*
a thing that you wear on your foot inside your shoe.

socket sockets *noun*
a thing in a wall with holes where you can push in an electric plug.

sofa sofas *noun*
a long, comfortable seat for two or more people, also called a settee.

soft softer softest *adjective*
1 not hard or rough. *Cats have soft fur.*
2 not firm or stiff. *soft snow.*
3 not loud, quiet and gentle. *He has a soft voice.*
4 too kind. *The teacher is too soft, so her class is always noisy.*
softly *adverb*, **soften** *verb*
The butter is very hard beacuse it has been in the refrigerator, we should leave it out to soften.

software *noun*
the part inside a computer or on a computer disk that has the instructions that make a computer work.

soil *noun*
the brown stuff, also called earth, that plants grow in.

solar *adjective*
to do with the Sun. *the Solar System.*

sold past of **sell**
My mum sold our old car and bought a new one.

soldier soldiers *noun*
a person in an army. ▲ Say *sole-jer*.

sole soles *noun*
the bottom of your foot or your shoe.

solid solids *noun*
an object that is hard and not a liquid or a gas. *Water is a liquid, but ice is a solid.*

solid *adjective*
1 hard. *a solid rock.*
2 with no space inside. *a solid brick wall.*
■ The opposite is **hollow**.

solution **solutions** *noun*
1 an answer to a sum or a problem. *I can't find the solution to this puzzle.*
2 a liquid that has some substance completely mixed into it. *This solution is made of sugar and water.*

solve **solves solving solved** *verb*
1 If you solve a problem, you find the answer to it.
2 If you solve a mystery, you find out why it happened. *The detective was trying to solve the mystery of the stolen necklace.*

somersault **somersaults** *noun*
When you do a somersault, you roll your body in a circle so that your feet go over your head.

son **sons** *noun*
Somebody's son is a boy or man who is their child. ● A word that sounds like **son** is **sun**.

song **songs** *noun*
a short piece of music with words that you sing.

soot *noun*
black powder that comes from smoke after a fire.
sooty *adjective*.

sore *adjective*
If a part of your body is sore, it hurts. *I've got a sore throat.*

sorrow *noun*
the feeling that you have when you are very sad. *He felt great sorrow when his mother died.* ■ The opposite is **joy**.

sort **sorts sorting sorted** *verb*
If you sort things, you put them into different groups. *He sorts the blocks into plain, coloured and patterned ones.*

sort **sorts** *noun*
a kind. *What sort of animal is it? It's a lizard.*

sought past of **seek**.

sound **sounds** *noun*
something that you can hear. *I can hear the sound of somebody playing a guitar.*

soup **soups** *noun*
a hot, liquid food that you make by boiling vegetables or meat in water. *tomato soup.* ◆ *chicken soup.*

sour **sourer sourest** *adjective*
1 Something that tastes sour is not sweet. *Lemons are sour.*
2 When milk is sour, it is not fresh.

source **sources** *noun*
1 the place, person or thing that something comes from. *The library is a good source of information.*
2 the place where a river starts. *The source of the river is in the mountains.*

south *noun*
the direction that is on your right if you face the Sun as it rises in the morning.
■ The opposite is **north**.
south *adjective*, **southern** *adjective*
Peru is in South America. ◆
Bournemouth is in southern England.
south *adverb*
The Arctic tern flies south from the Arctic to the Antarctic every winter.

souvenir **souvenirs** *noun*
something that you keep to remember a place or something that happened. *My friend bought me a Dutch doll as a souvenir of Holland.*

sow **sows sowing sown** *verb*
When you sow seeds, you put them in the soil so that they will grow into plants. ▲ Rhymes with *low*.

space **spaces** *noun*
1 an empty place with nothing in it. *There is space in this cupboard for your clothes.* ◆ *Mum couldn't find a space to park the car.*
2 the place above the Earth where the Sun, stars and planets are.

spacecraft *noun*
a vehicle that travels in space.

spade **spades** *noun*
a tool with a long handle and a wide, flat blade that you use for digging.

span **spans spanning spanned** *verb*
When something like a bridge spans a river, it goes across it.

spanner **spanners** *noun*
a tool for tightening and undoing bits of metal called nuts and bolts. *I need a spanner to fix the chain on my bike.*

spare *adjective*
Something that is spare is not being used now, but you can use it when you need. *When my friend stayed, he slept in the spare room.*

spark **sparks** *noun*
a tiny piece of fire. Sparks can be made by electricity. *Sparks from the fire flew up the chimney.*

sparkle **sparkles sparkling sparkled** *verb*
When something sparkles, it shines with little flashes of light. *sparkling objects.*

A B C D E F G H I J K L M N O P Q R S T U V W X Y Z

spat past of **spit**.

speak speaks speaking spoke spoken *verb*
When you speak, you say words. *Philippa was speaking to her friend on the telephone.* ◆ *Can you speak Spanish?*

spear spears *noun*
a weapon made from a long stick with a sharp point at one end.

special *adjective*
1 If something is special, it is not ordinary but better or more important than other things. *Today is a special day because it's my birthday.*
2 Special also means for a particular person or thing, or to do a particular job. *An ambulance is a special van for taking people to hospital.*
specially *adverb*
I bought a present specially for you.

species *noun*
a group of animals or plants that are the same in some way. *different species of hedgehog.*

European hedgehog

desert hedgehog

Mindanao moonrat

moonrat

spectator spectators *noun*
a person who watches something. *There were lots of spectators at the football match.*

speech speeches *noun*
1 the ability to talk. Speech is one of the main ways of communicating.
2 a special talk that you give to a group of people.

speed *noun*
how fast something goes or happens. *The car was travelling at a speed of 60 kilometres an hour.*

speedometer speedometers *noun*
an instrument that shows how fast a vehicle is travelling.

spell spells spelling spelt or spelled *verb*
When you spell a word, you say or write the letters in the right order. *"How do you spell tiger?" "T-i-g-e-r."*
spelling *noun*.

spend spends spending spent *verb*
1 When you spend money, you use it to buy something. *I must stop spending so much money on sweets.*
2 When you spend time with somebody, you stay with them. *I spent a week with my aunt and uncle.*

sphere spheres *noun*
a solid shape like a ball. *The Earth is a sphere.*
spherical *adjective*.

spice spices *noun*
powder or seeds from a plant that you put in food to give it a stronger taste. *Cinnamon, ginger and nutmeg are spices.*
spicy *adjective*.

spider spiders *noun*
a small creature with eight legs and no wings. *Spiders spin webs to catch insects.*

a bird-eating spider

spike spikes *noun*
a piece of metal or wood with a sharp point at one end. *The fence has spikes along the top.*

spill spills spilling spilt or spilled *verb*
If you spill a liquid, you let it flow out of a container by mistake. *I spilt my drink on the carpet.*

spin spins spinning span spun *verb*
1 When something spins, it turns around and around very fast. *The ball spun through the air.*
2 To spin also means to pull cotton or wool into long, thin pieces and twist them together to make thread.

spine spines *noun*
1 Your spine is the row of bones down your back.
2 one of the sharp points that cover some animals and plants. *Hedgehogs and cactuses have spines.*
3 The spine of the book is the part of the cover between the front and the back.

spiral spirals *noun*
a shape that goes round and round in circles like a spring.

spirit spirits *noun*
1 Your spirit is the part of you that some people believe does not die when the body dies.
2 a ghost.

spit spits spitting spat *verb*
If you spit, you send food or liquid out of your mouth. *We spat out the cherry stones.*

splash splashes splashing splashed *verb*
If you splash someone or something, you make them wet with drops of water or some other liquid.

split splits splitting split *verb*
1 When something splits, it breaks open. *The bag split and all the shopping fell out.*
2 To split also means to share something. *We split the sweets between us.*

spoil spoils spoiling spoilt or spoiled *verb*
1 If somebody spoils something, they make it less good than it was before. *I spoilt my shirt when I spilt paint all over it.*
2 If somebody spoils a child, they give it everything that it wants.

spoke, spoken past of **speak**
Clive spoke very good French.

sponge
sponges
noun

a natural sponge

1 a soft thing that is full of holes. You use a sponge to wash yourself or to clean things. *Wendy washed the car with a sponge.*

2 A sponge is also a sea creature with a soft part inside that is full of holes.

3 a kind of light cake. *a chocolate sponge.*

sponsor **sponsors** *noun*
a person or a company that gives money to somebody or a group of people for doing something special such as walking for a charity. *A famous chocolate company is a sponsor for the rugby competition.*

spooky **spookier spookiest** *adjective*
Something that is spooky is frightening. *I read a spooky ghost story.*

spoon **spoons** *noun*
a metal tool that you use for eating things such as soup and cereals.
spoonful *noun*
six spoonfuls of sugar.

sport **sports** *noun*
something that you do to keep your body strong and well and to have fun. *Football, tennis, cricket and swimming are all sports.*

spot **spots** *noun*
1 a small, round mark. *Leopards have yellow fur with dark spots.*
2 a small red mark on your skin.
3 a place. *This is the spot where I fell off my horse.*
spotted *adjective*
a spotted scarf.
spotty *adjective*
a spotty face.

spout **spouts** *noun*
a part of a container such as a teapot where the liquid comes out.

sprain **sprains spraining sprained** *verb*
When you sprain something such as your ankle or your wrist, you hurt it by twisting it suddenly.

sprang past of **spring**.

spray **sprays spraying sprayed** *verb*
When you spray something, you make lots of small drops of liquid fall on it. *Jenny sprayed the flowers with water.*

spread **spreads spreading spread** *verb*
1 If you spread something such as butter, you cover something else with it. *Freddie spread syrup on the cake.*
2 When something spreads, it moves all over a place. *The rain has spread to all parts of the country.*
3 When you spread your arms, you stretch them out. *The bird spread its wings.*

spring **springs** *noun*
1 the season of the year between winter and summer. *Plants start to grow in spring.*
2 A spring is a piece of wire that is twisted around in circles. *A spring will jump back into the same shape if you press or pull it and then let it go.*

spring **springs springing sprang sprung** *verb*
To spring is to jump. *The cat sprang on to the wall.*

sprinkle **sprinkles sprinkling sprinkled** *verb*
If you sprinkle something, you throw small drops or pieces of something on to it. *Angelina sprinkled the flowers with some water.*

sprung past of **spring**.

spun past of **spin**.

spy **spies** *noun*
a person who tries to find out secret information about another person or a country.

square **squares** *noun*
a flat shape with four straight sides that are the same length.
square *adjective*
a square table.

squash **squashes squashing squashed** *verb*
If you squash something, you press it hard and make it flat. *He sat on my hat and squashed it.*

squeak **squeaks squeaking squeaked** *verb*
To squeak is to make the small, high sound that a mouse makes. *The door squeaks when you open it.*

squeeze **squeezes squeezing squeezed** *verb*
If you squeeze something, you press it hard on the sides. *I squeezed the water out of the sponge.*

squirrel **squirrels** *noun*
a small, grey or red animal with a big, thick tail. *Squirrels can climb well and live in trees.*

squirt **squirts squirting squirted** *verb*
When something squirts, liquid comes out very fast. *I opened the bottle and lemonade squirted everywhere.*

A
B
C
D
E
F
G
H
I
J
K
L
M
N
O
P
Q
R
S
T
U
V
W
X
Y
Z

stab stabs stabbing stabbed *verb*
To stab is to stick a knife or weapon into somebody or something.

stable stables *noun*
a building where horses are kept.

stadium stadiums or stadia *noun*
a large area for sports such as football or athletics. There are usually seats around the edge so that people can watch the games. *an ancient stadium.*

stage stages *noun*
1 A stage is the part of the theatre where the actors perform.
2 If you do something in stages, you do it in parts. *It will take a long time to build the treehouse, so we'll have to do it in stages.*

stain stains *noun*
a dirty mark on something that is very difficult to get rid of. *Jo's football shorts were covered in grass stains.*

stair stairs *noun*
one of a set of steps for going up or down inside a building.

staircase staircases *noun*
a set of stairs inside a building.

stale staler stalest *adjective*
not fresh. *Sheri threw away the last piece of cake because it was stale.*

stalk stalks *noun*
the stem or long, thin part of a plant that flowers, leaves and fruit grow on.

stall stalls *noun*
1 A stall is a kind of open shop where things for sale are put on a big table. *a fruit and vegetable stall.*
2 A stall is also a place in a shed for one cow or in a stable for one horse.

stamp stamps *noun*
a small piece of paper with a picture and a price on it. *You have to stick a stamp on a letter before you post it.*

stamp stamps stamping stamped *verb*
1 If you stamp your foot, you put it down hard on the floor. *My sister stamps her foot when she is angry.*
2 If you stamp a passport, you make a mark on it with a special tool to show that you have come into a country or a place. Some stamps show that you have paid for something or that you have returned it.

stand stands standing stood *verb*
When you stand somewhere, you are on your feet.

standard standards *noun*
1 a measure of how good or bad something is. *Your drawing is of a very high standard.*
2 a flag.

stank past of **stink**.

star stars *noun*
1 a small, bright light that you can see in the sky on a clear night.
2 a shape with five or six points.
3 a famous person who sings, acts or plays a sport. *a film star.*

stare stares staring stared *verb*
If you stare at somebody or something, you look at them for a long time. *Freddie and James stared at each other.*

start starts starting started *verb*
1 When something starts, it begins. *What time does the film start?* ■ The opposite is **end** or **finish**.

2 When you start something like a car, you make it move.

start *noun*
the beginning. *the start of the play.*

startle startles startling startled *verb*
If somebody or something startles you, they surprise you in a frightening way. *You startled me when you jumped out from behind the curtain.*

starve starves starving starved *verb*
If a person or an animal starves, they become ill and can die because they do not have enough to eat. *Many birds starve during the winter months.* **starvation** *noun.*

state states *noun*
1 a country and its government. *Many schools are run by the state.*
2 a part of a country. *California is one of the states of the United States of America.*
3 A state is also how somebody or something looks or is. *Your clothes are in a terrible state!*

station stations *noun*
1 a place where trains and buses stop and pick up passengers. *a railway station.*
2 a building that is used for something special. *a police station.*

statue statues *noun*
a sculpture or model of a person or an animal that is made of stone or metal. *There is a statue of Horatio Nelson in Trafalgar Square in London.*

stay stays staying stayed *verb*
1 If you stay somewhere, you do not move from that place. *I told the puppy to stay in the garden.*
2 If you stay with somebody, you live in their house for a short time. *I'm staying with my friend Janet tonight.*

steady steadier steadiest *adjective*
Somebody or something that is steady is not moving about or shaking. *Hold the ladder steady while I climb it.* ■ The opposite is **unsteady**.

steal steals stealing stole stolen *verb*
To steal is to take something that does not belong to you and keep it. *Somebody stole my purse.*

a b c d e f g h i j k l m n o p q r s t u v w x y z

steam *noun*
Steam is the gas that water turns into when it boils. *Steam was coming out of the kettle.*

steel *noun*
a strong metal that is used for making such things as knives, tools and machines.

steep steeper steepest *adjective*
If something such as a hill is steep, it goes up or down sharply. *This hill is too steep to climb up.*

steer steers steering steered *verb*
When you steer a car, you turn the wheel so that it goes in the direction you want.

stem stems *noun*
the long, thin part of a plant that grows above the ground.

step steps *noun*
1 what you do when you lift your foot and put it down in a different place. *Try to follow these dance steps.*
2 the flat part of stairs where you put your foot for going up or down.

step steps stepping stepped *verb*
To step is to lift your foot and put it down in another place as you walk. *You stepped on my foot!*

stereo *noun*
music or sound that comes from two different loudspeakers at the same time. *Music sounds much better in stereo.*

stick sticks *noun*
a long, thin piece of wood. *The old man walked with a stick.*

stick sticks sticking stuck *verb*
1 When you stick two things together, you join them with glue. *Camilla stuck a picture in her book.*
2 If something sticks, it cannot be moved. *The car is stuck in the mud.*
3 When you stick a pointed thing into something else, you push it in. *If you stick a pin into a balloon it will burst.*
sticky *adjective*
Her fingers are sticky with jam!

sticker stickers *noun*
a small piece of paper with a picture or words on it that you can fix on to something. *My bag is covered in stickers.*

stiff stiffer stiffest *adjective*
1 If something is stiff, it does not bend easily. *a stiff piece of cardboard.*
2 not moving easily. *a stiff neck.*

still *adjective, adverb*
1 not moving. *Please stand still while I take your photo.*
2 going on and on. *It's still raining.*

sting stings stinging stung *verb*
If an insect or a plant stings you, a small sharp point goes into your skin and hurts you. *Bees, wasps and nettles can sting you.*
sting *noun.*

stink stinks stinking stank or stunk *verb*
If something stinks, it smells very bad. *That fish stinks!*

stir stirs stirring stirred *verb*
When you stir a liquid, you move a spoon around to mix it. *Rose stirred the soup.*

stitch stitches *noun*
a loop that you make when you put a needle and thread through a piece of material and bring it out again a little farther along.

stock stocks *noun*
all the things that a shop keeps ready to sell. *This shop has a large stock of children's shoes.*

stocking stockings *noun*
a piece of clothing like a long, thin sock that women and girls wear over their legs and feet.

stole, stolen past of **steal**.

stomach stomachs *noun*
Your stomach is the place in the middle of your body where food goes after you have eaten it.

stone stones *noun*
1 a small piece of rock.
2 a large mass of rock that is used for building. *a stone wall.*
3 A stone is also the hard, round seed in the middle of some fruits. Cherries, plums and peaches have stones.

stood past of **stand**.

stool stools *noun*
a kind of chair without a back or arms.

stop stops stopping stopped *verb*
1 If you stop what you are doing, you do not do it any more. *Stop talking and listen for a moment.*
2 When something that was moving stops, it stands still. *The bus stopped.*
3 If you stop somebody from doing something, you do not allow them to do it. *I tried to stop the dog from sitting on the sofa.*
4 When a machine stops, it does not work any more. *My watch has stopped.*

store stores *noun*
1 a large shop that sells lots of different kinds of things.
2 a number of things that you are keeping to use later. *We had a good store of food in the tent.*

store stores storing stored *verb*
If you store something somewhere, you put it there so that you can use it later. *The tins of food were stored in the cupboard.*

storey storeys *noun*
all the rooms on one floor of a building. *This office block has ten storeys.*

stork storks *noun*
a big, white bird with long legs and a large beak. *Storks live near water.*

storm storms *noun*
very bad weather with strong winds and a lot of rain or snow. *Many storms also have thunder and lightning.*
stormy *adjective.*

story stories *noun*
A story tells you about things that have happened. Some stories are about real things and others are made up. *I read a story about a boy who made friends with a ghost.*

stout stouter stoutest *adjective*
rather fat. *a stout woman.*

A
B
C
D
E
F
G
H
I
J
K
L
M
N
O
P
Q
R
S
T
U
V
W
X
Y
Z

stove stoves *noun*
something you can use for heating a room or for cooking. *a gas stove.*

straight **straighter straightest** *adjective*
If something is straight, it does not bend, curl or turn to the side. *You can use a ruler to draw a straight line.* ◆ *Ben's hair is curly, but mine is straight.*

strain **strains straining strained** *verb*
1 If you strain a part of your body, you hurt it by stretching a muscle too much.
2 If you strain food, you put it through a tool called a sieve to separate the solid part from the liquid. *James strained the tomatoes.*

strand strands *noun*
a long, thin piece of something. *strands of long, yellow hair.*

strange **stranger strangest** *adjective*
1 odd or unusual. *I read a story about a strange animal that could talk.*
2 not known or seen before. *a strange house.* ■ The opposite is **familiar.**

stranger strangers *noun*
a person that you do not know. *a complete stranger waved at me.*

strap straps *noun*
a long, thin piece of material that you use for fastening things, carrying things or for holding things. *How many kinds of straps can you see?*

straw straws *noun*
1 the dried stems of plants like wheat. Straw is used for animals such as horses and pet rabbits to lie on. You can make hats out of straw.
2 a long, thin tube made of paper or plastic for drinking through.

strawberry **strawberries** *noun*
a small, soft, red fruit that grows near the ground. ❖ *Look at page 69*

streak streaks *noun*
a long, thin line of something. *There are streaks of paint on the floor.*

stream streams *noun*
1 a small, narrow river.
2 a long line of things going in one direction. *a stream of traffic.*

street streets *noun*
a road in a town or village, with houses and other buildings along each side.

strength *noun*
how strong somebody or something is. *Do you have the strength to move the table?*

stress *noun*
too much worry or work. *Stress has caused his headaches.*

stretch **stretches stretching stretched** *verb*
1 If you stretch something, you make it longer or wider by pulling it. *Jordan's jumper is being stretched.*
2 If you stretch your body, you push your arms and legs out and make yourself as tall as you can.

strict **stricter strictest** *adjective*
A strict person expects people to do what they say and to obey rules.
strictly *adverb.*

stride **strides striding strode** *verb*
to walk or run with long steps. *He strode out of the room in a bad temper.*

strike **strikes striking struck** *verb*
1 If you strike somebody or something, you hit them. *The ball struck me on the back of the head.*
2 When lightning strikes, it hits and goes through somebody or something. *The tree was struck by lightning.*
3 When a clock strikes, it rings a bell to show the time. *The clock struck ten.*
4 When you strike a match, you rub it on something rough to make a flame.
5 When people strike, they stop work because they want more money or because they want to protest about something.

strike strikes *noun*
a time when people stop work because they want more money or because they want to protest about something.

string *noun*
1 very thin rope. You use string to tie up things such as parcels.
2 Musical instruments such as guitars and violins have thin wires called strings that you touch to make sounds.

strip strips *noun*
a long, thin piece of something such as paper or material.

stripe stripes *noun*
a coloured line on something. *My football shirt has red and white stripes.*
striped *adjective*
a striped dress.

stroke **strokes stroking stroked** *verb*
When you stroke an animal such as a cat, you move your hand gently over its body.
stroke *noun.*

strong **stronger strongest** *adjective*
1 If you are strong, you have a lot of power in your muscles. *Are you strong enough to lift these heavy bags?*
2 not easy to break. *These toys are made of strong plastic.*
3 If a taste or a smell is strong, you can notice it easily. *This cheese has a very strong smell.*

struck past of **strike**.

struggle struggles struggling
struggled *verb*
1 To struggle means to fight to get away
from somebody or something. *The
thief struggled with the policeman.*
2 If you struggle to do something that is
difficult, you try hard to do it. *Connie
and Joe had to struggle to get into the
same pair of trousers!*

stubborn *adjective*
A stubborn person does not change their
mind easily and does not like doing what
other people tell them to do.

stuck past of **stick**.

student students *noun*
a person who is learning something at a
university or a college.

studio studios *noun*
1 a room where an artist or a
photographer works.
2 a place where films, television or radio
programmes, or records are made.

study studies studying studied
verb
1 If you study something, you spend
time learning about it. *I am studying
history at school.*
2 To study something is to look at it very
carefully. *David was studying the stars
through his telescope.*
studious *adjective*
somebody who is studious spends a lot
of time studying. *a studious girl.*

stuff *noun*
a word we use for something when we
do not know what else to call it. *What's
this stuff on the floor?* ◆ *Please tidy up
all the stuff in your room.*

stumble stumbles stumbling
stumbled *verb*
If you stumble over something, you
nearly fall over it. *I stumbled over a pair
of shoes on the floor.*

stung past of **sting**.

stunk past of **stink**.

stupid stupider stupidest *adjective*
silly, not clever, bright or sensible. *Don't
ask stupid questions.*
stupidity *noun.*

style styles *noun*
the way something is done or made, or
how it looks. *a new style of shoe.*

subject subjects *noun*
1 something you learn about. *My best
subjects at school are English and
history.*
2 what something such as a story is all
about. *Animals are the subject of this
book.*
3 the subject of a sentence is the person
or thing that does the action. *In the
sentence, "Katie climbed a tree",
"Katie" is the subject.*

submarine submarines *noun*
a boat that can travel under water.

substance substances *noun*
something that you can see, touch or
use for making things. *This vegetable
contains a very sticky substance.*

subtract subtracts subtracting
subtracted *verb*
To subtract is to take one number away
from another number. *If you subtract
four from six, you are left with two.*
■ The opposite is **add**.
subtraction *noun*
Subtraction is harder than addition.

subway subways *noun*
a path that goes under a busy road so
that you can get to the other side safely.

succeed succeeds succeeding
succeeded *verb*
If you succeed, you do or get the thing
that you wanted. *Ben succeeded in
passing the swimming test.*

success successes *noun*
doing something well or getting what
you wanted. *We wish you success in the
race.* ◆ *The party was a great success.*
successful *adjective*, **successfully**
adverb.

suck sucks sucking sucked *verb*
1 When you suck, you pull liquid into
your mouth from something. *The
baby is sucking milk from a bottle.*
2 When you suck a sweet, you keep it in
your mouth and lick it without
chewing it.

sudden *adjective*
happening quickly when you are not
expecting it. *We ran inside to get out of
the sudden rain.*
suddenly *adverb.*

suffer suffers suffering suffered
verb
If you suffer, you feel pain because you
are ill or because you are unhappy. *Tom
suffers a lot from colds.*

suffocate suffocates suffocating
suffocated *verb*
If a person or an animal suffocates, they
die because they have no air to breathe.

sugar *noun*
something that you put in food and
drinks to make them sweet. Sugar
comes from sugar cane or sugar beet.

suggest suggests suggesting
suggested *verb*
If you suggest something to somebody,
you tell them about an idea that you
have for doing something. *Sophie
suggested that we go to the beach.*
suggestion *noun.*

A
B
C
D
E
F
G
H
I
J
K
L
M
N
O
P
Q
R
S
T
U
V
W
X
Y
Z

suicide *noun*
Suicide means killing yourself on purpose.

suit suits *noun*
a set of clothes made out of the same material and that you wear together. A suit can be a jacket and trousers, or a jacket and a skirt.

suit suits suited *verb*
1 If clothes suit you, they look good on you. *Does this dress suit me?*
2 If something suits you, it is right for what you want or need. *This bedroom would suit me.*

suitable *adjective*
right for somebody or something. *This coat is suitable for rainy weather.*

suitcase suitcases *noun*
a large bag or box with a handle that you carry your clothes in when you travel.

sulk sulks sulking sulked *verb*
If you sulk, you refuse to talk to anybody because you are angry about something. *Joe is sulking because he's not allowed to watch any more TV.*

sum sums *noun*
a problem in arithmetic. *Three plus two is an easy sum.* ● A word that sounds like **sum** is **some**.

summer *noun*
the season of the year between spring and autumn. *Summer is the hottest part of the year.*

summit summits *noun*
the top of a mountain.

summon summons summoning summoned *verb*
If you summon somebody, you call them and tell them to come. *We were summoned to the headmaster's office.*

sun suns *noun*
the bright star that you can see in the sky during the day. The Sun gives us light and heat. ● A word that sounds like **sun** is **son**.

sunbathe sunbathes sunbathing sunbathed *verb*
To sunbathe is to sit in the Sun and let it make your skin go darker.

sung past of **sing**.

sunglasses *noun*
special dark glasses that you wear to protect your eyes from the bright light of the Sun.

sunk past of **sink**.

sunny sunnier sunniest *adjective*
with the Sun shining brightly. *It's a sunny day – let's have a picnic!*

sunrise *noun*
the time when the Sun comes up (rises) in the morning.

sunset *noun*
the time when the Sun goes down (sets) at night.

sunshine *noun*
the light and heat from the Sun.

super *adjective*
very good and great fun. *a super party.*

superb *adjective*
wonderful. *We had a superb holiday in America last year.*

superior *adjective*
better than somebody or something else. *Suzanne's drawing is superior to mine.*

supermarket supermarkets *noun*
a big shop where you can buy food and lots of other things. You take what you want as you go round and pay for everything on your way out.

supersonic *adjective*
If an aircraft, rocket or bullet is supersonic, it goes faster than the speed of sound. *Concorde is a supersonic aeroplane.*

superstitious *adjective*
A superstitious person believes they will have bad luck if they do or do not do certain things. *Superstitious people think it is bad luck to walk under ladders.*
superstition *noun*.

supervise supervises supervising supervised *verb*
If you supervise somebody or something, you watch them to make sure they are doing things in the right way.
supervision *noun*.

supper suppers *noun*
a meal that people eat in the evening.

supply supplies *noun*
an amount of something that you need. *We took a large supply of food on the camping trip.*

support supports supporting supported *verb*
1 To support is to hold somebody or something up. *Joe supported Connie when she twisted her ankle.*
2 If you support a club, a team or some other group, you try to help and encourage them. *Which team do you support?*
support *noun* **supporter** *noun*.

suppose supposes supposing supposed *verb*
If you suppose that something is true, you think that it is probably true. *I suppose you are right.*

sure surer surest *adjective*
1 If you are sure about something, you know it is true. *I'm sure I packed my raincoat.*

2 If you are sure that something will happen, you know it will. *I'm sure it will snow tomorrow.*

surf *noun*
the foam or white part on top of the waves on the sea.

surf surfs surfing surfed *verb*
To surf is to ride on top of the waves by standing on a long piece of wood or plastic called a surfboard.

surface surfaces *noun*
the outside part of something.

surgeon surgeons *noun*
a doctor whose job is to do operations on people in a hospital.

surgery *noun*
1 a place where you go to see a doctor or a dentist. *a dental surgery.*
2 cutting somebody's body to take out or mend a part inside. *heart surgery.*

surname surnames *noun*
your last name that shows which family you belong to. *My first name is Ben and my surname is Smith.*

surprise surprises surprising surprised *verb*
If you surprise somebody, you do something that they do not expect. *You surprised me when you came home early.*
surprise *noun*
Don't tell Chris about the party - it's a surprise!
surprising *adjective.*

surrender surrenders surrendering surrendered *verb*
When an army surrenders, it stops fighting and gives in to the enemy.
surrender *noun.*

surround surrounds surrounding surrounded *verb*
To surround means to be or go all around something. *An island is surrounded by water.* ◆ *The police surrounded the office building.*

survive survives surviving survived *verb*
To stay alive after something very bad or dangerous has happened. *Our cat was lucky to survive after being hit by a car.*

suspect suspects suspecting suspected *verb*
If you suspect somebody of doing something wrong, you think they did it. *The police suspected her of stealing the money and gold.*
suspect *noun.*

suspense *noun*
a feeling of fear or excitement that you have when you do not know what is going to happen. *We waited with suspense for the results of the competition.*

suspicious *adjective*
If you are suspicious, you think that something is wrong, or you do not believe somebody. *I was suspicious when he said he had lost my money.*

swallow swallows swallowing swallowed *verb*
When you swallow food or drink, it goes down your throat.

swam past of **swim**.

swamp swamps *noun*
a marsh or an area of wet ground. There are many swamps in the southeast of the United States.

swan swans *noun*
a big, white bird with a long neck that lives on water. Young swans are grey and are called cygnets. *We saw swans swimming on the lakes in Cumbria.*

swap swaps swapping swapped *verb*
To swap means to change something for something else. *Can I swap my book for your camera?*
swap *noun.*

sway sways swaying swayed *verb*
When somebody or something sways, they move slowly from side to side for some time. *The daffodils were swaying on their long stems in the wind.*

swear swears swearing swore sworn *verb*
1 If somebody swears, they say bad or rude words.
2 If you swear, you promise something in a very serious way. *I swear I didn't break the window.*

sweat sweats sweating sweated *verb*
When you sweat, you lose liquid from your body through your skin. *Everybody was sweating because it was so hot.*
sweat *noun.*

sweep sweeps sweeping swept *verb*
When you sweep something, you clean it with a brush. *Would you please sweep the kitchen floor?*

sweet sweeter sweetest *adjective*
1 Sweet foods and drinks have a taste like sugar. *Honey is sweet.*
2 A sweet person is gentle and kind. *It was very sweet of you to help me.*

sweet *noun*
1 a small piece of sweet food made with sugar or chocolate. *a packet of sweets.*
2 a pudding or sweet food that you eat at the end of a meal. *You can have ice-cream or fruit for sweet.*

swell swells swelling swelled swollen *verb*
When something swells, it gets bigger and thicker. *My ankle swelled up when I twisted it.* ◆ *The insect bite made her fingers swell up.*
swelling *noun.*

swept past of **sweep**
Gerry swept the snow from the path.

swerve swerves swerving swerved *verb*
When something that is moving swerves, it goes quickly to one side. *The cyclist swerved to avoid the car.*

A B C D E F G H I J K L M N O P Q R S T U V W X Y Z

swim swims swimming swam **swum** *verb*
When you swim, you use your arms and legs to move along in water. *We are going swimming in the sea.* ◆ *We watched the fish swimming in the pond.* **swim** *noun*.

swimming pool swimming pools *noun*
a large indoor or outdoor water-filled tank for swimming and diving in.

swing swings swinging swung *verb*
When something swings, it moves backwards and forwards through the air. *The soldiers were swinging their arms as they marched.*

swing swings *noun*
a seat for swinging that hangs from two strong ropes or chains. People sit in swings and move backwards and forwards.

switch switches *noun*
a thing that you press or turn to stop or start something working. *You press this switch to turn the computer on.*

switch switches switching switched *verb*
1 To switch is to change one thing for another thing. *My friend and I switched places.*
2 When you switch something on, you press a switch to make it work. *Can I switch the TV on?*
3 When you switch something off, you press a switch to make it stop working. *How do you switch the computer off?*

swivel swivels swivelling swivelled *verb*
To swivels is to twist or turn around on the same spot.

swollen past of **swell**.

swoop swoops swooping swooped *verb*
to rush or fly downwards suddenly. *The bird swooped down to catch the worm.*

sword swords *noun*
a weapon with a handle and a long metal blade with a sharp point at the end. Soldiers used to fight with swords.
▲ Say *sord*.

Spelling tip:
....
Some words that start with the sound "s" as in "simple", are spelt with a "c" such as certain, city, cycle

swore, sworn past of **swear**.

swum past of **swim**.

swung past of **swing**.

syllable syllables *noun*
a word or part of a word that has one sound. The word "but" has one syllable, the word "butter" has two syllables and the word "America" has four syllables.

symbol symbols *noun*
1 a sign or mark that means something. The symbol + means add in maths.
2 A symbol is also a thing that stands for something else. *A dove is a symbol of peace.*

Do you know what these symbols mean? Look at page 190 for the answers.

symmetrical *adjective*
If a shape is symmetrical, both sides are the same. If you draw a line through the middle of a circle, you will see that both sides are symmetrical.
symmetry *noun*.

All these shapes are symmetrical

sympathy *noun*
If you feel or show sympathy to somebody, you are very kind to them because they are hurt or sad.
sympathetic *adjective*, **sympathize** *verb*.
Richard's friends were very sympathetic when he broke his arm.

symphony symphonies *noun*
a long piece of music written for a large orchestra.
symphonic *adjective*.

symptom symptoms *noun*
something that is wrong with you and shows that you are ill. *A sore throat and a temperature are symptoms of a cold.*

synagogue synagogues *noun*
a building where Jewish people go to pray. ▲ Say *sin-a-gog*.

synonym synonyms *noun*
a word that means nearly the same as another word. Little and small are synonyms. A word that means opposite is an **antonym** - big and small, for example.

synthetic *adjective*
created artificially using chemicals. Nylon is a synthetic fabric.
▲ Say *sin-thet-ik*.

syringe syringes *noun*
a special needle that doctors can push into your skin when they give you an injection of medicine or when they take blood out of your body.

syrup *noun*
a sweet, sticky food made from the juice of fruit boiled with sugar.

system systems *noun*
1 an organized way of doing something. *We have changed the system for taking books from the library.*
2 a group of machines or other things that work together.

T t

table tables *noun*
1 a piece of furniture with a flat top that you can put things on.
2 a set of numbers or words arranged in columns.
3 a list of all the multiplications of all the numbers between 1 and 12.

Telephone numbers:
1	Heather	370 1037
2	Jill	104 0075
3	John	321 0076
4	Freddie	254 3084
5	Flora	828 1928
6	Sue	262 0208
7	Ray	704 4146
8	Carol	263 8043
9	Judy	883 0040
10	Kay	104 7767

Conversion table
Litres		Gallons
4.546	1	0.222
9.092	2	0.440
13.638	3	0.660
18.184	4	0.880
22.730	5	1.100
27.277	6	1.320
31.823	7	1.540
36.369	8	1.760
40.915	9	1.980
45.460	10	2.220

1 x 9 =	9
2 x 9 =	18
3 x 9 =	27
4 x 9 =	36
5 x 9 =	45
6 x 9 =	54
7 x 9 =	63
8 x 9 =	72
9 x 9 =	81
10 x 9 =	90
11 x 9 =	99
12 x 9 =	108

tablet tablets *noun*
a small, round piece of medicine that you swallow.

table tennis *noun*
a game for two or four people who stand at each end of a table with a net across the middle and hit a very small ball to each other, bouncing it off the table, with small bats.

tackle tackles tackling tackled *verb*
1 When you tackle something, you do whatever is needed, even if it is difficult.
2 If you tackle somebody when playing a game such as rugby, you try to get the ball away from them.

tactful *adjective*
careful not to say anything that would hurt somebody's feelings.
tactfully *adverb*.

tadpole tadpoles *noun*
a tiny animal that lives in water and that will grow into a frog or toad. Tadpoles have tails.

tail tails *noun*
the part at the back end of an animal, bird or fish. *The dog wagged its tail.* ◆ *Aeroplanes have tails.* ● A word that sounds like **tail** is **tale**.

tailor tailors *noun*
a person who makes suits, jackets and coats.

take takes taking took taken *verb*
1 If you take something, you get hold of it or carry it. *Can you take these books to the library?*
2 If somebody takes you, they drive you or you go with them. *Dan took me to school on his way to work.*
3 If you take something, you remove it. *She took her purse out of her bag.* ◆ *Have you taken my bag?*
take off When a plane takes off, it leaves the runway and moves into the air. ■ The opposite is **land**.

tale tales *noun*
a story. *a tale of love and adventure.*
● A word that sounds like **tale** is **tail**.

talent talents *noun*
If you have a talent for something you have a natural ability for it and can do it well. *Clive's got a real talent for acting.*
talented *adjective*.

talk talks talking talked *verb*
When you talk, you say words. *We talked on the phone for hours.* ▲ Say **tawk**.

tall taller tallest *adjective*
1 higher than usual. *She's very tall.* ◆ *a tall building.* ■ The opposite is **short**.
2 having a certain height. *He's just over a metre tall.*

tambourine tambourines *noun*
a small, round musical instrument that you shake or tap with your fingers. ▲ Say *tam-ber-een*.

tame tamer tamest *adjective*
A tame animal or bird has become used to living with people and is not afraid of them. ■ The opposite is **wild**.

tan *noun*
If you have a tan, your skin is a darker colour than usual because you have been in the Sun.

tandem tandems *noun*
a special bicycle for two people.

tangled *adjective*
twisted together in knots or muddled up together untidily. *The wool is a tangled mess.*

tank tanks *noun*
1 a big container that holds liquid or gas.
2 a big, heavy vehicle with a gun in it that is used in a war.

tanker tankers *noun*
1 a very big, long ship that carries oil.
2 a big lorry that carries petrol or some other liquid.

tap taps *noun*
a thing that you turn on to make water or gas flow out of a pipe and turn off to stop it flowing.

tap taps tapping tapped *verb*
If you tap somebody or something, you hit them gently. *He tapped a few keys and information came up on the screen.*

tape tapes *noun*
1 a long, narrow piece of material. *a piece of sticky tape.*
2 a long strip of plastic that you can record sounds or pictures on and then play back on a tape-recorder or by using a video and television.
tape *verb*.

tape-recorder tape-recorders *noun*
a machine that you use to play a tape or to record sounds on to a tape.

tapestry tapestries *noun*
a piece of material that has a picture on it made from coloured threads.

A
B
C
D
E
F
G
H
I
J
K
L
M
N
O
P
Q
R
S
T
U
V
W
X
Y
Z

tar *noun*
a thick, black, sticky substance that is used mainly for making roads.

target **targets** *noun*
an object that people aim at or try to hit when they are shooting.

tart **tarts** *noun*
a piece of pastry with jam or fruit on it.

task **tasks** *noun*
a job that must be done.

taste **tastes tasting tasted** *verb*
1 When you taste something, you try a bit of it to see if you like the flavour. *Taste this fish and tell me if you like the sauce.*
2 If something tastes nice or nasty, you think the flavour is nice or nasty. *I like that ice-cream, it tastes lovely.* ◆ *This milk tastes a bit funny.*

taste **tastes** *noun*
1 the ability to recognize the flavour of something by touching it with your tongue. *Sugar has a sweet taste.*
2 the way something tastes. *This bread has no taste at all.*

tattoo **tattoos** *noun*
a permanent pattern on a person's skin made by putting coloured dyes under the skin using a needle.

taught past of **teach**
▲ Say *tort.*

tax **taxes** *noun*
money that people have to pay to the government so that it can pay for running the country. *income tax.*

taxi **taxis** *noun*
a car that will take you where you want to go if you pay the driver.

tea *noun*
a drink that you make by pouring boiling water on to the dried leaves of the tea plant.

teach **teaches teaching taught** *verb*
1 When somebody teaches you, they tell you about a subject and help you learn about it. *Mrs Jones teaches History.*
2 To teach also means to show somebody how to do something. *I'm trying to teach my sister how to ride a bicycle.*
teacher *noun.*

team **teams** *noun*
a group of people who work together or play a sport together. *the football team.*

teapot **teapots** *noun*
a container for making tea in with a spout for pouring it out.

tear **tears** *noun*
one of the drops of liquid that comes from your eyes when you cry. ▲ Rhymes with **here.** ● A word that sounds like **tear** is **tier.**

tear **tears tearing tore torn** *verb*
When you tear something, you pull one part away from the rest. *If you tear paper in a special way, you can make different shapes and patterns.*
▲ Rhymes with **chair.**

tease **teases teasing teased** *verb*
When you tease somebody, you laugh at them or make jokes about them.
▲ Say *teez.*

technology **technologies** *noun*
machines or systems that have been invented because of discoveries by scientists. ▲ Say *tek-nol-o-jee.*

teenage *adjective*
between 13 and 19 years old.
teenager *noun.*

teeth plural of **tooth.**

telephone
telephones *noun*
an instrument that you use to speak to another person who is not in the same place as you. ▲ Say *tel-e-fone.*

telescope **telescopes** *noun*
an instrument in the shape of a tube with a lens at each end that makes things that are far away look clearer and closer when you look through it.

television **televisions** *noun*
an instrument in the shape of a box that receives programmes that are broadcast and shows them in sound and pictures.

tell **tells telling told** *verb*
1 If you tell somebody something, you give them information in words about it. *I told him how to mend a puncture.* ◆ *She told me a very funny joke.*
2 If you tell somebody to do something, you say that they must do it.

temper *noun*
1 If you have a bad temper you get cross or angry easily. *Bill is always in a bad temper when he loses.*
2 If you lose your temper, you get very angry.

temperature *noun*
1 how hot or cold something is. *Water boils at a temperature of 100 degrees.*
2 If you have a temperature, your body is hotter than it should be.
▲ Say *temp-re-cher.*

temple temples *noun*
a building where people go to pray. *The Golden Temple is a famous in India.*

temporary *adjective*
lasting for a short time. *He's got a temporary job.* ■ The opposite is **permanent**.
temporarily *adverb*.

tempt tempts tempting tempted *verb*
If something tempts you, you really want it even if you know you should not have it. *I was really tempted by those shoes but they were too expensive.*
temptation *noun*.

tend tends tending tended *verb*
If something tends to happen, it usually happens or happens often. *I tend to miss the bus if I leave after 8 o'clock.* ◆ *He tends to get angry when he is tired or unhappy.*

tender tenderer tenderest *adjective*
1 easy to chew. *This is very tender meat.* ■ The opposite is **tough**.
2 a bit sore. *My ankle is still tender from when I fell over.*
3 gentle and loving. *He gave her a tender look.*
tenderly *adverb*
She spoke tenderly to the little girl.
tenderness *noun*.

tennis *noun*
a game for two or four players. The players hit a soft ball with rackets backwards and forwards to each other over a net that is stretched across the middle of an area called a court.

tense tenser tensest *adjective*
1 nervous and anxious about something. *I always get tense when I have to go to the dentist.*
2 If your muscles are tense, they are stiff and tight. *After running the marathon my legs were very stiff and tense.*
■ The opposite is **relaxed**.
tensely *adverb*
He waited tensely for the results of his medical tests.

tent tents *noun*
a shelter made of strong cloth that is held up by poles and ropes.

tepid *adjective*
slightly warm. *Babies have tepid baths so that they do not burn themselves.*

term terms *noun*
1 one of the periods of a school or university year when students are being taught.
2 a word or phrase. *"adagio" and "forte" are musical terms.*

terminal terminals *noun*
a building at an airport where passengers leave and arrive.

terrible *adjective*
very bad or unpleasant. *What a terrible noise.*
terribly *adverb*.

terrific *adjective*
very good indeed. *The video is terrific - I've seen it five times.*

terrify terrifies terrifying terrified *verb*
If you terrify somebody, you make them feel very frightened. *The explosion terrified the horses.* ◆ *Many dogs are terrified of thunder.*

territory territories *noun*
1 land that belongs to or is controlled by a country, army or ruler.
2 an area where an animal lives that it will fight for if another animal tries to come and live there.

terror *noun*
very great fear. *He screamed with terror when he thought he'd seen a ghost.*

test tests *noun*
1 a way of finding out what you know about something by asking you a set of questions or getting you to show what you can do. *a driving test.* ◆ *a spelling test.*
2 a check to see if part of your body is working properly. *an eye test.*

test tests testing tested *verb*
1 When you test something, you use or examine it to see if it works well. *I'm testing the brakes to make sure they're working properly.*
2 When you test somebody, you try to find out how much they know by using a test.

text texts *noun*
written words. *Books for very young children have lots of pictures and not much text.*

texture textures *noun*
the way that something feels. *This wool has a smooth texture almost like silk.*

thank thanks thanking thanked *verb*
When you thank somebody, you tell them how nice it was of them to do something for you or give you something. *Thank you very much for taking us all to the theme park.*

thaw thaws thawing thawed *verb*
When something frozen thaws, it becomes warm enough to melt. *The Sun's out and the snow has started to thaw.*

an eye test

theatre theatres *noun*
a building where people go to see plays. ▲ Say *thee-a-ter.*

theft thefts *noun*
the crime of stealing. *He was sent to jail for the crime of theft.*

theme park theme parks *noun*
a place you go to have fun where all the games and activities are to do with the same subject, for example, space.

A B C D E F G H I J K L M N O P Q R S T U V W X Y Z

thermometer thermometers *noun*
an instrument that shows how hot or cold it is.

thick thicker thickest *adjective*
1 Something that is thick measures a lot from one side to the other or from top to bottom. *The castle wall was a metre thick.* ■ The opposite is **thin**.
2 A thick liquid does not flow easily. *Honey is thick.* ■ The opposite is **thin**.
3 Something that is thick is not easy to get through or to see through. *The airport was closing because of thick fog.* ◆ *a thick forest.*
thicken *verb*
The fog thickened.
thickly *adverb*.

thief thieves *noun*
a person who steals something. *Thieves broke into the shop and stole all the silver and jewellery.* ▲ Say **theef**.

thigh thighs *noun*
Your thigh is the part of your leg above your knee. *Your thighs are the fattest part of your legs.* ▲ Rhymes with **by**.

thin thinner thinnest *adjective*
1 narrow from side to side or from top to bottom. *a thin slice of cake.* ◆ *There was a thin layer of ice on the pond.* ■ The opposite is **thick**.
2 A thin person does not have much flesh covering their bones and weighs less than most people. ■ The opposite is **fat**.
3 A thin liquid flows easily. *This soup is too thin.* ■ The opposite is **thick**.
thinly *adverb*.

think thinks thinking thought *verb*
1 When you think, you have ideas or words in your mind. *What are you thinking about?*
2 When you think something is true, you believe it. *I think Mike's plans for the party are super.*

thirsty thirstier thirstiest *adjective*
If you are thirsty, you need something to drink. *Exercise can make you thirsty.*

thistle thistles *noun*
a wild plant with very prickly leaves and purple or white flowers.

thorn thorns *noun*
a little, sharp point on the stem of a plant such as a rose.
thorny *adjective*.

This blackberry has a thorny stem

thorough *adjective*
complete or careful. *a thorough investigation.* ▲ Say **thur-a**.
thoroughly *adverb*.

thought thoughts *noun*
an idea or something that you think. *Any thoughts about what you'd like for your birthday?* ▲ Say **thort**.

thought past of **think**
▲ Say **thort**.

thoughtful *adjective*
1 quiet and serious while you are thinking about something carefully.
2 If you are thoughtful, you think about what other people want and try to behave in a way that makes them more comfortable or happy. ▲ Say **thort**-ful.
thoughtfully, thoughtless *adverbs*
thoughtless behaviour.

Jordan is looking thoughtful

thread threads *noun*
a long, thin piece of cotton, wool or nylon that you use for sewing or for weaving. ▲ Say **thred**.
thread *verb*.

threat threats *noun*
a warning that something nasty may happen. ▲ Say **thret**.

threaten threatens threatening threatened *verb*
If somebody threatens you, they say that they will do something nasty if you do not do what they want. *She threatened to hit me.* ▲ Say **thret**-en.

three-dimensional *adjective*
Something that is three-dimensional is like a real thing with height, width and depth, and not like a flat picture. A sculpture is three-dimensional.

threw past of **throw**
● A word that sounds like **threw** is **through**.

thrill thrills *noun*
a sudden feeling of excitement or pleasure.
thrilling *adjective*.

throat throats *noun*
Your throat is the front part of your neck and the tube that goes down from inside your mouth taking food and air into your body.

throb throbs throbbing throbbed *verb*
1 If part of your body throbs, it hurts a lot and beats with pain. *My head is throbbing.*
2 To throb is to beat in a regular way like your heart pumping blood.

throne thrones *noun*
a special chair for a king or queen.

through *preposition*
from one side to the other. *The train went through a tunnel.*◆ *Water is coming through a hole in the ceiling.* ▲ Say **throo**. ● A word that sounds like **through** is **threw**.

throw throws throwing threw thrown *verb*
When you throw something, you send it through the air from your hand. *Throw the ball up into the air and then hit it with your racket.*

thumb thumbs *noun*
Your thumb is the short, thick finger at the side of your hand. ▲ Say **thum**.

thump thumps thumping thumped *verb*
If you thump somebody or something, you hit them with your fist. *He thumped the door.*

thunder *noun*
the loud noise that you hear after a flash of lightning during a storm called a thunderstorm.

tick ticks *noun*
the mark (✔) used to show that something is correct.

ticket tickets *noun*
a small piece of paper that shows you have paid for something. *Have you bought the cinema tickets yet?* ◆ *a railway ticket.*

tickle tickles tickling tickled *verb*
When you tickle somebody, you touch them very softly in a place where it makes them laugh and wriggle away.

tide tides *noun*
the movement every day of the sea coming towards land and then away from land. *The tide is coming in.* ◆ *The tide is going out.*

tidy tidier tidiest *adjective*
with everything in its proper place. *a tidy room.* ◆ *tidy hair.*
tidy *verb*, **tidily** *adverb*.

tie ties tying tied *verb*
1 When you tie something, you fasten it using string or something similar. *The parcel was tied with red and white ribbons.* ◆ *She tied the dog to a tree.*
2 When two people or teams tie in a race or competition, they finish in an equal position. *They tied in second place.*
tie up *Ships were tied up at the dock.*

tie ties *noun*
a long, thin piece of material that you wear around the neck of a shirt with a knot at the front.

tier tiers *noun*
one of a series of rows or layers that are placed one above the other. *There are several tiers of seats in the theatre.* ◆ *a wedding cake with three tiers.* ▲ Rhymes with **here**. ● A word that sounds like **tier** is **tear**.

tiger tigers *noun*
a large, wild animal in the cat family which has orange fur with dark stripes. Tigers live in Asia.

tight tighter tightest *adjective*
1 fitting very close to your body. *Connie's shoes are very tight - Joe is trying to pull them off.*
2 When something is tight, it is firmly fastened so that it will not move. *Make sure the lid is tight.*
▲ Say **tite**. ■ The opposite is **loose**.
tightly *adverb*.

tighten tightens tightening tightened *verb*
If you tighten something, you make it tighter. If something tightens, it gets tighter. ▲ Say **tite-en**.

tightrope tightropes *noun*
a rope high up in the air that acrobats walk along in the circus. ▲ Say **tite-rope**.

tights *noun*
a piece of clothing made of thin material that tightly covers your legs, feet and bottom. ▲ Say **tites**.

tile tiles *noun*
a thin piece of hard material that you use to cover a wall, floor or a roof. *The bathroom tiles have pictures of fish and shells on them.*

till *preposition*
until. *We had to wait two weeks till we heard the exam results.*

time *noun*
1 what we measure in units such as minutes, hours, days, weeks and years.
2 a particular point in time. *What's the time?*
3 a period of time. *Did you enjoy your time in San Francisco?*

timetable timetables *noun*
a list that shows when things are going to happen. *a train timetable.* ◆ *a school timetable.*

timid *adjective*
shy and not very brave. *A mouse is a timid creature.*
timidly *adverb*.

tin tins *noun*
1 a kind of silver-coloured metal.
2 a can or metal container to store food in. *a tin of beans.* ◆ *a biscuit tin.*

tiny tinier tiniest *adjective*
very small. *Bacteria are so tiny that you can only see them through a microscope.* ■ The opposite is **huge** or **enormous**.

tip tips *noun*
1 the end of something long and thin. *the tips of your fingers.*
2 an extra amount of money that you give to somebody such as a waiter for helping you.
3 a place you can leave rubbish that you cannot get into the rubbish bin. *Take all these old boxes to the tip.*

A B C D E F G H I J K L M N O P Q R S T U V W X Y Z

tiptoe tiptoes tiptoeing tiptoed *verb*
If you tiptoe, you walk on your toes so that you do not make a noise.

tired *adjective*
If you are tired, you want to go to sleep or you want to rest.

tissue tissues *noun*
1 a thin piece of soft paper that you can use as a handkerchief.
2 thin, soft paper for wrapping things in to protect them from damage.
3 a lot of tiny cells of the same kind that make up part of the body. *muscle tissue.*

title titles *noun*
1 the name of something such as a book, film or picture.
2 a word such as Lord, Professor, Dr, Mrs or Princess that a person can have in front of their name.

toad toads *noun*
an animal like a big frog. It lives on land but lays its eggs in water.

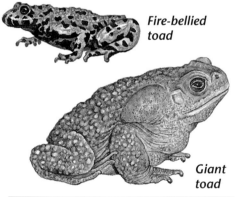

Fire-bellied toad

Giant toad

toadstool toadstools *noun*
a poisonous fungus that looks like a mushroom.

toast *noun*
a slice of bread that has been grilled on both sides to make it brown and crunchy.

tobacco *noun*
the cut and dried leaves of the tobacco plant that are used in cigarettes, cigars and pipes.

toboggan toboggans *noun*
a vehicle like a long seat fixed to two long strips of wood or metal called runners that you use to slide downhill on snow.

toddler toddlers *noun*
a very young child who is just learning to walk.

toe toes *noun*
Your toes are the five parts at the end of your foot. ● A word that sounds like **toe** is **tow**.

toilet toilets *noun*
1 a large bowl with a seat that you use to get rid of liquid and solid waste from your body.
2 the room where the toilet is.

token tokens *noun*
a card or piece of paper that you can use instead of money to buy something. *a record token.* ◆ *a book token.*

told past of **tell**.

tomato tomatoes *noun*
a soft, round, red fruit that you eat in salads or that can be used to make soup or ketchup.

tomb tombs *noun*
a grave or place where somebody is buried. ▲ Say *toom*.

tongue tongues *noun*
the long, pink part inside your mouth that you use to lick something and that helps you to taste things and to speak. ▲ Say *tung*.

tonsil tonsils *noun*
Your tonsils are the two small, soft lumps at the back of your throat. They sometimes swell and get painful in an illness called tonsillitis.

took past of **take**.

tool tools *noun*
anything that you use to help you to do a particular job. Hammers and saws are tools. Here are lots of different tools.

tooth teeth *noun*
1 one of the hard, white parts inside your mouth that you use to bite and to chew.
2 one of the thin parts that stick out in a row on such things as a comb, saw or zip.

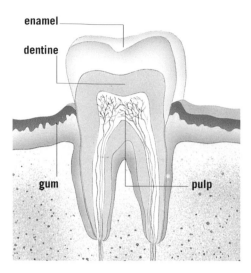

enamel

dentine

gum

pulp

toothbrush toothbrushes *noun*
a small brush with a handle that you use to clean your teeth with.

toothpaste *noun*
a paste that you put on your toothbrush to clean your teeth with.

top tops *noun*
1 the highest part of something. *We walked to the top of the hill.* ■ The opposite is **bottom**.
2 a lid or cover for something. *a milk bottle top.*

topic topics *noun*
something that is being talked about or written about. *The weather is his only topic of conversation.*

topple topples toppling toppled *verb*
If something topples, it falls over because it is too heavy at the top. *The tree toppled over in the wind.*

torch torches *noun*
a small, electric light that you can hold in your hand.

tore, torn past of **tear**.

tornado tornadoes *noun*
a very strong wind that travels in circles and that can do a lot of damage to buildings. ▲ Say *tor-nay-doh*.

a b c d e f g h i j k l m n o p q r s t u v w x y z

tortoise tortoises *noun*
a small animal that has a hard shell over its back and that moves very slowly. Tortoises are reptiles. ▲ Say *tor-tus.*

Giant Galapagos tortoise

torture tortures torturing tortured *verb*
to make somebody feel great pain on purpose, as a punishment or to get information from them. ▲ Say *tor-cher.* **torturer** *noun.*

toss tosses tossing tossed *verb*
1 If you toss something, you throw it upwards in a careless way. *She tossed me a pen and said "Write down this number".*
2 If something tosses, it moves about from side to side. *The boat tossed in the storm.*

total *adjective*
complete. *a total disaster.* **totally** *adverb.*

total totals *noun*
the amount that you get when you add everything together. *If you add 12, 17, and 8, you get a total of 37.*

touch touches touching touched *verb*
1 When you touch something, you feel it with your hand or another part of you. *Don't touch the iron - it's very hot.*
2 If two things touch, there is no space between them.
▲ Say *tuch.*

tough tougher toughest *adjective*
1 strong and hard to break or damage. *Plastic is a tough material.*
2 difficult. *a tough decision.*
3 difficult to chew. *This meat is tough.*
■ The opposite is **tender.**
▲ Say *tuff.*

tour tours *noun*
a journey to different interesting places. *a tour of Paris.* ▲ Say *toor.*

tourist tourists *noun*
a person who is visiting interesting places on holiday. ▲ Say *toor-ist.*

tournament tournaments *noun*
a competition in which a lot of matches are played until one person wins over all the others. ▲ Say *toor-na-ment.*

tow tows towing towed *verb*
To tow a vehicle is to pull it along behind another vehicle. *The car is towing a caravan.* ● A word that sounds like **tow** is **toe.**

towel towels *noun*
a large piece of soft, thick material that you use to dry yourself.

tower towers *noun*
a very tall, narrow building or part of a building. *the Eiffel Tower.* ◆ *the Leaning Tower of Pisa.*

the Leaning tower of Pisa

town towns *noun*
a place with streets, houses, shops and other buildings where a lot of people live and work.

toy toys *noun*
a thing for a child to play with.

trace traces tracing traced *verb*
1 When you trace a picture, you put a thin piece of paper over it and draw over the lines that show through.

2 If you trace somebody or something, you find them after looking for them. *He is trying to trace an uncle who nobody in the family has heard from for years.*

trace traces *noun*
a tiny amount. *Traces of poison were found in the soup.*

track tracks *noun*
1 footprints or other marks left by a person or animal that show where they have been.
2 a narrow path. *a mountain track.*
3 an area of ground where races take place.
4 the rails that a train runs on.
5 one of the songs or pieces of music on a record or tape.

tractor tractors *noun*
a powerful vehicle with very large back wheels used on a farm for pulling heavy machinery.

trade *noun*
buying and selling things. *Ireland does a lot of trade with Britain.*

tradition traditions *noun*
a way of doing something that has been the same for a very long time. **traditional** *adjective* *traditional songs.* **traditionally** *adverb.*

traffic *noun*
cars, lorries, buses and other vehicles that are moving along the roads. *A lot of traffic goes through the village.*

tragedy tragedies *noun*
1 a very sad event. *Two of his brothers and a sister died in the tragedy.*
2 a serious play with a sad ending.
▲ Say *traj-e-dee.* **tragic** *adjective* *a tragic accident.*

trail trails *noun*
1 a track or path for people to follow or go along in the country.
2 marks or other signs left behind where a person or animal has been. *He left a trail of muddy footprints on the floor.*

trailer trailers *noun*
1 a vehicle that is towed behind a car or lorry to carry very large or heavy things, such as a boat.
2 an advertisement that shows short scenes from a film or TV programme.

a b c d e f g h i j k l m n o p q r s t u v w x y z

train trains *noun*
a set of carriages that move along rails pulled by an engine. Some trains carry passengers and some trains carry freight.

train trains training trained *verb*
1 When you train, you practise a sport or do exercises to get fitter. *He's training for the Olympics.*
2 To train a person or animal is to teach them how to do something. *She's training the dog to shake a paw.*
3 If you train, you learn the skills you need to do a job. *Sue's training to be a doctor.*
trainer *noun.*

trainers *noun*
shoes with thick soles that can be worn for running and exercising.

trample tramples trampling trampled *verb*
If you trample on something, you walk on it and crush it. *They trampled the flowers.*

trampoline trampolines *noun*
a piece of very strong material fixed to a metal frame with springs that is used for jumping up and down in gymnastics. ▲ Say *tramp-o-leen.*

transfer transfers transferring transferred *verb*
To transfer a person or thing is to move them to a different place.

transform transforms transforming transformed *verb*
If you transform something, you change it completely. *With make up, a wig and good acting, he transformed himself into an old man.*

translate translates translating translated *verb*
If you translate something, you change

the same words in to a different language. *Richard translated the novel from English into French.*

transparent *adjective*
If something is transparent, you can see through it. *This plastic is transparent.*

transplant transplants *noun*
an operation in which a surgeon takes out a damaged part of the body and replaces it with one that is not damaged. *a heart transplant.*

transport *noun*
buses, trains and other vehicles that take people or goods from one place to another.

transport transports transporting transported *verb*
To transport people or goods is to take them from one place to another in a vehicle. *The parcels were transported by air.*

trap traps *noun*
a thing to catch an animal or bird. *a mouse trap.*
trap *verb.*

trapeze trapezes *noun*
a bar hanging from ropes high up in the air that acrobats swing from in a circus.

travel travels travelling travelled *verb*
When you travel, you go from one place to another. *We'll be travelling back to Scotland on Wednesday.*
travel *noun,* **traveller** *noun.*

trawler trawlers *noun*
a boat for catching fish by pulling a wide net behind it in the sea.

tray trays *noun*
a flat piece of wood, metal or plastic that you carry things on. *He put the cups and saucers on a tray.*

treacle *noun*
a thick, black liquid made from sugar.

tread treads treading trod trodden *verb*
When you tread on something, you put your foot down on it. *Ouch! You trod on my toe.* ▲ Say **tred.**

treasure treasures *noun*
a collection of very valuable objects such as gold, silver or jewels. *The pirates hid the treasure in a cave.* ▲ Say **tresh**-er.

treat treats treating treated *verb*
1 When you treat somebody in a particular way, you behave towards them like that. *He always treats me politely.*
2 To treat somebody is to give them medicine or to look after them in a way that will make them well. *The doctor treated her for an earache.*

treatment treatments *noun*
1 how a doctor treats somebody who is ill. *What's the right treatment?*
2 how somebody behaves towards a person, animal or thing. *cruel treatment.*

tree trees *noun*
a big plant that has a thick, hard stem of wood called a trunk and branches and leaves. ❖ *Look opposite.*

tremble trembles trembling trembled *verb*
If you tremble, you shake a little because you are frightened, cold or excited.

trend trends *noun*
the way things seem to be changing. *The trend is for people to save their money and spend less.*

trespass trespasses trespassing trespassed *verb*
If you trespass, you go on somebody's land without asking them if you can.

a trawler

TREES

Hornbeam

Douglas fir

Cedar of Lebanon

Common juniper

Golden weeping willow

Hybrid black-poplar

Sea black thorn

Red oak

Spindle

Box

Pendulculate oak

Common jujube

Guelder rose

Dragon tree

Petticoat palm

A B C D E F G H I J K L M N O P Q R S T U V W X Y Z

trial **trials** *noun*
1 a period of time in a law court when lawyers, judge and jury try to find out whether somebody is guilty or innocent of a crime.
2 a test to find out how good a thing is.

triangle **triangles** *noun*
1 a shape with three straight sides.
2 a small musical instrument with three metal sides that you play by hitting it with a short metal rod.
▲ Say *try-ang-gul*.
triangular *adjective*
a triangular shape.

tribe **tribes** *noun*
a group of people of the same race that speak the same language and live in the same area.

trick **tricks** *noun*
1 something that is done to cheat somebody or to try to make them believe something that is not true.
2 something that looks as if it could not be done. *a magic trick.*

trick **tricks tricking tricked** *verb*
To trick somebody is to cheat them or try to make them believe something that is not true. *We changed the time of the clock and tricked our teacher into sending us home early.*

trickle **trickles trickling trickled** *verb*
When liquid trickles, a small amount of it flows slowly. *Tears slowly trickled down his cheeks.*

tricycle **tricycle** *noun*
a vehicle like a bicycle with three wheels. ▲ Say *try-sik-ul*.

trim **trims trimming trimmed** *verb*
If you trim something, you cut small pieces off it so that it has a better shape and looks tidy. *The hairdresser is trimming Joe's hair.*

trip **trips** *noun*
a journey to a place and back again. *We went on a school trip to the museum.*

trip **trips tripping tripped** *verb*
If you trip, you knock your foot on something and fall over. *She tripped over the cat.*

triple *adjective*
having three parts or done three times. *He's a triple winner.* ◆ *A triple chocolate milkshake.*

triplet **triplets** *noun*
one of three people or animals who have the same mother and were born at the same time.

triumph **triumphs** *noun*
a great success at something you have had to try hard to do. ▲ Say *try-umf*.

trod, trodden past of **tread**.

trolley **trolleys** *noun*
an open container on wheels that you use to carry heavy things. *a supermarket trolley.*

trombone **trombones** *noun*
a large, brass musical instrument that you play by blowing into it and moving one tube in and out of another tube to change the notes.
trombonist *noun*.

trophy **trophies** *noun*
a prize such as a silver cup that is given to a person who has won a competition or tournament. *My baseball team got a huge silver trophy for winning the contest.* ▲ Say *troh-fee*.

tropical *adjective*
to do with the tropics, the very hot parts of the world near the Equator. *a tropical rainforest.*

trot **trots trotting trotted** *verb*
When a horse trots, it moves quite quickly.
trot *noun*.

trouble **troubles** *noun*
1 a problem or a difficult or worrying situation.
2 **in trouble** If you are in trouble, you have done something wrong and made somebody angry who might punish you. *If you break the window with that ball, you'll be in big trouble.*
▲ Say *trub-l*.

trough **troughs** *noun*
a long, narrow container that has food or water in for animals. ▲ Say *troff*.

trousers *noun*
a piece of clothing that covers the lower half of your body with separate parts for each leg. *a pair of trousers.*

trowel **trowels** *noun*
a tool like a very small spade with a curved blade and a short handle.

truck **trucks** *noun*
1 a lorry.
2 a railway carriage for carrying goods in rather than people.

trudge **trudges trudging trudged** *verb*
If you trudge somewhere, you walk slowly because you are tired or cross. *We trudged home through the mud.*
▲ Say *trudj*.

true **truer truest** *adjective*
If something is true, it is based on known facts and accurate, not made up or guessed at. *a true joke.* ■ The opposite is **false**.
truly *adverb*
very. *It was a truly funny story.*

trumpet **trumpets** *noun*
a brass musical instrument that you play by blowing into it.
trumpeter *noun*.

trunk **trunks** *noun*
1 the round, hard stem of a tree that the branches grow from.
2 the long nose of an elephant.
3 the main part of your body from the top of your legs to your shoulders.
4 a large, strong box for carrying things in on a long journey or for storing things in.
❖ *Look at page 173*

trust trusts trusting trusted *verb*
If you trust somebody, you believe that they are good and honest and will not do anything to hurt you.
trust *noun*.

truth *noun*
what is true, accurate and correct. *I'm sure she's telling the truth.*

try tries trying tried *verb*
1 If you try to do something, you do your best to do it.
2 If you try something, you test it to see what it is like. *Try this soup and tell me if it needs more salt.*

T-shirt T-shirts *noun*
a shirt made of cotton with short sleeves and no collar or buttons that you pull over your head.

tub tubs *noun*
a container for food. *a tub of ice-cream.*

tube tubes *noun*
1 a long, round, hollow thing, like a pipe.
2 a long, thin container that you squeeze to get the contents out. *a tube of toothpaste.*

tuck tucks tucking tucked *verb*
If you tuck something, you push the end of it under something or in something else. *He tucked his shirt into his trousers.*

tuft tufts *noun*
a clump of hair or grass.

tug tugs tugging tugged *verb*
If you tug something, you pull hard at it. *The baby kept tugging at her hair.*

tulip tulips *noun*
a plant that grows from a bulb and has a long stem and a bright flower in the shape of a cup.

tumble tumbles tumbling tumbled *verb*
If you tumble, you fall suddenly, rolling over and over. *The child tumbled down the stairs.*

tune tunes *noun*
a series of musical notes that are nice to listen to.

tunic tunics *noun*
a loose piece of clothing with no sleeves or collar.

tunnel tunnels *noun*
a long hole under the ground or through a hill. *the Channel Tunnel.*
tunnel *verb*
The moles have tunnelled under the lawn in the back garden.

turban turbans *noun*
a long strip of material wound around the head and especially worn by Sikh men.

turf *noun*
short, thick grass.

turkey turkeys *noun*
a large bird that does not fly and that is usually kept on a farm for its meat.

ocellated turkey

common turkey

turn turns turning turned *verb*
1 When something turns, it moves around so that it faces a different direction or goes in a different direction. *The car turned right at the traffic lights.* ◆ *He turned round and looked behind him.*
2 When something turns, it goes round. *The wheel turned.*
3 When you turn something, you turn it round. *She turned the handle.*
4 When something turns into something else, it changes to become that thing. *A caterpillar turns into a butterfly.*

turn turns *noun*
a time when you do something that other people have done before you and that other people will do after you. *It's my turn to use the computer.*

turtle turtles *noun*
a large reptile with a hard shell that lives in the sea.

tusk tusks *noun*
a long, pointed tooth that comes right outside the mouth of an animal such as an elephant.

TV TVs *noun*
short for television. *She's upstairs watching TV.*

twice *adverb*
two times. *I've been to see the film twice now. How many times have you seen it?*

twig twigs *noun*
a small branch of a tree.

twilight *noun*
a time after sunset before it gets completely dark. ▲ Say *twy-lite.*

twin twins *noun*
one of two people or animals who have the same mother and were born at the same time.

twinkle twinkles twinkling twinkled *verb*
When something twinkles, it shines with little flashes of light. *The stars were twinkling.*

A
B
C
D
E
F
G
H
I
J
K
L
M
N
O
P
Q
R
S
T
U
V
W
X
Y
Z

twirl twirls twirling twirled *verb*
to turn or spin round and round. *She twirled her hair around her fingers.* **twirl** *noun.*

twist twists twisting twisted *verb*
1 If you twist something, you turn it around and around. *She twisted the screwdriver to tighten the screw.*
2 When you twist something, you bend it or turn it around. *He twisted the wires together.*

twitch twitches twitching twitched *verb*
To twitch is to make a small, quick movement.

twitter *noun*
the high sounds made by small birds.

tycoon tycoons *verb*
A tycoon is a rich and powerful businessman or businesswoman.

type types typing typed *verb*
When you type, you press the keys on a keyboard to write something. ▲ Say **tipe.**

type types *noun*
1 a kind of thing. *What type of apple is that?*

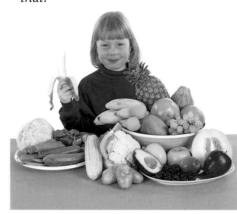

2 the size and style of printed letters and numbers.
▲ Say *tipe.*

typewriter typewriters *noun*
a machine with keys that you press to print letters and numbers on paper.

typhoon typhoon *noun*
a violent tropical storm of wind and rain.
▲ Say *tye-foon.*

typical *adjective*
A typical thing is the most usual of that kind of thing. *a typical English village.*
▲ Say *tip-i-cal.*

tyrant tyrants *noun*
a cruel and unfair ruler.

tyre tyres *noun*
a circle of rubber around the outside or rim of a bicycle or car wheel. ▲ Rhymes with *fire.*

tyrannosaur *noun*
a very large dinosaur with small front legs, a large head and sharp teeth.
❖ *Look at page 125*

U u

udder udders *noun*
the part of a cow, goat or sheep that hangs under its body, near the back legs, and that produces milk.

ugly uglier ugliest *adjective*
not nice to look at. *a monster's ugly face.* ■ The opposite is **beautiful.**

umbrella umbrellas *noun*
a thing that you hold over your head to stay dry when it rains. The frame of an umbrella is covered with a round piece of material and joined to a long handle.

uncle uncles *noun*
Your uncle is the brother of your mother or your father, or the husband of your aunt.

unconscious *adjective*
1 If you are unconscious, you are in a kind of sleep and you do not know what is happening. *When she fell downstairs and hit her head, she was unconscious for an hour.*
2 If you are unconscious of something, you do not know about it. *Rachel was unconscious that she had been rude.*

uncover uncovers uncovering uncovered *verb*
1 When you uncover something, you

take off the thing or things that cover it. *He uncovered the box and looked inside.*
2 To uncover also means to find something that was hidden or not known about. *A skeleton was uncovered by a farmer digging in a field.* ◆ *The plot to blow up the building was uncovered.*

underground *adjective, adverb*
under the ground. *Rabbits build their burrows underground below the surface of the earth.*

undergrowth *noun*
all the bushes and other plants that grow under trees. *They cleared a path through the thick undergrowth.*

underline underlines underlining underlined *verb*
If you underline something, you draw a line under it to make people notice it. *Please write the date and <u>underline</u> it with a ruler.*

underneath *preposition, adverb*
below or under something. *I found my shoes underneath the bed.* ◆ *He laughed, but underneath he was sad.*

understand understands understanding understood *verb*
If you understand something, you know what it means, how it works or why it happens. *I didn't understand what the teacher said.* ◆ *Mark can now understand computers.*

underwear *noun*
Underwear is clothes such as vests and pants that you wear under your other clothes.

undo undoes undoing undid undone *verb*
If you undo something like a parcel, you open it. *Can you undo this knot?*

undress undresses undressing undressed *verb*
When you undress, you take off your clothes. *It's time to undress and go to bed.* ■ The opposite is **dress**.

unemployed *adjective*
A person who is unemployed does not have a job and is not working. *She has been unemployed for six months.* **unemployment** *noun.*

unfold unfolds unfolding unfolded *verb*
When you unfold something like a piece of paper or material, you open it out so that it lies flat. *I unfolded the map and put it on the table.* ■ The opposite is **fold**.

uniform uniforms *noun*
a special set of clothes that people wear to show that they belong to the same group. *Pilots, nurses and security guards wear uniforms.*

union unions *noun*
a group of workers that come together to talk to their managers about any problems at work. *the National Union of Teachers.*

unique *adjective*
different from anybody or anything else and the only one of its kind. *Each person's voice is unique.* ▲ Say yoo-**neek**.

unit units *noun*
1 one part of something. *a kitchen unit.*
2 an amount used in measuring or counting. *A metre is a unit of length, a kilogram is a unit of weight and a minute is a unit of time.*
▲ Say **yoo**-nit.

unite unites uniting united *verb*
If things or people unite, they join together or do something together. *Children in the school are united in wanting to win the cup.* ▲ Say yoo-**nite**.
united *adjective*
the United States of America.

universe *noun*
the Earth, the Sun, the Moon and all the other planets and stars in space. *The Earth is a tiny spot in the universe.*
▲ Say **yoo**-ni-verse.

university universities *noun*
a place where people can go to study things when they have left school. *My sister is studying biology at university.*
▲ Say yoo-ni-**ver**-sit-ee.

unload, unloads, unloading, unloaded *verb*
To unload is to take goods off a ship or vehicle. ■ The opposite is **load**.

unlock unlocks unlocking unlocked *verb*
When you unlock something, you turn a key to open it. *I unlocked the door and went inside.* ■ The opposite is **lock**.

untidy *adjective*
in a mess and nothing in the proper place. *untidy hair.*

untie unties untying untied *verb*
If you untie something, you undo the knots that fasten it. *I untied my shoelaces.*

until *preposition*
up to a certain time or day. *Dad is in his office until six o'clock every evening.* ◆ *I can't come until tomorrow.*

unusual *adjective*
Something that is unusual is not ordinary, normal or usual. *It is unusual to see snow in summer.*

upper *adjective*
above or higher than another thing.

upright *adjective, adverb*
If something like a bottle is upright, it is standing up, with the top facing upwards. *Connie is standing upright and Joe is lying down.*

upset upsets upsetting upset *verb*
1 If you upset somebody, you make them unhappy. *She upset me when she said I was fat.*
2 If you upset something like a drink, you knock it over and spill it.

upside-down *adjective, adverb*
If something is upside-down, the bottom is at the top and the top is at the bottom. *This sloth is hanging upside-down.*

upstairs *adjective, adverb*
on or to an upper floor. *My bedroom is upstairs.*

A B C D E F G H I J K L M N O P Q R S T U V W X Y Z

up-to-date *adjective*
new and modern. *News is information that is up-to-date.*

upward, upwards *adverb*
from lower to higher.

urgent *adjective*
so very important that it must be done immediately. *She made an urgent phone call to the doctor.*
urgency *noun.*

use uses using used *verb*
1 If you use something, you do a job with it. *You use scissors to cut things with.*
2 To use also means to take something. *Don't use all the glue.*
▲ Say **yooz**.
used to *verb*
1 If you used to do something, you did it before, but you do not do it now. *I used to go swimming every Tuesday, but now I play tennis.*
2 Used to can also mean knowing somebody or something well. *We are all used to her jokes.*
▲ Say **yoost**-*too*.

use uses *noun*
what you can do with something. *This bag has many uses.* ▲ Say **yooss**.

useful *adjective*
If somebody or something is useful, they help you in some way. *Ben was very useful because he helped with the baby.*
■ The opposite is **useless**.

useless *adjective*
If something is useless, it is no good for anything and you cannot use it. *This bag is useless because the handle has broken.* ■ The opposite is **useful**.

usual *adjective*
If something is usual, it happens often or most of the time. *Seven o'clock is our usual time for breakfast.*
usually *adverb*
I usually go to school by bike.

utensil utensils *noun*
a tool or container, especially one used for cooking.

utter utters uttering uttered *verb*
To make a sound or to say something. *He uttered a cry of pain.*

The broken things above are useless – the others are useful, they will help you to do a job properly.

V v

vacant *adjective*
empty and not being used. *Do you have any vacant rooms in the hotel?*
▲ Say **vay**-*kant*.
vacancy *noun*

vaccination vaccinations *noun*
an injection that stops you getting an illness. *Joey had his vaccination against measels today.* ▲ Say *vak-si-***nay***-shun.*
vaccinate *verb*.

vacuum cleaner vacuum cleaners *noun*
a machine that sucks up dirt from floors and carpets.

vagina vaginas *noun*
The vagina is a part of a woman's body that leads to the womb.

vague vaguer vaguest *adjective*
not clear or definite. *I could see a vague shape in the mist.* ▲ Say **vayg**.
vaguely *adverb*.

vain vainer vainest *adjective*
Vain people are too proud of themselves, especially of how they look.

valley valleys *noun*
low land between hills or mountains.

valuable *adjective*
1 worth a lot of money. *a valuable necklace.*
2 useful and helpful. *He gave me some valuable advice.*

value *noun*
1 the amount of money that something is worth. *What is the value of your house?*
2 how useful and helpful something is. *The instructions you gave were of great value in helping me to make the machine work.*

vampire vampires *noun*
in stories, a dead person who sucks people's blood.

van vans *noun*
a small, covered lorry with doors at the back that is used for carrying goods.

vandal vandals *noun*
a person who breaks or damages property on purpose. *Vandals have smashed the telephone box.*

vanilla *noun*
a flavour that comes from the pod of a tropical plant and is used in sweet foods. *vanilla ice-cream.*

vanish vanishes vanishing vanished *verb*
If something vanishes, it suddenly disappears.

vanity *noun*
being vain and very proud of what you look like.

variety **varieties** *noun*
1 a number of different kinds of thing. *They had a variety of skirts and dresses in the sale.*
2 a kind or sort of thing. *There are lots of different varieties of breakfast cereal.*
3 a lot of different things happening. *I like a lot of variety in my life.*
▲ Say *var-eye-i-tee.*

different varieties of breakfast cereal

various *adjective*
several different things. *You can buy these towels in various colours.* ▲ Say *vair-ee-us.*

varnish *noun*
a clear liquid that you paint on wood to protect it and make it look shiny.

vary **varies varying varied** *verb*
If something varies, it keeps changing. *I take sandwiches to school every day but what goes in them varies.* ▲ Say *vair-ee.*

vase **vases** *noun*
a jar or container for putting flowers in. ▲ Say *varz.*

vast **vaster vastest** *adjective*
very, very large. *The Sahara is a vast desert.*

vegetable **vegetables** *noun*
a plant that people eat. Cabbages, carrots and potatoes are vegetables. ▲ Say *vej-te-bul.* ❖ **Look at page 178**

vegetarian **vegetarians** *noun*
a person who does not eat meat or fish. ▲ Say *vej-e-tair-ee-an.*

vehicle **vehicles** *noun*
a thing that takes people or goods from one place to another. Buses, cars, lorries, planes and trains are all vehicles. ▲ Say *vee-ik-ul.*

veil **veils** *noun*
a piece of very thin material that some women wear over their face or head.

vein **veins** *noun*
A vein is one of the tubes in your body that carries blood back to your heart.

velvet *noun*
cloth that is thick and soft on one side.

verb **verbs** *noun*
a word that tells you what somebody or something does or what is happening. "Think", "run" and "cut" are all verbs. *What are you thinking?*

verdict **verdicts** *noun*
what the judge and jury decide at the end of a trial in a law court.

verse **verses** *noun*
a part of a poem or song made of several lines.

version **versions** *noun*
1 a changed form of something. *We bought a new version of the computer game.*
2 one person's way of telling a story or what happened that is a little different from other people's. *In Harry's version of the story, the bull didn't chase her to the gate, she just ran because she was so scared.*

vertical *adjective*
standing straight up. *a vertical post.*
■ The opposite is **horizontal.**

vessel **vessels** *noun*
1 a ship or large boat.
2 a container for liquid.

vest **vests** *noun*
a piece of clothing that you wear under a shirt or blouse.

vet **vets** *noun*
a person whose job is to treat animals and help them to get well when they get ill or hurt.

via *preposition*
If you go somewhere via another place, you go to the other place first. *We went to the supermarket via the library.*

viaduct **viaducts** *noun*
a long bridge that carries a road or railway over a valley. ▲ Say *vye-a-dukt.*

vibrate **vibrates vibrating vibrated** *verb*
When something vibrates, it shakes very quickly. *The floor vibrated every time a train went past.* ▲ Say *vye-brate.* **vibration** *noun.*

vicious *adjective*
cruel and violent. *a vicious attack.*
▲ Say *vish-us.* **viciously** *adverb.*

victim **victims** *noun*
a person who has been attacked, hurt, robbed or killed.

victory **victories** *noun*
a success in winning a battle or game.
■ The opposite is **defeat.**

video **videos** *noun*
1 a machine that you use to record a television programme so that you can watch it later.
2 a tape that is used to record a film or television programme.

view **views** *noun*
1 what you can see from one place. *We had a good view of the mountains.*
2 a person's opinion or what they think about something. *In my view, he fell over because he wasn't looking where he was going.* ▲ Say *vyoo.*

vile **viler vilest** *adjective*
horrible. *This cheese has a vile taste.*

village **villages** *noun*
a group of houses and other buildings in the country. *Villages are smaller than towns.*

villain **villains** *noun*
a very bad person, especially in a film, story or play. *The villain was killed at the end of the film.* ▲ Say *vil-en.*

vine **vines** *noun*
a climbing plant that grapes grow on.

vinegar *noun*
a sour liquid that is used to add flavour to food.

A
B
C
D
E
F
G
H
I
J
K
L
M
N
O
P
Q
R
S
T
U
V
W
X
Y
Z

VEGETABLES

1 savoy cabbage	8 asparagus	16 French beans	24 celery
2 white cabbage	9 broccoli	17 parsnip	25 squash
3 cauliflower	10 globe artichoke	18 courgette	26 salad onion
4 pumpkin	11 sweet potato	19 carrot	27 cucumber
5 lollo rosso	12 iceberg lettuce	20 red onion	28 yam
lettuce	13 mange tout	21 Brussels sprout	29 swede
6 leek	14 peas	22 potato	
7 sweetcorn	15 flat beans	23 radish	

a
b
c
d
e
f
g
h
i
j
k
l
m
n
o
p
q
r
s
t
u
v
w
x
y
z

vineyard vineyards *noun*
a place where grape vines are grown for making wine. ▲ Say *vin-yard*.

violent *adjective*
1 a violent person uses force or weapons to hurt somebody.
2 very strong or rough. *a violent storm.*

violet violets *noun*
a small plant with small white or purple flowers.

violin violins *noun*
a musical instrument with strings stretched across a wooden frame. *You play a violin by holding it under your chin and moving a stick called a bow across the strings.*
violinist *noun*.

virtual reality *noun*
an image made by a computer that surrounds you and that looks real.

virtue *noun*
a kind of goodness. *Honesty is a virtue.*

virus viruses *noun*
1 a tiny germ that causes a disease. *Colds and flu are caused by viruses.*
2 a computer program that damages the data in a computer system.

visible *adjective*
If something is visible, you can see it. ▲ Say *viz-i-bul*. ■ The opposite is **invisible**.

vision *noun*
a person's ability to see. *He has excellent vision.* ▲ Say *vish-un*.

visit visits visiting visited *verb*
If you visit somebody or somewhere, you go to see them. *Matt visited his friend Tom in hospital.*
visitor *noun*.

vitamin vitamins *noun*
one of the substances that are in food naturally that you need to keep healthy.

vocabulary vocabularies *noun*
1 all the words somebody knows.
2 a list of words and what they mean.

voice voices *noun*
the sound that you make when you speak or sing.

volcano volcanoes *noun*
a mountain with an opening called a crater in the top from which very hot melted rock called lava and gases sometimes pour out.

ash and smoke

lava

magma chamber

Earth's layers

volume volumes *noun*
1 the amount of space inside something or the amount of space that something takes up. *What's the volume of that petrol can?*
2 a book in a set of books. *The first volume of a 20-volume encyclopedia.*
3 how loud a sound is. *Can you turn the volume of your radio down?*

volunteer volunteers *noun*
a person who does something without being paid and without being made to do it. *This work is done by volunteers.*
voluntary *adjective*
I do voluntary work for the homeless.

vote votes voting voted *verb*
If you vote for somebody or something you choose them by putting your hand up or by making a mark on a piece of paper. *Have you voted yet?*
vote *noun*
There were ten votes for my plan and eight votes against.

VOTE FOR
JOHN OLIVER

vowel vowels *noun*
the letters a, e, i, o and u and sometimes y are vowels.

voyage voyages *noun*
a long journey by sea or in space. ▲ Say *voy-ij*.

vulture vultures *noun*
a large, tropical bird that eats dead animals.

A
B
C
D
E
F
G
H
I
J
K
L
M
N
O
P
Q
R
S
T
U
V
W
X
Y
Z

W w

wade wades wading waded *verb*
To wade is to walk through deep water. *He waded across the stream.*

wag wags wagging wagged *verb*
When a dog wags its tail, it moves it quickly from side to side and up and down.

wages *noun*
the money that people are paid for the work they do.

wagon wagons *noun*
a cart that is used to carry people and things from one place to another. It has four wheels and is usually pulled along by horses.

wail wails wailing wailed *verb*
If somebody wails, they shout or make a sad cry because they are hurt or sad. *"You kicked me!" he wailed.*

waist waists *noun*
Your waist is the narrow, middle part of your body. *Jack is wearing a belt round his waist.*

waistcoat waistcoats *noun*
a short jacket with no sleeves or collar.

wait waits waiting waited *verb*
If you wait, you stay where you are because you are expecting something to happen. *We waited half an hour for the bus.*

waiter waiters *noun*
a person who brings you food in a café or a restaurant.

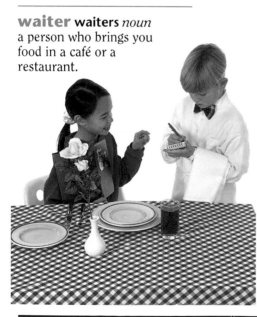

wake wakes waking woke woken *verb*
1 When you wake, you stop sleeping. *I woke up at seven o'clock this morning.*
2 When you wake someone, you make them stop sleeping.

walk walks walking walked *verb*
When you walk, you move along on your feet. *I walk to the park every day.*
walk *noun*
We took the dog for a walk.

wall walls *noun*
1 one of the sides of a building or a room. *I helped to paint my bedroom walls.*
2 A wall is also something made of bricks or stones that you can see around some fields and gardens. *We climbed over the wall into the secret garden.*

wallet wallets *noun*
a small, flat purse for keeping paper money in. *Dad had a £20 note in his wallet.*

wand wands *noun*
a stick that fairies and magicians wave when they do magic.

wander wanders wandering wandered *verb*
When you wander, you walk around slowly without going in any particular direction. *We wandered around in the woods looking for mushrooms.*

want wants wanting wanted *verb*
When you want something, you need it or you would like to have it. *Do you want an apple or an orange?*

war wars *noun*
a time when armies of different countries are fighting. ■ The opposite is **peace.**

ward wards *noun*
a big room in a hospital with beds in it for patients.

wardrobe wardrobes *noun*
a large cupboard where you can keep your clothes. *She hung her dress in the wardrobe.*

warehouse warehouses *noun*
a big building where goods are stored before they are taken to shops or other places. *a furniture warehouse.*

warm warmer warmest *adjective*
quite hot but not too hot. *The cat sat by the fire to keep warm.* ■ The opposite is **cool.**
warmth *noun*
I felt the warmth of the sun on my skin.

warn warns warning warned *verb*
If you warn somebody, you tell them about something dangerous or bad that may happen. *He warned us not to swim in the river because it was very deep.*
◆ *Dad warned us not to be late or he'd get cross.*

warning warnings *noun*
something that tells you about a danger that may happen. *The sign on the gate said, "Warning! Keep out - dangerous bull in field".*

wart warts *noun*
a hard lump on your skin. ▲ Rhymes with **sort.**

wash washes washing washed *verb*
When you wash something, you use soap and water to clean it.
He washed his face before going to bed.

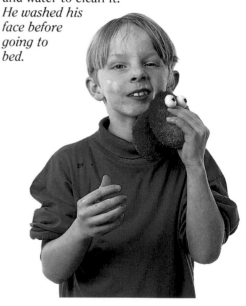

washing *noun*
clothes that you need to wash or that you have washed. *I put the washing in the washing machine.*

washing-up *noun*
When you do the washing-up, you clean the knives, forks, plates and cups after a meal. *I'll help you do the washing-up.*

wasp wasps *noun*
a flying insect with yellow and black stripes on its body. Wasps can sting.

waste *noun*
1 things that people throw away because they are old, broken, used up or not wanted.
2 What is left after you have digested your food and that is sent out of your body.
3 Something is a waste when you use too much of it, or do not use it carefully. *It's a waste to throw food away.*

waste **wastes wasting wasted** *verb*
1 If you waste something, you use more than you need. *Don't waste water.*
2 To waste also means not to make good use of something. *Don't waste time.*

watch **watches watching watched** *verb*
If you watch something, you look at it for a long time. *We watched the football match.* ◆ *Watch how I do this trick.*

watch
watches
noun
a small
clock that
you wear
around
your wrist.

water *noun*
the clear liquid that is in seas, lakes and rivers. *All living things need water.*

water **waters watering watered** *verb*
When you water plants, you pour water over them to help them grow.

waterfall **waterfalls** *noun*
a place on a river where a lot of water falls over high rocks or down a mountain. *Niagara Falls is a famous waterfall in North America.*

waterproof *adjective*
If something is waterproof, it does not let water go through it. *a waterproof jacket.*

wave **waves** *noun*
1 a curved line of water moving across a sea. *The waves crashed upon the shore.*
2 a vibrating movement like a wave on the sea that carries sound or light. *sound waves.*
3 a curving shape in your hair.
4 a movement with your hand that you make when you say "hello" or "goodbye" to somebody.

wave **waves waving waved** *verb*
When you wave, you move your hand up and down to say "hello" or "goodbye" to somebody. *Gran waved me goodbye as she got on the bus.*

wax *noun*
material that candles are made out of. Wax is hard when it is cold but it goes soft and melts when you heat it.

weak **weaker weakest** *adjective*
1 a weak person or thing has little power or strength. *She felt weak after her illness.* ◆ *weak knees.*
2 likely to break very easily. *That branch is too weak to support your weight.*
3 A weak drink has a lot of water or milk in it. *weak tea.*
● A word that sounds like **weak** is **week**.
■ The opposite is **strong** or **powerful**.

wealthy **wealthier wealthiest** *adjective*
rich and with a lot of money.

weapon **weapons** *noun*
something such as a gun, spear, a sword or a bow and arrow that people use to fight with.

wear **wears wearing wore worn** *verb*
1 When you wear clothes, you have them on your body. *Lindsay is wearing a blue dress.* ◆ *Steve wore jeans.*
2 When something wears out, you cannot use it any more because it is broken or too old. *These socks are worn out - they have holes in them.*
3 When something wears you out, it makes you very tired. *After running all the way to school, I was worn out.*

weather *noun*
The weather is how hot, cold, windy, rainy or dry it is outside. *The weather forecast tells you what the weather will be like for the next few days.*

weave **weaves weaving wove woven** *noun*
1 When you weave, you make a piece of cloth using a machine called a loom. *The loom has rows of thread fixed at each end and you move another thread in and out of these.*
2 To weave also means to make something like a basket or a mat by twisting thin strips of wood or straw in and out of each other.

web **webs** *noun*
a round net that a spider makes to catch flies in.
web-footed *adjective*
having feet with a piece of skin between the toes, such as geese and ducks have.

wedding **weddings** *noun*
When two people get married, they have a wedding.

A B C D E F G H I J K L M N O P Q R S T U V W X Y Z

a
b
c
d
e
f
g
h
i
j
k
l
m
n
o
p
q
r
s
t
u
v
w
x
y
z

weed **weeds** *noun*
a wild plant that grows in the garden
and that you do not want. *Daisies are
weeds.*

daisy

thistle

Blue whales

week **weeks** *noun*
a measure of time. There are seven days
in a week – Sunday, Monday, Tuesday,
Wednesday, Thursday, Friday and
Saturday. There are 52 weeks in a year.
● A word that sounds like **week** is **weak**.

weekend **weekends** *noun*
Saturday and Sunday.

weep **weeps weeping wept** *verb*
If somebody weeps, they cry. *She wept
because her cat had died.*

weigh **weighs
weighing
weighed** *verb*
1 You weigh
something on
scales to find out
how heavy it is.
2 Weigh also means how
heavy you are. *How
much do you weigh?*

weight **weights**
noun
1 how heavy somebody
or something is.
*What's the weight of
these apples?*
2 a piece of metal
weighing a certain
amount that you use
on scales to find
out how heavy
something is.
weighty *adjective*
a weighty problem.

weird **weirder weirdest** *adjective*
very strange. *I heard a weird noise last
night.*

welcome **welcomes welcoming
welcomed** *verb*
If you welcome somebody, you show that
you are happy to see them. *She came to
the door to welcome us.*

well **better best** *adjective, adverb*
1 When you do something well, you do
it in a good way. *Gerry plays the
guitar very well.*
2 If you are well, you feel healthy.

well **wells** *noun*
a well is a deep hole in the ground with
water or oil at the bottom.

wellingtons *noun*
long boots made of rubber or plastic that
you wear to keep your feet dry.

went past of **go**.

wept past of **weep**.

west *noun*
the direction in which the Sun sets in
the evening.
west *adjective*, **western** *adjective*
Senegal is in West Africa.
west *adverb*
The boat was sailing west.

western **westerns** *noun*
a film or a book about cowboys and the
Wild West of America.

wet **wetter wettest** *adjective*
Something that is wet is covered with or
full of water or other liquid. *You will get
wet if you go out in the rain.*
■ The opposite is **dry**.

whale **whales** *noun*
a very large mammal that lives in the
sea. Whales need air to breathe. A young
whale is called a calf.

wheat *noun*
a plant that farmers grow. We use its
seeds, called grain, to make flour.

wheel **wheels** *noun*
A wheel is a round thing on something
like a car, lorry or bicycle. Wheels turn
around and around to move things along
the ground.

wheelchair **wheelchairs** *noun*
a special chair with wheels for somebody
who cannot walk very well.

whether *conjunction*
If. *I don't know whether I can come
tonight.*

whine **whines whining whined**
verb
To whine is to make a long, miserable
sound because you want something.

whip **whips whipping whipped**
verb
1 If you whip a person or an animal you
hit them with a long piece of rope or
leather called a whip.
2 To whip also means to stir cream or
eggs very fast until they become stiff.

whisk **whisks whisking whisked**
verb
When you whisk things such as eggs or
cream, you beat them very quickly.
whisk *noun*.

whisker **whiskers** *noun*
one of the long hairs that cats, mice and
some other animals have on their faces.

whisper whispers whispering whispered *verb*
When you whisper, you speak very quietly so that other people cannot hear you. *She whispered in his ear.*

whistle whistles *noun*
1 an instrument that you blow into to make very high sounds. *He blew a whistle to end the football match.*
2 a high sound that you make when you blow through your lips.
whistle *verb*.

whole *adjective*
all of something. *He ate the whole cake.*
● A word that sounds like **whole** is **hole**.
whole *noun*
Two halves make a whole.

wick wicks *noun*
a piece of string that goes through the middle of a candle. When you light the wick, the candle burns.

wicked wickeder wickedest *adjective*
very bad or cruel. *That was a very wicked thing to do.*

wide wider widest *adjective*
1 Something that is wide measures a lot from one side to the other. *Motorways are very wide roads.*
■ The opposite is **narrow**.
2 Wide also means how much something measures. *The window is one metre wide.*

widow widows *noun*
a woman whose husband is dead.

widower widowers *noun*
a man whose wife is dead.

width *noun*
how wide something is. *He measured from side to side to find the width of the box.*

wife wives *noun*
A man's wife is the woman he is married to.

wig wigs *noun*
a thing made of hair that covers your head. Actors and bald people sometimes wear wigs.

wild wilder wildest *adjective*
1 Wild animals are animals that are not kept by people for food or as pets. Foxes and badgers are wild animals.
■ The opposite is **tame**.
2 Wild flowers and plants are not planted by people.

will wills *noun*
the part of your mind that makes you want to do things or decide what you want to do. *She has the will to win the race.* ◆ *He tidied his bedroom against his will.*

willing *adjective*
If you are willing, you are ready and happy to do what is wanted. *Are you willing to go to the shops for me?*

willow willows *noun*
a tree with long, narrow leaves that grows near water. Weeping willows have thin branches that hang downwards.

wilt wilts wilting wilted *verb*
If a plant wilts, it droops because it needs water.

win wins winning won *verb*
When you win a race or game you come first and do better than everybody else. *Kamran won the 100-metre race.*

wind winds *noun*
air that is moving very fast. *The wind blew the sailing boat along.* ▲ Rhymes with **tinned**.
windy *adjective*.
windy weather.

wind winds winding wound *verb*
1 When you wind a clock or a watch, you turn a key or a knob so that it starts working.
2 When you wind something like string around another thing, you twist it round and round. *They wound the wool into a ball.*
3 When a road or a river winds, it has lots of bends in it.
4 When you wind a film or a tape, you move it backwards or forwards. *Remember to wind the film on before you take the next picture.*
▲ Rhymes with **find**.

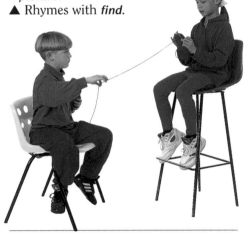

windmill windmills *noun*
a tall building with large pieces of wood, called sails, on top that turn around in the wind. As the sails turn, they make machines inside work to grind corn into flour.

A B C D E F G H I J K L M N O P Q R S T U V W X Y Z

a
b
c
d
e
f
g
h
i
j
k
l
m
n
o
p
q
r
s
t
u
v
w
x
y
z

window windows *noun*
a hole covered by glass in a wall of a building that lets in light and air.

windscreen windscreens *noun*
the window at the front of a car.

windsurf windsurfs windsurfing windsurfed *verb*
To windsurf is to ride over water on a special board with a sail.
windsurfer *noun*.

wine wines *noun*
Wine is an alcoholic drink usually made from grapes.

wing wings *noun*
1 Birds, bats and some insects, like bees, have wings which they flap when they fly.
2 The wings of an aeroplane are the two flat parts on each side that help it move through the air.

wink winks winking winked *verb*
If you wink at somebody, you close and open one eye very quickly. *She winked at me to show that it was a joke.*

winter *noun*
the season of the year between autumn and spring. Winter is the coldest part of the year.

wipe wipes wiping wiped *verb*
When you wipe something, you move a cloth over it to clean or dry it. *Freddie wiped the mess off the table.*

wire wires *noun*
a long, thin piece of metal that bends easily. Copper wire is used to carry electricity. Some fences are made of wire.

wise wiser wisest *adjective*
A person who is wise knows and understands a lot about many things. *Mum says you get wiser as you get older.*
wisdom *noun*.

wish wishes wishing wished *verb*
If you wish for something, you want to have it or you want it to happen very much. *I wish I was good at sport.*
wish *noun*.

witch witches *noun*
a woman in fairy stories who has magic powers. *The prince rescued the princess from the wicked witch.*

wither withers withering withered *verb*
When a plant withers, it becomes dry and dies. *The flowers withered in the hot sun and died.*

witness witnesses *noun*
a person who sees something important happen and can tell other people about it later. The *police are looking for a witness to the accident.*

wives plural of **wife**.

wizard wizards *noun*
a man in fairy stories who has magic powers.

wobble wobbles wobbling wobbled *verb*
When something wobbles, it shakes a little from side to side. *The jelly wobbled on the plate.*
wobbly *adjective*.

woke, woken past of **wake**.

wolf wolves *noun*
a wild animal that looks like a big dog, with a pointed nose and pointed ears. Wolves hunt in groups called packs. A young wolf is called a cub.

woman women *noun*
a grown-up female person.

womb wombs *noun*
The womb is the part of a woman or a female animal where a baby grows before it is born.
▲ Say **woom**.

won past of **win**.

wonder wonders wondering wondered *verb*
To wonder is to think about something that you do not know the answer to. *I wonder why snails move so slowly.*
wonder *noun*
They gazed with wonder at the fireworks.

wonderful *adjective*
very beautiful or very good. *We had a wonderful holiday.*

wood woods *noun*
1 the material that trees are made of. Tables and chairs are usually made of wood. You can also use wood to make paper.
2 A wood is a place where there are a lot of trees growing near each other.
wooden *adjective*
a wooden table.

wool wools *noun*
the soft, thick hair that grows on sheep. Wool is used for making cloth and for knitting. Jumpers and scarves are often made of wool.
woollen *adjective*
woollen gloves.
woolly *adjective*
a woolly hat.

word words *noun*
We use words when we speak or write. Words are made of letters of the alphabet and each word means something. *Angela looked up the meaning of a word in the dictionary.*

wore past of **wear**.

work works working worked *verb*
1 When you work, you do or make something as a job. *I work in a bank.*
2 To work also means to do something that takes a lot of time and effort. *I worked hard to finish the essay.*
3 When a machine works, it does what it should do. *The computer isn't working.*
work *noun*.

world *noun*
1 the planet that we live on, and all its countries and people.
2 the universe.

worm worms *noun*
a small creature with a long, thin body and no legs. Many worms live in the earth in gardens.

worn past of **wear**
worn socks.

worry worries worrying worried *verb*
If you worry, you keep thinking of bad things that might happen. *Dad worries if I'm late home from school.*

worship worships worshipping worshipped *verb*
To worship is to pray to God or Allah.

worth *adjective*
having a certain value. If something is worth £20, you could sell it for £20. *This bike is worth £20.*

wound wounds wounding wounded *verb*
To wound is to hurt or injure somebody. *He was shot and wounded in the leg.*
▲ Say **woond**.
wound *noun*.

wound past of **wind**.
▲ Rhymes with **found**.

wove, woven past of **weave**.

wrap wraps wrapping wrapped *verb*
If you wrap something, you cover it in paper or cloth. *He wrapped up the birthday present.*

wreck wrecks wrecking wrecked *verb*
To wreck is to break or destroy something completely so that you cannot use it. *The fire wrecked the house.*

wreck wrecks *noun*
a boat or an aircraft that has been badly damaged in an accident.

wreckage wreckages *noun*
the broken parts of something that has been badly damaged. *They found the wreckage of a plane.*

wrestle wrestles wrestling wrestled *verb*
To wrestle is to fight with somebody and try to push them onto the ground.

Sumo wrestlers

wriggle wriggles wriggling wriggled *verb*
If you wriggle, you keep twisting and moving about because you feel excited or uncomfortable. *The worm wriggled through the grass.*

wring wrings wringing wrung *verb*
If you wring something that is wet, you twist and squeeze it to get water out of it. *He wrung out the clothes and hung them out to dry.*

wrinkle wrinkles *noun*
a crease or line in your skin. *The old man's face was full of wrinkles.*
wrinkle *verb*
He wrinkled his forehead.
wrinkled *adjective*
wrinkled skin.

wrist wrists *noun*
Your wrist is the thin part of your arm just above your hand.

write writes writing wrote written *verb*
When you write, you make words with a pen or pencil. *Tom wrote his name at the top of the paper.* ● A word that sounds like **write** is **right**.
writer *noun*.

writing *noun*
the words that you make on paper with a pen or pencil. *Primrose has very neat writing.*

wrong *adjective*
1 If something is wrong, it is incorrect. *The answer to that sum is wrong.*
■ The opposite is **right**.
2 bad. *Being unkind to animals is wrong.*

wrung past of **wring**.

A B C D E F G H I J K L M N O P Q R S T U V W X Y Z

X x

X-ray **X-rays** *noun*
a picture of part of your body that shows the bones and other parts inside so that doctors can see if anything is broken or damaged.

xylophone **xylophones** *noun*
a musical instrument that has a row of wooden or metal bars of different lengths that you hit to give different notes. ▲ Say *zye-lo-fone*.

Y y

yacht **yachts** *noun*
a large boat with sails or an engine. Some yachts are used for racing.
▲ Say *yot*.

yawn **yawns yawning yawned** *verb*
When you yawn, you open your mouth wide and breathe in as you do when you are very tired.

year **years** *noun*
a measure of time. There are 12 months in a year.
yearly *adjective, adverb*
a yearly visit.

yeast *noun*
a substance that is used to make bread rise.

yell **yells yelling yelled** *verb*
If you yell, you shout very loudly.

yoghurt *noun*
a thick, slightly sour liquid made from milk. ▲ Say *yog-ert*.

yoke **yokes** *noun*
a wooden frame that goes across the back of two oxen pulling a plough or cart to make them stay together.
● A word that sounds like **yoke** is **yolk**.

yolk **yolks** *noun*
the yellow part inside an egg.
▲ Say *yoke*.

young **younger youngest** *adjective*
not having lived for many years or for as many years as somebody else. *I'm younger than my granddad.* ▲ Say *yung*. ■ The opposite is **old**.

youth **youths** *noun*
1 a time when a person is young. *He spent his youth in Australia.* ■ The opposite is **old age**.
2 a young man.
3 all young people. *the youth of today.*
◆ *a youth hostel.*
▲ Say *yooth*.

Z z

zap **zaps zapping zapped** *verb*
1 To zap is to shoot somebody or destroy something in a computer game.
2 To zap also means to keep changing quickly from one TV programme to another or from one section of a videotape to another.

zebra **zebras** *noun*
an animal like a horse with black and white stripes on its body. Zebras live in Africa.

zero **zeros** *noun*
the number 0. You write ten with a one and a zero – 10.

zest *noun*
orange, lemon or lime peel.

zigzag **zigzags** *noun*
a line that keeps changing direction and that bends sharply up and down.

zinc *noun*
a hard, blue-white metal.

zip **zips** *noun*
a long metal or plastic thing with two rows of teeth that fit together and that holds together two edges of material. *Trousers and bags often have zips.*
zip *verb*.

zombie **zombies** *noun*
in stories, a dead body brought back to life by witchcraft.

zone **zones** *noun*
an area in a town or a country used for a special purpose. *a danger zone.* ◆ *a no-parking zone.*

zoo **zoos** *noun*
a place where wild animals are kept so that people can look at them.
❖ **Look opposite**

zoology *noun*
the scientific study of animals.
▲ Say *zoo-ol-ogee*.
zoological *adjective*, **zoologist** *noun*
zoological gardens.

zoom **zooms zooming zoomed** *verb*
If something zooms, it moves very fast. *The rocket zoomed into space.*

Introduction

This book is called a thesaurus, which is a Latin word of Greek origin, meaning 'a treasury or storehouse of information', particularly when it deals with words and collections of words. If you examine what this book contains, you will see that is exactly what it is: a collection of words. It is a kind of dictionary, with a list of words in alphabetical order.

Instead of simply giving the *meaning* of a word, it tells you of other words that have a *similar* meaning. Suppose you began a letter to a friend with the sentence *I hope you have a nice time on your holiday*. The word *nice* sounds dull in this case. If you look up the word *nice* in this thesaurus, you will find that it gives you a short list of words that you could use instead: *pleasant, agreeable, amiable, charming, delightful.* Such words are known as **synonyms**. The word *nice* also has another meaning, which is quite different: *precise, accurate, fine, subtle.*

To go back to our letter, you could now write *I hope you have a **pleasant** time on your holiday*. Your friend could write back to you and tell you that *I am having a **delightful** time on my holiday!* As you can see, the thesaurus helps you to write in a better style, and to use words other than the very ordinary, perhaps even boring ones.

In addition to giving these alternative words, this thesaurus also shows you *opposite* words. In the case of *nice*, you will find the opposite word *nasty*. These opposite words are called **antonyms**. In many cases, there are cross-references to other words of similar meaning which are to be found elsewhere in the book. Below is a key to show you how to find the various words and their meaning.

Parts of speech: *adj.* = adjective; *adv.* = adverb; *conj.* = conjunction; *n.* = noun; *prep.* = preposition; *v.* = verb

Opposite words: These are shown with a star (★) and in ★**bold type.**

Cross-reference to other meanings: If a word is shown with an arrow ▷ and in *italics*, it means that you can look up that word to find further, similar meanings. For example, if you look up the word *ruffian*, you find, at the end of the list, the word ▷ *rascal.* So, if you look under *rascal* you will find other, similar words.

A **homonym** is a word that sounds the same as another, but means something quite different. Such words are shown in small capitals, like this: HERE.

If a word has a number of different meanings, each different meaning is shown by a figure in a circle: ①, ②, ③.

George Marshall

A
B
C
D
E
F
G
H
I
J
K
L
M
N
O
P
Q
R
S
T
U
V
W
X
Y
Z

A a

abandon *v.* forsake, give up, leave in the lurch, surrender, sacrifice ▷*leave, quit*

abate *v.* lessen, slacken, dwindle, fade

abbey *n.* monastery, priory, cloister, church

abbreviate *v.* shorten, cut, contract, reduce ▷*abridge* ★**expand**

abdicate *v.* resign, retire, renounce ▷*quit*

ability *n.* aptitude, knack, flair, talent, gift, skill ★**inability**

able *adj.* skilful, competent, talented, strong ▷*clever* ★**incapable**

abnormal *adj.* unusual, exceptional, erratic ★**normal**

abode *n.* home, residence, haunt, dwelling, lodging

abolish *v.* destroy, cancel, do away with, exterminate ★**restore**

abominable *adj.* detestable, foul, hateful, horrible, loathsome, atrocious, ▷*awful* ★**desirable**

about *prep. & adv.* near, nearly, touching, concerning, around

above *prep. & adv.* over, beyond, exceeding, on high, aloft ★**below**

abridge *v.* condense, compact ▷*abbreviate*

abroad *adv.* overseas, far, away, apart, adrift ★**home**

abrupt *adj.* ① sudden, curt, blunt, brusque ② steep, hilly ★**smooth**

absent *adj.* not present, away, elsewhere, missing ★**present**

absent-minded *adj.* distracted, heedless, forgetful ★**attentive**

absolute *adj.* perfect, complete, certain, positive ▷*utter* ★**imperfect**

absorb *v.* take in, soak up, assimilate, devour, pull in, swallow, consume ★**emit**

absorbed *adj.* intent, rapt, engrossed, preoccupied

abstain *adj.* refuse, refrain, give up, keep from, avoid, forbear ★**indulge**

abstract ① *adj.* theoretical, intangible ② *v.* withdraw, steal, remove, take away

absurd *adj.* preposterous, nonsensical, foolish ▷*silly* ★**sensible**

abundant *adj.* ample, profuse, rich, plentiful, overflowing ★**scarce**

abuse ① *v.* damage, injure, spoil, maltreat, hurt, misuse ★**protect** ② *n.* maltreatment, attack, exploitation

accelerate *v.* speed up, hasten, quicken, urge ▷*hurry* ★**delay**

accent *n.* ① stress, beat, rhythm, emphasis ② brogue *Eileen speaks with an Irish brogue,* drawl, pronunciation, twang

accept *v.* receive, take, admit, adopt, take on ★**refuse**

accident *n.* chance, casualty, disaster, calamity, mishap ★**purpose**

acclaim *v.* applaud, praise, approve ★**denounce**

accommodate *v.* oblige, lodge, receive, admit, adapt ★**deprive**

accompany *v.* be with, go with, escort, attend, convoy ★**abandon**

accomplice *n.* ally, confederate, helper, partner, conspirator, henchman

accomplish *v.* perform, fulfil, finish, complete ▷*achieve* ★**fail**

accord ① *v.* agree, consent, harmonize, allow ★**differ** ② *n.* agreement, harmony

account *n.* ① bill, invoice, record, score ② tale, story *Mary told us the story of her trip to Australia,* narrative, history

accumulate *v.* collect, grow, gather, hoard, increase, amass ★**scatter**

accurate *adj.* careful, exact, faithful, precise ▷*correct* ★**defective**

accuse *v.* charge, incriminate, taunt, denounce ★**defend**

accustom *v.* acclimatize, get used to, familiarize ★**estrange**

ache ① *n.* pain, twinge ② *v.* hurt, pain, sting, smart

achieve *v.* fulfil, accomplish, reach ▷*attain* ★**fail**

achievement *n.* accomplishment, attainment, exploit, deed, completion ▷*feat*

acid *adj.* sharp, vinegarish, acrid, sour, tart ★**sweet, mellow**

acknowledge *v.* admit, avow, recognize, own, accept, yield ★**disclaim**

acquaint *v.* inform, tell, teach, notify, advise ★**deceive**

acquaintance *n.* ① friend, pal, associate ② knowledge *You will need some knowledge of Spanish if you visit Mexico,* familiarity, experience

acquainted *adj.* aware, familiar, informed

acquire *v.* gain, earn, obtain, get, capture ★**forfeit, lose**

acquit *v.* discharge, release, exonerate, dismiss, liberate ★**accuse**

acrid *adj.* bitter, harsh, sour ▷*acid* ★**mellow**

across *adj. & prep.* crosswise, athwart, slantingly, over against ★**along**

act ① *n.* deed, performance, action, step, presentation ② *v.* operate, work, function, perform *Our class will perform a play by Ibsen*

action *n.* operation, movement, feat, deed, exercise ★**rest**

actual *adj.* correct, true, positive, certain ★**possible**

acute *adj.* sharp, pointed, keen, penetrating, severe, distressing ★**blunt**

adapt *v.* fit, adjust, accommodate, suit, conform

adaptable *adj.* flexible, usable, adjustable

add *v.* ① total, combine, tot up ★**subtract** ② affix, annex, connect ★**detach**

address ① *n.* residence, place, home, domicile ② *v.* talk to, speak to, accost, call

adept *adj.* expert, adroit, handy, skilful ▷*clever* ★**clumsy**

adequate *adj.* ① sufficient, ample *The boat was small, but there was ample room for two,* plenty ② equal, able, qualified

adjacent *adj.* near, neighbouring, next, bordering, touching ★**separate**

adjoin *v.* border, touch, verge, annex

adjust *v.* ① regulate, rectify, correct, amend, revise ② get used to *Our puppy quickly got used to her new home*

administer *v.* ① execute, perform, carry out, conduct, direct, manage ② give, dole out

The nurse doled out the pills each morning

admirable *adj.* praiseworthy, commendable, excellent ★**despicable**

admiration *n.* adoration, affection, approval, delight, respect ★**contempt**

admire *v.* approve, esteem, appreciate ▷*respect* ★**despise**

admit *v.* ① pass, permit, grant, concede, allow, let in, acknowledge ② confess, own up ★**deny**

ado *n.* hubbub, commotion, fuss *Let's start the meeting without any more fuss,* excitement

adopt *v.* assume, select, choose, employ, apply, take over

adore *v.* worship, idolize, admire, revere, venerate ★**despise**

adorn *v.* beautify, decorate, embellish, deck, garnish ★**deface**

adrift *adv.* loose, afloat, floating, distracted

adroit *adj.* handy, skilful, dexterous, expert ▷*adept* ★**awkward**

adult *adj.* grown-up, mature, full-grown ★**immature**

advance *v.* ① progress, increase, further, go,

Adequate

The boat was small, but there was ample room for two.

go on, proceed ★**retreat** ② lend *Helen said she will lend me the money,* loan

advanced *adj.* beforehand, ahead, modern

advantage *n.* benefit, upper hand, opportunity, assistance, boon ★**hindrance**

adventure *n.* experience, escapade, venture, undertaking

adversary *n.* foe, opponent, antagonist, rival ▷*enemy* ★**ally**

adverse *adj.* unfavourable, hard, hostile, unfortunate ▷*unlucky* ★**fortunate**

advice *n.* counsel, suggestion, guidance

advise *v.* counsel, urge, suggest, prompt, inform, persuade ★**deter**

afar *adv.* far, far off, away, abroad ★**near**

affable *adj.* courteous, gracious, easy, frank, open ★**haughty**

affair *n.* ① matter, business, concern ② romance, liaison, love affair

affect *v.* ① assume, adopt, feign, sham, put on airs ② influence, change, sway *Your argument did not sway my opinion*

affection *n.* desire, fondness, feeling, kindness, liking ▷*love* ★**indifference**

affectionate *adj.* warmhearted, fond, loving ▷*tender* ★**indifferent**

affirm *v.* assert, state, declare, endorse, maintain ★**deny**

affix *v.* attach, fasten, unite, append ★**detach**

afflict *v.* trouble, ail, distress, upset

afford *v.* ① be wealthy, be rich ② produce, provide *The stream provided good, clean water,* yield, bear ★**deny**

afraid *adj.* timid, cautious, frightened, alarmed ▷*fearful* ★**fearless**

after *prep.* behind, later, following, succeeding ★**before**

again *adv.* ① frequently, repeatedly, anew, afresh ② furthermore, moreover

against *prep.* opposite, over, opposing, resisting ★**for**

age ① *n.* period, date, time ② *n.* old age, senility ★**youth** ③ *v.* grow old, mature

aged *adj.* ancient, antiquated ▷*old* ★**youthful**

agent *n.* doer, actor, performer, operator,

Aircraft

Hot air balloon

Microlight

Seaplane

worker, representative, go-between

aggravate *v.* ① increase, make worse, worsen ★**mitigate** ② irritate, annoy

aggressive *adj.* offensive, warlike, military, pushy ★**peaceful**

aghast *adj.* astonished, dumbfounded, bewildered ★**calm**

agile *adj.* nimble, active, fleet, brisk, alert ▷*lithe* ★**clumsy**

agitate *v.* disturb, trouble, excite, stir, fluster ★**smooth**

ago *adv.* past, gone, since ★**hence**

agony *n.* torture, torment, distress, pangs,

Airship

VTOL (Vertical Take Off and Landing)

Airliner

Glider

Biplane

Helicopter

anguish, woe ▷*pain* ★**comfort**

agree *v.* accord, fit, harmonize, combine, tally, suit ★**differ**

agreeable *adj.* obliging, welcome, acceptable, grateful ▷*pleasant* ★**disagreeable**

agreement *n.* understanding, harmony, concord ★**dispute**

ahead *adv.* ① forward, onwards ② before, in advance ★**behind**

aid *v.* assist, support, encourage, serve ▷*help* ★**hinder**

aim *n.* object, goal, purpose, end, intention

aisle *n.* path, corridor, passage, way ISLE

akin *adj.* related, similar, allied, like ★**dissimilar**

alarm *v.* frighten, terrify, startle ▷*scare* ★**comfort**

alert *adj.* active, ready, wakeful, watchful ▷*agile* ★**drowsy**

alien ① *adj.* foreign, strange, remote ★**akin** ② *n.* foreigner, stranger

alike *adj.* similar, resembling, allied, like ★**unlike**

alive *adj.* living, breathing, warm, alert, brisk ★**dead**

all *adj.* whole, entire, complete, total ★**none**

allot *v.* apportion, give, allocate, dispense, grant ★**retain**

allow *v.* grant, permit, concede, owe, tolerate, entitle ★**forbid**

ally *n.* friend, companion, supporter, accomplice, colleague ★**foe**

almost *adj.* nearly, about, approximately, well-nigh

alone *adj.* lone, lonely, lonesome, forlorn ★**together**

aloud *adv.* loudly, noisily, clamorously, audibly ★**silently** ALLOWED

already *adv.* at this time, now, just now, previously

alter *v.* modify, vary, convert, transform ▷*change* ★**retain** ALTAR

altogether *adv.* completely, wholly, outright, totally ★**partially**

always *adv.* ever, forever, eternally ★**never**

amass *v.* collect, accumulate, heap, pile ★**scatter**

amaze *v.* astound, surprise, stun, dumbfound ▷*astonish*

ambition *n.* aspiration, desire, longing, zeal, aim ▷*goal*

amend *v.* revise, mend, correct, repair, improve, put right, remedy ▷*alter*

amiable *adj.* affable, kindly, pleasant, amicable ▷*agreeable* ★**unfriendly**

amount *n.* figure, volume, sum, number, total

ample *adj.* bountiful, liberal, sufficient, plentiful ▷*abundant* ★**insufficient**

amplify *v.* increase, raise, enlarge, elaborate *Our teacher explained the problem and went on to elaborate the details,* make louder ★**abbreviate**

amuse *v.* entertain, charm, beguile, please ★**bore**

ancestor *n.* forebear, parent, forefather, antecedent, predecessor ★**descendant**

ancient *adj.* aged, antique, primeval, time-honoured ▷*old* ★**modern**

anger *n.* wrath, ire, resentment, indignation, fury ▷*rage*

angry *adj.* wrathful, irate, resentful, furious, infuriated, indignant ★**good-tempered**

angle *n.* ① corner, bend, fork, branch ② aspect, phase, point of view *We quarrelled at first, but then I saw Tom's point of view*

anguish *n.* torment, torture, pain ▷*agony* ★**ease**

announce *v.* broadcast, declare, propound,

Alphabets

Arabic

Hebrew

АБВГДЕ

Cyrillic (Russian)

ลหรูต่๑๖อ้ำ

Thai

Egyptian hieroglyphs

A B C D E F

Latin

Sanskrit

Japanese

ABГΔEZ

Greek

Runes

reveal, herald ▷*proclaim* ★**conceal**

annoy *v.* tease, vex, irritate, disturb, harass ▷*upset* ★**soothe**

answer *n.* reply, response, solution *It was a difficult puzzle, but Emma came up with the solution* ★**question**

anticipate *v.* expect, prepare, hope for, foresee, predict

anxious *adj.* fearful, afraid, apprehensive, worried ★**carefree**

apart *adv.* away, separately, asunder, loosely ★**together**

aperture *n.* slit, hole, orifice, opening, cleft

apologize *v.* express regret, excuse, explain, plead, atone ★**insult**

apparel *n.* clothes, robes, vestments, raiment, trappings, attire

apparent *adj.* plain, conspicuous, unmistakable, clear ▷*obvious* ★**obscure**

appeal *v.* address, request, urge, entreat, invite, ask ▷*atttract*

appear *v.* emerge, become visible, seem, look, come into view ★**disappear**

appearance *n.* aspect, look, shape, form, impression, likeness

appease *v.* pacify, moderate, satisfy, stay, soften ★**provoke**

appetite *n.* hunger, palate, relish, liking

applaud *v.* clap, cheer, praise, approve, encourage ★**denounce**

apply *v.* ① use, utilize, employ ② devote, direct, dedicate *Sue was dedicated to her job and worked very hard*

appoint *v.* name, assign, nominate, engage

appreciate *v.* esteem, recognize, respect, value, enjoy

appropriate ① *v.* use, employ, adopt ② *adj.* fitting, proper *To do a job well, you should use the proper tools,* timely

approve *v.* acclaim, admire, appreciate, favour, agree ★**disapprove**

approximate *adj.* near, close, rough

apt *adj.* ① fit, apposite, appropriate, timely ★**unfitted** ② liable, prone, inclined *Jack and Meg are both inclined to be late.* ③ clever, intelligent, expert

ardent *adj.* passionate, warm, eager, fervent,

Apes

Gibbon
Gorilla
Orangutan
Chimpanzee

intense, keen, dedicated ★**indifferent**

arduous *adj.* hard, laborious, tough, strenuous ▷*difficult* ★**easy**

area *n.* district, region, place, expanse, tract

argue *v.* ① discuss, debate, talk over ② quibble, quarrel, disagree

arid *adj.* parched, sterile ▷*dry* ★**moist**

arise *v.* ① awaken, get up ② begin, come into existence, originate, crop up, take place

army *n.* troops, legion, force, soldiery

around *adv.* about, encircling, on every side ★**within**

arouse *v.* awaken, excite, disturb, alarm ★**pacify**

arrange *v.* sort, order, dispose, deal, classify ★**confuse**

arrest *v.* seize, take prisoner, hold, detain, stop ★**release**

arrive *v.* reach, attain, land, get to, appear ★**depart**

arrogant *adj.* supercilious, proud, haughty, disdainful, conceited ★**modest**

A
B
C
D
E
F
G
H
I
J
K
L
M
N
O
P
Q
R
S
T
U
V
W
X
Y
Z

a
b
c
d
e
f
g
h
i
j
k
l
m
n
o
p
q
r
s
t
u
v
w
x
y
z

art *n.* skill, artistry, cleverness, talent

artful *adj.* cunning, knowing, crafty, wily, sly ★**innocent**

article *n.* ① thing, object, substance ② essay, treatise, typescript

artificial *adj.* invented, fictitious, fabricated, man-made, synthetic ★**real**

ascend *v.* climb, rise, go up, get up, move up, scale, mount ★**descend**

ashamed *adj.* shamefaced, abashed, confused ★**proud**

ask *v.* demand, query, inquire, appeal ▷*request* ★**answer**

aspect *n.* front, face, side, appearance, presentation, look, expression

aspire *v.* wish, long, desire, aim, hope, crave

ass *n.* ① donkey, mule ② fool, dunce, idiot, dolt, wally, clot

assault *v.* attack, assail, set upon, charge, invade ★**defend**

assemble *v.* meet, gather, convene, come together, muster, collect ★**disperse**

assent *v.* agree, comply, accept, consent ★**dissent**

assert *v.* pronounce, maintain, state, aver ▷*declare* ★**deny**

assess *v.* estimate, evaluate, appraise

assign *v.* appoint, name, apportion, entrust

assist *v.* aid, support, protect, maintain, sustain ▷*help* ★**obstruct**

association *n.* union, connection, companionship, society, company, club

assortment *n.* variety, kind, sort, batch, parcel, collection

assume *v.* ① believe, accept, suppose, admit ② confiscate, take, possess oneself of

assure *v.* promise, guarantee, warrant, encourage ★**deter**

astonish *v.* startle, surprise, confound, alarm, scare ▷*amaze*

astound *v.* stagger, stupefy ▷*astonish*

astray *adj.* lost, gone, vanished, missing, loose ★**safe**

astute *adj.* shrewd, brainy, knowing, sharp, acute, crafty ★**simple**

atrocious *adj.* monstrous, enormous, shameful, cruel, abominable, vile

attach *v.* fasten, append, unite, tie ▷*connect* ★**unfasten**

attack *v.* assault, invade, set upon, pounce, descend upon ★**defend**

attain *v.* extend, master, obtain, acquire, grasp ▷*reach* ★**fail**

attempt *v.* endeavour, strive, seek, tackle ▷*try* ★**abandon**

attend *v.* ① listen, heed, notice, observe, follow ★**disregard** ② be present

attentive *adj.* mindful, particular, heedful, observant ★**careless**

attire *n.* costume, robes, clothes, garments ▷*apparel*

attitude *n.* disposition, bearing, outlook, posture, position, aspect

attract *v.* ① draw, influence, tempt, prompt, pull, drag ② fascinate, enchant, captivate ★**repel**

attractive *adj.* agreeable, beautiful, handsome, pretty, tempting ★**repellent**

avail *n.* benefit, advantage, use, help, profit

available *adj.* convenient, handy, ready, attainable, accessible, within reach

avenge *v.* retaliate, revenge, pay back, take vengeance for ★**pardon**

average *adj.* usual, ordinary, mediocre, so-so, normal, standard ★**extreme**

avid *adj.* eager, greedy, grasping

avoid *v.* shun, elude, quit, keep clear of, evade ▷*dodge* ★**seek**

awake *v.* wake, rouse, arouse, awaken, stir

award *v.* reward, give, bestow, grant, donate ★**withdraw**

aware *adj.* conscious, sensible, informed, assured ★**unaware oblivious**

away *adv.* absent, not present, afar, elsewhere ★**near**

awe *n.* fear, dread, shock, consternation, wonder

awful *adj.* fearful, terrible, alarming, dreadful ★**commonplace**

awkward *adj.* ungainly, unwieldy, uncouth, clownish, gawky ▷*clumsy* ★**dexterous**

awry *adj.* crooked, askew, amiss, twisted, wrong ★**straight**

B b

babble *v.* prattle, blab, cackle, chatter, gossip

baby *n.* babe, infant, child, toddler, tot

back ① *adj.* after, rear, hind, posterior ★**front** ② *v.* uphold, support *The party will support Tina Johnson at the next election,* endorse, be loyal to

backer *n.* supporter, ally, champion, sponsor

backward *adj.* slow, shy, reluctant, unwilling, retarded ▷*dull* ★**forward**

bad *adj.* ① imperfect, dreadful, unsound, awful, atrocious ② naughty, wrong, wicked, ill-behaved ③ rotten *This barrel is full of rotten apples,* spoiled ★**good**

badge *n.* emblem, hallmark, symbol, crest

badger *v.* bother, annoy, nag ▷*pester*

bad-mannered *adj.* impolite, boorish, uncivil ▷*rude* ★**polite**

baffle *v.* puzzle, perplex, frustrate, bewilder, mystify ▷*puzzle*

bag *n.* net, sack, pouch, purse, knapsack

bail *v.* scoop, ladle, dip

bait ① *v.* tease, bother, goad, rib, needle ▷*pester* ② *n.* decoy, lure, snare BATE

bake *v.* cook, roast, harden, fire

balance *v.* weigh, adjust, equalize, compare

bald *adj.* hairless, severe, stark, bare, unadorned

balk *v.* hinder, baffle, thwart, obstruct, foil ★**aid**

ball *n.* ① dance, masquerade ② globe, orb, sphere

ballad *n.* song, serenade, ditty

ballot *n.* vote, election, franchise, poll

ban *v.* prohibit, forbid, deny, stop

band *n.* ① stripe, strip, zone, belt ② orchestra, ensemble, group BANNED

bandit *n.* outlaw, robber, highwayman, thief, crook

bang *v.* crash, slam, smash, collide

banish *v.* expel, eject, exclude, exile, deport, cast out ▷*dismiss* ★**welcome**

bank *n.* ① shore, terrace, coast, embankment ② safe, vault, treasury

banner *n.* ensign, standard, streamer ▷*flag*

banquet *n.* meal, feast, repast

banter *v.* chaff, tease, ridicule, joke

bar *v.* ① obstruct, block, blockade, forbid, shut out ② fasten, bolt, lock, latch

bare *adj.* ① barren, empty, void ② naked, unclothed, severe, blunt *We expected a polite reply, but got a blunt refusal,* bald BEAR

barely *adv.* hardly, scarcely *The well had run dry, and there was scarcely enough water for all of us,* just, simply

bargain ① *n.* pact, deal ② *adj.* low-priced, cheap

bark *n.* ① rind, husk, peel ② yelp, growl, cry

barrel *n.* cask, keg, drum, tub, cylinder

barren *adj.* bare, unfertile, empty ▷*arid* ★**fertile** BARON

barrier *n.* obstruction, obstacle, block, fence

barter *v.* swap, exchange, trade

base ① *adj.* low, sordid, cheap, corrupt ② *adj.* dishonourable, vile ③ *adj.* humble, menial ④ *n.* bottom, foundation ⑤ *v.* found *The book* Robinson Crusoe *was founded on a true story* BASS

Band

Banned

bashful *adj.* shy, timid, modest, coy ★**bold**

basin *n.* bowl, pot, sink, tub, depression

batch *n.* lot, amount, assortment, collection

batter *v.* beat, strike, shatter, break, smash

battle *v.* clash, combat, fight, struggle, wrestle

bawl *v.* shout, yell, roar, bellow ★**whisper**

bay ① *n.* inlet, gulf, basin, bight ② *v.* bark, yelp BEY

be *v.* exist, live, breathe

beach *n.* shore, sands, seaside, strand BEECH

beacon *n.* signal, lamp, light, guide

beak *n.* snout, bill, nose

beam *n.* ① ray, light, streak ② plank, joist, girder

bear *v.* ① tolerate, put up with, endure, suffer ★**protest** ② bring, fetch, carry BARE

bearing *n.* manner, behaviour, appearance, attitude, posture *He was a tall man with a military bearing* BARING

bearings *n.* direction, whereabouts, location *In the storm we totally lost our bearings*

beat *v.* ① strike, pound, thrash ▷*batter* ② throb, flutter, thump *My heart thumped when I heard the sound of shouting in the street* BEET

beautiful *adj.* handsome, lovely, graceful, delicate, gorgeous ▷*pretty* ★**ugly**

beauty *n.* elegance, charm, loveliness, grace ★**ugliness**

because ① *conj.* for, owing to, by reason of, since *Since Tom and Jane are here, I will stay too, as* ② *adv.* consequently

beckon *v.* signal, call, nod, summon

becoming *adj.* graceful, suitable, comely, fitting, attractive

before ① *prep.* ahead, in front of, forward, preceding ② *adv.* earlier *Here is a pie that I baked earlier,* previously ★**after**

beg *v.* ask, request, entreat, beseech, plead, pray

begin *v.* commence, initiate, found, launch ▷*start* ★**end**

beginner *n.* novice, recruit, learner, pupil

beginning *n.* start, opening, origin, outset, foundation ★**end**

behaviour *n.* conduct, demeanour, manners

Bell

Handbell

Belfry
Bell tower
Bicycle bell
Church bell
Doorbell
Gong

▷*bearing* ★**misbehaviour**

behind ① *prep.* after, following *Bill arrived to meet us, with his dog following* ② *adv.* in the rear of, later, afterwards ★**before**

being *n.* creature, animal

belief *n.* faith, confidence, opinion, trust ★**disbelief**

believe *v.* trust, assent, have faith in, think, suspect ★**disbelieve**

bellow *v.* roar, shout, cry ▷*bawl*

belong *v.* relate to, pertain, be owned by

below *adv.* under, beneath, underneath ★**above**

belt *n.* strap, sash, girdle, strip

bend *v.* curve, incline, turn, yield, relax ★**straighten**

benefit *n.* advantage, profit, good, favour, aid, blessing ★**disadvantage**

beside *adv.* alongside, side by side, next to, abreast, together ★**apart**

besides *adv.* in addition, furthermore, also, moreover

best *adj.* choice, prime, unequalled, finest ★**worst**

bestow *v.* award, donate, confer, present ★**deprive**

betray *v.* deceive, dupe, expose, unmask, inform on, reveal ★**protect**

better *adj.* superior, finer, preferable *I think it would be preferable to visit the museum this afternoon instead of this morning* ★**worse**

between *prep.* amid, among, betwixt

beware *v.* be careful, refrain from, heed,

avoid, mind, watch out, guard against

bewilder *v.* confound, dazzle, mystify, confuse ▷*astonish* ★**enlighten**

beyond *adv.* over, farther, past, more, after ★**near**

bicker *v.* quarrel, dispute, wrangle, argue ★**converse**

bid *v.* proffer, present, tender, request, propose

big *adj.* ① large, great, wide, huge, bulky, fat, ② important ★**small**

bill *n.* ① statement *This is a statement of your investments with us,* account, invoice, score, chit, reckoning ② beak, mouth ③ poster, advertisement, notice

bin *n.* box, can, case, chest, crate, tub

bind *v.* tie, fasten, secure, lace, swathe ★**untie**

birth *n.* origin, beginning, source, creation ★**death** BERTH

bit *n.* morsel, piece, fragment, part, crumb ★**whole**

bite *v.* gnaw, chew, rend, chomp BIGHT

bitter *adj.* ① harsh, sour, tart ▷*acid* ② severe, stern ▷*sarcastic* ★**mellow**

blame *v.* chide, rebuke, reproach, criticize, accuse, condemn ★**praise**

bland *adj.* soft, mild, gentle, soothing, tasteless

blank *adj.* empty, bare, void, bleak ★**full**

blare *v.* blast, boom, clang, roar, sound

blast *v.* explode, split, discharge, burst

blaze *v.* burn, flare, glare, flicker

bleak *adj.* bare, open, exposed, dismal, stormy, chilly, raw, desolate *The farm was a cold and desolate place in winter* ★**sheltered**

blemish *n.* spot, stain, mark, speck, flaw, blotch, defect

blend *v.* mix, unite, harmonize, merge, fuse, combine ★**separate**

bless *v.* hallow, praise, exalt, endow, enrich, consecrate ★**curse**

blessing *n.* advantage, boon, approval, godsend ★**curse**

blight *n.* pest, plague, disease

blind *adj.* ① eyeless, sightless *These*

salamanders live in underground caves and are sightless, unsighted, unseeing ② ignorant, uninformed

blink *v.* wink, twinkle, glitter, gleam

bliss *n.* joy, ecstasy, rapture, blessedness, happiness ★**misery**

block ① *n.* lump, mass, chunk ② *v.* obstruct, bar, arrest BLOC

bloom ① *n.* flower, blossom, bud ② *v.* blossom, flourish, flower, thrive ★**decay**

blot *n.* stain, blotch ▷*blemish*

blow ① *v.* puff, gust, blast ② *n.* shock, stroke, impact, bang

blue *adj.* azure, turquoise, indigo, navy, ultramarine, cobalt BLEW

bluff ① *adj.* frank, brusque, abrupt, outspoken *Freda Jones will never be elected mayor; she's too outspoken* ② *v.* deceive, pretend *The lion closed its eyes, pretending it had not seen the antelope,* conceal

blunder ① *n.* mistake, error, slip, fault *It was my fault that the plates were broken,* oversight ② *v.* slip, err, bungle ★**correct**

blunt *adj.* ① plain, abrupt, curt ▷*bluff* ② dull, not sharp

blush *v.* redden, colour, crimson, flush

The Body

Head
Hair
Eyes
Ears
Back
Arm
Elbow
Nails
Leg
Knee
Ankle
Foot

A B C D E F G H I J K L M N O P Q R S T U V W X Y Z

board ① n. plank, table ② n. committee, council ③ v. live *The new teacher is going to live at our house,* lodge, accommodate BORED

boast v. swagger, swell, bluster ▷*brag*

boat n. ship, vessel, craft, bark, barge

body n. ① corpse, trunk, carcase ② corporation, company, society

bog n. swamp, morass, marsh, quagmire

bogus adj. fake, false, spurious, sham, counterfeit ★**genuine**

boil v. cook, steam, poach, seethe, foam

boisterous adj. tempestuous, stormy, uncontrolled, loud, noisy ★**serene**

bold adj. fearless, courageous, adventurous, valiant, daring ▷*brave* ★**fearful** BOWLED

bolt ① v. run away, take flight, flee *After the revolution, the queen had to flee the country* ② v. devour, gorge, eat ▷*gulp* ③ n. lock, latch, fastening

bond n. tie, link, joint, band, fastening

bonny adj. fair, handsome, healthy, shapely, buxom ▷*pretty* ★**plain**

bonus n. premium, benefit, award, prize

booby n. blockhead, noodle, oaf, chump, nincompoop, dunce, noodle, numbskull, blast ★**oracle**

boom n. ① thunder, roar, rumble ② prosperity *After the recession came years of prosperity*

boon n. blessing, windfall, advantage ▷*benefit* ★**drawback**

boorish adj. unrefined, loutish, bad-mannered, rude, clumsy ★**refined**

boost v. strengthen, raise up, heighten

border n. fringe, edge, margin, frontier

bore v. ① tire, weary, fatigue *We were fatigued by the long bus ride home* ② drill, punch, perforate BOAR

bored adj. uninterested, tired, jaded, fed-up BOARD

borrow v. take, imitate, adopt, assume, raise money ★**lend**

boss n. ① stud, knob ② chief, manager *Helen is manager of the new beauty salon,* employer

bossy adj. domineering, tyrannical, despotic, overbearing ▷*arrogant* ★**modest**

bother v. alarm, annoy, concern, distress ▷*disturb*

bottom n. underside, deepest part, floor ▷*base* ★**top**

bough n. branch, limb, shoot BOW

boulder n. rock, slab, stone

bounce v. leap, spring, bound, bump, jump

bound v. rebound, prance ▷*bounce*

boundary n. bounds, limits, border, frontier, verge, perimeter ▷*barrier*

bounty n. donation, gift, grant ▷*bonus*

bow v. bend, nod, stoop, kneel, incline, kowtow, yield, submit BOUGH

bowl n. plate, basin, dish, vessel, casserole BOLL

box ① n. carton, case, chest, coffer *The town's coffers were empty, so they had to raise taxes,* pack ② v. fight, spar, punch

boy n. lad, youth, child, youngster BUOY

brag v. crow, swagger, gloat ▷*boast*

braid v. entwine, weave, plait BRAYED

branch n. ① shoot, limb, twig ▷*bough* ② department, office, division

brand n. ① trade-mark, emblem, label ② blot, stigma, stain

brandish v. flourish, parade, shake, swing, wave, wield, flaunt

brash adj. brazen, foolhardy, hasty, impetuous, impudent ▷*rash*

brave ① adj. audacious, fearless, daring, dauntless, gallant, heroic, courageous ▷*bold* ★**cowardly** ② v. dare, defy, endure

break v. batter, burst, crack, snap, fracture, shatter BRAKE

breathe v. draw in, gasp, inhale, sniff, gulp, wheeze, emit

breed v. reproduce, produce, cause, bear, rear, bring forth, multiply, propagate

bribe v. corrupt, buy, grease the palm, fix

brief adj. short, little, concise, terse, crisp, curt ★**lengthy**

bright adj. ① clear, cloudless, fair, airy ② cheerful, genial *We were pleased to find so many genial members in the club* ③ clever, ingenious, acute ★**dull**

Bridges

Cantilever

Suspension

Beam

Arch

Bascule bridge
Drawbridge
Footbridge

Rope bridge
Swing span bridge
Viaduct

brilliant *adj.* ① lustrous, shining, radiant, dazzling, luminous ② clever, intelligent ★**dull**

brim *n.* edge, brink, rim, fringe

bring *v.* bear, fetch, deliver, carry, convey

bring about *v.* bring off, accomplish, achieve, cause, make happen

bring up *v.* breed, develop, raise, educate, foster

brink *n.* margin, border, boundary, limit

brisk *adj.* agile, alert, busy, energetic, active, nimble, invigorating ★**sluggish**

brittle *adj.* breakable, fragile, delicate ▷*frail*

broad *adj.* wide, expansive, roomy, open, vast, large ★**narrow**

brood *v.* sigh, agonize, dwell upon *You must try to forget your disappointment and not dwell upon it,* languish BREWED

brook *n.* stream, rivulet, watercourse, burn

brow *n.* forehead, face, front, brink, edge, summit

bruise *v.* damage, discolour, blemish, injure, wound BREWS

brusque *adj.* abrupt, discourteous, gruff ▷*blunt* ★**polite**

brutal *adj.* cruel, inhumane, savage, barbarous, bloodthirsty ★**humane**

bubble *n.* drop, droplet, blob, bead

buckle *n.* catch, clasp, clip, fastening

bud *n.* sprout, germ, shoot

budge *v.* move, propel, push, shift, slide

build *v.* make, form, assemble, construct, erect, put up ★**demolish** BILLED

bulge *n.* bump, swelling, lump, billow

bulky *adj.* big, huge, unwieldy, massive, cumbersome *I never liked that chair; it's too big and cumbersome to move*

bully ① *n.* ruffian, tormentor, bruiser, tyrant, tough ② *v.* cow, harass, oppress, terrorize

bump *v.* collide, hit, knock, strike, jab, jolt

bunch *n.* batch, bundle, cluster, collection, lot, clump, stack

bundle *n.* group, mass, heap, pack, parcel

bungle *v.* botch, blunder, mess up, ruin, fumble ★**succeed**

burden *n.* ① load, weight ② strain, hardship *We suffered great hardship during the war*

burly *adj.* beefy, big, hefty, brawny, husky, muscular ★**frail**

burn *v.* blaze, flare, glow, singe, scorch, char, incinerate, smoulder

burst *v.* break open, crack, explode, shatter, erupt

bury *v.* inter, conceal, cover up, hide, entomb, lay to rest BERRY

business *n.* ① occupation, career, profession, ② company, enterprise, firm ③ problem, duty, affair

busy *adj.* active, brisk, industrious, lively, bustling ★**lazy**

buy *v.* acquire, get, purchase, procure *If I can procure a computer, I'll do the job for you* ★**sell** BY, BYE

Cc

cab *n.* taxi, taxicab, hackney carriage

cabin *n.* ① hut, chalet, cottage, shack ② berth, compartment

cabinet *n.* ① cupboard, dresser, closet ② council, committee

cackle *v.* chuckle, giggle, snigger

café *n.* restaurant, coffee bar, snack bar

cage *v.* shut up, confine, imprison ★**free**

calamity *n.* catastrophe, disaster, misadventure ▷*mishap* ★**blessing**

calculate *v.* reckon, figure, estimate ▷*count*

call *v.* ① cry out, shout, hail ② name, designate ③ summon, telephone ④ visit *We will visit you next week,* drop in

calling *n.* occupation, job, profession

callous *adj.* unfeeling, harsh, hard-bitten ★**sensitive**

calm ① *v.* soothe, ease, pacify, comfort ② *adj.* easy, composed, mild ▷*peaceful* ★**excited**

can *n.* tin, jar, container, canister

cancel *v.* abolish, erase, put off, obliterate ★**confirm**

candid *adj.* fair, honest, open, sincere, truthful, blunt ▷*frank* ★**devious**

capable *adj.* talented, able, competent, ▷*clever* ★**incompetent**

capacity *n.* ① space, volume, extent ② ability, aptitude *Jenny has an aptitude for learning languages,* intelligence

caper ① *v.* dance, gambol, frolic ② *n.* (*old*) prank, joke, jest, lark

capital ① *n.* cash, assets, funds, finance ② *adj.* chief, excellent, important

captain *n.* chief, head, commander, master, skipper

capture *v.* seize, arrest, trap ▷*catch* ★**release**

car *n.* automobile, motor-car, vehicle, conveyance, carriage, coach

carcase *n.* body, corpse, skeleton

care ① *v.* take care, beware, heed, mind ② *n.* attention, protection ★**carelessness**

careful *adj.* heedful, prudent, watchful ▷*cautious* ★**careless**

careless *adj.* neglectful, slack, casual, thoughtless ★**careful**

carelessness *n.* inaccuracy, negligence, slackness ★**care**

caress *v.* hug, stroke, cuddle, embrace, pet, pat, fondle

carriage *n.* car, coach, cab, chariot

carry *v.* bring, convey, lift, support ▷*bear*

carry on *v.* continue, maintain, persist

carry out *v.* perform, achieve, fulfill, do

cart *n.* wagon, pushcart, handcart, wheelbarrow

carton *n.* bin, case, package, crate ▷*box*

carve *v.* sculpt, cut, chisel, fashion, whittle ▷*shape*

case *n.* chest, bin, suitcase, trunk ▷*box*

cash *n.* money, coins, funds, coinage CACHE

cask *n.* barrel, keg, drum

cast *v.* ① mould, form, shape ② fling, heave, sprinkle ▷*throw* CASTE

casual *adj.* accidental, chance, random ▷*occasional* ★**regular**

catch *v.* grasp, seize, arrest ▷*capture* ★**miss**

catching *adj.* infectious, contagious

cause ① *v.* bring about, create, provoke ② *n.* reason, source, origin CAWS

caution *n.* watchfulness, heed, vigilance, prudence ▷*care* ★**recklessness**

cautious *adj.* careful, discreet, prudent ▷*watchful* ★**heedless**

cavity *n.* dent, hole, gap, hollow

cease *v.* stop, conclude, end, refrain, terminate ★**begin**

celebrate *v.* commemorate, observe, honour, glorify, rejoice, praise

cell *n.* chamber, cavity, cubicle, compartment SELL

cellar *n.* basement, vault, crypt, cave SELLER

cement ① *v.* glue, stick, bind, gum, unite ② *n.* plaster, mortar, adhesive

censor *v.* cut, examine, take out CENSER

censure *v.* blame, rebuke, reprimand, chide ▷*scold* ★**praise**

centre *n.* middle, core, heart, nucleus

ceremony *n.* ritual, custom, performance

certain *adj.* ① decided, definite, undoubted ▷*sure* ★**dubious** ② particular *I had a particular reason for inviting you,* special

certainty *n.* confidence, assurance, trust, sureness ★**doubt**

certificate *n.* document, permit, decd, diploma, testimonial

chafe *v.* rub, rasp, grate, irritate

chain *v.* bind, fetter, shackle, tether, bond

challenge *v.* dare, demand, dispute, defy, object to

chamber *n.* room, apartment, bedroom, compartment, hollow

champion *n.* defender, victor, master, winner ★**loser**

chance *n.* ① fortune, hazard, luck, gamble, lottery, wager ② opportunity, occasion, risk ★**certainty**

change *v.* alter, vary, turn, shift, reform, transform ★**preserve**

chant *v.* intone, drone, croon, recite ▷*sing*

chaos *n.* turmoil, confusion, disorder, pandemonium ★**order**

chapter *n.* clause, division, part, period *It was a period in my life that I will never forget,* phase

character *n.* ① letter, mark, emblem, device ② reputation *She had the reputation of being very generous,* temperament, qualities

charge *n.* ① attack, stampede, advance ② cost, amount, price ③ accusation, blame *The men were all guilty, but it was Harry Smith who took the blame,* indictment

charm *v.* please, delight, enchant, bewitch, fascinate ▷*attract* ★**irritate**

charming *adj.* delightful, appealing, lovely, pleasant ▷*attractive* ★**disgusting**

chart *n.* map, sketch, diagram, plan

chase *v.* hunt, pursue, follow, run after, hurry, track

chaste *adj.* virgin, pure, virtuous, innocent ★**immodest** CHASED

chastise *v.* punish, whip, flog, beat, scold, tell off, reprove, berate

chat *v.* converse, gossip ▷*talk*

chatter *v.* babble, gossip ▷*talk*

Chest

Chest

cheap *adj.* inexpensive, low-priced, bargain, reasonable, inferior, ★**expensive**

cheat *v.* swindle, bilk, defraud, fleece, diddle, rip off ▷*trick*

check ① *v.* inspect, compare, examine *The customs officer examined our luggage,* make sure ② *n.* curb, setback, reverse

cheek *n.* audacity, boldness, impertinence, insolence

cheer *v.* ① comfort, console, elate, buck up ② applaud *The audience applauded the leading soprano,* clap, hail

cheerful *adj.* lively, bright, happy, merry, joyful ▷*happy* ★**sad**

cheery *adj.* blithe, breezy, bright, merry ★**downcast**

cherish *v.* caress, hold close, care for, shelter, treasure

chest *n.* ① case, coffer ▷*box* ② bosom, torso

chew *v.* bite, gnaw, grind, munch ▷*eat*

chide *v.* scold, criticize, blame, tell off

chief *adj.* main, principal, leading, foremost ★**minor**

child *n.* baby, infant, youth, juvenile, bairn

chilly *adj.* cool, crisp, brisk, cold, unfriendly ★**warm**

chip *v. & n.* crack, splinter, dent, flake

chirp *v. & n.* warble, trill, cheep, twitter

choice ① *n.* option *I had no option but to take the job,* preference, alternative ② *adj.* select, dainty, precious, cherished, special

choke *v.* throttle, suffocate, gag, strangle, smother ▷*stifle*

A B C D E F G H I J K L M N O P Q R S T U V W X Y Z

Churches and Places of Worship

Cathedral
Chapel
Church
Mosque
Oratory
Pantheon
Synagogue
Temple

choose v. pick, elect, decide, prefer ▷*select*
CHEWS

chop v. cut, hack, clip, cleave, sever, lop

chubby adj. plump, buxom, portly, round, stout ★**slim**

chum n. comrade, pal, friend, mate, companion, crony

chuck v. throw, toss, fling, heave, sling

chuckle v. cackle, chortle, snigger, giggle ★**laugh**

chunk n. piece, lump, mass, portion, slab

churlish adj. brusque, harsh, impolite, morose *Dad had a headache and was in a morose mood* ▷*surly* ★**polite**

circle n. ① ring, band, hoop ② company, group, class, clique

circular ① adj. round, disc-like ② n. handbill, notice, poster

circulate v. broadcast, distribute, publicize

cistern n. tank, sink, basin, reservoir

cite v. mention, specify, name, quote
SIGHT, SITE

civil adj. polite, courteous, polished ▷*affable* ★**churlish**

claim v. demand, ask, require, insist, call for

clamour n. babel, blare, din, row, hubbub, racket ▷*noise* ★**silence**

clamp v. fasten, fix, hold, grasp

clap v. applaud, acclaim, cheer

clarify v. ① make clear, explain, simplify ② cleanse, purify

clash v. ① battle, conflict, quarrel ② bang, crash, clang, clatter

clasp ① v. grasp, grip, seize, hold, fasten ② n. buckle, catch, pin

class n. category, type, sort, grade, group, species

classical adj. pure, refined, scholarly, elegant, polished, well-proportioned

classify v. grade, sort, arrange, catalogue

clean ① adj. pure, fresh, spotless, unsoiled ② v. cleanse, scrub ▷*wash* ★**dirty**

cleanse v. purify, scour ▷*clean* ★**defile**

clear adj. ① bright, fair, fine, light ★**dim** ② distinct, audible, lucid ★**vague** ③ free, open, empty

cleft n. crack, cranny, slit, split, aperture

clever adj. able, astute, apt, brainy, skilful, talented ▷*expert* ★**foolish**

cliff n. precipice, height, bluff, crag, overhang

climax n. crisis, head, summit, turning point

climb v. mount, scale, ascend, soar, go up

cling v. adhere, attach, embrace, grasp, hold

clip ① n. fastener, clasp ② v. trim, prune, snip, cut

clog v. block, dam up, hinder, jam, impede

close ① v. (kloz) shut, bolt, bar, obstruct *The curtains were thick and obstructed a lot of light,* end ② adj. (klos) near, neighbouring, adjacent ★**far** ③ adj. heavy, stuffy, uncomfortable

closet n. wardrobe, cabinet

clothing n. garments, dress, attire, raiment

cloud n. vapour, fog, billow, haze

clown n. buffoon, comedian, jester, joker

club n. ① cudgel, stick, truncheon ② company, group, society

clue n. evidence, inkling, lead, sign CLEW

clump n. cluster, group, bunch

clumsy adj. awkward, gawky, ungainly, blundering ★**graceful**

clutch v. snatch, clasp, grasp, seize, grip

clutter n. litter, muddle, mess

coach n. ① bus, car, carriage, vehicle ② trainer, tutor, instructor

Clothing

Dresses and trousers
Bermuda shorts
cocktail dress
dress
evening gown
jeans
jodhpurs
kilt
miniskirt
petticoat
sari
sarong
skirt

Coats and jackets
anorak
blazer
cloak
poncho
raincoat
suit
tuxedo

Tops
blouse
cardigan
pullover
sweater
sweatshirt
T-shirt

Headwear see page 56

Foot and legwear
boots
galoshes
moccasins
shoes
socks
stockings
tights
trainers

coarse *adj.* ① rough, unrefined, unpolished ② brutish, rude, uncivil ★**refined** COURSE

coat *n.* ① jacket, blazer, windcheater ② fleece, fur, skin, hide

coax *v.* cajole, wheedle, urge, persuade, beguile *We sat for hours as Aunt Anna beguiled us with stories* ★**dissuade** COKES

coddle *v.* pamper, spoil, indulge, baby, mollycoddle

coffer *n.* casket, case, chest, treasury

cog *n.* tooth, prong

coil *v.* twist, wind, loop, curl

coincide *v.* match, agree, accord, synchronize, tally

cold *adj.* cool, chilly, frigid, freezing, frosty, frozen ★**hot**

collapse *v.* founder, topple, break down, crumple, fall down

collect *v.* accumulate, amass, assemble, save ▷*gather* ★**scatter**

collide *v.* crash, smash, hit, strike, meet

colossal *adj.* enormous, gigantic, immense, massive ▷*huge* ★**tiny**

column *n.* ① pillar, post, shaft, support, upright ② file *The file of soldiers marched on parade,* line, procession, queue, rank

combat *v.* battle, contend, contest, oppose, defy ★**submit**

combine *v.* unite, join, link, fuse, merge, mix, bond, blend ★**separate**

come *v.* arrive, appear, enter, reach, advance ★**go**

come by *v.* get, procure, acquire *I acquired a new television set in the sale*

comfort *v.* cheer, hearten, calm, soothe, console ★**torment**

comfortable *adj.* restful, convenient, cosy, agreeable ★**uncomfortable**

comforting *adj.* cheering, encouraging, consoling

command *v.* ① order, dictate, direct, demand, require ② rule, dominate

commence *v.* start, begin, initiate, originate, embark on ★**finish**

comment *v.* mention, remark, observe, point out, note

commiserate *v.* sympathize, show pity, be sorry for

commit *v.* carry out, do, enact, perform, promise, entrust

common *adj.* ① ordinary, vulgar, habitual, customary ② public, social, communal

commonplace *adj.* everyday, humdrum, ordinary, obvious ★**rare**

commotion *n.* excitement, flurry, stir, uproar ▷*fuss*

communicate *v.* tell, disclose, impart, reveal

community *n.* society, partnership, association ▷*group*

compact *adj.* dense, close, tight, firm, condensed, concise

companion *n.* comrade, friend, chum, mate, colleague, comrade, escort ★**rival**

company *n.* association, league, alliance, business, firm

compare *v.* match, liken, equal, parallel

compartment *n.* cubicle, alcove, bay, cell, carriage

compassion *n.* kindness, mercy, sympathy, charity, understanding ▷*pity* ★**indifference**

compel *v.* make, coerce, drive, force *We could not understand the signs so we were forced to guess where to check in*, urge ★**coax**

compensate *v.* make good, refund, reimburse, repay, reward ★**injure**

compete *v.* contest, contend, rival, strive, oppose, challenge, emulate

Compel

We could not understand the signs so we were forced to guess where to check in.

competent *adj.* able, adapted, capable ▷*clever* ★**incompetent**

competition *n.* game, match, contest, rivalry, race, tournament

compile *v.* amass, put together, unite ▷*collect*

complacent *adj.* self-satisfied, contented ▷*smug* ★**diffident**

complain *v.* protest, gripe, grumble, grouse ▷*nag* ★**rejoice**

complement *v.* complete, round off, add to, supplement, match COMPLIMENT

complete ① *v.* finish, accomplish, achieve ② *adj.* finished, full, entire

complex *adj.* complicated, intricate, mixed, tangled ★**simple**

complicated *adj.* entangled, involved ▷*complex*

compliment *v.* flatter, admire, congratulate ▷*praise* ★**insult** COMPLEMENT

comply *v.* agree to, assent to, abide by, perform, yield ★**refuse**

compose ① *v.* make up, put together, form, construct, write ② calm, quell

composure *n.* assurance, calm, confidence ★**exuberance**

compound *n.* mixture, alloy, blend, combination

comprehend *v.* grasp, discern, take in ▷*understand* ★**misunderstand**

compress *v.* condense, contract, abbreviate ▷*squeeze* ★**expand**

comprise *v.* contain, consist of, include, embody, encompass

compromise *v.* ① meet halfway, strike a balance, adjust, agree ② imperil, weaken, jeopardize

compulsory *adj.* forced, necessary, obligatory *Everyone in the school has to go*

to the meeting; it's obligatory, required
★**voluntary**

compute *v.* calculate, figure, reckon,
estimate

computer *n.* calculator, word processor

comrade *n.* companion, pal, chum, mate
▷*friend* ★**enemy**

conceal *v.* bury, camouflage, cover ▷*hide*
★**reveal**

concede *v.* allow, admit, yield, acknowledge,
surrender ★**dispute**

conceit *n.* vanity, self-importance, arrogance
▷*pride* ★**modesty**

conceited *adj.* proud, vain, arrogant
★**modest**

conceive *v.* create, design, devise *We
devised a way to sharpen the scissors,*
form, think up, develop

concentrate *v.* focus on, centralize, heed,
pay attention

concept *n.* idea, thought, theory, view

concern ① *v.* affect, touch ② *n.* affair,
matter, interest, business

concerning *prep.* as regards, respecting,
about, with reference to

concise *adj.* brief, condensed, short
▷*compact* ★**expansive**

conclude *v.* ① finish, terminate ▷*end*
② deduce, judge, reckon, presume

conclusion *n.* result, termination, end

concoct *v.* contrive, hatch, plan, devise,
invent

concord *n.* agreement, understanding, goodwill, harmony ★**discord**

concrete ① *adj.* actual, definite, real ② *n.*
cement, mortar

concur *v.* approve, agree, coincide, consent
★**disagree**

condemn *v.* blame, denounce, reprove,
sentence, disapprove ★**approve**

condense *v.* compress, concentrate, abridge,
thicken ★**expand**

condition *n.* shape, way, state, position,
plight, situation ▷*predicament*

condone *v.* overlook, disregard, forgive,
excuse ★**censure**

conduct ① *n.* attitude, bearing, behaviour

② *v.* guide, direct, lead, pilot, steer, usher

confederate *n.* accomplice, ally, associate,
partner

confer *v.* bestow, grant, award, give, present

conference *n.* discussion, meeting, forum

confess *v.* admit, acknowledge, own up,
divulge ★**deny**

confide *v.* tell, divulge, reveal, whisper,
entrust, unburden

confidence *n.* assurance, belief, boldness,
firmness ★**doubt**

confident *adj.* certain, assured, poised,
fearless ★**diffident**

confine *v.* restrict, limit, detain, imprison,
constrain, intern ★**free**

confirm *v.* verify, assure, approve, endorse,
attest ★**deny**

confiscate *v.* seize, impound, commandeer
The house was commandeered by the army

conform *v.* agree with, comply with, yield,
adjust

confound *v.* perplex, mystify, puzzle, baffle,
fluster ▷*bewilder* ★**enlighten**

confront *v.* challenge, defy, face, oppose,
menace

confuse *v.* baffle, bemuse, mystify
▷*bewilder* ★**clarify**

congenial *adj.* companionable, natural,
sympathetic, agreeable ▷*friendly*
★**disagreeable**

congested *adj.* jammed, crowded, clogged,
packed, teeming ★**clear**

congratulate *v.* rejoice, compliment, praise,
wish well ★**commiserate**

congregate *v.* assemble, meet, come
together, converge ★**disperse**

congress *n.* meeting, assembly, council,
convention

conjecture *v.* guess, surmise, suspect,
imagine, assume

connect *v.* unite, join, combine, fasten, link
★**disconnect**

conquer *v.* beat, crush, overcome,
overpower, triumph ▷*defeat* ★**surrender**

conscientious *adj.* moral, scrupulous,
careful, diligent ▷*honest* ★**careless**

conscious *adj.* alert, alive, aware, sensible,

A
B
C
D
E
F
G
H
I
J
K
L
M
N
O
P
Q
R
S
T
U
V
W
X
Y
Z

mindful, responsible ★**unconscious**

consecutive *adj.* chronological, in sequence, successive, continuous

consent *v.* assent, permit, concur, approve, comply ▷*agree* ★**oppose**

conserve *v.* keep, preserve, protect, save, store up, safeguard ★**waste**

consider *v.* discuss, examine, ponder, reflect *Alone on the island, I reflected on all that had happened,* take account of ★**ignore**

considerable *adj.* abundant, ample, great, large, noteworthy, important ★**insignificant**

consist of *v.* comprise, be composed of, contain, include

consistent *adj.* uniform, constant, regular, steady ★**inconsistent**

console *v.* comfort, cheer, sympathize, soothe, solace ★**upset**

conspicuous *adj.* noticeable, marked, apparent, obvious, prominent ★**inconspicuous**

conspire *v.* intrigue, scheme, plot *He was gaoled for plotting against the government*

constant *adj.* ① regular, stable, uniform ▷*consistent* ② loyal, faithful, staunch, true ★**fickle**

consternation *n.* dismay, horror, fear, awe, stupefaction ▷*alarm* ★**composure**

constitute *v.* compose, comprise, set up, fix, form, establish ★**destroy**

constrict *v.* tighten, strain, tauten, draw together, choke, pinch ★**expand**

construct *v.* erect, compose, compound, assemble ▷*build* ★**demolish**

consult *v.* ask, seek advice, discuss, confer, debate, refer to

consume *v.* use up, absorb, eat up, devour

contact *n.* touch, connection, meeting, communication, association

contagious *adj.* catching, infectious

contain *v.* comprise, consist of, hold, accommodate, enclose

contaminate *v.* pollute, soil, stain, sully, taint, infect

contemplate *v.* think, reflect, deliberate, consider, ponder

contempt *v.* disdain, scorn, disregard, derision ★**admiration**

contend *v.* compete, contest, conflict, strive, struggle ★**concede**

content ① *adj.* (con-*tent*) satisfied, smug ② *v.* satisfy, delight, gratify ③ *n.* (*con*-tent) matter, text, subject

contest ① *n.* (*con*-test) competition, match, tournament ② *v.* (con-*test*) dispute, argue

continue *v.* go on, keep up, endure, last, persist ★**stop**

contract ① *v.* (con-*tract*) condense, lessen, shrink ② *n.* (*con*-tract) agreement, pact, understanding

contradict *v.* deny, dispute, challenge, oppose, gainsay

contrary *adj.* opposed, adverse, counter, opposite ★**agreeable**

contrast ① *n.* (*con*-trast) difference, disparity, comparison ② *v.* (con-*trast*) compare, differ, oppose, distinguish

contribute *v.* donate, present, bestow, provide, assist, help ★**withhold**

contrive *v.* form, fashion, construct, create, design, invent

control *v.* command, direct, dominate, lead, supervise, oversee, superintend

convene *v.* call together, rally, meet, muster *We mustered on the dock before boarding the ship,* assemble ★**dismiss**

convenient *adj.* handy, fit, helpful, suitable, accessible ★**awkward**

conversation *n.* talk, chat, communication, discussion, discourse, exchange

convert *v.* alter, change, transform, adapt

convey *v.* carry, transport, conduct, bear, transmit

convict ① *n.* (*con*-vict) prisoner, captive, criminal ② *v.* (con-*vict*) find guilty, condemn, sentence

convince *v.* assure, persuade, prove to, win over, sway, bring round

cook *v.* boil, broil, heat, warm, steam, fry, stew, bake, grill, roast

cool *adj.* ① chilly, frigid ▷*cold* ② self-composed, calm, relaxed

cooperate *v.* collaborate, combine, aid,

a b c d e f g h i j k l m n o p q r s t u v w x y z

assist, join forces, unite, conspire

cope (with) *v.* deal, handle, struggle, grapple, manage

copy *v.* duplicate, reproduce, imitate, mimic, simulate, crib, plagiarize

cord *n.* string, rope, twine, line CHORD

cordial *adj.* hearty, sincere, congenial, jovial, affable ★**hostile**

core *n.* heart, kernel, pith, crux *Now we're getting to the crux of the problem,* centre CORPS

corner *n.* angle, bend, crook, cavity, cranny, niche, compartment

corpse *n.* body, carcase, remains

correct *adj.* true, actual, accurate, exact, precise ★**wrong**

correspond *v.* ① fit, harmonize, agree, coincide ② write letters

corridor *n.* hallway, passage, aisle

corroborate *v.* confirm, certify, endorse, establish ★**contradict**

corrode *v.* erode, waste, eat away, rust

corrupt ① *adj.* dishonest, fraudulent, rotten

② *v.* bribe, deprave, entice, lead astray

cost *n.* ① charge, amount, price, outlay ② penalty, forfeit, sacrifice

costly *adj.* expensive, valuable, precious

costume *n.* suit, outfit, ensemble, attire, dress, uniform, get-up

cot *n.* bed, bunk, berth

cottage *n.* bungalow, cabin, chalet, shack, lodge

couch *n.* sofa, settee, chaise-longue

council *n.* assembly, committee, congress, convention COUNSEL

counsel ① *n.* lawyer, attorney, advocate ② *v.* advise, instruct, recommend COUNCIL

count *v.* add up, calculate, check, compute, reckon, tally

counter ① *n.* token, coin, disc ② *n.* bar, bench ③ *adj.* against, opposed

counterfeit *adj.* forged, fraudulent, fake, bogus *She entered the country on a bogus passport,* false

country ① *n.* nation, people, realm, state ② *adj.* rural, farmland, sticks

Cooking utensils

Blender	Grill	Rolling pin
Bottle	Jar	Saucepan
Bowl	Kettle	Sieve
Casserole	Ladle	Skillet
Colander	Lemon	Spatula
Cup	squeezer	Spoon
Cutting	Masher	Tureen
board	Measuring	Urn
Dish	jug	Whisk
Frying pan	Pan	Wok
Funnel	Peeler	
Grater	Plate	
Griddle	Pot	
	Ramekin	

A B C D E F G H I J K L M N O P Q R S T U V W X Y Z

couple ① *n.* pair, brace, two ② *v.* link, yoke, unite, join, connect

courage *n.* bravery, valour, boldness, gallantry, daring, pluck ★**cowardice**

courageous *adj.* brave, bold, fearless, valiant ▷*plucky* ★**cowardly**

course *n.* ① route, channel, path, road, track, trail ② policy, plan, manner COARSE

court ① *n.* alley, courtyard, atrium, quad ② *n.* bar, bench, tribunal ③ *n.* palace, retinue ④ *v.* make love, woo, flatter

courteous *adj.* considerate, polite, refined, elegant ★**discourteous**

courtesy *n.* politeness, civility, manners, gentility, gallantry, respect

cove *n.* inlet, bay, creek, firth

cover ① *v.* conceal, hide, secrete ② *v.* include, embody, incorporate ③ *n.* cap, case, lid, canopy

covet *v.* want, envy, fancy, hanker after, long for, crave

cow *v.* frighten, bully, terrorize, scare, subdue

coward *n.* weakling, craven, funk, sneak ★**hero** COWERED

cowardice *n.* fear, funk, faint-heartedness ★**courage**

cowardly *adj.* fearful, weak, scared,

Creature

It was a huge brute – the biggest crocodile I'd ever seen.

spineless, timorous ★**courageous**

cower *v.* cringe, grovel, flinch, crouch

coy *adj.* demure, skittish, blushing, bashful, shy ★**forward**

crack ① *n.* slit, split, cleft, cranny, crevice, breach ② *v.* snap, split, splinter

craft *n.* ① cunning, deceit ② ability, cleverness, expertise ③ occupation, business ④ boat, ship, plane

crafty *adj.* cunning, artful, wily, shrewd

cram *v.* ram, stuff, squeeze, press

cramp *v.* restrict, obstruct, hinder, confine

crash *v.* bang, clash, clatter, break, fall, topple, plunge, collapse

crass *adj.* stupid, oafish, boorish, obtuse, slow-witted ★**sensitive**

crave *v.* long for, hanker after, need, yearn for, beg, plead

crawl *v.* creep, drag, slither, grovel

crazy *adj.* insane, mad, beserk, deranged, idiotic ★**sane**

creak *v.* grate, grind, rasp, groan CREEK

crease *n.* fold, pucker, ridge, pleat, tuck

create *v.* bring into being, compose, concoct, make, invent, coin, devise

creation invention, handiwork, foundation, production ★**destruction**

creature *n.* animal, beast, being, brute *It was a huge brute – the biggest crocodile I'd ever seen,* person

credible *adj.* believable, likely, plausible ★**incredible**

credit *n.* ① acclaim, kudos, merit ② belief, faith, confidence

creek *n.* bay, cove, bight, stream, CREAK

creep *v.* crawl, slither, squirm, wriggle

crest *n.* top, crown, pinnacle

crestfallen *adj.* downcast, dejected, discouraged ★**elated**

crevice *n.* cleft, chink, crack, cranny, gap

crew *n.* team, company, party, gang

crime *n.* misdeed, offence, fault, felony

criminal ① *n.* culprit, convict, felon, crook ② *adj.* unlawful, wicked

cringe *v.* cower, flinch, duck, shrink, grovel

cripple *v.* disable, mutilate, paralyse, weaken, damage

Creek

Creak

crisis *n.* climax, turning point, catastrophe, disaster, crunch

crisp *adj.* brittle, crumbly, crunchy, firm, crusty ★**soggy**

critical *adj.* crucial, all-important, acute, grave, pressing, decisive

criticize *v.* find fault with, disapprove of, condemn ★**praise**

crony *n.* accomplice, ally, confederate, comrade, chum ▷*friend*

crooked *adj.* ① bent, bowed, distorted, twisted ② dishonest, criminal

crop ① *n.* harvest, gathering, yield ② *v.* graze, shorten, browse

cross ① *adj.* angry, annoyed, crusty ② *v.* bridge, pass over ③ *n.* crucifix

crouch *v.* stoop, squat, bow, cringe

crow ① *v.* gloat, shout, brag, bluster ② *n.* blackbird, raven

crowd *n.* mob, multitude, flock, assembly, swarm, throng

crowded *adj.* jammed, packed, congested, cramped

crucial *adj.* decisive, critical, acute

crude *adj.* raw, unrefined, rustic, unpolished ▷*coarse* ★**refined**

cruel *adj.* unkind, brutal, inhuman, ruthless ▷*savage* ★**kind**

cruise *n.* voyage, trip, sail, crossing CREWS

crumb *n.* bit, morsel, seed, grain, scrap, shred

crumble *v.* decay, grind, powder, crunch

crumple *v.* crinkle, crush, wrinkle, pucker

crunch *v.* chew, grind, masticate, munch ▷*crush*

crush *v.* squash, mash, pound, compress

cry *v.* ① exclaim, call, shout, shriek ② weep, bawl, blubber, sob

cuddle *v.* hug, embrace, fondle, cosset, pet, snuggle, fondle

cue *n.* hint, key, nod, sign, signal QUEUE

cull *v.* choose, pick, thin out, amass, collect

culprit *n.* criminal, convict, felon, offender, malefactor

cultivated *adj.* refined, civilized, cultured, educated, trained ★**neglected**

cumbersome *adj.* bulky, awkward, clumsy, hefty ★**convenient**

cunning *adj.* artful, astute, crafty

curb *v.* check, tame, restrain

cure ① *n.* remedy, medicine, drug ② *v.* heal, remedy, treat, attend

curious *adj.* ① odd, peculiar, singular ② inquisitive, prying, nosy

curl *v.* coil, twist, curve, crimp

current ① *adj.* present, contemporary, topical, fashionable ② *n.* stream, course, flow, electrical flow CURRANT

curse ① *v.* swear, condemn, damn ② *n.* oath, denunciation

curt *adj.* brusque, blunt, churlish, crusty, gruff ▷*terse* ★**polite**

curtail *v.* trim, shorten, clip, truncate ▷*abbreviate* ★**lengthen**

curve *n.* loop, hook, curl, twist, wind, coil ▷*bend*

cushion *n.* pillow, bolster, pad, support

custom *n.* habit, usage, convention, rite ▷*fashion*

customer *n.* purchaser, buyer, client, patron

cut *v.* carve, whittle, chisel, cleave, sever, gash, slice, shear, shave

cut off *v.* disconnect, interrupt, stop

cute *adj.* charming, attractive, pretty, dainty

cutting *adj.* sharp, biting, bitter, sarcastic

A B C D E F G H I J K L M N O P Q R S T U V W X Y Z

D d

dab *v.* blot, swab, touch, pat

dabble *v.* toy, meddle, tinker, trifle, potter

daft *adj.* crazy, silly, innocent, idiotic, cracked, dopey ★**bright**

dagger *n.* knife, dirk, bayonet, stiletto

daily ① *adj.* everyday, normal, common *It is quite common to see squirrels in the woods* ② *n.* newspaper

dainty *adj.* delicate, charming, exquisite, choice, tasty

dally *v.* play, trifle, dawdle, linger, loiter

damage *n.* harm, sabotage, vandalism, injury, hurt

damn *v.* curse, swear, condemn, criticize ★**bless**

damp *adj.* humid, clammy, dank ▷*moist* ★**dry**

damsel *n.* girl, maiden, lady, woman

dance *v.* hop, skip, jump, prance, frolic, gambol

danger *n.* peril, hazard, risk, jeopardy, menace ★**safety**

dangerous *adj.* perilous, precarious, unsafe, risky, hazardous, reckless, hairy ★**safe**

dangle *v.* hang, swing, sway

dank *adj.* sticky, muggy, moist, soggy ▷*damp*

dapper *adj.* spruce, natty, neat, stylish, trim ▷*smart* ★**scruffy**

dare *v.* brave, face, risk, defy, challenge, venture

daring *adj.* adventurous, dashing, bold, fearless ▷*brave* ★**timid**

dark *adj.* dusky, swarthy, shady, dim, dingy, shadowy ★**light**

darling *n.* pet, love, dear, favourite, beloved, precious

darn *v.* mend, sew, patch, repair

dart ① *n.* arrow, missile ② *v.* dash, hurtle *The express train hurtled through the tunnel*, charge, gallop

dash *v.* rush, gallop, run, career, fly, hasten

date ① *n.* time, point ② *n.* appointment *I have an appointment to see the doctor*, engagement ③ *v.* become old, become dated

daub *v.* plaster, spread, smear, coat, paint

daunt *v.* intimidate, terrify, scare, confront

dauntless *adj.* fearless, gallant, courageous ▷*brave* ★**discouraged**

dawdle *v.* linger, loiter, lag, waste time,

Dances

Ballet	Polonaise
Bolero	Quadrille
Bop	Quickstep
Cha-cha	Rumba
Charleston	Samba
Conga	Square dance
Country dance	Tango
Disco	Tarantella
Fandango	Two-step
Flamenco	Twist
Fox-trot	Waltz
Gavotte	
Highland fling	
Jitterbug	
Jive	
Mazurka	
Minuet	
Morris dance	
Polka	

a b c d e f g h i j k l m n o p q r s t u v w x y z

hang about, dilly-dally ▷*dally* ★**hurry**

dawn *n.* beginning, daybreak, daylight, morning, sunrise ★**dusk**

daze *v.* deaden, muddle, blind, dazzle ▷*bewilder* DAYS

dazzle *v.* blind, glare, confuse ▷*daze*

dead *adj.* deceased, departed, gone, lifeless, dull ★**alive**

deaden *v.* paralyse, blunt, muffle, drown

deadly *adj.* fatal, lethal, mortal, baleful, venomous

deaf *adj.* hard of hearing, unhearing, heedless

deal *v.* bargain, trade, market, communicate, traffic, give out

dealer *n.* merchant, trader, tradesman

dear ① *adj.* darling, beloved, loved, cherished *These old records are some of my cherished possessions* ② expensive, high-priced, costly DEER ★**cheap**

death *n.* decease, end of life, mortality ★**life**

debate *v.* argue, discuss, dispute, question, contend

debris *n.* trash, junk ▷*rubbish*

debt *n.* obligation, debit, dues, liability ★**credit**

decay *v.* ① decompose, rot *The potatoes had been left too long and had rotted,* spoil ② decline, sink, dwindle, waste

deceive *v.* dupe, hoax, trick, cheat, mislead ▷*betray* ★**enlighten**

decent *adj.* respectable, chaste, proper, fair, modest ★**indecent**

decide *v.* determine, rule, judge, resolve

declare *v.* avow, state, profess, proclaim, announce

decline ① *v.* descend, dwindle *The profits of the business had dwindled,* drop, fall ② *v.* refuse, say no ★**assent** ③ *n.* descent, slope, slant, dip, pitch

decorate *v.* embellish, adorn, ornament

decoy ① *v.* entice *We were enticed into the café by the smell of roasting coffee,* ensnare, mislead, tempt ② *n.* lure, bait

decrease *v.* diminish, lessen, wane, decline, reduce ★**increase**

decree *n.* law, edict, manifesto, rule, decision, order, statute, proclamation

decrepit *adj.* senile, infirm, crippled, feeble, frail ★**robust**

dedicate *v.* devote, apportion, assign, surrender, pledge

deduce *v.* draw, infer, conclude, glean, surmise, reason

deduct *v.* subtract, take from, remove, withdraw ★**add**

deed *n.* ① act, feat, stunt ② document, paper, contract *Michael was under contract to play rugby for the team for three years*

deep *adj.* ① profound *The accident taught us a profound lesson about friendship,* bottomless, low ② learned, wise, sagacious

deface *v.* disfigure, deform, injure, mar, blemish ★**adorn**

defeat *v.* beat, conquer, overcome, vanquish, overthrow, overwhelm ★**triumph**

defect *n.* flaw, fault, weak point, blemish, error, imperfection

defective *adj.* imperfect, faulty, deficient, insufficient ★**perfect**

defend *v.* protect, guard, fortify, support, sustain, uphold ★**attack**

defer *v.* postpone, put off, adjourn, waive, yield ★**hasten**

defiant *adj.* mutinous, rebellious, resistant, aggressive ★**submissive**

deficient *adj.* wanting, imperfect, defective, faulty ★**superfluous**

defile *v.* taint, infect, pollute, sully, disgrace ★**cleanse**

define *v.* explain, interpret, designate, mark out, specify ★**obscure**

definite *adj.* clear, certain, clear-cut, distinct ▷*sure* ★**vague**

deform *adj.* misshape, distort, contort, twist, warp

defraud *v.* fleece, swindle, embezzle, diddle ▷*cheat*

defy *v.* resist, withstand, disregard, challenge, disobey ★**obey**

degrade *v.* humble, debase, corrupt, downgrade, cheapen ★**improve**

degree *n.* grade, step, measure, rate, scale *Our answers were scored on a scale from*

A B C D E F G H I J K L M N O P Q R S T U V W X Y Z

one to ten, class, step, level, standard

dejected *adj.* depressed, downcast, crestfallen, disheartened, disconsolate ▷*gloomy* ★**elated**

delay *v.* postpone, put off, detain, halt, hinder, impede ★**hurry**

deliberate ① *adj.* wilful, calculated, intentional, planned ★**unintentional** ② *v.* reflect, contemplate, discuss

delicate *adj.* dainty, refined, soft, luxurious, modest, fragile, tender ★**harsh**

delicious *adj.* palatable, luscious, mellow, savoury, choice, mouth-watering ▷*scrumptious* ★**unpleasant**

delight *n.* enjoyment, pleasure, rapture, bliss ▷*happiness* ★**displease**

delightful *adj.* enjoyable, cheery, enchanting, lovely ▷*agreeable* ★**horrible**

deliver ① *v.* transfer, hand over, bear *She came bearing gifts for the whole family,* carry, convey ② free, liberate, release

delude *v.* cheat, hoax, hoodwink, mislead ▷*deceive* ★**guide**

deluge *n.* inundation, swamp, spate ▷*flood*

demand *v.* ① request, ask, appeal, entreat ② badger, pester, nag *My sister has been nagging me to take her to the park*

demeanour *n.* bearing, manner, conduct, air

demented *adj.* distracted, foolish, insane ▷*mad* ★**sane**

demolish *v.* destroy, wreck, ruin, smash, overthrow, knock down ★**build**

demon *n.* fiend, imp, devil, evil spirit

demonstrate *v.* prove, exhibit, illustrate ▷*show*

demote *v.* degrade, downgrade, relegate ★**promote**

demur *v.* hesitate, object, protest, doubt, waver ★**consent**

demure *adj.* coy, sedate, staid, sober, prudish, discreet ★**indiscreet**

den *n.* ① nest, cave, haunt, lair ② hideaway, retreat *This little room is my retreat, where I can sit and think,* study

denote *v.* designate, indicate, mean, show, point out

denounce *v.* decry, defame, attack, brand, condemn, vilify ▷*accuse* ★**praise**

dense *adj.* ① thick, solid, stout, compact ★**sparse** ② stupid, thick, stolid, obtuse ★**clever** DENTS

dent *n.* notch, cavity, chip, dimple, hollow

deny *v.* ① refuse, reject, repudiate ② disagree with *I am afraid that I disagree with what you say,* oppose, contradict ★**admit**

depart *v.* quit, go, retire, withdraw, vanish ▷*leave* ★**arrive**

department *n.* section, division, office, branch, province

depend on *v.* lean on, rely upon, trust in

depict *v.* describe, sketch, portray, outline, draw

deplorable *adj.* distressing, disastrous, shameful, scandalous ★**excellent**

deplore *v.* regret, lament, mourn ★**celebrate**

deport *v.* banish, exile, expel, oust

deposit *v.* drop, lay, place, put, bank, entrust, save ★**withdraw**

depot *n.* ① warehouse, storehouse ② terminus, station

depraved *adj.* corrupted, immoral, evil, sinful, vile *After calling me vile names, he left* ★**upright**

depreciate *v.* ① devalue, lessen, lose value *From the moment it was bought the car began losing value,* reduce ② belittle, disparage, deride ★**appreciate**

depress ① *v.* dishearten, dispirit, cast down ★**cheer** ② flatten, push down

depressed *adj.* dispirited, disheartened, despondent, fed up

deprive *v.* take away, rob, starve, divest *The traitor had been divested of all her honours* ★**bestow**

depth *n.* pit, shaft, well, chasm, gulf, abyss

deputy *n.* agent, delegate, lieutenant, assistant, councillor

derelict *adj.* abandoned, deserted *The Mary Celeste sailing ship was found deserted in the Atlantic,* forlorn

deride *v.* laugh at, jeer at, ridicule ▷*mock* ★**praise**

derive *v.* develop *Many English words developed from Norman-French,* obtain, arise from, originate

descend *v.* fall, drop, lower, decline, collapse ▷*sink* ★**ascend**

describe *v.* depict, portray, detail, define, tell

desert ① *n.* (*dez*-ert) wasteland, wilderness ② *adj.* desolate, arid, barren ③ *v.* (dez-*ert*) forsake, leave ▷*abandon* DESSERT

deserve *v.* be worthy of, merit, warrant, be entitled to ★**forfeit**

design *n.* drawing, painting, plan, pattern, scheme

desirable *adj.* ① agreeable, pleasing, good ② attractive, alluring, adorable

desire *v.* ① wish, require, need, want, crave ② long for, yearn after, pine for *My sister lived abroad, but always pined for home* ★**detest**

desist *v.* abstain, avoid, break off, cease, end

desolate *adj.* lonely, forlorn, miserable, wretched, alone ★**cheerful**

despair *n.* depression, misery, hopelessness, sorrow ▷*gloom* ★**hope**

desperate *adj.* drastic, reckless, frantic, rash, wild ★**hopeful**

despicable *adj.* contemptible, low, detestable, degrading ★**noble**

despise *v.* abhor, detest, loathe, look down upon ▷*hate* ★**prize**

despite *prep.* in spite of, notwithstanding

despondent *adj.* depressed, dispirited, broken-hearted ▷*miserable* ★**cheerful**

destination *n.* goal, terminus, end, objective, journey's end

destiny *n.* fate, lot, fortune, future, prospect, doom

destitute *adj.* poor, needy, bankrupt, penniless, poverty-stricken ★**wealthy**

destroy *v.* ruin, demolish, spoil, smash, exterminate ▷*wreck* ★**create**

destruction *n.* desolation, downfall, ruin, defeat, havoc ★**creation**

detach *v.* separate, part, divide, loosen, undo ★**attach**

detail *n.* item, fact, circumstance, point

detain *v.* delay, retard, restrain, arrest, hold

Dessert

Desert

up, hinder, impede, stop ★**release**

detect *v.* notice, discover, observe, scent, track down ★**miss**

deter *v.* prevent, hold back, check, stop ▷*detain* ★**encourage**

deteriorate *v.* become worse, worsen, corrode, decline, decompose ★**improve**

determine *v.* find out, decide, identify, choose, regulate

detest *v.* abhor *Lucy was a peaceful person and abhorred violence,* loathe, despise ▷*hate* ★**adore**

devastate *v.* lay waste, ravage, overwhelm ▷*destroy*

develop *v.* mature, ripen, grow up, evolve, extend ★**restrict**

deviate *v.* diverge, differ, vary, contrast, wander ★**conform**

device *n.* apparatus, contrivance, instrument, appliance

devil *n.* imp, evil spirit, demon, fiend, Satan

devious *adj.* tricky, sly, subtle, cunning, roundabout ★**forthright**

devise *v.* contrive, fashion, form, plan, conceive

devoid *adj.* barren, empty, free, without, lacking ★**endowed**

devote *v.* allocate, allot, give, assign, dedicate

A B C D E F G H I J K L M N O P Q R S T U V W X Y Z

devoted *adj.* dedicated, devout, loyal, caring, ardent ★**indifferent**

devour *v.* swallow, gulp, gorge, consume ▷*eat*

devout *adj.* pious, devoted, religious, faithful, passionate ★**insincere**

dexterous *adj.* able, active, deft, nimble ▷*skilful* ★**clumsy**

diagram *n.* outline, plan, sketch, draft, chart, drawing

dictate *v.* speak, utter, say, instruct, ordain, command

die *v.* expire, finish, end, pass away, perish, cease ★**live** DYE

differ *v.* ① vary, contrast, diverge *In this case, my views diverge strongly from yours* ② argue, conflict, clash

difference *n.* variance, distinctness, divergence, subtlety ★**agreement**

different *adj.* contrary, variant, distinct, original, unusual ★**same**

difficult *adj.* hard, puzzling, baffling, complex, laborious ★**easy**

difficulty *n.* trouble, bother, predicament ★**plight**

diffident *adj.* bashful, reserved, retiring, timid, unsure ▷*shy* ★**confident**

dig *v.* burrow, excavate, grub, delve, scoop

digest ① *v.* (di-*gest*) absorb, assimilate, dissolve ② *n.* (*di*-gest) abridgment, condensation, précis

digit *n.* ① number, figure, cipher ② finger, toe, thumb

dignified *adj.* grave, majestic, noble, lofty, grand ★**undignified**

dignity *n.* grandeur, merit, fame, gravity, nobility

dilapidated *adj.* neglected, unkempt, crumbling, decayed

dilemma *n.* quandary, plight, difficulty, predicament

dilute *v.* water down, weaken, reduce, thin

dim *adj.* dark, faint, pale, gloomy ▷*obscure* ★**bright**

diminish *v.* reduce, lessen, decrease, become smaller ★**enhance**

din *n.* uproar, racket, babble, pandemonium, commotion, hubbub ▷*noise* ★**quiet**

dingy *adj.* murky, dark, dreary, sombre, gloomy ▷*dismal* ★**bright**

dip *v.* sink, subside, immerse, plunge

dire *adj.* alarming, appalling, awful, horrible ▷*terrible* DYER

direct ① *adj.* straight, even, blunt, candid ② *v.* aim, level, train, point

direction *n.* course, trend, way, track, route

dirt *n.* impurity, filth, grime, muck, soil

dirty *adj.* unclean, impure, filthy, sordid, squalid, nasty ★**clean**

disable *v.* cripple, lame, maim, disarm

disadvantage *n.* inconvenience, burden, damage, loss, obstacle ★**advantage**

disagree *v.* differ, revolt, decline, refuse, dissent, argue ★**agree**

disagreeable *adj.* unpleasant, obnoxious,

Dogs

Afghan hound
Airedale
Bassett hound
Beagle
Bloodhound
Borzoi
Boxer
Bulldog
Chihuahua

unwelcome, offensive ★**agreeable**

disappear *v.* vanish, dissolve, fade, melt, depart, expire ★**appear**

disappoint *v.* frustrate, disillusion, let down, dismay, dissatisfy ★**please**

disapprove *v.* condemn, denounce, criticize, reproach ★**approve**

disaster *n.* calamity, catastrophe, accident, misfortune ★**triumph**

disbelief *n.* incredulity, distrust, doubt, suspicion ★**belief**

discard *v.* eliminate, get rid of, reject, scrap *Once we got a new car, I scrapped the old one,* throw away ★**adopt**

discern *v.* note, discover, distinguish

discharge *v.* ① dismiss, give notice to, expel ② detonate, emit, fire

disciple *n.* follower, learner, pupil, attendant

discipline *n.* correction, training, self-control, obedience

disclaim *v.* repudiate, disown, renounce, deny, reject ★**acknowledge**

disclose *v.* discover, show, reveal, expose, betray ▷*divulge* ★**conceal**

disconcert *v.* abash, confuse, confound, upset, bafflc ★**encourage**

disconnect *v.* separate, detach, cut off, sever, uncouple ★**connect**

disconsolate *adj.* distressed, sad, forlorn, melancholy, desolate ▷*unhappy* ★**cheerful**

discontented *adj.* displeased, disgruntled, unsatisfied, reluctant ★**content**

discord *n.* disagreement, strife ★**concord**

discourage *v.* depress, dismay, dispirit, dishearten *I don't want to dishearten you, but our holiday is cancelled,* put off ★**encourage**

discouraged *adj.* crestfallen, daunted, depressed, downcast ★**encouraged**

discourteous *adj.* blunt, crude, churlish,

Chow chow
Collie
Dachshund
Dalmatian
Doberman
 pinscher
Foxhound

German shepherd
Golden retriever
Great Dane
Greyhound
Irish setter
Labrador
Old English
 sheepdog
Pekinese
Pointer

Poodle
Pug
St. Bernard
Saluki
Spaniel
Terrier

A
B
C
D
E
F
G
H
I
J
K
L
M
N
O
P
Q
R
S
T
U
V
W
X
Y
Z

outspoken, abrupt ★**courteous**

discover *v.* locate, surprise, unearth, uncover ▷*find* ★**conceal**

discreet *adj.* prudent, cautious, careful, tactful, sensible ★**indiscreet** DISCRETE

discriminate *v.* distinguish, penetrate, favour, judge, assess ★**confound**

discuss *v.* confer, consider, talk over, debate, argue

disdain *n.* ridicule, scorn, contempt, derision ★**admiration**

disease *n.* infection, contagion, illness, plague, ailment, sickness

disfigure *v.* blemish, deface, deform, mar, scar, spoil ★**adorn**

disgrace *n.* scandal, dishonour, shame, infamy, stigma ★**honour**

disguise *v.* conceal, mask, falsify, cloak, deceive, fake

disgust ① *n.* revulsion, loathing, distaste *The room was messy, and I entered it with distaste* ② *v.* repel, revolt, nauseate ★**admire**

dish *n.* plate, platter, bowl

dishearten *v.* depress, cast down, deter, deject ▷*discourage* ★**encourage**

dishonest *adj.* deceitful, unscrupulous, shady, crooked ★**honest**

disintegrate *v.* crumble, moulder, decompose, rot, fall apart ★**unite**

dislike *v.* hate, loathe, detest, abhor, abominate ▷*despise* ★**like**

dismal *adj.* dreary, ominous, cheerless, depressing ▷*hopeless* ★**cheerful**

dismiss *v.* banish, discard, abandon, dispel, repudiate, release ★**appoint**

disobey *v.* rebel, transgress, resist, defy, ignore ★**obey**

disorder *n.* confusion, disarray, commotion, chaos ★**order**

dispel *v.* disperse, drive away, dismiss, allay, scatter ★**collect**

dispense *v.* distribute, arrange, allocate, supply, measure out ★**accept**

disperse *v.* scatter, separate, break up, spread abroad, distribute ★**gather**

display *v.* show, exhibit, unfold, expose,

flaunt *He flaunts his expensive clothes to his friends,* flourish ▷*reveal* ★**hide**

displease *v.* annoy, anger, irritate, upset, vex, offend, infuriate, incense ★**please**

dispose *v.* arrange, place, position, regulate, order

dispose of *v.* discard, dump, destroy, eliminate, throw away ★**keep**

dispute ① *n.* conflict, quarrel, argument ② *v.* argue, refute, contend

disregard *v.* overlook, misjudge, despise, ignore, snub ★**heed**

disreputable *adj.* discreditable, dishonourable, disgraceful ▷*shameful* ★**honourable**

dissect *v.* examine, scrutinize, analyse, dismember

dissent *n.* disagreement, difference, repudiation, opposition ★**assent**

dissimilar *adj.* different, diverse, unlike, various ★**similar**

dissolve *v.* melt, thaw, break up, fade

dissuade *v.* deter, discourage, warn, put off ★**persuade**

distance *n.* extent, remoteness, range, reach, span, stretch

distinct *adj.* ① separate, independent, detached ② clear, conspicuous, lucid ★**hazy**

distinguish *v.* discern, discover, differentiate

distinguished *adj.* important, notable, great, famed, celebrated ★**ordinary**

distort *v.* deform, misshape, twist, bend, buckle

distract *v.* ① beguile, bewilder, disturb, confuse ② entertain

distress *v.* harass, embarrass, trouble, grieve ▷*worry* ★**soothe**

distribute *v.* give out, deliver, disperse, circulate ▷*dispense* ★**collect**

district *n.* area, community, locality *Pat and Mike have moved to a new locality,* neighbourhood, region

distrust *v.* suspect, discredit, doubt, disbelieve ★**trust**

disturb *v.* annoy, bother, disquiet, unsettle, upset, confuse ★**calm**

a b c d e f g h i j k l m n o p q r s t u v w x y z

206

Domesticated Animals

Camel	Goat
Canary	Goose
Cat	Horse
Cattle	Parakeet
Chicken	Parrot
Dog	Pig
Donkey	Pigeon
Duck	Sheep
Elephant	

dither *v.* waver, hesitate, falter, oscillate

dive *v.* plunge, pitch, swoop, descend, drop

diverse *adj.* different, various, dissimilar, numerous, separate ★**identical**

divert *v.* ① alter, change, deflect ② entertain, gratify

divest *v.* disrobe, undress, strip

divide *v.* separate, dissect, part, divorce, distribute, apportion, split ★**join**

division *n.* portion, fragment, section, compartment, department

divorce *v.* annul, cancel, separate, divide, part, split up

divulge *v.* betray, disclose, tell, announce, broadcast, uncover

dizzy *adj.* giddy, confused, shaky, wobbling, muddled, staggering

do *v.* ① carry out, perform, act ② be adequate, suffice

do away with *v.* destroy, abolish, eliminate, kill

do up, *v.* fasten, tie, fix

docile *adj.* amenable, tame, meek, orderly, manageable ★**unco-operative**

doctrine *n.* article, belief, creed, dogma, teaching

document *n.* paper, deed, certificate, form

dodge *v.* avoid, parry, duck, elude, fend off

dogged *adj.* obstinate, morose, sullen, persistent, steadfast ★**docile**

doleful *adj.* dismal, woebegone, depressing, rueful, sad ▷*gloomy* ★**merry**

domestic ① *adj.* homely, household *The children always help with the household chores,* family, internal ② domesticated, tame

dominant *adj.* masterful, superior, supreme, prevalent ★**subordinate**

dominate *v.* rule, control, direct, tyrannize, overbear ★**yield**

donation *n.* gift, present, contribution

doom *n.* judgement, fate, verdict, destiny, destruction

door *n.* entrance, doorway, gate, gateway, portal

dose *n.* draught, potion, quantity, amount

doubt *v.* hesitate, waver, demur, suspect, mistrust, be dubious ★**trust**

doubtful *adj.* suspicious, dubious, indefinite, uncertain, unclear ★**certain**

dour *adj.* austere, dreary, grim, hard, severe ★**cheery**

dowdy *adj.* dull, plain, dingy, frumpish ▷*shabby* ★**elegant**

downcast *adj.* crestfallen, downhearted, dejected ▷*miserable* ★**happy**

downfall *n.* ruin, overthrow, misfortune, disgrace, failure

downright *adj.* blunt, candid, absolute, forthright, straightforward

doze *v.* snooze, slumber, sleep, nod off, drowse DOES

drab *adj.* colourless, cheerless, dull, gloomy, grey ▷*dreary* ★**bright**

draft *v.* sketch, outline, draw, design, plan

drag *v.* draw, pull, haul, tug, tow, lug

drain ① *v.* draw, strain, drip, percolate, empty, dry, drink up ② *n.* conduit, sewer, pipe

dramatic *adj.* theatrical, exciting, surprising, sensational ★**ordinary**

drape *v.* hang, suspend, droop, cover

drastic *adj.* extreme, dire, desperate, harsh, radical ★**mild**

draw *v.* ① pull, tug, drag, haul ② sketch, design, depict, portray

drawback *n.* weakness, shortcoming, failing, defect, handicap ★**advantage**

dread *n.* fear, terror, horror, alarm, awe, dismay ▷*fright* ★**confidence**

dreadful *adj.* fearful, terrible, horrible, alarming ▷*awful* ★**comforting**

dream *n.* trance, vision, fancy, reverie, fantasy, illusion

dreary *adj.* dingy, gloomy, sombre, cheerless ▷*dismal* ★**bright**

drench *v.* saturate, soak, steep, flood

dress ① *n.* clothing, vestments, costume, garb, apparel, attire ② *v.* wear, put on, don

dress up *v.* play-act, don, fancy-dress

drift *v.* float, flow, wander, stray, meander
The little stream meandered through lush countryside

drill ① *v.* teach, exercise, train, discipline ② bore, penetrate, pierce

drink *v.* imbibe, swallow, absorb, quaff, sip

drip *v.* drop, ooze, percolate, drizzle, trickle

drive *v.* ① make, compel, force, oblige, prod, goad ② propel, direct, operate, actuate

drivel *n.* nonsense, babble, twaddle, bunkum, gibberish

drizzle *v.* dribble, mizzle, shower, spit, spray ▷*rain*

droll *adj.* whimsical, comical, comic ▷*funny*

droop *v.* flag, sink, decline, languish, drop, bend, wilt

drop ① *v.* fall, sink, dip, plunge, plummet ② *n.* droplet, globule, drip

drown *v.* sink, immerse, swamp, submerge, extinguish

drowsy *adj.* sleepy, somnolent, dazed, tired

drudge *v.* toil, labour, struggle, plod, slave

drug *v.* dope, deaden, sedate, stupefy, poison

dry *adj.* ① arid, parched, moistureless, dried up ★**wet** ② uninteresting, boring, tedious, prosaic, dull

dubious *adj.* suspicious, fishy, suspect, untrustworthy ▷*doubtful* ★**trustworthy**

duck ① *n.* water fowl ② *v.* plunge, submerge, dip, dodge, lurch

due *adj.* ① owing, unpaid, payable ② just, fair, proper ③ scheduled, expected DEW

duel *n.* combat, contest, battle, swordplay

duffer *n.* blunderer, bungler, booby, dolt

dull *adj.* ① stupid, stolid, obtuse, dim-witted ② blunt, not sharp ③ boring, uninteresting, tedious, monotonous, lifeless

dumb ① *adj.* silent, speechless, mute ② foolish, stupid ▷*dull* ★**intelligent**

dummy ① *n.* mannequin, puppet, doll ② *n.* blockhead, dimwit ③ *adj.* artificial, fake, false

dump *v.* deposit, ditch, empty, throw away

dunce *n.* dimwit, dolt, blockhead, duffer, ignoramus ★**genius**

dungeon *n.* cell, prison, jail, vault, gaol

dupe *v.* cheat, defraud, deceive, outwit

duplicate *n.* copy, facsimile, replica, reproduction

durable *adj.* lasting, enduring, permanent, stable, reliable ★**fragile**

dusk *n.* twilight, nightfall, evening, gloaming ★**dawn**

dusty *adj.* grimy, dirty, filthy, grubby ★**polished**

duty *n.* ① obligation, responsibility, allegiance, trust, task ② impost, tax, excise

dwell *v.* stop, stay, rest, linger, tarry, live, reside

dwell on *v.* emphasize, linger over, harp on

dwindle *v.* diminish, decrease, decline, waste, shrink, become smaller ★**increase**

dye *n.* pigment, colouring matter, colour, stain, tint DIE

E e

eager *adj.* avid, enthusiastic, ambitious, ardent, zealous ▷*keen* ★**indifferent**

early *adj.* advanced, forward, soon ★**late**

earn *v.* make money, deserve, merit, rate, win, acquire ★**spend** URN

earnest *adj.* serious, sincere, determined, eager, zealous ★**flippant**

earth *n.* ① soil, dust, dry land world, globe, sphere

ease *n.* ① calm, repose, rest, quiet, peace ② dexterity, deftness ★**difficulty**

easy *adj.* effortless, smooth, simple, practicable ★**difficult**

eat *v.* consume, dine, chew, swallow, gorge

ebb *v.* flow back, fall back, recede, decline, wane ★**flow**

eccentric *adj.* queer, strange, odd, erratic, whimsical ▷*peculiar* ★**normal**

echo *v.* vibrate, reverberate, imitate

economical *adj.* moderate, reasonable, frugal ▷*thrifty* ★**expensive**

ecstasy *n.* joy, happiness, delight, elation ▷*bliss* ★**torment**

edge *n.* border, rim, brink, fringe, margin, tip ▷*end*

edible *adj.* eatable, comestible, safe, wholesome ★**inedible**

edit *v.* revise, correct, adapt, censor, publish

educate *v.* instruct, teach, tutor, coach, train

educated *adj.* learned, cultured, erudite, literate, well-bred ★**ignosant**

eerie *adj.* weird, unearthly, uncanny, awesome

effect ① *n.* outcome *What was the outcome of your interview?*, end, result ② *v.* cause, make, bring about, accomplish

effective *adj.* operative, serviceable, competent ★**useless**

efficient *adj.* competent, proficient, able ▷*effective* ★**inefficient**

effort *n.* exertion, toil, labour, accomplishment ▷*feat*

eject *v.* drive out, force out, expel, evict, oust, discharge

elaborate *adj.* complex, elegant, ornate, intricate ★**simple**

elated *adj.* excited, gleeful, joyous, overjoyed ▷*pleased* ★**downcast**

elderly *adj.* old, aged, ancient ★**youthful**

elect *v.* choose, determine, vote, select, pick

elegant *adj.* refined, luxurious, polished, classical ▷*graceful* ★**inelegant**

elementary *adj.* easy, effortless, basic, clear ▷*simple* ★**complex**

Eating verbs

bolt breakfast
chew chomp consume
devour dig in dine drink
eat eat up
feast feed finish off
gobble gorge gulp guzzle
imbibe
lap up lunch
masticate munch
nibble nosh
partake peck at pick at
quaff
relish
sample savour set to sip slurp
snack swallow sup swig swill
taste tuck in
wash down wine and dine
wolf down

A B C D E F G H I J K L M N O P Q R S T U V W X Y Z

elevate *v.* raise, erect, hoist, upraise ▷*lift* ★**lower**

eligible *adj.* qualified, suitable, acceptable, proper ▷*fit* ★**unfit**

eliminate *v.* do away with, abolish *The government has abolished many old laws,* exterminate, erase, delete ★**keep**

elude *v.* evade, avoid, depart, dodge, escape

embarrass *v.* abash, confuse, disconcert, fluster, shame

emblem *n.* badge, mark, brand, sign, crest, device

embrace *v.* ① hug, squeeze, cuddle, caress, hold ② include *The census figures include new arrivals this year,* encompass, enclose

emerge *v.* come out, exit, appear, arise, turn up ★**disappear**

emergency *n.* crisis, danger, extremity, predicament ▷*plight*

eminent *adj.* famous, noted, renowned, well-known, esteemed ▷*important* ★**unknown**

emit *v.* give off, belch, radiate, discharge, eject, vent ★**absorb**

emotion *n.* sentiment, feeling, fervour, passion

emotional *adj.* affected, sensitive, responsive, temperamental ★**cold**

emphasize *v.* accentuate, accent, intensify ▷*stress* ★**understate**

employ *v.* engage, hire, retain, apply, adopt ▷*use*

employee *n.* worker, workman, staff member, job-holder, hand

empty ① *adj.* bare, barren, vacant *That house has been vacant for months,* hollow, unoccupied ★**full** ② *v.* discharge, drain, unload, pour out ★**fill**

enchant *v.* enthral, bewitch, delight, gratify ▷*charm* ★**bore**

enclose *v.* surround, encircle, encompass, contain, include ★**open**

encounter *v.* come upon, meet, experience, face

encourage *v.* cheer, hearten, console, comfort, support ▷*urge* ★**dissuade**

encroach *v.* intrude, transgress, overstep, trespass, infringe, make inroads, invade

end ① *n.* conclusion, finish, limit, boundary *This river marks the boundary of the county* ② *v.* complete, close, terminate ▷*finish* ★**start**

endanger *v.* hazard, imperil, jeopardize ▷*risk* ★**protect**

endeavour *v.* aspire, aim, strive, struggle, try ▷*aim*

endless *adj.* ceaseless, continuous, everlasting, limitless

endorse *v.* undersign, uphold, support, guarantee, vouch for ★**disapprove**

endow *v.* settle upon, invest, award, bequeath, provide ▷*bestow* ★**divest**

endowed *adj.* talented, gifted, enhanced

endure *v.* bear, tolerate, suffer, go through, experience, cope with

enemy *n.* foe, adversary, rival, antagonist, opponent ★**friend**

energetic *adj.* dynamic, lively, vigorous, brisk ▷*active* ★**sluggish**

energy *n.* vigour, endurance, stamina, vitality, force, power

enforce *v.* apply, administer, carry out

engage *v.* ① employ, hire, charter, rent ② occupy *That new book has occupied my mind for weeks,* oblige, operate ③ pledge, betroth

engine *n.* machine, device, motor, turbine, appliance

engrave *v.* etch, stipple, incise, sculpture, carve, chisel

engrossed *adj.* absorbed, fascinated, enthralled ★**bored**

enhance *v.* intensify, strengthen, amplify, improve ★**decrease**

enigma *n.* riddle, puzzle, cryptogram, mystery, problem

enjoy *v.* like, be fond of, delight in, appreciate, savour ▷*relish* ★**detest**

enjoyable *adj.* likeable, amusing, delicious ▷*agreeable* ★**disagreeable**

enlarge *v.* amplify, make bigger, expand, extend, magnify, increase, broaden ▷*swell* ★**shrink**

enlighten *v.* inform, teach, explain to,

Engines

Diesel engine
Internal combustion
  engine
Jet engine
Piston engine
Steam engine
Turbojet engine
Turboprop
  engine
Wankel engine

educate, instruct ★**confuse**

enlist *v.* conscript, employ, engage, muster, sign up, volunteer

enmity *n.* animosity, acrimony, bitterness, hostility, antagonism, antipathy ▷*hatred* ★**friendship**

enormous *adj.* immense, vast, tremendous, massive ▷*huge* ★**tiny**

enough *adj.* sufficient, adequate, ample, plenty ★**insufficient**

enrage *v.* aggravate, incite, incense, infuriate ▷*anger* ★**soothe**

enrich *v.* decorate, embellish, adorn, improve ★**impoverish**

enrol *v.* sign up, enlist, register, accept, admit ★**reject**

enslave *v.* bind, conquer, dominate, overpower, yoke ★**free**

ensue *v.* develop, follow, result, arise ▷*happen* ★**precede**

ensure *v.* confirm, guarantee, insure, protect, secure

entangle *v.* tangle, snarl, ensnare, complicate ▷*bewilder* ★**extricate**

enter *v.* go in, arrive, enrol, invade, commence, penetrate ★**leave**

enterprise *n.* endeavour, adventure, undertaking, concern, establishment

entertain *v.* amuse, charm, cheer, please, divert, beguile ★**bore**

enthral *v.* captivate, charm, entrance, fascinate ★**bore**

enthusiasm *n.* fervour, ardour, interest, hobby, passion, eagerness

entice *v.* attract, beguile, coax, lead on, wheedle

entire *adj.* complete, intact, total, whole, full ★**partial**

entirely *adj.* absolutely, wholly, utterly *Our old dog came home, utterly tired and exhausted,* altogether ★**partially**

entitle *v.* ① allow, authorize, empower *As president, I am empowered to sign this document,* enable ② call, christen, term, name

entrance ① *n.* (*en*-trance) way in, access *There is an access to the garden on the far side,* doorway, gate, opening ② *v.* (en-*trance*) bewitch, captivate, charm ★**repel**

entreat *v.* beg, beseech, implore, ask

entry *n.* access, admission, admittance ▷*entrance* ★**exit**

envelop *v.* wrap, wind, roll, cloak, conceal, enfold

envious *adj.* jealous, grudging, covetous *Arlene cast a covetous eye at my new jacket,* resentful ★**content**

environment *n.* surroundings, neighbourhood, vicinity, background

envy *v.* covet, grudge, desire, crave, resent

episode *n.* occasion, affair, circumstance, happening, instalment

equal *adj.* ① matching, like, alike, same ★**different** ② fit *I'm not sure if Joe is really fit for this job*

equip *v.* furnish, provide, supply, fit out, rig

equipment *n.* stores, supplies, outfit, tackle *When we arrived at the lake, Sam found he'd left his fishing tackle behind,* gear

equivalent *adj.* equal, comparable, alike, similar, interchangeable ★**unlike**

era *n.* epoch, age, generation, period, time

eradicate *v.* uproot, weed out, remove, stamp out ▷*abolish*

erase *v.* cancel, rub out, obliterate, eliminate ▷*delete* ★**mark**

erect ① *adj.* upright, upstanding, rigid *The tent had a rigid metal frame* ★**relaxed** ② *v.* build, construct, put up ★**demolish**

err *v.* be mistaken, blunder, go astray,

mistake, misjudge, sin, slip up

errand *n.* mission, assignment, duty, job
▷*task*

erratic *adj.* eccentric, irregular, unstable,
unreliable ★**stable**

erroneous *adj.* untrue, false, faulty,
inaccurate ▷*wrong* ★**correct**

error *n.* mistake, fault, flaw, fallacy, untruth
▷*blunder* ★**truth**

erupt *v.* blow up, explode, burst, vent
▷*discharge*

escape *v.* break free, get away, dodge, elude,
evade ▷*flee* ★**capture**

escort ① *n.* (*es*-cort) guard, conductor, aide,
attendant, procession ② *v.* (es-*cort*)
accompany, conduct

especially *adv.* chiefly, principally, notably

essay *n.* ① effort, trial ② theme,
manuscript, composition *Whoever writes
the best composition gets a prize*

essence *n.* ① extract, juice, perfume
② substance *He spoke well, but there was
no substance to his speech,* core, pith,
character

essential *adj.* necessary, needed, vital,
requisite ★**superfluous**

establish *v.* situate, place, station, found,
organize, set up ★**upset**

estate *n.* property, land, fortune, inheritance

esteem *v.* honour, respect, admire ▷*like*
★**dislike**

estimate *v.* consider, calculate, figure,
assess, reckon

estrange *v.* alienate, antagonize, separate
★**unite**

eternal *adj.* endless, ceaseless, forever,
immortal, undying ★**temporary**

evacuate *v.* leave, desert, quit ▷*abandon*
★**occupy**

evade *v.* elude, avoid, get away from, escape
from ★**face**

evaporate *v.* vanish, dissolve, disappear,
condense, dry up

even *adj.* ① smooth, plane, flat, flush ②
balanced, equal ★**uneven** ③ yet, still

evening *n.* eve, eventide, sunset ▷*dusk*
★**morning**

event *n.* occurrence, incident, happening

ever *adv.* always, evermore, perpetually,
forever ★**never**

everlasting *adj.* continual, endless,
permanent, lasting ★**temporary**

everyday *adj.* common, frequent, daily,
familiar ★**occasional**

everything *n.* all, the whole, the lot

evict *v.* expel, eject, cast out, remove, kick
out

evidence *n.* appearance, proof, sign, token,
testimony

evident *adj.* obvious, apparent, plain,
visible, conspicuous ★**obscure**

evil *v.* wicked, sinister, wrong, bad, hurtful,
sinful ★**good**

exact *adj.* accurate, precise, definite, correct
▷*right* ★**inexact**

exaggerate *v.* magnify, overstate,
overestimate, amplify ★**minimize**

examine *v.* check, inspect, scrutinize, test,
quiz, question

example *n.* case, sample, specimen, pattern,
model, illustration

exasperate *v.* provoke, anger, annoy,
aggravate ★**soothe**

excavate *v.* mine, quarry, shovel, dig up,
discover, unearth ★**bury**

exceed *v.* excel, surpass, better, beat,
outstrip

excel *v.* outdo ▷*exceed*

excellent *adj.* admirable, good, superb,
exquisite ▷*splendid* ★**inferior**

except *prep.* with the exception of, barring,
save, saving, omitting

exceptional *adj.* unique, unusual, rare
Margaret has a rare gift for the piano,
uncommon ★**common**

excess *n.* too much, extreme, glut,
extravagance, extreme ▷*surplus*
★**scarcity**

exchange *v.* trade, barter, swap, convert,
change

excite *v.* inflame, inspire, provoke, rouse,
thrill ★**quell**

excited *adj.* ablaze, wild, ecstatic, frantic,
thrilled ★**bored**

exclaim *v.* state, say, utter, ejaculate, declare, cry out

exclude *v.* bar, shut out, prevent, boycott, forbid, leave out ★**include**

exclusive *adj.* only, personal, choice, particular, special ★**inclusive**

excuse *v.* forgive, pardon, absolve, exempt, release ★**accuse**

execute *v.* ① accomplish, do, carry out *The work was carried out just as I had expected,* achieve ② put to death, hang

exempt *v.* excuse, release, discharge, relieve, exonerate

exercise ① *n.* performance, lesson, lecture, training ② *v.* apply, train, practise *We have been practising our tennis for months*

exert *v.* apply, exercise, strain, struggle, toil

exhale *v.* breathe out, expel, expire ★**inhale**

exhaust ① *v.* use up *We have used up all our butter,* consume, deplete, empty ② overtire, fatigue, weaken

exhibition *n.* spectacle, show, fair, pageant, display

exhilarate *v.* invigorate, animate, stimulate, thrill ★**discourage**

exile *v.* deport, banish, relegate, transport, dismiss

exist *v.* be, live, breathe, subsist, stand

exit *n.* way out, outlet, egress, door

expand *v.* inflate, spread, dilate, extend, amplify ▷*swell* ★**contract**

expansive *adj.* affable, genial, friendly, open, comprehensive

expect *v.* look out for, anticipate, assume, foresee, contemplate

expedition *n.* ① outing, excursion, exploration, quest *As a child I spent long hours in the library in the quest for knowledge* ② speed, dispatch, alacrity

expel *v.* evict, eject, discharge, throw out ★**admit**

expend *v.* spend, lay out, waste, consume, use up ▷*exhaust* ★**save**

expensive *adj.* costly, high-priced, valuable, rich ★**cheap**

experience ① *n.* training, practice, wisdom, knowledge ② *v.* encounter, try, undergo, endure, meet, know, live through

experiment *n.* trial, test, check, venture

expert *n.* specialist, master, authority, professional ★**novice**

expire *v.* ① breathe out, exhale ② die, lapse *The lease on this house will lapse at the end of the year,* run out ★**begin**

explain *v.* elucidate, spell out, define, expound, teach ★**mystify**

explanation *n.* definition, outline, answer, meaning

explode *v.* detonate, blow up, go off, burst, discharge

exploit ① *n.* deed, feat, act, stunt ② *v.* take advantage of, profit by

export *v.* ship, send out, send abroad

expose *v.* show, reveal, exhibit, present, lay bare, betray ★**cover**

express ① *v.* phrase, voice, put into words, utter ② *v.* squeeze out ③ *adj.* speedy, fast

expression *n.* ① phrase, idiom, sentence, statement ② look, countenance, appearance

exquisite *adj.* dainty, subtle, fine, refined ▷*beautiful* ★**coarse**

extend *v.* stretch, reach, lengthen ▷*expand* ★**shorten**

extent *n.* breadth, expanse, width, bulk, mass, reach, duration

exterior ① *n.* outside, surface ② *adj.* external, outer, outdoor ★**interior**

extinct *adj.* defunct, dead, exterminated ★**living**

extinguish *v.* put out, blow out, abolish, destroy, quench ★**establish**

extract *v.* take out, select, remove, withdraw ★**insert**

extraordinary *adj.* unusual, incredible, strange, uncommon, marvellous ★**common**

extravagant *adj.* wasteful, reckless, prodigal, lavish ★**stingy**

extreme *adj.* ① excessive, outrageous, intense ★**moderate** ② farthest, final, remote

extricate *v.* loose, loosen, remove, retrieve, pull out

exultant *adj.* rejoicing, jubilant, joyous, triumphant ▷*elated* ★**depressed**

A
B
C
D
E
F
G
H
I
J
K
L
M
N
O
P
Q
R
S
T
U
V
W
X
Y
Z

F f

fable *n.* myth, legend, story, fantasy ★**fact**

fabric *n.* cloth, textile, material

fabulous *adj.* imaginary, legendary *Many tales have been passed down about the legendary deeds of Robin Hood,* mythical, marvellous ▷*wonderful*

face ① *n.* countenance, visage ② *n.* front, frontage, facade *The original facade was kept when the building was renovated* ③ *v.* confront, be opposite

facetious *adj.* frivolous, jocular, humorous, witty, comical ▷*funny* ★**serious**

facility *n.* ease, readiness, quickness, adroitness, knack

facsimile *n.* replica, copy, repro, photocopy

fact *n.* truth, deed, occurrence, event, reality, actuality ★**fiction**

factory *n.* plant, mill, works, shop

factual *adj.* true, actual, accurate, correct ▷*real* ★**false**

fad *n.* craze, fashion, passion, desire, mania *My sister has a mania for teddy bears,* vogue

fade *v.* discolour, bleach, dwindle, dim

fail *v.* collapse, fall, miss, trip, lose, flop ★**succeed**

failing *n.* frailty, weakness, fault, flaw ▷*defect*

failure *n.* collapse, crash, fiasco, downfall ★**success**

faint ① *adj.* indistinct *The writing was so indistinct that we could hardly read it,* soft, low, dim, feeble ② *v.* swoon, pass out, collapse FEINT

fair *adj.* ① just, equal, reasonable ★**unfair** ② mediocre *He was not a good piano player, just mediocre,* average, moderate ③ blonde, light-skinned, beautiful

faith *n.* trust, confidence, belief, fidelity, creed

faithful *adj.* ① loyal, constant, staunch, true ★**faithless** ② accurate, dependable *My watch is very dependable; it keeps accurate time,* exact, strict, close ★**inaccurate**

faithless *adj.* false, unfaithful, untrue ★**faithful**

fake *adj.* false, fictitious, pretended ▷*bogus* ★**genuine**

fall *v.* ① fall down, stumble, drop ② decline, dwindle *My mother's shares had dwindled and were worth much less,* lower ★**rise**

fall down *v.* stumble, lose one's balance

fall through *v.* collapse, fail, founder *The family business had foundered during the recession*

fallacy *n.* flaw, fault, mistake, illusion, deception

false *adj.* ① untrue, counterfeit, fake, inaccurate ② dishonest, disloyal ★**reliable**

falsehood *n.* lie, fiction, fable, fabrication, untruth, fib ★**truth**

falter *v.* reel, totter, stumble, waver, tremble

fame *n.* glory, distinction, honour, eminence, renown

familiar ① *adj.* common, frequent, well-known ② intimate *Joe and Mary are intimate friends of mine,* close, dear

famine *n.* scarcity, hunger, shortage, starvation

famished *adj.* hungry, starving, ravenous

famous *adj.* famed, well-known, celebrated, legendary *My grandmother was very attractive; her beauty was legendary,* notorious ★**unknown**

fan *v.* ventilate, cool, blow, stimulate

fanatic *n.* enthusiast, zealot, follower, fan

fanciful *adj.* romantic, fantastic, imaginary, unreal ★**ordinary**

fancy ① *adj.* decorative, beautiful, ornamental ② *v.* desire, hanker after *I had been hankering after a sea cruise all year,* yearn

fantastic *adj.* strange, bizarre, unfamiliar, romantic ▷*fanciful* ★**ordinary**

far *adj.* distant, faraway, remote ★**near**

fare ① *v.* manage *I managed quite well while my parents were abroad,* get along, happen ② *n.* charge, cost, fee, price ③ *n.* food, meals, menu, rations, provisions

farewell *interj.* goodbye, so long, adieu *We*

a b c d e f g h i j k l m n o p q r s t u v w x y z

bade our hosts adieu as we drove off

farm ① *v.* cultivate, raise, grow ② *n.* farmstead, homestead, ranch, holding *We owned a small holding of land in the west*

fascinate *v.* bewitch, beguile, enthral, engross ★**bore**

fashion ① *n.* style, fad, mode, manner ② *v.* form, carve, sculpt, devise

fast ① *adj.* rapid, quick, speedy, brisk ② *v.* starve, famish, go hungry

fasten *v.* fix, tie, attach, bind, hitch, truss ★**unfasten**

fat ① *adj.* stout, corpulent *Uncle Harry was a corpulent old man* ▷*plump* ★**thin** ② *n.* grease, oil, tallow

fatal *adj.* deadly, lethal, destructive, mortal ★**harmless**

fate *n.* fortune, destiny, future, lot, portion

fathom *v.* unravel, understand, follow, comprehend

fatigue ① *n.* tiredness, weariness ② *v.* tire, exhaust, languish *The survivors of the shipwreck languished in an open boat*

fault *n.* ① defect, flaw, imperfection ② blame, responsibility, error

faulty *adj.* imperfect, defective, unreliable, unsound, broken ★**perfect**

favour ① *n.* kindness, courtesy, benefit ② *v.* indulge, prefer, approve ★**disapprove**

favourite ① *n.* choice, darling, preference ② *v.* best-liked, chosen, preferred

fawn *v.* crouch, crawl, grovel FAUN

fear ① *n.* fright, alarm, terror, panic, shock ★**courage** ② *v.* dread, be afraid, doubt

fearful *adj.* timid, anxious, alarmed, worried ▷*afraid* ★**courageous**

fearless *adj.* gallant, courageous, daring, valiant *My ailing mother made a valiant effort to keep working* ▷*brave* ★**timid**

feast *n.* banquet, repast, dinner

feat *n.* deed, exploit, achievement, performance, stunt FEET

feature *n.* mark, peculiarity, distinction, characteristic

fee *n.* charge, commission, cost

feeble *adj.* frail, faint, flimsy, puny ▷*weak* ★**strong**

Feat

Feet

feed *v.* nourish, sustain, foster, nurture *These plants must be nurtured if they are to survive*

feel *v.* touch, handle, perceive, comprehend, know, suffer

feign *v.* fake, pretend, act, sham FAIN

feint *n.* bluff, pretence, dodge, deception FAINT

fellow *n.* companion, comrade, associate, colleague, mate

female *adj.* feminine, womanly, girlish, maidenly ★**male**

fence ① *n.* barrier, paling, barricade ② *v.* dodge, evade, parry *The sudden attack was parried by the defenders,* duel

ferocious *adj.* fierce, savage, brutal, grim, vicious ★**gentle**

fertile *adj.* fruitful, productive, rich, abundant ★**barren**

fervent *adj.* warm, passionate, enthusiastic, zealous ▷*ardent*

festival *n.* celebration, carnival, fête, jubilee

festive *adj.* convivial, jovial, sociable, gleeful, cordial ★**sombre**

fetch *v.* bear, bring, carry, deliver, convey

fête *n.* bazaar, carnival, fair, festival FATE

fetter *v.* manacle, handcuff, shackle, restrain

feud *n.* dispute, grudge, conflict, discord ★**harmony**

fever *n.* illness, infection, passion, excitement, heat ecstasy

few *adj.* scant, scanty, meagre, paltry, not many

fiasco *n.* washout, calamity, disaster, failure

fib *n.* lie, falsehood, untruth

fickle *adj.* unstable, changeable, faithless, disloyal ★**constant**

fiction *n.* stories, fable, myth, legend, invention ★**fact**

fidelity *n.* faithfulness, loyalty, allegiance *I owe allegiance to my family and my country* ★**treachery**

fidget *v.* be nervous, fret, fuss, jiggle, squirm

field *n.* farmland, grassland, green, verdure, meadow, prairie, paddock, pitch

fiend *n.* devil, demon, imp, beast, brute

fiendish *adj.* atrocious, cruel, devilish, diabolical

fierce *adj.* barbarous, cruel, brutal, merciless ▷*savage* ★**gentle**

fiery *adj.* passionate, inflamed, excitable, flaming ★**impassive**

fight *n. & v.* conflict, argument, encounter, combat, contest, battle

figure ① *n.* symbol, character, numeral ② *n.* form, shape, model ③ *v.* calculate, reckon *Bella has reckoned the amount correctly*

filch *v.* steal, thieve, sneak, purloin *Someone has purloined the letters from our mailbox*

file ① *v.* scrape, grind, grate, rasp ② *n.* binder, case, folder

fill *v.* load, pack, cram, replenish, occupy ★**empty**

filter *v.* sieve, sift, refine, clarify, screen, percolate PHILTRE

filth *n.* impurity, dirt, soil, slime, smut, grime, muck, squalor, dung ★**purity**

filthy *adj.* unclean, impure, nasty, foul ▷*dirty* ★**pure**

final *adj.* terminal, closing, ultimate, conclusive ▷*last*

find *v.* discover, achieve, locate, obtain, perceive, meet with *Our plans met with the approval of the committee* ★**lose** FINED

fine ① *adj.* thin, minute, smooth, slender ② *adj.* excellent, sharp, keen, acute ③ *n.* forfeit, penalty

finesse *n.* skill, competence, deftness

finger ① *v.* feel, grope, handle, touch ② *n.* digit, thumb, pinkie

finish *v.* accomplish, complete, close, conclude ▷*end* ★**begin**

fire ① *n.* blaze, conflagration, heat ② *v.* ignite, light, discharge, shoot

firm ① *adj.* stable, steady, solid, substantial ② *n.* company, business

first *adj.* beginning, earliest, initial, chief, principal

fishy *adj.* suspicious, dubious, doubtful ★**honest**

fissure *n.* breach, cleft, crack, cranny FISHER

fit *adj.* ① suitable, fitting, able, apt, eligible ② trim, hale, healthy, sturdy,

fitting *adj.* proper, suitable, appropriate, correct ★**unsuitable**

fix ① *v.* repair, mend, attach, fasten ② *n.* predicament, jam, pickle, plight *After the earthquake, the town was in a desperate plight*

flabby *adj.* baggy, drooping, feeble, sagging, slack

flag ① *v.* droop, languish, dwindle, fail ② banner, ensign, colours *The regimental colours were flying at half-mast*

flagrant *adj.* blatant, bold, brazen, arrant ★**secret**

flair *n.* knack, talent, faculty, ability, gift FLARE

flame *n.* fire, blaze, radiance

flap *v.* agitate, flutter, wave, swing, dangle

flare ① *v.* blaze, burn, glare, flash, glow ② *n.* signal, beacon FLAIR

flash *v.* ① gleam, glimmer, sparkle, twinkle,

Flags

Jack

Banner

Burgee

Signalling flags

Streamer

Standard

Ensign

Pennant

Jolly Roger

Bunting

scintillate, beam ② streak, dash

flat ① *adj.* level, smooth, even, horizontal ② *n.* apartment, chambers

flatter *v.* blandish, toady, soft-soap, butter up, curry favour *He gives me presents, but only to curry favour with me* ★**criticize**

flavour *n.* taste, savour, tang, aroma, quality

flaw *n.* fault, defect, blemish, mark, weakness

flawless *adj.* perfect, immaculate, faultless, sound ★**imperfect**

flee *v.* escape, abscond, run away, bolt, vanish ★**stay** FLEA

fleet ① *adj.* rapid, speedy, quick, nimble ▷*swift* ★**slow** ② *n.* navy, armada, flotilla *A flotilla of yachts sailed up the river*

fleeting *adj.* passing, brief, momentary, temporary ★**lasting**

flexible *adj.* pliant, pliable, supple, elastic

flicker *v.* blaze, glitter, flare, burn, sparkle

flimsy *adj.* slight, meagre, fragile, trivial, rickety, weak, makeshift, feeble ★**sturdy**

flinch *v.* cower, cringe, shrink, wince *I had twisted my ankle, and winced with pain as I climbed the hill*

fling *v.* throw, pitch, cast, heave ▷*hurl*

flippant *adj.* saucy, pert, brash, impudent, glib ★**earnest**

float *v.* drift, glide, hover, sail, swim

flock *n.* herd, drove, crush, group

flog *v.* beat, chastise, flay, lash, spank

flood *v.* deluge, engulf, inundate *The town was inundated when the river overflowed*, drown, swamp

floor *n.* deck, base, bottom, platform, level, storey

flop *v.* flap, fall, drop, droop, fall flat

florid *adj.* ruddy, flushed, red, ornate ★**pale**

flounce *v.* bounce, fling, jerk, spring, bob

flounder ① *v.* bungle, fail, falter, fumble ② *n.* flatfish

flour *n.* meal, bran, farina FLOWER

Flower

Flour

flourish *v.* ① shake, brandish, flaunt ② blossom, bloom, prosper ▷*thrive*

flow *v.* run, stream, glide, sweep, swirl ▷*gush* FLOE

flower *n. & v.* blossom, bloom, bud FLOUR

fluent *adj.* vocal, facile, articulate *Sally is very articulate and has a great command of language,* flowing, fluid

fluid *adj.* watery, flowing, liquid, runny ★**solid**

flummox *v.* baffle, confuse, fluster, confound ▷*bewilder* ★**enlighten**

flush ① *v.* glow, bloom, blush ② *v.* swab, drench, rinse ③ *adj.* level, even, flat

fluster *v.* bother, confuse, perturb, ruffle ▷*fuss* ★**calm**

flutter *v.* wave, flap, flop, flitter, hover, flit

fly ① *v.* take flight, glide, soar, float ② *v.* escape, hasten ③ *n.* winged insect

foam *n.* froth, scum, lather, suds, surf

foe *n.* enemy, opponent, rival, adversary ★**friend**

fog *n.* mist, vapour, haze, cloud

foil ① *v.* defeat, overcome, elude ② *n.* sheet metal, tinfoil, film, flake

fold *n. & v.* crease, hem, seam, crimp, pleat FOALED

follow *v.* ① pursue, succeed, come after ② understand, catch on to, comprehend

folly *n.* silliness, foolishness, absurdity, craziness ▷*nonsense* ★**wisdom**

fond *adj.* tender, loving, caring ▷*affectionate* ★**hostile**

fondle *v.* pet, stroke, cuddle, caress, coddle

food *n.* nourishment, nutriment, provender, provisions, fare, sustenance

fool ① *n.* idiot, dunce, clown, blockhead, simpleton ② *v.* deceive, trick, swindle

foolhardy *adj.* reckless, impetuous, madcap ▷*rash* ★**cautious**

foolish *adj.* absurd, ridiculous, daft ▷*silly* ★**wise**

for *prep.* on behalf of, towards, because of ★**against** fore, four

forbid *v.* bar, ban, prohibit, deter, hinder, prevent ★**allow**

force ① *n.* energy, strength, might, power ② *v.* make, compel, coerce *It's no use, you can't coerce me into flying home,* push

fore *adj.* first, front, leading FOR, FOUR

forecast *v.* foresee, predict, foretell, prophesy

foreign *adj.* alien, strange, remote, exotic, outlandish ★**domestic**

foremost *adj.* chief, leading, principal, uppermost

forfeit *v.* abandon, give up, lose, relinquish, sacrifice ★**reward**

forge *v.* ① counterfeit, falsify, copy, imitate ② construct, form, make, fashion

forgery *n.* fake, dud, counterfeit, imitation, phoney, sham, fraud

forget *v.* overlook, neglect, lose sight of, let slip ★**remember**

forgive *v.* pardon, absolve, reprieve, let off, overlook ★**blame**

forlorn *adj.* lonely, desolate, miserable, wretched ★**hopeful**

form ① *v.* make, fabricate, fashion, contrive, create ② *n.* manner, fashion, style ③ *n.* shape, figure *I made a clay figure of a pirate*

formal *adj.* stiff, solemn, ceremonial, ritualistic, aloof ★**informal**

former *adj.* earlier, previous, prior ★**later**

formidable *adj.* awful, terrible, alarming, terrifying, serious ★**trivial**

forsake *v.* abandon, give up, desert, discard, leave ▷*quit* ★**resume**

forth *adv.* ahead, forward, onward, outward

forthright *adj.* frank, candid, direct, bald, blunt ★**devious**

forthwith *adv.* immediately, directly, at once, instantly ★**soon**

fortify *v.* ① strengthen, confirm, corroborate, hearten ② garrison, protect, buttress *The old house was crumbling and the walls needed to be buttressed* ★**weaken**

fortitude *n.* courage, endurance, bravery, composure ▷*strength* ★**cowardice**

fortunate *adj.* happy, felicitous, auspicious, rosy ▷*lucky* ★**unfortunate**

fortune *n.* ① affluence, wealth, treasure ② chance, destiny, fate

forward ① *adv.* onward, forth, ahead, before ② *adj.* progressive, bold, audacious ★**modest** ③ *v.* advance, send, transmit

foster *v.* ① help, promote, aid ② care for, cherish, nurse

foul *adj.* mucky, nasty, filthy, dirty, murky ★**fair** FOWL

found *v.* create, build, erect, establish

foundation *n.* establishment, base, basis, groundwork *You will pick up Spanish easily, for you already have the groundwork*

fountain *n.* spring, well, reservoir, source

fowl *n.* bird, chicken, poultry FOUL

foxy *adj.* crafty, slick, cunning, tricky ▷*artful* ★**naive**

fraction *n.* portion, part, division ▷*fragment*

fracture *n.* break, cleft, crack, fissure, rupture, breach, opening ▷*split*

fragile *adj.* brittle, frail, delicate, dainty ▷*flimsy* ★**robust**

fragment *n.* portion, bit, chip, morsel, piece ▷*fracture*

fragrance *n.* aroma, smell, odour ▷*scent*

frail *adj.* weak, feeble, infirm ▷*fragile*

frame *n.* framework, casing, shape, mount, chassis

frank *adj.* sincere, candid, open, honest, blunt ▷*truthful* ★**insincere**

frantic *adj.* excited, furious, distracted, wild, mad ▷*frenzied* ★**calm**

fraud *n.* deceit, fake, extortion, swindle ▷*forgery*

fraudulent *adj.* sham, fake, counterfeit ▷*bogus* ★**genuine**

fray *n.* combat, contest, battle, brawl ▷*rumpus*

freak *adj.* abnormal, bizarre *A snowstorm in the tropics would be bizarre,* odd, unusual ★**common**

free ① *adj.* unhindered, at liberty, liberated, unrestricted ② *adj.* gratuitous, gratis, without cost ③ *v.* let loose, unleash, release, liberate, emancipate

freeze *n.* ice, frost, refrigerate FREES, FRIEZE

frenzied *adj.* agitated, excited, furious, hysterical *Lisa became hysterical when she saw the house on fire* ▷*frantic* ★**placid**

frequent *adj.* repeated, numerous, recurrent, common ▷*regular* ★**rare**

frequently *adv.* often, many times, commonly ★**rarely**

fresh *adj.* new, young, vigorous, blooming, recent, wholesome ★**stale**

fret *v.* worry, harass, irritate, torment ▷*vex* ★**calm**

friction *n.* ① rubbing, grating, contact, abrasion ② ill-feeling, discord, dispute

friend *n.* companion, associate, ally, crony *On Saturdays, my father plays golf with some of his cronies,* pal ▷*chum*

friendly *adj.* affable, amicable, kindly, cordial ▷*genial* ★**hostile**

friendship *n.* affection, fellowship, fondness, harmony ▷*concord* ★**enmity**

A
B
C
D
E
F
G
H
I
J
K
L
M
N
O
P
Q
R
S
T
U
V
W
X
Y
Z

fright *n.* alarm, dread, dismay, terror ▷*fear* ★**calm**

frighten *v.* daunt, dismay, scare, alarm ▷*terrify* ★**reassure**

frightful *adj.* alarming, shocking, ghastly ▷*horrible* ★**pleasant**

frigid *adj.* cool, chilly, icy, frozen, wintry ★**warm**

fringe *n.* edge, border, limits, outskirts

frisky *adj.* lively, spirited, playful, active ★**quiet**

frivolous *adj.* frothy, facetious, flippant, foolish ▷*trivial* ★**serious**

frock *n.* robe, dress, gown, smock

frolic *v.* gambol, caper, frisk, sport

front *n.* fore, brow, forehead, face, facade, beginning ★**back**

frontier *n.* border, boundary, edge, limit

frosty *adj.* chilly, frigid, frozen, freezing ▷*cold* ★**warm**

froth *n.* scum, bubbles ▷*foam*

frown *v.* glower, grimace, glare ▷*scowl* ★**smile**

frugal *adj.* thrifty, economical, careful, sparing *We were poor in the old days and needed to be sparing with our money* ▷*meagre* ★**wasteful**

fruitful *adj.* fertile, productive, flourishing,

Futile

It was hopeless, the bear was too big for Zak to carry.

plentiful, abundant, profitable ★**barren**

fruitless *adj.* unprofitable, sterile, barren, pointless ★**fruitful**

frustrate *v.* thwart, balk, foil, hinder, defeat ★**fulfil**

fugitive *n.* escapee, runaway, deserter

fulfil *v.* perform, render, please, accomplish, achieve ★**frustrate**

full *adj.* loaded, packed, laden, charged, abundant, complete ★**empty**

fumble *v.* grope, spoil, mismanage, flail ▷*bungle*

fun *n.* sport, frolic, gaiety, jollity, entertainment, amusement

function ① *n.* service, purpose, activity ② *n.* affair, party, gathering ③ *v.* act, operate, work

fund *n.* stock, supply, pool, store, treasury *The city treasury has a small surplus this year*, kitty, reserve

fundamental *adj.* basic, essential, primary, rudimentary ★**unimportant**

funny *adj.* comical, droll, amusing, ridiculous ▷*humorous* ★**solemn**

furious *adj.* agitated, angry, fierce, intense ▷*frantic* ★**calm**

furnish *v.* ① supply, provide, offer ② equip

furrow *n.* groove, channel, hollow, seam, rib

further ① *adj.* extra, more, other, supplementary, ② *v.* advanced, aid, hasten

furtive *adj.* secretive, sly, hidden ▷*stealthy* ★**open**

fury *n.* anger, frenzy, ferocity, passion ▷*rage* ★**calm**

fuse *v.* melt, smelt, combine, merge, solder, weld, integrate ▷*join*

fuss *n.* stir, excitement, tumult, bustle, bother, palaver, commotion ▷*ado* ★**calm**

fussy *adj.* busy, faddish, fastidious, finicky, exacting ★**plain**

futile *adj.* useless, in vain, hopeless *It was hopeless, the bear was too big for Zak to carry*, barren, forlorn, ineffective ★**effective**

future *adj.* forthcoming, coming, impending, eventual

fuzzy *adj.* murky, foggy, misty, unclear

G g

gain *v.* get, win, acquire, attain, profit

gale *n.* storm, wind, hurricane, tornado, cyclone

gallant *adj.* courageous, noble, chivalrous ▷*brave*

gallop *v.* dash, run, career, rush

gamble *v.* bet, risk, wager, chance GAMBOL

gambol *v.* prance, romp, frisk, frolic ▷*jump* GAMBLE

game *n.* ① sport, pastime, contest, competition ★**work** ② quarry, prey

gang *n.* crew, team, troop, crowd, cluster, party

gap *n.* space, blank, hole, break, cranny, chink, opening, crack, interval

gape *v.* yawn, stare, gaze, gawk ▷*look*

garbage, *n.* trash, rubbish, refuse, waste, slops

garden *n.* flower bed, vegetable patch, patio, park, allotment

garment *n.* clothes, dress, attire, robe, costume ▷*clothing*

garret *n.* attic, loft, cupola

gas *n.* vapour, fume, mist, smoke

gasp *v.* gulp, pant, choke ▷*breathe*

gate *n.* door, portal, gateway GAIT

gather *v.* ① collect, pick up, pick, draw, amass, assemble, flock, hoard, acquire ★**disperse** ② understand *I understand that you have been elected treasurer of the club,* assume, judge

gathering *n.* meeting, assembly, function, affair, company, collection

gaudy *adj.* flashy, cheap, tawdry, loud, showy

gaunt, *adj.* thin, lean, skinny, spare ▷*haggard* ★**robust**

gauge ① *n.* measure, meter, rule ② *v.* judge, measure, estimate *We must estimate the number of beans in the jar,* probe

gaze *v.* stare, look, regard, contemplate

gear *n.* tackle, array, accessories, machinery, harness, equipment

gem *n.* jewel, stone, treasure

general *adj.* normal, usual, habitual, customary, total, whole ★**local**

generous *adj.* free, liberal, kind ★**selfish**

genial *adj.* cheerful, cheery, sunny, hearty, cordial, pleasant ▷*jolly* ★**cold**

genius *n.* brilliance, prowess, talent, power, skill, cleverness, brains ★**stupidity**

genteel *adj.* refined, polished, civil, courteous, well-bred, polite, elegant ★**boorish**

gentle *adj.* ① easy, mild, soft, kind, moderate, tender, humane ② gradual, faint, feeble, slight *The field had a slight slope as it came down to the river*

genuine *adj.* ① real, authentic, true, sound ② sincere, honest, candid, frank ★**false**

germ *n.* microbe, seed, embryo, nucleus

gesture *n.* sign, signal, motion, nod, shrug, movement

get *v.* ① acquire, obtain, gain, win, receive, secure, achieve, inherit ★**forfeit** ② understand, catch on *It took Johnny quite a while to catch on to what I meant,* fathom, figure out, learn

get up *v.* arise, awake, awaken

get rid of *v.* discard, reject, throw away, scrap

ghastly *adj.* shocking, hideous, horrible, fearful, terrible, frightful

ghost *n.* spook, spirit, spectre, banshee, phantom, apparition

ghostly *v.* uncanny, haunted, eerie, weird

giant *adj.* mammoth, huge, colossal, enormous, tremendous, immense ▷*big, gigantic* ★**tiny**

gibber *v.* gabble, prattle, jabber

gibberish *n.* nonsense, drivel, rubbish

gibe *v.* jeer, sneer, scoff, deride ▷*taunt*

giddy *adj.* dizzy, whirling, reeling, unsteady, wild, reckless

gift *n.* ① present, donation, bounty, boon ② talent, skill *Her skill was so great that I knew she must have been born with it,* ability, power

gigantic *adj.* stupendous, titanic, colossal ▷*giant* ★**minute**

giggle v. chuckle, chortle, cackle, snigger
▷*laugh*

gingerly adv. carefully, daintily, warily,
cautiously

girder n. rafter, joist, beam

girl n. maid, maiden, miss, damsel, young
woman, lass, wench

girlish adj. maidenly, dainty, feminine

girth n. circumference, perimeter, fatness,
breadth

gist n. essence, substance, kernel,
nub, pith, significance

give v. ① donate, grant, distribute, bestow
② bend, yield *The wooden footbridge
suddenly yielded under his weight and
crashed into the stream,* relax, recede
③ produce, yield ④ pronounce, utter, emit
★**take**

give back v. return, restore

give forth v. emit, send out, radiate

give in v. surrender, quit, yield

give off v. belch, emit, exude

give up v. surrender, give in, relinquish,
hand over

giver n. donor, bestower, presenter

glad adj. joyful, joyous, delighted, pleased
▷*happy* ★**sorry**

gladden v. make happy, gratify, delight,
elate ▷*please* ★**grieve**

gladly adv. freely, readily, cheerfully,
willingly

glamour n. romance, interest, fascination,
attraction, enchantment

glance ① n. look, glimpse, peep ② v. peer,
notice ③ brush, shave, graze, *The bullet
merely grazed his head*

glare ① v. blaze, glow, flare, sparkle, dazzle
② frown, glower, stare

glaring adj. ① sparkling, dazzling ②
blatant, notorious, conspicuous

glass n. tumbler, goblet, beaker, mirror,
looking-glass

glaze v. polish, gloss, burnish, varnish

gleam v. sparkle, glitter, flash, glisten,
twinkle

glee n. jollity, gaiety, elation, triumph
▷*happiness*

glib adj. fluent, slick, smooth, facile,
talkative, plausible

glide v. slide, slither, slip, soar, sail, skate,
skim

glimmer v. sparkle, scintillate, flicker, glow,
gleam

glimpse v. spy, spot, glance, view

glisten v. shine, glitter, glow, gleam

glitter v. gleam, sparkle, flash, glint, glisten,
scintillate

gloat v. whoop, exult, crow, revel, triumph

globe n. ball, sphere, planet, earth, world

gloom n. darkness, gloaming, dusk, shadow,
dimness, bleakness ★**light**

gloomy adj. cheerless, black, dark, bleak,
cloudy, overcast, dismal, dour, glum,
melancholy ▷*dreary* ★**happy**

glorious adj. brilliant, lustrous, noble,
exalted, renowned ▷*splendid*

glory n. brilliance, radiance, pride
▷*splendour*

gloss n. lustre, sheen, shimmer, polish
▷*glaze*

glossy adj. shiny, burnished, sleek, slick,
polished

glow n. & v. glare, glitter, bloom, blush,
flush, shine, gleam, twinkle

glower v. frown, stare, scowl, glare

glue ① n. paste, gum, cement, mucilage,
adhesive, size ② v. stick, fasten

glum adj. sullen, sulky, morose, miserable,
dejected, downcast ▷*gloomy*

glut n. abundance, plenty, too much, surplus

glutton n. gorger, stuffer, crammer, pig,
gormandizer, gourmand

gnash v. grind, chomp, bite, crunch

gnaw v. chew, nibble, bite, consume

go v. ① walk, pass, move, travel, depart,
proceed ② stretch, reach, extend *The
prairie extended as far as the mountain
range*

go after v. pursue, chase, follow

go ahead v. progress, proceed, continue

go away v. leave, depart, vanish, disappear

go back v. return, resume, withdraw

go by v. pass, elapse, vanish

go in v. enter, advance, invade, penetrate

go in for *v.* enter, take part, participate, compete

go off *v.* explode, blow up, depart

go on *v.* continue, advance, proceed, move ahead, keep up

go up *v.* climb, mount, rise ▷*ascend*

goad *v.* prod, incite, impel, drive, urge, sting, worry

goal *n.* target, ambition, aim, object, destination

gobble *v.* devour, gorge, swallow, gulp, bolt

goblin *n.* sprite, demon, gnome, elf

God *n.* the Creator, the Father, the Almighty, Jehovah, the Divinity, the Holy Spirit, King of Kings, the Supreme Being

godless *adj.* unholy, unclean, wicked, savage, profane ★**righteous**

golden *adj.* excellent, precious, brilliant, bright

good *adj.* ① excellent, admirable, fine ② favourable, *The calm weather provides favourable conditions for water-skiing,* advantageous, profitable ③ righteous, moral, true *A true friend can forgive your mistakes* ④ clever, skilful, expert ⑤ fit, proper, suited ★**bad**

goodness *n.* excellence, merit, worth, honesty, kindness ▷*virtue* ★**evil**

goods *n.* wares, commodities, cargo, load, material, belongings

gorge ① *v.* swallow, gulp, devour ▷*eat* ② *n.* canyon, glen, valley

gorgeous *adj.* beautiful, ravishing, stunning, superb, magnificent

gossip *v.* chat, chatter, prattle, tittle-tattle

gouge *v.* excavate, groove, dig out

govern *v.* rule, reign, manage, direct, guide, control, conduct, command

government *n.* rule, administration, supervision, parliament, council

governor *n.* director, manager, leader, chief, overseer, head of state

gown *n.* robe, dress, frock

grace *n.* elegance, refinement, polish, symmetry ▷*beauty*

graceful *adj.* beautiful, lovely, shapely, refined ▷*elegant*

Great

Grate

gracious *adj.* amiable, kind, suave, urbane, affable, elegant ★**churlish**

grade *n.* ① class, rank, degree ② slope, gradient, incline, slant

gradual *adj.* by degrees, step-by-step, continuous, little by little ★**sudden**

graft ① *v.* splice, insert, bud, plant ② *n.* bribery, corruption

grain *n.* fibre, crumb, seed, particle, atom, bit, drop

grand *adj.* splendid, impressive, stately, magnificent, wonderful, superb

grandeur *n.* magnificence, splendour, majesty, lordliness

grant ① *n.* bounty, award, subsidy ② *v.* bestow, donate *We all donated some money to help the earthquake victims,* confer, give

grapple *v.* struggle, tussle, wrestle, seize, grasp, clutch

grasp *v.* ① grip, seize, take, grab, hold ② understand, comprehend

grasping *adj.* greedy, avaricious, covetous, miserly ★**generous**

grate ① *v.* rasp, file, jar, clash, rub, grind

② annoy, irritate, vex ③ *n.* fireplace GREAT

grateful *adj.* thankful, appreciative, obliged, indebted

gratify *v.* delight, satisfy, please, content, enchant, indulge, favour ★**displease**

gratitude *n.* thankfulness, appreciation, obligation

grave ① *adj.* solemn, sober, momentous, dignified, majestic ② essential, important *I have important news to tell* ③ *n.* tomb, vault, shrine

gravity *n.* ① seriousness, solemnity, importance, significance ② force, gravitation, weight

graze *v.* ① scrape, brush, shave, glance ② browse, crop, bite GREYS

grease *n.* fat, suet, tallow, oil

great *adj.* ① large, considerable, bulky, huge, ample ② important, elevated, noted *Here is a list of noted citizens of this town* ③ main, chief, principal GRATE

greedy *adj.* gluttonish, voracious, grasping, selfish, acquisitive ★**unselfish**

green *adj.* ① emerald, jade, turquoise ② ungrown, immature, raw *During the war, many raw recruits were drafted into the army,* untrained ★**expert**

greet *v.* welcome, accost, hail, salute, salaam, address

grief *n.* woe, sadness, regret, distress, anguish ▷*sorrow* ★**joy**

grievance *n.* injury, hardship, complaint, wrong, trial ★**boon**

grieve *v.* lament, deplore, mourn, sorrow, be sad, afflict, hurt ★**rejoice**

grievous *adj.* lamentable, deplorable, grave, critical, severe; mortal

grill ① *v.* fry, broil ② *n.* grating, grid

grim *adj.* ① serious, stern, harsh, solemn, dour, forbidding ② horrid, dreadful, terrible ▷*sombre* ★**mild**

grime *n.* filth, soil, dust, soot ▷*dirt*

grin *n. & v.* smile, beam, smirk, simper

grind *v.* ① scrape, file, crush, powder ② sharpen, whet, grate

grip *v.* grasp, grab, snatch, clasp, seize ▷*hold* ★**loosen**

Groups of Animals

a drove of cattle
a flock of birds
a herd of elephants
a mob of kangaroos
a pack of wolves
a pride of lions
a school of porpoises
a sloth of bears
a swarm of bees
a troop of monkeys
a colony of seals
a cete of badgers
a skulk of foxes

grisly *adj.* horrid, horrible, dreadful, ghastly ▷*grim*

grit *n.* ① powder, dust, sand, gravel ② nerve, mettle, pluck ▷*courage*

groan *v.* moan, complain, grumble, creak GROWN

groom ① *n.* husband, bridegroom ② *n.* stable-boy, servant, ostler ③ *v.* spruce, tidy, preen

groove *n.* furrow, ridge, corrugation, channel, rut, score

grope *v.* feel, handle, finger, manipulate, touch, pick

gross *adj.* ① large, bulky, unwieldy, massive ② coarse, vulgar, crude ③ outrageous,

Growls, grunts, and other animal noises

Bees buzz	Horses neigh
Cats meow	Lions roar
Cockerels crow	Mice squeak
Cows moo	Owls hoot
Dogs bark	Pigs grunt
Dogs also growl	Snakes hiss
Ducks quack	Wolves howl

glaring, flagrant *The driver was arrested for a flagrant disregard of the speed limit*

grotesque *adj.* deformed, malformed, misshapen, freakish, abnormal, bizarre

ground *n.* ① dry land, soil, earth, dust ② bottom, base, foundation

grounds *n.* ① foundation, cause, basis, excuse ② dregs, sediment, silt ③ gardens, parkland, estate

group *n.* ① division, section, branch ② gang, throng, cluster, bunch, class, set

grovel *v.* fawn, crouch, crawl, toady, cringe, wallow, cower

grow *v.* ① increase, advance, expand, extend, develop, raise ② sprout, germinate, shoot

growl *v.* snarl, snap, threaten, thunder

growth *n.* expansion, development, advance ▷*increase*

grow up *v.* mature, develop, ripen

grubby *adj.* messy, dirty, mucky

grudge *n. & v.* hate, envy, dislike, spite

gruesome *adj.* frightful, hideous, ghastly ▷*grisly*

gruff *adj.* husky, throaty, croaky, blunt, churlish, crusty, curt ★**affable**

grumble *v.* complain, snivel, murmur, growl, protest

grumpy *adj.* disgruntled, dissatisfied, surly, sour, irritable, sullen ★**affable**

grunt *n. & v.* snort, groan ★**growl**

guarantee *n.* warranty, assurance, security, pledge

guard ① *n.* protector, sentry, guardian, watchman ② *v.* protect, defend, watch over, shelter, shield

guess *v.* surmise, conjecture, judge, think, suspect, suppose

guest *n.* visitor, caller GUESSED

guide ① *n.* pilot, director, leader, controller ② *v.* steer, navigate, lead, direct, manage, conduct *Our teacher conducted us to the bus and we all climbed aboard*

guild *n.* club, trade union, association, federation, fellowship, band, society

guile *n.* knavery, foul play, trickery, deceit, cunning, fraud ★**honesty**

guilty *adj.* blameworthy, sinful, wicked, wrong ★**innocent**

guise *n.* garb, pose, posture, role, aspect *The motel manager's aspect was a little too friendly; we did not trust him,* appearance GUYS

gulch *n.* valley, gully, ravine

gulf *n.* ① bay, basin, inlet ② chasm, opening, abyss, depths

gullible *adj.* credulous, innocent, naive, trusting, suggestible

gully *n.* trench, ditch, channel, ravine

gulp *v.* swallow, consume, guzzle, devour

gun *n.* rifle, cannon, revolver, pistol, automatic, shotgun

gurgle *v.* ripple, murmur, purl, babble

gush *v.* stream, spurt, spout, flow, run, pour out

gust *n.* blast, blow, squall, wind

gusto *n.* relish, zest, eagerness, zeal, pleasure

gutter *n.* moat, ditch, dike, drain, gully, channel, groove

guzzle *v.* gulp, imbibe, drink, swill, quaff

A B C D E F G H I J K L M N O P Q R S T U V W X Y Z

H h

habit *n.* ① custom, practice, routine, way, rule ② mannerism *One of his annoying mannerisms is drumming his fingers on the table,* addiction, trait

hack *v.* chop, mangle, gash, slash

hackneyed *adj.* stale, trite, commonplace, tired ★**new**

hag *n.* crone, harridan, witch, virago *I know I have a temper, but Julia is a real virago*

haggard *adj.* drawn, wan, pinched, thin ▷*gaunt* ★**hale**

haggle *v.* bargain, barter, bicker, dispute ★**yield**

hail ① *v.* salute, call to, accost, welcome, greet ② *n.* sleet, frozen rain, ice storm HALE

hair *n.* locks, mane, tresses, strand

hale *adj.* hearty, robust, sound, fit ▷*healthy* ★**ill** HAIL

half *n.* division, fraction, segment, share

hall *n.* entrance, foyer, corridor, lobby, vestibule *There is a coat rack and an umbrella stand in the vestibule of her house* HAUL

hallow *v.* sanctify, consecrate, bless, dedicate, make holy

hallucination *n.* illusion, fantasy, delusion, mirage, dream ★**reality**

halt *v.* end, pause, rest, cease ▷*stop* ★**start**

halting *adj.* faltering, hestitating, wavering, awkward ★**fluent**

hammer ① *v.* beat, pound, bang ② *n.* mallet, gavel *The leader banged his gavel on the desk and called for order*

hamper ① *v.* hinder, interfere, impede, curb ★**aid** ② *n.* basket, creel, *The fisherman carried a creel to put his catch in*

hand ① *v.* give, pass, present, yield ② *n.* fist, palm, paw, mitt

handicap *n.* defect, disability, drawback, restriction ★**advantage**

handicraft *n.* skill, hobby, art, workmanship, craft, occupation

handle ① *n.* shaft, holder, grip ② *v.* feel,

Habitations

Apartment	Igloo
Bungalow	Lodge
Cabin	Mansion
Castle	Palace
Chalet	Ranch
Chateau	Shack
Cottage	Shanty
Duplex	Villa
Estate	
Flat	
Hacienda	
Hut	

touch, finger, work, wield, grasp, fondle

handsome *adj.* ① good-looking, graceful, attractive ② generous, lavish *Aunt Betsy is always lavish with presents for the children* HANSOM

handy *adj.* ready, convenient, deft, skilled ★**clumsy**

hang *v.* dangle, suspend, sag, droop, swing

hanker for *v.* long for, yearn for, crave, desire ★**dislike**

haphazard *adj.* accidental, random, aimless, casual ▷*chance* ★**deliberate**

hapless *adj.* ill-fated, luckless, unlucky ▷*miserable* ★**lucky**

happen *v.* occur, take place, come about, result, transpire

happening *n.* event, incident, occurrence, occasion, phenomenon

happiness *n.* delight, ecstasy, gaiety, joy, enjoyment ▷*bliss* ★**unhappiness**

happy *adj.* cheerful, blithe, content, joyous, jubilant ▷*merry* ★**unhappy**

harass *v.* beset, annoy, upset, bother, pester,

badger, hassle ▷*distress* ★**assist**

harbour ① *n.* port, anchorage, mooring ② *n.* refuge, shelter, safety *At last we were back in the safety of our home* ③ *v.* give shelter to

hard *adj.* ① firm, stony, rocky, solid ★**soft** ② difficult, tough *I had a very tough problem to solve,* perplexing ★**easy** ③ stern, severe, callous, ruthless

hardly *adv.* seldom, rarely, scarcely, slightly

hardship *n.* trouble, suffering, want ▷*difficulty* ★**ease**

hardy *adj.* rugged, sturdy, tough, healthy, sound ▷*robust* ★**weak**

hark *v.* listen, hear ▷*listen*

harm ① *n.* damage, mischief, ruin, wrong, abuse, sin ② *v.* abuse, blemish, hurt *I'm sorry, I didn't mean to hurt you,* injure ★**benefit**

harmful *adj.* injurious, evil, wicked, damaging ★**harmless**

harmless *adj.* safe, gentle, innocuous, innocent ★**harmful**

harmony *n.* agreement, conformity, accord, unity, goodwill ★**discord**

harp ① *n.* lyre, stringed instrument ② *v.* harp on, dwell on *I tried to forget our quarrel, but Carol continued to dwell on it,* allude to

harrow *v.* agonize, taunt, distress, torture, harry ▷*harass* ★**hearten**

harsh *adj.* ① jarring, coarse, rasping, rough ② severe, strict, ruthless ★**mild**

harvest *v.* plough, harrow, reap, pluck

hash *n.* ① mess, confusion, muddle ② stew, goulash, hotpot

hassle *n.* argument, bother, difficulty, squabble, struggle

haste *n.* rush, bustle, dispatch, urgency, swiftness ▷*hurry* ★**delay**

hasten *v.* hurry, hustle, quicken, accelerate, speed up ★**dawdle**

hasty *adj.* hurried, rushed, abrupt, indiscreet ★**deliberate**

hate *v.* abhor, detest, loathe ▷*despise* ★**love**

hateful *adj.* abominable, loathsome, odious, despicable ★**pleasing**

haughty *adj.* arrogant, disdainful, scornful, snobbish ★**humble**

haul *v.* pull, draw, tug, drag, heave HALL

have *v.* possess, occupy, own, receive, take in

haven *n.* harbour, port, refuge, retreat, sanctum, shelter

havoc *n.* wreckage, ruin, destruction, disorder, mayhem

hay *n.* pasture, silage, grass, straw HEY

haze *n.* cloud, vapour, fog, mist HAYS

hazy *adj.* foggy, misty, murky, vague, uncertain ★**clear**

head ① *n.* visage, skull, cranium, pate ② *adj.* chief, main, principal

heading *n.* caption, headline, title, inscription

headlong *adj.* rough, dangerous, reckless ▷*rash*

heal *v.* soothe, treat, cure, mend, restore HEEL, HE'LL

healthy *adj.* fine, fit, hearty, sound, vigorous ▷*hale* ★**sick**

heap *n.* pile, mass, mound, collection

hear *v.* listen to, hearken, overhear HERE

hearten *v.* assure, encourage, embolden, inspire ★**dishearten**

heartless *adj.* brutal, callous, cold ▷*unkind* ★**kind**

hearty *adj.* cordial, sincere, earnest, honest, jovial ★**cold**

heat *n.* ① warmth, temperature ② passion, ardour, fervour *She spoke with great fervour about what she believed*

heave *v.* fling, cast, hurl, hoist, pull, tug

heavenly *adj.* beautiful, blessed, divine, lovely ★**hellish**

heavy *adj.* weighty, hefty, ponderous, loaded ★**light**

hectic *adj.* excited, fast, frenzied, wild ▷*frantic* ★**leisurely**

heed *v.* listen, pay attention, follow, respect, obey ★**ignore**

heedless *adj.* thoughtless, reckless, unwary, rash ▷*careless*

height ① *n.* altitude, stature ② top, apex, peak, zenith, climax ★**depth**

Headgear

Balaclava	Helmet	Stetson
Beret	Homburg	Tam-o'-shanter
Boater	Hood	Top hat
Bonnet	Kepi	Toque
Cap	Panama	Trilby
Glengarry	Shako	Turban
Fedora	Sombrero	Tyrolean hat
Fez	Sou'wester	Yarmulke

hellish *adj.* abominable, awful, inhuman, fiendish ★**heavenly**

help ① *n.* aid, support, assistance ② *v.* lend a hand *We all lent a hand in building the hut,* aid, assist ★**hinder**

helpful *adj.* caring, considerate ▷*useful* ★**useless**

helping *n.* ration, portion, piece, serving, helping *Mike would like a second helping. He's still hungry,* share, dollop

helpless *adj.* incapable, powerless, unfit, forlorn ▷*weak* ★**strong**

hem *n.* edge, border, fringe, margin

hence *adv.* accordingly, thus, therefore, henceforward

herd *n.* crowd, crush, flock, group, mass, mob, horde HEARD

here *adv.* present, attending, hereabouts, in this place HEAR

heritage *n.* inheritance, legacy, birthright, tradition

hermit *n.* recluse, solitary, monk

hero *n.* champion, daredevil, star, idol, conqueror, celebrity, superstar ★**villain**

heroic *adj.* bold, fearless, lion-hearted, gallant ▷*brave* ★**cowardly**

heroine *n.* celebrity, goddess *Marilyn Monroe was a goddess of the screen,* idol, star, lead

hesitate *v.* falter, dither, doubt, wait

hew *v.* chop, cut, fashion, carve, sculpt HUE

hidden *adj.* concealed, covered, veiled, unseen ★**open**

hide *v.* conceal, cover, obscure, bury, cloak ★**reveal** HIED

hideous *adj.* repulsive, unsightly, gruesome, horrible ▷*ugly* ★**beautiful**

hiding *n.* beating, thrashing, caning

high ① *adj.* tall, towering, lofty, elevated ② shrill *The referee blew a shrill blast on his whistle,* treble, strident ③ expensive, costly, exorbitant, excessive ★**low**

highbrow *adj.* brainy, educated, intellectual

hijack *v.* raid, kidnap, seize, snatch, steal

hike *v.* walk, ramble, tramp

hilarious *adj.* amusing, gleeful, jocular,

entertaining ▷*funny* ★**serious**

hill *n.* hummock, rise, climb, height, elevation, slope

hinder *v.* hamper, impede, obstruct, retard, frustrate ▷*handicap* ★**help**

hindrance *n.* impediment, obstruction, check, barrier ★**aid**

hint *n.* clue, inkling *We had just an inkling of what was in store,* whisper, tip, suggestion, pointer

hire *v.* charter, rent, lease, retain, engage ★**dismiss** HIGHER

hiss *v.* boo, hoot, jeer, deride, whistle ▷*ridicule* ★**applaud**

history *n.* narration, account, saga, story, chronicle *The new book is a chronicle of the progress of equal rights*

hit ① *v.* strike, slap, beat, batter, whack ② *v.* collide, strike, clash ★**miss** ③ *n.* stroke, collision, blow ④ success, triumph

hitch ① *v.* attach, connect, fasten ② *n.* delay, hold-up, problem, snag *The work went smoothly for hours, until we hit a snag*

hoard *v.* accumulate, save, collect, treasure ★**squander** HORDE

hoarse *adj.* raucous, croaky, husky, throaty ★**mellow** HORSE

hoax *n.* trick, deception, fraud, joke, spoof, lie, cheat, swindle

hobble *v.* dodder, falter, shuffle, stagger

hobby *n.* pastime, amusement, recreation, interest, pursuit

hoist *v.* lift, raise, erect, heave, winch up

hold ① *v.* have, possess, own, retain, keep, grasp ② *v.* contain, accommodate *This cabin can accommodate four people* ③ *v.* stop, arrest ④ *n.* fortress, keep, storeplace HOLED

hole *n.* aperture, slot, perforation, opening, cavity, gap WHOLE

hollow ① *adj.* concave, empty, vacant ② *adj.* insincere, artificial ③ *n.* basin, depression *Water had accumulated in a small depression,* crater, channel

holy *adj.* sacred, pure, consecrated, blessed, hallowed ★**wicked** WHOLLY

home *n.* house, dwelling, homestead

homely *adj.* ① humble, unpretentious, comfortable, modest ② ordinary, plain, simple, unpretentious

honest *adj.* upright, fair, sincere, honourable ★**devious**

honesty *n.* integrity, honour, sincerity, morality ★**dishonesty**

honour *n.* morality, honesty, reputation, integrity, uprightness ★**disgrace**

honourable *adj.* honest, respectable, high-minded, virtuous ★**dishonest**

hook *n.* clasp, link, catch, fastener, barb *The fishhook ended in a number of small barbs*

hoop *n.* loop, ring, band, circle

hoot *v.* call, cry, howl, shout, shriek, yell

hop *v.* jump, leap, skip, spring, vault, caper

hope *v.* anticipate, envision, envisage, desire, expect, foresee ★**despair**

hopeful *adj.* expectant, confident, optimistic ★**pessimistic**

hopeless *adj.* despairing, desperate, downhearted, unattainable ★**hopeful**

horde *n.* crowd, gang, band, throng, swarm *We were suddenly attacked by a swarm of hornets,* HOARD

horrible *adj.* awful, atrocious, frightful, ghastly ▷*horrid* ★**agreeable**

horrid *adj.* beastly, bloodcurdling, dreadful, frightening ▷*horrible* ★**pleasant**

horror *n.* dread, fear, fright, outrage, panic, loathing ★**attraction**

horse *n.* mount, charger, hack, stallion, mare, filly, colt, foal HOARSE

hose *n.* ① tubing, pipe ② socks, stockings HOES

hospitable *adj.* sociable, neighbourly, charitable, welcoming ★**hostile**

host *n.* ① entertainer, master-of-ceremonies, landlord ② army, band, legion, horde

hostile *adj.* unfriendly, antagonistic, alien, malevolent ★**friendly**

hot ① *adj.* warm, fiery, scalding, roasting, heated ★**cold** ② pungent, peppery, sharp

hotel *n.* inn, hostelry *The stagecoach pulled in to a local hostelry for refreshment,* tavern, motel, resort, public house

house *n.* home, residence, dwelling, abode

A
B
C
D
E
F
G
H
I
J
K
L
M
N
O
P
Q
R
S
T
U
V
W
X
Y
Z

Hue

A hue is a tint or variety of a colour.
Blue: aquamarine beryl turquoise indigo azure sapphire ultramarine
Brown: amber chocolate dun fawn beige khaki auburn chestnut
Green: apple emerald jade moss olive pea sea
Purple: violet lilac heliotrope amethyst mauve magenta
Orange: carrot tangerine sandy
Red: crimson scarlet cherry cerise terracotta salmon pink cardinal
Yellow: sulphur primrose apricot saffron citron canary lemon

hovel *n.* cabin, shed, den, shack, shanty

hover *v.* fly, float, hang, dally, linger

howl *v.* hoot, cry, bellow, shriek ▷*scream*

hub *n.* centre, axis, focal point, pivot

hubbub *n.* racket, bedlam, chaos, clamour, uproar ▷*row* ★**calm**

huddle *v.* cluster, flock, gather, herd, nestle ★**separate**

hue *n.* colour, dye, shade, tinge, tint HEW

huff *n.* anger, passion, mood, pique *My cousin stormed off in a fit of pique* ▷*sulk*

hug *v.* clasp, embrace, enfold ▷*cuddle*

huge *adj.* enormous, monstrous, colossal, immense ▷*vast* ★**tiny**

hum *v.* drone, croon, buzz, pulsate, throb

human *adj.* reasonable, understandable, mortal ▷*humane* ★**inhuman**

humane *adj.* benign, forgiving, gentle, lenient, kind ★**inhumane**

humble *adj.* low, lowly, meek, unassuming, respectful, servile ▷*modest* ★**arrogant**

humbug *n.* bluff, bunkum, claptrap *The salesman's goods were cheap and he talked a lot of claptrap about them,* quackery, trickery, eye-wash, bluff

humdrum *adj.* monotonous, commonplace, everyday, boring ▷*dreary* ★**exceptional**

humid *adj.* clammy, damp, moist, wet, vaporous ★**dry**

humiliate *v.* embarrass, humble, abash, degrade, deflate ★**boost**

humorous *adj.* amusing, droll, comical, whimsical ▷*funny* ★**serious** HUMERUS

humour ① *n.* comedy, fun, banter, whimsy ② *v.* flatter, coax, pamper, spoil

hunch ① *n.* feeling, guess, idea, inkling ② *v.* crouch, curl up, squat *We squatted in the long grass, where we were out of sight*

hunger ① *n.* craving, desire, starvation ② *v.* crave, desire, hanker

hungry *adj.* famished, starving, voracious

hunt *v.* chase, seek, scour, search, stalk, trail

hurdle *n.* barrier, fence, hedge, obstruction

hurl *v.* cast, fling, heave, pitch, throw, propel, toss

hurry *v.* dash, hustle, quicken, accelerate ▷*hasten* ★**dally**

hurt ① *v.* harm, wound, pain, sting, suffer ② *v.* upset, annoy, distress ③ *adj.* rueful, sad, offended

hurtful *adj.* cutting, cruel, distressing, wounding ★**kind**

hurtle *v.* chase, charge, dash, rush, speed, tear, race, fly

hush *v.* calm, quiet down, soothe ★**disturb**

husky *adj.* croaking, gruff, harsh ▷*hoarse*

hustle *v.* bustle, speed, hasten ▷*hurry*

hut *n.* cabin, shelter, shanty, shack

hymn *n.* anthem, chant, carol, psalm HIM

hypnotize *v.* mesmerize, fascinate, spellbind *We stood spellbound as we watched the trapeze artist,* bewitch

hypocrite *n.* fraud, deceiver, impostor, mountebank

hysterical *adj.* ① distraught, mad, delirious, beside oneself ② comical, hilarious, farcical ★**calm**

I i

icy *adj.* freezing, frozen, cold, frigid, frosty

idea *n.* notion, thought, belief, fancy, impression, image

ideal *adj.* perfect, absolute, supreme, best, model, complete

identical *adj.* same, alike, twin, duplicate, equal ★**different**

identify *v.* detect, recognize, know, distinguish, spot

identity *n.* existence, self, singularity, individuality

idiot *n.* imbecile, moron, fool, dimwit, dolt

idiotic *adj.* crazy, stupid, simple, fatuous ▷*foolish* ★**sane**

idle *adj.* ① unoccupied, unemployed, unused ② lazy, frivolous, sluggish ★**active** IDOL

idol *n.* ① image, icon, god, fetish ② hero, favourite, star *Buster Keaton was a star of the silent films* IDLE

ignite *v.* kindle, set light to, spark off, catch fire, burn

ignorant *adj.* unknowing, ill-informed, unread, stupid, thick ★**wise**

ignore *v.* disregard, neglect, omit, overlook, pass over ★**note**

ill *adj.* ① ailing, diseased, frail, infirm, sick, poorly ★**well** ② hostile, malicious *Cinderella's sisters were cruel and malicious,* evil, harmful

ill-mannered *adj.* coarse, crude, boorish, uncivil ▷*rude* ★**polite**

ill-tempered *adj.* bad-tempered, curt, irritable ★**good-tempered**

ill-treat *v.* abuse, harm, injure, neglect, oppress ★**care for**

ill will *n.* animosity, hard feelings, dislike, hatred, hostility ▷*malice* ★**good will**

illegal *adj.* unlawful, wrong, villainous, illicit, contraband ★**legal**

illegible *adj.* unreadable, indecipherable, obscure, indistinct ★**legible**

illegitimate *adj.* illegal, unlawful, improper, wrong ★**legitimate**

illiterate *adj.* uneducated, unlearned, unlettered, unread, untaught ★**literate**

illness *n.* ailment, attack, complaint, disease, disorder

illuminate *v.* brighten, clarify, enlighten, light up ★**darken**

illusion *n.* apparition, fancy, fantasy, mirage, deception ★**reality**

illustration *n.* picture, drawing, explanation, sketch

image *n.* likeness, effigy, portrait, replica, reflection, double

imaginary *adj.* unreal, fanciful, fictitious, visionary ★**real**

imagination *n.* idea, notion, thought, illusion, conception, fancy, vision, impression ★**reality**

imagine *v.* assume, believe, invent, pretend, think up ▷*visualize*

imbecile *n.* blockhead, fool, idiot, bungler, dolt

imitate *v.* emulate, follow, reproduce, simulate, mock ▷*copy*

immaculate *adj.* clean, spotless, faultless, stainless ▷*pure* ★**soiled**

immature *adj.* callow, raw, crude, childish, unripe, green ★**mature**

immediate *adj.* ① instant, instantaneous, prompt ② nearest, next, neighbouring *As children, my mother and father lived in neighbouring houses* ★**distant**

immediately *adv.* at once, directly, without delay, forthwith

immense *adj.* tremendous, enormous, vast ▷*huge* ★**tiny**

immerse *v.* plunge, dip, douse, submerge, duck ▷*sink*

imminent *adj.* impending, approaching, looming, close, forthcoming

immobile *adj.* at rest, at a standstill, motionless ★**moving**

immodest *adj.* shameless, barefaced, indelicate, improper ★**modest**

immoral *adj.* evil, unscrupulous, vicious, vile, depraved ▷*wicked* ★**moral**

immortal *adj.* undying, eternal, everlasting, constant ★**mortal**

A B C D E F G H I J K L M N O P Q R S T U V W X Y Z

immune *adj.* exempt, resistant, safe, protected ★**susceptible**

imp *n.* rascal, urchin, elf

impact *n.* blow, shock, stroke, collision, crash, knock

impair *v.* damage, spoil, devalue, cheapen, harm ▷*hinder* ★**enhance**

impart *v.* communicate, render, bestow, disclose *I am unable to disclose where I heard that story* ▷*tell*

impartial *adj.* unbiased, candid, fair-minded, impersonal ★**biased**

impatient *adj.* intolerant, irritable, hasty, curt ★**patient**

impede *v.* hamper, interfere with, obstruct ▷*hinder* ★**aid**

impel *v.* goad, incite, urge, actuate, push ▷*drive* ★**dissuade**

impending *adj.* approaching, coming, forthcoming, looming ★**remote**

imperfect *adj.* defective, unsound, blemished, flawed ▷*faulty* ★**perfect**

imperial *adj.* august, majestic, lofty, regal, royal, sovereign, grand

imperious *adj.* arrogant, domineering, overbearing ★**humble**

impersonal *adj.* aloof, detached, remote, neutral, cold ★**friendly**

impersonate *v.* imitate, mimic, masquerade as, pose as, portray

impertinent *adj.* insolent, impudent, discourteous ▷*cheeky* ★**polite**

impetuous *adj.* sudden, unexpected, impulsive, spontaneous ▷*hasty* ★**careful**

implement ① *v.* accomplish, bring about, fulfil *I was able to fulfil my dream of going to Japan* ② *n.* instrument, tool, gadget

implicate *v.* connect, entangle, involve, throw suspicion on ★**absolve**

implicit *adj.* implied, indicated, understood, tacit, insinuated

implore *v.* beseech, entreat, beg, crave, plead

imply *v.* hint at, intimate, insinuate ▷*suggest* ★**declare**

impolite *adj.* discourteous, ill-mannered ▷*rude* ★**polite**

import ① *v.* bring in, carry in ② *n.* meaning, purport *When I grew old enough I realized the purport of my mother's advice,* sense

important *adj.* significant, essential, serious, substantial ▷*great* ★**trivial**

imposing *adj.* impressive, massive, magnificent ▷*stately* ★**modest**

impossible *adj.* hopeless, not possible, unworkable, unacceptable ★**possible**

impostor *n.* impersonator, masquerader, deceiver, fraud, pretender, bluffer

impoverish *v.* bankrupt, diminish, weaken, ruin, beggar ★**enrich**

impractical *adj.* impossible, unworkable, idealistic, unusable ★**practical**

impress *v.* ① influence, affect, sway, inspire ② emboss *She wore a crown of gold embossed with diamonds,* engrave, indent

impression *n.* ① belief, concept, fancy, effect ② dent, imprint, stamp, printing *The book had sold 5,000 copies, and a new printing was planned*

imprison *v.* jail, lock up, confine ★**free**

improbable *adj.* doubtful, unlikely, implausible ▷*dubious* ★**probable**

impromptu *adj.* improvised, spontaneous, ad lib, unrehearsed ★**planned**

improper *adj.* ① erroneous, false, unsuitable ② immoral *My parents always taught me that lying and cheating were immoral,* indecent ▷*wrong* ★**proper**

improve *v.* make better, repair, restore, improve upon, refine ★**diminish**

impudent *adj.* impertinent, audacious, brazen, disrespectful ▷*rude* ★**polite**

impulse *n.* motive, drive, force, inclination, urge, notion, wish

impulsive *adj.* sudden, unexpected, reckless ▷*impetuous* ★**cautious**

impure *adj.* contaminated, corrupted, foul, corrupt ★**pure**

inaccessible *adj.* remote, isolated, unattainable ★**accessible**

inaccurate *adj.* erroneous, incorrect, imprecise ▷*faulty* ★**accurate**

inactive *adj.* inert, static, dormant, quiet, unoccupied ★**active**

inadequate *adj.* deficient, unequal, incapable ▷*unfit* ★**adequate**

inane *adj.* absurd, ridiculous, stupid, senseless ▷*silly* ★**sensible**

inappropriate *adj.* improper, wrong, incorrect, unsuitable, unfitting ★**appropriate**

inattentive *adj.* unheeding, indifferent, careless, neglectful ★**attentive**

incapable *adj.* helpless, inadequate, unable, unfit, weak ★**capable**

incense ① *v.* (in-*cense*) enrage, infuriate, annoy ② *n.* (*in*-cense) fragrance *We walked through fields where the fragrance of wild flowers was wonderful,* aroma, perfume

incentive *n.* motive, impulse, drive, spur, lure

incident *n.* event, happening, episode, circumstance, occurrence

incidental *adj.* casual, chance, accidental, random, minor

incite *v.* encourage, urge, drive, goad, impel, provoke ▷*prompt* ★**restrain**

incline ① *n.* (*in*-cline) slant, slope, grade, gradient ② *v.* (in-*cline*) tend, verge, lean to, bias, favour

inclined *adj.* liable, prone, disposed, favourable

include *v.* contain, cover, incorporate, embody, comprise ★**exclude**

inclusive *adj.* comprehensive, all-embracing ★**exclusive**

income *n.* earnings, royalty, revenue, receipts, profits ★**expenses**

incomparable *adj.* brilliant, first-class, superb ▷*unrivalled* ★**ordinary**

incompetent *adj.* incapable, inadequate, inept, helpless ▷*clumsy* ★**competent**

incomplete *adj.* unfinished, partial, imperfect, wanting ★**complete**

incomprehensible *adj.* unintelligible, perplexing, puzzling ★**comprehensible**

inconceivable *adj.* incredible, unlikely, strange, unthinkable, unheard of ▷*extraordinary* ★**comprehensible**

inconsiderate *adj.* tactless, careless, insensitive ▷*thoughtless* ★**considerate**

inconsistent *adj.* incongruous, unstable, unpredictable ★**consistent**

inconspicuous *adj.* indistinct, faint, hidden, ordinary ★**conspicuous**

inconvenient *adj.* annoying, awkward, difficult, troublesome ★**convenient**

incorrect *adj.* erroneous, imprecise, mistaken ▷*wrong* ★**correct**

increase ① *v.* add to, boost, magnify, heighten ② *n.* addition *We heard the news today that Emily has had an addition to her family,* rise, enhancement ★**decrease**

incredible *adj.* unbelievable, amazing, far fetched, wonderful ★**ordinary**

incriminate *v.* implicate, accuse, indict ▷*blame* ★**acquit**

indecent *adj.* immodest, improper, impure, coarse ★**decent**

indeed *adv.* actually, truly, really, very much, positively

indefinite *adj.* uncertain, unsure, unreliable, dubious ▷*vague* ★**certain**

indelicate *adj.* coarse, immodest, indecent ▷*unseemly* ★**delicate**

independent *adj.* free, self-reliant, separate, self-governing ★**dependent**

indicate *v.* show, point out, denote, suggest, symbolize, specify, signal

indifference *n.* disinterest, unconcern, apathy, coldness ★**interest**

indifferent *adj.* uninterested, cold, casual, apathetic, listless ★**interested**

indignant *adj.* annoyed, resentful, wrathful ▷*angry* ★**pleased**

indirect *adj.* devious, roundabout, incidental ★**direct**

indiscreet *adj.* incautious, thoughtless, ill-advised ▷*hasty* ★**discreet**

indiscriminate *adj.* confused, bewildered, careless ▷*random* ★**deliberate**

indispensable *adj.* necessary, crucial, vital ▷*essential* ★**unnecessary**

indistinct *adj.* faint, dim, unclear, obscure, murky ▷*vague* ★**distinct**

individual ① *adj.* single, odd, special, exclusive ② *n.* person, being *Sharon enjoys the company of other human beings,*

A
B
C
D
E
F
G
H
I
J
K
L
M
N
O
P
Q
R
S
T
U
V
W
X
Y
Z

creature, body, soul, fellow

indulge *v.* gratify, humour, pamper, satisfy, spoil

industrious *adj.* busy, hard-working, diligent, conscientious ★**lazy**

inedible *adj.* deadly, poisonous, harmful, uneatable ★**edible**

inefficient *adj.* negligent, incapable ▷*incompetent* ★**efficient**

inelegant *adj.* awkward, ungainly, crude, coarse ▷*clumsy* ★**elegant**

inept *adj.* awkward, absurd, unskilled ▷*clumsy* ★**skilful**

inert *adj.* inactive, passive, static, sluggish, listless, dead ★**alive**

inevitable *adj.* unavoidable, certain, sure, necessary ★**uncertain**

inexact *adj.* imprecise, inaccurate ▷*erroneous* ★**exact**

inexpensive *adj.* low-priced, reasonable, economical ▷*cheap* ★**expensive**

inexperienced *adj.* inexpert, unskilled, untrained ▷*inept* ★**experienced**

infallible *adj.* perfect, unerring, faultless ▷*reliable* ★**faulty**

infamous *adj.* notorious, shady, scandalous, shameful, disgraceful ★**glorious**

infant *n.* baby, child, little one, toddler

infatuated *adj.* in love, beguiled, charmed, fascinated, smitten

infect *v.* contaminate, blight, defile, pollute

infectious *adj.* catching, contagious

infer *v.* reason, conclude, judge, understand

inferior *adj.* second-rate, lesser, lower, poor, mediocre, imperfect ★**superior**

infinite *adj.* eternal, unending, endless, immense, unbounded

infirm *adj.* weak, feeble, frail, senile, decrepit ★**healthy**

inflame *v.* inspire, provoke, excite, stimulate, arouse ★**cool**

inflate *v.* expand, dilate, swell, pump up, blow up ★**deflate**

inflict *v.* apply, burden, deal, deliver, force

influence ① *n.* authority, control, guidance, force ② *v.* affect, impress, inspire *After Annie visited the old city, she was inspired to write a poem,* prejudice

inform *v.* tell, let know, acquaint, warn, enlighten

informal *adj.* casual, easy, familiar, relaxed, simple ★**formal**

information *n.* knowledge, news, intelligence, advice

infrequent *adj.* unusual, uncommon, occasional ▷*rare* ★**frequent**

infringe *v.* disobey, violate, encroach, trespass, flout

infuriate *v.* anger, enrage, madden, incense, vex ▷*annoy* ★**calm**

ingenious *adj.* clever, resourceful, shrewd, adroit, inventive ★**clumsy**

ingenuous *adj.* honest, open, simple, trusting, sincere ★**artful**

ingratiate *v.* curry favour, flatter, grovel, toady *We distrusted Tim, as he was always trying to ingratiate himself with the teacher*

Ingratiate

We distrusted Tim, as he was always trying to ingratiate himself with the teacher.

ingredient *n.* component, element, part, factor, constituent

inhabit *v.* live in, dwell in, reside in, dwell, occupy, stay

inhale *v.* breathe in, inspire, sniff, suck in ★**exhale**

inherit *v.* succeed to, acquire, take over, receive, come into

inhospitable *adj.* unfriendly, desolate, unkind, unsociable ★**hospitable**

inhuman *adj.* barbaric, brutal, beastly, heartless, savage

inhumane *adj.* callous, cruel, pitiless, ruthless ▷*inhuman* ★**humane**

initiate *v.* start, launch, teach, instruct, train ▷*begin*

initiative *n.* ambition, drive, enterprise, resourcefulness

inject *v.* inoculate, infuse, vaccinate

injure *v.* hurt, mar, spoil, wound, blemish, deform, disfigure

inkling *n.* suspicion, impression, notion, clue

inlet *n.* bay, gulf, basin, bight, estuary, harbour, fjord

inn *n.* hotel, motel, lodge, tavern IN

innocent *adj.* guiltless, faultless, stainless, virtuous, blameless ★**guilty**

inoffensive *adj.* harmless, safe, gentle, quiet ▷*innocent* ★**malicious**

inquire *v.* ask, examine, inspect, check, question, look into, probe

inquisitive *adj.* nosy, snooping, eager, inquiring, ▷*curious*

insane *adj.* demented, mad, frenzied, crazy, wild, lunatic ★**sane**

inscribe *v.* write, stamp, cut, carve, etch

inscription *n.* heading, caption, legend, epitaph, label

insecure *adj.* perilous, unsafe, hazardous, dangerous, unconfident, uncertain ★**secure**

insensible *adj.* ① unconscious, stunned, knocked out *The reigning champion was knocked out in the third round* ② insensitive, numb, stupefied

insensitive *adj.* impassive, indifferent, thick-skinned, unruffled, insensible ★**sensitive**

inseparable *adj.* indivisible, devoted, intimate, close

insert *v.* put in, inset, introduce, place, interleave ★**remove**

inside *adv.* indoors, inner, inward, within, core, middle ★**outside**

insight *n.* awareness, intelligence, judgement, knowledge ▷*wisdom*

insignificant *adj.* unimportant, non-essential, meagre, irrelevant ▷*humble* ★**important**

insincere *adj.* pretended, deceptive, dishonest, two-faced, false ★**sincere**

insinuate *v.* suggest, imply, signify, get at, intimate, indicate

insipid *adj.* tasteless, flat, flavourless, bland, banal ★**tasty**

insist *v.* assert, maintain, request, require, demand, persist ★**waive**

insolent *adj.* impudent, impertinent, discourteous, insulting, fresh, rude, cheeky ★**respectful**

inspect *v.* examine, check, oversee, supervise, superintend

inspiration *n.* motive, stimulus, brain wave, revelation ▷*encouragement*

inspire *v.* hearten, prompt, provoke, excite ▷*encourage* ★**deter**

instal *v.* establish, plant, set, position, fix, introduce, locate

instance *n.* example, case, occasion, occurrence INSTANTS

instant ① *adj.* immediate, instantaneous *I pressed the button, and there was an instantaneous explosion,* rapid ② *n.* moment, minute, flash, jiffy

instantly *adv.* at once, right away, immediately, now ▷*forthwith* ★**later**

instead *adv.* alternatively, preferably, rather

instead of *adv.* in place of, in one's place, on behalf of, preferably

instinct *n.* ability, knack, intuition, feeling, sixth sense

institute ① *n.* association, college, establishment, organization ② *v.* begin, start *The people raised enough money to start a new programme to help the poor,* found

A B C D E F G H I J K L M N O P Q R S T U V W X Y Z

Musical Instruments

Accordion
Bagpipes
Balalaika
Banjo
Bassoon
Bells
Bugle
Castanets
Cello
Clarinet
Cornet
Cymbals
Didgeridoo
Double bass
Drum
Dulcimer
Electric
  guitar

Fiddle
Fife
Flute
French horn
Glockenspiel
Guitar
Harmonica
Harp
Harpsichord
Hurdy-gurdy
Kazoo
Kettledrum
Lute
Lyre
Mandolin
Maraca
Oboe

Organ
Piano
Piccolo
Recorder
Saxophone
Synthesizer
Tambourine
Triangle
Trombone
Trumpet
Tuba
Ukulele
Viola
Violin
Whistle
Xylophone
Zither

instruct *v.* teach, direct, order, educate, coach, drill, train

instrument *n.* device, gadget, implement, contraption, tool, utensil

insufferable *adj.* unbearable, intolerable, impossible ★**tolerable**

insufficient *adj.* inadequate, lacking, scanty, wanting ▷*sparse* ★**sufficient**

insulate *v.* protect, shield, isolate, set apart

insult *n. & v.* slander, slight, snub, abuse, outrage ★**compliment**

insure *v.* guarantee, protect, warrant, assure

intact *adj.* whole, unharmed, uncut, complete, in one piece, sound ★**damaged**

integrity *n.* honour, uprightness, honesty, goodness, purity ★**dishonesty**

intellectual *adj.* scholarly, studious, thoughtful ▷*intelligent* ★**foolish**

intelligent *adj.* acute, astute, brainy, brilliant, intellectual ▷*clever* ★**stupid**

intend *v.* mean, aim, determine, ordain, plan, project, resolve

intense *adj.* extreme, ardent, earnest, forcible, passionate ▷*keen* ★**mild** INTENTS

intention *n.* aim, intent, project, design, notion, end, goal

intercept *v.* stop, arrest, confiscate, delay, obstruct ▷*thwart*

interest *n.* appeal, fascination, zest, activity, concern ★**boredom**

interesting *adj.* appealing, fascinating, absorbing, entertaining ★**boring**

interfere *v.* meddle, intrude, interrupt, butt in, tamper ★**assist**

interior *adj.* internal, inner, inside, inward ★**exterior**

interlude *n.* pause, interval, intermission, spell, recess

internal *adj.* inner, inward ▷*interior* ★**external**

interpret *adj.* explain, define, construe

interrogate *v.* question, examine, ask, inquire, quiz ▷*investigate*

interrupt *adj.* break in, butt in, interject, disturb, hold up, suspend

interval *n.* space, period, term, intermission ▷*interlude*

intervene *v.* break in, interrupt, intrude, mediate, arbitrate ▷*interfere*

interview *n.* conference, inquiry, meeting, consultation, talk

intimate ① *adj.* near, close, familiar, private, secret ★**distant** ② *v.* hint at, suggest *The evidence suggests that the defendant has not been telling the truth* ▷*insinuate*

intimidate *v.* daunt, overawe, cow, bully, frighten, browbeat ★**persuade**

intolerant *adj.* bigoted, unfair, small-minded, dogmatic ★**tolerant**

intoxicated *adj.* drunk, inebriated, tipsy

intrepid *adj.* daring, heroic, unafraid, bold, gallant ▷*fearless*

intricate *adj.* complex, complicated, elaborate, tricky ★**simple**

intrigue ① *n.* plot, scheme, affair, liaison ② *v.* attract, enchant *The old man enchanted us with his stories,* captivate, scheme

introduce *v.* ① put in, insert, inject ② acquaint, present ③ propose, offer

intrude *v.* interrupt, interfere, invade, trespass ★**withdraw**

inundate *v.* flood, deluge, engulf, immerse, submerge, swamp *We advertised for a new assistant and were swamped with replies*

invade *v.* break in, penetrate, assault, assail ▷*enter* ★**withdraw** INVEIGHED

invalid ① *adj.* (in-*val*-id) null, void *These tickets are void, for they are more than a year old,* useless ② *n.* (*in*-val-id) patient, sufferer, sick person, disabled person

invaluable *adj.* precious, costly, priceless, valuable ★**worthless**

invent *v.* fabricate, conceive, devise, make up, originate, concoct

invention *n.* creation, gadget, contrivance, discovery

investigate *v.* explore, examine, research, inquire, search, study

invisible *adj.* hidden, concealed, out of sight, unseen, masked ★**visible**

invite *v.* ask, beckon, attract, summon, urge, encourage ★**force**

involve *v.* comprise, complicate, entangle, include, take in, entail

inward *adj.* hidden, inner, internal, secret, inside ★**outward**

irate *adj.* incensed, cross, annoyed, furious, infuriated ▷*angry* ★**calm**

irksome *adj.* annoying, irritating, disagreeable ★**pleasing**

ironic *adj.* satirical, derisive, mocking, scornful

irregular *adj.* uncertain, unsettled, disordered, singular ▷*odd* ★**regular**

irrelevant *adj.* immaterial, unnecessary, unrelated ★**relevant**

irresistible *adj.* charming, compelling, overpowering, fascinating ★**resistible**

irresponsible *adj.* undependable, unreliable, feckless, flighty ★**responsible**

irritable *adj.* bad-tempered, edgy, fretful, peevish ▷*cross* ★**cheerful**

irritate *v.* annoy, vex, irk, offend, provoke ▷*bother* ★**please**

island *n.* isle, islet, key, atoll, cay

issue ① *v.* flow, ooze, bring out, circulate, publish ② *n.* edition, printing, publication *My book of poems was ready for publication,* impression ③ problem, question, affair, concern

itch ① *v.* prickle, tingle, irritate ② *n.* impulse, motive, desire *I have always had a strong desire to work in a hospital*

item *n.* point, particular, thing, object, article

A B C D E F G H I J K L M N O P Q R S T U V W X Y Z

J j

jab *v.* poke, prod, push, stab, dig

jabber *v.* chatter, gabble, mumble, babble

jacket *n.* coat, jerkin, cover, case, sheath

jagged *adj.* rough, broken, snagged, notched, uneven ★**smooth**

jail *n.* prison, penitentiary, lock-up, brig

jam ① *n.* jelly, preserves, conserve, marmalade ② *v.* crowd, pack *All the buses were full, and we were packed in like sardines,* crush, squeeze JAMB

jar ① *n.* jug, beaker, ewer, vase, pitcher, pot ② *v.* jog, rattle, grate *That singer's voice really grates on me,* grind

jaunt *n. & v.* trip, journey, cruise, travel, tour

jaunty *adj.* light-hearted, showy, dapper, spruce, debonair, perky

jealous *adj.* envious, covetous, grudging

jealousy *n.* envy, covetousness, distrust, spite

jeer *v.* laugh at, deride, mock, ridicule, insult ▷*taunt*

jeopardy *n.* peril, risk, hazard, plight ▷*danger* ★**safety**

jerk *n. & v.* yank, pull, drag, jog, jolt, tug

jersey *n.* pullover, sweater, jumper

Jewels

Agate
Amethyst
Aquamarine
Bloodstone
Carbuncle
Carnelian
Coral
Diamond
Emerald
Garnet
Jasper
Moonstone
Onyx
Opal
Ruby
Sapphire
Topaz
Turquoise
Zircon

jest *n.* joke, jape, spoof, banter, chaff

jester *n.* clown, buffoon, merry-andrew, prankster, comedian

jet *n. & v.* spurt, squirt, flow, gush

jetty *n.* wharf, dock, quay, pier

jewel *n.* gem, stone, trinket, charm, locket

jibe *v.* mock, scoff, scorn, sneer, taunt ▷*jeer*

jiffy *n.* instant, flash, minute, moment

jilt *v.* abandon, brush off, desert, drop, forsake

jingle *v.* tinkle, clink, chink, ring, jangle

job *n.* task, work, chore, place, office, post, position, situation, profession, trade

jocular *adj.* gleeful, hilarious, witty, humorous, jolly ▷*funny* ★**serious**

jog *v.* ① prod, nudge, shove, shake ② run, sprint, canter, trot, exercise

join *v.* ① unite, link, combine, connect, attach ★**separate** ② enlist, sign up *Gaby and Bill have signed up for tennis lessons*

joint ① *n.* junction, knot, union, connection ② *adj.* shared, united, mutual *It's in our mutual interest to keep expenses down*

joke *n.* gag, trick, frolic, lark, jape, game, prank ▷*jest*

jolly *adj.* jovial, cheerful, blithe, frisky ▷*merry* ★**sad**

jolt *n. & v.* jar, shock, shove, rock, jerk, bump

jostle *v.* push, shove, shoulder, thrust, elbow

jot ① *n.* atom, bit, grain, particle ② *v.* note, scribble, take down

journal *n.* ① ledger, account book ② diary, newspaper, magazine *I've just become editor of the natural history society's magazine*

journey *n.* excursion, trip, tour, jaunt, ramble

jovial *adj.* jolly, festive, cordial, affable, cheerful ▷*merry* ★**sad**

joy *n.* rapture, enchantment, delight, pleasure, charm ▷*bliss* ★**sorrow**

joyful *adj.* joyous, enjoyable, pleasurable, happy, jovial, delighted ★**sorrowful**

jubilant *adj.* exultant, gleeful, happy, overjoyed, excited ★**depressed**

judge ① *n.* justice, magistrate, referee, umpire ② *v.* assess *We can ask the jeweller to assess the value of these pearls,* decide, find, appraise, estimate

judgement *n.* ① decision, opinion, verdict *The*

Key

Keys

jury gave a verdict of 'not guilty', decree, finding ② intelligence, understanding, valuation

judicious *adj.* prudent, shrewd, discreet, expedient, wise ★**indiscreet**

jug *n.* beaker, ewer, urn, vase ▷*jar*

juggle *v.* conjure, manipulate

juice *n.* essence, extract, sap, fluid, nectar

jumble *n.* medley, mixture, muddle, tangle, clutter, hotch-potch

jump *v.* spring, bound, hop, skip, vault, ▷*leap*

junction *n.* ① union, combination, joint, connection ② crossroads, intersection, juncture, crossing

jungle *n.* forest, bush, wilderness

junior *adj.* lesser, lower, younger, subordinate ★**senior**

junk *n.* trash, debris, rubbish, waste, clutter, litter, scrap, garbage, refuse

just ① *adj.* sound, regular, orderly, exact, fair, honest, impartial ② *adv.* exactly, precisely ③ *adv.* only, merely, simply

justice *n.* equity, impartiality, fairness, right ★**injustice**

justify *v.* vindicate, acquit, condone, uphold, legalize

jut *v.* bulge, extend, stick out, overhang, project *We took shelter where the cliff projects over the path* ★**recede**

juvenile ① *adj.* adolescent, youthful, young, childish ★**mature** ② *n.* boy, girl, child, youngster, youth

K k

keen ① *adj.* eager, ardent, earnest, diligent ② sharp *Her wit is as sharp as a razor,* acute, fine ★**dull**

keep ① *v.* hold, retain, collect, possess ★**abandon** ② *v.* care for, maintain, shelter *We have arranged to shelter the refugees* ③ *n.* tower, dungeon, castle, fort, stronghold

keeper *n.* jailer, warden, attendant, caretaker, janitor, curator, guardian

keeping *n.* compliance, obedience, accord

keep on *v.* continue, go on, endure, persist ★**give up**

keepsake *n.* souvenir, token, memento, reminder, relic

keg *n.* barrel, cask, tub, drum, container

ken *n.* grasp, grip, understanding, mastery, knowledge

kerchief *n.* scarf, headscarf, shawl, neckcloth

kernel *n.* core, heart, hub, centre, gist, nub COLONEL

kettle *n.* boiler, cauldron, cooking pot, tea-kettle

key ① *n.* opener ② *n.* solution, clue, answer ③ *n.* cay, isle, inlet, atoll ④ *adj.* essential, fundamental, vital, crucial QUAY

kick *v.* ① boot, strike with the foot, punt, hit ② complain, grumble, rebel *The people rebelled against the harsh rule of the new king,* resist

kidnap *v.* abduct, capture, seize, snatch, steal, hijack

kill *v.* slay, assassinate, destroy, massacre, slaughter ▷*murder*

killjoy *n.* spoil-sport, wet blanket *I don't want to be a wet blanket, but I'm too tired to play,* grouch, complainer ★**optimist**

kin *n.* race, kindred, offspring, kind, family, relation

kind ① *adj.* gentle, kindly, genial, good-natured, amiable ★**unkind** ② *n.* style, character, sort, variety

kindle *v.* ① light, ignite, set fire to ② inflame

A
B
C
D
E
F
G
H
I
J
K
L
M
N
O
P
Q
R
S
T
U
V
W
X
Y
Z

A Little Knowledge is a Dangerous Thing – and Other Misquotes

Many of the familiar quotations we use from literature, history or the world of entertainment are incorrect adaptations of the original. Greta Garbo did not say 'I want to be alone'. Her true words were: 'I like to be alone', Shakespeare did not say 'Discretion is the better part of valour'. The correct quotation is: 'The better part of valour is discretion'. Here are some more, with the correct original version printed in italic type:

From Shakespeare
Alas, poor Yorick: I knew him well.
Alas, poor Yorick; I knew him,
Horatio: a fellow of infinite jest.
(Hamlet)

O Romeo. Romeo! wherefore art thou, Romeo?
O Romeo. Romeo! wherefore art thou
Romeo? (Romeo and Juliet)
(Note the position of the comma.
'Wherefore' means 'why' not 'where'.)

To gild the lily . . .
to gild refined gold, to paint the lily . . .
(King John)
Screw your courage to the sticking-point
But screw your courage to the sticking-
place (Macbeth)

All that glitters is not gold
All that glisters is not gold
(The Merchant of Venice)

Discretion is the better part of valour.
The better part of valour is discretion.
(King Henry IV, part I)

From the King James Bible
Pride goes before a fall
Pride goeth before destruction and an
haughty spirit before a fall (Proverbs)

Money is the root of all evil
For the love of money is the root of
all evil (Timothy)

To go the way of all flesh
And, behold, this day I am going the
way of all the earth (Joshua)

The mayor's words only inflamed the
people even more, excite, provoke, rouse

kindness *n.* good nature, charity, amiability, affection, tenderness **★cruelty**

king *n.* monarch, sovereign, majesty, ruler, emperor

kink *n.* ① knot, loop, bend, coil ② freak, eccentricity, whim *This strange tower was built as the result of a whim by the eccentric designer*

kiss *v.* salute, embrace, buss, smooch

kit *n.* set, outfit, baggage, effects, gear, rig

knack *n.* flair, talent, ability, genius, gift ▷*skill*

knave *n.* cheat, rascal, villain, scamp, scoundrel ▷*rogue* NAVE

knead *v.* form, squeeze, mould, shape, press NEED

kneel *v.* bend the knee, genuflect *The nun genuflected before the altar, then said her rosary,* bow down, worship

knife *n.* scalpel, blade, dagger, cutter

knight *n.* cavalier, champion, soldier, warrior, baronet NIGHT

knit *v.* weave, crochet, spin, twill, link, loop

knob *n.* boss, bump, handle, opener, button

knock *v.* hit, slap, punch, bang, smite, strike

knock out ① *v.* stun, make insensible,

Other sources
Water, water, everywhere, and not a drop to drink
Water, water, everywhere, Nor any drop to drink (The Rime of the Ancient Mariner)

A little knowledge is a dangerous thing *A little learning is a dang'rous thing (Alexander Pope)*

Tomorrow to fresh fields and pastures new *Tomorrow to fresh woods, and pastures new (Paradise Lost)*

They shall not grow old as we that are left grow old
They shall grow not old, as we that are left grow old (Laurence Binyon)

Play it again, Sam (Humphrey Bogart, in the film *Casablanca*)

Play it, Sam. Play "As Time Goes By" (Ingrid Bergman, in the film *Casablanca*)

render unconscious ② *n.* success, hit
knoll *n.* barrow, hill, mound, hillock
knot *n.* ① tie, bond, join, loop, kink, ② cluster, group NOT
know *v.* perceive, discern, notice, identify ▷*understand* NO
know-how *n.* skill, knowledge, talent
knowing *adj.* astute, knowledgeable, intelligent, perceptive ★**ignorant**
knowledge *n.* understanding, acquaintance, learning, wisdom, scholarship, information, sapience ★**ignorance**
kudos *n.* prestige, distinction, fame, glory, recognition

L l

label *n.* badge, tag, ticket, sticker, docket, slip
laborious *adj.* ① hard-working, diligent ② strenuous, arduous *Digging potatoes is arduous work,* hard ★**easy**
labour *n. & v.* toil, work, drudge, strain, struggle, slog, sweat
lack ① *n.* need, want, absence, deficiency, scarcity *During the hot weather there was a scarcity of water* ② *v.* need, require, want, miss
laconic *adj.* terse, curt, brief, concise ★**wordy**
lad *n.* boy, fellow, kid, youth, chap
laden *adj.* loaded, burdened, hampered, weighed down ★**empty**
ladle *v.* dip, scoop, dish, shovel
lady *n.* woman, female, dame, damsel, matron, mistress
lag *v.* dawdle, loiter, tarry, saunter ▷*linger* ★**lead**
lagoon *n.* pool, pond, lake, basin
lair *n.* den, nest, retreat, hideout, hole
lake *n.* lagoon, loch, pond, spring, reservoir
lam *v.* beat, hit, clout, knock ▷*strike*
lame *adj.* ① crippled, hobbled, disabled ② weak, feeble *That's a feeble excuse for missing school,* inadequate, unconvincing
lament *v.* deplore, mourn, grieve, sorrow ▷*regret* ★**rejoice**
lamp *n.* lantern, light, flare, torch
lance ① *n.* spear, pike, javelin, shaft ② *v.* puncture, pierce, cut
land ① *n.* country, district, tract, area, nation, region ② *v.* alight, arrive, carry, touch down *We had engine trouble, so the aircraft touched down in the desert*
landlord *n.* host, hotelier, innkeeper, owner
landmark *n.* milestone, milepost, beacon, monument, signpost
landscape *n.* scenery, view, prospect, countryside, panorama
lane *n.* alley, drive, passage, way LAIN

A
B
C
D
E
F
G
H
I
J
K
L
M
N
O
P
Q
R
S
T
U
V
W
X
Y
Z

language *n.* tongue, speech, utterance, dialect, jargon

languid *adj.* leisurely, unhurried, sluggish, slow, easy ★**lively**

languish *v.* decline, droop, flag, pine, suffer, yearn ★**flourish**

lanky *adj.* tall, rangy, gangling, scrawny, weedy ★**squat**

lantern *n.* lamp, flashlight, torch

lap ① *v.* lick, drink, sip, sup ② *n.* circuit, course, distance ③ *n.* thighs, knees

lapse *v.* expire, die, pass, elapse, go by, deteriorate LAPS

larder *n.* pantry, storeroom, cellar

large *adj.* big, ample, substantial, great, broad ▷*huge* ★**small**

lark *n.* adventure, escapade, spree, joke, frolic, gambol

lash ① *v.* beat, cane, whip, flay, flog ② *n.* prod, goad, drive, whip

lass *n.* girl, maiden, maid, young woman

last ① *adj.* final, concluding, latest, utmost, aftermost ★**first** ② *v.* remain, linger *The foggy weather lingered for most of the morning,* endure, stay

latch *n.* bolt, bar, padlock, fastener

late *adj.* tardy, behindhand, departed, slow ★**early**

lately *adv.* recently, latterly, formerly

lather *n.* suds, foam, bubbles, froth

latter *adj.* final, last, latest, recent, closing ★**former**

laud *v.* compliment, praise, applaud, glorify ★**blame**

laugh *v.* chuckle, giggle, guffaw, snigger, titter, fall about ★**cry**

launch ① *v.* start, begin, commence, establish, initiate ② *n.* motorboat

lavish ① *adj.* abundant, generous, liberal, extravagant ② *v.* waste, squander *My parents left me a small fortune, but I squandered it all,* give

law *n.* rule, ordinance, regulation, edict, decree

lawful *adj.* legal, legitimate, rightful ★**illegal**

lawyer *n.* attorney, counsel, jurist, barrister, solicitor, advocate, QC

lax *adj.* careless, casual, slack, relaxed, vague ★**strict** LACKS

lay ① *v.* put, set *It's time for dinner; let's set the table,* deposit, place, spread ② *v.* impute, charge ③ *adj.* non-professional, amateur; *amateur actors*

layer *n.* seam, sheet, thickness, tier

lazy *adj.* idle, inactive, slothful, slow, sluggish ★**active**

lead *v.* conduct, guide, escort, direct, command ★**follow**

leader *n.* guide, pilot, conductor, chief, head, master, captain, boss

leaf *n.* frond, blade, sheet LIEF

league *n.* band, association, society, guild, group, federation, coalition

leak *v.* trickle, ooze, seep, exude, flow out, percolate LEEK

lean ① *adj.* spare, slim, thin, skinny *Lina has no flesh on her; she is very skinny,* ② *v.* bend, curve, tilt, incline LIEN

leap *v.* spring, bound, jump, hop, skip

learn *v.* find out, ascertain, determine, acquire knowledge, understand

learned *adj.* cultured, educated, scholarly, literate ★**ignorant**

learning *n.* scholarship, education, knowledge ▷*wisdom* ★**ignorance**

least *adj.* fewest, smallest, slightest, lowest, tiniest ★**most** LEASED

leave ① *v.* abandon, desert, forsake, quit, go ② bequeath, bestow ③ *n.* vacation, furlough *Jack is on a furlough from the army,* permission

lecture *n.* talk, speech, address, sermon

ledge *n.* shelf, ridge, step

legacy *n.* bequest, inheritance, gift

legal *adj.* legitimate, lawful, valid, sound, authorized, rightful ★**illegal**

legend *n.* ① fable, myth, tale, fiction ② inscription *The box bore a brass plate with an inscription,* heading, caption

legible *adj.* clear, readable, understandable, distinct ★**illegible**

legitimate *adj.* legal, lawful, proper, rightful ▷*genuine* ★**illegal**

Lights

Arc lamp
Candle
Chandelier
Desk lamp
Electric light
Flashlight
Fluorescent lamp
Footlights
Gaslight
Headlight
Lantern
Nightlight
Reading light
Spotlight
Sunlamp
Table lamp
Torch

leisurely *adj.* unhurried, slow, easy, carefree, tranquil ★**hectic**

lend *v.* loan, advance, provide, supply, grant, lease ★**borrow**

lengthen *v.* extend, elongate, stretch, draw out, prolong ★**shorten**

lengthy *adj.* long, drawn out, long-winded ▷*tedious* ★**short**

lenient *adj.* tolerant, merciful, sparing, forbearing, indulgent ★**severe**

less *adj.* lesser, smaller, inferior, lower

lessen *v.* reduce, cut, become smaller, diminish, decrease ★**increase** LESSON

lesson *n.* instruction, lecture, information, teaching, exercise LESSEN

let ① *v.* allow, permit, suffer, authorize *The mayor authorized our school to hold the celebrations in the park,* grant ② lease

let down *v.* ① lower, take down ② betray, abandon, disappoint ★**satisfy**

letter *n.* ① dispatch, communication, epistle, message ② character *The book was printed in Hebrew characters,* sign, symbol

level ① *n.* plane, grade ② *adj.* even, flat, smooth ★**uneven** ③ *v.* aim, direct, point ④ *v.* demolish *Many houses were demolished during the earthquake,* destroy

liable ① *adj.* answerable, accountable, responsible ② apt *My parents are apt to be annoyed if I play loud music,* prone, inclined

liar *n.* deceiver, fibber, teller of tales LYRE

libel *v.* slander, malign, blacken, defame, slur ★**praise**

liberal *adj.* open-handed, generous, open-hearted, free, lavish

liberate *v.* set free, save, release, ★**restrict**

liberty *n.* freedom, independence ★**slavery**

license *v.* allow, permit, entitle ★**ban**

lie ① *n.* untruth, falsehood ② *v.* recline *I shall recline on the sofa for the afternoon,* lounge, repose ▷*loll* ③ *v.* tell a lie, fib, invent LYE

life *n.* being, existence, activity, energy, ★**death**

lift *v.* raise, erect, hoist, elevate, hold up ★**lower**

light ① *n.* radiance, glow, shine, glare, brightness ② *n.* lamp, beacon, flame ② *v.* ignite, illuminate, kindle *The scouts kindled a fire to cook their food* ③ *adj.* fair, light-coloured, sunny ★**dark** ④ lightweight, buoyant, airy ★**heavy**

like ①*adj.* similar, resembling, akin ★**unlike**

② v. admire, love, adore, cherish, prize ★**dislike**

likely adj. probable, expected, possible

likeness n. ① resemblance, appearance ② photograph *That's a wonderful photograph of my grandmother,* portrait

likewise adv. also, too, furthermore, further

limb n. leg, arm, extension, branch, shoot, bough

limit ① n. barrier, boundary, border, edge, end, restraint ② v. reduce, restrict *The heavy rain was restricted to the hilly country,* confine ★**free**

limited adj. restricted, reduced, narrow, confined ★**unrestricted**

limp ① adj. flabby, flimsy, flexible ② v. hobble, falter, shuffle

line n. ① stripe, streak, dash, bar ② cord, thread ③ row, queue, file ④ calling *Being an opera singer is a noble calling but a difficult one,* occupation

linger v. loiter, lag, dally, tarry, delay ▷*dawdle* ★**speed**

link ① n. bond, tie, connection, joint ② v. unite, join, couple, bracket ★**separate**

liquefy v. liquidize, melt

liquid n. fluid, liquor, solution, juice, sap

list ① n. schedule, table, catalogue, register ② v. tilt, lean, heel *The yacht heeled over as it turned into the wind,* careen, slope

listen v. hear, hearken, hark, heed

listless adj. languid, dull, lethargic, lifeless ▷*sluggish* ★**lively**

literally adv. actually, faithfully, precisely, really ★**loosely**

literate adj. educated, well-educated, learned, lettered ★**illiterate**

lithe adj. agile, nimble, flexible, supple ★**stiff**

litter n. clutter, jumble, rubbish, mess, refuse

little ① adj. small, tiny, short, slight, trivial, petty ▷*small* ★**large** ② adv. hardly, rarely, seldom

live ① adj. alive, living, existing, active, alert ★**dead** ② v. be, subsist, breathe, exist

lively adj. active, brisk, vivacious, animated, agile ★**listless**

livid adj. ① angry, enraged, furious, mad ② ashen *We were really scared, and Bob's face was ashen,* greyish, pale, leaden

living ① adj. alive, existing ② n. job, occupation, work, livelihood

load ① n. freight, cargo, goods, burden ② v. fill, pack, burden, pile up, stack LODE, LOWED

loaf ① v. waste time, idle, dally, dawdle ② n. block, cube, lump, cake

loan ① n. credit, advance, allowance ② v. allow, lend, advance *The bank advanced me the money to pay the mortgage* LONE

loath or **loth** adj. reluctant, disinclined, opposed

loathe v. abhor, detest, despise, dislike ▷*hate* ★**like**

lobby n. hallway, entrance, vestibule, foyer

local adj. regional, district, provincial

locate v. find, discover, detect, unearth

lock ① n. bolt, fastener, latch, clasp ② v. bolt, fasten, secure ③ n. floodgate, weir ④ n. curl, braid, tress *I kept a tress of her hair in a locket*

lodge ① v. stay at, put up, shelter, get stuck *A fishbone got stuck in his throat,* remain ② n. inn, hotel

lofty adj. ① tall, high, noble, great ② proud, exalted, arrogant ★**modest**

logical adj. fair, justifiable, reasonable, sound ★**illogical**

loiter v. lag, trail, linger, dally, dawdle, hang around, dilly dally

loll v. recline, sprawl, lounge, lie, rest, flop

lone adj. single, sole, lonely, separate, unaccompanied LOAN

lonely adj. alone, forsaken, friendless, remote, forlorn, lonesome

long ① adj. lengthy, extended, expanded ★**short** ② v. crave, hanker, yearn, desire

look ① v. appear, seem ② v. peer, glance, watch, behold ③ n. appearance, glance, gaze *Her gaze fell upon me, and I had to answer the next question*

loom v. menace, portend, rise, emerge, appear

loop n. bend, circle, coil, noose, twist

loophole n. escape, way out, excuse, get-out

loose *adj.* ① slack, separate, apart, flimsy, flabby, baggy ② free, relaxed, ③ vague, indefinite

loosely *adv.* freely, separately, vaguely

loosen *v.* slacken, relax, undo, detach, release, unfasten ★**tighten**

Loot　　**Lute**

loot *n.* booty, haul, swag, spoils, prize, plunder LUTE

lord *n.* noble, ruler, duke, marquess, earl, viscount, baron

lose *v.* ① mislay, misplace, miss ★**find** ② be defeated, suffer defeat *The rebels suffered defeat at the hands of the army,* fail ★**win**

loser *n.* failure, dud, flop ★**winner**

loss *n.* damage, harm, forfeit, ruin, misfortune ★**gain**

lost *adj.* mislaid, missing, gone, vanished, strayed, ruined ★**found**

lot *n.* ① group, batch, assortment ② fate, portion, fortune ③ plot, patch, land

lotion *n.* balm, salve, ointment, cream, liniment

loud *adj.* ① noisy, blatant, shrill, blaring, deafening ② gaudy, vulgar, tasteless ★**quiet**

lounge ① *v.* recline, lie, loll, sprawl, laze ② *n.* parlour *Step into my parlour said the spider to the fly,* reception room, sitting room

lout *n.* oaf, clod, boor, lummox

lovable *adj.* winsome, charming, attractive, fascinating ★**hateful**

love ① *v.* adore, idolize, worship, dote on, cherish, treasure ② *n.* affection, passion, devotion, ardour ★**hate**

lovely *adj.* charming, delightful, beautiful, adorable ★**hideous**

low *adj.* ① base, vulgar, crude, improper ② not high, flat, level ③ soft, faint, muffled, deep ④ humble, modest, lowly ⑤ cheap, inexpensive ★**high** LO

lower ① *v.* let down, fall, descend ② *v.* debase, disgrace, degrade ③ *adj.* inferior, lesser, smaller, minor

loyal *adj.* constant, staunch *Bill was Kathy's staunch friend for years,* true ▷*faithful* ★**disloyal**

lucid *adj.* clear, obvious, intelligible, bright ▷*transparent* ★**murky**

luck *n.* chance, fortune, success, windfall ★**misfortune**

lucky *adj.* fortunate, successful, blessed, charmed, favoured ★**unlucky**

ludicrous *adj.* absurd, foolish, silly, outlandish, ▷*ridiculous*

lug *v.* pull, draw, drag, haul, tow, heave

luggage *n.* baggage, suitcases, trunks, boxes

lull ① *v.* calm, dwindle, cease, slacken, subside ② *n.* calm, hush, respite

lumber ① *n.* timber, wood, boards, logs ② *v.* plod, shuffle, clump ③ clutter, jumble

luminous *adj.* shining, radiant, bright

lump *n.* bit, piece, chunk, block, knob, swelling *I noticed a rather mysterious swelling on my arm*

lunatic *n.* insane person, maniac, psychopath

lunge *v.* push, thrust, plunge, charge, pounce

lurch *v.* lean, list, reel, rock, stagger, stumble

lure *v.* attract, draw, decoy, ensnare, invite ▷*tempt* ★**repulse**

lurid *adj.* ghastly, disgusting, grim, grisly, melodramatic, sensational

lurk *v.* slink, skulk, crouch, hide, prowl, snoop

luscious *adj.* juicy, succulent, mellow, delicious, scrumptious ★**nauseous**

lush *adj.* wild, luxuriant, green, rich, abundant

lust *n.* desire, passion, craving, greed

lustre *n.* brightness, brilliance, gleam, sheen

lusty *adj.* hale, hearty, vigorous, energetic, rugged, tough ★**weak**

luxury *n.* affluence, wealth, richness, comfort, bliss

lyre *n.* harp, zither LIAR

A B C D E F G H I J K L M N O P Q R S T U V W X Y Z

M m

macabre *adj.* ghastly, grisly, hideous, horrible ▷ *ghostly*

machine *n.* engine, contrivance, device

mad *adj.* ① angry, furious ② lunatic, crazy ▷ *insane* ★**sane**

madcap *adj.* flighty, reckless, thoughtless, impulsive

magazine *n.* ① periodical, publication ② storehouse, depot, arsenal

magic ① *n.* wizardry, witchcraft, sorcery, conjuring ② *adj.* bewitching *She greeted me with a bewitching smile,* fascinating, miraculous

magician *n.* conjuror, wizard, witch, sorcerer, juggler

magistrate *n.* judge, justice, bailiff

magnanimous *adj.* forgiving, generous, charitable, liberal ★**paltry**

magnate *n.* industrialist, merchant, tycoon, VIP, leader MAGNET

magnet *n.* lodestone, attraction, bait, draw MAGNATE

magnetic *adj.* attracting, attractive, absorbing, entrancing, alluring, mesmerizing ▷ *charming* ★**repulsive**

magnificent *adj.* majestic, noble, grand, brilliant, superb ▷ *splendid* ★**modest**

magnify *v.* enlarge, increase, exaggerate ▷ *enhance* ★**diminish**

maid *n.* ① maiden, virgin, miss, damsel ② maidservant, domestic help, waitress MADE

mail *n.* ① letters, post, correspondence, epistles ② armour *The knight's armour was made of breastplates and chain mail,* shield MALE

maim *v.* mutilate, injure, mangle, crush ▷ *disable* ★**heal**

main ① *adj.* leading, principal, central, chief, head *Such important matters are dealt with at our head office,* ② *n.* channel, duct, line, pipe

mainly *adv.* chiefly, generally, mostly, on the whole, usually

Mail

Mail

maintain *v.* ① sustain, keep, support, provide for ② affirm, advocate *The chairman advocated an increase in charges,* assert

majestic *adj.* dignified, grand, noble, august, elevated ▷ *magnificent* ★**unimportant**

major ① *adj.* senior, chief, leading, more important, greater ★**minor** ② *n.* officer, soldier

majority *n.* greater number, most part, bulk, mass ★**minority**

make *v.* ① build, construct, fabricate, fashion ② compel, drive, coerce ③ designate *Two days after her boss retired Liz was designated as the new head of the department,* appoint

make up *v.* ① invent, fabricate, create ② forgive and forget, bury the hatchet *At last, my brother and sister stopped arguing and decided to bury the hatchet*

makeshift *adj.* improvised, temporary, stop-gap *I fixed the car engine, but it was only a stop-gap repair* ★**permanent**

malady *n.* illness, sickness, ailment, affliction, disease

malevolent *adj.* malign, baleful, venomous, malicious ▷ *hostile* ★**benevolent**

246

malice *n.* bitterness, rancour, spite, enmity ▷*hatred* ★**kindness**

malicious *adj.* malignant, spiteful, resentful, bitter ▷*hateful* ★**kind**

maltreat *v.* bully, harm, abuse, injure ▷*hurt* ★**assist**

mammoth *adj.* giant, colossal, massive, enormous ▷*huge* ★**small**

man ① *n.* male, sir, mankind, gentleman ② *n.* valet, manservant ③ *v.* equip, fit out, arm, crew

manage *v.* ① direct, control, administer ② get along *I get along quite well on my own,* fare, cope with ★**fail**

manager *n.* director, superintendent, overseer, supervisor, boss

mandate *n.* authority, command, instruction, warrant

mangle *v.* crush, deform, destroy, maul ▷*maim*

mania *n.* madness, delirium, craze, fad, enthusiasm, passion, craziness

manifest *v.* signify, suggest, demonstrate, display ▷*show* ★**hide**

manipulate *v.* work, handle, wield, use conduct, control ▷*operate*

manly *adj.* male, masculine, brave, bold, strong, ▷*fearless*

manner *n.* fashion, style, form, mode, demeanour, bearing, way MANOR

manoeuvre *v.* direct, drive, guide, handle ▷*manipulate*

manor *n.* estate, country house, château, hall MANNER

mansion *n.* house, castle, residence ▷*manor*

mantle *n.* canopy, cape, covering, hood, shroud, cloak MANTEL

mantel *n.* fireplace shelf, mantelpiece MANTLE

manual ① *adj.* hand-operated, physical *We found the electric typewriter easier to use than the manual typewriter* ② *n.* guide, guidebook, handbook

manufacture *v.* make, build, fabricate, create, produce ▷*construct*

manuscript *n.* ① script, article, essay, theme ② handwriting, autograph

many *adj.* numerous, varied, various, frequent, countless ★**few**

map *n.* chart, plan, diagram, outline

mar *v.* deface, disfigure, injure, blemish, damage ▷*spoil* ★**enhance**

march *v.* stride, walk, pace, step, file, trek

margin *n.* edge, border, rim, side, boundary, brim, brink ★**centre**

mariner *n.* seaman, sailor, seafarer, deckhand, tar, seadog

mark ① *n.* feature, emblem, impression *The letter had a hand-stamped impression on it,* blemish ② *v.* scratch, blemish, stain ③ *v.* take notice of, observe

marked *adj.* noticeable, conspicuous, apparent, clear, striking ★**slight**

market *n.* supermarket, bazaar, fair, mart

maroon *v.* desert, beach, strand, abandon, cast away ★**rescue**

marry *v.* wed, get married, espouse, mate, unite ★**separate**

marsh *n.* swamp, mire, moor, morass, bog

marshal *v.* gather, group, deploy, assemble MARTIAL

martial *adj.* military, militant, hostile, warlike ★**peaceful** MARSHAL

marvel *n.* miracle, wonder, spectacle, sensation

marvellous *adj.* wonderful, wondrous, fabulous, spectacular, superb, astounding ▷*remarkable* ★**ordinary**

masculine *adj.* manlike, manly, strong, robust, strapping ▷*male* ★**feminine**

mash *v.* crush, squash, pulverize, grind

mask ① *n.* camouflage, veil, domino ② *v.* conceal, disguise *Aladdin went to the market-place disguised as a beggar,* shield ★**uncover**

mass *n.* batch, combination, hunk, load, quantity, lump

massacre *v.* exterminate, butcher, murder, slaughter, kill

massive *adj.* big, large, bulky, enormous ▷*huge* ★**small**

master ① *n.* controller, director, leader, captain, champion ② *v.* tame *Our job on*

A B C D E F G H I J K L M N O P Q R S T U V W X Y Z

ranch was to tame the wild horses, control, defeat, subdue

match ① *n.* light, fuse, taper, lucifer ② *v.* copy, pair, equal, tone with

mate ① *n.* spouse, husband, wife, companion, chum, comrade ② *v.* breed, join, wed, yoke

material ① *n.* fabric, textile, cloth, stuff, matter ② *adj.* actual, real, concrete *There was concrete evidence of the prisoner's innocence*

maternal *adj.* motherly, parental, kind, affectionate, protective

matter ① *n.* affair, concern, subject, topic ② *n.* stuff, material, substance *This rock contains some sort of mineral substance* ③ *n.* trouble, distress ④ *v.* signify, count, affect *What does it matter?*

mature *adj.* ripe, mellowed, seasoned, developed, grown-up, adult ★**immature**

maul *v.* batter, beat, molest, paw ▷*mangle*

maxim *n.* saying, motto, axiom, proverb

maximum *adj.* supreme, highest, most, greatest, top, largest ★**minimum**

maybe *adv.* possibly, perhaps, perchance

maze *n.* labyrinth, puzzle, tangle, confusion ▷*muddle* MAIZE

meadow *n.* grassland, field, mead, pasture

meagre *adj.* thin, spare, slight, flimsy, sparse ▷*scanty* ★**substantial**

meal *n.* repast, dinner, lunch, breakfast, supper ▷*feast*

mean ① *v.* signify, denote, express, suggest ② *adj.* cruel, base, low, paltry, miserly ★**generous** ③ average, medium mien

meaning *n.* significance, explanation, sense

means *n.* ① resources, money, wealth ② technique, ability *She has the ability to become a professional player,* method

measure ① *n.* meter, gauge, rule ② *n.* limit, extent, amount ③ *v.* estimate, value, quantify *It is hard to quantify how much damage has been done*

meat *n.* flesh, viands, victuals, food MEET

Measurements

Inch
Foot
Yard
Mile
Pint
Quart
Gallon
Ounce
Pound
Ton

Millimetre
Centimetre
Metre
Kilometre
Millilitre
Litre
Milligram
Gram
Kilogram
Tonne

Measuring cup

Ruler

Callipers

Bathroom scales

mechanical *adj.* ① automatic, machine-driven ② routine, unthinking

medal *n.* award, decoration, ribbon, prize, trophy MEDDLE

meddle *v.* interfere, intervene, intrude, tamper, butt in MEDAL

medicine *n.* remedy, cure, physic, medicament, nostrum, drug, prescription

mediocre *adj.* average, common, inferior, middling ▷*ordinary* ★**excellent**

meditate *v.* ponder, puzzle over, think, reflect, contemplate

medium ① *n.* means, agency, centre ② *n.* conditions, setting, atmosphere *I like school because it has such a wonderful atmosphere of learning* ③ *adj.* average, fair ▷*mediocre*

medley *n.* assortment, jumble, collection, hotchpotch

meek *adj.* docile, humble, quiet, patient, uncomplaining ▷*mild* ★**arrogant**

meet *v.* come together, converge, join, flock, assemble, encounter MEAT, METE

meeting *n.* gathering, assembly, convention

melancholy *adj.* glum, gloomy, unhappy, sad ▷*miserable* ★**cheerful**

mellow *adj.* ① ripe, rich, full-flavoured ★**unripe** ② jovial, cheerful ③ smooth, soothing, delicate *The wine had a smooth, delicate flavour*

melodious *adj.* sweet, mellow, silver-toned, rich, resonant ★**harsh**

melody *n.* tune, air, lay, song, chant, theme

melt *v.* dissolve, liquefy, soften, thaw ★**solidify**

member *n.* ① fellow, associate, comrade, fellow, representative ② limb, part, portion, leg, arm

memorable *adj.* unforgettable, fresh, indelible, noticeable, striking, noteworthy ▷*conspicuous*

memorial *n.* monument, memento, relic, mausoleum *The emperor was buried in the state mausoleum*

memorize *v.* learn, commit to memory, remember, learn by heart

memory *n.* recall, recapture, recollection, remembrance, renown ▷*fame*

menace *v.* threaten, intimidate, frighten, alarm ▷*bully*

mend *v.* restore, correct, promote, improve, rectify, heal ▷*repair* ★**damage**

menial ① *adj.* servile, ignoble, base ② *n.* skivvy, dog's body , underling, lackey

mental *adj.* intellectual, theoretical *Edward's knowledge of music is purely theoretical; he can't play or sing,* abstract ★**physical**

mention *v.* declare, announce, observe, disclose, speak of, say

mercenary ① *adj.* acquisitive, grasping, greedy ▷*selfish* ② *n.* soldier of fortune *The men who were killed were not patriots, but soldiers of fortune,* freelance, hireling

merchandise *n.* wares, goods, commodities, cargo, freight, stock

merchant *n.* dealer, trader, marketeer, vender, retailer, tradesman

merciful *adj.* humane, clement, lenient, compassionate, sparing, forgiving ★**merciless**

merciless *adj.* callous, cruel, pitiless, unrelenting, inhuman ★**merciful**

mercy *n.* compassion, clemency, forgiveness, forbearance, grace ▷*pity* ★**cruelty**

Metals

Aluminium
Brass
Bronze
Chromium
Copper
Gold
Iron and Steel
Lead
Manganese
Mercury
Nickel
Platinum
Silver
Tin
Zinc

Trophy

Girder

A B C D E F G H I J K L M N O P Q R S T U V W X Y Z

mere *adj.* pure, unmixed, absolute, unaffected, simple, paltry

merge *v.* mix, mingle, combine, fuse, blend, weld ▷*unite*

merit ① *n.* excellence, quality, virtue, worth, calibre ▷*talent* ★**failing** ② *v.* deserve, be worthy of

merry *adj.* jolly, gleeful, cheerful, mirthful, sunny ▷*happy* ★**melancholy**

mesh *n.* net, lattice, snare, netting, tangle, trap, web

mess ① *n.* muddle, confusion, clutter, jumble, chaos ▷*plight* ★**order** ② dining hall, mess hall, dining-hall

message *n.* communication, letter, missive, notice, note, dispatch *The reporter sent a dispatch to her paper in Lisbon*

messenger *n.* courier, runner, agent, bearer, carrier, herald

mete *v.* measure, apportion, distribute, divide, deal MEAT, MEET

method *n.* routine, usage, way, means, system, rule, manner ▷*mode*

metre *n.* ① measure, gauge, rule ② cadence *He recited some of his poems, which had a peculiar cadence to them,* rhythm, lilt, swing

mettle *n.* spirit, life, fire, animation, ardour, boldness ▷*courage*

middle ① *n.* centre, heart, midst ② *adj.* medium, average, normal

midget ① *n.* dwarf, gnome, pygmy ② *adj.* little, miniature, small ▷*tiny* ★**giant**

mien *n.* appearance, air, look, manner, expression MEAN

miffed *adj.* annoyed, nettled, offended, hurt ▷*upset* ★**delighted**

might ① *n.* strength, ability, power, force, energy ② *v. past tense of* **may** *She might not have gone had she known it would snow* MITE

mighty *adj.* strong, powerful, potent, stupendous ▷*hefty* ★**weak**

mild *adj.* moderate, calm, gentle, genial, docile ▷*meek* ★**harsh**

military *adj.* martial, soldierly, warlike

mill ① *n.* grinder, works, factory, plant ② *v.* crush, grind, pulverize *The rock was pulverized to make roads,* pound, grate

mimic *v.* impersonate, copy, simulate, imitate

mince *v.* shred, chop, crumble, grind, hash, dice MINTS

mind ① *n.* brain, intellect, soul, spirit ② *v.* listen to, obey, follow orders ③ *v.* take care of, look after ④ *v.* be careful, watch out for

mine ① *n.* quarry, colliery, shaft, deposit, tunnel ② *n.* bomb, explosive ③ *v.* excavate, dig out ④ *pron.* belonging to me *This shop is mine*

mingle *v.* mix, blend, combine ▷*merge*

miniature ① *adj.* tiny, small, dwarf, midget, minute ② *n.* small portrait

minimum *adj.* least, smallest, lowest, slightest ★**maximum**

minister ① *n.* clergyman, vicar, priest ② *n.* ambassador, diplomat *My aunt was a diplomat working in the Brazilian embassy* ③ *n.* secretary, cabinet member ④ serve, give aid

minor *adj.* lesser, smaller, lower, junior, trivial, trifling ★**major** MINER

mint ① *v.* stamp, forge, cast ② *adj.* new, perfect, untarnished ③ *n.* peppermint, plant

minute ① *n.* (*min*-it) flash, instant, moment ② *adj.* (my-*nyute*) slight, tiny, small ▷*miniature* ★**huge**

miracle *n.* marvel, wonder, phenomenon

miraculous *adj.* supernatural, amazing, wondrous, prodigious ★**ordinary**

mire *n.* slime, muck, ooze, mud

mirror ① *n.* looking glass, reflector ② *v.* imitate, simulate, reflect *The essay reflected my feelings about my old home,* copy

mirth *n.* hilarity, laughter, jocularity, fun, frolic, jollity ★**melancholy**

misbehave *v.* do wrong, disobey, offend, be naughty ★**behave**

miscellaneous *adj.* various, varied, divers, sundry, mixed, jumbled

mischief *n.* roguery, pranks, damage, hurt, annoyance, harm

mischievous *adj.* rascally, villainous, naughty, destructive, spiteful ★**good**

misconduct *n.* misbehaviour, wrong-doing, naughtiness, rudeness

miser *n.* niggard, skinflint, scrooge, penny-pincher, tightwad ★**spendthrift**

miserable *adj.* forlorn, wretched, pitiable, desolate, suffering ★**cheerful**

misery *n.* sorrow, woe, grief, anguish, distress ▷*unhappiness* ★**happiness**

misfit *n.* eccentric *Professor Jones is something of an eccentric and comes to lectures in her slippers,* drop-out, oddball, nonconformist

misfortune *n.* adversity, bad luck, hardship, evil, calamity ▷*disaster* ★**luck**

misgiving *n.* distrust, mistrust, doubt, apprehension, anxiety ▷*qualm* ★**confidence**

mishap *n.* misadventure, blow, accident, setback ▷*misfortune*

misjudge *v.* underestimate, overestimate, overrate, underrate ▷*mistake*

mislay *v.* lose, misplace, miss

mislead *v.* deceive, lead astray, hoodwink, take in, outwit, fool ▷*bluff*

miss ① *v.* fail, fall short of, skip, pass over, mistake ② *v.* grieve over, yearn for, lament ③ *n.* girl, young woman, damsel

missile *n.* projectile, arrow, dart, pellet, shot, rocket, torpedo

mission *n.* errand, task, assignment, object, objective, end, aim ▷*quest*

mist *n.* moisture, dew, vapour, fog, cloud, smog, haze MISSED

mistake ① *n.* error, fault, lapse, blunder, oversight ② *v.* slip up, misunderstand, confuse, confound, blunder

mistaken *adj.* erroneous, untrue, false, fallacious ▷*wrong* ★**correct**

mistrust *v.* disbelieve, distrust, doubt, fear ▷*suspect* ★**trust**

misunderstand *v.* mistake, misinterpret, take wrongly ★**grasp**

misuse *v.* exploit, abuse, corrupt, harm

mite *n.* ① grain, atom, morsel, particle ② bug, parasite *The plants were infested with parasites* MIGHT

mitigate *v.* allay, ease, abate, moderate, justify, vindicate ★**aggravate**

mix *v.* blend, whip, mingle, combine ▷*stir*

mix up *v.* confuse, confound, muddle, jumble ▷*bewilder*

mixture *n.* miscellany, medley, jumble, blend

moan *v.* wail, groan, grouse, grumble, grieve, whinge

mob *n.* crowd, mass, gang, flock, rabble, company, throng

mobile *adj.* active, portable, wandering, movable ★**immobile**

mock ① *v.* mimic, imitate, jeer at, laugh at, ridicule ▷*flatter* ② *adj.* pretended, artificial, sham, false, fake

mode *n.* fashion, style, vogue, manner, way, form ▷*method* MOWED

model *n.* ① pattern, original, prototype *This car is a prototype, and we will produce many like it* ② mannequin ③ replica, representation

moderate *adj.* reasonable, medium, gentle, mild, quiet, modest ▷*fair*

modern *adj.* new, up-to-date, modish, stylish, recent, current, contemporary, state-of-the art, trendy ANTIQUATED

modest *adj.* bashful, demure, diffident, unassuming, humble ★**vain**

modesty *n.* humility, diffidence, reserve, shyness, decency ★**vanity**

modify *v.* transform, convert, change, alter, revise, redesign

moist *adj.* damp, humid, watery, clammy, dank ▷*wet* ★**dry**

moisture *n.* damp, dampness, liquid, wetness, dew, dankness

molest *v.* annoy, bother, pursue, attack, pester, plague, tease, torment ▷*harry*

moment *n.* ① second, instant, twinkling ② importance, worth, weight *I think your argument has some weight, and I agree with you*

momentous *adj.* notable, outstanding, decisive, important, significant, weighty, grave ★**insignificant**

monarch *n.* king, sovereign, ruler, emperor, prince *The head of state in Monaco is a prince*

A
B
C
D
E
F
G
H
I
J
K
L
M
N
O
P
Q
R
S
T
U
V
W
X
Y
Z

World Money

afghani	*Afghanistan*	lek	*Albania*
balboa	*Panama*	leu	*Romania*
bolivar	*Venezuela*	lev	*Bulgaria*
cedi	*Ghana*	lira	*Italy, Turkey*
colón	*Costa Rica, El Salvador*	mark	*Germany*
cruzeiro	*Brazil*	markka	*Finland*
dinar	*Algeria, Bahrain, Iraq,*	naira	*Nigeria*
	Jordan, Kuwait	peseta	*Spain*
dollar	*Australia, Bahamas,*	peso	*Argentina,*
	Canada, USA, etc		*Chile, Cuba*
drachma	*Greece*	pound	*United Kingdom*
escudo	*Portugal*	rand	*South Africa*
forint	*Hungary*	rial	*Iran, Oman, Yemen*
franc	*Belgium, France, etc*	rouble	*Russia*
guarani	*Paraguay*	rupee	*India*
guilder	*Netherlands*	schilling	*Austria*
kip	*Laos*	sol	*Peru*
krona	*Iceland, Sweden*	sucre	*Ecuador*
krone	*Denmark, Norway*	yen	*Japan*
		yuan	*China*
		zloty	*Poland*

money *n.* wealth, cash, coin, legal tender

mongrel *n.* hybrid, mixed, crossbreed, dog

monitor ① *n.* listener, auditor, watchdog, prefect ② *v.* check, supervise, oversee

monologue *n.* lecture, oration, speech, recitation, sermon

monopolize *v.* control, take over, appropriate ▷*dominate* ★**share**

monotonous *adj.* tedious, uninteresting, dull, prosaic *His speech was so prosaic that I almost dropped off to sleep,* repetitive ▷*tiresome*

monstrous *adj.* hideous, frightful, dreadful, terrible, criminal ▷*wicked*

mood *n.* state of mind, humour, temper, disposition *My grandmother's gentle disposition won her many friends*

moody *adj.* morose, sulky, sullen, peevish, cantankerous *I didn't like Uncle Harry; he was a cantankerous old man* ★**cheerful**

moor ① *v.* tether, picket, tie, chain, anchor, secure ② *n.* heath, moorland MORE

mop *n.* ① sponge, swab, towel ② hair, tresses, locks, mane

mope *v.* grieve, moon, pine, sulk

moral *adj.* virtuous, good, honest, honourable ▷*upright* ★**immoral**

morbid *adj.* gruesome, macabre, melancholy, grisly, putrid

more ① *adj.* in addition, also, beyond, extra, further ② *adv.* better, again, longer

morning *n.* dawn, daybreak, daylight, cockcrow *I rose at cockcrow, saddled my horse, and was off to Richmond,* sunrise ★**evening** MOURNING

morose *adj.* glum, sullen, sulky, broody, taciturn ▷*moody* ★**cheerful**

morsel *n.* bit, bite, piece, scrap, nibble

mortal *adj.* ① human, feeble, ephemeral ② fatal, final, deadly, severe

most ① *adj.* greatest nearly all ② *adv.* mostly, chiefly, mainly, utmost

mostly *adv.* as a rule, principally, usually, normally

mother ① *n.* female parent, ma, mummy, mama ② *v.* nurse, protect, rear, care for

motherly *adj.* caring, comforting, loving, maternal, gentle

motion *n.* ① movement, locomotion, action, passage ② proposal *I vote that we accept the proposal,* suggestion

motionless *adj.* stationary, still, transfixed, stable, inert ★**moving**

motive *n.* reason, purpose, occasion, impulse, cause ▷*spur*

mottled *adj.* speckled, spotted, pied, piebald

motto *n.* saying, slogan, watchword, maxim *My mother's maxim was 'Always look on the bright side'.* proverb

mould ① *v.* form, shape, fashion, cast, create ② *n.* pattern, matrix ③ *n.* earth, loam

mouldy *adj.* mildewed, putrid, bad

mound *n.* hillock, pile, knoll, rise, mount

mount *v.* ascend, climb, rise, vault

mourn *v.* lament, deplore, sorrow, regret, weep ▷*grieve* ★**rejoice**

mournful *adj.* doleful, sombre, cheerless, sorrowful ▷*melancholy* ★**joyful**

mouth *n.* aperture, opening, entrance, orifice, inlet, jaws

mouthful *n.* bite, morsel, sample, taste, titbit

move *v.* ① march, proceed, walk, go ② propose, suggest, recommend ③ propel, drive, impel

moving *adj.* touching, affecting, stirring *The band played a stirring rendition of 'Amazing Grace',* emotional

much ① *adj.* abundant, considerable, ample ② *adv.* considerably, greatly, often ③ *n.* lots, loads, heaps, plenty

muck *n.* dirt, filth, mire, ooze, mud, scum

muddle ① *n.* confusion, clutter, jumble, mix-up ② *v.* bungle, tangle, confound ▷*bewilder*

muff *v.* botch, mismanage, miss, spoil ▷*muddle*

muffle *v.* ① deaden, mute, muzzle, silence ② wrap, envelop, wind, swaddle

mug ① *n.* innocent, simpleton ② *n.* cup, beaker, tankard ③ *v.* attack, beat up, rob

muggy *adj.* clammy, dank, damp, humid, close ★**dry**

mull *v.* meditate *I meditated over the weekend before deciding what to do,* consider, study, think about

multiply *v.* increase, spread, grow, extend, intensify ★**decrease**

multitude *n.* crowd, legion, throng, swarm, horde ★**handful**

munch *v.* crunch, chew, bit, nibble ▷*eat*

murder *v.* slay, assassinate, butcher, destroy, slaughter ▷*kill*

murky *adj.* foggy, cloudy, dark, gloomy, dull, misty ★**bright**

murmur *n.* & *v.* whisper, mutter, mumble, drone

muscular *adj.* brawny, athletic, burly, beefy, powerful ▷*robust* ★**puny**

muse *v.* meditate, ponder, puzzle over, brood, deliberate

must ① *v.* ought to, should, be obliged to ② *n.* duty, necessity, requirement

muster *v.* marshal, collect, assemble, rally *The troops rallied and prepared to attack again,* enrol

musty *adj.* mouldy, rank, mildewy, decayed

mute *adj.* silent, speechless, voiceless, soundless ★**loud**

mutilate *v.* injure, hurt, cut, damage ▷*maim*

mutiny *n.* & *v.* protest, revolt, strike, riot

mutter *v.* mumble, grouse, grumble ▷*murmur* ★**exclaim**

mutual *adj.* common, reciprocal, interchangeable ▷*joint* ★**one-sided**

mysterious *adj.* obscure, unrevealed, unexplained, secret ▷*hidden* ★**clear**

mystery *n.* puzzle, enigma, secrecy, riddle, problem

mystify *v.* confuse, bamboozle, hoodwink, puzzle, mislead ▷*baffle* ★**enlighten**

myth *n.* fable, legend, supposition, fabrication, tradition, fantasy ★**fact**

mythical *adj.* fabulous, fabled, legendary, traditional, imaginary ★**true**

A
B
C
D
E
F
G
H
I
J
K
L
M
N
O
P
Q
R
S
T
U
V
W
X
Y
Z

N n

nab *v.* arrest, apprehend, seize, catch, capture, grab

nag ① *v.* pester, hector, heckle, badger, annoy, henpeck, scold *My parents scolded me for coming home late* ② *n.* horse, pony

nail ① *n.* pin, peg, pin, spike, tack ② *v.* hammer, fix, tack, peg

naive *adj.* innocent, unworldly, unsophisticated, simple, trusting, artless, natural, childlike, unaffected, ingenous, credulous ★**cunning, sophisticated**

naked *adj.* nude, bare, unclothed, undressed ★**clothed**

name ① *n.* title, description, designation ② *n.* character, reputation *A good reputation is very important to me,* distinction ③ *v.* christen, style, term, entitle

nap ① *v.* sleep, doze, drowse, rest ② *n.* down, fibre, fuzz *Velvet is a cloth with a kind of fuzz on the surface*

narrate *v.* describe, tell, recite, relate

narrow *adj.* slender, fine, small ▷*thin* ★**wide**

nasty *adj.* dirty, mucky, foul, offensive, unpleasant ▷*squalid* ★**nice**

national *adj.* civil, governmental, public, general, nationwide

native *adj.* natural, inborn, aboriginal, domestic, local

natural *adj.* frank, genuine, innate, instinctive, ordinary, usual

naturally *adj.* absolutely, certainly, frankly, normally

nature *n.* ① temper, personality, disposition ② the world, the outdoors, landscape

naughty *adj.* mischievous, rascally, wicked, disobedient ▷*bad* ★**well-behaved**

nauseous *adj.* disgusting, sickening, repulsive, revolting ★**pleasant**

nautical *adj.* maritime *Ancient Greece was a great maritime nation,* seamanlike, naval, sailing, seafaring

navigate *v.* voyage, cruise, sail, guide, pilot

navy *n.* ships, fleet, armada, flotilla

near *adj.* close, nearby, adjacent, bordering, neighbouring, beside ▷*nigh* ★**remote**

nearly *adv.* about, almost, all but, thereabouts, roughly

neat *adj.* ① tidy, spruce, smart, stylish ★**untidy** ② skilful, clever, adroit *I admire your adroit handling of that tricky situation,* ingenious

necessary *adj.* needed, essential, basic, required, compulsory ★**optional**

need ① *v.* require, want, crave ▷*demand* ★**have** ② *n.* distress, want, necessity, deprivation *During the long war, the people suffered many deprivations* KNEAD

needed *adj.* wanted, desired, lacking ▷*necessary* ★**unnecessary**

needless *adj.* pointless, unnecessary, superfluous, useless ★**necessary**

needy *adj.* destitute, down-and-out, deprived ▷*poor* ★**well-off**

neglect *v.* overlook, ignore, scorn, slight, disregard ▷*spurn* ★**cherish**

neglected *adj.* unkempt, abandoned, dilapidated, uncared for ★**cherished**

negligent *adj.* neglectful, forgetful, slack, indifferent ▷*careless* ★**careful**

negotiate *v.* bargain, deal, treat, haggle, mediate, transact

neighbourhood *n.* vicinity, surroundings, district, area, locality *There are many fine houses in this locality*

neighbourly *adj.* hospitable, friendly, kind, obliging ▷*helpful*

nerve *n.* ① mettle, guts, pluck, courage ② audacity, impudence *Mr Thompson already owes us money and yet he has the impudence to ask for more*

nervous *adj.* tense, taut, jumpy, flustered, jittery, anxious, timid ★**confident**

nest *n.* den, burrow, haunt, refuge, resort

nestle *adj.* cuddle, snuggle, huddle, nuzzle

net ① *v.* catch, trap, lasso, capture ② *n.* mesh, lattice, trap, web, lace *I have some new lace curtains* ③ *adj.* clear *I made a clear £15,000 after taxes,* final, lowest

nettle *v.* exasperate, annoy, ruffle ▷VEX

National and Religious Holidays

Advent, All Saints' Day, Anzac Day, Ascension Day, Ash Wednesday, Australia Day, Bastille Day, Boxing Day, Canada Day, Candlemas, Carnival, Christmas, Commonwealth Day, Diwali, Day of the Dead, Easter, Father's Day, Gandhi's Birthday, Good Friday, Guy Fawkes Day, Halloween, Hanukkah, Independence Day, Kwanzaa, Labour Day, Lent, Mardi Gras, Martin Luther King Day, Memorial Day, Mother's Day, Muhammad's

Birthday, New Year's Day, Palm Sunday, Passover, Pentecost, Purim, Ramadan, Rosh Hashanah, Saint Patrick's Day, Shavuot, Sukkot, Thanksgiving Day, Valentine's Day, Yom Kippur

A puppet from the Mexican Day of the Dead Festival.

neutral *adj.* impartial, unbiased, fair-minded, unprejudiced ★**biased**

never *adv.* at no time, not at all, under no circumstances ★**always**

new *adj.* recent, just out, current, latest, fresh, unused ▷*novel* ★**old** GNU, KNEW

news *n.* information, intelligence, tidings, account, bulletin, rumour

next *adj.* ① following, succeeding, after, later ② adjacent, adjoining *I live on Park Street, and my friend lives on the adjoining street,* beside

nibble *v.* bite, peck, gnaw, munch ▷*eat*

nice *adj.* ① pleasant, agreeable, amiable, charming, delightful ★**nasty** ② precise, accurate, fine, subtle

niche *n.* compartment, hole, corner, recess, place

nick *v.* ① dent, score, mill, cut, scratch ② prison, gaol, police station

nigh *adj.* next, close, adjacent, adjoining ▷*near* ★**distant**

night *n.* dark, darkness, dusk, evening ★**day** KNIGHT

nimble *adj.* active, agile, spry, lithe, skilfull ▷*deft* ★**clumsy**

nip *v.* cut, snip, pinch, twinge, bite

no ① *adj.* not any, not one, none ② *adv.* nay, not at all KNOW

noble *adj.* ① dignified, lofty *My aunt is very important and has a lofty position on the council,* generous, grand, stately, elevated ★**base** ② aristocrat, peer

nod *v.* ① beckon, signal, indicate, salute ② sleep, doze, nap

noise *n.* din, discord, clamour, clatter, hubbub, tumult, uproar ★**silence**

noisy *adj.* loud, boisterous, turbulent, rowdy, clamorous ★**quiet**

nominate *v.* appoint, assign, elect, choose, propose, suggest

nonchalant *adj.* casual, unperturbed, calm, blasé *We enjoyed the new musical, but Sue has been to so many shows she was very blasé about it,* cool, detached ★**anxious**

nondescript *adj.* commonplace, colourless, dull, ordinary ▷*plain* ★**unusual**

none *pron.* not one, not any, not a part, nil, nobody NUN

nonsense *n.* absurdity, balderdash, drivel, rot, garbage, twaddle ★**sense**

nook *n.* compartment, hole, corner, alcove,

crevice, cranny, cavity, hide-out ▷*niche*

noose *n.* loop, bight, snare, rope, lasso

normal *adj.* usual, general, average, sane, lucid, rational, standard ★**abnormal**

nose *n.* ① beak, bill, neb, snout ② prow, stem, bow, front

nosy *adj.* inquisitive, curious, prying, snooping, intrusive

nostalgia *n.* homesickness, longing, pining, regret, remembrance, yearning

notable *adj.* eventful, momentous, marked, outstanding, great, celebrated, eminent ▷*famous* ★**commonplace**

notch *n.* dent, nick, score, cut, cleft, indentation

note *n.* ① letter, message, communication ② remark, record, report ③ fame, renown, distinction ④ banknote, bill

noted *adj.* eminent, renowned, celebrated, great ▷*famous* ★**obscure**

nothing *n.* zero, naught, null, nil, zilch ★**something**

notice ① *n.* announcement, advice, sign, poster ② *v.* note, remark, observe *After observing that his bike had a flat tyre, Jo knew he would have to walk to school*, perceive, make out, see ★**ignore**

notify *v.* inform, tell, intimate, announce, declare ★**withhold**

Notice

After observing that his bike had a flat tyre, Jo knew he would have to walk to school.

notion *n.* idea, conception, opinion, belief, view, judgement

notorious *adj.* infamous, questionable, scandalous, blatant

notwithstanding *adv.* nevertheless, nonetheless, however, despite

nourish *v.* feed, sustain, nurture, comfort, cherish, support ★**starve**

nourishing *adj.* beneficial, healthful, nutritious, wholesome

novel ① *adj.* fresh, unusual, original, unique, rare, uncommon ② *n.* fiction, story, book, romance, tale

novice *n.* beginner, learner, apprentice, tiro, pupil, trainee ★**expert**

now *adv.* at this moment, at present, at once, instantly, right away

now and then *adv.* from time to time, sometimes, occasionally

nude *adj.* bare, naked, unclothed, stripped, undressed

nudge *v.* poke, push, prod, jog, shove, dig

nuisance *n.* offence, annoyance, plague, trouble, bore, pest, irritation

nullify *v.* annul, invalidate, cancel, quash ▷*abolish* ★**establish**

numb *adj.* deadened, insensible, dazed, stunned, unfeeling ★**sensitive**

number ① *n.* figure, amount, volume, quantity, sum ② *n.* crowd, throng, multitude *The new president's visit to the town was watched by a multitude of people* ③ *n.* figure, symbol ▷*numeral* ④ *v.* count, reckon, tally

numeral *n.* symbol, figure, character, cipher

numerous *adj.* many, divers, several, plentiful ▷*abundant* ★**few**

nun *n.* sister, abbess, prioress NONE

nurse ① *v.* attend, care for, foster, support, sustain ② *n.* hospital sister, matron, nanny

nursery *n.* ① children's room, creche ② greenhouse, hothouse, garden

nurture *v.* feed, nourish, cherish, foster, tend, care for ▷*nurse*

nutritious *adj.* healthful, substantial, health-giving ▷*nourishing* ★**bad**

O o

oaf *n.* brute, lout, blockhead, dolt, ruffian,

obedient *adj.* respectful, obliging, law-abiding, servile, dutiful, deferential, yielding ★**rebellious**

obey *v.* comply, conform, submit, heed, mind, behave ★**disobey**

object ① *v.* (ob-*ject*) protest, complain, argue, oppose, refuse ★**agree** ② *n.* (*ob-*ject) thing, article, commodity, item ③ *n.* mission, purpose *The purpose of my visit is to end this conflict,* end,

objectionable *adj.* displeasing, distasteful, disagreeable, repugnant ★**pleasant**

obligation *n.* responsibility, liability, commitment ★**choice**

oblige *v.* ① require, compel, force, make ② gratify, please, help ▷*assist* ★**displease**

obliging *adj.* helpful, polite, agreeable, courteous ▷*willing* ★**unkind**

obliterate *v.* blot out, efface, erase, wipe out, destroy, annihilate

oblivious *adj.* unmindful, absent-minded, heedless, unaware ★**aware**

obnoxious *adj.* repulsive, revolting, offensive ▷*unpleasant* ★**pleasant**

obscene *adj.* dirty, unclean, vile, filthy, nasty, immoral, indecent ★**decent**

obscure ① *adj.* indistinct, dim, vague, hidden, confusing *The language of a legal document can be very confusing* ▷*doubtful* ★**clear** ② *v.* conceal, hide, cloud, darken, cover ▷*hide* ★**clarify**

observant *adj.* attentive, watchful, heedful ▷*alert* ★**inattentive**

observation *n.* ① attention, study, supervision ② utterance, comment, remark, statement *The police issued a statement*

observe *v.* ① abide by *I intend to abide by the laws of this country,* adhere to, carry out, keep up ② note, notice, perceive, watch ▷*see* ③ utter, remark, mention

obsolete *adj.* dated, outmoded, unfashionable, out-of-date ★**current**

obstacle *n.* obstruction, barrier, bar, hindrance ▷*drawback* ★**advantage**

obstinate *adj.* determined, dogged, unyielding, perverse *As a child I upset my parents by my perverse behaviour* ▷*stubborn* ★**docile**

obstruct *v.* hinder, impede, block, bar, choke ▷*restrain* ★**help**

obstruction *n.* hindrance, restraint, impediment, snag

obtain *v.* acquire, achieve, gain, procure, attain ▷*get* ★**lose**

obtuse *adj.* dull, stupid, unintelligent, stolid, thick, blunt ★**bright**

obvious *adj.* plain, evident, self-evident, explicit, apparent ▷*clear* ★**obscure**

occasion *n.* ① affair, episode, occurrence, circumstance ② reason, purpose, motive

occasional *adj.* casual, rare, infrequent, periodic ★**frequent**

occult *adj.* hidden, unrevealed, secret, mysterious, supernatural *Edgar Allan Poe wrote tales of the supernatural* ★**open**

occupant *n.* owner, resident, proprietor, tenant, inmate, inhabitant

occupation *n.* ① activity, employment, calling, job ② possession, tenancy, residence

occupied *adj.* ① busy, employed, active ② settled, populated, peopled ★**unoccupied**

occupy *v.* ① inhabit, live in, reside, dwell in, own, possess, hold ② invade, overrun

occur *v.* take place, befall, turn out, come to pass, result ▷*happen*

occurrence *n.* happening, affair, circumstance, incident, occasion ▷*event*

ocean *n.* sea, main *The pirates of the Spanish Main were the curse of shipping,* deep, tide

odd *adj.* ① single, unmatched ② singular,

Oceans and Waters

Antarctic	Bay	Sound
Arctic	Fjord	Straits
Atlantic	Gulf	
Indian	Lagoon	
Pacific	Loch	

A B C D E F G H I J K L M N O P Q R S T U V W X Y Z

peculiar, quaint, queer ★**ordinary**
③ surplus, left over, remaining

odds and ends *n.* leavings, debris *The police found the debris of the crashed aircraft,* leftovers, oddments, remains

odious *adj.* hateful, offensive, detestable ▷*abominable* ★**pleasant**

odorous *adj.* fragrant, perfumed, aromatic, sweet-smelling

odour *n.* ① scent, aroma ▷*fragrance* ② stink, stench, reek ▷*smell*

off ① *adv.* away from, over, done ② *prep.* along, against, opposite, distant ★**on** ③ *adj.* bad, mouldy, rotten

offence *n.* insult, outrage, attack, crime, hurt

offend *v.* ① insult, hurt, wound, outrage, displease ② transgress, sin ★**please**

offensive *adj.* insulting, offending, rude, repugnant, hurtful, distasteful

offer ① *v.* propose, proffer, present, tender, attempt ② *n.* bid, endeavour, proposal

offering *n.* sacrifice, donation, gift, present

offhand *adj.* ① brusque, casual, curt, informal, abrupt ② informal, improvised, impromptu *My sister, who is a singer, gave an impromptu performance* ★**planned**

office ① *n.* bureau, department, room ② position, appointment, post

officer *n.* ① official, administrator, functionary, executive ② military rank, policeman, minister *A minister from the French Embassy called*

official ① *adj.* authorized, authentic, proper, formal ★**unofficial** ② *n.* executive, office-holder, bureaucrat *The city bureaucrats take months to get a job done*

officious *adj.* interfering, meddlesome, self-important

offspring *n.* child, children, descendant, heir, family, issue, progeny

often *adv.* frequently, regularly, recurrently, time after time, repeatedly ★**seldom**

ointment *n.* lotion, salve, cream, balm, embrocation, liniment

old *adj.* ① ancient, antique, aged, antiquated ② crumbling, decayed *Beneath the ivy were the decayed remains of the castle wall,*

decrepit ★**new** ③ out-of-date, old-fashioned, passé ④ aged, mature, elderly ★**young**

ominous *adj.* menacing, threatening, foreboding, sinister

omit *v.* leave out, neglect, let go, overlook, miss out, skip ★**include**

once *adv.* formerly, at one time, previously

one ① *adj.* sole, alone, lone, whole ② *n.* unit, single thing

one-sided *adj.* unequal, unfair, unjust, biased

only ① *adj.* exclusive, single, sole, lone, solitary ② *adv.* solely, barely, exclusively

onset *n.* start, outbreak, assault, attack, onslaught, onrush

onslaught *n.* charge, attack, bombardment

ooze ① *n.* mire, muck, slime ② *v.* bleed, discharge, emit, exude, leak

open ① *v.* uncover, unlock, unfasten ② *v.* start, commence, begin ③ *adj.* uncovered, clear, evident, apparent ★**closed** ④ *adj.* frank, honest, candid, fair

opening *n.* ① aperture, mouth, crevice, recess, hole ② commencement, beginning

openly *adv.* candidly, frankly, plainly, sincerely ★**secretly**

operate *v.* function *Despite its age, the old millwheel continued to function,* work, manipulate, drive, ▷*perform*

operation *n.* performance, movement, action, motion, proceeding

opinion *n.* view, concept, judgement, belief, point of view, stance

opponent *n.* antagonist, rival, competitor, contestant, foe ▷*enemy* ★**ally**

opportune *adj.* timely *It had started to rain, thus the timely arrival of the bus was welcome,* convenient, fortunate, suitable ★**untimely**

opportunity *n.* occasion, chance, opening, scope, moment

oppose *v.* withstand, resist, obstruct, confront, hinder ▷*defy* ★**support**

opposite *adj.* ① facing, fronting ② conflicting, opposing, contrary, adverse ★**same**

a b c d e f g h i j k l m n o p q r s t u v w x y z

opposition *n.* antagonism, defiance, hostility, difference ▷*resistance* ★**co-operation**

oppress *v.* crush, depress, harass, overpower, overwhelm, subdue

optimist *n.* hopeful person, perfectionist ★**pessimist**

optimistic *adj.* hopeful, cheerful, confident, positive ★**pessimistic**

option *n.* preference, choice, alternative

optional *adj.* possible, voluntary, unforced, open ★**compulsory**

opulent *adj.* rich, affluent, prosperous, well-to-do ▷*wealthy* ★**poor**

oration *n.* sermon, lecture, speech, discourse

orb *n.* globe, ball, sphere

orbit *n.* ① path, passage, trajectory ② province, realm, domain *The river, the forest, and the castle were all within her domain*

ordeal *n.* trial, nightmare, torment, agony

order ① *n.* arrangement, pattern, grouping, organization ② *n.* command, law, rule, decree *A decree was issued forbidding the killing of deer* ③ *n.* shipment, consignment ④ *v.* direct, instruct, command ⑤ *v.* arrange, control, conduct

orderly *adj.* regular, methodical, trim, neat, well-mannered ★**messy**

ordinary *adj.* common, usual, commonplace, general, customary ★**extraordinary**

organization *n.* ① association, group, institute, establishment ② structure, arrangement, system

organize *v.* arrange, form, structure, establish, classify ★**disorganize**

origin *n.* beginning, start, basis, foundation, root, source ★**end**

original *adj.* ① first, aboriginal, ancient, former, primary ② fresh, new, novel *Travelling by camel was a novel experience*

originate ① *v.* create, conceive, compose ② arise, begin ▷*start* ★**end**

ornament ① *n.* decoration, adornment, tracery, pattern ② trinket, curio, knick-knack

ornate *adj.* decorated, adorned, flowery,

Original

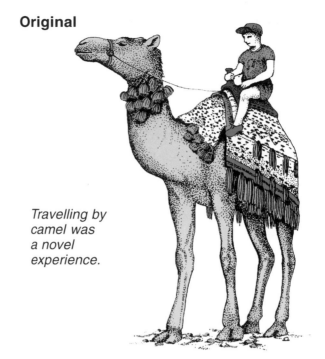

Travelling by camel was a novel experience.

embellished, showy, garish ★**plain**

oust *v.* expel, eject, evict, dismiss, throw out ▷*overthrow*

out ① *adj.* away, outside, absent ★**in** ② *adj.* open, revealed, uncovered ③ *adv.* loudly, aloud, audibly

out of order *adj.* broken, not working

out of sorts *adj.* sick, ill, poorly, gloomy, fed up

outbreak *n.* epidemic *An epidemic of cholera had hit the village,* rebellion, eruption, explosion, flare-up

outburst *n.* eruption, explosion ▷*outbreak*

outcast *n.* exile, castaway *Robinson Crusoe was a castaway on a desert island,* derelict, refugee, reject

outcome *n.* effect, consequence, conclusion, result, upshot

outcry *n.* commotion, row, uproar, tumult, shouting, hue and cry ▷*clamour*

outdated *adj.* old, antique, old-fashioned, unfashionable, obsolete ★**modern**

outdo *v.* surpass, excel, beat, outclass, eclipse, exceed, outshine

outfit *n.* ensemble, set *My mother bought a new set of dishes in the sale for half price,* rig, equipment, gear

outing *n.* excursion, picnic, expedition, trip, ramble

A
B
C
D
E
F
G
H
I
J
K
L
M
N
O
P
Q
R
S
T
U
V
W
X
Y
Z

outlandish *adj.* strange, erratic, odd, queer, quaint, bizarre ★**ordinary**

outlaw *n.* bandit, highwayman, hooligan, desperado *Billy the Kid was a desperado in the Wild West*, robber

outlet *n.* exit, egress, way out, vent, spout, nozzle, opening ★**inlet**

outline ① *n.* diagram, plan, blueprint, sketch, framework, summary ② *v.* draw, sketch, describe

outlook *n.* view, prospect, forecast, attitude, aspect, prognosis

output *n.* yield, product, produce, achievement, manufacture

outrage ① *n.* disgrace, injury, offence, affront ② *v.* offend, insult, shock, violate

outrageous *adj.* insulting, offensive, exorbitant, monstrous ★**acceptable**

outright ① *adj.* complete, thorough, absolute, wholesale ② *adv.* at once, completely, entirely, altogether

outset *n.* first, opening, beginning, inauguration, kick-off ▷*start* ★**finish**

outside ① *n.* exterior, surface, front ② *adj.* exterior, external, outward, surface

outsider *n.* stranger, foreigner, alien, misfit *Gulliver was something of a misfit in the land of the tiny Lilliputians*

outskirts *n.* limits, bounds, boundary, outpost, suburb

outspoken *adj.* frank, open, straightforward, blunt, direct ▷*candid* ★**tactful**

outstanding *adj.* striking, pronounced, conspicuous, notable ▷*exceptional* ★**ordinary**

outward *adj.* exterior, outside, outer, superficial *From a distance, my father and Bill Jones look alike, but it's really just superficial*

outwit *v.* get the better of, swindle, defraud, dupe ▷*cheat*

over ① *adj.* concluded, ended, done with, settled ② *prep.* above, more than, exceeding ③ *adv.* aloft, above, beyond, extra

overall ① *adj.* complete, inclusive, total, broad ② *adv.* by and large, on the whole

overbearing *adj.* domineering, dictatorial, haughty, pompous ▷*arrogant* ★**modest**

overcast *adj.* cloudy, heavy, dark, murky, dull ★**bright**

overcome *adj.* overwhelm, conquer, crush, defeat, vanquish ▷*subdue*

overdo *v.* overwork, exaggerate, go too far *I didn't mind your eating one of my apples, but taking all four was going too far*

overdue *adj.* delayed, belated, late, behindhand ★**early**

overflow *v.* swamp, deluge, inundate, submerge, soak, spill

overhaul *v.* ① repair, mend, fix, inspect, examine ② overtake, pass, gain on

overhead *adv.* above, upward, aloft, on high ★**below**

overhear *v.* listen, eavesdrop, snoop, spy

overjoyed *adj.* elated, jubilant, rapturous ▷*delighted* ★**disappointed**

overlap *v.* overrun, go beyond, coincide, overlay

overlook *v.* ① disregard, pardon, condone, ignore ② neglect, miss, pass over ③ inspect, check, examine

overpower *v.* conquer, crush, master, subdue, vanquish ▷*defeat*

overseas *adj.* abroad, foreign ★**domestic**

overseer *n.* inspector, supervisor, boss, manager, master, mistress

oversight *n.* omission, blunder, error, fault, lapse ▷*mistake*

overtake *v.* catch up, pass, outdo, outstrip, pass ▷*overhaul*

overthrow *v.* defeat, beat, topple ▷*overpower*

overture *n.* ① (in music) prelude, opening, introduction ② offer, proposal, invitation

overwhelm *v.* overcome, stun, shock, overpower, deluge, inundate *The reply to our advertisement was huge; we were inundated with letters*

overwhelming *adj.* all-powerful, formidable, breathtaking, shattering ★**insignificant**

owe *v.* be in debt, incur, be due

own ① *v.* possess, occupy, hold ② *v.* admit, confess, grant ③ *adj.* individual, personal, private

owner *n.* proprietor, possessor, landlord

Pp

pace ① *n. & v.* step, tread, stride ② *n.* speed, rate, velocity, tempo

pacify *v.* appease, calm, moderate, tranquilize ▷*soothe* ★**aggravate**

pack ① *n.* bundle, bunch, swarm, crowd, group ② *v.* cram, load, fill, throng

package *n.* parcel, packet, bundle, box, carton, bale, consignment

packet *n.* bag, pack, container, parcel ▷*package*

pact *n.* contract, treaty, agreement, arrangement, deal, understanding PACKED

pad ① *n.* tablet, notepad, jotter ② *n.* foot, paw ③ *v.* fill, pack, shape, stuff, cushion

paddle ① *n.* oar, sweep, scull ② *v.* row, steer, propel ③ *v.* wade, splash, swim

pagan *n.* heathen, idol-worshipper, infidel

page *n.* ① sheet, leaf, paper ② boy, attendant, bell-boy, messenger

pageant *n.* fair, parade, procession, exhibition, masque ▷*show*

pail *n.* bucket, churn, tub, container PALE

pain ① *n.* ache, pang, throb, twinge, spasm, cramp ② *v.* hurt, sting, ache ▷*ail* PANE

painful *adj.* aching, throbbing, sore, agonizing ★**painless**

painstaking *adj.* scrupulous *Carly kept a scrupulous record of all she spent,* careful, diligent, particular ★**negligent**

paint *v.* colour, draw, daub, varnish, stain

painting *n.* drawing, illustration, picture, mural, design, fresco

pair *n.* couple, brace, two, twins, twosome, duo PARE, PEAR

pal *n.* chum, friend, mate, buddy, crony ▷*comrade* ★**enemy**

palace *n.* castle, château, stately home *In Britain you can visit stately homes belonging to the aristocracy,* mansion

pale *adj.* pallid, ashen, pasty, colourless, faint, feeble, white ★**ruddy** PAIL

pallid *adj.* ashen, colourless, livid *The man had a livid scar across his forehead,*

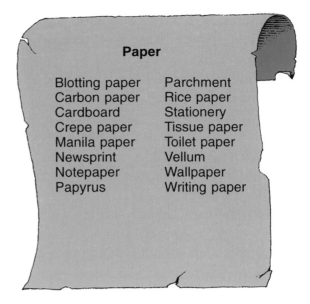

Paper

Blotting paper	Parchment
Carbon paper	Rice paper
Cardboard	Stationery
Crepe paper	Tissue paper
Manila paper	Toilet paper
Newsprint	Vellum
Notepaper	Wallpaper
Papyrus	Writing paper

waxen, chalky, wan, sallow ▷*pale*

paltry *adj.* petty, mean, shabby, trifling, pitiable, trashy ★**significant**

pamper *v.* humour, indulge, coddle, fondle ▷*spoil* ★**neglect**

pan *n.* container, saucepan, casserole ▷*pot*

pandemonium *n.* uproar, clatter, row, turmoil, bedlam, rumpus, din, chaos *The ice storm reduced the airline schedule to total chaos* ▷*noise* ★**calm**

pander *v.* indulge, pamper, please, give in to

pane *n.* panel, glass, window PAIN

panel *n.* ① pane, rectangle, insert ② jury, group, committee, forum *There will be a forum of all the candidates before the election*

pang *n.* ache, throe, twinge, throb ▷*pain*

panic ① *n.* fright, alarm, fear, terror ② *v.* scare, frighten, startle, stampede ★**relax**

pant *v.* puff, snort, blow, gasp, heave

pantry *n.* larder, buttery, storeroom, cupboard

paper *n.* stationery, document, deed, article, dossier *The police have a dossier on all known criminals in this town*

parade ① *n.* procession, march, display ▷*pageant* ② *v.* display, exhibit, flaunt, show off

paralyse *v.* cripple, disable, incapacitate, deaden, stun

paramount *adj.* leading, chief, supreme, outstanding ▷*foremost* ★**minor**

paraphernalia *n.* baggage, equipment, gear

parasite *n.* sponger, hanger-on, leech, scrounger

parcel *n.* batch, bundle, lot ▷*package*

parched *v.* arid, scorched, withered, dry, thirsty, dehydrated

pardon *v.* excuse, forgive, acquit, condone, absolve ★**condemn**

pare *v.* skin, peel, uncover, strip, scrape, shave PAIR, PEAR

parent *n.* father, mother, guardian, begetter

park ① *n.* garden, green, grounds, pleasureground, woodland ② *v.* leave *You can leave your car outside our house,* position, station

parlour *n.* drawing-room, living-room, sitting room

parody *n.* caricature, burlesque, satire, imitation, lampoon, skit

parry *v.* avoid, avert, fend off, rebuff, repel

parsimonious *adj.* niggardly *The factory workers received a niggardly sum for their work,* sparing, miserly, stingy ▷*frugal* ★**generous**

part ① *n.* piece, fragment, portion, scrap ② *n.* character, role *My sister has a leading role in the play,* duty ③ *v.* separate, divide, detach ④ *v.* depart, quit, leave

partial *adj.* ① imperfect, limited, part, unfinished ② biased, favourable to, inclined

partially *adv.* incompletely, somewhat, in part

participate *v.* take part, share, co-operate

particle *n.* morsel, atom, bit, seed, crumb, grain, scrap, sliver

particular *adj.* ① choosy, fastidious, scrupulous ② strange, odd, peculiar ③ special, distinct, notable *Old John Cotton was one of the notable citizens of our city*

partly *adv.* in part, incompletely, to some degree, up to a point ★**totally**

partner *n.* colleague, associate, ally, helper

party *n.* ① function, celebration, festivity, rave-up, social ② group, faction *A small faction on the committee wanted the park to be closed,* body, rave-up

pass ① *v.* exceed, overstep, outstrip ② *v.* go by, elapse, proceed, flow, run, move, vanish ③ *v.* neglect, ignore ④ *n.* permit, ticket, passport ⑤ *n.* defile, gap, notch, passage

passage *n.* ① corridor, pathway, alley ② journey, cruise, voyage ③ sentence, paragraph, clause

passenger *n.* traveller, commuter, wayfarer

passing *adj.* casual, fleeting, hasty, temporary, brief ★**permanent**

passion *n.* desire, ardour, warmth, excitement, zeal ▷*emotion* ★**calm**

passionate *adj.* ardent, impetuous, fiery, earnest, enthusiastic ★**indifferent**

past ① *adj.* finished, ended, former, gone ★**present** ② *prep.* after, exceeding, beyond ③ *n.* history, yesterday ★**future** PASSED

paste *n.* glue, cement, gum, adhesive

pastime *n.* recreation, sport, fun, hobby, amusement, distraction, activity

pasture *n.* grass, field, meadow, mead

pat ① *v.* tap, caress, fondle, stroke, touch ② *adv.* timely, exactly *Celia arrived at exactly the right moment,* precisely

patch *v.* mend, repair, sew, darn, cobble

path *n.* way, track, road, route, course, footway, lane, bridleway

pathetic *adj.* pitiable, sad, wretched, miserable, poor, puny *We picked out the*

Paths and Passageways

Alley	Highway	Path
Avenue	Lane	Pavement
Boulevard	Mountain	Road
Freeway	pass	Street
Drive	Passage	Thoroughfare

puniest pup in the litter for a pet

patience *n.* endurance, perseverance, composure, calmness, restraint, fortitude ★**impatience** PATIENTS

patient *adj.* forbearing, long-suffering, persevering, understanding ★**impatient**

patriotic *adj.* loyal, nationalistic, public-spirited, jingoistic

patrol *v.* police, watch, guard, protect, tour

patronize *v.* ① assist, encourage, foster, buy from ② talk down to, condescend

pattern *n.* ① model, standard, prototype ② arrangement, decoration, ornament

pause ① *v.* halt, cease, suspend, stop, delay ② *n.* lull, intermission, break, interruption, breathless, stoppage PAWS

pay ① *v.* reward, award, support, compensate, discharge ② *n.* payment, salary, wages, compensation

peace *n.* harmony, calm, concord, serenity, quiet, tranquillity *We spent the day in total tranquillity down by the lake* ★**tumult** PIECE

peaceful *adj.* serene, quiet, restful, harmonious ▷*tranquil* ★**disturbed**

peak *n.* summit, apex, top, crown, pinnacle

peal *v.* ring, strike, toll, knell, clang, chime, resound PEEL

peasant *n.* farmer, rustic, bumkin, countryman, yokel

peculiar *adj.* ① singular, odd, curious, unusual, uncommon, strange ② unique, private, special, distinctive

peddle *v.* sell, hawk, canvas, trade, vend, retail, tout

pedestal *n.* base, stand, plinth, support

pedlar *n.* hawker, street-trader

peel ① *v.* skin, strip, pare, scale ② *n.* skin, covering, rind, coat PEAL

peep *n. & v.* glimpse, blink, look ▷*peer*

peer ① *v.* peep, stare, look, gaze ② *n.* aristocrat, lord, noble ③ *n.* equal, fellow, counterpart PIER

peerless *adj.* unequalled, unique, beyond compare, unbeatable

peevish *adj.* cross, childish, grumpy, crusty, irritable ▷*testy* ★**good-tempered**

peg *n.* hook, knob, pin, post, hanger, fastener

pelt ① *v.* beat, bombard, thrash, throw ② *v.* rain cats and dogs, teem, pour ③ *n.* skin, hide, fleece, fur

pen ① *n.* quill, ballpoint ② *n.* cage, coop, hutch, stall ③ *v.* write, autograph, scribble

penalty *n.* fine, forfeit, punishment, price ★**reward**

pending *adj.* awaiting, unfinished, doubtful, uncertain, undecided, in the balance

penetrate *v.* ① pierce, perforate, stab, permeate *The aroma of lilacs and roses permeated the house* ② discern, see through, comprehend

penetrating *adj.* ① sharp, perceptive, understanding ② shrill, stinging

pennant *n.* flag, streamer, bunting, banner

penniless *adj.* destitute, needy, poverty-striken ▷*poor* ★**wealthy**

pensive *adj.* thoughtful, reflective, wistful, preoccupied, meditative

people ① *n.* folk, society, the public, populace, inhabitants ② *v.* populate, inhabit, settle

pep *n.* punch, energy, high spirits, vigour ▷*vitality*

peppery *adj.* ① biting, caustic *I'm afraid your essay wasn't very good; the teacher made some very caustic comments,* hot-tempered, angry ② hot, pungent, sharp

perceive *v.* feel, sense, observe, notice, make out, understand ▷*see*

perch ① *v.* alight, settle, sit, squat, roost ② *n.* rod, pole, staff, roost ③ *n.* fish

perfect ① *adj.* (*per*-fect) absolute, ideal, sublime, excellent, splendid, faultless ★**imperfect** ② *v.* (per-*fect*) complete, finish, fulfil, refine

perforate *v.* puncture, drill, punch, penetrate

perform *v.* ① carry out, do, fulfil, accomplish ② play, act, stage, present *The local drama group will present a new play next week*

performer *n.* actor, player, singer, entertainer, artist

perfume *n.* scent, essence, aroma, odour

perhaps *adv.* possibly, perchance, maybe, conceivably

peril *n.* hazard, jeopardy, menace, risk, insecurity ▷*danger* ★**safety**

period *n.* spell, time, duration, term, interval, course, span, age

periodical ① *n.* magazine, publication, journal, gazette, review ② *adj.* regular, routine, recurring, repeated

perish *v.* die, pass away, wither, disintegrate, expire, shrivel

perky *adj.* bouncy, bright, cheerful, lively ▷*sprightly* ★**dull**

permanent *adj.* endless, ageless, timeless, constant ▷*durable* ★**fleeting**

permission *n.* authorization, sanction, privilege, warrant *The police have a warrant for your arrest* ★**prohibition**

permit ① *v.* (per-*mit*) allow, grant, agree, empower ② *n.* (*per*-mit) warrant, licence, pass

perpendicular *adj.* upright, erect, sheer, steep, vertical ★**horizontal**

perpetrate *v.* commit, do, inflict, perform, practise, execute, carry out

perpetual *adj.* everlasting, ceaseless, eternal, never ending ▷*endless* ★**fleeting**

perplex *v.* mystify, baffle, bewilder, confound ▷*puzzle* ★**enlighten**

persecute *v.* harass, molest, plague, badger ▷*bother* ★**pamper**

persevere *v.* persist, hold out, hang on, endure, continue ★**give up**

persist *v.* remain, stand fast, abide, carry on ▷*persevere* ★**stop**

persistent *adj.* tenacious, relentless, stubborn, obstinate ★**weak**

person *n.* individual, human, being, type, somebody, personage, character

personal *adj.* individual, intimate, private, special, peculiar

personality *n.* individuality, character, disposition, nature

perspective *n.* outlook, aspect, proportion

perspire *v.* sweat, exude, ooze

persuade *v.* convince, wheedle, blandish, entice, cajole *I cajoled my mother into buying me a new swimsuit,* induce ▷*coax* ★**discourage**

pert *adj.* saucy, flippant, jaunty, cheeky, brash ★**shy**

perturb *v.* upset, disturb, trouble, distress, fluster ▷*bother* ★**reassure**

peruse *v.* read, study, pore over, browse, inspect, scrutinize, examine

pervade *v.* penetrate, permeate, spread, saturate, suffuse

perverse *adj.* contrary, wayward, opposite, disobedient ▷*stubborn* ★**reasonable**

pessimist *n.* defeatist, killjoy, wet blanket, cynic *Uncle Bert is a real cynic; he even thinks the lottery is fixed* ★**optimist**

pessimistic *adj.* cynical, dismal, fatalistic, defeatist, downhearted ★**optimistic**

pest *n.* nuisance, plague, blight, curse, vexation, bug, scourge

pester *v.* nag, hector, badger, annoy, disturb, harass ▷*bother*

pet ① *v.* fondle, caress, baby, cosset, cuddle ② *n.* favourite, beloved, dear ③ *adj.* endearing, cherished, dearest

petition *n.* plea, appeal, entreaty, round robin, request

petrified *adj.* spellbound, frightened, scared, terrified

petty *adj.* ① paltry, cheap, inferior, trifling ▷*trivial* ★**important** ② mean, measly, stingy

petulant *adj.* fretful, displeased, querulous, irritable ▷*peevish*

phantom ① *n.* apparition, spectre, spook, ghost ② *adj.* spooky, ghostly, imaginary

phase *n.* aspect, appearance, angle, view, period, point FAZE

phenomenal *adj.* remarkable, outstanding, marvellous, miraculous, incredible

phenomenon *n.* marvel, rarity, curiosity, sensation, spectacle

philanthropic *adj.* charitable, kind, generous, humane, benevolent, bountiful, public-spirited ★**selfish**

philosophical *adj.* calm, cool, logical, thoughtful, impassive, unruffled

phobia *n.* dread, fear, awe, neurosis, hang-

Pine

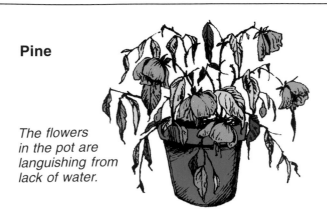

The flowers in the pot are languishing from lack of water.

up *My father has a hang-up about bats; he can't stand them,* horror

phrase *n.* expression, idiom, saying, utterance, sentence FRAYS

physical *adj.* ① material, substantial, solid, concrete ② bodily, personal, sensible

pick ① *v.* select, choose, single out, gather ② *n.* pike, pickaxe

picket ① *n.* patrol, scout, sentinel, lookout, guard ② *n.* post, rail, panel, fence ③ *v.* strike, demonstrate, blockade

pickle ① *n.* preserve ② *n.* difficulty, predicament ③ *v.* cure, salt, preserve, souse

picture ① *n.* painting, tableau, portrait, illustration, drawing ② *n.* movie, film ③ *v.* illustrate, imagine, fancy

picturesque *adj.* attractive, artistic, pictorial, scenic

piece *n.* portion, fragment, lump, morsel, bit ▷*scrap* PEACE

pier *n.* wharf, dock, quay, jetty PEER

pierce *v.* perforate, drill, bore ▷*penetrate*

piercing *adj.* ① loud, deafening, shrill, penetrating ② keen, sharp, cutting

pigment *n.* colour, dye, hue, paint, stain

pile *n. & v.* heap, mass, stack, load, store

pilfer *v.* purloin, rifle, rob, filch ▷*steal*

pilgrim *n.* traveller, wanderer, wayfarer

pilgrimage *n.* excursion, journey, mission, tour, trip, crusade

pillage *v.* plunder, ravage, loot, ransack *Thieves broke into the museum and ransacked all the cases,* rifle

pillar *n.* column, shaft, tower, obelisk, monument

pillow *n.* cushion, bolster, support

pilot *n.* ① guide, steersman, coxswain, helmsman ② aviator, flyer

pimple *n.* zit, blemish, swelling, boil

pin ① *n.* fastener, clip, spike, peg ② *v.* fix, fasten, attach, join, tack

pinch ① *v.* nip, squeeze, crush, tweak ② *v.* pilfer, steal ③ *n.* dash, drop, splash ④ *n.* crisis, difficulty, jam

pine *v.* hanker, yearn, long for, languish *The flowers in the pot are languishing from lack of water,* sicken

pinnacle *n.* summit, top, crest, peak, apex

pioneer *n.* founder, leader, trail-blazer, explorer, innovator

pious *adj.* devout, godly, holy, moral, religious, virtuous, reverent

pipe ① *n.* tube, duct, passage, hose, conduit ② whistle, flute

piquant *adj.* appetizing, spicy, tangy, savoury, pungent

pique *v.* annoy, displease, irritate, affront, VEX PEAK

pirate ① *n.* corsair *In days of old the ships in the Mediterranean were often raided by corsairs,* buccaneer, privateer, sea-rover ② *v.* copy, plagiarize, steal

pistol *n.* gun, revolver, automatic PISTIL

pit *n.* ① hole, hollow, crater, trench, mine ② dent, dimple, depression

pitch ① *v.* fling, throw, cast, sling, toss ② *v.* fall, drop, descend ③ *v.* raise, set up, erect ④ *n.* angle, slope, degree ⑤ *v.* sales message

pitcher *n.* jar, beaker, crock, jug, ewer, vessel

piteous *adj.* pitiful, heartbreaking, mournful ▷*pathetic*

pitiless *adj.* merciless, unmerciful, cruel, unrelenting ★**merciful**

pity ① *n.* mercy, compassion, charity, tenderness ② *v.* spare, forgive, grieve for, sympathize with

pivot ① *n.* axle, axis, hinge, turning point, spindle, swivel ② *v.* revolve, rotate, turn, spin

placate *v.* appease, pacify, soothe, satisfy ▷*humour* ★**infuriate**

place ① *n.* spot, locality, site, situation, position ② *n.* house, apartment, residence

A
B
C
D
E
F
G
H
I
J
K
L
M
N
O
P
Q
R
S
T
U
V
W
X
Y
Z

Planets

The nine planets of our solar system travel around a star we call the Sun.

Earth
Jupiter
Mars
Mercury
Neptune
Pluto
Saturn
Uranus
Venus

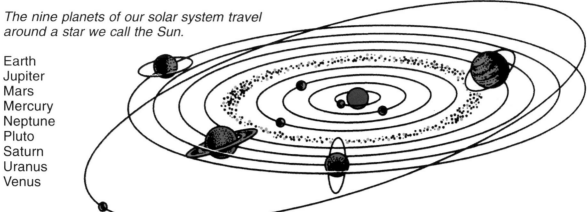

③ *v.* put, deposit, establish, allocate, arrange

placid *adj.* peaceful, quiet, serene, mild ▷*restful* ★**ruffled**

plague ① *n.* epidemic, disease, contagion, pest, blight ② *v.* persecute, pester *We were pestered by flies,* infest, annoy ▷*badger*

plain ① *adj.* unadorned, simple ② *adj.* obvious, clear, apparent ③ *adj.* blunt, direct, candid ④ *adj.* smooth, level, flat ⑤ *n.* prairie, plateau, tableland PLANE

plan ① *n.* design, chart, diagram, drawing ② *n.* project, proposal, arrangement, scheme ③ *v.* design, prepare, arrange, invent

plane ① *adj.* level, even, flat, smooth ② *n.* aircraft ③ *n.* smoothing tool PLAIN

planned *adj.* prepared, ready, arranged

plant ① *v.* sow, scatter, implant ② *v.* place, set, establish ③ *n.* herb, shrub, vegetable ④ *n.* equipment, machinery, factory

plaster ① *n.* cement, mortar, paste ② *n.* bandage, dressing ③ *v.* spread, smear, daub

plastic ① *adj.* mouldable, pliable, malleable, soft, supple ② *n.* thermoplastic

plate ① *n.* dish, platter, palette ② *n.* sheet, panel ③ *v.* laminate, cover, gild, anodize

platform *n.* rostrum *I was called up to the rostrum to receive my prize,* stage, stand, dais, podium

plausible *adj.* believable, credible, convincing, glib, persuasive ★**unlikely**

play ① *v.* sport, gambol, frisk, romp, frolic ② *v.* perform, act, represent ③ *n.* drama, performance ④ *n.* sport, amusement, recreation, diversion, pastime, hobby

player *n.* actor, sportsman, artist, musician, performer, contestant

playful *adj.* frisky, frolicsome, larky, lively, sportive ★**serious**

plead *v.* appeal, argue, ask, implore, request, beseech, entreat, beg

pleasant *adj.* affable, agreeable, cheerful, nice ▷*charming* ★**unpleasant**

please *v.* ① gratify, enchant, amuse, entertain ▷*delight* ② like, choose, wish, prefer, desire

pleased *adj.* delighted, gratified, satisfied ▷*contented* ★**annoyed**

pleasing *adj.* agreeable, enchanting, entertaining ▷*satisfying* ★**unpleasant**

pleasure *n.* delight, joy, amusement, entertainment, enjoyment ▷*fun* ★**trouble**

pledge ① *n.* promise, vow, undertaking, warrant, oath ② *v.* bind, contract, promise, undertake, vow

plentiful *adj.* lavish, ample, profuse, bountiful ▷*abundant* ★**scanty**

plenty *n.* enough, profusion, plethora ▷*abundance* ★**scarcity**

pliable *adj.* supple, flexible, pliant, malleable, mouldable, bendy ★**rigid**

plight *n.* predicament, difficulty, condition, dilemma *We made it to the railway station on time, but when we realized we had forgotten our tickets we were in a real dilemma,* jam

plod *v.* toil, labour, drudge, slog, grind

plot ① *n.* scheme, plan, intrigue ② *n.* story, narrative ③ *v.* hatch, intrigue, scheme

pluck ① *v.* gather, pick, pull, yank, catch ② *n.* courage, determination, bravery

plucky *adj.* courageous, daring, heroic, hardy ▷*brave* ★**feeble**

plug ① *n.* stopper, cork, bung ② *v.* stop, block, choke, cork ③ *v.* publicize, boost, promote, push

plum ① *n.* prize, bonus, treasure ② *adj.* best, choice, first-class

plump *adj.* buxom, stout, chubby, rotund, pudgy ★**skinny**

plunder ① *n.* booty, loot, swag, spoils ② *v.* fleece, rob, ransack, pillage, loot

plunge *v.* dive, pitch, submerge, duck, immerse, swoop, hurtle

poach *v.* ① pilfer, steal, filch, purloin ② steam, cook

pocket ① *n.* compartment, pouch, sack, bag ② *v.* filch, pinch, steal

poem *n.* ode, verse, rhyme, ballad, lyric

poetic *adj.* artistic, elegant, graceful, flowing, lyrical

poignant *adj.* moving, touching, pathetic, biting, penetrating

point ① *n.* spike, barb, pike, prong, end, tip ② *n.* locality, place, spot ③ *n.* aspect, object, aim, purpose ④ *n.* headland, cape, ness ⑤ *v.* aim, direct, level, train

pointless *adj.* meaningless, senseless, silly, vague, feeble ▷*absurd* ★**significant**

poise ① *n.* confidence, assurance, dignity, self-possession, balance ② *v.* stand, hover, brood over

poison ① *n.* venom, virus, toxin ② *v.* taint, fester, corrupt, infect

poisonous *adj.* deadly, evil, lethal *Don't touch those red berries; they're lethal,* noxious, toxic, venomous

poke *v.* jab, push, nudge, jostle, ram, thrust, stab, prod ▷*shove*

pole *n.* stick, stave, stake, rod, post, bar, mast, shaft, spar

policy *n.* rules, guidelines, course, action, practice, rule, procedure

polish ① *v.* burnish, buff, smooth, brighten, clean ② *n.* gloss, glaze, shine ③ *n.* refinement, grace, culture

polished *adj.* ① glossy, burnished, shiny ② refined, cultivated, cultured

polite *adj.* courteous, attentive, civil, well-bred, elegant, discreet ★**impolite**

poll ① *n.* election, vote, count, census, ballot ② *v.* survey, canvas, vote

pollute *v.* adulterate, debase, befoul, taint, poison, corrupt ★**purify**

pomp *n.* ceremony, show, splendour, pageantry, magnificence ★**simplicity**

pompous *adj.* showy, self-important, bombastic ▷*pretentious* ★**modest**

ponder *v.* meditate, consider, reflect, deliberate, think about

pool ① *n.* lagoon, pond, lake ② *n.* accumulation, funds, reserve, kitty ③ *v.* combine, contribute, share

poor *adj.* ① destitute, penniless, miserable ★**rich** ② low quality, faulty, feeble, shoddy *That shirt may be cheap, but it's shoddy and won't last* ★**superior**

poorly ① *adj.* ailing, ill, sick, seedy ② *adv.* badly, inexpertly, crudely ★**well**

pop *v.* ① bang, burst, crack, explode, go off ② slide, slip, insert

popular *adj.* ① well-liked, favourite, in favour, fashionable ② current, common, vulgar, prevailing

Poisonous Plants

Aconite
Baneberry
Belladonna
Black nightshade
Deadly nightshade
Foxglove
Hellebore
Hemlock
Henbane
Larkspur
Nux vomica
Poison ivy

A B C D E F G H I J K L M N O P Q R S T U V W X Y Z

pore *v.* scan, examine, peruse, scrutinize
POUR

portable *adj.* lightweight, convenient, transportable ▷*handy* ★**awkward**

portion *n.* piece, fragment, share, fraction, quota, ration, bit, measure ▷*part*

portly *adj.* plump, stout, fat, burly, bulky

portrait *n.* likeness, painting, picture, profile

portray *v.* describe, depict, represent, picture, illustrate, impersonate

pose ① *v.* stand, poise, posture, position ② *n.* position, stand, guise, stance *If you want to learn to play golf well, you need a good stance*

position *n.* ① spot, situation, location, place, site ② job, post ③ posture, attitude ④ rank, standing, status

positive *adj.* ① certain, sure, confident ★**doubtful** ② real, true, absolute ★**negative** ③ precise, definite, irrefutable, unmistakable, conclusive, explicit

possess *v.* have, own, hold, occupy ★**lose**

possessions *n.* wealth, assets, property, goods, belongings

possible *adj.* conceivable, imaginable, likely, feasible, attainable ★**impossible**

possibly *adv.* perhaps, maybe, perchance conceivably

post *n.* ① rail, pole, beam, banister, stake ② position, employment, job ③ mail

poster *n.* placard, bill, advertisement, sign

posterior *adj.* hind, behind, after, rear ★**front**

postpone *v.* put off, defer, shelve, adjourn ▷*delay* ★**advance**

posture *n.* bearing, stance, attitude, pose carriage, deportment

pot *n.* basin, bowl, pan, vessel, container, jar

potential ① *adj.* possible, probable, latent *The professor discovered that I had a latent talent for languages,* dormant, budding ② *n.* ability, talent, capacity, aptitude, power ▷*flair*

potion *n.* beverage, medicine, mixture, tonic, brew, draught

pouch *n.* bag, poke, sack, purse, pocket, wallet

pounce *v.* strike, lunge, spring, swoop, fall upon ▷*attack*

pound ① *v.* beat, batter, crush, hammer ② *n.* enclosure, compound, pen ③ *n.* sterling

pour *v.* spout, jet, gush, spill, cascade, rain
PORE

pout *v.* grimace, glower, sulk, scowl, mope ★**smile**

poverty *n.* ① distress, need, bankruptcy, privation ▷*want* ② scarcity, shortage ★**plenty**

powder ① *n.* dust, sand, ash, grit, bran ② *v.* pulverize, crunch, grind

power *n.* ① authority, command, control, ability ② energy, force, strength

powerful *adj.* mighty, vigorous, forceful ▷*strong* ★**weak**

practical *adj.* ① useful, effective, workable ② experienced, qualified, trained ▷*skilled* ★**impractical**

practice *n.* custom, ① habit, usage ② work, conduct, performance, action ★**theory**

practise ① *v.* carry out, apply, do, execute, implement ② rehearse, train ▷*perform*

praise ① *v.* acclaim, applaud, glorify, exalt ★**criticize** ② *n.* applause, flattery, compliment, approval ★**criticism** PRAYS, PREYS

prance *v.* gambol *I love to watch the lambs gambol in the spring,* frolic, romp, caper, swagger

prank *n.* trick, joke, antic, lark, jape, stunt

prattle *n. & v.* chatter, jabber, gossip, drivel, babble, witter

pray *v.* beg, beseech, entreat, implore, crave, solicit, request PREY

prayer *n.* petition, entreaty, worship, devotion, supplication

preach *v.* lecture, moralize, advocate *The president advocated a programme to feed the poor,* urge, proclaim

precarious *adj.* perilous, hazardous, insecure, dangerous ▷*risky* ★**safe**

precaution *n.* forethought, provision, anticipation, care, providence ▷*prudence*

precede *v.* lead, head, usher, go before, preface ★**follow**

Prey

Pray

precious *adj.* valuable, cherished, treasured, dear, beloved ▷*costly* ★**worthless**

precise *adj.* ① definite, exact, pointed, accurate, meticulous ② formal, particular, strict, rigid ★**vague**

precisely *adv.* absolutely, just so, exactly, correctly, literally

precision *n.* exactness, accuracy, care, detail, correctness

precocious *adj.* forward, fast, smart, clever ★**backward**

predicament *n.* situation, state, condition, embarrassment, fix ▷*plight*

predict *v.* foresee, foretell, prophesy, presage, divine

predominant *adj.* leading, main, powerful, superior, ruling, controlling ★**minor**

preen *v.* prance, swagger, strut, spruce up, doll up, groom

preface *n.* introduction, prelude, prologue, preamble, foreword

prefer *v.* choose, select, desire, like better, fancy ▷*favour* ★**reject**

prejudice ① *n.* bigotry, intolerance, bias, discrimination ② *v.* influence, warp, twist, distort, undermine ★**benefit**

prejudiced *adj.* biased *My opinion of Jessica is biased; she was very cruel to me once*, bigoted, one-sided, unfair, intolerant, narrow-minded, racist, sexist ★**fair**

preliminary *adj.* introductory, preparatory, opening, initial ★**final**

premature *adj.* untimely, previous, early, immature ★**late**

premeditated *adj.* calculated, planned, prearranged, intentional ★**spontaneous**

premier ① *n.* prime minister, first minister, head of government ② *adj.* chief, first, head, leading, principal

premises *n.* grounds, house, building, lands

prepare *v.* arrange, adapt, provide, get ready, concoct, plan ★**demolish**

preposterous *adj.* absurd, ridiculous, laughable ▷*unreasonable* ★**reasonable**

prescribe *v.* indicate, order, propose, recommend, specify

presence *n.* ① existence, appearance, aspect ② nearness, neighbourhood, proximity
PRESENTS

present ① *n.* (*pres*-ent) gift, donation, bounty, favour ② (*pres*-ent) *adj.* here, on the spot, ready, current ③ *v.* (pre-*sent*) offer, tender, bestow, award, exhibit

presently *adv.* soon, shortly, before long, immediately

preserve ① *v.* protect, safeguard, conserve, shield ▷*keep* ② *n.* jam, jelly, pickle

press ① *v.* bear down, depress, clamp, jam, compress, flatten ② *n.* printing machine ③ *n.* newspapers, reporters, journalism

pressure *n.* ① strain, tension, stress, urgency ② weight, compression, force

prestige *n.* repute, authority, weight, power

presume *v.* infer *I infer from your smile that you have passed your exam,* suppose, grant, take for granted, assume

presumptuous *adj.* arrogant, bold, audacious, insolent ▷*forward* ★**modest**

pretend *v.* ① make believe, simulate, sham, feign, masquerade ② aspire, claim, strive for ③ allege, profess

pretext *n.* excuse, pretence, guise, device

pretty *adj.* attractive, beautiful, comely,

A B C D E F G H I J K L M N O P Q R S T U V W X Y Z

dainty, bonny ▷*lovely* ★**ugly**

prevail *v.* obtain, overcome, predominate ▷*triumph* ★**lose**

prevalent *adj.* current, common, popular, in use, accepted ★**uncommon**

prevent *v.* avert, forestall, ward off, discourage, stop ▷*hinder* ★**help**

previous *adj.* former, prior, earlier, premature, untimely ★**later**

prey *n.* quarry, chase, booty, victim PRAY

prey on *v.* plunder, fleece, oppress, terrorize

price *n.* cost, amount, expense, payment, value, worth

priceless *adj.* ① invaluable, precious, cherished, costly ② amusing, comic, humorous, hilarious *The clown's antics were hilarious*

prick *v.* jab, jag, puncture, stab, pierce

pride *n.* conceit, vanity, egotism, self-importance, honour, exaltation, pleasure PRIED

prim *adj.* puritanical, demure, starchy, priggish ★**informal**

primary *adj.* first, original, chief, essential, fundamental

prime *adj.* ① principal, chief, basic, original ② best, finest, choice

primitive *adj.* ① simple, austere, crude ② uncivilized, savage, barbarous

principal ① *adj.* main, chief, head, leading, foremost ② *n.* head, leader, boss, director, manager, superintendent PRINCIPLE

principle *n.* ① law, regulation, rule, doctrine ② virtue, worth, integrity, rectitude *The president of the club was honoured by the mayor as a 'person of high moral rectitude'* ★**wickedness** PRINCIPAL

print ① *v.* impress, stamp, brand, publish ② *n.* impression, printing, imprint

prior ① *adj.* previous, former, earlier, preceding ② *n.* abbot, monk

prison *n.* jail, penitentiary, dungeon, lock-up

private *adj.* ① particular, personal, special, own ② solitary, remote *He spent his holidays on a remote island,* quiet ★**public**

privilege *n.* ① advantage, benefit, exemption

Printing

Collotype
Computer-setting
Cylinder press
Flatbed press
Intaglio
Letterpress
Linotype
Lithography
Monotype
Photogravure
Rotary press
Silk screen
Type
Web offset

② right, authority, entitlement, prerogative *It was the emperor's prerogative to pardon offenders*

prize ① *n.* reward, premium, trophy, honour ② *n.* booty, spoils, plunder ③ *adj.* best, champion, winning ④ *v.* value, appreciate, cherish ⑤ *v.* force, lever, pry, lift, raise PRIES

probable *adj.* likely, presumable, reasonable, possible ★**improbable**

probe *v.* ① poke, prod ② examine, investigate, scrutinize

problem ① *n.* puzzle, question, riddle, poser, quandary ② difficulty, dilemma, snag, complication, predicament

proceed *v.* ① advance, continue, go on, progress ★**recede** ② arise, flow, spring, emanate *A strong sulphurous odour emanated from the crater of the volcano*

process ① *n.* procedure, operation, movement, system, method ② *v.* convert, alter, handle, refine

procession *n.* parade, pageant, march, cavalcade, cortege

proclaim *v.* declare, announce, advertise, publish, expound

procure *v.* secure, acquire, win, gain, attain, get ★**lose**

prod *v.* goad, poke, nudge, incite, urge, shove, egg on

prodigal *adj.* extravagant, reckless, lavish ▷*spendthrift* ★**thrifty**

prodigious *adj.* ① miraculous, abnormal, amazing, remarkable ▷*extraordinary*

★**ordinary** ② huge, mighty ▷*enormous*
★**tiny**

produce ① *n.* (*pro*-duce) product, output, yield, crop, harvest ② *v.* (pro-*duce*) provide, yield, create, deliver, put forward

product *n.* output, crop, harvest, return, merchandise, commodity

profane *adj.* impious, blasphemous, unholy, worldly, sinful ★**sacred**

profess *v.* declare, avow, acknowledge, own

profession *n.* ① occupation, career, job, calling, employment ② avowal, admission

professional *adj.* skilled, efficient, experienced ▷*expert* ★**amateur**

proffer *v.* present, offer, tender, submit

proficient *adj.* competent, able, skilled, trained ▷*expert* ★**clumsy**

profit ① *n.* benefit, gain, advantage, acquisition ★**loss** ② *v.* improve, gain, reap, acquire ★**lose** PROPHET

profound ① *adj.* deep, penetrating, fathomless ② wise, shrewd, learned, sagacious *The leader of the tribe was old, wise and sagacious* ★**shallow**

profuse *adj.* bountiful, extravagant, exuberant, prolific, sumptuous ▷*lavish* ★**sparse**

progress ① *n.* (*prog*-ress) advancement, growth, development ★**decline** ② *v.* (pro-*gress*) advance, proceed, go, forge ahead, travel, grow, make headway

prohibit *v.* forbid, bar, deny, ban, obstruct, hinder ▷*prevent* ★**permit**

project ① *n.* (*pro*-ject) work, affair, plan, scheme, undertaking ② *v.* (pro-*ject*) propel, hurl, jut, protrude ③ *v.* contrive, scheme, plan ④ *v.* protrude, bulge out

prolific *adj.* fruitful, creative, productive, fertile ★**scarce**

prolong *v.* lengthen, stretch, draw out, spin out ▷*extend* ★**shorten**

prominent *adj.* ① famous, notable, distinguished ★**minor** ② projecting, standing out, bulging, jutting

promise ① *n.* commitment, undertaking, warrant, pledge ② *v.* agree, guarantee, vow

promote *adj.* ① cultivate, advance, assist

▷*encourage* ② dignify, elevate, upgrade, honour ★**degrade**

prompt ① *adj.* punctual, timely, quick, smart, ready ★**tardy** ② *v.* hint, remind, urge ▷*encourage* ★**deter**

prone *adj.* ① inclined, apt, liable, disposed ★**unlikely** ② prostrate *The poor fellow lay prostrate on the ship's deck,* face down, recumbent ★**upright**

pronounce *v.* ① speak, utter, say, articulate ② declare, decree, proclaim

pronounced *adj.* outstanding, striking, noticeable ▷*distinct* ★**vague**

proof *n.* evidence, testimony, confirmation, criterion, scrutiny ★**failure**

prop *n.* & *v.* stay, brace, truss, support

propel *v.* start, push, force, impel, send ▷*drive* ★**stop**

proper *adj.* ① correct, without error, right, accurate, exact ② respectable, decent, becoming, seemly ★**improper** ③ personal, own, special ★**common**

property ① *n.* possessions, wealth, chattels, buildings, belongings ② quality, virtue, characteristic, peculiarity

prophecy *n.* forecast, divination, prediction, prognostication

prophesy *v.* predict, foretell, foresee, declare

proportion ① *n.* ratio, percentage, part, fraction ② adjustment, arrangement

proposal *n.* proposition, offer, outline

propose *v.* ① put forward, offer, suggest ② ask for the hand of *Sir, I have the honour to ask you for the hand of your daughter in marriage,* pop the question

proprietor *n.* owner, possessor, landlady, landlord, leaseholder

prosaic *adj.* tedious, uninteresting, boring, dull, mundane, ordinary ★**interesting**

prosecute *v.* ① indict, put on trial, summon, sue ② continue, pursue, carry on, conduct ★**abandon**

prospect *n.* ① outlook, forecast, promise, expectation ② view, landscape, vista, aspect

prosper *v.* succeed, flourish, grow ★**fail**

prosperous *adj.* affluent, wealthy, rich, successful, thriving ★**unsuccessful**

protect v. defend, preserve, guard, secure, shelter, support ★**endanger**

protest ① v. (pro-*test*) complain, object, dispute, challenge ★**accept** ② n. (*pro*-test) objection, complaint, dissent, outcry

protracted adj. extended, drawn out, lengthy, prolonged ★**shortened**

protrude v. project, bulge, jut ★**recede**

proud ① adj. arrogant, haughty, supercilious, boastful ★**humble** ② lofty, majestic, noble, splendid ★**mean**

prove v. show, demonstrate, authenticate, confirm, verify ★**disprove**

provide v. supply, furnish, equip, contribute, afford ★**withhold**

province n. ① realm, sphere, orbit, place, department ② region, state, county

provoke v. prompt, incite, excite, enrage, inflame ▷*aggravate* ★**appease**

prowess n. ability, strength, might, bravery ▷*valour* ★**clumsiness**

prowl v. stalk *Somewhere in the darkness a large grey cat stalked its prey,* roam, slink

prudent adj. careful, cautious, discreet, shrewd ▷*thrifty* ★**rash**

prudish adj. strait-laced, narrow-minded, demure, priggish ▷*prim*

prune ① v. cut, shorten, trim, crop ② n. dried plum

pry v. snoop, peep, meddle, intrude

public ① adj. communal, civil, popular, social, national ② n. the people, the populace, society, the nation

publish v. broadcast, distribute, circulate, communicate, bring out, issue

pucker v. fold, crease, cockle, furrow, wrinkle ★**straighten**

puerile adj. callow, immature, juvenile

puff v. inflate, swell, blow, pant, distend

pull v. ① haul, drag, tow, heave ★**push** ② gather, pluck, detach, pick

pump v. ① inflate, expand, swell, fill, inject, siphon, draw ② interrogate, question, grill

punch v. ① strike, beat, hit, cuff ② puncture, pierce, perforate, bore

punctual adj. prompt, on time, precise, in good time, timely ★**tardy**

puncture n. perforation, hole, leak, wound

pungent adj. sharp, bitter, poignant, biting ▷*acrid* ★**mild**

punish v. chastise, correct, discipline, chasten, reprove, scold

puny adj. feeble, weak, frail, small, petty, stunted, insignificant ★**large**

pupil n. student, scholar, schoolchild, learner

puppet n. ① doll, marionette ② cat's-paw *The prisoner was not the true culprit, but only the ringleader's cat's-paw,* figurehead, pawn

purchase ① v. buy, procure, secure, obtain, get ▷*buy* ★**sell** ② n. bargain, investment

pure adj. ① immaculate, spotless, stainless, clear ▷*clean* ★**impure** ② virtuous, chaste, honest, blameless

purely adv. simply, barely, merely, only

purge v. ① purify, clean, scour, cleanse ② liquidate, exterminate, kill

purify v. clean, clarify, wash, purge

purloin v. rob, thieve, take, filch, pilfer ▷*steal*

purpose n. intent, design, will, goal, target

purse ① n. wallet, pouch, reticule, ② v. pucker, crease, compress, wrinkle

pursue v. ① follow, track, trace ▷*chase* ② practise, maintain, work for

pursuit n. ① hunt, chase, hue and cry ② occupation, hobby, interest *Stamp collecting has always been one of my main interests*

push ① v. shove, thrust, press, drive, propel ② n. advance, assault, drive

put v. ① set, place, deposit, repose, lay ② express, propose, state

put down v. ① write, jot down, record, note ② crush, humiliate, subdue ③ kill

put off v. ① postpone, defer, delay, adjourn ② dishearten, unsettle, perturb

putrid adj. decomposed, rotten, rancid, rank, stinking ★**wholesome**

puzzle ① v. baffle, confuse, mystify, perplex ▷*bewilder* ② n. conundrum, brainteaser, problem, dilemma

puzzling adj. baffling, curious, strange, bewildering ▷*peculiar*

pyromaniac n. arsonist, incendiary

Q q

quack *n.* impostor, charlatan *She pretended to tell fortunes by cards, but she was nothing but a charlatan,* humbug, fake

quaff *v.* imbibe, swallow ▷*drink*

quagmire *n.* bog, mire, marsh ▷*swamp*

quail *v.* tremble, flinch, shrink, cower, succumb ★**withstand**

quaint *adj.* curious, whimsical, fanciful, singular, old-fashioned, droll

quake ① *v.* tremble, quaver, shiver, quiver, shudder ② *n.* shock, convulsion, tremor *The tremors from the earthquake were felt hundreds of miles away*

qualification *n.* ① fitness, capacity, ability, accomplishment ② restriction, limitation, modification *The engineer's design was accepted with certain modifications*

qualify *v.* ① empower, enable, fit, suit ② moderate, limit, restrict

quality *n.* ① characteristic, condition, power ② excellence, worth, goodness

qualm *n.* doubt, misgiving, hesitation

quandary *n.* difficulty, doubt ▷*dilemma*

quantity *n.* amount, number, volume, sum

quarrel ① *n.* dispute, squabble, wrangle, disagreement ★**harmony** ② *v.* argue, bicker, brawl, squabble ★**agree**

quarry ① *n.* game, prey, object, victim, target ② mine, excavation, pit

quarter *n.* ① area, territory, place, district ② one-fourth ③ mercy *The commander of the invading army showed no mercy to the local defenders,* grace, lenience

quarters *n.* lodgings, dwelling, billet, rooms

quash *v.* abolish, nullify, suppress, overthrow, subdue

quaver *v.* shake, tremble, shiver, shudder, vibrate, oscillate, quake

quay *n.* pier, dock, wharf, landing, jetty KEY

queasy *adj.* bilious, squeamish, sick, faint

queer *adj.* strange, odd, whimsical, peculiar

quell *v.* crush, stifle, extinguish, defeat

quench *v.* ① douse *We carefully doused our campfire before leaving the site,* put out, cool, check ② slake *The cattle rushed to the river and slaked their thirst,* cool, allay

query ① *n.* question, doubt, objection ② *v.* ask, inquire, question, doubt ★**accept**

quest *n.* chase, hunt, search, pursuit, venture

question ① *n.* query, inquiry, interrogation, ② *n.* topic, problem, issue ③ *v.* ask, inquire, interrogate ★**answer**

questionable *adj.* doubtful, uncertain, undecided, unbelievable ★**certain**

queue *n.* ① row, line, procession, line-up ② pigtail, coil, braid, ponytail CUE

quibble *v.* argue, trifle, split hairs, carp *If you like our plan, don't carp about the details*

quick *adj.* ① speedy, rapid, express, swift ▷*fast* ② alert, active, agile, lively ★**slow** ③ clever, intelligent, acute ★**dull** ④ hasty, sharp, touchy ★**mild**

quicken *v.* accelerate ▷*hasten* ★**delay**

quiet ① *adj.* silent, soundless, noiseless, hushed ★**noisy** ② *adj.* placid, smooth, undisturbed ★**busy** ③ *n.* peace, rest, tranquillity, silence ★**tumult**

quilt *n.* blanket, cover, duvet, eiderdown

quip *n.* joke, gag, gipe, jest, wisecrack, retort

quirk *n.* pecularity, curiosity, foible *Despite his age and one or two foibles, old Uncle Fred was very agile,* mannerism ▷*habit*

quit *v.* ① cease, desist, stop ② leave, depart, relinquish ③ give up, surrender

quite *adv.* absolutely, altogether, wholly

quits *adj.* even *If I pay what I owe, it makes us even,* all square, level, equal

quiver ① *v.* tremble, quake, shiver, shudder ② *n.* holster, scabbard, sheath

quiz ① *v.* question, ask, examine, grill ② *n.* test, examination, contest *Barbara was the winner in the spelling contest*

quizzical *adj.* ① incredulous, sceptical, suspicious ② whimsical, teasing, amused

quota *n.* allowance, allocation, ration

quotation *n.* ① extract, selection, passage ② cost, estimate, price

quote *v.* recite, cite, recount, recollect, tell, mention

A
B
C
D
E
F
G
H
I
J
K
L
M
N
O
P
Q
R
S
T
U
V
W
X
Y
Z

R r

rabble *n.* crowd, mob, scum, riffraff

race ① *n.* competition, contest, chase, dash ② *n.* people, nation, folk, stock, breed, tribe ③ *v.* run, speed, hurry, scamper, gallop, sprint

rack ① *n.* shelf, stand, frame, framework ② *v.* distress, strain, torment, pain WRACK

racket *n.* ① uproar, noise, hubbub, tumult ▷*din* ② fraud, deception, swindle

racy *adj.* ① pungent, piquant, zestful ② spirited, smart, lively

radiant *adj.* ① brilliant, bright, luminous, shining ② splendid, glorious, happy ★**dull**

radiate *v.* ① gleam, sparkle, beam, shine ② emit, spread, diffuse

radical *adj.* ① extreme, fanatical, deep-seated ② original, fundamental *The new teacher made some fundamental changes in our lessons,* natural ★**superficial**

raffle *n.* draw, sweepstakes, lottery

rafter *n.* joist, girder, beam, support

ragamuffin *n.* scarecrow, urchin ▷*waif*

rage ① *n.* wrath, fury, ferocity, passion, madness ▷*anger* ② *v.* rave, fret, fume *The mad bull was fuming with rage as we leapt over the fence,* storm, flare up

ragged *adj.* shabby, seedy, shaggy, rough, torn ★**smart**

raid ① *n.* invasion, attack, strike, sortie ② *v.* attack, invade, ransack, maraud, descend on, plunder *The ship was attacked and plundered by pirates* RAYED

rail ① *n.* post, picket, fence, railing ② *v.* scold, rant, blast, reproach

rain *n. & v.* deluge, drizzle, flood, shower, torrent REIGN, REIN

raise *v.* ① elevate, lift, erect, hoist *The flag was hoisted as the ship came into port* ★**lower** ② excite, awaken, rouse ③ promote, increase, advance ④ cultivate, grow, breed RAZE

rake *v.* grope, scrape, collect, gather, assemble

rally *v.* ① meet, assemble, convene *The members of the club will convene next month* ★**disperse** ② encourage, restore, reunite

ram *v.* ① cram, crowd, push, pack, stuff, poke, wedge ② charge, beat, crash, drive

ramble *v.* ① stroll, meander, saunter, roam, rove ② chatter, digress *Joe's speech was very long, as he kept digressing from the point,* dodder

ramp *n.* gradient, slope, incline, grade

rampage ① *n.* storm, rage, riot, uproar, tumult ② *v.* rave, rush, run wild *Someone left the gate open, and the pigs ran wild in the cabbage patch*

ramshackle *adj.* unstable, shaky, unsteady, flimsy, rickety ▷*decrepit* ★**stable**

rancid *adj.* sour, curdled, rank, putrid, musty

rancour *n.* spite, grudge, animosity, hatred ▷*malice* RANKER

random *adj.* haphazard, vague, casual, accidental ▷*chance* ★**deliberate**

range ① *n.* extent, length, span, magnitude, area ② *n.* kind, sort, class, order ③ *v.* wander, rove, roam, stray

rank ① *n.* grade, class, position, level ② *adj.* foul, musty, offensive, coarse ③ *adj.* luxuriant, fertile, dense ④ utter, total, complete, absolute, out and out

rankle *v.* burn, smoulder, fester, be embittered

ransack *v.* plunder, pillage, search, scour

ransom ① *n.* release, deliverance, payoff, price ② *v.* rescue, redeem *Jill was lazy at school to begin with, but later redeemed herself with hard work,* liberate

rant *v.* rave, declaim, bluster, roar, shout

rap *v.* tap, pat, strike, knock

rape *v.* violate, abuse, assault, attack

rapid *adj.* speedy, quick, swift ▷*fast* ★**slow**

rapt *adj.* engrossed, intent, captivated, fascinated, delighted RAPPED, WRAPPED

rapture *n.* bliss, ecstasy, delight ▷*joy* ★**sorrow**

rare *adj.* ① unusual, uncommon, scarce, occasional ② valuable, fine, precious ★**common** ③ underdone, lightly cooked

rascal *n.* rogue, knave, villain, scamp, scoundrel, blackguard ★**gentleman**

rash ① *adj.* headstrong, audacious, hasty,

foolhardy ▷*reckless* ★**cautious** ② *n.*
eruption, outbreak, epidemic *There has
been an epidemic of chickenpox in our
neighbourhood*

rashness *n.* audacity, carelessness,
hastiness, recklessness ★**carefulness**

rasp ① *v.* file, grate, grind ② *v.* irk, irritate,
vex ③ *n.* file, tool

rate ① *n.* pace, tempo *It took us a while to
get used to the tempo of life in the city,*
velocity, speed ② *n.* tax, charge, cost ③ *v.*
appraise, assess, estimate, merit, value

rather *adv.* ① somewhat, to some extent, sort
of ② first, preferably, sooner

ration ① *n.* portion, share, allotment, helping
② *v.* allocate, allot, restrict, control

rational *adj.* ① sensible, sound, wise,
intelligent, sane ★**irrational** ② reasonable,
fair, proper ★**absurd**

rattle *v.* ① jangle, jingle, vibrate ② muddle,
confuse, daze ▷*bewilder*

raucous *adj.* harsh, hoarse, rough, strident,
gutteral, rasping, jarring

ravage *v.* devastate, destroy, pillage,
ransack, desolate, wreck

rave *v.* ① rant, ramble *The old man rambled
on for hours about his youth,* roar, rage,
storm ② favour, be ecstatic about

ravenous *adj.* hungry, starving, famished,
voracious ▷*greedy*

ravishing *adj.* beautiful, bewitching,
delightful, charming ▷*enchanting*

raw *adj.* ① uncooked ② unripe, green *I was
pretty green during the first six months in
the job,* inexperienced ③ sensitive, painful,
tender ④ cold, exposed, chilly

ray *n.* beam, gleam, glimmer, shaft, stream

raze *v.* demolish, destroy, flatten, obliterate,
ruin RAISE, RAYS

reach ① *v.* arrive at, gain, get to, attain,
grasp ② *v.* stretch, extend ③ *n.* extent,
length, grasp, distance, scope

react *v.* respond, reverberate *The sound of
the church bell reverberated through the
village,* behave, respond

read *v.* ① peruse, pore over, study, browse,
understand ② recite ③ record, register REED

Read

Reed

readily *adv.* easily, eagerly, freely, gladly,
promptly ★**reluctantly**

ready *adj.* ① prepared, alert, prompt, willing
★**reluctant** ② convenient, handy ★**remote**
③ skilful, facile, expert ★**clumsy**

real *adj.* ① genuine, authentic, factual
★**false** ② substantial, existent, actual
★**imaginary** REEL

realistic *adj.* ① authentic, lifelike
② practical, down-to-earth *Sue is a real
romantic type, but her boyfriend is much
more down-to-earth,* unromantic,
businesslike, matter of fact ★**fanciful**

realize *v.* ① understand, comprehend, feel
② earn, gain, obtain, acquire

really *adv.* truly, indeed, actually, absolutely

realm *n.* domain, province, sphere *My
mother has taken up writing and is very
involved in the sphere of books,* region,
territory, orbit, field

reap *v.* harvest, gather, obtain, realize,
derive, gain ★**squander**

rear ① *n.* back, end, tail, behind, posterior
② *adj.* hind, after, following ③ *v.* foster,
breed, educate ④ *v.* lift, raise, elevate

reason ① *n.* purpose, motive, basis, cause,
explanation ② *n.* wisdom, sense, intellect
③ *v.* consider, think, argue

reasonable *adj.* ① sensible, valid, rational
★**absurd** ② moderate, fair, just, modest
③ inexpensive, low-priced *Everything in
the new supermarket is low-priced*
★**excessive**

reassure *v.* inspire, hearten, convince ▷*encourage* ★**discourage**

rebate *n.* refund, repayment, discount, allowance, deduction

rebel ① *v.* (re-*bel*) revolt, mutiny, disobey, resist ② *n.* (*reb*-el) revolutionary, mutineer *Fletcher Christian was the leader of the mutineers on the* Bounty, traitor

rebellious *adj.* defiant, disobedient, mutinous, resistant ★**obedient**

rebuke *v.* reprimand, reproach, scold, tell off ★**praise**

recall *v.* ① recollect, remember ② cancel, overrule, countermand *We were just about to pull down the building when our orders were countermanded,* call back

recede *v.* ebb, retreat, flow back, decline, shrink, withdraw, return ★**proceed**

receipt *n.* acknowledgement, voucher

recent *adj.* late, new, fresh, novel, modern, current, up-to-date ★**out-of-date**

recently *adv.* lately, currently, latterly

receptacle *n.* container, holder, vessel, bowl

reception *n.* ① entertainment, function, party ② acceptance, acknowledgement

recess *n.* ① alcove, corner, socket, niche, slot, nook ② intermission, interlude, pause

recession *n.* slump, stagnation, depression, downturn ★**boom**

recipe *n.* formula, method *I'll show you my mother's method of making chocolate sponge cake; it never fails,* prescription

recite *v.* recount, chant, speak, declaim, relate, describe

reckless *adj.* unwary, incautious, daring, brash, heedless ▷*rash* ★**cautious**

reckon ① *v.* calculate, figure, count, tally *I have checked the accounts and my figures tally with yours,* account ② judge, expect, believe, fancy, surmise, guess

reclaim *v.* recover, redeem, reform, retrieve, restore, salvage

recline *v.* lounge, sprawl, lie, rest, loll, repose

recognize *v.* ① recall, recollect, remember, identify, know ② see *I will explain my idea slowly and you will see what I mean,* comprehend, understand

recoil *v.* ① rebound, backfire, boomerang ② falter, flinch, shrink, quail *My little brother quailed at the sound of the thunder*

recollect *v.* recall, recognize, place ▷*remember* ★**forget**

recommend *v.* suggest, advise, propose, commend, approve ★**veto**

recompense ① *n.* payment, compensation, remuneration ② *v.* reimburse, repay ▷*reward*

reconcile *v.* ① accept, harmonize, pacify, placate ★**estrange** ② adjust, settle, square

record ① *v.* (re-*cord*) note, register, enter, inscribe, list ② *n.* (*rec*-ord) album, disc, platter, CD, LP ③ chronicle, archive, almanac *We'll get hold of the almanac and check the time of high tide,* register ④ performance, championship

recount *v.* ① (re-*count*) relate, tell, recite, describe ② (*re*-count) count again

recover *v.* ① reclaim, retrieve, redeem, regain ② get better, recuperate, revive ★**worsen**

recreation *n.* pastime, sports, amusement, fun

recruit ① *n.* trainee, beginner, apprentice ② *v.* enlist, enrol, draft, mobilize

rectify *v.* correct, put right, repair, remedy, restore, mend, adjust

recuperate *v.* get better, rally, improve, mend ▷*recover* ★**worsen**

recur *v.* return, reappear, come back, repeat, revert, persist

redden *v.* crimson, colour, flush ▷*blush*

redeem *v.* ① buy back, compensate for, exchange ② save, liberate, free

reduce *v.* ① lessen, diminish, curtail, contract ② overcome, defeat, humiliate

reek *v.* smell, stink, fume, exhale, smoke

reel ① *v.* roll, rock, shake, stagger, falter, totter ② *n.* spool, bobbin, spindle REAL

refer *v.* relate, connect, associate, assign, belong, pertain

referee *n.* umpire, arbitrator, judge

reference *n.* ① allusion, insinuation, innuendo *From your innuendo, it seems that you think I'm joking!* ▷*hint* ② testimonial, recommendation, credentials

refine *v.* clarify, purify, filter, process, cultivate

refined *adj.* ① civilized, cultivated, cultured ▷*polite* ② purified, pure, clarified ★**coarse**

reflect *v.* ① think, contemplate, deliberate, consider ② mirror, copy, imitate, image

reform *v.* ① improve, correct ▷*rectify* ② remodel, reorganize, revamp

refrain ① *v.* avoid, abstain, forbear, resist, keep from ② *n.* chorus, melody, tune

refresh *v.* rejuvenate, renew, restore, cheer, enliven ★**exhaust**

refrigerate *v.* chill, cool, freeze

refuge *n.* haven, harbour, asylum, sanctuary ▷*shelter*

refugee *n.* exile, fugitive, emigrant

refund *v.* repay, rebate, reimburse *I must reimburse you for everything you spent on my behalf,* pay back, return

refuse ① *v.* (re-*fuze*) decline, say no, demur, repudiate ② *n.* (*ref*-use) trash, garbage, rubbish, waste

refute *v.* deny, dispute, disprove, discredit ★**prove**

regain *v.* recover, get back, retrieve, redeem

regal *adj.* royal, princely, majestic, noble, stately

regard ① *v.* esteem, revere, honour, respect ★**dislike** ② *v.* notice, observe, see, gaze ③ *n.* affection, esteem, fondness, repute ★**contempt**

regardless ① *adj.* heedless, neglectful, indifferent ★**careful** ② *adv.* anyhow, anyway, in any case

region *n.* area, zone, territory, locality, province, country

register ① *n.* roll, roster, record, archives *We can trace the town's history from the ancient archives* ② *v.* enter, record, inscribe, enrol, sign on

regret ① *v.* repent, rue, deplore, lament, mourn, apologize ★**welcome** ② *n.* remorse, sorrow, apology, grief

regular *adj.* ① normal, customary, periodical, formal ★**unusual** ② orderly, steady, unchanging ★**variable**

regulate *v.* ① control, manage, govern, determine ② adjust, measure, time, correct

regulation *n.* ① rule, law, command, bylaw

Rain

Rein

The club bylaws require us to elect a new secretary ② order, control, government

rehearse *v.* repeat, practise, drill, prepare, run through

reign ① *n.* rule, sway, power, control ② *v.* govern, rule, dominate, command RAIN, REIN

rein *v. & n.* bridle, hold, check, harness RAIN, REIGN

reinforce *v.* support, strengthen, toughen, harden, stiffen ★**weaken**

reject ① *v.* (re-*ject*) discard, get rid of, throw out, refuse, repel, deny ② *n.* (*re*-ject) cast-off, scrap

rejoice *v.* glory, exult, cheer, please, triumph ▷*delight* ★**lament**

relapse ① *v.* revert, backslide, turn back, recede ② *n.* repetition, recurrence, setback

relate *v.* describe, recount, tell, mention, detail

related *adj.* associated, allied, connected, linked, akin ★**different**

relative ① *n.* kinsman, kinswoman, cousin, relation, sibling *I have four siblings – three sisters and one brother* ② *adj.* comparative, approximate, relevant

relax *v.* diminish, loosen, ease, reduce, relieve, unwind ★**tighten**

relaxed *adj.* composed, cool, easy-going, mellow ▷*casual* ★**tense**

release *v.* let go, loose, liberate, acquit, discharge ▷*free* ★**detain**

relent *v.* relax, soften, yield, ease, give in, unbend ★**harden**

relentless *adj.* unmerciful, remorseless, grim, pitiless ▷*cruel* ★**humane**

relevant *adj.* applicable, pertinent, appropriate, apt ▷*suitable* ★**irrelevant**

reliable *adj.* dependable, trustworthy, responsible, honest ▷*sound* ★**unreliable**

relic *n.* fragment, vestige, antique, keepsake, memento *This brooch is a memento of my great-grandmother; she wore it often*

relief *n.* aid, assistance, respite, support, succour ▷*help* ★**aggravation**

relieve *v.* release, support, comfort, lighten, relax, console ★**aggravate**

religious *adj.* pious, devout, orthodox, devoted, God-fearing, faithful

relinquish *v.* renounce, let go, waive, disclaim, give up ▷*abandon* ★**retain**

relish ① *v.* enjoy, like, approve ▷*appreciate* ★**loathe** ② *n.* savour, flavour, tang, gusto *The fried chicken was a great success; everyone ate with gusto,* zest, sauce

reluctant *adj.* hesitant, averse, loth, disinclined, squeamish ★**willing**

rely on *v.* depend on, count on, believe in

remain *v.* ① stay, tarry, dwell, wait, rest ★**depart** ② persist, last, endure

remainder *n.* remnant, residue, leavings

remark *v.* ① utter, observe, state, mention ▷*say* ② notice, perceive, note ▷*see*

remarkable *adj.* unusual, surprising, curious, prominent ▷*outstanding* ★**ordinary**

remedy ① *n.* cure, restorative, medicine ② *n.* relief, solution, treatment, corrective ③ *v.* relieve, heal, cure, put right

remember *v.* recollect, recognize, think back ▷*recall* ★**forget**

remind *v.* suggest, hint, cue, prompt

remit *v.* ① relax, desist, slacken, modify, excuse, forgive ② pay, square, settle up

remnant *n.* residue, remains, rest, scrap, leftover ▷*remainder*

remorse *n.* regrets, contrition, pity

remote *adj.* ① distant, far, isolated ★**near** ② unrelated, alien, foreign ★**significant**

remove *v.* take away, transfer, withdraw, carry off

rend *v.* split, fracture, tear apart, sever, break

render *v.* ① give, present, surrender, deliver ② play, execute, perform

renew *v.* ① modernize, mend, prolong, renovate ② reissue *Next week we start to reissue some of the old silent films,* revive

renounce *v.* disown, disclaim, give up, repudiate, forsake ★**retain**

renowned *adj.* eminent, noted, famed, notable ▷*celebrated* ★**obscure**

rent ① *v.* hire, lease, let, charter ② *n.* tear, rip, break, crack, fissure ③ *n.* fee, payment

repair ① *v.* fix, mend, correct, remedy, rectify *We are sorry there was an error in your account; we will rectify it right away* ② *n.* restoration, adjustment

repast *n.* meal, food, snack, spread

repay *v.* ① refund, reimburse, pay ② avenge, retaliate, revenge, punish

repeal *v.* revoke, annul, abolish, quash *The man's innocence was proved and his sentence was quashed* ▷*cancel* ★**establish**

repeat *v.* duplicate, renew, reiterate, do again

repel *v.* ① repulse, deter, reject, push back ② revolt, disgust, nauseate ★**attract**

repellent *adj.* distasteful, hateful, discouraging ▷*repulsive* ★**attractive**

repent *v.* sorrow, deplore, grieve ▷*regret*

replace *v.* ① supersede, succeed, follow, substitute ② put back, reinstate, restore

replenish *v.* fill, refill, restock, furnish, provide, top up ★**empty**

replica *n.* facsimile, copy, likeness, duplicate

reply ① *v.* answer, respond, rejoin, retort, acknowledge ② *n.* answer, response, acknowledgement, riposte

report ① *n.* statement, account, message, communication, tidings ② *n.* noise, explosion, bang ③ *v.* tell, disclose, reveal, expose

repose ① *v.* rest, settle, lie down, sleep, recline ② *n.* ease, peace, quiet, tranquillity ★**tumult**

represent *v.* ① depict, picture, portray, illustrate ② stand for, mean, denote

a b c d e f g h i j k l m n o p q r s t u v w x y z

representative ① *n.* agent, delegate, envoy, deputy ② *adj.* typical, figurative

repress *v.* restrain, suppress, bottle up, smother, stifle

reprimand ① *v.* admonish, blame, rebuke ▷*chide* ② *n.* reproach, talking-to, scolding, telling off, dressing down ★**praise**

reproach *v.* scold, reprove, reprimand, blame ▷*rebuke* ★**approve**

reproduce *v.* ① copy, duplicate, imitate, simulate ② breed, multiply, generate

reprove *v.* reproach, reprimand ▷*rebuke* ★**approve**

repudiate *v.* renounce, disown, disavow, disclaim ★**acknowledge**

repugnant *adj.* unattractive, disagreeable, offensive ▷*repulsive* ★**pleasant**

repulse *v.* repel, rebuff, drive back, reject ▷*spurn* ★**attract**

repulsive *adj.* obnoxious, disgusting, loathsome ▷*repugnant* ★**attractive**

reputation *n.* standing, position, esteem, honour, good name

request ① *v.* demand, beg, entreat, beseech ▷*ask* ② *n.* petition, entreaty, invitation

require *v.* ① need, want, demand, crave ② expect, cause, instruct

rescue ① *v.* save, set free, liberate, recover, release ② *n.* liberation, deliverance, salvation *Salvation for the shipwrecked crew came when the coastguard lifted them to safety* ★**capture**

research *v.* examine, explore, investigate, inquire ▷*study*

resemble *v.* look like, mirror, take after, be like ★**differ**

resent *v.* resist, begrudge, dislike, take exception to ★**like**

resentful *adj.* offended, bitter, piqued, huffy ▷*indignant* ★**contented**

reserve ① *v.* hoard, retain, withhold ▷*keep* ② *n.* modesty, shyness, restraint ③ *n.* supply, backlog, stock

reservoir *n.* lake, spring, pool, container

reside *v.* live, occupy, inhabit, lodge ▷*dwell*

residence *n.* house, home, habitation, dwelling, mansion RESIDENTS

resign *v.* retire, abdicate, step down, give notice, abandon ▷*quit* ★**join**

resign oneself to *v.* accept, comply, reconcile *Robinson Crusoe became reconciled to loneliness on his island,* yield, give in ▷*submit* ★**resist**

resist *v.* withstand, oppose, defy, refrain, hinder ▷*thwart* ★**submit**

Rescue

Salvation for the shipwrecked crew came when the coastguard lifted them to safety.

resistance *n.* defiance, obstruction, opposition, hindrance ★**acceptance**

resolute *adj.* determined, resolved, obstinate, stubborn, dogged *Despite the bad weather, the climbers were dogged in their will to reach the peak* ★**weak**

resolve ① *v.* determine, intend, decide ② *v.* decipher, unravel, disentangle ③ *n.* resolution, purpose, will

resort ① *v.* frequent, haunt, visit ② *n.* alternative, chance, course ③ *n.* spa, watering place, hotel, holiday centre

resourceful *adj.* clever, ingenious, bright

respect ① *n.* esteem, honour, regard, repute, dignity ② *v.* esteem, honour, revere, venerate *The names of the pioneers and explorers will always be venerated*

respectable *adj.* decent, admirable, honest, honourable, proper ★**disreputable**

respectful *adj.* deferential, courteous, polite, dutiful ★**disrespectful**

respite *n.* break, halt, interval, lull, recess, let-up

respond *v.* answer, reply, retort, tally, accord, agree ★**differ**

A B C D E F G H I J K L M N O P Q R S T U V W X Y Z

responsible *adj.* ① accountable, dependable, sensible ▷*reliable* ★**unreliable** ② liable, guilty

rest ① *n.* repose, relaxation, peace, tranquillity ② *n.* break, pause, respite, spell ③ *n.* remainder, residue, balance ④ *v.* repose, settle, sleep, relax wrest

restful *adj.* peaceful, quiet, calm, placid ★**disturbing**

restless *adj.* uneasy, fitful, agitated, nervous, fretful ★**calm**

restore *v.* ① replace, reinstate, return ② refurbish, recondition, renovate *We renovated this old sofa which we found in a junk shop*

restrain *v.* stop, prevent, hold back, subdue ▷*check* ★**encourage**

restrict *v.* confine, limit, cramp, handicap ▷*regulate* ★**free**

result ① *n.* effect, consequence, outcome, end ★**cause** ② *v.* ensue, happen, turn out, follow, emerge, occur

resume *v.* renew, recommence, start again, go back to ▷*continue* ★**interrupt**

retain *v.* hold, restrain, withhold, detain ▷*keep* ★**relinquish**

retaliate *v.* avenge, reciprocate, fight back, repay, retort ★**submit**

retire *v.* ① retreat, go back ▷*withdraw* ★**advance** ② abdicate, resign, relinquish

retort ① *n.* riposte, reply, rejoinder ② *v.* return, answer, reply

retract *v.* recant, deny, disavow, take back, repudiate, revoke ★**maintain**

retreat ① *v.* retire, depart, shrink ▷*withdraw* ★**advance** ② *n.* sanctuary *This section of the park is being made into a bird sanctuary,* shelter, den, haven

retrieve *v.* redeem, recover, regain, rescue ▷*salvage* ★**lose**

return ① *v.* rejoin, come back, reappear ② *v.* restore, give back, repay, refund ③ *n.* form, tax form, document, list

reveal *v.* disclose, expose, show, display, uncover, divulge ★**hide**

revel ① *v.* make merry, celebrate, have fun ② *n.* celebration, gala, party, spree

revenge ① *n.* vengeance, reprisal, retaliation ② *v.* avenge, get one's own back

revenue *n.* income, receipts, earnings

revere *v.* honour, esteem, regard, adore, venerate, respect ★**despise**

reverse ① *v.* cancel, change, overrule, repeal, revoke ② *n.* adversity, disaster, bad luck, misfortune ③ *adj.* backward, contrary, opposite *We turned the car around and drove back in the opposite direction*

review ① *v.* reconsider, examine, survey ② *n.* inspection, examination ③ *n.* synopsis, journal, magazine REVUE

revise *v.* edit, amend, improve, rewrite, alter

revive *v.* awaken, rally, recover, refresh, restore, invigorate ▷*rouse*

revoke *v.* repeal, abolish *The principal refuses to abolish the school dress code,* cancel, quash, reverse, withdraw

revolt ① *v.* rebel, mutiny, riot ② *v.* nauseate, sicken, disgust ③ *n.* rebellion, uprising, revolution

revolting *adj.* obnoxious *The chemical factory's chimney was giving off obnoxious fumes,* repulsive, offensive ▷*repugnant* ★**pleasant**

revolve *v.* rotate, spin, gyrate, turn

reward ① *n.* award, payment, benefit, bonus, profit ★**punishment** ② *v.* compensate, repay, remunerate ★**punish**

rhyme *n.* verse, poem, ditty, ode RIME

rhythm *n.* beat, pulse, throb, stroke, timing

ribald *adj.* smutty, vulgar, coarse, gross

rich *adj.* ① wealthy, prosperous, affluent, opulent ★**poor** ② fertile, loamy, fruitful, abundant ★**barren** ③ delicious, sweet, luscious, delicate

rid *v.* get rid of, unburden, expel, free

riddle ① *n.* puzzle, cryptogram, enigma ② *v.* puncture, bore, perforate, pierce

ride ① *v.* sit, travel, drive, journey ② *n.* journey, jaunt, lift, trip

ridge *n.* ① groove, furrow, fold ② highland, chain, range *A range of hills could be seen in the distance*

ridicule ① *n.* scorn, derision, travesty, sarcasm, mockery ② *v.* deride, mock, jeer,

a b c d e f g h i j k l m n o p q r s t u v w x y z

Rivers and Waterways

Brook
Canal
Channel
Creek
Lake
Loch
Pool
Pond
Mere
River
Spring
Strait
Stream
Surf
Tide
Waterfall

banter *His banter can be amusing, but he doesn't know when to stop and sometimes offends people*

ridiculous *adj.* laughable, absurd, foolish, preposterous ▷*silly* ★**sensible**

rife *adj.* common, current, frequent, prevalent ▷*widespread* ★**scarce**

rifle ① *v.* loot, rob, plunder ▷*ransack* ② *n.* gun, musket, firearm

rift *n.* ① fissure, breach, crack, spilit, cleft ② disagreement, clash, break

right ① *adj.* correct, proper, true ★**incorrect** ② *adj.* honest, upright, fair ③ *adj.* seemly, fit, suitable, becoming ★**improper** ④ *n.* truth, justice, honesty ★**wrong** RITE, WRITE

righteous *adj.* honourable, upright, moral

rigid *adj.* ① stiff, firm, inflexible ② stern, austere, harsh ★**flexible**

rigorous *adj.* stern, severe, strict, rigid

rim *n.* border, margin, edge, verge *We knew we were on the verge of disaster,* brink

ring ① *n.* circle, band, collar ② *n.* bell, chime, tinkle ③ *v.* chime, strike, jingle, sound WRING

riot ① *n.* uproar, tumult, brawl, broil ★**calm** ② *v.* revolt, rampage, rebel

ripe *adj.* ① mellow, mature, seasoned ② developed, adult, full-grown

rise ① *v.* ascend, mount, soar, arise, grow ★**fall** ② *v.* appear, occur, happen ★**vanish** ③ *n.* ascent, advance, increase ★**fall**

risk ① *v.* chance, dare, hazard, gamble ② *n.* adventure, peril, danger, jeopardy ★**safety**

risky *adj.* perilous, chancy, dangerous, tricky, uncertain ★**safe**

rite *n.* custom, ritual, practice RIGHT

rival ① *adj.* opposing, competing, conflicting ② *n.* opponent, adversary ★**associate**

river *n.* stream, waterway, brook, torrent *Before the rains came, this torrent was only a trickle*

road *n.* street, avenue, drive, lane, highway, motorway, route, way RODE, ROWED

roam *v.* rove, ramble, range, stroll, wander

roar *v.* bellow, bawl, yell, blare, cry

rob *v.* cheat, defraud, loot, plunder ▷*steal*

robber *n.* bandit, brigand, thief, crook

robe *n.* costume, dress, gown, habit

robust *adj.* strong, healthy, lusty, sturdy ▷*vigorous* ★**delicate**

rock ① *n.* stone, boulder, cobble, pebble, crag, reef ② *v.* totter, reel, sway, falter ③ *v.* quiet, still, tranquillize, soothe

rod *n.* baton, stick, stave, pole, perch, cane

rogue *n.* rascal, blackguard, scamp, knave ▷*scoundrel* ★**gentleman**

role *n.* character, post, duty, function *At the end of the party, my function will be to clear up*

roll ① *n.* record, register, list ② *n.* spool, scroll, reel ③ *v.* revolve, rotate, turn ④ *v.* smooth, level, press ⑤ *v.* lurch, reel, pitch, ROLE

romance *n.* ① love story, novel, love affair ② adventure, excitement, fantasy, glamour

romantic *adj:* ① amorous, passionate, loving ② visionary, fanciful *Many people have a fanciful idea of how things were in the old days,* fantastic, extravagant ★**ordinary**

romp *v.* gambol, caper, frolic, prance, play

roof *n.* ceiling, covering, cover, canopy

room *n.* ① apartment, chamber, area, compartment, salon ② space, capacity

A
B
C
D
E
F
G
H
I
J
K
L
M
N
O
P
Q
R
S
T
U
V
W
X
Y
Z

root *n.* ① seed, source, radicle ② basis, element, stem, origin

rope *n.* cable, cord, hawser, line, lasso

rosy *adj.* ① cheerful, encouraging, hopeful, optimistic ② pink, flesh-coloured

rot ① *v.* corrupt, crumble, decay, perish ② *n.* bunkum *The last speaker at the meeting was talking a lot of bunkum,* balderdash, bosh, poppycock, claptrap

rotate *v.* revolve, turn, spin, pivot, gyrate

rotten *adj.* ① decayed, putrid, decomposed, fetid ② deplorable, despicable, nasty, vicious ③ ill, poorly, grotty

rough *adj.* ① wrinkled, craggy, coarse, shaggy, broken ② rude, crude, imperfect ③ blunt, gruff, brusque, discourteous RUFF

round ① *adj.* circular, rotund, spherical ② *n.* ring, circle, loop

rouse *v.* ① waken, arouse, excite, disturb ② anger, inflame, incite ★**calm**

rout *v.* crush, defeat, conquer, overthrow

route *n.* road, track, way, journey, direction

routine *n.* usage, practice, formula, technique, method, habit *After being alone for so long, I have got into the habit of talking to myself*

rove *v.* tramp, roam, wander, stroll, drift

row ① *n.* (ro) string, line, queue, rank, column ② *v.* paddle, scull ROE ③ *n.* (rhymes with *now*) fight, squabble, noise, quarrel, dispute, tiff ★**calm**

rowdy *adj.* rough, unruly, boisterous, noisy, wild, riotous ★**quiet**

royal *adj.* sovereign, princely, stately, majestic ▷*regal*

rub *v.* stroke, brush, scrub, wipe, polish

rubbish *n.* debris, trash, junk, garbage, refuse, waste

rude *adj.* ① coarse, primitive, ill-bred, impolite, boorish, bad-mannered ② crude, formless ★**polished** ROOD, RUED

rue *v.* be sorry for, deplore, grieve ▷*regret*

ruffian *n.* hoodlum, hooligan, lout, scoundrel, rogue, ▷*rascal*

ruffle *v.* ① fluster, worry, excite, agitate ② crumple, rumple, crease

ruffled *adj.* upset, worried, flustered

Rulers, Monarchs, and Leaders

Caesar	Prime
Czar	Minister
Czarina	Prince
Emperor	Princess
Empress	Queen
King	Rajah
Mikado	Sultan
Mogul	
Pharaoh	
President	

rugged *adj.* ① rough, craggy, shaggy, ragged ② rigorous, robust, strong, strenuous

ruin *v.* ① demolish, wreck, damage, smash ② bankrupt, impoverish, overwhelm

rule ① *v.* control, govern, command, manage, direct ② *v.* decide, determine, judge ③ *n.* law, regulation ④ *n.* straight-edge

ruler ① *n.* leader, director, king, queen, monarch, governor ② rule, straight-edge

rumble *v.* roar, thunder, boom, roll

rumour *n.* hearsay, report, gossip, scandal *The bribery scandal, added to high taxes, brought down the government*

rumpus *n.* uproar, racket, riot, commotion, hurly-burly ★**calm**

run ① *v.* hurry, hasten, speed, sprint ★**saunter** ② *v.* leak, flow, ooze ③ *v.* operate, propel, drive ④ *n.* race, sprint, spurt, dash, rush

run away *v.* escape, flee, bolt, abscond ★**stay**

rupture *v. & n.* break, burst, puncture, split

rural *adj.* rustic, countrified, pastoral, agrarian ★**urban**

ruse *n.* dodge, hoax, scheme, trick, ploy RUES

rush *v. & n.* dash, speed, hurry, scramble, stampede, rampage ★**saunter**

rust *n.* corrosion, mould, blight, mildew, stain, deterioration

rustic *adj.* rural, pastoral, country, homely, simple, sylvan

rustle *n. & v.* crackle, swish, murmur, whisper

rut *n.* furrow, channel, groove, score, track

ruthless *adj.* cruel, savage, harsh, ferocious, pitiless ★**merciful**

S s

sack ① *n.* bag, pouch, pack ② *v.* rob, plunder, pillage ③ discharge, dismiss, lay off SAC

sacred *adj.* holy, blessed, hallowed, spiritual, consecrated, review ★**profane**

sacrifice ① *n.* offering ② *v.* forfeit, give up, relinquish ▷*abandon*

sad *adj.* sorrowful, melancholy, unhappy, mournful, woeful ▷*sorry* ★**happy**

sadden *v.* mourn, grieve, distress, lament, dismay, dishearten ★**please**

safe ① *adj.* secure, protected, sure ★**unsafe** ② *n.* vault, coffer, cash-box, strongbox

safety *n.* shelter, security, sanctuary, protection, refuge ★**danger**

sag *v.* bend, curve, bow, decline, flag, slump ▷*droop* ★**bulge**

sage ① *adj.* wise, sensible, shrewd, sagacious ★**foolish** ② *n.* wise person, savant *We were taught by an old savant of the university, Professor Hankins, philosopher* ★**fool**

said *adj.* expressed, stated

sail *v.* cruise, voyage, navigate, float, skim, weigh anchor SALE

sailor *n.* seaman, seafarer, mariner, jack tar, seadog, yachtsman, yachtswoman

sake *n.* motive, reason, purpose, object, principle

salary *n.* pay, earnings, reward, wages, income, emolument

sale *n.* auction, transaction, selling, trade, disposal SAIL

sally *n.* jest, joke, crack, riposte ▷*quip*

salute ① *v.* greet, accost, welcome, hail, honour ② *n.* greetings, welcome, acknowledgement

salvage *v.* save, conserve, rescue, restore, reclaim ▷*preserve* ★**abandon**

same *adj.* ① identical, duplicate, alike, similar ② aforesaid, aforementioned *I leave all my possessions to my wife, the aforementioned Angela Gomez*

sample ① *n.* specimen, example, model, pattern, illustration ② *v.* inspect, try, taste

sanction *v.* permit, allow, authorize, approve

sanctuary *n.* retreat, shelter, shrine, asylum, haven ▷*refuge*

sane *adj.* normal, rational, reasonable, lucid ▷*sensible* ★**insane**

sap *v.* bleed, drain, exhaust, reduce, weaken ★**strengthen**

sarcastic *adj.* biting, cutting, sardonic, cynical, ironic, caustic *My cousins made some caustic remarks after I played the violin*

satire *n.* invective, sarcasm, burlesque, ridicule, parody

satisfaction *n.* contentment, delight, gratification, compensation ★**grievance**

satisfy *v.* gratify, fulfil, appease, suit, please ▷*delight* ★**disappoint**

saturate *v.* soak, steep, drench, souse, waterlog *I am afraid that old canoe is too waterlogged ever to be used again*

saucy *adj.* forward, pert, impudent, cheeky, disrespectful ★**civil**

saunter *v.* roam, loiter, wander, linger, dawdle, amble ▷*stroll* ★**hasten**

savage ① *adj.* barbaric, wild, uncivilized, ferocious, brutal ★**civilized** ② *n.* brute, oaf, barbarian

save *v.* ① liberate, set free, rescue, protect,

Sacred Books

Apocrypha	Koran
Bhagavad-Gita	Talmud
Bible	Torah
Book of Mormon	Tripitaka
Book of Common Prayer	Upanishad
Granth	Veda

A
B
C
D
E
F
G
H
I
J
K
L
M
N
O
P
Q
R
S
T
U
V
W
X
Y
Z

guard ② keep, preserve, salvage, hoard, put aside ★**squander**

savoury *adj.* appetizing, flavourful, luscious, agreeable ★**tasteless**

say *v.* speak, utter, state, pronounce, talk, tell, assert

saying *n.* proverb, statement, adage, idiom, maxim, aphorism

scale ① *n.* measure, balance, calibration ② *n.* crust, plate, flake ③ *n.* clef, key *I will play this next piece in the key of C,* mode ④ *v.* climb, ascend, clamber up

Scales

Scale

scamp *n.* knave, rogue, rascal, scoundrel, scallywag *Someone rang our doorbell, but when I opened the door, the scallywag had gone*

scamper *v.* hurry, run, scurry, hasten, sprint, scoot, fly ▷*rush*

scan *v.* examine, glance at, scrutinize, pore over ▷*check*

scandal *n.* disgrace, libel, slander, offence, infamy, rumour, discredit ★**honour**

scanty *adj.* meagre, insufficient, sparse, inadequate, poor, scant ★**plenty**

scar ① *n.* blemish, mark, stigma, wound ② *v.* brand, damage, disfigure

scarce *adj.* rare, infrequent, sparse, scanty, uncommon ★**common**

scarcity *n.* lack, deficiency, dearth, rarity, infrequency ★**abundance**

scare *v.* frighten, startle, shock, alarm, dismay ★**reassure**

scatter *v.* spread, disperse, strew, broadcast, sow, shower, disseminate ▷*sprinkle* ★**collect**

scene *n.* sight, spectacle, vision, view, exhibition, landscape SEEN

scent ① *n.* aroma, tang, fragrance, smell, odour ② *v.* detect, sniff, smell CENT, SENT

sceptical *adj.* doubtful, unbelieving, incredulous ▷*dubious* ★**convinced**

schedule *n.* timetable *We checked the timetable before buying our train tickets,* programme, catalogue, diary

scheme *n.* plot, plan, project, design, proposal, idea

scholar *n.* ① pupil, student, schoolchild, learner ② intellectual *That café is a favourite gathering place for intellectuals,* savant, academic

scholarly *adj.* learned, educated, literate, cultured ★**illiterate**

scoff *v.* sneer, mock, deride, jeer, ridicule

scold *v.* rebuke, admonish, reprove, find fault with ▷*chide* ★**praise**

scoop ① *v.* bail, ladle, spoon, excavate, gouge, hollow ② exclusive, coup, inside story

scope *n.* extent, margin, compass, range, latitude, field

scorch *v.* sear, burn, singe, blister, shrivel

score *v.* ① cut, mark, scratch ② register, record, win

scorn ① *n.* mockery, disdain, ridicule, disregard ② *v.* despise, mock, spurn, slight

scoundrel *n.* rascal, knave, thief, rogue, villain ▷*vagabond* ★**gentleman**

scour *v.* ① cleanse, rinse, scrub, purge ② search, seek, ransack, rake

scourge ① *v.* beat, whip, thrash, cane ② *n.* curse, evil, misfortune, plague ★**blessing**

scowl *v. & n.* frown, glower, grimace, glare ★**smile**

scramble ① *v.* clamber, climb ② *v.* jostle, struggle, swarm, push ③ *n.* turmoil, bustle, confusion ★**order**

scrap ① *n.* piece, morsel, bit, portion, fragment, grain ② *v.* abandon, discard, junk

scrape ① *v.* scratch, groove, abrade, file, grate, scour ② *n.* predicament, fix, difficulty

scratch *v. & n.* wound, cut, mark, score

scream *v. & n.* screech, cry, shriek, howl, yell

screen ① *n.* awning *Before the ceremony, an awning was erected over the entrance to the hotel,* canopy, shade, protection ② *v.* protect, hide, conceal, veil

screw *v.* twist, turn, wrench, tighten, compress

scribble *v.* write, scrawl, scratch, doodle

scribe *n.* writer, penman, clerk, historian

script *n.* handwriting, manuscript, text, words, libretto *Sir Arthur Sullivan wrote the music for* The Mikado, *and W. S. Gilbert wrote the lyrics and libretto*

scrub ① *v.* scour, brush, mop, cleanse ② *n.* brushwood, undergrowth

scruffy *adj.* messy, dirty, frowzy, seedy, shabby, sloppy ▷*slovenly* ★**neat**

scrumptious *adj.* delightful, delicious, appetizing, exquisite

scrupulous *adj.* painstaking, particular, rigorous, strict, conscientious ★**careless**

scrutinize *v.* examine, inspect, peruse, study

scuffle *v. & n.* tussle, skirmish, fight, struggle, squabble

scum *n.* dross, foam, froth, dregs, crust

scuttle *v.* ① scramble, scamper, scoot, hurry ② destroy, smash, wreck

seal ① *n.* signet, stamp ② *n.* cork, bung, closure ③ *n.* sea mammal ④ *v.* fasten, close, shut, stop

seam ① *n.* ridge, scar, lode, furrow ② hem, pleat, tuck SEEM

search ① *v.* seek, quest, hunt, trail, track, scour, explore ② *n.* exploration, probe investigation, quest, pursuit

season ① *n.* period, time, occasion, term ② *v.* accustom, acclimatize, mature ③ *v.* flavour, spice, salt

seat ① *n.* bench, chair, stool, sofa, couch, throne ② *n.* headquarters, place, site ③ *v.* accommodate, locate, place

secret *adj.* mysterious, hidden, concealed, obscure, private ★**public**

section *n.* division, group, department, segment, portion

secure ① *adj.* safe, protected ② *adj.* confident, certain, sure, stable ★**uncertain** ③ *v.* fasten, protect, close, lock ★**unfasten** ④ *v.* acquire, procure, obtain ★**lost**

sedate *adj.* staid, sober, demure, earnest ▷*steady* ★**flippant**

see *v.* ① behold, witness, sight, observe ② heed, examine, watch, note ③ understand, comprehend, know SEA

seedy *adj.* shabby, squalid, poor, grubby, unkempt ▷*slovenly* ★**spruce**

seek *v.* look for, search, inquire, endeavour, hunt, strive

seem *v.* appear, look like, sound like, look as if SEAM

seemly *adj.* fit, suitable, proper, decent, decorous ★**unseemly**

seethe *v.* simmer, fizz, bubble, boil, foam

seize *v.* grasp, snatch, take, clutch, arrest ▷*grab* ★**abandon** SEAS, SEES

seldom *adv.* rarely, infrequently, hardly, scarcely ★**often**

select ① *adj.* choice, preferred, fine, prime *All the fruit on the trees in the orchard is in its prime,* first-class ★**common** ② *v.* choose, pick out, single out, prefer

selfish *adj.* greedy, self-centred, narrow, illiberal ▷*stingy* ★**generous**

sell *v.* vend, market, retail, trade, peddle, barter, deal in ★**buy**

send *v.* transmit, dispatch, forward, mail, direct ★**detain**

send for *v.* command, order, summon, request ★**dismiss**

sensation *n.* ① feeling, perception, impression, awareness ② excitement, commotion, scandal

sensational *adj.* exceptional, scandalous, lurid ▷*exciting* ★**ordinary**

sense *n.* ① sensation, impression, feeling ② understanding, mind, tact, intellect ③ wisdom, significance, meaning CENTS

senseless *adj.* silly, stupid, absurd, unwise ▷*foolish* ★**sensible**

sensible *adj.* ① wise, intelligent, astute, shrewd ② reasonable, rational ③ conscious, aware, mindful ★**senseless**

sensitive *adj.* ① susceptible, responsive, acute, impressionable *Because Rachel is at such an impressionable age, her mother does not want her to see the film* ② thin-skinned, touchy, irritable, tender

sentence *n.* ① phrase, clause ② judgement, decision, condemnation, doom, irritable

sentimental *adj.* romantic, tender, emotional

separate ① *adj.* disconnected, apart, detached ★**united** ② *v.* detach, part, divide, break, disconnect ★**unite**

sequel *n.* continuation, consequence, result, outcome, follow-up

serene *adj.* tranquil, calm, peaceful, undisturbed, clear ★**tempestuous**

series *n.* sequence, progression, succession, run, string

serious *adj.* grave, earnest, solemn, thoughtful, severe, grim ★**trivial**

serve *v.* attend, assist, aid, oblige, help, officiate, act

service *n.* ① aid, help, assistance, attendance, employment ② ceremony, rite *Stuart is at college studying the marriage rites of the Incas*

set ① *n.* group, pack, outfit, series ② *v.* settle, put, place, seat, locate ③ *v.* stiffen, congeal, harden ④ *adj.* decided, resolved, determined, fixed

setback *n.* defeat, delay, problem, snag, hold-up ★**advantage**

settle *v.* ① establish, regulate, fix ② pay, liquidate, finish ③ populate, colonize ④ live, dwell, reside

several *adj.* various, numerous, sundry, separate, assorted

severe *adj.* strict, rigid, unkind, hard, austere ▷*stern* ★**lenient**

sew *v.* stitch, tack, baste, fasten sow

shabby *adj.* torn, ragged, mean, shoddy, tacky ▷*squalid* ★**neat**

shack *n.* hut, cabin, shanty, shed, hovel

shackle *v.* & *n.* manacle, handcuff, chain, rope, fetter

shade *n.* ① shadow, gloom, darkness, dusk ② blind, awning, screen ③ colour, tint, hue, tone ④ ghost, spirit, wraith *Out of the darkness, a wraithlike figure loomed up before us*

shadow ① *n.* shade ② *v.* follow, stalk, tail

shady *adj.* ① shadowy, shaded ★**sunny**

② crooked, infamous, disreputable ★**honest**

shaft *n.* ① pillar, column, support ② hilt, handle, rod ③ mine, pit, well, tunnel

shaggy *adj.* hairy, tousled, unkempt, rough, dishevelled ★**smooth**

shake *v.* flutter, tremble, throb, shudder ▷*quiver*

shallow *adj.* ① not deep ② trivial, empty, silly, empty-headed ★**profound**

sham *adj.* false, imitation, counterfeit, forged, fake ▷*bogus* ★**genuine**

shame *n.* & *v.* dishonour, discredit ▷*disgrace*

Ships and Boats

Gondola

Catamaran

Kayak

shameful *adj.* disgraceful, scandalous, outrageous ▷*disreputable* ★**honourable**

shape ① *n.* form, structure, outline, pattern ② *v.* form, fashion, make, create

share ① *v.* allot, divide, participate, co-operate ② *n.* portion, allotment, allowance

sharp *adj.* ① acute, keen, pointed ② clear, distinct, clean-cut ③ painful, severe, intense ④ pungent, acrid, acid ⑤ alert, shrewd, acute ▷*clever* ★**dull**

shatter *v.* smash, wreck, break, fracture, ruin ▷*destroy*

shave *v.* shear, crop, slice, shred, graze, trim

shear *v.* fleece, strip, cut ▷*shave* SHEER

sheath *n.* scabbard, quiver, holster, holder, case, casing

shed ① *n.* hut, barn, lean-to, shanty ② *v.* cast off, moult *Our parrot is moulting and is leaving feathers all over the carpet,* spill ③ *v.* beam, radiate

sheepish *adj.* timid, diffident, foolish, embarrassed, shamefaced ★**unabashed**

sheer *adj.* ① absolute, simple, pure, unmixed ② transparent, filmy, thin ③ steep,

Ferry

Motorboat

Liner

abrupt, perpendicular *The trail ended at the foot of a huge, perpendicular cliff* SHEAR

shell *n.* pod, case, husk, hull, shuck, crust

shelter ① *n.* roof, sanctuary, safety, home, retreat, cover ② *v.* shield, cover, protect, screen ★**expose**

shield *n. & v.* guard, screen, safeguard ▷*shelter*

shift ① *v.* alter, move, change, displace, remove ② *n.* turn, spell, stint

shifty *adj.* untrustworthy, devious, treacherous ▷*wily* ★**honest**

shine *v. & n.* glow, gleam, glitter, sparkle, flash

ship ① *n.* boat, barge, craft, vessel ② *v.* export, send, transport *(see page 114)*

shirk *v.* dodge, avoid, shun, evade, slack

shiver *v.* quaver, quiver, shake, shudder ▷*tremble*

shock ① *n.* blow, jolt, clash, collision ② *n.* scare, start, turn ③ *v.* stupefy, daze, stun

shocking *adj.* scandalous, awful, frightful ▷*horrible* ★**agreeable**

shoot *v.* ① fire, discharge, bombard, propel ② *v.* germinate *We grew some beans in a glass jar and watched them germinate,* grow, bud, sprout ③ *n.* bud, twig, sprout CHUTE

shop ① *n.* store, market, emporium ② *v.* buy, market, purchase

shore ① *n.* beach, coast, strand, seashore, seaside ② *v.* prop, support, bolster up

short *adj.* ① brief, concise, condensed ★**long** ② deficient, incomplete, scanty ★**full** ③ sharp, severe, bad-tempered ④ small, puny, squat, diminutive, tiny ★**tall**

shortcoming *n.* defect, fault, flaw, inadequacy, ▷*weakness*

shorten *v.* cut, crop, abbreviate, lessen ▷*diminish* ★**lengthen**

shortened *adj.* abbreviated, abridged, condensed ★**enlarged**

shortly *adj.* presently, soon, before long, directly

shout *n. & v.* cry, scream, roar, shriek, cheer, whoop, bellow

shove *v.* push, jostle, prod, nudge, move, propel ★**pull**

show ① *v.* display, parade, exhibit, flaunt, reveal ★**hide** ② *v.* prove, testify to, demonstrate ③ *v.* explain, teach, instruct ④ *n.* exhibition, display, ceremony, play

shower ① *v.* scatter, spray, sprinkle, rain ② *n.* downpour, cloudburst ③ *n.* barrage, volley, discharge

shred ① *n.* particle, piece, scrap, tatter, fragment ② *v.* tear, rip, strip

shrewd *adj.* profound, deep, discerning ▷*wise* ★**obtuse**

shriek *n. & v.* screech ▷*shout*

shrill *adj.* treble, high-pitched, screeching, ear-piercing

shrink *v.* ① contract, dwindle, shrivel, become smaller ② flinch, cringe, recoil, withdraw

shrivel *v.* wither, contract, wrinkle, decrease, pucker, parch ▷*wilt*

shudder *v.* shake, quake, tremble ▷*quiver*

shuffle *v.* ① mix, jumble, rearrange ② hobble, limp

shun *v.* avoid, elude, ignore, spurn, steer clear of ★**accept**

shut *v.* fasten, close, secure, slam, bar, latch, lock ★**open**

shut up *v.* ① imprison, cage, intern ② be silent, hold one's tongue, be quiet

shy ① *adj.* bashful, diffident, timid, wary, shrinking ★**bold** ② *v.* flinch, quail, recoil

sick *adj.* ① ill, poorly, ailing, unwell, feeble ② weary, fed up, displeased ③ nauseated

side *n.* ① border, edge, flank, margin, half ② party, sect, group, team SIGHED

sift *v.* strain, drain, separate, screen, sieve, riddle

sigh *v.* ① grieve, lament, moan, complain ② wheeze, breathe

sight ① *n.* appearance, spectacle, scene, mirage ② *n.* seeing, perception, visibiity ③ *v.* behold, glimpse, observe CITE, SITE

sign ① *n.* symbol, emblem, mark ② *n.* omen, token ③ *n.* signboard, signpost, placard ④ *v.* endorse, autograph, inscribe

signal ① *n.* beacon *As soon as the ships*

were sighted, beacons were lit all along the coast, sign, flag, indicator ② *adj.* distinguished, impressive, outstanding

significant *adj.* symbolical, meaningful, weighty ▷*important* ★**unimportant**

signify *v.* denote, indicate, suggest, imply ▷*mean*

silence *n.* quiet, hush, peace, tranquillity ★**noise**

silent *adj.* hushed, noiseless, soundless, still, mute ▷*quiet* ★**noisy**

silly *adj.* absurd, senseless, stupid, fatuous, childish, puerile ▷*foolish* ★**wise**

similar *adj.* resembling, alike, harmonious, common ▷*like* ★**different**

simple *adj.* ① elementary, plain, uncomplicated ▷*easy* ② trusting, open, naive ★**intricate**

simply *adv.* ① merely, purely, barely, solely, only ② easily, directly

sin ① *n.* misdeed, wrong, vice, evil, wickedness ② *v.* err, offend, trespass, stray, do wrong

since ① *conj.* because, as, for, considering ② *prep.* subsequently, after

sincere *adj.* true, unaffected, frank, open, truthful ▷*genuine* ★**insincere**

sing *v.* vocalize, warble, yodel, trill, croon, chant, carol, hum, chirp

singe *v.* scorch, burn, scald, sear, char

singer *n.* vocalist, minstrel, songster, chorister, crooner

single *adj.* ① one, only, sole ② solitary, alone, separate ③ unmarried, celibate *The priests of the Roman Catholic Church are celibate*

singular *adj.* odd, peculiar, curious, surprising ▷*unusual* ★**ordinary**

sinister *adj.* menacing, threatening, unlucky, disastrous ▷*evil* ★**harmless**

sink ① *v.* drop, dip, descend, decline ▷*fall* ★**rise** ② *n.* basin, drain

sit *v.* perch, seat, squat, roost, rest, settle

site *n.* spot, plot, locality, place, station, post ▷*situation* CITE, SIGHT

situation *n.* ① position, location, place, site, whereabouts, standpoint ② predicament,

Singers

Alto
Baritone
Bass
Basso profundo
Cantor
Chorister
Contrabass
Contralto
Countertenor
Mezzo-soprano
Prima donna
Soprano
Tenor
Treble
Vocalist

plight, state of affairs, condition

size *n.* ① dimensions, proportions, measurement ② magnitude, bulk, volume, weight SIGHS

sketch ① *n.* drawing, picture, cartoon ② *n.* draft, blueprint, outline ③ *v.* draw, portray, depict, outline, delineate

skilful *adj.* adroit, able, adept, dexterous, expert, competent ▷*clever* ★**clumsy**

skill *n.* ability, expertness, knack, facility ▷*talent*

skim *v.* brush, touch, graze, float, glide

skimp *v.* stint, scrimp, economize, scrape

skin *n.* peel, rind, hide, husk, pelt

skinny *adj.* thin, lean, scraggy, weedy ★**fat**

skip *v.* ① jump, hop, dance, caper ② pass over, miss, disregard, omit

skirmish *n. & v.* scuffle, fight, affray, scrap, combat, clash, set-to

skirt ① *n.* petticoat, kilt ② *n.* border, hem, edge, margin ③ *v.* border, flank, evade, avoid

skulk *v.* lurk, hide, cower, slink, sneak

slab *n.* board, stone, boulder, piece, chunk

slack *adj.* ① limp, flabby, loose, relaxed ★**tight** ② lazy, sluggish ▷*idle* ★**busy**

slander *v.* libel, malign, accuse, abuse ▷*defame* ★**praise**

slaughter ① *v. & n.* incline, angle, list ▷*slope*

slap *v.* smack, whack, strike, hit, spank

slash *v. & n.* cut, slit, gash, hack, rip

slaughter *v.* slay, butcher, massacre ▷*kill*

slave ① *n.* bondsman, bondswoman, serf, vassal, drudge, captive ② *v.* drudge, toil, labour, grind

slavery *n.* bondage, enslavement, serfdom, servility, drudgery, captivity ★**freedom**

slay *v.* murder, massacre ▷*kill* SLEIGH

sleek *adj.* shiny, smooth, glossy, slick

sleep *v. & n.* snooze, nap, doze, drowse, repose, slumber

slender *adj.* ① narrow, thin, fine, slight ▷*slim* ★**thick** ② trivial, inadequate, meagre, scanty

slice ① *v.* shred, shave, cut, strip, segment ② *n.* segment, piece, cut, slab

slick *adj.* ① shiny, smooth ▷*sleek* ② glib, suave, plausible

slide *v.* slip, slither, glide, skim, skate

slight ① *adj.* delicate, tender ▷*slender* ② *adj.* small, little, meagre, trifling, trivial ★**significant** ③ *n. & v.* snub, insult, disdain

slim *adj.* fine, slight, thin ▷*slender* ★**fat**

slime *n.* mire, ooze, mud, filth

sling ① *v.* hurl, toss, throw ② *n.* loop, bandage, strap, support

slink *v.* prowl, creep, sidle, sneak ▷*skulk*

slip ① *v.* slide, slither, glide ② *v.* fall, lurch, drop, slip over ③ *v. & n.* blunder, slip up

slippery *adj.* ① smooth, glassy ② cunning, untrustworthy, tricky ▷*shifty* ★**trustworthy**

slit *v.* gash, cut, rip ▷*slash*

slogan *n.* motto, catchword, war cry, saying

slope ① *n.* slant, grade, gradient, incline, ascent, descent, rise ② *v.* lean, incline, descend, ascend

sloppy *adj.* ① careless, slipshod, inattentive ▷*slovenly* ② dowdy, messy, tacky ③ dingy, dirty ④ schmaltz, sentimental, slushy

slot *n.* recess, opening, hole, groove

slovenly *adj.* slipshod, careless, negligent, disorderly, sloppy, untidy, dowdy

slow ① *adj.* inactive, tardy, late, slack, leisurely ▷*sluggish* ★**fast** ② *v.* slow down, slacken, lose speed, relax ★**accelerate** SLOE

sluggish *adj.* slothful, lazy, inactive, languid, indolent, lifeless ▷*idle* ★**brisk**

slumber *v.* snooze, doze ▷*sleep* ★**awaken**

sly *adj.* cunning, tricky, furtive, sneaky, artful ▷*wily* ★**frank**

smack *v.* slap, strike, spank ▷*hit*

small *adj.* ① minute, tiny, slight, diminutive ▷*little* ★**large** ② trivial, petty, feeble, paltry, inferior

smart ① *adj.* alert, bright ▷*intelligent* ② *adj.* elegant, neat, spruce, dressy ★**dull** ③ *v.* sting, burn, throb ▷*ache*

smash *v.* break, hit, destroy, wreck, demolish, destroy, defeat, crush

smear *v.* plaster, daub, coat, varnish, cover, spread, smudge

smell *n.* aroma, fragrance, scent, perfume, stink, stench, odour, tang

smile *v.* grin, simper, smirk, beam ▷*laugh*

smoke ① *n.* vapour, mist, gas ② *v.* fume, reek, whiff, smoulder, vent

smooth ① *adj.* level, even, flat, plain, sleek ★**rough** ② *v.* flatten, level, press

smother *v.* choke, throttle, stifle, restrain

smudge *n. & v.* mark, smear, blur, stain, blight, daub

smug *adj.* self-satisfied, content, holier-than-thou, complacent, conceited

smut *n.* dirt, smudge, blot, spot, smear

snack *n.* lunch, repast, morsel, bite

snag *n.* catch, complication, drawback, hitch

snap *v.* ① break, crack, snip ② snarl, growl

snare ① *v.* trap, catch, seize, net ② *n.* trap, noose, pitfall

snatch *v.* seize, grab, clutch, grip, take, pluck, grasp

sneak ① *v.* slink, prowl, crouch ▷*skulk* ② *n.* wretch, coward, informer

sneer *v.* jeer, scoff, gibe, scorn, ridicule, taunt, deride

sniff *v.* smell, breathe in, inhale, scent

snivel *v.* weep, cry, blub, sniffle,

snobbish *adj.* condescending, snooty, lofty, patronizing, stuck-up

snoop *v.* pry, eavesdrop, peep, peek, sneak

snooze *v.* doze, nap, slumber ▷*sleep*

snub *v.* slight, slur, spurn, cut ▷*humiliate*

snug *adj.* cosy, sheltered, secure, safe,

restful, close-fitting ▷*comfortable*

so *adv.* accordingly, thus, therefore, likewise SEW, SOW

soak *v.* moisten, wet, douse, saturate, steep

soar *v.* glide, fly, rise, hover, tower SORE

sob *v.* lament, cry, sigh ▷*weep*

sober *adj.* temperate, abstemious *Uncle Arthur was very abstemious and never drank anything alcoholic,* calm, composed, serious, sombre ★**excited**

sociable *adj.* companionable, affable, friendly, genial ★**withdrawn**

social *adj.* neighbourly, civic, public ② convivial ▷*sociable*

soft *adj.* ① pliable, plastic, flexible, supple ★**hard** ② kind, gentle, mild ▷*tender* ★**harsh** ③ low, faint, quiet ★**loud**

soften *v.* ① melt, dissolve, mellow ★**solidify** ② moderate, diminish, quell

soil ① *n.* earth, dirt, mould, clay, loam ② *v.* foul, dirty, sully, taint

sole *adj.* only, single, lone, one SOUL

solemn *adj.* ① grim, serious ▷*sombre* ② impressive, stately, sedate ★**frivolous**

solid *adj.* ① steady, firm, stable, sturdy ② dense, compact, hard ★**soft**

solidify *v.* congeal, harden, clot, cake, set ★**soften**

solitary *adj.* alone, lonely, remote, separate, only

solution *n.* ① blend, mixture, brew, fluid ② answer, explanation, key

solve *v.* unravel, untangle, elucidate ▷*explain* ★**complicate**

sombre *adj.* dark, serious, solemn, grim, gloomy, funereal ★**bright**

some *adj.* any, more or less, about, several SUM

sometimes *adv.* at times, from time to time, occasionally

somewhat *adv.* in part, a little, not much

song *n.* air, tune, carol, ballad, ode, ditty *The new pop song was based on an old sailors' ditty*

soon *adv.* presently, shortly, before long

soothe *v.* pacify, appease, mollify, ease, lull, comfort ★**irritate**

Soar

Sore

sordid *adj.* shabby, miserable, dirty, base, sleazy, tawdry ▷*squalid*

sore ① *adj.* tender, aching, painful, inflamed ② *adj.* annoyed, upset, grieved ③ *n.* ulcer, boil, carbuncle SOAR

sorrow ① *n.* grief, woe, remorse, anguish ★**joy** ② *v.* mourn, grieve, lament ★**rejoice**

sorrowful *adj.* sad, disconsolate, mournful, dejected ★**joyful**

sorry *adj.* ① pained, grieved, hurt, dejected, doleful ★**glad** ② wretched, mean, poor, shabby ★**delighted**

sort ① *n.* kind, type, variety, group, class ② *v.* sift, arrange, catalogue, classify

soul *n.* spirit, substance, mind, vitality, fire, essence SOLE

sound ① *n.* noise, din, tone ★**silence** ② *v.* blare, blast *We were startled by a blast from the trumpets,* blow ③ *adj.* hearty, virile, whole, perfect ▷*healthy* ★**unfit**

sour *adj.* ① tart, rancid, bitter, acid ★**sweet** ② morose, peevish ▷*harsh* ★**genial**

source *n.* origin, spring, fount, cause, beginning, wellhead

souvenir *n.* token, memento, keepsake, reminder, relic

sow ① *n.* (rhymes with *how*) female pig ② *v.* (rhymes with *mow*) *v.* plant, scatter, strew SEW, SO

space *n.* ① extent, expanse, capacity, room, accommodation ② the universe, the heavens, firmament

spacious *adj.* roomy, extensive, commodious, broad, wide ★**restricted**

span ① *n.* stretch, reach, extent, length ② *v.*

A B C D E F G H I J K L M N O P Q R S T U V W X Y Z

cross, bridge, link, connect, traverse

spare ① *adj.* extra, reserve, surplus ② *adj.* bare, meagre poor, scanty ▷*sparse* ③ *v.* afford, preserve, give, allow

sparkle *v.* glitter, glow, gleam, glint, twinkle

sparse *adj.* scanty, thin ▷*meagre* ★**dense**

spate *n.* flood, flow, deluge, rush, torrent

speak *v.* say, utter, talk, pronounce, lecture, express, articulate, enunciate

spear *n.* pike, javelin, lance

special *adj.* distinct, different, unique, individual ▷*particular* ★**common**

species *n.* breed, kind, sort, class, family

specific *adj.* definite, exact, precise ▷*special*

specimen *n.* sample, example, type, model, pattern

speck *n.* dot, speckle, spot, particle

spectacle *n.* sight, scene, exhibition, pageant, presentation ▷*display*

spectacles *n.* glasses, eyeglasses

spectacular *adj.* wonderful, fabulous, surprising ▷*marvellous*

spectator *n.* onlooker, witness, observer

speech *n.* ① talk, tongue *The people spoke a strange tongue we had never heard,* language ② address, lecture

speed *n.* velocity, rapidity, dispatch, pace, tempo *The tempo of life in the quiet seaside town was much too slow for us*

speedy *adj.* swift, rapid, fleet, quick, lively ▷*fast* ★**slow**

spell ① *n.* charm, magic, witchcraft ② *n.* period, term, space, time ③ *v.* form words, write out

spend *v.* ① expend, lay out, lavish, pay, disburse ② exhaust, use up

spendthrift *n.* wastrel, squanderer, prodigal ★**miser**

sphere *n.* ① globe, ball, orb, planet ② realm, orbit, domain, field, province

spice *n.* seasoning, flavouring, zest, relish, savour

spill *v.* pour, stream, run, overflow, spurt, upset, overturn, shed

spin *v.* revolve, rotate, turn, whirl, make thread, pirouette

spine *n.* backbone, needle, quill *The porcupine is covered in sharp quills,* ridge

spirit *n.* ① essence, substance, nature, character ② soul, air, breath ③ vigour, energy, courage ④ phantom, spectre, ghost

spiritual *adj.* ① religious, divine, unworldly, holy ② pure, immaterial

spite ① *n.* malice, rancour, hostility, hatred ② *v.* grudge, annoy, offend, injure

spiteful *adj.* vicious, malicious, vindictive ▷*hateful* ★**kind**

splash *v.* wet, spatter, shower, sprinkle

splendid *adj.* grand, brilliant, magnificent, showy, glorious ▷*sumptuous* ★**ordinary**

splendour *n.* glory, pageantry, brilliance, show, magnificence ▷*pomp*

split *v.* cleave, sever *Our family quarrelled with our cousins and severed relationships for years,* crack, snap, splinter

spoil *v.* ① hurt, injure, harm ② deface, disfigure, destroy ③ rot, decompose, decay

spoiled *adj.* decayed, rotten, broken up, corroded

spontaneous *adj.* natural, impulsive, self-generated, voluntary

spoof *n.* ① hoax, joke, bluff, prank, satire ② quip, jest, wisecrack

sport ① *n.* game, amusement, fun, athletics, recreation ② *v.* play, frolic, gambol, romp

Spices

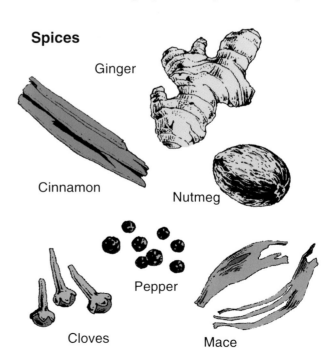

Ginger

Cinnamon

Nutmeg

Pepper

Cloves

Mace

spot ① *n.* dot, speck, mark, stain, blemish ②
v. espy, notice, recognize, distinguish

spotless *adj.* pure, clean, unstained,
faultless, perfect, immaculate

sprawl *v.* recline, stretch, extend, lie
▷*lounge*

spray *v.* sprinkle, squirt, splash, shower

spread *v.* ① scatter, strew, sow, circulate
② extend, stretch, expand, open

sprightly *adj.* lively, vivacious, cheerful,
agile ▷*brisk* ★**sluggish**

spur *v.* arouse, drive, urge, incite, encourage

spurious *adj.* fake, counterfeit, false
▷*bogus* ★**genuine**

spurn *v.* reject, scorn, disdain, disregard
▷*snub* ★**respect**

spurt *v.* ① stream, squirt, emerge, gush
② hurry, hasten, rush

spy ① *n.* agent, detective, observer, snooper,
scout ② *v.* see, glimpse, pry, peek, spot

squabble ① *n. & v.* quarrel, clash, fight,
row ▷*dispute*

squad *n.* group, company, troop, force,
band, team

squalid *adj.* foul, dirty, untended, poverty-
stricken ▷*sordid* ★**clean**

squall ① *n.* blast, gust, blow, tempest ② *v.*
blubber, cry, bawl, howl

squander *v.* misspend, waste, fritter, lavish

squash *v.* ① mash, crush, squelch, pound
② quell, suppress, humiliate

squat ① *adj.* dumpy, stocky, tubby, plump
② *v.* crouch, sit, roost, perch

squeal *v.* squawk, squeak, cheep, grunt, cry

squeamish *adj.* fastidious, delicate, finicky,
nauseous

squeeze *v.* compress, press, constrict, force,
pinch, clasp, cuddle

squirm *v.* wriggle, fidget, twist, flounder
▷*writhe*

squirt *v.* spray, splash ▷*spurt*

stab *v. & n.* cut, jab, puncture, wound, thrust

stable ① *adj.* firm, steady, solid, constant,
durable, lasting ★**unstable** ② *n.* barn,
cowshed, shed, stall

stack ① *n.* pile, pack, bundle, sheaf, heap
② *v.* assemble, pile up, amass, hoard

staff *n.* ① stick, cane, pole, rod ② team,
workers, force, personnel, crew

stage ① *n.* platform, dais, scaffold, podium
*The famous conductor stood on the podium
and raised his baton,* arena ② *n.* step,
degree, position ③ *v.* perform, produce,
present, put on

stagger *v.* reel, totter, waver, lurch

stagnant *adj.* motionless, inactive, still,
quiet, sluggish

staid *adj.* serious, steady, earnest, sober,
demure ▷*sedate* ★**frivolous** STAYED

stain ① *n.* blemish, blur, spot, blot ② *n.*
disgrace, shame ③ *v.* tarnish, sully, defile,
blemish

stair *n.* step, rung, spoke, footrest STARE

stake ① *n.* stick, stave, paling, spike, pole
▷*staff* ② *n.* bet, claim, wager, involvement
③ *v.* prop, secure, support STEAK

stale *adj.* ① musty, old, tasteless, faded
② common, trite, banal, flat ★**fresh**

stalk *v.* hunt, chase, follow, pursue, shadow,
tail, haunt, track

stall ① *v.* tarry, delay, hedge, obstruct,
hamper ★**advance** ② *n.* compartment,
booth, stand, bay

stalwart *adj.* rugged, sturdy, stout, lusty
▷*valiant* ★**timid**

stamina *n.* endurance, vitality, strength,
power, energy ★**weakness**

stammer *v.* stutter, falter, hesitate, stumble

stamp ① *v.* print, imprint, mark, impress
② *n.* impression, mark, print, brand ③ *n.*
kind, make, genus, cast ④ *n.* seal, sticker

stand ① *n.* board, counter, table, platform
▷*stall* ② *v.* rest, put, locate, place ③ *v.*
tolerate, put up with, abide, endure
★**oppose** ④ *v.* arise, get up, be erect ★**sit**

standard ① *adj.* normal, regular, uniform
② *n.* pattern, criterion, norm ③ *n.* flag,
banner, ensign

staple *adj.* main, principal, important,
leading, key, chief

stare *v.* gaze, gape, look, peer STAIR

stark *adj.* severe, plain, downright, bare,
absolute

start ① *v.* commence, begin, found, initiate

A
B
C
D
E
F
G
H
I
J
K
L
M
N
O
P
Q
R
S
T
U
V
W
X
Y
Z

② v. depart, set out, leave ③ v. startle, jump, wince ④ n. beginning, commencement ⑤ n. shock, scare, fit

startle v. frighten, alarm, scare, surprise ▷ *start*

starve v. be hungry, famish, want

state ① n. condition, situation, position ② n. country, nation, commonwealth ③ v. declare, say, express, utter ▷ *speak*

stately adj. imposing, grand, dignified ▷ *magnificent* ★**commonplace**

statement n. ① declaration, utterance, remark, motto ② bill, account, invoice

station ① n. post, spot, site, position, terminal ② v. park, place, put, establish *We got there early to establish our place in the queue* post, garrison

stationary adj. still, unmoving, standing, fixed, motionless ★**mobile** STATIONERY

stationery n. paper, envelopes, ink, pens, pencils STATIONARY

statue n. carving, bust, figure, effigy

staunch adj. constant, faithful, true, firm,

Stationery

Stationary

reliable, dependable ▷ *loyal* ★**unfaithful**

stay ① v. endure, last, remain, stand, linger ② v. check, curb, prevent ③ n. halt, wait, pause ▷ *stop*

steady ① adj. firm, fixed, established, constant ▷ *staunch* ★**uncertain** ② v. brace, stabilize, stiffen

steal v. ① thieve, pilfer, filch, swipe ▷ *rob* ② slink, flit, creep ▷ *prowl* STEEL

stealthy adj. furtive, sneaky, sly, secret ▷ *underhanded* ★**open**

steep ① adj. sheer, sharp, hilly, precipitous ② v. bathe, soak, souse, submerge

steer v. guide, direct, pilot, control

stem ① n. stalk, shoot, stock, trunk ② v. arise from, flow from ③ v. check, restrain

step ① n. pace, tread, stride, gait ② n. action, method, deed ③ v. walk, skip, trip, pace STEPPE

sterile adj. ① barren, unfertile, arid ② sanitary, disinfected, antiseptic

stern ① adj. strict, severe, harsh, grim ▷ *austere* ★**mild** ② n. aft end, rear, poop *The name of the ship was displayed in large letters on the poop*

stew v. ① cook, simmer, boil ② worry, fuss

stick ① n. stave, pole, rod, cane, staff ② v. adhere, cling, cleave, glue, paste, seal

sticky adj. gluey, gummy, adhesive

stick out v. project, bulge, protrude, extrude ▷ *jut* ★**recede**

stiff adj. ① inflexible, firm, stable, unyielding ▷ *rigid* ★**flexible** ② formal, stilted, prim, precise ★**yielding**

stifle v. suffocate, throttle, gag, muzzle ▷ *smother*

stigma n. ① blot, blur, scar ▷ *blemish* ② disgrace, dishonour ▷ *shame* ★**credit**

still ① adj. fixed, stable, static ② adj. calm, quiet, serene, tranquil, noiseless, hushed ▷ *peaceful* ★**agitated** ③ v. quiet, hush, muffle ▷ *calm* ★**agitate**

stimulate v. inspire, provoke, arouse, motivate ▷ *excite* ★**discourage**

sting v. prick, wound, pain, hurt, injure

stingy adj. miserly, tight-fisted, selfish,

niggardly, mean ▷*tight* ★**generous**

stink *v.* smell, whiff, reek

stint ① *n.* job, task, chore ② *n.* turn, spell, share, quota ③ *v.* limit, stop, scrimp, restrict ★**squander**

stir ① *v.* move, excite, spur, agitate ▷*stimulate* ② *v.* whisk, mix, blend ③ *v.* waken, arouse ★**calm** ④ *n.* flurry, fuss, uproar

stock ① *adj.* standard, regular, established, normal ② *n.* reserve, hoard, supply ③ *v.* provide, supply, equip, hoard

stocky *adj.* thickset, chunky, sturdy, pudgy ▷*squat* ★**willowy**

stodgy *adj.* dull, heavy, tedious, boring

stolid *adj.* stupid, dull, mindless, unintelligent ▷*stodgy* ★**quick**

stoop *v.* bend, crouch, kneel, bow

stop ① *v.* cease, desist, end, terminate, halt ★**start** ② *v.* prevent, forestall, avoid ③ *v.* arrest, hold, fix ④ *n.* pause, end, cessation *A cessation of hostilities came into force after the peace agreement*

store ① *v.* put by, reserve, hoard, save ★**use** ② *n.* stock, supply, reserve ③ *n.* market, shop, emporium

story *n.* ① yarn, tale, narrative, account, anecdote ② untruth, lie, fib ③ floor,

storey *n.* floor, landing, level, flight deck

storm ① *n.* tempest, gale, cyclone, hurricane, tornado ★**calm** ② *n.* turmoil, upheaval, attack ③ *v.* rage, rant, fume, attack

stout *adj.* ① sturdy, tough, robust ▷*strong* ★**weak** ② fat, corpulent ▷*plump* ★**thin**

stow *v.* deposit, store ▷*pack*

straight *adj.* ① right, undeviating, unswerving ▷*direct* ② frank, candid, truthful ▷*honest* ★**crooked** STRAIT

straightforward *adj.* open, outspoken, reliable, trustworthy ★**devious**

strain ① *n.* tension, fatigue, exertion ▷*stress* ★**relaxation** ② *n.* melody, tune, air ③ *v.* struggle, labour ▷*toil* ★**relax** ④ *v.* wrench, injure ⑤ *v.* filter, sift, separate

strait *n.* channel, sound, narrows

STRAIGHT

strait-laced *adj.* prim, prudish, strict, puritanical *My family was rather puritanical and we were not allowed to play any games on Sundays*

strand ① *n.* coast, beach, shore ② *n.* hair, fibre, tress, lock ③ *v.* desert, maroon, abandon

strange *adj.* ① unusual, incredible, extraordinary, curious ▷*odd* ★**commonplace** ② foreign, alien, remote

stranger *n.* outsider, foreigner, visitor, newcomer ▷*alien* ★**acquaintance**

strangle *v.* constrict, choke, garrote, throttle

strap *n.* belt, harness, thong, leash

stray *v.* ① wander, deviate, depart, rove ② sin, err, do wrong

streak *n.* stroke, stripe, band, line, bar, strip

stream ① *n.* current, course, drift, brook, creek, run ② *v.* flow, gush, spurt, pour

strength *n.* ① power, force, might ▷*energy* ② boldness, nerve, intensity ★**weakness**

strenuous *adj.* laborious, resolute, determined ▷*earnest* ★**weak**

stress ① *n.* tension, force, effort ▷*strain* ② *n.* accent, emphasis ③ *v.* emphasize, accentuate, highlight

stretch *v.* expand, reach, lengthen, elongate ▷*extend* ★**shorten**

strict *adj.* ① severe, rigorous, rigid, austere ▷*stern* ★**lenient** ② scrupulous, thorough, punctilious, accurate ▷*precise* ★**inaccurate**

stride *n. & v.* walk, step, tread, march

strife *n.* struggle, contest, quarrel, friction ▷*conflict* ★**peace**

strike ① *v.* beat, smite, collide, knock ▷*thump* ② *v.* discover, unearth ③ *n.* assault, thrust, attack ④ *n.* walkout, boycott

striking *adj.* eye-catching, wonderful ▷*extraordinary* ★**commonplace**

strip ① *v.* take off, peel, skin, shave, remove ② *n.* ribbon, stroke, streak, line

stripe *n.* streak, band, bar, chevron *Soldiers in the army have chevrons on their sleeves to indicate their rank,* rule ▷*strip*

strive *v.* endeavour, attempt, aim, compete, contend, struggle ▷*try* ★**yield**

A
B
C
D
E
F
G
H
I
J
K
L
M
N
O
P
Q
R
S
T
U
V
W
X
Y
Z

stroke ① *n.* shock, blow, knock, thump ② *n.* seizure, fit, convulsion ③ *v.* pat, rub, caress, smooth, comfort

stroll *v. & n.* walk, promenade, saunter, tramp, ramble

strong *adj.* ① powerful, vigorous, hardy, muscular ▷*robust* ② solid, secure, fortified ★**weak** ③ potent, hot, spicy ▷*pungent*

structure *n.* ① building, edifice, erection ② construction, organization, composition

struggle ① *v.* endeavour, labour, battle, wrestle ★**yield** ② *n.* conflict, battle ▷*fight* ③ *n.* distress, trouble ▷*effort*

strut ① *n.* support, mainstay, prop ② *v.* parade, prance, swagger

stubborn *adj.* ① dogged, persistent, tenacious ② pig-headed, perverse, wilful ▷*obstinate* ★**docile**

stuck-up *adj.* vain, conceited ▷*snobbish* ★**modest**

studious *adj.* scholarly, learned, thoughtful ▷*diligent* ★**thoughtless**

study ① *v.* read, peruse, scrutinize, examine, train ▷*learn* ② *n.* learning, meditation, thought, contemplation ▷*research*

Structures

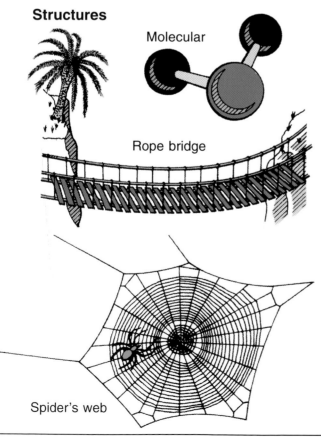

Molecular

Rope bridge

Spider's web

stuff ① *v.* fill, congest, pack, crowd ② *n.* textile, fabric, material, goods

stumble *v.* ① stagger, lurch, fall ▷*trip* ② stammer, falter ▷*stutter*

stump ① *v.* perplex, mystify, confuse ▷*bewilder* ② *n.* stub, tip, log, root

stun *v.* knock out, overpower, stupefy, dumbfound ▷*confound*

stunt *n.* deed, feat, achievement, deed, act, performance ▷*exploit*

stupefy *v.* daze, muddle, bewilder, astonish, flabbergast ▷*shock* ★**revive**

stupendous *adj.* astounding, amazing, overwhelming ▷*wonderful* ★**ordinary**

stupid *adj.* simple, stolid, dull, senseless ▷*foolish* ★**clever**

stupidity *n.* inanity, silliness, feebleness, foolishness ★**brilliance**

sturdy *adj.* rugged, stalwart, tough, robust, well-built, durable, strapping ▷*hardy* ★**weak**

stutter *v.* stumble, falter ▷*stammer*

style ① *n.* mode, vogue, fashion, way, manner, form ② *v.* name, call, christen STILE

suave *adj.* agreeable, elegant, polite, pleasant, sophisticated *After living in the city for many years, my sister had developed very sophisticated tastes*

subdue *v.* suppress, soften, tame, tone down, moderate, mellow ▷*repress*

subject ① *n.* (*sub*-ject) matter, topic, theme ② *n.* subordinate, dependant ③ *adj.* dependent, subordinate, liable ④ *v.* (sub-*ject*) rule over, subdue, subjugate

submerge *v.* plunge, immerse, sink ★**raise**

submissive *adj.* yielding, servile, meek ▷*obedient* ★**obstinate**

submit *v.* ① yield, give in, accede, surrender, hand over ② offer, tender, present

subordinate *adj.* junior, minor, subject, dependent, secondary ★**superior**

subscribe *v.* sign, enrol, register, agree, assent

subsequent *adj.* later, following, succeeding, after ★**former**

subside *v.* decline, peter out, decrease, diminish, wane, recede, ease *I used to go* *mountaineering but my interest waned after some years* ▷ *abate* ★**rise**

substance *n.* ① matter, object, stuff, material ② essence, kernel, meaning ▷ *gist*

substantial *adj.* ① steady, sturdy, firm ▷ *stable* ② ample, large, real, solid ★**imaginary**

substitute ① *n.* alternative, makeshift, stopgap ② *v.* swap, change, replace, duplicate, exchange, switch

subtle *adj.* ① shrewd, fine, delicate ② clever, crafty, perceptive

subtract *v.* take away, withdraw, deduct, remove ★**add**

succeed *v.* ① flourish, prosper, thrive, triumph ★**fail** ② follow, inherit, replace ★**precede**

success *n.* prosperity, triumph, victory, achievement ★**failure**

successful *adj.* victorious, prosperous, fortunate, thriving ★**unlucky**

suck *v.* inhale, take in, draw in, imbibe

sudden *adj.* unexpected, abrupt, impulsive, swift, prompt ★**gradual**

suffer *v.* ① bear, endure, put up with ② encounter, undergo ▷ *sustain*

sufficient *adj.* adequate, ample, plenty ▷ *enough* ★**deficient**

suffocate *v.* smother, choke ▷ *stifle*

suggest *v.* recommend, advise, submit, hint, intimate, propose

suit ① *v.* fulfil, gratify, please, suffice, accommodate, befit ② *n.* ensemble, outfit, costume

suitable *adj.* fitting, appropriate, correct, proper, becoming ★**unsuitable**

suite (*sweet*) *n.* ① set, series, succession ② apartment, rooms

sulk *v.* pout, grouch, brood, mope

sulky *adj.* glum, morose, churlish, moody ▷ *sullen* ★**genial**

sullen *adj.* gloomy, heavy, dismal, cheerless ▷ *sulky* ★**cheerful**

sum *n.* amount, total, whole, entirety SOME

summary *n.* synopsis, précis, abstract, summing-up, outline, analysis

summit *n.* peak, pinnacle, top, apex, zenith, acme, culmination ★**base**

summon *v.* call, beckon, command, invite, muster ★**dismiss**

sumptuous *adj.* profuse, costly, gorgeous, splendid ▷ *lavish* ★**frugal**

sundry *adj.* different, separate, several, diverse, assorted ▷ *various*

sunny *adj.* bright, cheerful, light, clear ▷ *radiant* ★**gloomy**

superb *adj.* magnificent, stately, gorgeous ▷ *grand* ★**commonplace**

supercilious *adj.* contemptuous, haughty, arrogant ▷ *snobbish* ★**modest**

superficial *adj.* slight, imperfect, shallow, skin-deep ▷ *trivial* ★**profound**

superfluous *adj.* in excess, inessential, extra, spare ▷ *surplus* ★**essential**

superior *adj.* ① better, greater, higher, loftier ▷ *excellent* ② eminent, conspicuous, principal ★**inferior**

supersede *v.* succeed, replace, displace, suspend, usurp *The president's authority was usurped by the military* ★**continue**

supervise *v.* superintend, control, manage, run, administer, handle ▷ *direct*

supple *adj.* lithe, pliable, flexible, bending

supplement ① *n.* addition, complement, sequel, postscript ② *v.* supply, add, fill

supply ① *v.* provide, furnish, yield, contribute, purvey ★**retain** ② *n.* hoard, reserve ▷ *stock*

support ① *v.* uphold, bear, sustain, maintain, help ▷ *favour* ★**oppose** ② *v.* hold up, prop, strut, brace ③ *v.* endure, tolerate, suffer ④ *n.* maintenance, upkeep

suppose *v.* assume, presume, believe, imagine, imply ▷ *consider*

suppress *v.* restrain, extinguish, destroy, stop ▷ *quell* ★**incite**

supreme *adj.* dominant, highest, greatest, maximum ★**lowly**

sure *adj.* ① certain, positive, definite ② secure, steady, safe ③ permanent, abiding, enduring ★**uncertain**

surface *n.* ① area, expanse, stretch ② outside, exterior, covering, façade, veneer ★**interior**

surge ① *v.* swell, rise, heave, rush ② *n.* ripple, billow, wave SERGE

surly *adj.* morose, cross, testy, touchy, crusty ▷*sullen* ★**affable**

surmise *v.* guess, speculate, conjecture, suspect ▷*presume* ★**know**

surpass *v.* eclipse, outdo, outstrip, excel, exceed ▷*beat*

surplus *n.* excess, remainder, balance, residue ★**shortcoming**

surprise ① *v.* startle, astonish, amaze ▷*astound* ② *n.* amazement, astonishment ▷*wonder*

surrender *v.* quit, give up, yield, submit ▷*relinquish*

surround *v.* enclose, encircle, encompass

survey ① *v.* (sur-*vey*) look at, examine, scrutinize ▷*study* ② *v.* estimate, measure ③ *n.* (*sur*-vey) assessment, appraisal

survive *v.* live, exist, continue, outlast, abide

susceptible *adj.* sensitive, impressionable, inclined, capable ★**insensitive**

suspect ① *v.* (sus-*pect*) disbelieve, doubt, distrust ② *adj.* (*sus*-pect) unbelievable, questionable, dubious, iffy

suspend *v.* ① interrupt, delay, adjourn, postpone, arrest ▷*stop* ★**continue** ② swing, dangle ▷*hang* ★**drop**

suspense *n.* anticipation, waiting, abeyance *The club couldn't decide on a new leader, so the matter was left in abeyance,* stoppage, uncertainty ▷*tension* ★**decision**

suspicious *adj.* incredulous, sceptical, doubtful, suspecting ★**trustful**

sustain *v.* ① uphold, keep, maintain, provide for ② suffer, undergo, experience ③ nourish, nurture, feed

swagger *v.* ① parade, prance, arrogance ▷*strut* ② brag, bluster ▷*boast*

swallow ① *v.* absorb, consume, eat, digest, devour, knock back, drink, ▷*gulp* ② *n.* mouthful, gulp ③ *n.* bird

swamp ① *n.* fen, bog, marsh, morass, quagmire ② *v.* submerge, submerse, overflow, deluge ▷*drench*

swap *v.* exchange, switch, trade, barter

swarm ① *n.* throng, horde, shoal, flock, crowd ② *v.* teem, abound, jam, mass, crowd, cluster

swarthy *adj.* dusky, dark, brown, tawny

sway ① *v.* swing, rock, totter, lean, incline ▷*waver* ② *n.* rule, authority, control ▷*influence*

swear *v.* ① promise, warrant, affirm, attest ② curse, damn, blaspheme

sweat *v.* perspire, ooze, leak, exude, swelter *During that time of the year it was very hot and we sweltered all day*

sweep *v.* brush, scrub, clean, scour

sweet *adj.* ① sugary, syrupy, luscious ★**sour** ② melodic, tuneful, musical, mellow ★**discordant** ③ gentle, tender, mild, lovable ★**unpleasant** ④ fragrant, pure, clean, fresh, wholesome, aromatic ★**putrid**

swell *v.* expand, distend, inflate, bulge ▷*enlarge* ★**contract**

swerve *v.* veer, deviate, skid, skew, lurch ▷*waver*

swift *adj.* speedy, rapid, quick ▷*fast* ★**slow**

swill ① *v.* swig, consume, imbibe, tipple ▷*gulp* ② *n.* refuse, garbage, waste

swim *v.* bathe, wade, paddle, float, glide

swindle ① *n.* trick, fraud, blackmail, racket ② *v.* hoodwink, deceive, hoax, dupe, fleece, rip off, bamboozle ▷*cheat*

swine *n.* pig, boar, sow, porker, hog

swing ① *v.* hang, suspend, dangle, lurch, reel ② *n.* tempo, time

switch ① *v.* change, exchange, alter, trade, substitute, swap ② *n.* lever, pedal, control

swivel *v.* pivot, spin, rotate, revolve, turn

swoop *v.* pounce, descend, stoop, plummet, plunge

sword *n.* rapier, blade, foil, épée, cutlass, sabre, steel SOARED

symbol *n.* character, figure, numeral, letter, sign, token, emblem CYMBAL

sympathetic *adj.* thoughtful, understanding, kind, affectionate ★**indifferent**

synopsis *n.* outline, summary, résumé, digest, review

system *n.* ① method, plan, order, scheme, arrangement, routine ② network, organization: *a hierarchical system*

T t

table *n.* ① board, stand, slab, tablet, counter, stall ② list, catalogue, schedule, index, statement

tablet *n.* ① pill, capsule, lozenge ② board, table, pad

tack ① *n.* drawing-pin, thumbtack, nail, pin, brad ② *n.* aim, direction, set ③ *v.* affix, fasten, join, stitch

tackle ① *n.* outfit, gear, rig, harness ② *v.* grasp, halt, intercept, seize ③ *v.* deal with *I dealt with the problem of the school fund shortage,* undertake, set about

tact *n.* diplomacy, judgement, skill, discretion *If you want your secret to be kept, you had better not rely on his discretion* TACKED

tactful *adj.* diplomatic, wise, subtle, prudent ▷*discreet* ★**tactless**

tactics *n.* strategy, campaign, method, procedure

tactless *adj.* inconsiderate, gauche, clumsy, boorish ▷*inept* ★**tactful**

tag *n.* label, ticket, docket, slip, sticker

taint *v.* sully, tarnish, infect, stain, soil, contaminate ▷*defile* ★**purify**

take *v.* ① grasp, grab, seize, procure ② receive, accept, obtain ③ carry, convey, lead, conduct ④ interpret, understand

take place *v.* occur, happen, befall *Our parents were concerned about what might befall us when we left school*

tale *n.* story, fable, anecdote, yarn, narrative TAIL

talent *n.* knack, genius, gift, ability, aptitude ★**stupidity**

talk ① *v.* speak, say, utter, gossip ② *v.* describe, comment on, talk about ③ *n.* speech, chatter, conversation ④ *n.* lecture, speech, discourse

tall *adj.* lanky, lofty, big, high, towering, giant ★**short**

tally *v.* ① count, enumerate, compute ② agree, conform, coincide ★**disagree**

tame ① *adj.* domesticated, gentle, mild, docile *Although we found it in the woods, the kitten was docile* ★**savage** ② *adj.* flat, dull, boring, tedious ③ *v.* train, discipline, domesticate

Tame

Although we found it in the woods, the kitten was docile

tamper with *v.* meddle, interfere, damage, tinker, fiddle

tang *n.* smell, scent, aroma, flavour, savour, taste, smack

tangible *adj.* concrete, solid, substantial, real, material ★**spiritual**

tangle *n. & v.* twist, muddle, jumble, knot

tantalize *v.* tease, taunt, thwart, disappoint ▷*frustrate* ★**satisfy**

tantrum *n.* rage, fit, hysterics, storm

tap ① *v.* pat, hit, knock, rap, strike ② *n.* spout, cock, nozzle, bung, faucet

tape *n.* ribbon, filament, braid, strip, riband

taper *v.* dwindle, narrow, contract, decline, wane, narrow ★**widen** TAPIR

tardy *adj.* slow, sluggish, reluctant, slack ▷*late* ★**prompt**

target *n.* goal, aim, ambition, purpose, butt, end, victim, prey

tariff *n.* tax, rate, toll, duty, payment, price list, levy

tarnish *v.* stain, sully *Mark's reputation at school was sullied after he was accused of stealing,* spot, darken, blemish, rust ★**brighten**

tarry *v.* delay, stall, wait, loiter ▷*linger* ★**hurry**

tart ① *adj.* acid, sour, sharp, pungent ② *n.* pie, quiche, pastry, flan

task *n.* job, stint, chore, assignment, undertaking

taste ① *n.* bite, mouthful, flavour, savour, tang ② *v.* try, sip, sample, relish

tasteful *adj.* artistic, graceful, elegant, smart ▷*refined* ★**tasteless**

tasteless *adj.* ① flavourless, insipid ② gaudy, inelegant ▷*vulgar* ★**tasteful**

tasty *adj.* appetizing, piquant, savoury ▷*delicious* ★**disgusting**

tattle *v.* gossip, tittle-tattle, blab, prattle

taunt *v.* jibe, reproach, rebuke, ridicule, scoff at ▷*sneer* ★**compliment**

taut *adj.* tense, tight, stretched ▷*rigid* ★**relaxed** TAUGHT

tawdry *adj.* flashy, loud, gaudy, showy ▷*vulgar* ★**superior**

tax ① *n.* levy, duty, impost, tithe, toll ② *v.* load, oppress, overburden TACKS

teach *v.* instruct, educate, tutor, coach, guide, train, drill

teacher *n.* educator, professor, lecturer, schoolmaster, schoolmistress, coach, tutor

team *n.* party, group, gang, crew, company TEEM

tear *v.* ① rip, rend, tatter, shred ② dash, bolt, rush, sprint TARE

tearful *adj.* weepy, moist, wet, sobbing, sad

tease *v.* annoy, harass, vex, irritate, torment ▷*tantalize* ★**soothe** TEAS, TEES

tedious *adj.* wearisome, tiresome, irksome, exhausting ▷*boring* ★**fascinating**

teem *v.* abound, swarm, overflow, increase, be full ★**lack** TEAM

tell *v.* ① disclose, speak, state, talk, utter ② discern, discover, distinguish

temper ① *n.* temperament, disposition, nature, humour ② *n.* anger, annoyance, passion ③ *v.* moderate, soften, weaken, restrain, soothe, assuage

temporary *adj.* short, limited, impermanent, brief ★**permanent**

tempt *v.* entice, invite, attract, persuade ▷*lure* ★**deter**

tenacious *adj.* ① stubborn, firm, obstinate, unwavering ★**weak** ② adhesive, glutinous

tenant *n.* occupant, householder, occupier

tend *v.* ① take care of, manage, serve, guard, nurse, cultivate, nurture, attend ★**neglect**

② affect, lean, incline, verge ★**diverge**

tendency *n.* disposition, leaning, inclination, bent ★**aversion**

tender ① *adj.* delicate, soft ▷*fragile* ② *adj.* mild, kind, sympathetic ▷*gentle* ③ *adj.* raw, painful, sore ④ *v.* proffer *Charlotte proffered her services as a babysitter,* present, volunteer, bid

tense *adj.* tight, strained, taut, nervous, edgy ★**relaxed** TENTS

tension *n.* strain, stress, rigidity, suspense, worry ★**relaxation**

term ① *n.* expression, denomination, title, phrase ② *n.* time, season, spell *We stayed in Hong Kong for a spell during our trip to the Far East,* duration ③ *v.* entitle, call, dub

terminate *v.* cease, stop, end, conclude ▷*finish* ★**begin**

terrible *adj.* frightful, terrifying, fearful, dreadful ▷*horrible* ★**superb**

terrify *v.* petrify, shock, appal, alarm ▷*frighten* ★**reassure**

territory *n.* region, area, expanse, dominion, land ▷*country*

terror *n.* alarm, panic, horror, dismay ▷*fright* ★**confidence**

terse *adj.* brief, concise, short, pithy, abrupt ▷*curt* ★**long-winded**

test ① *n.* examination, trial, check, proof, experiment ② *v.* examine, try out, check, quiz, analyse

testy *adj.* irritable, bad-tempered, touchy, peevish ▷*cross* ★**genial**

tether *n.* rope, cord, lead, leash, chain

text *n.* contents, reading, passage, clause

thanks *n.* gratitude, credit, appreciation

thaw *v.* ① melt, fuse, liquefy, soften ★**freeze** ② unbend, relax

theft *n.* robbery, fraud, larceny, plundering

theme *n.* subject, text matter, topic

theory *n.* idea, supposition, concept, hypothesis, surmise, speculation

therefore *adv.* consequently, hence, accordingly, thus

thick *adj.* ① dense, solid, bulky, compact ② stiff, set, congealed ③ viscous, gummy, stodgy ★**thin**

a b c d e f g h i j k l m n o p q r s t u v w x y z

thief *n.* crook, robber, burglar, bandit, pirate

thin *adj.* ① slender, slim, slight, lean, skinny ★**fat** ② wafer-like, delicate, flimsy ③ watery, dilute, unsubstantial ★**thick**

thing *n.* article, object, something, being, substance

think *v.* ① ponder, consider ▷*reflect* ② conceive, imagine ▷*fancy* ③ surmise, conclude ▷*reckon*

thirsty *adj.* parched, dry, craving, burning

thorn *n.* barb, prickle, bramble, thistle

thorough *adj.* outright, absolute, complete, utter ★**haphazard**

though *conj.* although, even though, notwithstanding, however, yet

thought *n.* reflection, consideration, study, concept, deduction

thoughtful *adj.* ① pensive, studious, contemplative ② considerate, kind, heedful, careful ★**thoughtless**

thoughtless *adj.* heedless, careless, rash, neglectful ▷*indiscreet* ★**thoughtful**

thrash *v.* ① whip, flog, hit ② stir, pitch *The sea was rough – each wave pitched the small boat closer to the rocks,* toss

thread *n.* filament, twist, yarn, fibre

threadbare *adj.* ① shabby, ragged, worn ② commonplace, hackneyed, stale ★**fresh**

threaten *v.* intimidate, bully, blackmail ▷*menace* ★**reassure**

Thrash

The sea was rough – each wave pitched the small boat closer to the rocks.

thrifty *adj.* frugal, careful, economical, saving, sparing ★**wasteful**

thrilling *adj.* exciting, gripping, stimulating

thrive *v.* prosper, flourish, succeed, grow, increase ★**decline**

throb ① *n.* tick, beat, palpitation ② *v.* beat, palpitate, vibrate

throng ① *n.* crowd, horde, mob ② *v.* pack, crowd, swarm, fill

throttle *v.* choke, smother, gag ▷*strangle*

through *prep.* by way of, by means of, as a result of

throw *v.* fling, cast, hurl, project, propel, thrust ★**keep** THROE

thrust *v. & n.* push, project, drive, force, prod, jab, lunge

thug *n.* hoodlum, bandit, assassin, mugger, ruffian, tough, hooligan

thump *v. & n.* beat, hit, knock, bang, wallop

thunderstruck *adj.* open-mouthed, amazed, astounded, staggered

thus *adv.* accordingly, so, therefore, consequently

thwart *v.* frustrate, balk, baffle, hinder, obstruct ★**assist**

ticket *n.* pass, label, card, coupon, token

tickle *v.* ① caress, stroke, pat, brush ② titillate, convulse, amuse ③ delight, gratify

tide *n.* stream, current, drift, ebb, flow TIED

tidings *n.* information, intelligence, report, advice ▷*news*

tidy *adj.* ① neat, well-kept, spruce, orderly ② ample, large, substantial, sizable

tie ① *v.* join, attach, secure *Be sure to secure the gate so the dogs can't get out,* unite ▷*fasten* ② *n.* cravat, necktie, bow tie ③ *n.* bond, connection ④ deadheat, stalemate

tight *adj.* ① fast, close, compact, tense ▷*taut* ★**loose** ② miserly, tightfisted, mean ▷*stingy* ★**generous**

tighten *v.* strain, tauten, constrict, cramp, crush ▷*squeeze* ★**loosen**

till ① *prep.* until, up to, as far as ② *v.* plough, cultivate, tend ③ *n.* cash-drawer, cash-register

tilt *v. & n.* slant, slope, incline, lean, list, tip

time *n.* ① period, duration, season, age, era, term, span ② metre, measure, tempo, rhythm THYME

timid *adj.* fearful, afraid, timorous, diffident, modest ▷*shy* ★**bold**

tinge *v. & n.* colour, tincture, tint, stain, shade

tingle *v.* thrill, throb, tickle, vibrate

tinker *v.* meddle, fiddle *Bill fiddled with the old clock for ages, trying to make it work,* patch up, potter, trifle

tinkle *v.* jingle, jangle, ring, clink

tint *n.* dye, hue, tinge, shade ▷*colour*

tiny *adj.* small, diminutive, puny, wee ▷*little* ★**huge**

tip ① *n.* apex, peak, point, extremity ▷*top* ② *n.* gratuity, gift, donation, reward ③ *n.* information, hint, tip-off ④ *v.* list, lean, tilt ▷*slope*

tipsy *adj.* inebriated, drunk, drunken

tire *v.* exhaust, bore, fatigue, harass, weaken

tiresome *adj.* wearisome, tedious, boring ▷*humdrum* ★**interesting**

titbit *n.* delicacy, morsel, dainty, snack, treat, scrap

title *n.* ① name, denomination, term, style, designation ② claim, interest *When my father died, I was left an interest in his business,* ownership

toady *v.* fawn, crawl, grovel, crouch, cringe

toast ① *n.* pledge, compliment, salutation ② *v.* brown, roast, heat

together *adv.* collectively, jointly, as one, simultaneously, at the same time, collectively ★**separately**

toil ① *v. & n.* struggle, labour, travail ▷*work* ★**relaxation**

token *n.* memento, keepsake, symbol, omen ▷*souvenir*

tolerable *adj.* endurable, supportable, bearable, passable ★**unbearable**

tolerant *adj.* forbearing, indulgent *Sally's parents are very indulgent with her and buy her whatever she wants,* liberal, easy-going ▷*lenient* ★**intolerant**

tolerate *v.* accept, bear with, put up with, endure, suffer ▷*allow* ★**resist**

toll ① *v.* ring, strike, chime, clang ② *n.* charge, duty, tax, levy

tone *n.* ① pitch, loudness, noise, note ② emphasis, accent, inflection ③ temper, manner, attitude ④ colour, cast, hue, shade

too *adv.* ① also, as well, besides ② extremely, very, unduly

tool *n.* ① implement, utensil, machine, agent ② pawn, puppet, cat's-paw, stooge TULLE

top *n.* ① summit, pinnacle, peak ② lid, cover, stopper, cap ③ upper surface ★**bottom** ④ *n.* spinning toy ⑤ *adj.* highest, topmost, best, uppermost *After climbing for four days, we reached the uppermost part of the range*

topic *n.* subject, motif, question ▷*theme*

topical *adj.* contemporary, popular, up-to-date, current

topple *v.* collapse, founder, overturn, totter ▷*fall*

topsy-turvy *adj.* upside-down, overturned, confused, chaotic

torment *v. & n.* pain, distress, plague ▷*torture* ★**ease**

torrent *n.* flood, stream, cascade, cataract, waterfall ★**trickle**

torture *v.* agonize, rack, anguish ▷*torment*

toss *v.* fling, hurl, pitch, cast, project, heave ▷*throw*

total ① *n.* aggregate, whole, sum, completion ② *v.* add, tot up, reckon ③ *adj.* complete, entire

totally *adv.* completely, absolutely, entirely, utterly ★**partially**

touch ① *v.* feel, finger, fondle, handle, stroke ② *v.* move, affect, concern ③ *v.* beat, hit, collide with ④ *v.* adjoin *Our house is situated at a spot where three counties adjoin,* meet, border ⑤ *n.* tinge, hint, suspicion

touchy *adj.* peevish, petulant, snappish ▷*moody* ★**genial**

tough ① *adj.* hard, strong, vigorous, rugged, sturdy ② *adj.* arduous, difficult ③ *n.* hooligan, bruiser, bully

tour *n.* trip, journey, jaunt, excursion, voyage, ride, visit

a
b
c
d
e
f
g
h
i
j
k
l
m
n
o
p
q
r
s
t
u
v
w
x
y
z

Titles

admiral
ambassador
archbishop
baron baroness
brigadier
cardinal
chancellor colonel
commodore
constable count
countess czar
czarina
dame deacon
dean don doña
duchess duke
earl emir emperor
general governor
graf
infanta
kaiser khan king
knight
lady laird lama
lieutenant lord
madame
maharajah
maharani
major mandarin

marchioness
margrave marshal
master mayor
mikado miss
mogul monsieur
monsignor
pasha pope priest
prince
princess provost
queen
rabbi regent
senator señor
señora señorita
sergeant signor
signora signorina
shah sheik shogun
sheriff sir sultan
sultana
taoiseach
vicar viceroy
viscount viscountess

Toys

Wheeled toy
ancient Egypt

Top and whip
1700s

Doll
1800s

Electronic game
1900s

tournament *n.* contest, championship, competition ▷*match*

tow *v.* haul, drag, tug, haul, heave ▷*pull* TOE

tower ① *v.* soar, dominate, surmount ② *n.* turret, spire, belfry

toy ① *n.* plaything, doll, game ② *v.* play, tinker, fiddle, twiddle

trace ① *v.* trail, track, follow, pursue, discover ② *v.* sketch, draw, copy ③ *n.* trail, track, spoor ④ *n.* drop, speck, vestige

track *v.* search out, follow ▷*trace*

tract *n.* ① area, space, extent, plot ② booklet, leaflet, pamphlet TRACKED

trade ① *v.* barter, exchange, buy, sell, patronize ② *n.* occupation, work, livelihood, business

tradition *n.* custom, convention, practice

traffic ① *n.* business, barter ▷*trade* ② transport, vehicles, movement

tragedy *n.* catastrophe, disaster, adversity ▷*calamity* ★**comedy**

tragic *adj.* disastrous, catastrophic, miserable, wretched ▷*deplorable* ★**comic**

trail *n.* spoor, track ▷*trace*

train ① *v.* teach, educate, instruct, drill, school ② *n.* chain, procession, series

traitor *n.* rebel, mutineer, renegade, quisling, betrayer

tramp ① *n.* vagabond, wanderer, vagrant, dosser, hobo ▷*beggar* ② *n.* jaunt, stroll, ramble ③ *v.* roam, rove, range, walk, travel

trample *v.* tread on, walk on, flatten ▷*crush*

tranquil *adj.* peaceful, placid, serene, restful ▷*calm* ★**restless**

transaction *n.* business, performance, dealing, negotiation, proceeding

transfer *v.* move *My sister is being moved to the head office after her promotion,* displace, change ▷*exchange*

transmit *v.* dispatch, forward, relay ▷*send* ★**receive**

transparent *adj.* clear, lucid, crystal, diaphanous, see-through, evident

transport ① *v.* carry, convey, conduct, transfer ▷*move* ② *n.* transportation

trap ① *v.* ensnare, catch, net ② *n.* snare, pitfall, noose, decoy ▷*ambush*

trash *n.* junk, debris, rubble, garbage ▷*rubbish* ★**treasure**

travel ① *v. & n.* trek, voyage, cruise ▷*journey*

treacherous *adj.* ① traitorous, unfaithful, false, deceptive ▷*disloyal* ★**faithful**

tread *v.* ① dangerous, risky, precarious, tricky ★**reliable** ② step, walk, tramp, march, go ③ stride, gait, walk, step

treason *n.* treachery, betrayal, sedition

treasure ① *n.* hoard, fortune, riches, wealth ② *v.* appreciate, esteem ▷*value*

treat ① *v.* deal with, handle, manage, serve ② *v.* regale, entertain ③ *v.* doctor, attend ④ *n.* banquet, entertainment, fun

treaty *n.* agreement, covenant, alliance

tremble *v.* quake, quaver, shudder, flutter ▷*shake*

tremendous *adj.* ① immense, enormous ▷*huge* ② terrible, dreadful, awful

tremor *n.* quiver, shake, flutter, ripple ▷*vibration*

trench *n.* ditch, moat, trough, gully, gutter

trend *n.* tendency, inclination, direction

trespass ① *v.* infringe, overstep, intrude ② *n.* offence, sin, transgression

trial *n.* ① endeavour, testing, experiment ② ordeal, grief, suffering ③ essay, proof ④ hearing, lawsuit

tribe *n.* clan, family, race, group, set

tribute *n.* ① ovation, compliment, praise ② dues, toll, tithe, tax

trick ① *n.* fraud, artifice, wile, cheat, deception ② *n.* jape, prank, frolic ③ *n.* juggling, stage magic, conjuring ④ *v.* deceive, defraud

trickle *v.* leak, ooze, seep, drip, drop, dribble

trifle ① *n.* bauble, plaything, foolishness, nonsense ② *v.* dabble, idle, play with

trifling *adj.* paltry, petty, worthless, slight ▷*trivial* ★**important**

trim ① *v.* prune, clip, shorten, crop ② *v.* ornament, smarten, decorate ③ *adj.* tidy, neat, orderly ★**scruffy**

trinket *n.* bauble, bead, jewel, ornament, toy

trip *n.* ① journey, excursion, jaunt ▷*tour* ② *v.* stumble, fall, slip

tripe *n.* rubblish, trash, nonsense, twaddle *This is a silly story; I've never read such twaddle*

trite *adj.* hackneyed, ordinary, corny ▷*stale* ★**novel**

triumph *n.* victory, success, achievement ▷*conquest* ★**defeat**

trivial *adj.* trifling, common, unimportant, ordinary, useless ▷*trite* ★**important**

troop ① *n.* band, gang, group, pack, team, unit ② *v.* flock, crowd, swarm TROUPE

trophy *n.* prize, award, cup, souvenir

trot *v.* canter, jog, scamper, scurry

trouble ① *n.* disturbance, annoyance, calamity, misfortune ▷*misery* ② *v.* disturb, annoy, harass ▷*distress* ★**delight**

true *adj.* ① accurate, precise, factual, correct. ★**inaccurate** ② faithful, loyal, constant ③ pure, real ▷*genuine* ★**false**

trunk *n.* ① body, torso, stem, stalk ② chest, case, box ③ proboscis *The tapir's proboscis is not as large as the elephant's trunk,* nose, snout

trust ① *n.* faith, confidence, belief ② *v.* believe in, credit, depend on ★**doubt** TRUSSED

trustful *adj.* trusting, innocent, naive ▷*gullible* ★**cautious**

trustworthy *adj.* dependable, credible, honourable ▷*reliable* ★**unreliable**

truth *n.* ① reality, fact, precision ▷*accuracy* ★**falsehood** ② integrity, faith, honour ▷*fidelity* ★**deceit**

truthful *adj.* reliable, frank, open, candid, straight ▷*honest* ★**false**

try ① *v.* endeavour, attempt ▷*strive* ② *v.* examine, try out ▷*test* ★**abandon** ③ *n.* trial, attempt, effort

trying *adj.* bothersome, annoying, irritating, troublesome ▷*irksome*

tub *n.* basin, bowl, pot, barrel, keg, tun

tube *n.* pipe, spout, duct, hose, shaft

tuck *v.* insert, stuff, fold, pack, pleat, hem

tug *v.* drag, tow, haul, heave ▷*pull* ★**push**

tumble *v.* drop, descend, trip, topple, stumble ▷*fall*

tumult *n.* noise, rumpus, racket, uproar, disturbance, disorder ★**peace**

tune *n.* melody, harmony, air, strain ▷*song*

tunnel *n.* subway, shaft, passage, gallery

turn ① *v.* spin, revolve, whirl ▷*rotate* ② *v.* bend, curve ▷*twist* ③ *v.* change, alter ▷*convert* ④ *v.* spoil ▷*sour* ⑤ *n.* stint, spell, chance ⑥ *n.* rotation, cycle, gyration ▷*revolution* TERN

twaddle *n.* balderdash, nonsense, drivel, rigmarole, piffle ▷*bunkum* ★**sense**

twinge *n.* pain, pang, spasm, gripe ▷*ache*

twinkle *v.* glitter, gleam, glisten, glimmer ▷*sparkle*

twist *v.* ① bend, curve, turn ② warp, contort, writhe ③ wind, intertwine *The octopus intertwined its legs around the large clam*

twitch *v.* jerk, jump, jiggle, blink, flutter

type ① *n.* kind, sort, character, description ② *n.* prototype, model, pattern ③ *n.* letter, symbol ④ *v.* typewrite, keyboard

typical *adj.* characteristic, symbolic, regular, stock, representative ★**abnormal**

tyrant *n.* despot, autocrat, dictator, martinet

A
B
C
D
E
F
G
H
I
J
K
L
M
N
O
P
Q
R
S
T
U
V
W
X
Y
Z

U u

ugly *adj.* unsightly, ungainly, frightful, ghastly, hideous, horrid, nasty ★**beautiful**

ultimate *adj.* furthest, farthest, most distant, extreme, eventual ▷*final*

umpire *n.* referee, judge, mediator

unabashed *adj.* brazen, unconcerned, undaunted ▷*composed* ★**sheepish**

unable *adj.* helpless, incapable, powerless ★**able**

unaccustomed *adj.* inexperienced, unfamiliar ▷*strange* ★**familiar**

unaffected *adj.* natural, sincere, true, artless ▷*naive* ★**impressed**

unafraid *adj.* courageous, dauntless, intrepid ▷*fearless* ★**afraid**

unanimous *adj.* harmonious, consenting, agreeing ▷*united*

unassuming *adj.* diffident, reserved, quiet, simple ▷*modest* ★**forward**

unattached *adj.* single, free, loose ▷*separate* ★**committed**

unattended *adj.* alone, unwatched, ignored ▷*abandoned* ★**escorted**

unavoidable *adj.* inevitable, irresistable, certain ▷*necessary* ★**uncertain**

unaware *adj.* ignorant, unheeding, unknowing, forgetful ▷*oblivious* ★**aware**

unbalanced *adj.* ① top-heavy, lopsided, uneven ② insane, unhinged *He seems to have become unhinged ever since he lost his job,* crazy, eccentric

unbearable *adj.* unacceptable, intolerable ▷*outrageous* ★**acceptable**

unbiased *adj.* impartial, fair, just ▷*neutral* ★**prejudiced**

uncanny *adj.* weird, ghostly, unearthly, creepy ▷*eerie*

uncertain *adj.* doubtful, vague, chancy, indefinite ▷*dubious* ★**certain**

uncivilized *adj.* primitive, barbaric, coarse, gross ▷*vulgar* ★**civilized**

uncomfortable *adj.* awkward, embarrassed, cramped, self-conscious ★**comfortable**

uncommon *adj.* rare, scarce, infrequent, extraordinary ▷*unusual* ★**common**

unconscious *adj.* ① ignorant, unheeding ▷*unaware* ② insensible, senseless, stunned ★**conscious**

unconventional *adj.* unorthodox, peculiar *I have my own peculiar way of looking at things,* individualistic ▷*eccentric* ★**conventional**

uncouth *adj.* crude, coarse, clumsy, vulgar ▷*boorish* ★**polite**

uncover *v.* expose, discover, show, divulge ▷*reveal* ★**conceal**

under ① *adv.* underneath, below, beneath ② *prep.* less than, lower than, subject to

undergo *v.* endure, tolerate, bear, suffer ▷*sustain*

underground *adj.* secret, private, hidden, subversive

underhand *adj.* stealthy, undercover, deceitful ▷*sneaky* ★**honest**

underneath *adj.* beneath, under ▷*below* ★**above**

underrate *v.* undervalue, understate, disparage, belittle ★**exaggerate**

understand *v.* comprehend, appreciate, grasp, sympathize, take in, follow ▷*realize* ★**misunderstand**

understudy *n.* stand-in, deputy, substitute, reserve, replacement

undertake *v.* attempt, commence, contract, embark on ▷*tackle*

undesirable *adj.* objectionable, distasteful ▷*unpleasant* ★**desirable**

undignified *adj.* improper, inelegant, clumsy ▷*unseemly* ★**graceful**

undo *v.* unfasten, disentangle, unravel, free ▷*release* ★**fasten**

undress *v.* disrobe, strip, remove, take off ▷*divest* ★**dress**

unearthly *adj.* eerie, uncanny, supernatural ▷*ghostly*

uneasy *adj.* uncomfortable, restive, self-conscious, edgy ★**calm**

unemployed *adj.* unoccupied, redundant, out of work

uneven *adj.* irregular, rough, bumpy,

lopsided, unequal ★**even**

unexpected *adj.* abrupt, impulsive, chance, surprising ▷*sudden* ★**normal**

unfair *adj.* prejudiced, one-sided, partial, unjust ★**fair**

unfaithful *adj.* faithless, untrue, dishonest ▷*false* ★**faithful**

unfamiliar *adj.* alien, obscure, fantastic, bizarre ▷*strange* ★**familiar**

unfasten *v.* release, open, unlatch, untie ▷*undo* ★**fasten**

unfinished *adj.* incomplete, imperfect, lacking, crude ★**finished**

unfit *adj.* unqualified, unsuitable, incapable, unsuited ★**suitable**

unfold *adj.* open, expand, develop, reveal, disclose, unwrap ★**withhold**

unforeseen *adj.* surprising, sudden, accidental ▷*unexpected* ★**predictable**

unforgettable *adj.* memorable, impressive, noteworthy, exceptional

unfortunate *adj.* deplorable, lamentable, adverse, hapless ▷*unlucky* ★**fortunate**

unfriendly *adj.* antagonistic, surly, cold ▷*hostile* ★**friendly**

ungainly *adj.* gawky, awkward, graceless, unwieldly ▷*clumsy* ★**graceful**

ungrateful *adj.* thankless, selfish, ungracious, ill-mannered ★**grateful**

unhappiness *n.* depression, misery, sadness

unhappy *adj.* miserable, dismal, luckless *Try as he might, the luckless Tom was almost last in the race*, melancholy ▷*sad* ★**happy**

unhealthy *adj.* ① unwholesome, harmful ② sick, ill, diseased ★**healthy**

uniform ① *n.* regalia, livery *It was a very grand affair, with the footmen in full livery*, costume, dress ② *adj.* stable, steady, unchanging, level ★**varied**

unimportant *adj.* puny, trivial, insignificant ▷*petty* ★**important**

unintentional *adj.* inadvertent, involuntary, unwitting ▷*accidental* ★**deliberate**

union *n.* ① alliance, association, league ② agreement, accord, harmony ③ fusion, blend, compound

unique *adj.* original, exceptional, exclusive,

single, sole ★**commonplace**

unit *n.* entity, single, one, individual

unite *v.* join, combine, connect, merge, blend, fuse ★**separate**

united *adj.* joined, combined, undivided ▷*unanimous* ★**separated**

unity *n.* union, harmony, uniformity, agreement ★**disagreement**

universal *adj.* general, all-embracing, entire, worldwide *Our company has products that are sold worldwide*

unjust *adj.* partial, prejudiced, unfair, wrong ▷*biased* ★**just**

unkempt *adj.* dishevelled, shabby, sloppy, slovenly, ungroomed ▷*scruffy* ★**neat**

unkind *adj.* inhuman, heartless, brutal, callous ▷*cruel* ★**kind**

unknown *adj.* hidden, mysterious, undiscovered, dark ★**familiar**

unless *conj.* if not, except when

unlike *adj.* unrelated, dissimilar, distinct ▷*different* ★**similar**

unlikely *adj.* rare, improbable, doubtful, incredible, unheard of ▷*dubious* ★**likely**

unlucky *adj.* unfortunate, luckless, ill-fated, unhappy ★**lucky**

unnatural *adj.* ① artificial, stilted, strained

Uniform

It was a very grand affair, with the footmen in full livery.

② inhuman, cruel ▷*heartless* ★**natural**

unnecessary *adj.* non-essential, excess, superfluous ▷*needless* ★**necessary**

unoccupied *adj.* ① uninhabited, empty, deserted ▷*vacant* ② idle, spare ▷*unemployed* ★**occupied**

unpleasant *adj.* disagreeable, displeasing, objectionable ▷*offensive* ★**pleasant**

unpopular *adj.* obnoxious *I was glad to leave the party, for I had been forced to talk to some obnoxious people,* detested, shunned, rejected ▷*disliked* ★**popular**

unqualified *adj.* ① unable, incompetent, inadequate ▷*unfit* ② complete, thorough, absolute

unreal *adj.* imaginary, fictional, artificial, false, fanciful ★**real** UNREEL

unreasonable *adj.* ① extravagant, excessive, extreme ★**moderate** ② far-fetched, absurd, foolish ★**rational**

unreliable *adj.* untrustworthy, undependable, irresponsible ▷*fickle* ★**reliable**

unrest *n.* ① defiance, disquiet, protest, rebellion ② anxiety, distress, worry ★**calm**

unrestricted *adj.* unrestrained, unlimited, open, free, unhindered ★**limited**

unripe *adj.* green, immature, callow *I was just a callow youth in those days, but I hope I have learned something since then,* unseasoned, unready ★**ripe**

unrivalled *adj.* inimitable, unequalled, matchless, peerless ★**inferior**

unruly *adj.* disorderly, troublesome, restive ▷*rowdy* ★**orderly**

unseemly *adj.* incorrect, indecent, improper, unbecoming, shocking ★**seemly**

unselfish *adj.* generous, liberal, charitable, hospitable ▷*kind* ★**selfish**

unstable *adj.* unsteady, shaky, inconstant, fickle, volatile ★**stable**

unsuitable *adj.* improper, unacceptable, unfitting, inconsistent ★**suitable**

untidy *adj.* bedraggled, disorderly, muddled, messy ▷*slovenly* ★**tidy**

untie *v.* unfasten, unravel, free, release ▷*undo* ★**tie**

until *prep.* till, as far as, up to

untimely *adj.* inopportune, ill-timed, premature ★**opportune**

unusual *adj.* strange, queer, exceptional, quaint, curious ▷*odd* ★**normal**

unwilling *adj.* averse, disinclined, grudging, opposed ▷*reluctant* ★**willing**

upheaval *n.* disturbance, disruption, overthrow, turmoil, shake-up

uphold *v.* sustain, keep up, endorse ▷*support*

upkeep *n.* maintenance, care, conservation, support, expenses ★**neglect**

upper *adj.* higher, superior, elevated, uppermost ★**lower**

upright *adj.* ① sheer, steep, perpendicular ★**horizontal** ② honourable *Josephine was one of the most honourable people I ever met,* ethical, virtuous ★**dishonest**

uproar *n.* hubbub, noise, disorder, tumult, turmoil ▷*clamour*

upset ① *v.* bother, perturb, unsettle, annoy ② *v.* overthrow, overturn, topple ③ *adj.* disturbed, confused, worried

upside-down *adj.* ① overturned, upturned ② chaotic, muddled, jumbled

urge ① *v.* goad, plead, spur, beseech ★**deter** ② *n.* encouragement, compulsion ▷*impulse*

urgent *adj.* important, earnest, intense, vital ★**trivial**

use ① *v.* employ, practise, apply ② *v.* consume, exhaust, deplete, expend ③ *n.* usage, wear

useful *adj.* valuable, favourable, practical, beneficial ★**useless**

useless *adj.* trashy, paltry, futile *Trying to train a cat to fetch is a futile activity,* inefficient ▷*worthless* ★**useful**

usual *adj.* common, general, habitual, familiar ▷*normal* ★**exceptional**

utensil *n.* tool, implement, instrument, apparatus, device

utilize *v.* employ, apply, exploit ▷*use*

utmost *adj.* extreme, supreme, greatest, ultimate, last, distant

utter ① *adj.* thorough, absolute, complete ② *v.* declare, pronounce, speak ▷*say*

utterly *adv.* extremely, completely, entirely, fully, wholly

V v

vacant *adj.* ① empty, unoccupied, exhausted ★**occupied** ② stupid, blank, expressionless, mindless

vacation *n.* holiday, rest, recess

vagabond *n.* vagrant, tramp, loafer, beggar, rover, hobo

vague *adj.* indefinite, imprecise, inexact, uncertain ▷*obscure* ★**certain**

vain *adj.* ① conceited, arrogant ▷*proud* ★**modest** ② fruitless, useless, worthless ▷*futile* VANE, VEIN

valiant *adj.* stout, valorous, worthy, gallant ▷*brave* ★**cowardly**

valid *adj.* genuine, authentic, official *No one is allowed into the meeting without an official pass,* proper

valley *n.* gorge, dale, dell, glen, vale

valour *n.* courage, fortitude, heroism, gallantry ▷*bravery* ★**cowardice**

valuable *adj.* ① costly, precious, priceless, expensive ★**worthless** ② meritorious *She was awarded the medal for meritorious service during the war,* righteous, worthy

value ① *n.* worth, benefit, merit, price ② *v.* appreciate, esteem, prize, treasure ③ *v.* appraise, assess, rate, estimate

van *n.* truck, vehicle, wagon, cart

vandalize *v.* damage, sabotage, harm, ruin

vanish *v.* ① disappear, fade, dissolve ★**appear** ② exit, depart, go

vanity *n.* pride, conceit, pretension, egotism ★**modesty**

vanquish *v.* conquer, defeat, overpower, subdue ▷*beat*

vapour *n.* steam, fog, mist, moisture, smoke

variable *adj.* changeable, fickle, unsteady, fitful, wavering ★**invariable**

varied *adj.* various, diverse *She was a woman of diverse interests,* miscellaneous, mixed, assorted ★**uniform**

variety *n.* ① assortment, array, mixture, medley *The singers entertained us with a medley of popular songs* ② sort, type,

Vehicles

Ambulance	Rickshaw	Train
Automobile	Scooter	Trap
Bicycle	Sedan	Trolley bus
Bulldozer	Stagecoach	Truck
Bus	Surrey	
Cab	Tank	
Car	Taxi	
Cart	Tractor	
Chariot	Tram	
Coach		
Fire engine		
Go-cart		
Hearse		
Jeep		
Limousine		
Lorry		
Motorcycle		

kind, class, category, species, breed, brand

various *adj.* mixed, different, many ▷*varied*

vary *v.* differ, alter, change, diversify, diverge

vase *n.* jug, jar, beaker ▷*pitcher*

vast *adj.* great, enormous, extensive, huge, wide ▷*immense* ★**narrow**

vault ① *n.* grave, mausoleum, cellar, crypt, dungeon ② *v.* jump, clear, bound, leap, hurdle, spring

veer *v.* swerve, skid, turn, tack, deviate, change, tack

vehement *adj.* impassioned, fiery, passionate, ardent, eager, zealous ▷*strong* ★**indifferent**

vehicle *n.* ① car, conveyance, automobile, carriage, cart ② agency, means, expedient

veil ① *n.* cloak, cover, wimple, curtain ② *v.* hide, conceal, shade, screen ★**expose** vale

vein *n.* ① seam, strain, streak, stripe, thread, course ② disposition, mood, style, phrasing VAIN

velocity *n.* rate, pace, tempo, rapidity, impetus *After I won the school prize, I had greater impetus to follow my studies* ▷*speed*

venerable *adj.* respectable, revered, august,

dignified, honoured, wise, grave ▷*sage*

vengeance *n.* reprisal, retaliation ▷*revenge* ★**pardon**

venomous *adj.* ① poisonous, toxic, vitriolic ② spiteful, malicious, hostile ▷*vindictive*

vent ① *v.* discharge, emit, express, let fly, release ② *n.* aperture, duct, opening, outlet

ventilate *v.* ① aerate, cool, fan, blow ② express, debate, discuss, examine

venture ① *n.* enterprise, undertaking, endeavour ② *v.* risk, bet, hazard ▷*chance*

verbal *adj.* stated, said, expressed, spoken, unwritten, word-of-mouth ★**written**

verdict *n.* decision, judgement, finding, conclusion, opinion

verge ① *n.* border, brink, edge, boundary ② *v.* incline, tend, border, come close to

verify *v.* confirm, declare, authenticate, corroborate *The witness corroborated the story told by the defendant* ★**discredit**

versatile *adj.* adaptable, variable, adjustable, handy ★**inflexible**

verse *n.* poem, rhyme, stave, canto, jingle, doggerel *Call this stuff poetry? It's just doggerel!*

version *n.* account, form, interpretation, adaptation, type

vertical *adj.* upright, erect, sheer, perpendicular, steep ★**horizontal**

very ① *adv.* extremely, exceedingly, greatly, intensely, absolutely ② *adj.* exact, real, true, actual, genuine

vessel *n.* ① bowl, pot, canister, container, basin, jar ② craft, ship, boat

vestige *n.* remains, remnant, hint, glimmer, residue, trace

veteran ① *n.* old-timer, master, old hand, expert ★**novice** ② *adj.* experienced, practised, adept ★**inexperienced**

veto ① *v.* ban, reject, prohibit, stop, forbid ★**approve** ② *n.* embargo *The United Nations placed an embargo on the selling of arms to the two countries,* prohibition, disapproval ★**assent**

vex *v.* annoy, provoke, trouble, irritate, harass ▷*displease* ★**soothe**

vibrate *v.* shake, quiver, oscillate, fluctuate,

throb, shudder, resonate ▷*tremble*

vice *n.* evil, failing, fault ▷*sin* ★**virtue**

vicinity *n.* area, environs, neighbourhood ▷*surroundings*

vicious *adj.* evil, sinful, malignant, immoral, vile ▷*wicked* ★**virtuous**

victim *n.* sufferer, scapegoat, martyr, prey, pawn, dupe

victor *n.* winner, conqueror, champion, prize-winner ★**loser**

victory *n.* success, triumph, achievement ▷*conquest* ★**defeat**

view ① *n.* landscape, sight, panorama, spectacle ② *n.* estimation, belief, theory, opinion ③ *v.* watch, see, behold, witness

vigilant *adj.* attentive, wary, alert, guarded ▷*watchful* ★**lax**

vigour *n.* energy, vim, stamina, might, power ▷*strength* ★**weakness**

vigorous *adj.* forceful, energetic, powerful, dynamic ▷*active* ★**weak**

vile *adj.* low, wretched, contemptible, miserable, nasty, evil ▷*despicable* ★**noble**

villain *n.* blackguard, knave *You are nothing but a knave who is out to steal my money,* sinner, rascal ▷*rogue* ★**hero**

vim *n.* stamina, zip, strength ▷*vigour*

vindicate *v.* warrant, sustain, support, defend, establish ▷*justify* ★**accuse**

vindictive *adj.* vengeful, unforgiving, grudging, spiteful ▷*malicious* ★**merciful**

violate *v.* ① disobey, oppose, defy, resist, infringe ★**obey** ② abuse, defile, outrage, desecrate

violent *adj.* furious, rabid, rampant, forcible, tempestuous ★**calm**

virile *adj.* manly, masculine, vigorous, vibrant ▷*strong* ★**weak**

virtually *adv.* almost, nearly, practically, substantially

virtue *n.* goodness, honesty, chastity, purity ▷*quality* ★**vice**

virtuous *adj.* chaste, innocent, honourable, moral ▷*righteous* ★**wicked**

visible *adj.* perceptible, discernible, apparent, exposed, obvious ★**invisible**

W w

vision *n.* ① apparition, spectre, ghost, mirage ② concept, revelation, foresight

visit ① *n.* call, sojourn, stay, excursion ② *v.* call on, drop in, tarry, stay

visitor *n.* guest, company, tourist, caller

visual *adj.* seeable, observable, visible

vital *adj.* ① essential, indispensible, crucial ▷*necessary* ② alive, vibrant, virile, dynamic *Our team won a number of games after we had been trained by the new dynamic coach*, vivacious, energetic

vitality *n.* stamina, virility ▷*strength*

vivacious *adj.* lively, spirited, vital, animated, merry ▷*sprightly* ★**languid**

vivid *adj.* ① clear, bright ▷*brilliant* ② vigorous, strong, lucid ★**dull**

vocal *adj.* articulate, eloquent, spoken, strident, vociferous ★**quiet**

vocation *n.* occupation, calling, job, mission, career, pursuit

vogue *n.* style, fashion, mode, popularity

voice ① *n.* speech, articulation, utterance ② *n.* choice, preference, opinion ③ *v.* utter, express, proclaim, pronounce

void ① *adj.* bare, barren, empty ② *adj.* invalid, cancelled, useless ③ *n.* cavity, chasm, space, opening, nothingness

volatile *adj.* ① lively, changeable, fickle, giddy ② elusive, fleeting, evaporable

volley *n.* discharge, fusillade, barrage, shower

volume *n.* ① bulk, capacity, mass, quantity ▷*amount* ② loudness, amplitude ③ book, edition, tome

voluntary *adj.* free-willed, optional, intended, gratuitous ★**compulsory**

vomit *v.* spew, disgorge, puke, throw up

vote ① *n.* ballot, election, poll, referendum ② *v.* ballot, poll, choose, elect

vow ① *v.* promise, swear, assure, vouch, testify ② *n.* oath, pledge, promise

voyage *n.* journey, cruise, passage, trip

vulgar *adj.* ① common, coarse, crude, indelicate, rude ★**elegant** ② native, ordinary, common

vulnerable *adj.* unprotected, unguarded, exposed, defenceless, tender ★**strong**

wad *n.* bundle, chunk, block, plug

waddle *v.* wobble, totter, shuffle, toddle

wag ① *v.* waggle, shake ▷*vibrate* ② *n.* wit, humorist, joker

wage ① *n.* fee, pay, salary, remuneration ② *v.* carry out, fulfil, undertake

wager ① *v.* gamble, bet, speculate, chance, hazard ② *n.* pledge, stake, bet

wagon *n.* cart, truck, van ▷*vehicle*

waif *n.* orphan, stray, foundling *In the old days, children were abandoned in the streets, but some people set up homes for such foundlings*

wail ① *v.* deplore, weep, grieve, lament ▷*cry* ★**rejoice** ② *n.* lamentation, weeping, grief, moan, howl

wait *v.* ① expect, await, bide, stay, stop ▷*linger* ② attend, serve WEIGHT

waive *v.* relinquish, disclaim, disown, forego, defer ▷*renounce* WAVE

wake *v.* awaken, stimulate, excite ▷*arouse*

wakeful *adj.* ① restless, awake ② alert, wary, watchful

walk ① *v.* advance, march, step, progress, move ② *n.* stroll, hike ▷*ramble* ★**run** ③ *n.* lane, alley, way ④ *n.* sphere, field, career *I started my career in the field of journalism, but I later went into politics*

wallow *v.* ① flounder, stagger, tumble ② delight, enjoy, revel

wan *adj.* pale, ashen, feeble, sickly, pallid ▷*weak* ★**robust**

wand *n.* mace, baton, stick, sceptre, rod

wander *v.* stray, meander, roam, stroll, deviate, saunter

wane *v.* droop, decline, decrease, lessen, ebb *As the little boat neared the rocks, Fred's courage ebbed away*, sink ★**wax** WAIN

wangle *v.* fiddle, contrive, fix, arrange

want ① *v.* desire, covet, crave, need, require ② *n.* need, necessity, demand ③ *n.* dearth, deficiency ▷*scarcity* ★**plenty**

wanton *adj.* ① unscrupulous, irresponsible

A B C D E F G H I J K L M N O P Q R S T U V W X Y Z

② playful, frolicsome, wild ③ dissolute, immoral

war *n.* hostilities, fighting, bloodshed, enmity, strife, combat ★**peace** WORE

ward *n.* ① pupil, minor, charge ② district, quarter WARRED

ward off *v.* prevent, forestall, avoid, stop ▷*avert*

wardrobe *n.* ① locker, cupboard, closet ② outfit, clothes, apparel

warm ① *adj.* tepid, hot, lukewarm ② *adj.* sympathetic ▷*warmhearted* ③ *adj.* eager, hot, zealous ④ *v.* heat, bake, cook, prepare

warn *v.* caution, admonish, advise, alert, apprise WORN

warning *n.* caution, admonition, forewarning, alarm, tip

warp *v.* contort, bend, twist, kink, deform, distort ★**straighten**

warrant ① *v.* guarantee, certify, justify, permit, allow ② *n.* assurance, permit, licence, authority *She produced documents that showed her authority on the board of directors*

wary *adj.* cautious, alert, careful, heedful ▷*prudent* ★**rash**

wash ① *v.* bathe, scrub, rinse, cleanse, wet ② *n.* washing, cleaning

waste ① *n.* rubbish, debris, trash, garbage ② *v.* squander, spend, lavish, fritter ③ *v.* wither, decay, shrivel, perish WAIST

wasteful *adj.* lavish, prodigal, spendthrift ▷*extravagant* ★**economical**

watch ① *v.* note, observe, guard ★**ignore** ② *v.* inspect, look at, oversee ③ *n.* timepiece ④ *n.* guard, sentry, watchman

watchful *adj.* attentive, observant, vigilant ▷*wary* ★**inattentive**

water *v.* wet, bathe, wash, douse, drench, sprinkle, spray

wave ① *v.* brandish, flourish, waft, swing ② *n.* breaker, billow, undulation WAIVE

waver *v.* falter, hesitate, vacillate *There's no time to vacillate; make up your mind* ★**decide**

wax *v.* increase, rise, grow, expand, enlarge ★**wane**

way *n.* ① route, road, path, passage, track ② technique *The company introduced a new technique for making glass,* procedure, method, style WEIGH

wayward *adj.* contrary, perverse, obstinate ▷*stubborn* ★**docile**

weak *adj.* ① feeble, frail, puny, helpless, delicate ② foolish, soft, senseless, stupid ③ thin, watery, insipid ④ fragile, flimsy, tumbledown ★**strong** WEEK

weaken *v.* enfeeble, relax, sag, flag ▷*languish* ★**strengthen**

weakness *n.* defect, fault, frailty, flaw ★**strength**

wealth *n.* riches, luxury, prosperity, money, opulence ★**poverty**

wealthy *adj.* rich, affluent, prosperous, opulent ★**poor**

wear *v.* ① dress in, don ② rub, scrape, waste, consume ③ last, endure, remain WARE

weary ① *adj.* exhausted, tired, fatigued ★**fresh** ② *v.* exhaust, tire, bore ★**refresh**

weather *n.* climate, clime, conditions

weave *v.* braid, plait, unite, blend

web *n.* net, tissue, webbing, textile, netting

wed *v.* marry, join, link, splice, tie the knot

wedge ① *n.* block, chock, lump, chunk ② *v.* crowd, force, jam, push, thrust, squeeze

wee *adj.* little, small, minute ▷*tiny* ★**large**

weep *v.* blubber, snivel, sob, whimper *The lost puppy was found at last, whimpering in a corner* ▷*cry* ★**rejoice**

weigh *v.* balance, estimate, ponder, examine, consider WAY

weight *n.* ① load, pressure, burden, heaviness ② importance, onus, significance, gravity WAIT

weighty *adj.* heavy, hefty, ponderous, onerous ★**trivial**

weird *adj.* eerie, supernatural, unearthly, mysterious ▷*uncanny*

welcome ① *adj.* pleasing, desirable ▷*agreeable* ② *v.* greet, accost, hail, salute ③ *n.* greeting, salutation, acceptance

welfare *n.* well-being, comfort, happiness, benefit, advantage ★**harm**

well ① *adj.* robust, healthy, hearty, sound

Weather Conditions

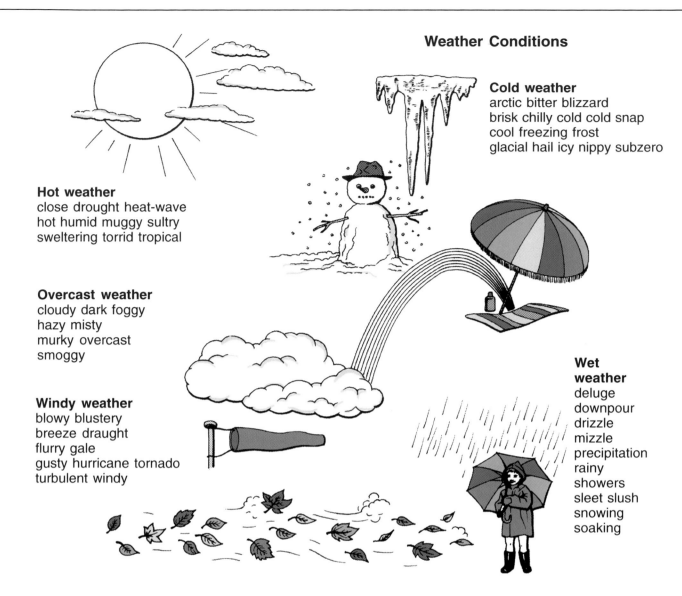

Cold weather
arctic bitter blizzard
brisk chilly cold cold snap
cool freezing frost
glacial hail icy nippy subzero

Hot weather
close drought heat-wave
hot humid muggy sultry
sweltering torrid tropical

Overcast weather
cloudy dark foggy
hazy misty
murky overcast
smoggy

Wet weather
deluge
downpour
drizzle
mizzle
precipitation
rainy
showers
sleet slush
snowing
soaking

Windy weather
blowy blustery
breeze draught
flurry gale
gusty hurricane tornado
turbulent windy

★**ill** ② *adv.* properly, suitable, adequately, accurately ★**badly** ③ *n.* fountain, spring

well-off *adj.* comfortable, prosperous ▷*wealthy* ★**poor**

wet *adj.* ① moist, damp, watery, drenched ② *adj.* drizzling, showery, raining ③ *v.* soak, moisten, dampen

wheedle *v.* coax, cajole, inveigle *We were inveigled into buying some of the local lace,* persuade ★**coerce**

whet *v.* ① sharpen, hone, strop ★**blunt** ② excite, stimulate, rouse ★**dampen**

whim *n.* fancy, humour, desire, urge, notion, impulse

whine *v.* ① howl, wail, whimper, moan ② complain, grouse, grumble, whinge

whip *v.* ① flog, lash, thrash, chastise, spank ② whisk, mix, blend

whirl *v.* pirouette, twirl, spin, rotate, revolve, whir, gyrate ▷*twist*

whisk *v.* beat, brush, hasten, hurry, sweep ▷*whip*

whisper ① *n.* murmur, hint, suggestion, breath ② *v.* breathe, murmur, divulge, buzz, intimate ★**shout**

whistle *n. & v.* cheep, chirp, warble, call

whole *adj.* ① all, entire, total, intact ② sound, complete, unbroken ★**part** HOLE

wholesome *adj.* healthful, nutritious, beneficial, sound, good ★**noxious**

wicked *adj.* infamous, corrupt, depraved, unrighteous, sinister, sinful ▷*evil* ★**virtuous**

wickedness *n.* corruption, depravity, iniquity, sinfulness, villainy ▷*evil*

wide *adj.* broad, ample, extended, spacious,

roomy, extensive, vast ★**narrow**

widespread *adj.* prevalent, far-flung, extensive, sweeping, universal *The use of a universal language would be of great help in the United Nations* ★**limited**

wield *v.* ① brandish, flourish, manipulate ② control, command, exert, maintain

wild *adj.* ① savage, ferocious, fierce, untamed ★**tame** ② violent, unrestrained, boisterous ★**civilized** ③ careless, insane, reckless ★**sane**

wilderness *n.* desert, jungle, wasteland, wilds, outback

will ① *n.* resolution, decision, zeal, accord ② *n.* order, wish, command, request, demand ③ *n.* legacy, testament ④ *v.* choose, desire, elect

wilful *adj.* temperamental, headstrong, deliberate ▷*obstinate* ★**docile**

willing *adj.* disposed, zealous, ready, earnest ▷*agreeable* ★**unwilling**

wilt *v.* wither, waste, sag, dwindle ▷*ebb*

wily *adj.* cunning, sly, tricky, deceitful ▷*crafty* ★**sincere**

win *v.* succeed, gain, get, acquire, procure ▷*triumph* ★**lose**

wince *v.* shrink, quail, flinch *My little sister didn't flinch once when she had her vaccination,* start ▷*cringe*

wind (rhymes with *pinned*) *n.* breeze, blast, gust, gale

wind (rhymes with *mind*) *v.* coil, turn, twist, bend WINED

wink *n.* & *v.* blink, flutter, flicker, glint

winner *n.* champion, master ▷*victor*

wipe *v.* clean, brush, mop, remove, swab

wire *n.* ① cable, telegraph, telegram ② cable, cord, flex

wisdom *n.* judgement, discretion, tact, thought, reason ★**folly**

wise *adj.* sensible, profound, astute, subtle, discreet ▷*sage* ★**foolish**

wish ① *v.* desire, crave, want, hanker for, long for ② *n.* command, will, desire, liking

wistful *adj.* ① pensive, musing, wishful ② forlorn, melancholy, soulful

wit *n.* ① fun, humour, levity, pleasantry,

banter, ② brains, sense, judgement, intelligence ★**stupidity**

witch *n.* enchantress, sorceress, crone, hag

withdraw *v.* ① retire, retreat, depart, leave ▷*flee* ② extract, take out

withdrawn *adj.* unsociable, retiring, reclusive, aloof, solitary ★**sociable**

wither *v.* waste, fade, pine, languish, shrivel, wilt ▷*shrivel*

withhold *v.* retain, reserve, restrain, hold back ▷*keep* ★**grant**

within *adj.* inside, interior, inner

withstand *v.* resist, oppose, confront, stand up to ▷*defy* ★**support**

witness ① *n.* spectator, onlooker, bystander *One of the bystanders at the accident came forward to give evidence,* signatory ② *v.* behold, observe, see, attest

witty *adj.* funny, jocular, waggish, amusing ▷*comical* ★**dull**

wizard *n.* sorcerer, magician, conjurer

woe *n.* sorrow, sadness, grief, misery, trouble ★**joy**

woman *n.* lady, girl, female, wife

wonder ① *n.* marvel, miracle, rarity, curiosity ② *n.* bewilderment, surprise, amazement ▷*awe* ③ *v.* speculate, question, marvel, muse, conjecture

wonderful *adj.* marvellous, fabulous, spectacular, superb ▷*splendid* ★**commonplace**

woo *v.* make love, court, pursue, chase

wood *n.* ① timber, planks, lumber ② forest, woods, copse, woodland, grove, thicket WOULD

word *n.* ① expression, term, utterance ② pledge, promise ③ tidings, news, information, bulletin, statement

work ① *n.* toil, drudgery, labour, grind ② *n.* task, job, stint, chore ③ *v.* operate, function, manipulate, run, drive

world *n.* globe, earth, sphere, planet

worry ① *v.* bother, annoy, disturb ▷*trouble* ★**soothe** ② *n.* vexation, anxiety, concern, fear ★**delight**

worsen *v.* aggravate, decline, deteriorate, degenerate ★**improve**

Borrowed Words

Boomerang

lemming
ombudsman
ski

Italian
balcony
cameo
fiasco
influenza

Dutch
boss
brandy
decoy
landscape

Modern French
police
rendezvous
liaison
menu

Scandinavia
fjord
geyser

German
blitz
delicatessen
dollar
kindergarten

Chinese
kowtow
sampan
typhoon
wok

Japanese
bonsai
judo
karate
origami

Turkish
coffee
kiosk

Spanish
armada
fiesta
macho
patio
siesta
sombrero

Afrikaans
aardvark
apartheid

boer
trek
veldt

Inuit
anorak
igloo
kayak
parka

Gaelic
blarney
bog
brat
brogue
smithereens

Aztec
avocado
cocoa
tomato

Arabic
admiral
alcohol
algebra
alkali
sherbet
sofa
zero

Aboriginal languages
boomerang
dingo
budgerigar
kangaroo

Persian
bazaar
caravan
divan
paradise

tulip
turban

Hindi
bungalow
chintz
cot
pyjamas
thug
veranda

Native American
chipmunk
moccasin
moose
papoose
wigwam

---

worship ① *v.* revere, adore, esteem, honour, praise ★**despise** ② *n.* adoration, devotion, reverence

worth *n.* value, benefit, merit, calibre *This year's students were of a high calibre,* dignity

worthless *adj.* valueless, paltry, trifling, useless ▷*cheap* ★**valuable**

worthwhile *adj.* valuable, helpful, useful, beneficial ★**useless**

worthy *adj.* upright, admirable, excellent, honest, fine ★**vile**

wound ① *v.* hurt, injure, gash, pain, distress ▷*harm* ★**heal** ② *n.* injury, bruise, harm

wrangle *v. & n.* squabble, fight, row, scrap ▷*quarrel* ★**accord**

wrap *v.* fold, envelop, enclose, cover, clothe, conceal ★**unfold** RAP

wrath *n.* fury, ire, rage, passion ▷*anger* ★**pleasure**

wreck ① *v.* demolish, smash, ruin, destroy, spoil, ravage ★**repair** ② *n.* derelict, hulk, shipwreck, ruin

wrench *v.* twist, wring, strain, sprain, pull

wrestle *v.* struggle, battle, combat, grapple, tussle ▷*fight*

wretch *n.* vagabond, blackguard, villain, rogue, ruffian, rascal ▷*scoundrel*

wretched *adj.* ① dejected, abject, miserable ▷*despicable* ② saddening, pathetic ▷*pitiful* ★**joyful**

wriggle *v.* twist, writhe, squirm, worm *My hamster wormed his way under the couch and it took some time before we could get him back out,* dodge

wring *v.* choke, squeeze, throttle, strangle, twist RING

wrinkle *n. & v.* crease, pucker, ruffle, rumple, crinkle, furrow

write *v.* inscribe, pen, sign, scrawl, scribble RIGHT, RITE, WRIGHT

writer *n.* ① scribe, penman, clerk ② author, essayist, narrator, playwright, poet, dramatist, columnist, hack

writhe *v.* wind, twine, weave, twist, squirm ▷*wriggle*

written *adj.* recorded, set down, documentary, transcribed

wrong ① *adj.* unjust, unfair, immoral, wicked ② *adj.* false, mistaken, erroneous ③ *v.* injure, hurt, abuse ④ *n.* offence, atrocity, iniquity, sin, injustice ★**right**

wry *adj.* crooked, askew, awry, aslant, twisted, distorted ★**straight** RYE

Y y

yank *v.* draw, pull, snatch ▷*jerk*

yap *v.* ① bark, yelp ② prattle, blather, gossip, jaw

yard ① *n.* courtyard, court, quadrangle, garden ② three feet

yarn *n.* ① story, account, tale, narrative ② thread, wool, linen, twist

yawn *v.* gape, open

yearly *adj.* ① annual, perennial, per annum *We shall pay a salary of £50,000 per annum* ② *adv.* every year, annually

yearn *v.* ache, crave, desire, pine, hunger for ★**dislike**

yell *v.* shriek, squawk, whoop, screech, shout ▷*bellow* ★**whisper**

yield ① *v.* produce, provide, furnish, supply ② *v.* surrender, give in, submit ★**withstand** ③ *v.* abdicate, resign, renounce ④ *n.* crop, harvest, product, output

yielding ① *adj.* obedient, submissive, unresisting ★**stubborn** ② plastic, malleable, flexible ★**solid**

yoke ① *v.* join, couple, link, harness ② *n.* chain, bondage *The children of Israel moved out of bondage in the land of Egypt,* enslavement YOLK

yokel *n.* bumpkin, rustic, boor, peasant

young *adj.* youthful, tender, juvenile, junior, little ★**old**

youngster *n.* child, youth, boy, girl, kid, teenager, lad, adolescent

youth *n.* ① adolescence, prime, salad days ★**age** ② lad, boy ▷*youngster*

youthful *adj.* boyish, girlish, young, spry, juvenile, lively ★**aged**

Yule *n.* Christmas

Z z

zany *adj.* crazy, daft, droll, goofy, eccentric, wacky, loony ▷*funny* ★**serious**

zeal *n.* devotion, eagerness, enthusiasm, keenness, ardour ★**apathy**

zealous *adj.* devoted, fervent *Dave was a fervent supporter of the school's football team,* fanatical, earnest ▷*eager* ★**apathetic**

zenith *n.* climax, height, apex, peak

zero *n.* nothing, nought, nil, nullity, zip, aught

zest *n.* ① relish, gusto, appetite, keenness ② flavour, piquancy, taste ③ rind, peel

zone *n.* area, district, region, tract, sector

zoom *v.* flash, fly, shoot, streak, hurtle, whizz

Countries and People

Some countries and the people or adjective that go with them.

Austria

Belarus

Brazil

China

Fiji

Greece

Guatemala

Nepal

Country	People/Adjective
Afghanistan	Afghan
Albania	Albanian
Algeria	Algerian
Angola	Angolan
Argentina	Argentinian
Austria	Austrian
Australia	Australian
Bangladesh	Bangladeshi
Belgium	Belgian
Belarus	Belarussian
Benin	Beninese
Bhutan	Bhutanese
Bolivia	Bolivian
Brazil	Brazilian
Burma	Burmese
Cambodia	Cambodian
Cameroon	Cameroonian
Canada	Canadian
Chad	Chadian
Chile	Chilean
China	Chinese
Colombia	Colombian
Congo	Congolese
Costa Rica	Costa Rican
Cuba	Cuban
Cyprus	Cypriot
Czech Republic	Czech
Denmark	Dane/Danish
Ecuador	Ecuadorean
Egypt	Egyptian
England	English
Ethiopia	Ethiopian
Fiji	Fijian
Finland	Finn/Finnish
Gambia	Gambian
Greece	Greek
Guatemala	Guatemalan
Guinea	Guinean
Guyana	Guyanese
Haiti	Haitian
Honduras	Honduran
Hungary	Hungarian
Iceland	Icelander/Icelandic
India	Indian
Indonesia	Indonesian
Iran	Iranian
Iraq	Iraqi
Ireland	Irish
Israel	Israeli
Italy	Italian
Jamaica	Jamaican
Japan	Japanese
Jordan	Jordanian
Kenya	Kenyan
Korea	Korean

Country	People/Adjective
Kuwait	Kuwaiti
Lebanon	Lebanese
Liberia	Liberian
Libya	Libyan
Luxembourg	Luxembourger
Malawi	Malawian
Malaysian	Malaysian
Mali	Malian
Mauritania	Mauritanian
Mexico	Mexican
Mongolia	Mongolian
Morocco	Moroccan
Namibia	Namibian
Nepal	Nepalese
Netherlands	Dutch
New Zealand	New Zealander
Nicaragua	Nicaraguan
Niger	Nigerien
Nigeria	Nigerian
Norway	Norwegian
Pakistan	Pakistani
Panama	Panamanian
Paraguay	Paraguayan
Peru	Peruvian
Philippines	Filipino
Poland	Pole/Polish
Portugal	Portuguese
Romania	Romanian
Russia	Russian
Saudi Arabia	Saudi Arabian
Scotland	Scot/Scottish
Senegal	Senegalese
Slovakia	Slovak/Slovakian
South African	South African
Spain	Spanish
Sri Lanka	Sri Lankan
Sudan	Sudanese
Sweden	Swede/Swedish
Switzerland	Swiss
Syria	Syrian
Tanzania	Tanzanian
Thailand	Thai
Tunisia	Tunisian
Turkey	Turk/Turkish
Uganda	Ugandan
United States of America	American
Uruguay	Uruguayan
Venezuela	Venezuelan
Vietnam	Vietnamese
Wales	Welsh
Yemen	Yemeni
Zambia	Zambian
Zimbabwe	Zimbabwean

New Zealand

Slovakia

Syria

Tunisia

Turkey

Uganda

Venezuela

Zimbabwe

A B C D E F G H I J K L M N O P Q R S T U V W X Y Z

Spellcheck

Words we use all the time and how to spell them. The words in **heavy black type** are some words which are difficult to spell.

a
about
ache
address
advertisement
after
ago
all
already
also
always
am
an
and
any
anybody
anyone
anything
anyway
anywhere
are
aren't = are not
as
at
away

b
be
became
because
become
been
being
best
better
business
but
by
bye

c
calendar
came
can
cannot = can not
can't = can not
career
ceiling
come
could
couldn't = could not

d
did
didn't = did not
do
does
doesn't = does not
doing
done
don't = do not
down
Dr = Doctor
during

e
each
either
else
ever
every
everybody
everyone
everywhere

f
few
first
for
friend
from

g
gave
get
getting
give
go
goes
going
gone
gorilla
got

h
had
hadn't = had not
handkerchief
has
have
haven't = have not
he
he'll
her
here
hers
herself
he's = he is
him
himself
his

how
hurrah

i
I
I'd = I had
if
I'll = I shall, I will
I'm = I am
in
into
is
isn't = is not
it
its
it's = it is
itself
I've = I have

j
jewellery
just

k
kilogram
kilometre

l
last
least
less
let's = let us
lot

m
made
make
many
may
me
might
mile
mine
Miss
more
most
Mr
Mrs
Ms
much
mum
must
mustn't = must not
my
myself

n
needn't
neither
nephew
next
niece

nobody
none
nonsense
no one
nothing
now
nowhere

o
o'clock
of
off
OK
on
once
only
or
other
our
ours
ourselves
out
over

p
perhaps
probably
put
putting

s
same
shall
shan't
she
she'll = she will
she's = she is
should
shouldn't = should not
since
sir
so
some
somebody
someone
something
sometime
somewhere
soon
sorry
success
such

t
than
that
the
their
theirs
them
themselves
then
there

these
they
they'd =they had
they'll = they will
they're = they are
they've = they have
this
those
to
today
tomorrow
tongue
tonight
too

u
up
upon
us

v
very

w
was
wasn't = was not
way
we
we'd = we had
we'll = we shall, we will
went
were
we're = we are
weren't = were not
what
when
where
which
while
who
who'll = who will
whom
who's = who is
whose
why
will
with
won't = will not
worst
would
wouldn't = would not

y
yet
you
you'd = you had
you'll = you will
your
you're = you are
yours
yourself
you've = you have

a
b
c
d
e
f
g
h
i
j
k
l
m
n
o
p
q
r
s
t
u
v
w
x
y
z